UXD and UCD Approaches for Accessible Education

Ricardo Mendoza-González
Tecnológico Nacional de México, Instituto Tecnológico de Aguascalientes, Mexico

Huizilopoztli Luna-García
Universidad Autónoma de Zacatecas, Mexico

Alfredo Mendoza-González
Universidad Autónoma de Zacatecas, Mexico

A volume in the Advances in Educational Technologies and Instructional Design (AETID) Book Series

IGI Global
DISSEMINATOR OF KNOWLEDGE

Published in the United States of America by
IGI Global
Information Science Reference (an imprint of IGI Global)
701 E. Chocolate Avenue
Hershey PA, USA 17033
Tel: 717-533-8845
Fax: 717-533-8661
E-mail: cust@igi-global.com
Web site: http://www.igi-global.com

Library of Congress Cataloging-in-Publication Data

Names: Mendoza-Gonzalez, Ricardo, 1979- editor. | Luna-García, Huizilopoztli, 1976- editor. | Mendoza-González, Alfredo, 1985- editor.

Title: UXD and UCD approaches for accessible education / Ricardo Mendoza-González, Huizilopoztli Luna-García, and Alfredo Mendoza-González, editors.
Description: Hershey, PA : Information Science Reference, 2020. | Includes bibliographical references and index. | Summary: "This book explores the use of User Centered-Design (UCD) and User eXperience Design (UXD) approaches in support of accessible and equity education"-- Provided by publisher.
Identifiers: LCCN 2019039289 (print) | LCCN 2019039290 (ebook) | ISBN 9781799823254 (hardcover) | ISBN 9781799823261 (paperback) | ISBN 9781799823278 (ebook)
Subjects: LCSH: Computer assisted instruction--Design. | User-centered system design. | User interfaces (Computer systems)--Design. | People with disabilities--Education.
Classification: LCC LB1028.5 .U94 2020 (print) | LCC LB1028.5 (ebook) | DDC 371.33/4--dc23
LC record available at https://lccn.loc.gov/2019039289
LC ebook record available at https://lccn.loc.gov/2019039290

This book is published in the IGI Global book series Advances in Educational Technologies and Instructional Design (AE-TID) (ISSN: 2326-8905; eISSN: 2326-8913)

British Cataloguing in Publication Data
A Cataloguing in Publication record for this book is available from the British Library.

Advances in Educational Technologies and Instructional Design (AETID) Book Series

Lawrence A. Tomei
Robert Morris University, USA

ISSN:2326-8905
EISSN:2326-8913

Mission

Education has undergone, and continues to undergo, immense changes in the way it is enacted and distributed to both child and adult learners. In modern education, the traditional classroom learning experience has evolved to include technological resources and to provide online classroom opportunities to students of all ages regardless of their geographical locations. From distance education, Massive-Open-Online-Courses (MOOCs), and electronic tablets in the classroom, technology is now an integral part of learning and is also affecting the way educators communicate information to students.

The **Advances in Educational Technologies & Instructional Design (AETID) Book Series** explores new research and theories for facilitating learning and improving educational performance utilizing technological processes and resources. The series examines technologies that can be integrated into K-12 classrooms to improve skills and learning abilities in all subjects including STEM education and language learning. Additionally, it studies the emergence of fully online classrooms for young and adult learners alike, and the communication and accountability challenges that can arise. Trending topics that are covered include adaptive learning, game-based learning, virtual school environments, and social media effects. School administrators, educators, academicians, researchers, and students will find this series to be an excellent resource for the effective design and implementation of learning technologies in their classes.

Coverage

- Collaboration Tools
- Instructional Design
- Bring-Your-Own-Device
- Virtual School Environments
- Online Media in Classrooms
- K-12 Educational Technologies
- Hybrid Learning
- E-Learning
- Higher Education Technologies
- Educational Telecommunications

IGI Global is currently accepting manuscripts for publication within this series. To submit a proposal for a volume in this series, please contact our Acquisition Editors at Acquisitions@igi-global.com or visit: http://www.igi-global.com/publish/.

The Advances in Educational Technologies and Instructional Design (AETID) Book Series (ISSN 2326-8905) is published by IGI Global, 701 E. Chocolate Avenue, Hershey, PA 17033-1240, USA, www.igi-global.com. This series is composed of titles available for purchase individually; each title is edited to be contextually exclusive from any other title within the series. For pricing and ordering information please visit http://www.igi-global.com/book-series/advances-educational-technologies-instructional-design/73678. Postmaster: Send all address changes to above address.

Titles in this Series

https://www.igi-global.com/book-series/advances-educational-technologies-instructional-design/73678

Challenges and Opportunities for Transforming From STEM to STEAM Education
Kelli Thomas (University of Kansas, USA) and Douglas Huffman (University of Kansas, USA)
Information Science Reference • © 2020 • 300pp • H/C (ISBN: 9781799825173) • US $195.00

Transforming Music Education in P-12 Schools and the Community
Taichi Akutsu (Okayama Prefectural University, Japan & Seisa University, Japan)
Information Science Reference • © 2020 • 230pp • H/C (ISBN: 9781799820635) • US $175.00

Preparing 21st Century Teachers for Teach Less, Learn More (TLLM) Pedagogies
Pradeep Kumar (Taylor's University, Malaysia) Michael James Keppell (Taylor's University, Malaysia) and Chee Leong Lim (Taylor's University, Malaysia)
Information Science Reference • © 2020 • 332pp • H/C (ISBN: 9781799814351) • US $195.00

Developing Technology Mediation in Learning Environments
Filomena Soares (Polytechnic of Porto, Portugal) Ana Paula Lopes (Polytechnic of Porto, Portugal) Ken Brown (Letterkenny Institute of Technology, Ireland) and Anne Uukkivi (TTK University of Applied Sciences, Estonia)
Information Science Reference • © 2020 • 330pp • H/C (ISBN: 9781799815914) • US $195.00

Global Perspectives on Gameful and Playful Teaching and Learning
Matthew Farber (University of Northern Colorado, USA)
Information Science Reference • © 2020 • 330pp • H/C (ISBN: 9781799820154) • US $195.00

Handbook of Research on Integrating Computer Science and Computational Thinking in K-12 Education
Jared Keengwe (University of North Dakota, USA) and Patrick Wachira (Cleveland State University, USA)
Information Science Reference • © 2020 • 385pp • H/C (ISBN: 9781799814795) • US $265.00

Personalization and Collaboration in Adaptive E-Learning
Mouenis Anouar Tadlaoui (Abdelmalek Essaâdi University, Morocco) and Mohamed Khaldi (Abdelmalek Essaâdi University, Morocco)
Information Science Reference • © 2020 • 348pp • H/C (ISBN: 9781799814924) • US $195.00

Recent Developments in Technology-Enhanced and Computer-Assisted Language Learning
Bin Zou (Xi'an Jiaotong-Liverpool University, China) and Michael Thomas (University of Central Lancashire, UK)
Information Science Reference • © 2020 • 454pp • H/C (ISBN: 9781799812821) • US $195.00

IGI Global
DISSEMINATOR OF KNOWLEDGE

701 East Chocolate Avenue, Hershey, PA 17033, USA
Tel: 717-533-8845 x100 • Fax: 717-533-8661
E-Mail: cust@igi-global.com • www.igi-global.com

Editorial Advisory Board

Table of Contents

Detailed Table of Contents

populations, idiosyncratic populations, right to privacy, and an understanding of ADA-compliant accommodations by UX researchers and participants. This chapter will introduce these principles as well as demonstrate one possible application in an undergraduate design classroom.

The objective of this chapter was to assess the impact that haptic tools have on the experience of people with some kind of visual impairment when accessing a building. The analysis was performed through the application of a case study carried out in the facilities of the Center for Teleinformatics and Industrial Production of the National Learning Service in Popayán, Colombia with the participation of five people. Taking into account the principles of universal design, the analysis considered people with total blindness, partial blindness, and people without visual limitation. Participants provided feedback and insights on their experience locating the designated area with and without the support of defined haptic tools. The study resulted in a set of drawbacks that influence the location of visually impaired people. Such findings can be taken into account by people who wish to make projects of access to physical spaces of visually impaired people.

This chapter was intended to emphasize the need of user-centered technology for the current generation of learners: "Multipotentielites." The scenario suggests that fostering attention in Multipotentialites is required for effective learning being empathy and emotions the key to achieve it. Important concepts such as user experience design (UXD) and learning experience design (LXD) where analyzed here as pivotal aspects to envision both new educational/learning processes and the environments/technologies that support them. Under this context, the chapter summarized several perceptions from experts by highlighting those Multipotentialites' qualities and skills that should be strengthen and exploited during learning processes where attention appears to be the new IQ.

Reading is an important competency to be developed for children in the first years of elementary school. Reading becomes a mechanism that allows the children to interact with the world and identify their characteristics. Dyslexia is one learning disability frequently manifested in elementary school, and to identify it, teachers require extra educative resources, in particular educational applications. This work proposes a process model to design and develop educational applications considering the learning needs of children with dyslexia. It involves a user-centered approach because different perceptions of several actors are considered. The performance of the proposed model is explored in a case study and an evaluation, taking into account usability and accessibility factors.

The inclusion of people with disabilities in society is an issue that is currently becoming relevant. This is why technology is in a constant struggle to develop tools that meet the needs of this sector of the population and with it fulfill this objective. One of these disabilities is blindness. Therefore, this chapter shows an analysis of the application of virtual reality (VR) and haptic devices as support tools in the teaching-learning of people with such disabilities through the study of various projects that have implement these technologies, obtaining the advantages and disadvantages offered by these resources. For this, an analysis is made from the point of view of accessibility that it presents as well as the approach of the user-centered design (UCD).

Virtual reality has captured the attention of people. Since virtual reality has become more realistic, with the evolution of the technology like the innovation of smartphones, it has been more accessible for society, and many industries have begun research on the application of VR for training and for learning about certain specific topics as it allows reducing accidents and maximizes safety. Their use in the education industry has been best seen as a tool to complement certain issues that may be difficult to understand since it can allow one to virtually move to certain areas from safe areas. However, the development virtual environments is not fully specialized to implicitly include and promote learning, much less the consideration of people with disabilities. The main objective of this chapter is the presentation of a design process for the development of virtual learning environments that allows accessibility.

The objective of this chapter is to identify web accessibility problems in order to fulfill the design guidelines. According to the proposal, accessibility is assessed through easy checks of the implementation of the social engineering educational platform. As a first phase, the developer carries out this evaluation and his results are analyzed. The second phase solves the identified problems or at least tries to give them a solution implementing a redesign on the platform; in the same way, the results are analyzed. In the third phase, a proposal is made of the improvements that can be introduced in the redesign of the user interface in a way that best complies with the web accessibility. The problem identified shows the difficulty of implementing the accessibility guides and the need to propose accessibility implementation guidelines that guarantee their compliance.

Evaluating software implies challenging users' abilities during a period, applying several assessments, and analyzing their evolution. This process might turn unpleasant and stressful, especially to those susceptible to anxiety and stress, such as Down syndrome users. The poor performance of unpleasant users generates unreal results. A gamified approach for software testing is proposed that maintains user motivation and engagement and reduces anxiety and stress. Common behaviors expected are anxiety, stress, unwilling to work, and in general, lack of motivation. Using gamification, makes it possible to succeed in controlling these common negative behaviors and stimulating the positive ones including the MDA framework into a generic learnability evaluation process, linking these two elements with the psychological approach of gestalt therapy. Gamifying the testing experience increased the quality of communication between users and applicators; provided a friendly, motivational, and engaging environment; and increased the rate of testing success and the range of potential participants.

This chapter described an analysis and those derived design improvements for an accessibility course offered by Tecnológico Nacional de México/IT Aguascalientes (ITA). The course is addressed to train professors for awareness and implementation of educational strategies that allow an accessible and inclusive learning environment. Enhancements found were oriented to makes easier teachers' tasks when generating strategies for the creation of accessible educational content. All suggestions were derived from a usability analysis of both interactive elements and the structure of the course on the on-line learning platform Moodle. The study was performed by implementing several international standards and design guides such as the traditional web content accessibility guidelines (WCAG).

Preface

Standard ISO 9241-11 (2018) defines Usability as "The extent to which a product can be used by specified users to achieve specified goals with effectiveness, efficiency and satisfaction in a specified context of use", in this context, it is easy to perceive a strong relation between usability and accessibility. Nonetheless, accessibility is not naturally integrated in usable environments. (Lee & Lee, 2019) explain that accessibility "tends to emphasize objective features of a product and its use by people of all abilities. Accessibility pertains to a variety of components in the environment and requires guidelines for specific contexts". There are many guidance intended to achieve accessibility goals in a wide range of products including web and virtual environments; e.g. Web Content Accessibility Guidelines (WCAG2, n.d.) which states that "people with disabilities can perceive, understand, navigate, and interact with the Web, and that they can contribute to the Web". Another example is the well-known Web Accessibility Initiative (WAI, n.d.) which summarize essential principles of accessibility: perceivable content and interface, operable interface components for navigation and control, robust content compatible with other/future systems, and understandable content and interface.

Said context becomes particularly important in learning and educative processes, since education is a human right. People should have plenty access to education in every level (Dowden & Dowden, 2019; Elder, 2019). There are many barriers that people with disabilities face when they try to access to physical educative spaces including buildings, classrooms, and laboratories (Hamburg & Lütgen, 2019; Kim, Bessho, & Sakamura, 2019; Ackah-Jnr, & Danso, 2019). In this scenario, several technological solutions have emerged; web and virtual environments becomes popular alternatives, but many times, the proposals are not well designed since developers do not consider needs of people with disabilities (Kurt, 2019). It is crucial to ensure quality in new virtual environments for learning and to improve it in those currently available being essential both accessibility and usability (Lee & Lee, 2019; Ng, 2020; Ozdemir, Preast, & Duffy, 2018).

To realize and implement a robust need finding process that bear in mind a wide range of users is not easy and requires adequate guidance and flexibility to integrate successful approaches from other fields (Mourão & Netto, 2019; Smith & Abrams, 2019). Additionally, it is necessary to consider current technology in order to take advantage of available devices, services, software, and hardware (Kim, Bessho, & Sakamura, 2019; Lee & Lee, 2019).

In order to put together all these pieces concepts like User Centered Design (UCD) and User eXperience (UX) are mandatory. According to the Interaction Design Foundation (n.d.) "is an iterative design process in which designers focus on the users and their needs in each phase of the design process. In UCD, design teams involve users throughout the design process via a variety of research and design techniques, to create highly usable and accessible products for them". On the other hand, UX "focuses on having a deep understanding of users, what they need, what they value, their abilities, and also their limitations. It also takes into account the business goals and objectives of the group managing the project. UX best practices promote improving the quality of the user's interaction with and perceptions of your product and any related services", (Interaction Design Foundation, n.d.) Said approaches could be coherently integrated into strategies that help designers and developers to conform truly accessible and inclusive learning environments.

WHAT ABOUT THIS BOOK?

The main intention of this book is to provide a set of strategies based on principles and approaches from User eXperience Design (UXD), Human-Computer Interaction (HCI), and User Centered Design (UCD) to contribute in improving accessibility in learning environments. Here are described meaningful insights focused in aspects that could benefit accessibility and inclusiveness in learning environments by strategies to structure and convey of information, design, assessment, and redesign interactions with technology and spaces not only in the virtual context but physical. In this vein, the book integrates proposals oriented to foster awareness and ethics to design learning environments that support all students in their learning process. Insights, guidance, approaches, implementations, and even venues to explore as future work where provided here by experienced academics, practitioners, independent researchers, and postgraduate students.

As mentioned in Introduction, the book could be helpful for a wide range of target audiences:

- **Academy:** Researchers and students from related fields could use the book to reinforce, document, and/or justify their current research works and/or projects. The book could be inspirational for future academic works and could encourage initiatives for accessible governance in Institutions.
- **Government:** Accessible and equity in education represent a primary Government-goal. This book could represent a starting point for new strategies or redesign the existing ones.
- **Industry:** The book would foster improvements on design/development processes for accessible learning technology and provide guidance for implementation strategies.
- **Enthusiasts:** This book would be inspirational for many people interested in the covered topics.

ORGANIZATION OF THE BOOK

The book was organized in two sections and 15 chapters. A brief description of the chapters is presented below:

Section 1: Thoughts, Reflections, and Strategies on Accessible Education

- **Chapter 1**. This chapter presents in a descriptive and graphic way the evolution of accessibility metadata in educational resources, considering the different organisms and projects that contributed in investigations and establishment of standards for their implementation. The purpose is to justify the importance of its application in the optimal search of educational resources that responds to the needs and preferences of the user, considering the variability of learning and emphasizing the even greater requirements when dealing with students with disabilities. Accessibility is an issue that is developed optimally and its adoption is increasing, however, in the area of virtual environments and digital educational resources, the use of accessibility metadata is still incipient and requires to be understood from its implementation of comprehensive manner and the suitability of its application.

- **Chapter 2**. The chapter discuss some similarities in developing distance education online courses and Massive Open Online Courses (MOOCs), using the basis of eLearning instructional design. Authors emphasize some controversies such as the fact that the task of converting an online course into a MOOC is not as simple as direct migration of eLearning materials and assessment resources into a MOOC platform. In online learning learners should be continually influenced by information, social interaction and learning experiences, providing them with the knowledge to come up with new ideas to develop within an engaging course. In this chapter, the process of MOOCification a distance education online course on "Design for All for an Inclusive and Accessible Society" is explained and contextualized. The re-factorization process has been based upon the quality model used for MOOCs at UNED Abierta and the instructional design based on Gagné's events of instruction. The eLearning activities were completely refactored, along with the content itself, the interaction events and the online assessment following the Gardner's Multiple Intelligences product grid.
- **Chapter 3**. Authors considered the term Accessibility as the ability of an object to be used despite the condition or disability of a person; and argued that accessibility it is a feature that often has not been taken into account in the design of products or services and the mobile serious game market is no exception. They analyzed and defined some Accessibility guidelines defined through the consolidation of different initiatives and good practices of video game developers as well as groups interested in providing accessibility to video games. Once the guidelines were defined, a method for evaluating the accessibility of mobile serious games was developed and applied in a mobile serious game. The purpose of this document is to propose an evaluation tool for those who wish to develop accessible mobile serious games for people with impairments and improve inclusive education.
- **Chapter 4**. This chapter discusses universal design strategies that could be implemented in online courses. In the addition, the author discusses the application of universal design (UD) principles in a large (180 students) online Computer Applications in Sport and Entertainment Management course. A survey was completed by students to determine the impact of UD strategies that were incorporated in the course. The results showed the ability to use learning aids when completing assignments, receiving instant feedback on assignments and the ability to complete course assignments unlimited times before the due date are impactful to student learning. The purpose of this chapter is to provide educators with a bank of UD strategies that can be used in online courses.
- **Chapter 5**. Authors stated that a thorough and robust understanding of responsible and ethical practices in UX are essential to user experience designers. They also explain that Ethical UX practices include: authentic inclusion, vulnerability in participants, the inclusion of IRB-protected groups in research, tolerance for risk and motivation, truth in research, fair and respectful conduct, informed consent, cultural sensitivity, accessibility in UX processes, stigmatized populations, idiosyncratic populations, right to privacy, and an understanding of ADA-compliant accommodations by UX researchers and participants. This chapter will introduce these principles as well as demonstrate one possible application in an undergraduate design classroom.

- **Chapter 6**. The objective of this chapter was to assess the impact that haptic tools have on the experience of people with some kind of visual impairment when accessing a building. The analysis was performed through the application of a case study carried out in the facilities of the Center for Teleinformatics and Industrial Production of the National Learning Service in Popayán - Colombia with the participation of 5 people. Taking into account the principles of Universal Design, the analysis considered people with total blindness, partial blindness and people without visual limitation. Participants provided feedback and insights on their experience locating the designated area with and without the support of defined haptic tools. The study resulted in a set of drawbacks that influence the location of visually impaired people, such findings can be taken into account by people who wish to make projects of access to physical spaces of visually impaired people.
- **Chapter 7**. This chapter was intended to emphasize the need of user-centered technology for current generation of learners: "Multipotentielites". The scenario suggests that fostering attention in Multipotentialites is required for effective learning being empathy and emotions the key to achieve it. Important concepts such as User eXperience Design (UXD) and Learning eXperience Design (LXD) where analyzed here as pivotal aspects to envision both new educational / learning processes, and the environments / technologies that support them. Under this context, the chapter summarized several perceptions from experts by highlighting those Multipotentialites' qualities and skills that should be strengthen and exploited during learning processes where attention appears to be the new IQ.
- **Chapter 8**. The chapter emphasized reading as an important competency to be developed for children in the first years of elementary school since reading becomes a mechanism that allows the children to interact with the world and identify their characteristics. Author explained why Dyslexia is one of learning disability frequently manifested at elementary school, and how teachers require identify extra educative resources such as educational applications. This work proposes as solution a process model to design and develop educational applications considering the learning needs of children with dyslexia. It involves a user-centered approach because different perceptions of several actors are considered since the early phases of the process. The performance of the proposed model is thorough out a case study and an evaluation considering usability and accessibility factors.
- **Chapter 9**. Authors of this chapter argued that the inclusion of people with disabilities in society is an issue that is currently becoming relevant, this is why technology is in a constant struggle to develop tools that meet the needs of this sector of the population and with it fulfill this objective. They considered that one of said disabilities is blindness, therefore, this chapter shows an analysis of the application of Virtual Reality (VR) and haptic devices as support tools in the teaching-learning of people with such disabilities through the study of various projects that has implement these technologies, Obtaining the advantages and disadvantages offered by these resources. For this, an analysis is made from the point of view of accessibility that it presents as well as the approach of the User Centered Design (UCD).

Section 2: Design, Assessment, and Redesign of Technology for Accessible Education

- **Chapter 10**. Author of this chapter describe how Virtual Reality has captured the attention of people. Since the Virtual Reality has become more realistic, with the evolution of the technology like the innovation of smartphones, the VR has been more accessible for society, many industries have begun research on the application of VR for training, for learning about certain specific topics as it allows reducing accidents and maximizes safety. Author emphasize that the use of VR in Education Industry has been best seen as a tool to complement certain issues that may be difficult to understand since it can allow to virtually move to certain areas from safely areas. And identified the lack of design and development strategies fully specialized to implicitly include the promote learning, much less the consideration of people with disabilities. In this vein, the main objective of this chapter is the presentation of a design process for the development of Virtual Learning Environments that allows accessibility.
- **Chapter 11**. The objective of this chapter is to identify web accessibility problems in order to fulfill the design guidelines. According to the proposal, accessibility is assessed through easy checks of the implementation of the social engineering educational platform. As a first phase, the developer carries out this evaluation and their results are analyzed. In the second phase, solves the identified problems or at least tries to give them a solution implementing a redesign on the platform; in the same way the results are analyzed. In the third phase, a proposal is made of the improvements that can be introduced in the redesign of the user interface in a way that best complies with the web accessibility. The problem identified shows the difficulty of implementing the accessibility guides and the need to propose accessibility implementation guidelines that guarantee their compliance.
- **Chapter 12**. Author explained how evaluating software implies challenging users' abilities during a period, applying several assessments and analyzing their evolution. He described why this process might turn unpleasant and stressful, especially to those susceptible to anxiety and stress, such as Down syndrome users. Additionally, analyze how the poor performance of unpleasant users generates unreal results. A gamified approach for software testing is proposed here, which maintains user's motivation and engagement, and reduces anxiety and stress. Common behaviors expected are anxiety, stress, unwilling to work and, in general, lack of motivation. The proposal showed how using gamification, makes possible succeed in controlling common negative behaviors mentioned and stimulating the positive ones. The process included the MDA framework into a generic learnability evaluation process, linking these two elements with the psychological approach of Gestalt therapy. Founds showed how gamifying the testing experience increased the quality of communication between users and applicators, provided a friendly, motivational, and engaging environment, and increased the rate of testing success and the range of potential participants.
- **Chapter 13**. The chapter described an analysis and those derived design improvements for an Accessibility course offered by Tecnológico Nacional de México / IT Aguascalientes (ITA). The course is addressed to train professors for awareness and implementation of educational strategies that allow an accessible and inclusive learning environment. Enhancements found was oriented to makes easier teachers' tasks when generating strategies for the creation of accessible educational content. All suggestions derived from a usability analysis of both: Interactive elements and the structure of the course on the on-line learning platform Moodle. The study was performed by im-

plementing several international standards and design guides such as the traditional Web Content Accessibility Guidelines (WCAG).

- **Chapter 14**. Authors explained that concept of inclusive education goes beyond considering the needs of people with disabilities; it refers to the process of recognizing the students' learning needs and to act according to such needs. They discussed why people with visual limitations do not necessarily require more attention and dedication than other people; since many times just an initially guided and to have accessible information were required. The chapter emphasize that one of the main challenges of the universal education is to generate inclusive and assistive educational technologies, which can be used for the teaching and learning of people with disabilities. In this chapter the development and assessment of haptic-enabled virtual reality learning systems for the education of non-sighted people are presented and discussed. These virtual systems represent the research work conducted to promote the accessible education of blind people, and to determine the effectiveness of virtual touch in the education of blind people.
- **Chapter 15**. This chapter was intended to describe the insights towards a proposal to integrate a procedural content generation strategy in a computer role-playing usable and accessible learning video game for gaining replayability to encourage engagement and motivation in learners. In order to explain the contextual issues of the topic, authors included a discussion on how computer role-playing video games impact on the skills considered as crucial for the work in the future abstraction, system thinking, experimentation and collaboration emphasizing the importance of usability and accessibility to ensure effectiveness of the proposal. A first approach of a computer role-playing video game is presented to provide an illustrative example and to establish a starting point for future evaluations with people for usability and accessibility.

REFERENCES

Ackah-Jnr, F. R., & Danso, J. B. (2019). Examining the physical environment of Ghanaian inclusive schools: How accessible, suitable and appropriate is such environment for inclusive education? *International Journal of Inclusive Education, 23*(2), 188–208. doi:10.1080/13603116.2018.1427808

Dowden, M., & Dowden, M. (2019). Why Should I Care About Accessibility? In Approachable Accessibility (pp. 1-18). Apress. doi:10.1007/978-1-4842-4881-2_1

Elder, A. (2019). *Accessibility and Usability*. OER Starter Kit.

Hamburg, I., & Lütgen, G. (2019). Digital Divide, Digital Inclusion and Inclusive Education. *Advances in Social Sciences Research Journal, 6*(4).

Interaction Design Foundation. (n.d.). *User Centered Design*. Retrieved from: https://www.interaction-design.org/literature/topics/user-centered-design

ISO 9241-11. (2018). *Ergonomics of human-system interactions – Part 11: Usability: Definitions and concepts.* Retrieved from http://www.iso.org/obp/ui/#iso:std:iso:9241:-11:ed-2:v1:en

Kim, J. E., Bessho, M., & Sakamura, K. (2019, March). Towards a Smartwatch Application to Assist Students with Disabilities in an IoT-enabled Campus. In *2019 IEEE 1st Global Conference on Life Sciences and Technologies (LifeTech)* (pp. 243-246). IEEE. 10.1109/LifeTech.2019.8883995

Kurt, S. (2019). Moving toward a universally accessible web: Web accessibility and education. *Assistive Technology*, *31*(4), 199–208. doi:10.1080/10400435.2017.1414086 PMID:29219749

Lee, Y., & Lee, J. (2019). A checklist for assessing blind users' usability of educational smartphone applications. *Universal Access in the Information Society*, 1–18.

Mourão, A. B., & Netto, J. F. D. M. (2019). Inclusive Model Application Using Accessible Learning Objects to Support the Teaching of Mathematics. *Informatics in Education*, *18*(1), 213–226. doi:10.15388/infedu.2019.10

Ng, W. S. (2020). Enhancing the quality of educational website design through assessment for learning strategies. In Learning and Performance Assessment: Concepts, Methodologies, Tools, and Applications (pp. 1106-1133). IGI Global. doi:10.4018/978-1-7998-0420-8.ch052

Ozdemir, D., Preast, V., & Duffy, P. A. (2018). Systematic approach for improving accessibility and usability in online courses. In *Handbook of research on human development in the digital age* (pp. 258–280). IGI Global. doi:10.4018/978-1-5225-2838-8.ch012

Smith, K., & Abrams, S. S. (2019). Gamification and accessibility. *The International Journal of Information and Learning Technology*, *36*(2), 104–123. doi:10.1108/IJILT-06-2018-0061

Web Accessibility Initiative. (n.d.). *WAI*. Retrieved from: https://www.w3.org/WAI

Web Content Accessibility Guidelines. (n.d.). *WCAG2*. Retrieved from: https://www.w3.org/TR/WCAG20

Acknowledgement

Editors would like to acknowledge the help of all the people involved in this project and, more specifically, to the colleagues that took part in the review process ensuring the improvement of quality, coherence, and content presentation of chapters. Without their support, this book would not have become a reality.

Our sincere gratitude goes to the chapter's authors and coauthors who contributed their invaluable time, knowledge, and expertise to this book.

Introduction

UNESCO (n.d.) states that "Ensuring that each individual has an equal opportunity for educational progress remains a challenge worldwide" and emphasize that inclusion and equity are fundamentals in education quality. Education is a human right, and no one should be excluded from, or limited to educational opportunities.

In this context, institutions, educators, students, and many other stakeholders will require technology that support inclusion and promote equity for both learning processes and governance in educational institutions.

This scenario has been encouraging the development and implementation of guidelines for accessible education, particularly for learning through technology since virtual education appear to be the learning modality for the future. Alternatives are oriented to adapt and generate educational programs and solutions compatible with inclusive and accessible learning, e.g. the UNESCO Guidelines for inclusion: ensuring access to education for all (UNESCO, n.d.) Guidelines on accessible education, of Ontario Human Rights Commission (n.d.), among others.

Initiatives as those mentioned above states a general frame for accessibility but should be complemented by specific approaches addressed to ensure good designs (those that help people do things that they care about). According to the Design Council (n.d.) "The central premise of User Centered Design is that the best designed products and services result from understanding the needs of the people who will use them"; so, a well understanding of users needs its imperative to achieve adequate learning technology. Traditionally, User Centered-Design Process, Human-Computer Interaction, and User eXperience Design represent the way to do this job. Nevertheless, many of the available proposals in these fields tend to focus on integrating ease of use and aesthetic design on technological solutions leaving aside accessibility aspects. Professionals around the world are very concerned about this; e.g. Sheena Lyonnais, Writer and digital specialist, wrote on the Billy Gregory's (Web accessibility developer, Director of Training with The Paciello Group) perception "It's a UX designer's job to think of all users, not some Users" to avoid the concept "SOME Users eXperience, a.k.a. SUX" that refers to "user experiences that suit the larger population overall, but do not go the extra step to ensure they're usable and accessible for all users" ("Why Designing", n.d.).

It is true that design is a crucial piece of the puzzle and demand guidance to be perceived as good design, e.g. by implementing User Centered-Design and /or User eXperience Design; but should consider accessibility aspects from early stages of design processes. This integration allows to understand users' needs from an inclusive perspective. In this way; to be usable in educational technology is not enough and have a tremendous impact in designing accessible technology for education since education is a Human right (UNESCO, n.d.) and every resource should be accessible and usable for all people.

Integration of usability and accessibility in learning technology could be a complicated endeavor and need to be structured over a controlled and evolutive process oriented to design solutions that could offer adequate experiences for users.

This book is intended to promote in readers the importance of considering the User eXperience Design, User Centered-Design processes, and accessibility criteria by means of guidance and frameworks in order to develop technology (Hardware, Software, or Services) for truly accessible and equity education. This book describes and discusses the perception of practitioners, researchers, academics, organizations, institutions, students, industrial, and enthusiasts on design and development of accessible and equity learning technology. This thoughts and background come from Human Computer-Interaction, User Centered-Design, User eXperience Design, Learning User eXperience, User Research, Technology Education, Design Thinking, among other related knowledge fields. provided by to contributing from our "trench" to mitigate this global challenge.

In this way, the book could be helpful for a wide range of target audience:

- **Academy:** Researchers and students from related fields could use the book to reinforce, document, and/or justify their current research works and/or projects. The book could be inspirational for future academic works and could encourage initiatives for accessible governance in Institutions.
- **Government:** Accessible and equity in education represent a primary Government-goal. This book could represent a starting point for new strategies or redesign the existing ones.
- **Industry:** The book would foster improvements on design/development processes for accessible learning technology and provide guidance for implementation strategies.
- **Enthusiasts:** This book would be inspirational for many people interested in the covered topics.

On the other hand, it is true that other books in the market address brilliantly (but separately) the project's topics A) User eXperience Design and User Centered Design approaches; and B) Designing Accessible Educational Technology; such as *End-User Considerations in Educational Technology Design* by Roscoe, R. D., Craig, S. D., & Douglas (2017) where editors put together knowledge on "usability testing techniques and user-centered design methodologies in the development of technological tools for learning environments"; and *Design for Inclusivity: A Practical Guide to Accessible, Innovative and User-Centered Design (Design for Social Responsibility)* by Coleman, Clarkson and Cassim (2016); here, authors emphasize that "inclusive design not only ensures that products, services, interfaces and environments are easier to use for those with special needs or limitations, but in doing so also makes them better for everyone." User eXperience and User Centered Design Approaches for Accessible Education is intended to integrate both topics to conform a coherent reference for academics, students, researchers, and practitioners on designing, developing, and implementing accessible learning technology by putting together knowledge from the *trenches*.

Ricardo Mendoza-González
Tecnológico Nacional de México IT Aguascalientes, Mexico

REFERENCES

Adobe Blog. (n.d.). *Why Designing Only For Some Users "SUX"*. Retrieved from: https://xd.adobe.com/ideas/perspectives/social-impact/designing-users-sux/

Coleman, R., Clarkson, J., & Cassim, J. (2016). *Design for Inclusivity: A Practical Guide to Accessible, Innovative and User-Centred Design*. Abingdon, UK: Taylor and Francis. doi:10.4324/9781315576626

Design Council UK. (n.d.). Retrieved from: https://www.designcouncil.org.uk/

Ontario Human Rights Commission. (n.d.). *Guidelines on Accessible Education*. Retrieved from: http://www.ohrc.on.ca/sites/default/files/attachments/Guidelines_on_accessible_education.pdf

Roscoe, R. D., Craig, S. D., & Douglas, I. (2018). *End-User Considerations in Educational Technology Design*. Hershey, PA: IGI Global. doi:10.4018/978-1-5225-2639-1

UNESCO. (n.d.). *Inclusion in Education*. Retrieved from: https://en.unesco.org/themes/inclusion-in-education

Section 1
Thoughts, Reflections, and Strategies on Accessible Education

Chapter 1
Evolution of Accessibility Metadata in Educational Resources

Salvador Otón Tortosa
https://orcid.org/0000-0002-6417-1779
Universidad de Alcalá, Spain

Paola Cristina Ingavélez-Guerra
https://orcid.org/0000-0003-3250-6156
Universidad Politécnica Salesiana, Ecuador

Sandra Sánchez-Gordón
https://orcid.org/0000-0002-2940-7010
Escuela Politécnica Nacional, Ecuador

Mary Sánchez-Gordón
https://orcid.org/0000-0002-5102-1122
Østfold University College, Norway

ABSTRACT

This chapter presents in a descriptive and visual way the evolution of accessibility metadata in educational resources, considering the different organizations and projects that contributed in investigations and establishment of standards for their implementation. The purpose is to justify the importance of its application in the optimal search of educational resources that responds to the needs and preferences of the user, considering the variability of learning and emphasizing the even greater requirements when dealing with students with disabilities. Accessibility is an issue that is developed optimally, and its adoption is increasing; however, in the area of virtual environments and digital educational resources, the use of accessibility metadata is still incipient and requires to be understood from its implementation of comprehensive manner and the suitability of its application.

DOI: 10.4018/978-1-7998-2325-4.ch001

INTRODUCTION

Advances in information and communication technologies, and specifically in multimedia, networking and software engineering have promoted a new generation of online learning environments. Currently, the Internet is the ubiquitous supporting environment for virtual and distributed learning environments. In fact, the adoption and implementation of e-learning innovations have become more demanding in recent years (Valiente et al., 2015). As a result, many organizations, both public and private, take advantage of new technologies to offer educational and training products and services at all levels (Anido et al., 2002). In particular, the wide availability of educational resources is a common objective for universities, libraries, archives and other knowledge-intensive institutions. There is also growing empowerment of instructors to collaborate with their students and other instructors in order to produce, share and reuse educational resources (Valiente et al., 2015). In this context, educational metadata has been recognized as one of the most fruitful fields in the standardization of education technologies (Anido et al., 2002), (Solomou, Pierrakeas, & Kameas, 2015). However, the emergence of large collections of learning resources created through the harvesting and aggregation of metadata have raised important concerns on the suitability of educational resource descriptions as provided in metadata schemas (Valiente et al., 2015). Thus, the ability to effectively manage educational resources in terms of findability, reusability, interoperability and accessibility lies in the adoption of an appropriate metadata schema, able to adequately describe them (Solomou et al., 2015). Despite this fact, only a little research has been done in this area and even more, to the best of our knowledge, there is not a comprehensive solution for the management of accessibility metadata. Accessibility is a key feature to promote inclusive education and training in virtual and distributed learning environments where there is a great diversity in the accessibility needs and preferences of students (Sanchez-Gordon & Luján-Mora, 2018). In this context, this chapter is devoted to better understand the evolution of the accessibility metadata in educational resources by reviewing the most relevant milestones up to date.

BACKGROUND

Historically, technology and its functionality in the teaching-learning process had offered students a variety of possibilities regarding interaction experiences according to their learning needs and preferences. The first attempt at using educational resources in the context of distance education dates from 1728. It was via printed correspondence. In 1971, the British Broadcasting Corporation (BBC) began airing on television Open University´s educational materials in the format of recorded lectures. In the 1990s, several universities developed technologies to manage digital educational resources given birth to Learning Content Management Systems (LCMS) and later to Learning Management Systems (LMS). In 2002, the Massachusetts Institute of Technology (MIT) launched the OpenCourseWare initiative, now Open Education Consortium, to provide free online access to educational resources from MIT courses. In the same year, the United Nations Educational, Scientific and Cultural Organization (UNESCO) coined Open Educational Resources (OER) to refer to teaching-learning materials released under an open license that permits no-cost access, use, adaptation and redistribution (Sanchez-Gordon & Luján-Mora, 2018b). In 2012, Massive Open Online Courses (MOOC) debuted to complement regular university courses. MOOCs differ from traditional online courses hosted in LMS platforms in that MOOC can have an unlimited number of participants, MOOC do not have enrollment requirements, and MOOC can be taken for free by optionally paying only for official certificates or extra services, such as instructor feedback. By 2018, the global MOOC offer included 11,400 online courses offered by 900 institutions, with 101 million students. The massive and open nature of MOOC implies heterogeneity in students. The accessibility of MOOC and the educational resources contained in them must be guaranteed, since the probability that students with different types of disabilities participate in a MOOC is much greater than in traditional face-to-face, distance or online courses. MOOC can greatly facilitate the education of people with some type of disability. However, in order for a student with a specific disability to be able to use a MOOC, the educational resources must be available in accessible formats and there have to be metadata mechanisms to identify which accessible educational resource is best suited for different accessibility needs and preferences, as well as different learning styles. When we approach accessibility, we respond to several questions that have been generated from a mythical "typical student" without considering the variability of each person's own learning, characteristics that enrich the educational process and constitute constant challenges for developers and consumers of educational resources. Despite the opportunities that educational technology presents, it is still used to support objectives, methods and evaluations of a traditional curriculum. This excludes students who are in the margins, such as people with disabilities.

The MOOCs life cycle proposed by (Sanchez-Gordon & Luján-Mora, 2018c) includes the selection of educational resources from repositories such as OER Commons and MERLOT. The use of these types of repositories offers some guarantee of quality, since the educational resources hosted have gone through a process of validation. On educational resources repositories, high findability is a desirable condition and metadata are essential for findability. "The lack of information or metadata about objects places a critical and fundamental constraint on our ability to discover, manage, and use OERs." (IEEE, 2002).

When we create educational resources and describe their accessibility characteristics through some metadata specification, it is just one of the steps to make those resources understandable by students with disabilities. In order for educational resources to be located, we will have to incorporate them into a repository or a virtual learning platform (for example Moodle). In both, we can store a set of educational resources to share with the educational community or for creating a course. In general, one of the most important tool that has a repository or a virtual learning platform is to bring the possibility of search in their educational content. If the educational resource has been described with accessibility metadata and the student has a description of its personal needs and preferences, the tool can choose the most adequate educational resources so that the student can understand its content (Batanero et al., 2017).

A virtual learning platform uses a technology that focuses on the development, management and publication of the contents and activities that contribute to the teaching-learning process. Virtual learning platforms work with web technology through a client-server model and currently with a tendency to provide services distributed through the "cloud". If it is an accessible virtual learning platform (Otón et al., 2015), it must be guaranteed that all the functionality can be used by any user, including users with functional diversity.

Several recommendations, standards and vocabularies had been proposed to enhance the management of the metadata of online objects. Few of them focus on educational resources and less deal with accessibility metadata. Among them we have (ISO/IEC 24751-1, 2008) Information technology - Individualized adaptability and accessibility in e-learning, education and training, defines Accessibility as "Usability of a product, service, environment or installation by individuals with the broadest spectrum of possible aptitudes", and to the adaptability as the "capacity of a digital resource of a system of provision to adjust the presentation, the methods of control, the structure, the way of access and the support to the user, in his presentation".

Relevant regulations such as (ISO 9241-11, 2018) Ergonomics of human-system interaction -- Part 11: Usability: Definitions and concepts", (ISO / IEC 19796-3, 2009) Learning, education and training - Quality management, assurance and metrics - Part 3: Reference methods and metrics, Information technology, (ISO/IEC 19778-3, 2015) Learning, education and training - Collaborative technology - Collaborative workplace - Part 3: Collaborative group data model, (ISO/IEC 24751-3, 2008) Information technology - Individualized adaptability and accessibility in e-learning, education and training - Part 3", Access for all "digital resource description without forgetting Information Technology - W3C Web Content Accessibility Guidelines (WCAG, 2018) 2.0 (ISO/IEC 40500, 2012), now 2.1, contribute significantly in the issue of accessibility and usability. However, these specifications contain a large amount of information that often discourages most developers of educational resources when trying to apply accessibility.

Some relevant metadata specifications and standards are the Dublin Core Metadata Initiative Element Set (DCMES) evolved in the Learning Resource Metadata Initiative (LRMI) (DCMI, 2012), the IEEE 1484.12.1 Learning Object Metadata (LOM) (IEEE, 2002) and the schema.org vocabulary, which are detailed in the next section.

STATE OF THE ART

In this section, the authors review the most important elements related to accessibility in online education, in particular, we focus on the specifications and standards related to accessibility metadata in educational resources and their evolution.

Metadata

In this chapter, the term "metadata" is related to data that describes other data. According to DAMA (2009), metadata are "data on data". The metadata provide relevant information about the object they describe, thus one can see structured information in various areas such as: bibliographic, geospatial objects, visual resources, museums, software implementations, educational resources, and so on. In other words, metadata are the basic information blocks for the development of applications and electronic government systems. Once the metadata is defined, such metadata can be shared and reused on multiple occasions. This reuse entails the following benefits:

- To increase interoperability among different systems that share data and services.
- To reduce the cost in the development of interoperable systems, since the reuse avoids the treatment of ambiguities within the applications.
- To facilitate the processing of data in information systems in general, and in particular in those that integrate and share data, for example, support systems for decision making.

Another broader definition was done by NISO (2004) as follows "structured information that describes, explains, locates or facilitates recovery, uses or manages an information resource". Moreover, in this case, the different use of the term in different communities is qualified. Thus, it is sometimes used to refer to information that can be interpreted by computers while it is used only to describe electronic resources, in other contexts. In the library environment, metadata are normally used for any formal scheme or description of resources, which can be applied to any type of object, digital or non-digital.

MARC21 (2010), the traditional cataloguing of libraries is a form of metadata because its set of rules is based on metadata standards. Furthermore, other metadata schemas have been developed to describe various types of textual and non-textual objects, such as published books, electronic documents, search help tools, art objects, educational and training materials, and scientific sets. A similar approach was proposed by Sicilia (2006), who identified the relationships between the purpose for which they were conceived and the own description of the nature of the metadata. Thus, the metadata can be focused on facilitating recovery, establishing an intellectual property, directing the behavior of an online system, facilitating the combination of various resources, and so on.

In turn, the metadata can be grouped or structured as "metadata schemes", a set of metadata for a specific purpose or to make a standard (NISO, 2004). These are sets of elements designed for a specific purpose, such as describing a specific type of information about a resource. The definition or meaning of the elements in itself is known as the semantics of the scheme. The values given to the elements of the metadata are its content. Metadata schemas usually specify the names of the elements and their semantics. Optionally, they can specify content rules on how their content can be established (such as establishing the main title) and the possible values for the content. Thus, for example, the terms may come from a specific controlled vocabulary. There may also be syntax rules about how elements and their content should be encoded. A metadata schema without established syntax rules is called independent syntax. The metadata can be encoded in any definable syntax such as SGML, XML or JSON.

History

The first reference to the concept of metadata can be found in the 1960s (Manso-Callejo et al., 2010). The term was coined by Myers and appears in the field of library management. However, the value of metadata repositories began to be recognized in the 90s. In the middle of this decade, they became more relevant especially in companies that tried to understand what their information resources were. Its extension is also associated with the appearance of the Web (Anastasiou, 2010) and in parallel, with the need to scale and filter information. Tim Berners Lee defined the metadata in 1997 as "information understandable by the machine for the Web".

The first workshop took place in Dublin (Ohio, 1995) and the set of elements "Dublin Core Metadata" (DCMI, 2009) was created. They were extended mainly by the commitment of the deadline of the year 2000, which made emerge very specific initiatives that demanded standardization within the applications of companies. For example, the "CASE Definition Interchange Facility" developed by the Electronics Industries Alliance in 1995, as well as the aforementioned Dublin Core initiative, which will be discussed at length later on. In turn, the Object Management Group (OMG) developed the "Common Warehouse Metadata Model (CWM)" in 1998. On the other hand, Microsoft supported the alternative called "Metadata Coalitions" in 1995. In the year 2000, the two standards were melted in CWM.

The first years of the 21st century were characterized by the updating of the repositories of existing metadata for issues related to the Web. The history of metadata management tools is characterized by the lack of methodological focus on information management that prevails in organizations. The lack of standards and the very nature of most metadata management solutions are the reasons why many organizations have not used them. However, the growing importance of information is leading the products for metadata management to standardization and to follow a more methodological approach.

Dublin Core

The set of metadata elements of Dublin Core (DCMI, 2009) is a vocabulary of fifteen properties or semantic definitions for the description of resources. It is described in ISO 15836: 2017 (ISO, 2017) as part of a set of broader vocabulary metadata and technical specifications maintained by the Dublin Core Agency (DCMI).

In addition to these basic elements (none mandatory and all repeatable), there are other mechanisms that serve to adapt the Dublin Core to the specific information needs and make this metadata model applicable to any system project or digital information service. These mechanisms are fundamentally:

- Application profiles, developed for the use of Dublin Core associated with different disciplines. An example is the application profile for libraries: DC-Lib.
- The terms of metadata (metadata terms), which include both the new elements that are incorporated into the DC vocabulary, and the qualifications of existing elements, coding schemes (formerly known as "qualifiers") as well as the terms of controlled vocabularies. All these metadata terms help to adapt and identify the value and usefulness of the meta information expressed through DC.

Dublin Core implementations generally use XML and are based on the Resource Description Framework (RDF). The Dublin Core metadata is being used as the basis for descriptive systems for various interest groups, such as:

- Government institutions.
- Scientific research sector.
- Authors of web pages.
- Businesses that require more researchable places.
- Corporations with extensive management systems in knowledge.

Educational Resources

In this section, the most important specifications and standards related to educational resources metadata will be reviewed.

LOM

The IEEE LOM or LOM (Learning Object Metadata) standard (IEEE, 2002) is an open standard that specifies syntax and semantics of the required attributes for metadata of learning objects. LOM standard Includes rules to control the identification of data elements and their attributes. It also provides principles, rules and structures for the specification of those same resources. Its objective is to facilitate the search, evaluation, recovery and use of learning objects. Moreover, IEEE LOM is considered the most accepted and implemented standard in multiple repositories of learning objects (Otón, et al.,, 2014). There are numerous versions and extensions of LOM that have been developed from IEEE LOM. It is organized into 9 categories, where each of them contains subcategories that can share basic characteristics (Pons et al., 2016), (Vizoso, 2017)

IEEE LOM was developed and formalized through the IEEE and the Learning Technology Standards Committee. Finally, it is worth noting that the ISO/IEC 19788 Metadata Learning Resource, published in January 2011, is closely related to it as well as its set of elements has an equivalence with those elements of Dublin Core.

LRMI (Learning Resource Metadata Initiative)

This initiative began in 2011, its aim was to develop a specification as an educational extension for Schema.org. LRMI Properties are intended to describe educational resources by adding specific properties so that they can be easily located through search engines and services (Navarrete & Lujan-Mora, 2018). The specifications are based on the vocabulary given by Schema.org and other standards. Therefore, there are LRMI terms not included in Schema.org. With the support of Association of Educational Publishers (AEP), Association of American Publishers, Creative Commons (CC), division 501, Bill & Melinda Gates, and the William and Flora Hewlett Foundation, LRMI has developed a metadata framework to tag web learning resources. The LRMI 1.1 scheme was adopted by Schema.org in 2013, which makes it possible for resources, through their LRMI metadata, to be recognized by the main search engines (DCMI: LRMI Terms, 2012). The properties considered are:

LRMI to Schema.org/CreativeWork

- **educationalAligment:** Established educational framework
- **educationalUse:** Purpose of work in the context of education
- **timeRequired:** Approximate time it takes to work on the resource
- **typicalAgeRange:** End-user age range
- **interactivityType:** Active, exhibition or mixed
- **learningResourceType:** Predominant type of resource, for example: presentation, brochure, etc.
- **useRightsUrl:** URL where the resource use permissions are established. Schema adopted the License property instead of useRightsUrl
- **isBasedOnUrl:** Resource that was used for the creation

LRMI to Schema.org/Intangibles/AligmentObject

- **aligmentType:** Alignment between the learning resource and the framework node. Recommended values include: 'evaluate', 'teach', 'require', 'textComplexity', 'readingLevel', 'educationalSubject', and 'educationLevel'
- **educationalFramework:** Resource description framework
- **targetDescription:** Description of the node of an educational framework
- **targetName:** Name of the node of an educational framework
- **targetUrl:** URL of a node of the educational framework

LRMI to Schema.org/Audence/EducationalAudience

- **EducationalRole:** Target Audience

AEP and CC requested that the administration of the LRMI specification is assigned to DCMI. Being adopted by Schema.org, it is possible to standardize a tag that allows LRMI to adopt trusted resources while its metadata are recognized by the main search engines.

IMS AfA

The main goal of IMS Access for All (AfA) v3.0 (IMS, 2012) was to simplify the ISO/IEC 24751 standard (ISO, 2008a, b, c), due to the difficulties that arose in practice. Both, ISO/IEC 24751 standard and AfA v3.0, cover the entire process from the reading of the user's needs to the search mechanism that is necessary to find the learning objects which satisfies those needs or preferences. It has two data models (figure 1) for description:

- **Personal Needs and Preferences (PNP):** A model for the description of the needs and preferences of the users to access and interact with digital resources.
- **Digital Resource Description (DRD):** A model for the description of the accessibility metadata for digital learning resources.

The AfA DRD specification (see figure 1) defines accessibility metadata for a resource that will be used for the search and use of the most fitting learning resource for each user according to PNPs. The LOMPAD tool was enabled to introduce accessibility metadata (besides ordinary metadata) according to the IMS 3.0 specification (Otón et al., 2014).

The way of working with accessible learning objects requires the creation of original and adapted learning objects. There are different tools that facilitate their creation (Mirri et al., 2006; Di Iorio et al., 2006; The Xerte project, 2008). An original resource corresponds to an initial resource, while an adapted resource presents the same educational information that the initial or original resource. However other characteristics change, such as the sensorial manner of access to the resource, the language, etc. For example, a file with a pdf format as an original resource and an audio description of its content as an adapted resource. The first presents textual access while the adaptation presents auditory access to the same educational content. Therefore, the original resources can have any number of adaptations, which can be total or partial, it means they are either adaptations of the entire educational content or only of a part of it.

Metadata can support the adequate information of original resources, such as access mode (vision, hearing, alphabetization, presentation, transformation feasibility, control, flexibility, adaptations, help tools, etc.), and information that is relevant about adapted resources, such as type of adaptation (subtitles, sign language), extension, description, among others. A fusion of resources + descriptive metadata + accessibility metadata means to consolidate a source of accessible repositories which strengthens the search for learning objects according to the special educational needs.

The accessible online education research work started with the Web-4-All (2003) and TILE (2004) projects, which respectively made internet connection possible in workstations located in public places in Canada, and permitted access to a learning objects repository by following IMS AfA v1.0 (IMS, 2003; IMS, 2004). Likewise, Mirri et al. (2011) presented the adaptation of the aTutor learning platform, following the IMS v1.0 standards (IMS, 2003; IMS, 2004) and ISO/IEC 24751-1-2-3 (ISO, 2008 a-b-c). There is another work based on IMS AfA v2.0 (IMS, 2009) related to the accessibility of the learning environments, in particular, the Moodle learning platform (Brahim et al., 2013; Laabidi et al., 2014). In

Figure 1. IMS Access For All 3.0 digital resource description properties

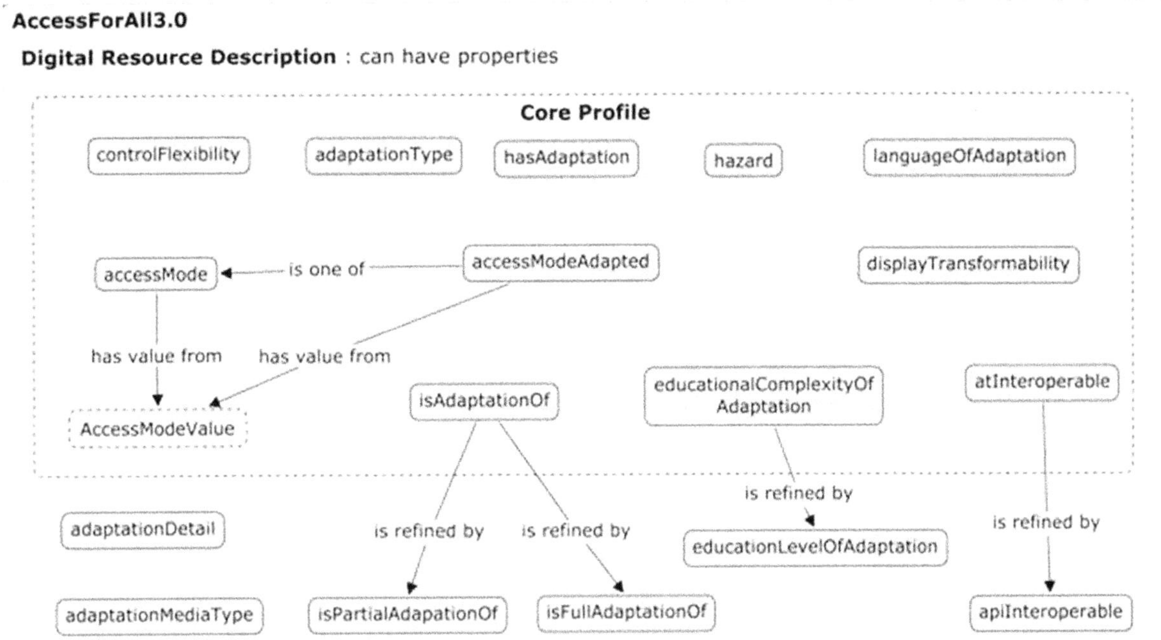

relation to the IMS v3.0 (IMS, 2012), the adaptation of the Moodle platform carried out by (Batanero et al., 2017) deserves to be mentioned.

The aim of the AfA PNP specification (figure 2) is to enable the definition of the personal needs of the students (or those related to disability environments). The PNPs are used in combination with the AfA DRD specification to deliver digital resources that satisfy the needs of a user and/or his or her preferences. The PNPs of the student or user define his or her preferences in the use of different sensorial modes for the perception of information. The suggested method to generate the PNPs of the student is the presentation of a form with different options about the preferred sensorial mode for the access of information. The PNPs will be generated from the student's responses to the questions in the form.

The principles of accessibility on e-learning are focused on providing personalization options based on the preferences of the user, content equivalents and compatibility with technical help, and complete keyboard access, as well as giving information about the context and offering support so the user can follow specifications on directives and/or norms of governing bodies such as IMS. A method that assesses the accessibility of virtual learning environments was published by Batanero et al. (2014). The method establishes a relation between the accessibility metadata introduced in the learning objects and the levels of compliance (A, AA and AAA) established in the accessibility norms for Web content (WCAG 2.0).

Another tool that should be considered in accessible online education are accessible repositories of learning objects. In this vein, the TILE (2004) repository deserves to be mentioned, however, there are other experiences building the architectures of distributed repositories of learning objects (Otón et al., 2010) and their application to accessible learning repositories based on IMS AfA v3.0 (Otón et al., 2015).

Figure 2. IMS Access For All 3.0 personal needs and preferences properties

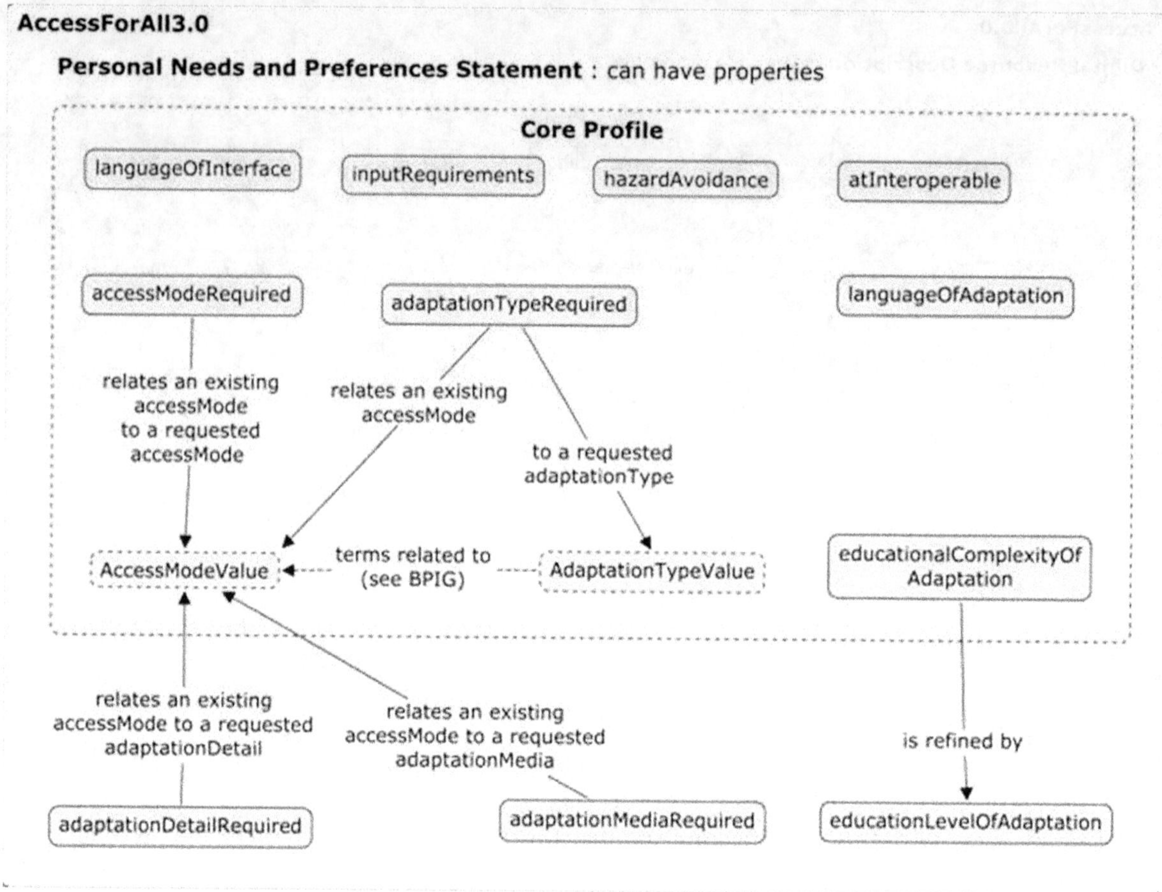

Schema.org

Schema.org is a community that is responsible for creating, maintaining and promoting metadata schemas for structured data that are published on the Internet. These schemes are constantly evolving, in fact, specific ones have been developed for accessibility. The most interesting aspect about Schema.org is that it receives the support of large companies such as Google, Microsoft and Yahoo. This means that the incorporation of metadata to the content published on the Internet is essential in order to be able to categorize them and describe their accessibility characteristics.

The most used formats for making semantic annotations are microdata, microformats, JSON-LD and RDFa (Sikos, 2015). Undoubtedly microdata is the most popular and most popular (Meusel et al., 2014). The microdata format has been developed in the context of the standardization of HTML5 for the marking of web content. Microdata consists of a group of name-value pairs; the groups are called elements and each pair name-value is a property. The elements are defined by the following five attributes: itemscope, itemtype, itemid, itemprop and itemref. These annotations provide semantics through the terminology and properties of a knowledge representation domain including its relationships.

Figure 3. Accessibility metadata from CreativeWork on Schema.org

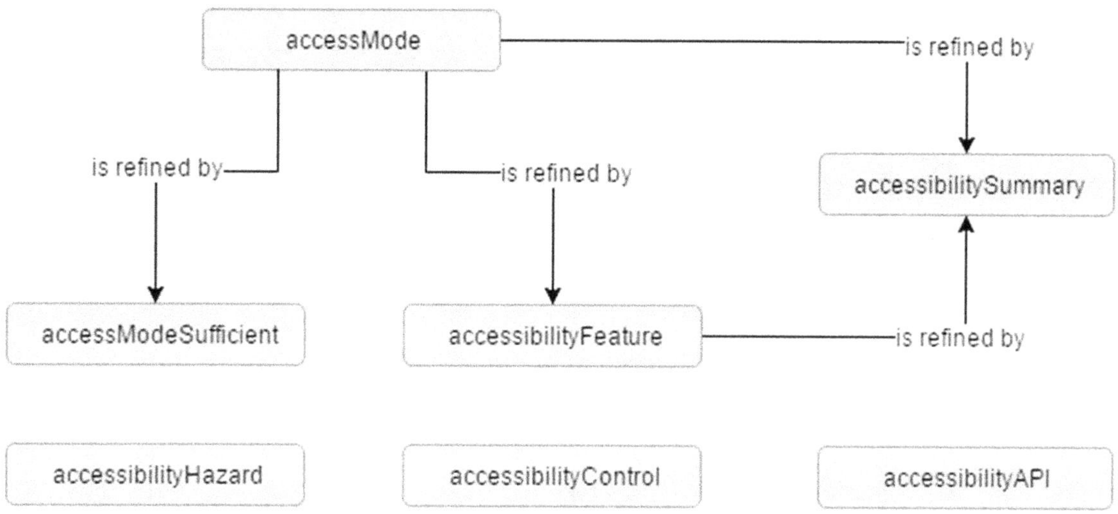

The Schema.org specification establishes a collection of shared vocabularies that include properties to describe some characteristics of different types of web content. These descriptions can be understood by the main search engines. In the case of Google, its search engine uses the HTML5 microdata of Schema.org to improve the results of its searches, and even more allows anyone to make a custom search using Schema.org's different schemes to restrict searches.

Accessibility on Shema.org

To define accessibility metadata in Schema.org, different types of web content are defined and can be classified using metadata schemas. Figure 3 shows an example of this approach, the "CreativeWork" type is the objective, which would include resources such as books, films, photographs, videos, etc. The types can have subtypes, for example, "CreativeWork" has the type "MediaObject" and this in turn "VideoObject".

The accessibility metadata defined by Schema.org are based on those specified for the IMS AfA v3.0 DRD, but a significant subset of them has been selected. Each of these metadata may have a possible value that is defined in the specification. In this way, one can determine the accessibility characteristics of any digital resource that is published on the web.

Table 1 describes all the accessibility metadata of the CreativeWork type proposed by Schema.org. They are accessModeRequired, accessModeAvoidance, accessibilityFeatureRequiered, accessibility-HazardAvoidance and accessibilityControl

Figure 4 shows accessibility metadata for a VideoObject in Schema.org. To understand some of the accessibility metadata that Schema.org proposes, we will label a "VideoObject", which is an introductory video about the Java programming language.

Table 1. CreativeWork accessibility metadata

PROPERTY	DESCRIPTION
accessModeRequired	The access mode that a user looks for in a digital resource to understand its content.
accessModeAvoidance	The access mode that a user wants to avoid in a digital resource.
accessibilityFeatureRequiered	The detailed characteristics of the content of the resource that a user searches for a complete understanding of the resource.
accessibilityHazardAvoidance	A resource that has such a feature should not be delivered to a user with this preference.
accessibilityControl	Identifies input methods that are sufficient to fully control a resource.

Figure 4. Accessibility metadata for a VideoObject in Schema.org

```
<video itemprop="video" itemscope itemtype="http://schema.org/VideoObject">
    <source itemprop="url" src="http://example.org/IntroJava.mp4" type="video/mp4">
    <meta itemprop="accessMode" content="visual">
    <meta itemprop="accessMode" content="auditory">
    <meta itemprop="accessMode" content="textual">
    <meta itemprop="accessModeSufficient" content="visual, auditory">
    <meta itemprop="accessModeSufficient" content="visual, textual">
    <meta itemprop="accessibilityFeature" content="captions">
    <meta itemprop="accessibilityHazard" content="noFlashingHazard">
    <meta itemprop="accessibilityControl" content="fullKeyboardControl">
    <meta itemprop="accessibilityControl" content="fullMouseControl">
    <span itemprop="name">Introduction to Java programming</span>
    <span itemprop="description">Introduction to the basic concepts of object-oriented programming
                                through the Java language</span>
    <span itemprop="uploadDate">2018-01-15</span>
    Duration: <span itemprop="duration">T10M30S</span>
    <meta itemprop="thumbnail" content="java.jpg" />
    <meta itemprop="thumbnailURL" content="http://example.org/java.jpg" />
    Autor:
    <div itemprop="author" itemscope itemtype="http://schema.org/Person">
        <span itemprop="name">Salvador Otón</span>
    </div>
</video>
```

In this example, certain accessibility features are described using “accessMode”. “accessMode” details three sensory forms in which one can understand the content: visual, auditory and textual (for subtitles). In turn, “accessModeSufficient” specifies the combination of forms necessary to understand all the content. In this case, it would be the combination of visual with auditory and textual. “accessibilityFeature” describes more detailed accessibility features such as the inclusion of subtitles in the video, the non-use of flashes because some people can be sensitive, and the total control of the video by using the keyboard and the mouse.

Evolution

After reviewing the literature, one can find a few standards and specifications that are part of the evolution of metadata. However, there are some isolated initiatives that have not evolved through time. The Figure 5 shows the evolution and relationships among the most relevant initiatives in this field. At first glance, one can distinguish the following four periods.

The first one started with the emergence of digital libraries (e-print) in the XX. At the beginning of the 90s, the Web development allowed new possibilities of sharing information, especially informational resources. As a result, repositories of electronic preprints (known as e-prints) emerged, e.g. arXiv.org (1991), RePEc and Cogprints (1997). In the second period, concerns about the representation and recovery of these resources became the focus of the study of many researchers. In 1995, Dublin Core (DC) (available from http://www.dublincore.org/specifications/dublin-core/) was proposed to locate and identify web pages, textual content and other resources on the Web. Although it seems that Dublin Core does not have predecessors, is endorsed in the following standards documents: IETF RFC 5013, ISO Standard 15836-1:2017, NISO Standard Z39.85. In turn, the Open Archives Initiative Protocol for Metadata Harvesting (OAI-PMH) was developed as a low-barrier mechanism for repository interoperability (available from https://www.openarchives.org/pmh/). Moreover, an implementation of OAI-PMH must support representing metadata in Dublin Core, but may also support additional representations. There are two protocol versions 1.1 and 2.0 that were published in 2001 and 2002, respectively. In 2003, the IMS Learner Information Package Accessibility for LIP (AccLIP) and the IMS AfA MetaData Specification (AccMD) v1.0 (available from http://www.imsglobal.org/accessibility/) were developed to work together so that metadata descriptions of content in IMS AccMD were associated with descriptions in IMS AccLIP of user preferences to allow learning content to be delivered to meet the needs of the user. This approach became known as the IMS Access For All (IMS AfA) v1.0 to accessibility. However, the ideas and technological approaches of IMS AfA were originally formulated as part of the Web-4-All project (http://web4all.atrc.utoronto.ca/), which began in 2002. The IMS AccLIP is based on the IMS LIP v1.0 Specification, it extends descriptive material that defines accessibility preferences. The interest in standardization is also revealed by the publication in 2002 of the IEEE 1484.12.1 standard, better known as LOM (available from https://ieeexplore.ieee.org/document/1032843).

The third period is boosted by the publication of the ISO/IEC 24751:2008 Individualized Adaptability and Accessibility in E-learning, Education and Training. The first three parts are: Part 1, a framework for definitions and rules within other parts, including the idea that parts should be in pairs, with one part for a description of the relevant user needs and preferences and the other part for matched resource descriptions (available from https://www.iso.org/standard/41521.html); Part 2, the Access For All Personal Needs and Preferences (PNP) - originally IMS AccLIP v1.0 (available from https://www.iso.org/standard/43603.html); Part 3, the Access For All Digital Resource Description (DRD) - originally IMS AccMD v1.0 (available from https://www.iso.org/standard/43604.html). It is worth noting that ISO/IEC 24751-1:2008 standard was last reviewed and confirmed in 2019. Therefore, this version remains current. The ISO editors made a set of changes recommended for IMS AfA. In consequence, IMS released IMS AfA v2.0, which adopted the improvements in late 2009 and early 2010. The Access For All metadata and user preferences specifications were developed for some years. As a result, a public draft of IMS AfA v3.0 was released in 2012. However, to the best of our knowledge, there is no other official version published.

Figure 5. The evolution of the accessibility metadata

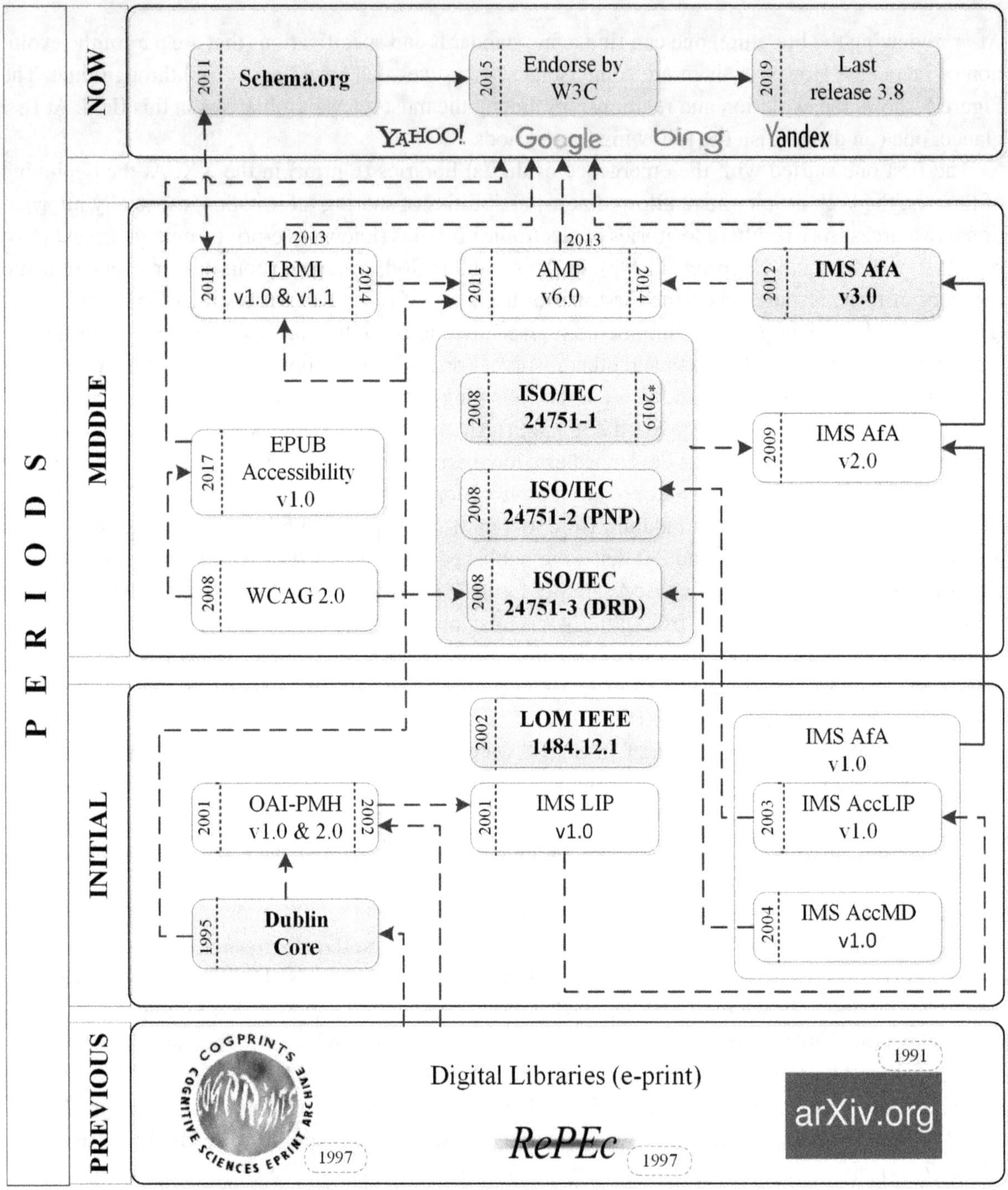

The Learning Resource Metadata Initiative (LRMI) began in 2011 shortly after the announcement of Schema.org, its initial goal was developed a set of properties and classes to augment Schema.org for the description of learning resources (available from http://www.lrmi.net/). The specification builds on the extensive vocabulary provided by Schema.org and other standards. The resulting LRMI specification version 1.1 was accepted as an official extension of Schema.org in 2013. In 2014, curation and further development of the initial LRMI v1.1 was transferred from the Association of Educational Publishers and Creative Commons to the Dublin Core Metadata Initiative (DCMI). At the same time, the root of the Accessibility Metadata Project (AMP) was the announcement in 2011 of Schema.org. AMP extends LRMI, using the work of IMS AfA to integrate information on the media types and features, whether captions, ebooks, audio, and so on into the web fabric to be reachable by all (available from http://www.a11ymetadata.org/). That means the development of an accessibility component of the educational metadata in order to find accessible educational materials that fit the specific learning needs of specific students, including students with disabilities. The AMP proposal was officially submitted to the W3C Schema.org process in 2013. Another relevant initiative is EPUB accessibility v1.0 (http://www.idpf.org/epub/a11y/accessibility.html) that was published in 2017. Every conformant EPUB Publication must include some Schema.org accessibility metadata (https://www.w3.org/Submission/2017/SUBM-epub-a11y-20170125/). EPUB Publications must meet WCAG 2.0 Level A to be conformant with this specification, but it is recommended that they meet Level AA.

The fourth period corresponds to the current evolution of this field. Schema.org is the most relevant initiative in this period. Schema.org has integrated four initiatives that emerged in the previous period: LRMI, IMS AfA v3.0, AMP v6.0 and EPUB accessibility v1.0. The continuous evolution of Schema.org is revealed by its releases. The most recent version 3.8 was published in 2019. One important milestone of the evolution of Schema.org was the endorsement by W3C in 2015. Moreover, three well-known search engine providers, Google, Yahoo and Microsoft (Bing), were involved and later a Russian search company, Yandex joined them. The key concept here is "metadata" which might be defined as data about data. However, Schema.org is not a standard itself but a vocabulary. In addition, Schema.org is not specific to educational resources but, in general, to semantic extraction. Therefore, it raises the question of how Schema.org is related to learning resources. Although Schema.org does include accessibility, the main contributor of Schema.org for educational resources is LRMI, as mentioned above. However, LRMI is not only insufficient but also its notation makes it difficult to understand and use out of the context of the education system of the USA.

Finally, despite the efforts made it is clear that further research is needed to mature this field.

CONCLUSION

Several concerns arise regarding the accessibility metadata needed to successfully find, evaluate and select online educational resources. There are many repositories that offer tens of thousands of online educational resources, for example, OER Commons and MERLOT. The use of these types of online educational resources offers some guarantee of quality, since the online educational resources hosted in these repositories have gone through a process of selection, filtering and validation. Nevertheless, the online educational resources found in repositories should be evaluated and selected with the goal of identifying those that best meet the educational requirements and the accessibility needs and preferences of the students (Sanchez-Gordon & Luján-Mora, 2018). To do so, the quality of the accessibility metadata is key.

The understanding of standards in the use of metadata constitutes a barrier when applying them. The learning curvature is still complex. Quality assessments in virtual environments have focused their efforts to determine support parameters through the use of metadata, but we must consider that there are diverse points of view that respond to institutional, local or regional particularities, because the metadata is unlimited and could be interpreted as different way depending on context. Although the panorama seems daunting, the universality of the web and the advances in accessibility could facilitate the adoption of basic guidelines, avoiding semantic inconsistency and subjective opinion. It is necessary to strengthen the use of metadata that is simple to process both by people and by machines, contributing significantly to the task of search engines. Identifying a resource by the need or preference of a user, ensures a result of satisfactory interaction. The contribution of accessibility standards in the design of interfaces strengthens the attention to a population that uses different access modes for their interaction.

The learning process and the diversity of needs and preferences of students with disabilities opens a range of diverse needs. The variability of learning with emphasis on students who are in the margins justifies the need to develop accessible educational material. All educational material is developed for a mythical "standard student" which limits the accessibility of many students with different ways of learning. It is necessary to provide alternatives that allow students to interact with multiple educational digital resources, considering their mode of access. These actions are consistent with the universal design for learning (UDL). Under this educational framework based on neuroscience (Rose & Meyer, 2006), flexible educational environments are strengthened in which students can make their own choices to use a material that considers usability, adaptability and accessibility by removing barriers.

Analyzing a virtual learning environment from accessibility with all the resources it has, requires going from the external (perception) to the internal (comprehension). The apprentices of online courses demand resources that potentialize their autonomy (be self-directed), mastery (be better and feel satisfaction) and purpose (why do I want to do it?). Research shows that students who follow online courses are more concerned with mastery and their desire to be self-directed.

In general, people with disabilities face many barriers to learning. By not having information about accessible online courses, they are limited in their learning. Therefore, the need to provide clear and timely information such as metadata accessibility is imminent.

We are aware of the importance of accessible online educational resources and aim to propose a study focused on reporting the availability and suitability of accessibility metadata for online learning resources to use in collaborative virtual learning environments. Therefore, this chapter aims to benefit the readers (both researchers and practitioners alike) by providing a comprehensive and balanced view of the area based on the analysis of learners accessibility needs and preferences. To achieve accessibility in learning environments and learning resources, it is important to comply with the Web Content Accessibility Guidelines 2.1 (WCAG) published in 2018 by the Web Accessibility Initiative of the World Wide Web Consortium (World Wide Web Consortium, 2018).

We believe that the use of accessibility metadata in educational resources published on the Internet is important in order to provide the semantic meaning that current search engines need. By reviewing the literature, it is clear that Schema.org is an initiative that promotes the use of metadata despite the fact that it is not a standard but a vocabulary. However, if we focus on other more concrete accessibility metadata specifications for educational resources such as IMS AfA, we realize that they have not updated since 2012. This does not happen with other accessibility specifications such as WCAG, which was updated in 2018 with the 2.1 version. With this comparison we want to highlight that on the one hand, both web pages and mobile applications can verify their degree of accessibility compliance with very current specifications, and yet digital resources or educational resources do not have a simple, clear and current specification for achieving the desired inclusion goal. What is the use of having an accessible web page if the resources published in it are not properly described in order to be understood by different disability profiles? Taking Schema.org as the most current proposal, we find that we can describe the accessibility metadata of a CreativeWork, however, we can not create a profile of a user using the Person type since there is no metadata to describe their accessibility preferences and needs.

REFERENCES

Anastasiou, D., & Vázquez, L. M. (2010). Localisation Standards and Metadata. In S. Sánchez-Alonso & I. N. Athanasiadis (Eds.), *Metadata and Semantic Research. MTSR 2010. Communications in Computer and Information Science* (Vol. 108). Berlin: Springer.

Anido, L. E., Fernández, M. J., Caeiro, M., Santos, J. M., Rodríguez, J. S., & Llamas, M. (2002). Educational metadata and brokerage for learning resources. *Computers & Education, 38*(4), 351-374. doi:10.1016/S0360-1315(02)00018-0

Barritt, C., & Alderman, F.L. (2004). *Creating a reusable learning objects strategy: Leveraging information and learning in a knowledge economy*. Pfeiffer & Company Editorial.

Batanero, C., Fernández-Sanz, L., Piironen, A. K., Holvikivi, J., Hilera, J. R., Otón, S., & Alonso, J. (2017). Accessible platforms for e-learning: A case study. *Computer Applications in Engineering Education, 25*(6), 1018–1037. doi:10.1002/cae.21852

Batanero, C., Karhu, M., Holvikivi, J., Otón, S., & Amado-Salvatierra, H. R. (2014, July). A method to evaluate accessibility in e-learning education systems. In *Advanced Learning Technologies (ICALT), 2014 IEEE 14th International Conference on* (pp. 556-560). IEEE. 10.1109/ICALT.2014.163

Brahim, H. B., Jemaa, A. B., Jemni, M., & Laabidi, M. (2013, July). Towards the design of personalised accessible e-learning environments. In *Advanced Learning Technologies (ICALT), 2013 IEEE 13th International Conference* (pp. 419-420). IEEE. 10.1109/ICALT.2013.128

DAMA. (2009). *The DAMA Guide to the Data Management Body of Knowledge*. Technics Publications, LLC.

DCMI. (2009). *Dublin Core Metadata Initiative*. Retrieved from http://dublincore.org/

DCMI. (2012). *Learning Resource Metadata Initiative (LRMI)*. Retrieved from http://lrmi.dublincore.net/

DCMI. (2012). *LRMI Terms*. Retrieved from http://dublincore.org/specifications/lrmi/lrmi_terms/1.1/

Di Iorio, A., Feliziani, A. A., Mirri, S., Salomoni, P., & Vitali, F. (2006). Automatically producing accessible learning objects. *Journal of Educational Technology & Society*, *9*(4), 3–16.

IMS. (2003). IMS Global Learning Consortium (2003). *IMS Learner Information Package Accessibility for LIP. Version 1.* Retrieved from http://www.imsglobal.org/accessibility/#acclip

IMS. (2004). IMS Global Learning Consortium (2004). *IMS AccessForAll Meta-data Specification. Version 1*. Retrieved from http://www.imsglobal.org/accessibility/#accmd

IMS. (2009). IMS Global Learning Consortium (2012). *IMS AccessForAll v2.0 Final Specification*. Retrieved from http://www.imsglobal.org/accessibility/#accDRD

IMS. (2012). IMS Global Learning Consortium, Inc. (2012). *IMS Access For All Version 3.0*. Retrieved from http://imsglobal.org/accessibility

Institute of Electrical and Electronics Engineers (IEEE). (2002). *IEEE 1484.12.1-2002 Learning Object Metadata (LOM)*. Retrieved from http://ltsc.ieee.org

International Standard Organization. (2008). *ISO/IEC 24751:2008, Information technology -- Individualized adaptability and accessibility in e-learning, education and training*. Author.

International Standard Organization. (2008a). *ISO/IEC 24751-1:2008, Information Technology -- Individualized Adaptability and Accessibility in e-Learning, Education and Training -- Part 1: Framework and Reference Model*. Retrieved from http://www.iso.org/cms/render/live/en/sites/isoorg/contents/data/standard/04/15/41521.html

International Standard Organization. (2008b). *ISO/IEC 24751-2:2008, Information Technology -- Individualized Adaptability and Accessibility in e-Learning, Education and Training -- Part 2: "Access for All" Personal Needs and Preferences for Digital Delivery*. Retrieved from http://www.iso.org/cms/render/live/en/sites/isoorg/contents/data/standard/04/36/43603.html

International Standard Organization. (2008c). *ISO/IEC 24751-3:2008, Information Technology -- Individualized Adaptability and Accessibility in e-Learning, Education and Training -- Part 3: "Access for All" Digital Resource Description*. Retrieved from http://www.iso.org/cms/render/live/en/sites/isoorg/contents/data/standard/04/36/43604.html

International Standard Organization. (2009). *ISO/IEC 19796-3:2009, Information Technology -- Learning, Education and Training -- Quality Management, Assurance and Metrics -- Part 3: Reference Methods and Metrics*. Retrieved from http://www.iso.org/cms/render/live/en/sites/isoorg/contents/data/standard/04/61/46159.html

International Standard Organization. (2012). *ISO/IEC 40500:2012, Information Technology -- W3C Web Content Accessibility Guidelines (WCAG) 2.0*. Retrieved from http://www.iso.org/cms/render/live/en/sites/isoorg/contents/data/standard/05/86/58625.html

International Standard Organization. (2015). *ISO/IEC 19778-3:2015, Information technology -- Learning, education and training -- Collaborative technology -- Collaborative workplace -- Part 3: Collaborative group data model*. Retrieved from http://www.iso.org/cms/render/live/en/sites/isoorg/contents/data/standard/06/50/65099.html

International Standard Organization. (2018). *ISO 9241-11:2018, Ergonomics of human-system interaction -- Part 11: Usability: Definitions and concepts*. Retrieved from https://www.iso.org/standard/63500.html

Laabidi, M., Jemni, M., Ayed, L. J. B., Brahim, H. B., & Jemaa, A. B. (2014). Learning technologies for people with disabilities. *Journal of King Saud University-Computer and Information Sciences*, *26*(1), 29–45. doi:10.1016/j.jksuci.2013.10.005

Manso-Callejo, M., Wachowicz, M., & Bernabé-Poveda, M. (2010). The Design of an Automated Workflow for Metadata Generation. In S. Sánchez-Alonso & I. N. Athanasiadis (Eds.), *In Metadata and Semantic Research. MTSR 2010. Communications in Computer and Information Science* (Vol. 108). Berlin, Heidelberg: Springer. doi:10.1007/978-3-642-16552-8_25

MARC21. (2010). *MARC 21 format for bibliographic records*. NIPO: 032-15-027-1. Retrieved from http://www.bne.es/es/Micrositios/Guias/

Meusel, R., Petrovski, P., & Bizer, C. (2014). The WebDataCommons Microdata, RDFa and microformat dataset series. In *13th International Semantic Web Conference (ISWC '14) - Part I,* 277-292. DOI: 10.1007/978-3-319-11964-9_18

Mirri, S., Pantieri, D., Roccetti, M., & Salomoni, P. (2006). A multimedia broker for accessible learning objects transcoding. In Information and Communication Technologies, 2006. ICTTA'06 (Vol. 1, pp. 641-646). IEEE. doi:10.1109/ICTTA.2006.1684447

Mirri, S., Salomoni, P., Roccetti, M., & Gay, G. R. (2011). *Beyond standards: unleashing accessibility on a learning content management system. In Transactions on edutainment V* (pp. 35–49). Berlin: Springer.

Navarrete, R., & Lujan-Mora, S. (2018). Microdata with Schema vocabulary: Improvement search results visualization of open educational resources. *13th Iberian Conference on Information Systems and Technologies (CISTI)*, 1-6. 10.23919/CISTI.2018.8399222

NISO. (2004). Understanding Metadata. NISO Press.

Otón, S., Amado-Salvatierra, H., Hilera, J. R., García, E., & García, A. (2015). Considerations on Barriers to Effective E-learning toward Accessible Virtual Campuses. In *E-learning - Instructional Design, Organizational Strategy and Management*. IntechOpen. Retrieved from https://www.intechopen.com/books/e-learning-instructional-design-organizational-strategy-and-management/considerations-on-barriers-to-effective-e-learning-toward-accessible-virtual-campuses

Otón, S., Batanero, C., García, E., García, A., & Barchino, R. (2014). Description of accessible learning resources by using metadata. *16TH International Conference on Enterprise Information Systems Vol. 2 (ICEIS 2014),* 620-626. DOI:10.5220/0004895606200626

Otón, S., García, A., García, E., Barchino, R., & Amado-Salvatierra, H. R. (2014). Transforming LOMPad to Support IMS Access for All v3.0. *2014 IEEE 14th International Conference on Advanced Learning Technologies*, 599-600. 10.1109/ICALT.2014.175

Otón, S., Gutiérrez de Mesa, J. A., & Batanero C. (2015). Una implementación de afa para la educación virtual accesible. *Revista Vínculos, 12*(1).

Otón, S., Ortiz, A., Hilera, J. R., Barchino, R., Gutiérrez, J. M., Martínez, J. J., & Gutiérrez, J. A. (2010). Service oriented architecture for the implementation of distributed repositories of learning objects. *International Journal of Innovative Computing, Information & Control, 6-3*(A), 843-854.

Pons, D., Hilera, J. R., Fernández, L., & Pagés, C. (2016). A Learning Quality Metadata Approach: Automatic Quality Assessment of Virtual Training from Metadata. *Computer Standards & Interfaces*, *45*, 45–61. doi:10.1016/j.csi.2015.12.001

Sanchez-Gordon, S., & Luján-Mora, S. (2018). Research challenges in accessible MOOCs: A systematic literature review 2008-2016. *Universal Access in the Information Society*, *17*(4), 775–789. doi:10.100710209-017-0531-2

Sanchez-Gordon, S., & Luján-Mora, S. (2018b). Technological Innovations in Large-Scale Teaching: Five Roots of MOOCS. *Journal of Educational Computing Research*, *56*(5), 623–644. doi:10.1177/0735633117727597

Sanchez-Gordon, S., & Luján-Mora, S. (2018c). Lifecycle for MOOC Development and Management. In R. Queirós (Ed.), *Emerging Trends, Techniques, and Tools for Massive Open Online Course (MOOC) Management* (pp. 24–48). IGI Global. doi:10.4018/978-1-5225-5011-2.ch002

Schema.org. (2019). Retrieved from https://schema.org/

Sicilia, M. A. (2006). Metadata, semantics and ontology: Providing meaning to information resources. *International Journal of Metadata, Semantics and Ontologies*, *1*(1), 83–86. doi:10.1504/IJMSO.2006.008773

Sikos, L. F. (2015). *Mastering Structured Data on the Semantic Web: From HTML5 Microdata to Linked Open Data*. New York: Apress. doi:10.1007/978-1-4842-1049-9

Solomou, G., Pierrakeas, C., & Kameas, A. (2015). Characterization of Educational Resources in e-Learning Systems Using an Educational Metadata Profile. *Journal of Educational Technology & Society*, *18*(4), 246–260.

The Xerte Project. (2008). *Learning Technology*. University of Nottingham. Retrieved from http://www.nottingham.ac.uk/xerte/index.aspx

TILE. (2004). *The Inclusive Learning Exchange*. University of Toronto. Retrieved from http://inclusivelearning.ca/tile/servlet/showtemplate?template=rswi/AboutTILE

Valiente, M.-C., Sicilia, M.-A., Garcia-Barriocanal, E., & Rajabi, E. (2015). Adopting the metadata approach to improve the search and analysis of educational resources for online learning. *Computers in Human Behavior*, *51*, 1134–1141. doi:10.1016/j.chb.2014.12.059

Vizoso, S. (2017). Metadatos de accesibilidad en recursos educativos: análisis y propuesta. *Palabra Clave; Ensenada, 7*(1). doi:10.24215/18539912e040

Web-4-All. (2003). *Web Accessibility through sight, sound and touch*. Adaptative Technology Resource Centre, ATRC. University of Toronto. Retrieved from http://www.web4all.ca

World Wide Web Consortium. (2018). *Web Content Accessibility Guidelines (WCAG) 2.1*. Retrieved from https://www.w3.org/TR/WCAG21/

Chapter 2
Reflections on Instructional Design Guidelines From the MOOCification of Distance Education:
A Case Study of a Course on Design for All

Covadonga Rodrigo
Universidad Nacional de Educación a Distancia (UNED), Spain

Francisco Iniesto
https://orcid.org/0000-0003-3946-3056
The Open University, UK

Ana García-Serrano
Universidad Nacional de Educación a Distancia (UNED), Spain

ABSTRACT

There are some similarities in developing distance education online courses and Massive Open Online Courses (MOOCs) using the basis of eLearning instructional design. However, the task of converting an online course into a MOOC is not as simple as direct migration of eLearning materials and assessment resources into a MOOC platform. In online learning, learners should be continually influenced by information, social interaction, and learning experiences, providing them with the knowledge to come up with new ideas to develop within an engaging course. In this chapter, the process of MOOCification a distance education online course on "Design for All for an Inclusive and Accessible Society" is explained and contextualized. The re-factorization process has been based upon the quality model used for MOOCs at UNED Abierta and the instructional design based on Gagné's events of instruction. The eLearning activities were completely refactored, along with the content itself, the interaction events, and the online assessment following the Gardner's multiple intelligences product grid.

DOI: 10.4018/978-1-7998-2325-4.ch002

INTRODUCTION

Massive Open Online Courses (MOOCs) have been a turning point in online learning delivery, in some cases being positioned as an alternative to traditional higher education (HE) courses (Yuan & Powell, 2013). It offers teachers, researchers and practitioners the opportunity to experiment with different pedagogies, trying different possibilities using their materials in either face to face or online campus settings, such as in flipped classroom or blended learning approaches (Hoyos et al., 2019; Hill, 2012). The pedagogical and visual design of MOOCs, their information architecture, usability and interaction design, is having a variable impact on learner engagement, retention and completion rates, as previously analyzed in adult learning (Montgomery & Mallette, 2018; Jordan, 2015; Yang et al., 2013; Liyanagunawardena et al., 2014). For instance, Jordan (2015) confirms that completion rates vary significantly, from 0.7% to 52.1%, with an average value of 12.6%, according to course length (longer courses having lower completion rates), start date (recent courses having higher percentage completion) and assessment type (courses using auto-grading having higher completion rates).

Recent innovations in MOOCs include the creation of new educational approaches (both from the pedagogical and technological point of view) that can be used to rethink education, also renewing calls for inclusive education to reach all citizens. Social inclusion can only be obtained by embedding inclusive strategies, leading to targeting and including vulnerable groups, such as people with disabilities, being emphasized (de Waard et al., 2014), although there has been limited progress to date in either producing accessible MOOCs, or tailoring MOOCs to meet individual learners' needs (Iniesto et al., 2016).

MOOCs are usually developed and delivered as independent online courses, but some pedagogical experiments have been reported by teachers and researchers on how to integrate MOOC into HE (Sandeen, 2013). From being video courseware repositories to dynamically adaptive eLearning models, the MOOC ecosystem has matured significantly leading to a wider taxonomy of MOOCs (as explained originally in the taxonomy of 8 types of MOOC developed by Clark (2013). Transfer MOOCs are created with recordings of existing classroom video lectures and engage learners by different motivating factors (Sooryanarayan & Gupta, 2015). Other researchers wrap formal university courses around existing MOOCs (Koller, 2012; Bruff, 2012; Bruff et al., 2013; Caufield et al., 2013; Holotescu et al. 2014), while some have attempted a different approach, where the participation of learners in different MOOCs was integrated into a blended course run on a social mobile Learning Management System (LMS) (Conole, 2008). More recently, Defaweux et al. (2019) combined a MOOC with a face-to-face course using blended pedagogical patterns.

Integration of MOOCs into HE appears to be converging on content licensing to support hybrid or flipped classes, an incremental change from current practice rather than a fundamental transformation (Sandeen, 2013; Rodrigo et al., 2016). As revealed by Gasevic et al. (2014), the design of MOOCs and their integration into formal curricula was one of the main research themes within the framework of future MOOC research. Gasevic also stated the need to increase efforts towards enhancing multi-disciplinarily. According to Desarathy et al. (2014), MOOCs could enhance crowd-sourcing multi-institutional degrees and competence-based education by improving the quality and personalization of the learner experience.

MOOC design can be addressed from the perspective of eLearning design (Conole, 2014), a research field that provides tools and methods for both articulating and representing the design process of learning experiences, making them more explicit and shareable while assisting educators in planning and organizing pedagogically educational actions (Conole, 2010). The focus is placed on the educational aspects of new technologies and, particularly, what might be the most appropriate "schema" for describing the ways in which technologies are used. Learning design methods and tools have been shown to be especially beneficial when employed to design complex learning contexts, as is the case of MOOCs, in which a significant number of resources and stakeholders are involved.

Our main contribution in the chapter is to contextualize and explain both methodologically and in a practical way, how to re-factorize a distance education online course into a MOOC. This MOOC needs to be designed as an engaging online course, following the quality model used for MOOCs at UNED Abierta and the instructional design based on Gagné's events of instruction. The transformation process is named MOOCification. This chapter is structured as follows. First, quality issues regarding MOOC pedagogical design and content production are analyzed, followed by a description of the hybrid approach to MOOC quality established at the university. Then, the MOOC design process on Design for All is presented, along with the mapping of new re-factored learning activities using Gardner's Multiple Intelligences Product Grid. Finally, future work and the main conclusions of the research are outlined.

BACKGROUND

There are some successful experiences of converting courses into MOOCs: Ostashewski et al. (2017) explored enhancing university course activities using MOOCs, Combéfis et al. (2014) remodeled a course into a Small Private Online Course (SPOC), Nuñez et al. (2016) transformed a small private traditional online course into a massive one. Nonetheless, distance learners are different from on-campus students. Early MOOC research tells us that the majority of MOOC learners are adult learners (Zweifler, 2013; Emanuel, 2013), such as those that enroll in distance HE (Richardson, 2017). When (Universidad Nacional de Educación a Distancia – The National Distance Education University (UNED) took the decision in 2011 to start producing MOOCs, launching its own MOOC platform (UNED Abierta)), it was evident that there were several online university courses that could be prepared and started rapidly as Transfer MOOCs, based on materials produced for the undergraduate courses. These online courses were used by many participants, ranging from 500 to 10,000 learners in the first run, depending on the subject. It soon became clear that it was not rational to apply the same specifications used for standard online undergraduate courses to the MOOCs development at the university. At the same time, every teaching team wanted to design them differently (e.g. engaging activities, peer-to-peer interaction and assessment methods). Therefore, a strategic decision was taken to follow a standard approach to structure the MOOCs, using design templates to provide a similar "look and feel", but allowing pedagogical differences between them, as if each course was one specific type of MOOC (Clark, 2013). Given the heterogeneous nature of the subjects being covered in the courses and the way in which each teaching team wanted to deliver a course, simple systematic quality control was undertaken, based upon previous experience in online learning (Read & Rodrigo, 2014).

MOOCs Quality issues

While there is an abundance of quality models for online course, they do not cater specifically to MOOCs. While research on MOOC quality has appeared in the literature, there is currently no consensus on how the quality assessment of these courses should be undertaken (Haggard, 2013) or even if it makes any sense to try to measure it (Weller, 2013). MOOCs have gained a lot of attention in the last decade as a new Technology Enhanced Learning (TEL) approach in HE, but further research is needed to identify the elements that drive a successful MOOC. Yousef et al. (2014) developed an empirical examination of criteria to assure design quality, identifying 74 criteria distributed into 6 categories - from both technological and pedagogical perspectives - that need to be considered when designing and implementing MOOCs. Curiously, although there is almost universal agreement that usability, content, collaboration, and instructional design play a major role in achieving effective MOOCs, these categories were identified in this study as less important compared to the learning analytics and assessment categories. In fact, the latter two categories are highly challenging tasks in MOOCs and are still less explored than the former ones. The MOOC Quality Project (Creelman et al., 2014), undertaken by the European Foundation for Quality, found that it was difficult to define what quality means for MOOCs since their very nature is constantly changing, with new types and variants of courses appearing all the time. Creelman et al. highlighted some factors that are related to the perception of MOOC quality, such as the notion of choice, what pre-course information is provided, the pedagogical approaches supported in a course, the level of learner commitment required, whether a course is scheduled or not, its technical requirements, the role of the teaching team, its availability, and level of interaction, whether certification is available or not, etc.

Downes (2015), as part of his contribution to The MOOC Quality Project, differentiates between the quality of a MOOC in terms of its platform and the related tools (functionality, stability, etc.). He also pointed out the difficulty in assessing the success of a specific MOOC in a given context with a given learner body, noting that *"measuring drop-out rates, counting test scores, and adding up learner satisfaction scores will not tell us whether a MOOC was successful, only whether this particular application of this particular MOOC was successful in this particular instance" (pp.72)*. Daniel (2012) even suggested that one approach could be for the courses to be evaluated by learners and educators, leading to league tables that rank the courses by the quality of the offering. In this case, the most relevant form of quality assurance and enhancement comes from the reflections and informal evaluations of the enthusiasts who put on the courses, and comments from participants using social media. Mudler (2013) proposed the 5 Five Components for Open Education (COE) quality model, focused on the application of Open Education components at MOOCs. It establishes that the use of Open Education components is not Open Education by itself, it needs three supply-side components: Open Educational Resources (OERs), Open Learning Services (OLS) and Open Teaching Efforts (OTE), and two demand-side components: Open to Learner's Needs (OLN) and Open to Employability & Capabilities development (OEC). The measurement of these five items reflects the course quality *"fingerprint"* in the model.

Another quality initiative suggested in the literature is considering MOOCs through the lens of the Quality Code at the QAA (Quality Assurance Agency for Higher Education at the UK) (Rosewell & Barefoot, 2013), which has influenced the OpenupEd label (Rosewell, 2013), based around the EADTU E-xcellence framework approach of using benchmarks for quality assessment that has been already tested at UNED Abierta MOOCs (Rodrigo et al., 2014). OpenupEd is the first MOOC Europe-wide initiative with the support of the European Commission. Its name refers indirectly to the European program Opening up Education. OpenupEd was initiated and is currently coordinated by the European Association of Distance Teaching Universities (EADTU), a group comprised mostly of open universities, but focused on reaching new partners that perform MOOCs and are keen on opening up education for all. It aims to be a quality brand embracing the diversity in (institutional) approaches to open up education by the use of MOOCs. Although there is a diversity of institutional approaches, the partnership has agreed on a framework of 8 common features; the 32 benchmarks represent the first step toward MOOC quality control (Kear et al., 2016).

MOOCs Instructional Design

MOOCification refers to a pedagogical approach used when a closed or small-format traditional online course is re-factored into a MOOC. There are several possibilities to do so successfully. Some authors explore the possibility of finding new formulas for connecting formal and informal learning (Dabbagh & Kitsantas, 2012). For instance, massive courses can be blended with existing units offered in universities allowing for links and connections between study programs and the outside world (Howell & Ostashewski, 2015). Ostashewski et al. (2017) presented evidence in their study that blending MOOCs with classroom-based or online learning provides HE learners with personalized learning opportunities.

Some of the reasons to re-factorize HE courses into a single MOOC or even a collection of NOOCs (Nano-MOOCs or pill-based courses) might be:

- To reach a wider audience with the subject,
- To deepen the learning of the learners through engagement in an informal learning context,
- To encourage significant peer interaction beyond forum posts and functionalities of regular and eLearning platforms,
- To learn small pieces of information in a short time by presenting pieces of information in an attractive and engaging way,
- And to make learners draw upon the open-content already present in the field and get both a realistic experience of the field and make first real connections with it.

In relation to learner's engagement, knowledge absorption and retention, Robert Gagné (1992) stated that different types of learning exist, and that different instructional conditions are most likely to bring about these different types of learning:

1. **Intellectual Skills:** Create individual competence and ability to respond to stimuli.
2. **Cognitive Strategies:** Capability to learn, think, and remember.
3. **Verbal information:** Rote memorization of names, faces, dates, phone numbers, etc.
4. **Motor Skills:** Capability to learn to drive, ride a bike, draw a straight line, etc.
5. **Attitudes:** Approach to ideas, people, or situations that affects how one acts towards these things.

Gagné suggested that certain mental conditions must be present for knowledge absorption and retention to occur. He proposed a series of events which follow a systematic instructional design process that shares the behaviorist approach to learning, with a focus on the outcomes or behaviors of instruction or training (see Table 1).

In relation to the process of making the learning to be a realistic experience and make real connections with the context, Gardner's Multiple Intelligences theory (1983) differentiates human intelligence into specific 'modalities', rather than seeing intelligence as dominated by a single general ability. Gardner argued that the broad spectrum of learners would be better served if disciplines could be presented in a different number of ways and learning could be assessed through a variety of means. The learning styles are as follows (Gardner & Hatch, 1989):

Table 1. Gagné's nine events of instruction

	Event
G.1	Gain the attention of the learners by using a compelling introduction. Even online learners who are distracted or possibly unmotivated to participate create an emotional connection about the topic.
G.2	Inform learners about the objectives and the outcomes of the course. When possible, they can be tied into real-world applications and benefits, as pursued in adult's learning, where learners know they are going to take something valuable away from the course are more likely to engage in the online learning process.
G.3	Stimulate recall of prior knowledge or learning, helping learners make sense of new information by relating it to something they already know or something they have already experienced. This gives learners the chance to commit it to long-term memory, rather than forgetting it right after reading it.
G.4	Create goal-centered online content, presenting it in a meaningful way: every activity, exercise, and piece of online content will be tied in directly to the goals and objectives. Information can be better grouped together along with concepts based on the specific goal.
G.5	Online learners need support and specific coaching to develop favorable online learning behaviors, or else they might be committing incorrect information to their long-term memory.
G.6	Activate learner processing to help them internalize new skills and knowledge and to confirm correct understanding of these concepts.
G.7	Give learners timely and constructive feedback they have the power to improve learning behaviors and identify their weaknesses and strengths.
G.8	Performance should be based on previously stated objectives and assessed early and often.
G.9	Enhance retention and transfer of knowledge by tying it into real-world situations and applications.

1. **Visual-Spatial:** Think in terms of physical space, as do architects and sailors. Very aware of their environments. They like to draw, do jigsaw puzzles, read maps, and daydream.
2. **Bodily-Kinesthetic:** Use the body effectively, like a dancer or a surgeon. Keen sense of body awareness. They like movement, making things, touching.
3. **Musical**: Show sensitivity to rhythm and sound. They love music, but they are also sensitive to sounds in their environments. They may study better with music in the background.
4. **Interpersonal**: Understanding, interacting with others. These learners learn through interaction. They have many friends, empathy for others, street smarts. They can be taught through group activities, seminars, and dialogues.
5. **Intrapersonal**: Understanding one's own interests, goals. These learners tend to shy away from others. They're in tune with their inner feelings; they have wisdom, intuition, and motivation, as well as a strong will, confidence, and opinions. They can be taught through independent study and introspection.
6. **Linguistic**: Using words effectively. These learners have highly developed auditory skills and often think in words. They like reading, playing word games, making up poetry or stories. They can be taught by encouraging them to say and see words, read books together.
7. **Logical-Mathematical**: Reasoning, calculating. Think conceptually, abstractly and are able to see and explore patterns and relationships. They like to experiment, solve puzzles, and ask cosmic questions. They can be taught through logic games, investigations, and inquiries.

It seems impossible to teach using all learning styles, however, but it becomes apparent that a mix of multimedia resources is more effective; it satisfies the many types of learning preferences that one learner may embody as refuted by Lane (2008). Specifically, Guàrdia et al. (2013) present a set of principles drawn from the learner's perspective for the case of MOOCs. Authors focus on empowering learners in networked environments for fostering critical thinking and collaboration, developing competency-based outcomes, encouraging peer assistance and assessment through social appraisal, providing strategies and tools for self-regulation, and finally using a variety of media to create and publish learning resources and outputs.

MAIN FOCUS OF THE CHAPTER

Issues, Controversies, Problems

The main focus of this chapter is to contextualize and explain both methodologically and in a practical way, the process of MOOCification used to re-factorize a traditional online course into a MOOC as a case study of UNED considering its learning design and quality issues. The MOOC has been designed with the idea of connecting formal and informal learning, and it will be blended with the existing units offered by the traditional online course at the university, "Accessibility and Usability", and offered in the 3rd level of Computer Science bachelor degree. The first two sections of the course content deal with Design For All principles and the barriers of people with disabilities when working with technology. This content will be delivered through an open and massive environment, as it can be used as an introductory course by itself, empowering the university open curricula and advance in inclusion awareness.

UNED Abierta Quality Issues

In June 2012, when UNED started its MOOC program at UNED Abierta, relatively few guidelines on MOOC quality existed. Specific guidelines were then created in the university to provide quality control during the creation of MOOCs, protecting the university's brand and ensuring a level of performance. The initial quality model was based upon the one used for the online undergraduate programs, which had been developed and refined over more than 15 years. Designing a MOOC is expected to be simpler for distance university staff than for their face-to-face counterpart since the former had been using eLearning platforms for years as part of their daily activities and they are familiar using the developing tools. The OpenupEd label and E-xcellence approach of using benchmarks for quality self-assessment process was applied to UNED Abierta quality model (Rodrigo et al., 2014). The process facilitated large-scale implementation (Gil-Jaurena, 2015), including several specific guidelines such as:

- Course syllabus divided into N modules (overall workload of 1-5 ECTS),
- A short introductory video per module,
- A self –paced methodology,
- Interactive user forums to help to build a community for the learners, teachers, and facilitators,
- Peer-review and group collaboration,
- And automated feedback through online assessments (e.g. quizzes and tests).

Based upon the quality process used at the university for online courses, a model was defined in terms of two types of control:

- **Coherence**: The structural and functional coherence of a given course, based upon the objectives defined by the teaching team which would be matched to a set of characteristics that could be used to evaluate the initial design of the course (Creelman et al., 2013, Morrison, 2013).
- **Flexibility:** The establishment of a flexible certification model (freemium model), that would demonstrate through a standard test-like evaluation, that the course had achieved its objectives and the learners had achieved the learning goals intended by the teaching staff.

Regarding the former, the establishment of a variable metric for each MOOC made it possible to control how each course was structured, what kind of resources were included and how activities, interaction and assessment was included. Specifically, the metric contemplates seven specific characteristics (Read & Rodrigo 2014):

1. **Topic:** Each course should be as specific as possible.
2. **Contents:** Educational resources could be reused from HE courses, although they had to be adapted to the MOOC format (e.g. videos with a maximum duration of 5 minutes, guidelines that would be understandable without the support of teaching staff, activities that either finished with self-evaluation or involved some kind of forum-based collaboration or interaction, etc.).
3. **Duration**: Between 25 and 125 hours of workload (equivalent to 1 ECTS to 5 ECTS).
4. **Structure:** UNED MOOCs are typically divided into 4 to 8 modules, depending upon duration and objectives. Each module would typically have between 4 to 8 videos with associated activities and evaluations. The latter is used to consolidate acquired knowledge and foster interaction between the learners.
5. **Specific Instructional Design Guidelines:** As stated in the next section. Self-assessment methodology required learners to reflect on their own work and judge how well they have performed.
6. **Social Channels:** Forums are the main interaction tool provided, although other associated web tools could also be included depending on the methodology. The forum tool present in the MOOC platform enables stakeholders to vote on any post, therefore posts with higher ranks will appear higher up in the relevant thread in the forum.
7. **Teaching Roles**: In UNED Abierta, teaching roles are restricted to facilitators and content curators. These last being a "*critical knowledge broker*", someone who seeks the forums continuously trying to maintain the relevance of the information that flows freely by learners for creating information environments.

Design for All Learning Objectives

As for the content of the MOOC, Spanish Legislative Decree 1/2013 establishes that the Government encourages universities to include new curricula regarding Access for All matters. This provision has been developed in universities across the Organic Law 4/2007, which has the aim of developing official curricula and programs according to the general lines emanating from the European Higher Education Area (EHEA) directives. It has been a breakthrough as it requires the inclusion of courses related to Human Rights and the principles of Design for All in the curricula. The main objectives of the initiative are as follows:

1. **Inclusion:** Advancing in inclusion awareness and dissemination of the Design for All criteria to learners in undergraduate levels.
2. **Empowerment:** Empower university curricula bearing in mind that any professional activity must be performed from the respect and promotion of human rights and equal opportunities for all.
3. **Good Practices:** Meet examples of good practices and successful experiences of the inclusion of Design for All in the curricula of university degrees.
4. **Relevance:** Analyze the importance of studying this subject as a way for specialization and doing research activities at the university.
5. **Awareness:** Raise awareness of the importance of Design for All as a necessary precondition for improving the life quality of people with disabilities.

The MOOC content was selected to achieve the Inclusion and Awareness objectives.

SOLUTIONS AND RECOMMENDATIONS

The course was defined to be an extended MOOC (xMOOC, similar to standard online courses but with larger learner numbers) that could focus on knowledge creation by collaborative work trying to engage learners in online activities as explored by Ostashewski et al. (2016). The interaction through the forum and its ordered message system is run by content curators. Curators give valuable feedback to learners undertaking the courses, not only on specific course-related content but also on general platform-related and associated topics (Rodrigo et al., 2016).

Authors share the vision for a new approach to curricula design that responds to the challenges of education and personalization aspects for learners with disabilities. Design for All provides an excellent approach for the development of products and services by considering the needs of all potential users, including those with disabilities. Raising stakeholders' awareness of Design for All concepts and their application is necessary in order to apply these principles in the design of products and services (Persson et al., 2015). Therefore, the design of the course had the objective of familiarizing the learner with an accessible use of the Internet as a way to reduce barriers for people with disabilities. Assistive technology is any tool that helps a user to perform tasks that he or she may not otherwise be able to do. Therefore, the course also includes the process used in selecting, obtaining, and using these tools.

As an overall, the MOOC provides learners with an introduction to:

- The barriers users with disabilities may face in accessing Internet services,
- Sample strategies for improving accessibility,
- The principles of Universal Design, Access For All and User-Centered Design,
- A framework for web accessibility to remove barriers,
- And assistive technologies used for accessing Internet services.

MOOC learning design process

Little guidance is available for educators to address the design of MOOCs from scratch (Papathoma, 2019), therefore, the teaching staff tried to keep a balance between the following aspects:

- A general description of the course (name, duration and field/area),
- The target learners,
- The pedagogical approaches that will be followed,
- The specific objectives and competencies pursued within the course,
- The learning contents that will be delivered,
- The assessment activities employed,
- And the complementary technologies that will support the MOOC.

As previously discussed, online learners include a significant percentage of adult learners with a degree of autonomy, self-direct learning, potential linguistic or spatial capabilities and inter-intrapersonal skills (Littlejohn et al., 2016). For the content, most of the learning activities belonging to the traditional online course were actualized and adapted to the new open environment. For this process, we have used Gardner's learning styles (Gardner & Hatch, 1989) in conjunction with Gagné's nine events (1992) to design an engaging and meaningful MOOC type of instruction. From the nine intelligences, the following five have been selected for the Design for All MOOC taking into account the variety of potential learners:

1. **Linguistic Intelligence:** New activities on reading texts and explaining their thoughts about through forum posts have been encouraged.
2. **Logical:** New activities that foster investigation and inquiries on assistive technologies have been developed.
3. **Spatial Intelligence:** New resources have been included implementing graphics, charts, maps and links to video.
4. **Interpersonal Intelligence:** Tools have been included for video-conferencing and writing activities have been reinforced.
5. **Intrapersonal Intelligence:** Distance learners are used to be taught through independent study and introspection. New textual materials have been included.

As for the relationship with Gagné's interaction events (1992), some new activities and related learning resources have been implemented or re-factored as explained below:

- New online lessons (modules) that focus on one core objective, which allows the learner to master that topic before moving onto the next,
- More explanations after demonstrations,
- Online learning guidance,
- Concept mapping as a method to provide learning guidance,
- Provision of case studies for real-world application,
- Visual images to make visual associations,
- Self-practice for accessible web development,
- Timely feedback: confirmatory, informative, analytical and remedial,

- And real-world scenarios.

As examples, an interactive video (HTML5 Package, H5P) has been re-factored for presenting types of disabilities (Activity A.5), an old presentation video was converted into a modular mini-video (Letón & Molanes-Lopez, 2014) for implementing spatial learning style in activity A.5 and an inquiry-based design activity, searching for assistive technologies, has been developed for logical learning in Activity A.9. Table 2 shows the complete correlation between the 14 re-factored or new-designed learning activities, the pre-selected Gardner's Learning Styles and the Gagné's events.

FUTURE RESEARCH DIRECTIONS

Future work will focus on the practical use of the developed course in differentiated educational environments, as it will be delivered in the next academic year in UNED Abierta. Regarding the MOOCification process, authors will gather and analyze quantitative data to differentiate between the course being taught as a blended MOOC and the traditional online course to identify where learners achieve better results, taking the research done by Parry & Baird (2013) as a reference.

A second objective is to evaluate this MOOC learning design within the framework developed in the YourMOOC4all project (Iniesto & Rodrigo, 2018). This project provides a framework for registered learners evaluating MOOCs based on Universal Design for Learning (UDL). Learners will provide direct feedback on the course's UDL characteristics, autonomously, through a web form specifically designed to assess Design for All quality of the course, along with information about their accessibility needs. In that sense, the course content links relevant concepts such as User eXperience Design (UXD) and User-Centered Design (UCD) and the importance they have in inclusive design and accessibility (Persson, et al., 2015). It is relevant to consider the evolution of design approaches with a more user-centered focus such as the UCD, or a Universal Design (UD) perspective like Design for All. Inclusive Design (ID) is suitable in a massive online environment such as MOOCs where an individualized learning experience can be achieved through the personalization of the learning environment (García-Peñalvo et al., 2018).

CONCLUSION

The task of converting introductory sections of a HE traditional online course into a MOOC has been shown to be not as simple as just transferring the online learning materials to a different platform. Teaching staff can take advantage of the similarities from HE online delivery while developing MOOCs, mainly due to the use of eLearning instructional design, but differences arise because, in MOOCs, learners should be continually influenced by information, social interaction and learning experiences keeping it as an engaging course.

In this chapter, an example of MOOCification of an online course based on Design for All has been detailed and explained. The standard quality model for online courses was complemented with the OpenupEd label features. The specific MOOC instructional design was based on a variable metric that facilitates the control on the way each course is structured, the kind of resources that are included and the way the activities, the interaction points with the learners and the assessment process are integrated.

Table 2. Gardner's Multiple intelligences product grid mapping with re-factored learning activities for MOOC adjusted to Gagné's nine events of instruction

	RE-FACTORED LEARNING ACTIVITY			
	GARDNER'S LEARNING STYLE	**TEACHING ACTIVITIES**	**TEACHING MATERIALS**	**INSTRUCTIONAL STRATEGIES (A – N, Activity) (T – N, Assessment test) (G – N, Gagné's event)**
Study Guide				(G.2) Inform learners of the objectives of the course, the outcomes and the assessment methods
MODULE 1. BASIC CONCEPTS ON USABILITY AND WEB ACCESSIBILITY				
1.1. Understanding Design for All, facing barriers and challenges ahead	Spatial	Visual presentations	Video presentation	(A.1) Video (G.4) Present the course
	Linguistic	Read about it, write about it	Source documents on the web	(A.2) Forum participation (first interaction) (G.5) Provide learning guidance
1.2. Usability and accessibility: somewhat distinct design concepts	Intrapersonal	Independent study	Self-checking material	(A.3) Personal activities (G.7) Provide feedback
	Intrapersonal	Independent study	Self-checking material	(T.1) Self-assessment test (G.3) Stimulate recall of prior learning
1.3. Types of disabilities	Interpersonal	Roleplay, social gatherings	Accessibility software	(A.4) Social empathy, case studies (G.1) Gain the attention of the learners
	Spatial	Visual presentations with interaction and assessments	Interactive H5P-based video	(A.5) Video (G.4) Present the content
MODULE 2. WORKING ALONG WITH UNIVERSAL DESIGN, DESIGN FOR ALL AND USER-CENTERED DESIGN				
2.1. Universal Design and Access For All	Spatial	Visual presentations	Graphs, maps, slides	(A.6) Conceptual maps, organizational charts (G.4) Present the content
	Spatial	Visual presentations with interaction	Modular Mini-video	(A.7) Video (G.4) Present the content
2.2. User-Centered Design	Linguistic	Lectures, discussions, read about it, write about it	Source documents on the web	(A.8) Debate, forum participation (G.5) Provide learning guidance
	Intrapersonal	Individualized instruction	Project materials, web accessibility checker	(A.9) Practice (G.6) Elicit performance
	Intrapersonal	Independent study	Self-checking material	(T.2) Self-assessment test (G.8) Assess performance
2.3. Assistive technologies and reasonable accommodations	Interpersonal	Cooperative Learning, a feedback technique	Fill-in tables	(A.10) Brainstorming, team learning (G.7) Provide feedback
	Logical	Independent study	Web navigation	(A.11) Object searching (inquiry) (G.6) Elicit performance
	Intrapersonal	Independent study	Audio-description development	(A.12) Self-designed project (G.8) Assess performance
	Intrapersonal	Independent study	Self-checking material	(T.3) Self-assessment test (G.8) Assess performance
MODULE 3. INTERFACE AND CONTENT ACCESSIBLE DESIGN				
3.1 Web access for people with disabilities	Linguistic	Read about it, write about it	Source documents on the web	(A.13) Debate, forum participation (G.5) Provide learning guidance
	Intrapersonal	Independent study	Self-checking material	(T.4) Self-assessment test (G.8) Assess performance
3.2 Adapted and personalized design	Intrapersonal	Independent study	Self-checking material	(A.14) Personal activities (G.9) Enhance retention and transfer to the job

Specifically, metrics measured seven aspects: topic, contents, duration, structure, specific instructional design guidelines, social channels, and teaching roles. The learning activities were completely refactored, adapted to MOOC learners, along with the content itself and the online assessments. The subject of the course is based on Design for All and reinforces current legislation regarding the need to include educational curricula focused on inclusion awareness.

ACKNOWLEDGMENT

This research was supported by the Research Chair on "Technology and Accessibility" UNED - Fundación VODAFONE and the MUSACCES project [S2015/HUM-3494]. Covadonga and Francisco thank the Global OER Graduate Network (GO-GN), which is supported by the William and Flora Hewlett Foundation. Francisco's research is supported by OpenTEL and a Leverhulme Trust Doctoral Scholarship in Open World Learning based in the Institute of Educational Technology (IET) at The Open University (OU).

REFERENCES

Bruff, D. (2012). *Teaching with MOOCs: Four Cases.* Retrieved from http://cft. vanderbilt. edu/2012/11/ teaching-with-moocs—four-cases

Bruff, D. O., Fisher, D. H., McEwen, K. E., & Smith, B. E. (2013). Wrapping a MOOC: Student perceptions of an experiment in blended learning. *Journal of Online Learning and Teaching / MERLOT*, *9*(2), 187.

Caulfield, M., Collier, A., & Halawa, S. (2013). Rethinking online community in MOOCs used for blended learning. *Educause Review*. Retrieved from http://www.educause.edu/ero/article/rethinking-online-community-moocs-used-blended-learning

Clark, D. (2013). *MOOCs: taxonomy of 8 types of MOOC.* Retrieved from http://donaldclarkplanb.blogspot.com/2013/04/moocs-taxonomy-of-8-types-of-mooc.html

Combéfis, S., Bibal, A., & Van Roy, P. (2014). Recasting a Traditional Course into a MOOC by Means of a SPOC. *Proceedings of the European MOOCs Stakeholders Summit*, 205-208.

Conole, G. (2008). Capturing practice: the role of mediating artefacts in learning design. In L. Lockyer, S. Bennett, S. Agostinho, & B. Harper (Eds.), *Handbook of Research on Learning Design and Learning Objects: Issues, Applications and Technologies* (pp. 187–207). Hersey, PA: IGI Global. doi:10.4018/978-1-59904-861-1.ch008

Conole, G. (2010). An overview of design representations. In *Proceedings of the 7th International Conference on Networked Learning* (pp. 482-489). Academic Press.

Conole, G. (2014). A new classification schema for MOOCs. *The International Journal for Innovation and Quality in Learning, 2*(3), 65-77.

Creelman, A., Ehlers, U., & Ossiannilsson, E. (2014). Perspectives on MOOC quality-An account of the EFQUEL MOOC Quality Project. *INNOQUAL-International Journal for Innovation and Quality in Learning*, *2*(3), 78–87.

Dabbagh, N., & Kitsantas, A. (2012). Personal Learning Environments, social media, and self-regulated learning: A natural formula for connecting formal and informal learning. *The Internet and higher education, 15*(1), 3–8. doi:10.1016/j.iheduc.2011.06.002

Daniel, J. (2012). Making sense of MOOCs: Musings in a maze of myth, paradox and possibility. *Journal of Interactive Media in Education, 2012*(3), 18. doi:10.5334/2012-18

Dasarathy, B., Sullivan, K., Schmidt, D. C., Fisher, D. H., & Porter, A. (2014). The past, present, and future of MOOCs and their relevance to software engineering. In *Proceedings of the on Future of Software Engineering* (pp. 212-224). ACM. 10.1145/2593882.2593897

de Waard, I., Gallagher, M. S., Zelezny-Green, R., Czerniewicz, L., Downes, S., Kukulska-Hulme, A., & Willems, J. (2014). Challenges for conceptualising EU MOOC for vulnerable learner groups. *Proceedings of the European MOOC Stakeholder Summit, 2014*, 33–42.

Defaweux, V., Delbrassine, D., Dozo, B. O., Etienne, A. M., Centi, V., D'Anna, V., ... Wagener, A. (2019). To combine a MOOC to a regular face-to-face course–A study of three blended pedagogical patterns. *Proceedings of Work in Progress Papers of the Research. Experience and Business Tracks at EMOOCs, 2019*, 210–217.

Downes, S. (2015). The Quality of Massive Open Online Courses. In International Handbook of E-Learning. Academic Press.

Emanuel, E. J. (2013). MOOCs taken by educated few. *Nature, 503*, 342.

Gagné, R. M., Briggs, L. J., & Wager, W. W. (1992). *Principles of instructional design* (4th ed.). Fort Worth, TX: Harcourt Brace Jovanovich College Publishers.

García-Peñalvo, F. J., Fidalgo-Blanco, Á., & Sein-Echaluce, M. L. (2018). An adaptive hybrid MOOC model: Disrupting the MOOC concept in higher education. *Telematics and Informatics, 35*(4), 1018–1030. doi:10.1016/j.tele.2017.09.012

Gardner, H. (1983). Frames of Mind: The Theory of Multiple Intelligences. New York: Academic Press.

Gardner, H., & Hatch, T. (1989). Educational implications of the theory of multiple intelligences. *Educational Researcher, 18*(8), 4–10.

Gasevic, D., Kovanovic, V., Joksimovic, S., & Siemens, G. (2014). Where is research on massive open online courses headed? A data analysis of the MOOC Research Initiative. *The International Review of Research in Open and Distributed Learning, 15*(5). doi:10.19173/irrodl.v15i5.1954

Gil-Jaurena, I. (2015). MOOCs in Spain: preliminary lessons from UNED MOOCs experience. *MOOCs and educational challenges around Asia and Europe*, 191-204.

Guàrdia, L., Maina, M., & Sangrà, A. (2013). MOOC design principles: A pedagogical approach from the learner's perspective. *eLearning Papers*, (33).

Haggard, S. (2013). Massive open online courses and online distance learning: review. *GOV. UK. Research and analysis, 18.*

Hill, P. (2012). Online educational delivery models: A descriptive view. *EDUCAUSE Review, 47*(6), 84–86.

Holotescu, C., Grosseck, G., Creţu, V., & Naaji, A. (2014). Integrating MOOCs in blended courses. *Elearning & Software for Education*, (1).

Howell, J., & Ostashewski, N. (2015). MOOCifying courses: real and authentic learning in higher education. In EdMedia+ Innovate Learning (pp. 1663-1668). Association for the Advancement of Computing in Education (AACE).

Hoyos, C. A., Ayres, I. M. E., Kloos, C. D., Román, J. V., Merino, P. J. M., & Pérez, E. L. (2019). Redesigning a freshman engineering course to promoteactive learning by flipping the classroom through thereuse of MOOcs. *International Journal of Engineering Education*, *35*(1), 385–396.

Iniesto, F., McAndrew, P., Minocha, S., & Coughlan, T. (2016). Accessibility of MOOCs: Understanding the Provider Perspective. *Journal of Interactive Media in Education*, *2016*(1), 20. doi:10.5334/jime.430

Iniesto, F., & Rodrigo, C. (2018). YourMOOC4all: a MOOCs inclusive design and useful feedback research project. In 2018 Learning With MOOCS (LWMOOCS) (pp. 147-150). IEEE. doi:10.1109/LWMOOCS.2018.8534644

Jordan, K. (2015). Massive open online course completion rates revisited: Assessment, length and attrition. *The International Review of Research in Open and Distributed Learning*, *16*(3). doi:10.19173/irrodl.v16i3.2112

Kear, K., Rosewell, J., Williams, K., Ossiannilsson, E., Rodrigo, C., Sánchez-Elvira, P., … Mellar, H. (2016). *Quality assessment for e-learning: A benchmarking approach*. Academic Press.

Koller, D. (2012). How online courses can form a basis for on-campus teaching. *Forbes*. Retrieved from http://www.forbes.com/sites/coursera/2012/11/07/how-online-courses-can-form-a-basis-for-on-campus-teaching/

Lane, C. (2008). *The distance learning technology resource guide*. Retrieved from https://www.tecweb.org/styles/gardner.html

Letón, E., & Molanes-Lopez, E. M. (2014). Two New Concepts in Video Podcasts-Minimalist Slides and Modular Teaching Mini-videos. *CSEDU*, (2), 292-297.

Littlejohn, A., Hood, N., Milligan, C., & Mustain, P. (2016). Learning in MOOCs: Motivations and self-regulated learning in MOOCs. *The Internet and Higher Education*, *29*, 40–48. doi:10.1016/j.iheduc.2015.12.003

Liyanagunawardena, T. R., Parslow, P., & Williams, S. (2014). Dropout: MOOC participants' perspective. *Proceedings of the European MOOC Stakeholder Summit*, *2014*, 95–100.

Montgomery, A., & Mallette, L. (2018, October). Massive Open Online Courses: Misperceptions of Completion Rates The Misalignment of Measurements and Actual Participation. In *E-Learn: World Conference on E-Learning in Corporate, Government, Healthcare, and Higher Education* (pp. 850-857). Association for the Advancement of Computing in Education (AACE).

Morrison, D. (2013). *A MOOC Quality Scorecard applied to Coursera Course*. Retrieved from http://onlinelearninginsights.wordpress.com/2013/06/15/a-mooc-quality-scorecard-applied-to-courseracourse

Mudler, F. (2013). OER reflections on Opening up Education (OuE). In Neth-ER Seminar, EU Parliament, Brussels, Belgium.

Nunez, J. L. M., Caro, E. T., & Gonzalez, J. R. H. (2016). From higher education to open education: Challenges in the transformation of an online traditional course. *IEEE Transactions on Education*, *60*(2), 134–142. doi:10.1109/TE.2016.2607693

Ostashewski, N., Howell, J., & Dron, J. (2016). *Crowdsourcing MOOC Interactions: Using a Social Media Site cMOOC to Engage Students in University Course Activities*. Academic Press.

Ostashewski, N., Howell, J., & Dron, J. (2017). MOOCifying Courses: Delivery of a MOOC to Enhance University Course Activities. *Journal of Learning for Development.*, *4*(2), 184–195.

Papathoma, T. (2019). *MOOC educators: who they are and how they learn* (Doctoral dissertation). The Open University.

Parry, Z., & Baird, C. (2013). Should I, Could I MOOCify my course? In *INTED2013 Proceedings* (pp. 3669-3679). IATED.

Persson, H., Åhman, H., Yngling, A. A., & Gulliksen, J. (2015). Universal design, inclusive design, accessible design, design for all: Different concepts—one goal? On the concept of accessibility—historical, methodological and philosophical aspects. *Universal Access in the Information Society*, *14*(4), 505–526. doi:10.100710209-014-0358-z

Read, T., & Rodrigo, C. (2014). Toward a quality model for UNED MOOCs. *eLearning Papers*. Retrieved from http://www. openeducationeuropa. eu/en/elearning_papers

Richardson, J. T. (2017). Academic attainment in students with autism spectrum disorders in distance education. *Open Learning: The Journal of Open, Distance and e-Learning, 32*(1), 81-91.

Rodrigo, C., García-Serrano, A., Delgado, J. L., & Iniesto, F. (2016). Challenges while MOOCifying a HE eLearning course on Universal Accessibility. In *Proceedings of the XVII International Conference on Human Computer Interaction* (p. 44). ACM. 10.1145/2998626.2998659

Rodrigo, C., Read, T., Santamaria, M., & Sánchez-Elvira, A. (2014). OpenupEdLabel for MOOC quality assurance: UNED COMA initial self-evaluation. In *Actas del V Congreso Internacional sobre Calidad y Accesibilidad en la Formación Virtual (CAFVIR 2014)* (pp. 551-555). Academic Press.

Rosewell, J. (2013). *E-xcellence / OpenupEd Quality benchmarks for MOOCs*. Retrieved from http://www.openuped.eu/images/docs/e-xcellence-MOOC-benchmarks-v09.pdf

Rosewell, J., & Barefoot, H. (2013). MOOCs and Quality Issues – QAQE Steering Group. *QAA*. Retrieved from http://www.slideshare.net/J.P.Rosewell/rosewell-barefootmoo-csandqualityissues

Sandeen, C. (2013). Integrating MOOCs into traditional higher education: The emerging "MOOC 3.0" era. *Change: The Magazine of Higher Learning, 45*(6), 34-39.

Sooryanarayan, D. G., & Gupta, D. (2015). Impact of learner motivation on mooc preferences: Transfer vs. made moocs. In *2015 International Conference on Advances in Computing, Communications and Informatics (ICACCI)* (pp. 929-934). IEEE. 10.1109/ICACCI.2015.7275730

Weller, M. (2013). *MOOCs & Quality*. MOOC Quality Project, week 7. Retrieved from http://mooc.efquel.org/week-7-moocs-quality-by-martin-weller

Yang, D., Sinha, T., Adamson, D., & Rosé, C. P. (2013, December). Turn on, tune in, drop out: Anticipating student dropouts in massive open online courses. In *Proceedings of the 2013 NIPS Data-driven education workshop* (*Vol. 11*, p. 14). Academic Press.

Yousef, A. M. F., Chatti, M. A., Schroeder, U., & Wosnitza, M. (2014). What drives a successful MOOC? An empirical examination of criteria to assure design quality of MOOCs. In *2014 IEEE 14th International Conference on Advanced Learning Technologies* (pp. 44-48). IEEE. 10.1109/ICALT.2014.23

Yuan, L., & Powell, S. (2013). MOOCs and disruptive innovation: Implications for higher education. *eLearning Papers, In-Depth, 33*(2), 1-7.

Zweifler, S. (2013). Study: MOOC students are highly educated, job-oriented. *The Daily Pennsylvanian*. Retrieved from http://www.thedp.com/article/2013/11/new-penn-study-moocs-far-from-revolutionizing-higher-education

KEY TERMS AND DEFINITIONS

Accessibility: All learners can use courses in a range of contexts of use, including mainstream and assistive technologies; to achieve this, courses need to be designed and developed, considering technical and learning design aspects, to support usability across these contexts.

Design for All: Design of products, services and systems by as many people as possible without the need for adaptation.

eLearning: A learning system that we can obtain through the internet using an electronic device. I can also be called online learning or online education.

Instructional Design: The instructional design process consists of determining the needs of learners, defining the end goals and objectives of instruction, designing and planning assessment tasks, and designing teaching and learning activities to ensure the quality of instruction.

MOOC: MOOCs are courses designed for large numbers of participants, which can be accessed by anyone anywhere as long as they have an internet connection, are open to everyone without entry qualifications, and offer a complete course experience online for free.

MOOCification: The process of converting a distance education online course into a MOOC.

Multiple Intelligences: The theory of multiple intelligences differentiates human intelligence into specific 'modalities', rather than seeing intelligence as dominated by a single.

Quality Model: Is the framework of a product quality evaluation system, it determines which quality characteristics will be taken into account when evaluating the properties of an educational product.

Chapter 3
Inclusive Education Through Accessible Mobile Serious Games

Angel Jaramillo-Alcázar
https://orcid.org/0000-0003-4143-2515
Universidad de Las Américas, Ecuador

Santiago Criollo-C
https://orcid.org/0000-0001-7212-5513
Universidad de Las Américas, Ecuador

Sergio Luján-Mora
https://orcid.org/0000-0001-5000-864X
University of Alicante, Spain

ABSTRACT

Accessibility has been defined as the ability of an object to be used despite the condition or disability of a person. However, it is a feature that often has not been taken into account in the design of products or services, and the mobile serious game market is no exception. Accessibility guidelines were defined through the consolidation of different initiatives and good practices of video game developers as well as groups interested in providing accessibility to video games. Once the guidelines were defined, a method for evaluating the accessibility of mobile serious games was developed and applied in a mobile serious game. The purpose of this document is to propose an evaluation tool for those who wish to develop accessible mobile serious games for people with impairments and improve inclusive education.

DOI: 10.4018/978-1-7998-2325-4.ch003

INTRODUCTION

Nowadays, technology is an active part of people's daily lives, including teaching-learning processes. Many educational institutions use technology as a tool to reinforce the teaching process, specially by the inclusion of smart devices. Cisco (2017) announced that 563 million mobile devices and connections to the Internet were added in 2015. According to The Radicati Group (2014) the number of worldwide mobile users is expected to increase over 6.2 billion at the end of 2018 and than roughly 84% of the world population will be using mobile technology. This is because people prefer to purchase a mobile device to access the Internet instead of a computer. In education, mobile devices offer a variety of ways to learn, communicate and collaborate (Gikas & Grant, 2013). For example, mobile learning (m-learning) allows users of mobile devices to be able to learn from any device at anytime, anywhere (Removed for blind review).

On the other hand, education is one of the essential factors for success in life, but if education is not inclusive then Stephen Hawking's words "Disability need not be an obstacle to success", which begins with the prologue of World Report on Disability of the World Health Organization (WHO), cannot be fulfilled (2011). Around the world, people with disabilities have grown in number. More than one billion people live with some type of disability, what is about 15% of the world population (World Health Organization, 2011). These people usually live with social, educational and entertainment limitations because their impairments. All of them require equal conditions in their education.

Furthermore, Accessible University (2016) defines accessibility as the ability of an object to be used in spite of the condition or disability of a person. Accessibility in video games is a factor that is beginning to be considered by software developers and some video game players have benefited from it. The growth of people with disabilities has led to initiatives that promote accessibility as an important feature in the world around us. In addition, thanks to technology a variety of study techniques have been developed to ease learning. Some examples are different serious games whose objective includes teaching, practice and reinforce of what was learned in the classroom. Serious games is a category of video games designed with the purpose of supporting the educational process (Michael & Chen, 2006). One of the main advantages of serious games is that they enable learning through entertainment (Koster, 2013). It is estimated that the development of this kind of games will reach $5,400 million in 2020, at a compound annual growth rate of 16.38 % between 2015 and 2020 (Markets and Markets, n.d.). In many cases, serious games allow teachers to apply new teaching methods (Sauve, Senecal, Kaufman, Renaud, & Leclerc, 2011). This kind of video games are designed to understand the necessities of students in the acquisition of skills, knowledge (Ghannem, 2014) and the achieving of learning outcomes (Guillén-Nieto & Aleson-Carbonell, 2012).

Likewise, user experience (UX) and usability are terms that had to be coined in the design of technological products and services (Rusu, Rusu, Roncagliolo, & González, 2015). UX is defined in ISO 9241-210:2019 as a "person's perceptions and responses resulting from the use and/or anticipated use of a product, system or service" (International Standard Organization, 2019). On the other hand, usability is defined in ISO 9241-11:2018 as "the extent to which a system, product or service can be used by specified users to achieve specified goals with effectiveness, efficiency and satisfaction in a specified context of use" (International Standard Organization, 2018). Both, UX and usability, seems to be a tendency and this work tries to reinforce their adoption in the design of video games.

Serious games have been applied in different knowledge areas: medicine, engineering, training and education, programming, business and industry, nursing education, among others. In spite of efforts that has been made in create and develop serious games, there still exist a gap in the accessibility field (Sik, David, & Brown, 2010; Torrente, del Blanco, Moreno-Ger, & Fernández-Manjón, 2012). This gap can be mitigated through the development of accessibility guidelines and an evaluation tool used in different platforms and applied to education on people with some disorder. Therefore, considering the growth of the mobile video games market, the increase of smart devices in the daily life of people, as well as the number of people with disabilities in the world, it is important to determine an accessibility evaluation tool for mobile serious games. A tool that allows identifying the accessibility that a mobile video game can present for people with different disabilities.

Some initiatives to design mobile serious games have emerged recently. In engineering for example, in a study by Salvador-Ullauri, Jaramillo-Alcázar, & Luján-Mora (2017), the authors have presented a serious game to learn the Ohm's law. In addition, in a study by Callaghan, Savin-Bane, McShane and Eguiluz (2017) a serious game based on Learning Mechanics-Game is proposed. There are some studies about accessibility in video games, its design and importance in different fields. Grammenos (2009) introduces the concept of *universally accessible games*, that is, games proactively designed to optimally fit and adapt to individual gamer characteristics and to be concurrently played among people with diverse abilities, without requiring particular adjustments or modifications. Another study by Grammenos (2007) describes how the Unified Design method, originally conceived as a means for developing universally accessible user interfaces, can be adapted and applied to the development of universally accessible games. Also, a study by Yuan (2011) describes a state-of-the-art in research and practice in the accessibility of video games and points out relevant areas for future research. Finally, Pérez-Castilla (2012) seek to raise awareness and support developers and designers, to take into account the accessibility from the beginning, to ensure that the games will be accessible and that they can be used by as many players as possible, with the advantages derived from it.

There are also initiatives that come from governmental institutions. This is the case of the Government of Spain, who through its Ministry of Finance and Public Function has developed an accessibility guide for mobile applications (Aguado & Estrada, 2017). This guide aims to help developers / evaluators of mobile applications in terms of accessibility. In addition, this government has defined that all the companies that develop applications for the public sector must be accessible (La Presidencia & Con Las Cortes Igualdad, 2018). In previous works, the authors of this research analyzed several accessibility guidelines for mobile video games development according to four principal impairments: visual (Removed for blind review), hearing (Removed for blind review), motor (Removed for blind review) and cognitive (Removed for blind review). The focus of this article is based in these previous works. In this work, the authors propose to review the guidelines and the best accessibility practices that different developers or interest groups have proposed, as well as to define a evaluation tool that allows measuring the accessibility of a video game and to support the improvement of the learning of the people with disabilities through mobile serious games.

BACKGROUND

In the research presented in this article, the authors analyze several accessibility guidelines for mobile video games development for people with impairments. The scientific community has not given much interest to the accessibility of video games so far. This group of people have not proposed guidelines for the development of accessible video games. Guidelines, for the most part, originate from video games development groups. The scientific community focus their work on proposing accessibility features so that people with disabilities have the opportunity to have fun through video games.

Mobile Video Games in Education

There are works that confirm that the use of mobile video games in the educational field is evident and is increasing. Sánchez and Olivares (2011) obtained results about the implementation of a series of learning activities based on Mobile Serious Games for the development of problem solving and collaborative skills in elementary students. On the other hand, a study by Akkerman, Admiraal and Huizenga (2009) was developed with the aim of using a mobile video game to teach medieval history of Amsterdam to high school students. Likewise, DeShazo, Harris and Pratt proposed a study about a review of mobile video games for diabetes education (2010). These researches are examples about the use of mobile video games for education.

There are also mobile video games that are aimed at people with disabilities to facilitate their use and improve their experience. It is the case of BrailePlay (Milne, Bennett, Ladner, & Azenkot, 2014), a suite of accessible games for smartphones that teach Braille character encodings to promote Braille literacy. Also, Song, Karimi and Kim propose to design a mobile learning game for visually impaired children to improve they spatial ability and executive function (Donggil Song, Karimi, & Kim, 2011). This type of initiative improves the inclusion of people with disabilities in the educational sectors and the labor market.

Impairments Description

The characteristics of the different types of disabilities should be taken into account when developing accessibility guidelines and their combination could be a challenge. However, the main ones are identified with the visual, auditory, motor and cognitive areas of the human body. These disabilities are described below to identify the area of analysis of this article.

Visual Impairments

In 2010 around 285 million people had some kind of visual impairment, and of these, 39 million were blind (World Health Organization, 2016b). According to the International Classification of Functioning, Disability and Health (ICF) (World Health Organization, 2001), the visual function is divided into four levels of severity:

- Normal vision.
- Moderate visual impairment.
- Severe visual impairment.

- Blindness.

Both moderate visual impairment and severe visual impairment are grouped under the term *low vision*; *low vision* and *blindness* together represents the total number of cases of visual impairments. Another vision alteration is *color blindness* which is defined as inability to detect certain colors or distinguish between red and green or yellow and blue correctly (Colour Blind Awareness, n.d.).

Hearing Impairments

Also, in 2010 around 360 million people worldwide had disabling hearing loss, and 32 million of these were children (World Health Organization, 2016a). According to WHO, there are four grades of hearing impairment based on a decibel scale representing hearing loss:

- Slight/mild hearing loss (26 - 40dB).
- Moderate hearing loss (41 - 60dB).
- Severe hearing loss (61 - 80dB).
- Profound hearing loss (over 81dB).

People with mild, moderate and severe hearing loss are grouped under the term *hard of hearing*, whereas people with profound hearing are *deaf*. Both, hard of hearing and deaf together represents the total number of cases of hearing impairments.

Motor Impairments

According to the ICF (World Health Organization, 2001), body structures related to movement are divided as follows:

- Structure of head and neck region.
- Structure of shoulder region.
- Structure of upper extremity.
- Structure of pelvic region.
- Structure of lower extremity.
- Structure of trunk.

These body structures give rise to some motor disabilities, such as quadriplegia, paraplegia, among others.

Cognitive Impairments

Likewise, the ICF (World Health Organization, 2001) divides mental functions in global and specific. Global mental functions consider functions like consciousness, orientation, intellectual, global psychosocial, temperament and personality, energy and drive, sleep and other specified and unspecified. Specific mental functions instead take into accounts the following functions: attention, memory, psychomotor, emotional, perceptual, thought, higher-level cognitive, language, calculation, sequencing complex movements, experience of self and time, and other specified and unspecified.

These mental functions give rise to some cognitive disorders, such as: autism, Down syndrome, traumatic brain injury, attention deficit disorder, memory loss dyslexia, dyscalculia and learning disabilities in general.

MAIN FOCUS OF THE CHAPTER

Accessibility Guidelines Review

Taking into account all these impairments, it is important to determine what accessibility parameters should be taken into account for the development of mobile video games. There are organisms that define accessibility guidelines to be applied in mobile devices. The World Wide Web Consortium (W3C) defines, through the Web Content Accessibility Guidelines (WCAG) 2.1 (World Wide Web Consortium, 2018), a wide variety of recommendations to improve the accessibility of applications in different types of devices. Rather than having technology specific techniques in WCAG 2.0, the guidelines and Success Criteria themselves have been written in a technology neutral fashion. WCAG 2.1 provides four layers of guidance:

- **Principles:** There are four principles of accessibility perceivable, operable, understandable, and robust.
- **Guidelines:** Under the principles are guidelines. There are 13 guidelines that provide the basic goals in order to make content more accessible to users with different disabilities.
- **Success Criteria:** There are 78 success criteria for each guideline that could be used where requirements and conformance testing are necessary. Three levels of conformance are defined A (lowest), AA, and AAA (highest).
- **Sufficient and Advisory Techniques:** For each of the guidelines and success criteria there are a wide variety of techniques. These techniques may be sufficient or advisory. Sufficient for meeting the success criteria and advisory to go beyond what is required by the individual success criteria and to better address the guidelines.

Guidelines and success criteria are structured according to the four principles and also define the necessary bases for anyone to access and use the web content. Users with disabilities cannot use the web if any of the following is not met:

- **Perceivable:** Users must be able to perceive the information and user interface components in different ways.
- **Operable:** Users must be able to operate the user interface and navigation components.
- **Understandable:** Users must be able to understand the information and the operation of the user interface.
- **Robust:** Users must be able to access content as technologies advance.

Table 1: Guidelines and success criteria per principle (WCAG)

	Perceivable	Operable	Understandable	Robust
Guidelines	4	5	3	1
Success Criteria	29	29	17	3
Success Criteria for mobile devices	4	5	6	3

WCAG 2.1 includes guidelines that address the particular problems of people with disabilities. It means, those that block or interfere with access to the web more severely for people with disabilities. However, the W3C in its draft (World Wide Web Consortium, 2016), developed by the Mobile Accessibility Task Force (Mobile A11Y TF), describes how the WCAG and its principles, guidelines, and success criteria can be applied to mobile web content, mobile web apps, native apps, and hybrid apps using web components inside native apps. Taking this into account, the authors presents in Table 1 the number of guidelines and success criteria for each principle of WCAG 2.1, including those that can be applied on mobile devices.

On the other hand, there are some videos game developers' groups that propose accessibility guidelines. Below is a description of those authors that have been considered representative for this work. The AbleGamers Foundation (2012) explains some important accessibility features that can be included into a video game . It defines three levels of accessibility, from a minimal scenario to an ideal one:

- **Level one (Good):** Minimum level, many things already being included as standard-practice.
- **Level two (Better):** Mix the need for greater accessibility and the easiness of implementation.
- **Level three (Best):** Maximum level, the result of covering all the accessibility barriers.

This study presents several accessibility guidelines depending on the disability. These parameters cover from basic to advanced accessibility items that should be considered in development of video games. This study also presents a section that describes six guidelines specifically to mobile gaming accessibility:

- **Touch:** Allow the largest area possible to be pressed in case of an involuntary shaking, tremors or low precision hitting.
- **Multi-Touch:** If the game requires pressing multiple places at the same time, group them together to make press the buttons simultaneously.
- **Alternative Buttons:** If the game requires a special feature such as tapping on the back of the device, rotating it, etc., allow for alternative means to be used to accomplish the same goal.
- **High Contrast:** It is important for those with visual impairments to see important areas of the game and navigation menus.
- **Colorblind Options:** It is convenient that mobile game have options for those with color deficiency or who are colorblind.
- **Speed Settings:** It is adequate that the game has the ability to slow down the game to allow the gamer to play at a rate comfortable for their needs.

On the other hand, the International Game Developers Association (IGDA) with its Game Accessibility Special Interest Group (2004), describes the importance and the benefits of accessible games. Among them, the most relevant benefits are: user satisfaction, reach the largest possible audience and the opportunity to learn new skills.

The Game Accessibility Guidelines (2017) propose a list of parameters for the development of video games for people with disabilities. For the proposed guidelines, three categories are defined: basic, intermediate and advanced. These levels try to balance the number of people who benefit, the impact or difference made for those people and the cost to implement. A step-by-step guide to work with these guidelines is also provided in this paper.

Finally, the MediaLT company in its Game accessibility UPS-project defines a list of guidelines for the development of entertaining software for people with disabilities (MediaLT, 2004). This company determines five categories: level/progression, entries, graphics, sounds, installation and configuration, which have some guidelines to consider.

All these works have been proposed in isolation and each group or developer that has been interested in providing accessibility in video games for people with disabilities has not defined an accessibility evaluation model. All the initiatives have been kept as good practices and for this reason it has become important and necessary the proposal of an accessibility evaluation tool for video games and especially mobile video games. This article proposes a novel accessibility evaluation tool for mobile video games.

METHODOLOGY

In this section, the authors will analyze the guidelines for video games in mobile devices for people with impairments. It is important to note that most guidelines come from video games development groups. They have focused their work on proposing best practices that provide the opportunity for people with disabilities to enter this world and have fun. Likewise, it will be determined those that are required in the mobile devices and their respective levels. Once the authors have presented an overview of accessibility guidelines, it is necessary to analyze and group them into a categorization. Duplicates will be deleted as part of the process.

First, the authors consider appropriate to propose accessibility categories. These categories will group the guidelines according to the complexity of applying them and the benefit they provide to people with disabilities. The perspective of complexity is given from the point of view of the developer while the benefit is defined by the player view.

The categories and guidelines proposed by the cited authors are reviewed and this leads to the definition of three categories or levels. Three levels are proposed to be able to differentiate the simplest levels of accessibility compliance: low, medium and high. These categories cover the full range of guidelines that have been considered:

- **Low Level - Good:** It refers to simple implementation complexity and good accessibility features.
- **Medium Level - Better:** It refers to a medium implementation complexity and better accessibility features.
- **High Level - Best:** It refers to a high implementation complexity and the best accessibility features.

Table 2. Mobile video games guidelines for visual impairments per level

Low Level-Good	Medium Level-Better	High Level-Best
-Use simple language -Customizable fonts (color, sizes) -Enemy marking -Accessible menus -Allow interfaces to be resized -Color-blind options -Adequate distributed virtual controls -No essential information in a color alone	-High-contrast mode -Use explicit auditory feedback -Possibility for repetition -No information outside the player's eye-line -Customized head-up display -Save settings -Turn off/hide background animation -Pause while text is being read -Switch off/on Graphic Elements	-Simple to difficult progression -Speed settings -Sound Compass o voiced GPS -Text to speech capability -Auto aim, ability to lock on a target -Adjustable sensitivity -No 3D graphics mode -In-game tutorials

Table 3. Mobile video games guidelines for hearing impairments per level

Low Level-Good	Medium Level-Better	High Level-Best
-Subtitles -Customizable fonts (color, sizes) -Switch on/off graphic elements -Use simple language -No essential information in audio alone -Adequate interface for the player age -Appropriate words-per-minute -Vibratory alerts	-Use explicit auditory feedback -Background noise to minimum during speech -Possibility for repetition -Ambient noise and information as text output -Save settings -Visual indication of who is currently speaking -Pause while text is being read -Simple evaluation system grades	-Simple to difficult progression -Speed settings -Sound compass or voiced GPS -Provide separate volume controls -Provide a stereo/mono toggle -Adjustable sensitivity/error tolerance -In-game tutorials -Sign language

Table 4. Mobile video games guidelines for motor impairments per level

Low Level-Good	Medium Level-Better	High Level-Best
-Alternative configurations -Camera controls -Accessible menus -Simple and well-spaced game controls -Use simple language -Switch on/off graphic elements -In-game tutorials -Customizable fonts (color, sizes)	-Movable/resizable user interface -Macroability -Difficulty settings and fail safes -Save points -Sensitivity sliders -Click-to-move -Assists (aim, puzzle, etc.) -Use explicit visual rewards -Possibility for repetition -Pause while text is being read -Save settings	-Input devices -Speed settings -Auto aim, ability to lock on a target -Vertical and horizontal orientation -No timing essential to gameplay -Simple to difficult progression

Once the levels have been defined, each guideline is analyzed to assign it to the appropriate level. In this process, it is important to assess ease of implementation and the benefit for people with disabilities.

With the guidelines mapped in their respective category, the authors proceed to eliminate existing duplicates. The process for removing duplicates is done by carefully comparing the descriptions of each guideline. Every author handles their own descriptive language and a thorough review of each guideline is necessary.

Table 5. Mobile video games guidelines for cognitive impairments per level

Low Level-Good	Medium Level-Better	High Level-Best
-Use simple language -Customizable fonts (color, sizes) -Switch on/off graphic elements -Subtitles -In-game tutorials -Simple to difficult progression -Accessible menus -Sandbox modes	-Training levels -Objectives reminder during gameplay -Controls reminder during gameplay -Alternative sound files setup -Use explicit visual rewards -Possibility for repetition -Pause while text is being read -Save settings	-Auto aim, ability to lock on a target -Speed settings -Self-voicing capability -Adjustable sensitivity / error tolerance -Auto-pass

After this analysis, the authors proceed to verify those guidelines that can be used for the assessment of mobile video games. This process is carried out considering the characteristics and nature of mobile devices, for example Android (Android Developers, n.d.) and iOS (Apple Developer, n.d.) accessibility features. The result for visual, hearing, motor and cognitive impairments are showed in Table 2, Table 3, Table 4 and Table 5, respectively. It is important to specify that all the guidelines are ordered in each table by the three levels defined before.

There are several considerations that arise from this analysis. Thus, there are guidelines that apply to several or all disabilities. This is the case of "use simple language" or "customizable fonts", which are parameters to be considered in the development of mobile video games for any type of impairment. On the other hand, it can be seen that a guideline can be present in different disabilities at different levels. The proposal tries to maintain an adequate order of the guidelines for the respective accessibility assessment.

Accessibility Evaluation Tool

With the mobile guidelines determined for each impairment, an indicator is defined for each accessibility level. This indicator allows quantifying the accessibility of a serious game at each of the proposed levels. Each guideline should be analyzed in the video game and its compliance should be scored. The indicator for each level will be given by equation 1:

$$L_j = \sum_{i=0}^{i=n} x_i$$

where n refers to the number of guidelines that are available for each category and x_i takes the value of "1" or "0" taking into account if the game complies with it or not. The authors also include a value of "n/a" for guidelines that do not apply in the type of video game. For a general indicator of a specific impairment accessibility the authors propose the summation of each level indicator as follows in equation 2:

$$L_T = \sum_{j=1}^{j=3} L_j$$

In this case, j corresponds to the number of levels proposed (1 - low, 2 - medium, 3 - high) and L_j is the value scored in each level by equation 1. As result, the authors will have a value that will allow them to have a general accessibility rating of the video game for a specific impairment (L_T). It means that a video game could be assessed depending of a selected impairment.

SOLUTIONS AND RECOMMENDATIONS

Data Analysis and Results

The next step in this work is to present an evaluation as proof of concept of the tool developed to assess its feasibility. For that, the authors assess a mobile video game called Serious Games CEOE. This app, developed by the Confederación Española de Organizaciones Empresariales (CEOE), contains five games to promote healthy life in the daily and especially in the workplace (Confederación Española de Organizaciones Empresariales (CEOE), n.d.). This game was downloaded from Apple Store and installed in an iPhone SE with IOS 12.3.1 for its analysis.

Figure 1 shows the initial screen of the mobile game which allows access to the five games, each one with different purpose:

- **Stress Management:** It is a game of awareness about the importance of stress management in the workplace.
- **Healthy Life:** This game is about consciousness to the player about healthy eating habits.
- **Move It:** It is a game of awareness of healthy habits.
- **The Office Room:** This game allows the player to solve the riddles to end its workday of the healthiest fashion.
- **Business Up:** It is a real-time game whose goal is to grow a company through actions of health and safety at work.

Once the games were identified, the assessment was carried out considering the guidelines in Table 2, 3, 4 and 5. Equation 1 was used to quantify the level of accessibility of each game. For this, each accessibility guideline was analyzed in each game and it was scored whether or not complies with it. To finalize the assessment, it was necessary to determine the total value of accessibility of the video games for each impairment.

In order to reduce the ambiguity in the evaluation, two evaluators were considered (E1, E2). They used the equation 2 and both applied the same evaluation process. The results of all the assessment process are presented in Figure 2, Figure 3, Figure 4 and Figure 5 for visual, hearing, motor and cognitive impairments, respectively.

The total value of accessibility, in parentheses, is obtained by adding the value reached by the video game in each level. Additionally, within the process of analysis of guidelines there is a number of them categorized as "not applies". This consideration is made taking into account the nature of the mobile video game analyzed and would vary from one type of video game to another.

Each graph shows the value of accessibility reached in each level per impairment. It is important to take into account that the maximum value of accessibility that can be reached depends of the impairment analyzed due to the number of guidelines that were determined.

Figure 1. Serious Games (CEOE) initial screen
Source: CEOE, 2019

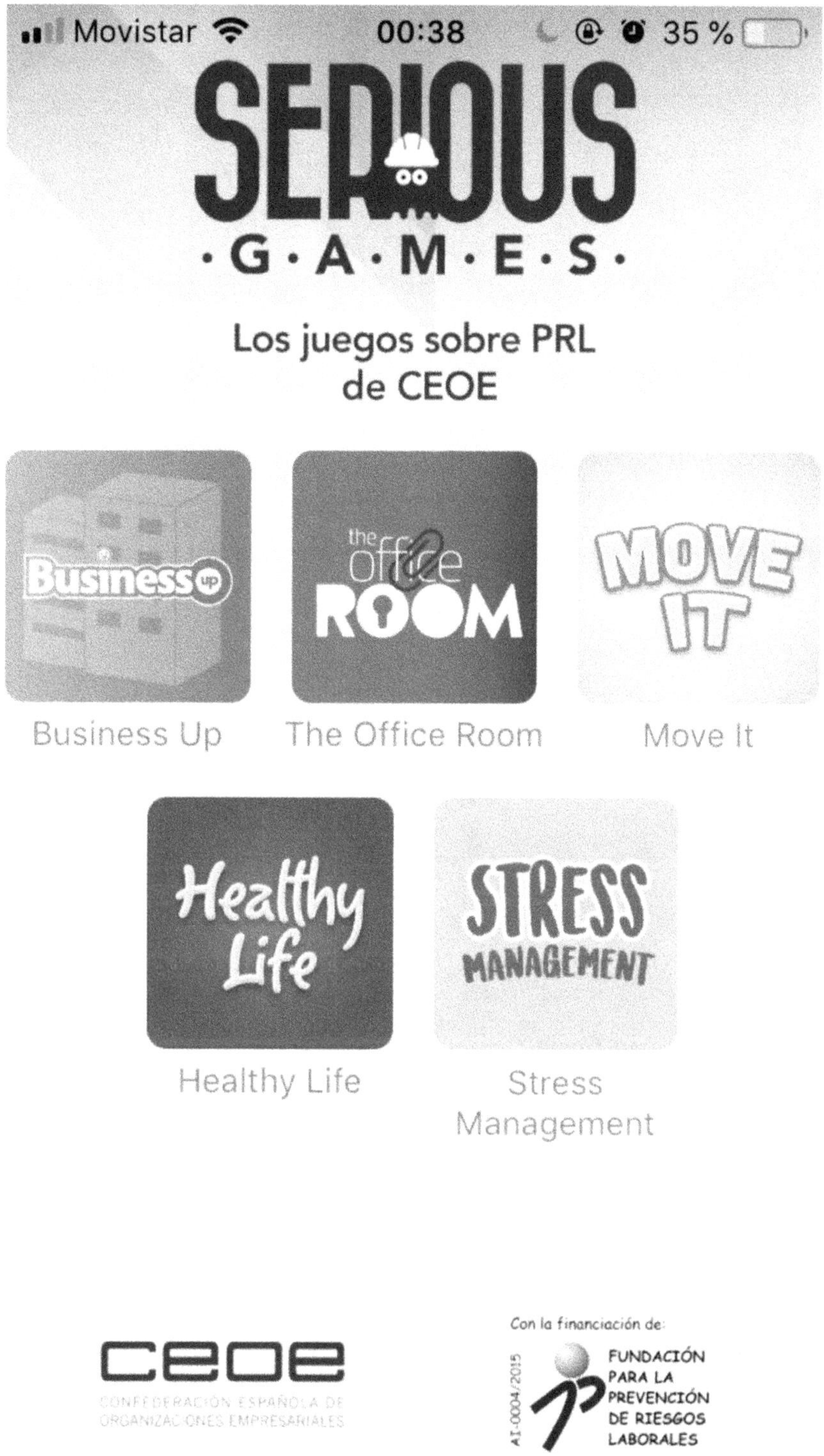

Figure 2. Visual accessibility assessment
Source: Authors, 2019

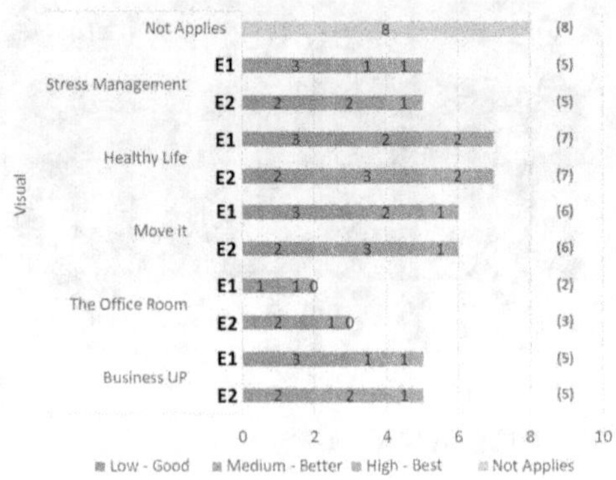

Figure 3. Hearing accessibility assessment
Source: Authors, 2019

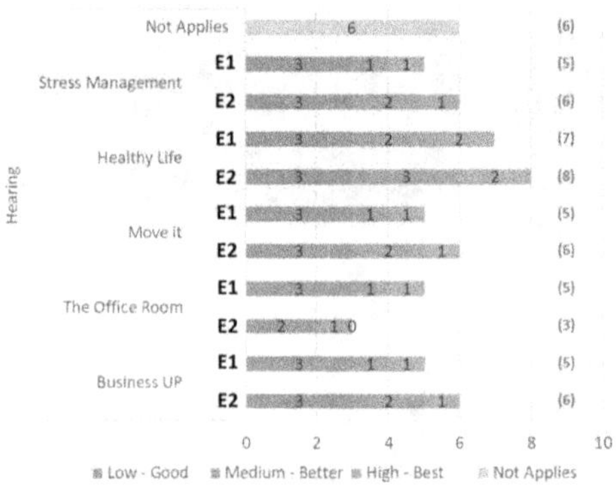

Figure 4. Motor accessibility assessment
Source: Authors, 2019

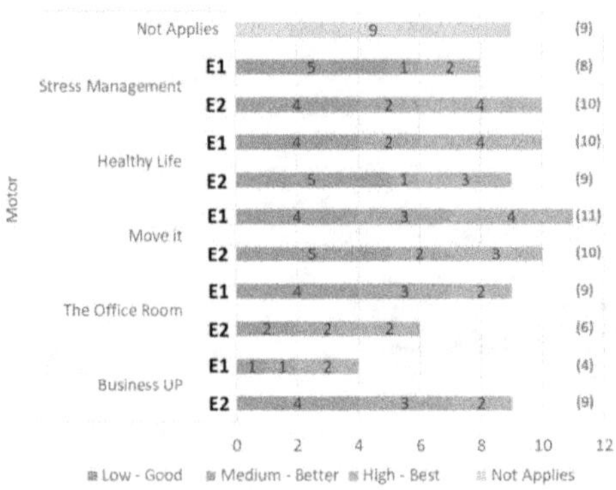

Figure 5. Cognitive accessibility assessment
Source: Authors, 2019

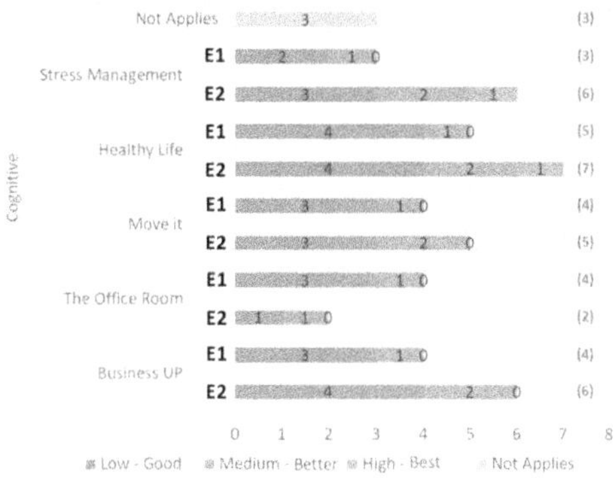

Table 6. Cohen's Kappa - visual impairments guidelines

Game	Good	Better	Best	All Levels
Business UP	0.78	0.82	1.00	0.87
The Office Room	0.74	1.00	1.00	0.93
Move it	0.78	0.83	1.00	0.87
Healthy Life	0.78	0.83	1.00	0.88
Stress Management	0.78	0.82	0.57	0.74

Table 7. Cohen's Kappa - hearing impairments guidelines

Game	Good	Better	Best	All Levels
Business UP	0.58	0.23	1.00	0.66
The Office Room	0.35	0.38	0.77	0.56
Move it	0.58	0.23	1.00	0.66
Healthy Life	0.58	0.35	1.00	0.68
Stress Management	0.58	0.23	0.58	0.53

Table 8. Cohen's Kappa - motor impairments guidelines

Game	Good	Better	Best	All Levels
Business UP	0.81	0.39	0.74	0.64
The Office Room	0.79	0.54	1.00	0.75
Move it	0.79	0.55	0.74	0.70
Healthy Life	0.79	0.70	0.71	0.76
Stress Management	0.79	0.85	0.50	0.76

Table 9. Cohen's Kappa - cognitive impairments guidelines

Game	Good	Better	Best	All Levels
Business UP	0.75	0.74	1.00	0.83
The Office Room	0.39	1.00	1.00	0.79
Move it	1.00	0.74	1.00	0.91
Healthy Life	1.00	0.74	0.67	0.84
Stress Management	0.71	0.74	0.67	0.73

Figure 6. Assessment percentage of agreement (%) per disability
Source: Authors, 2019

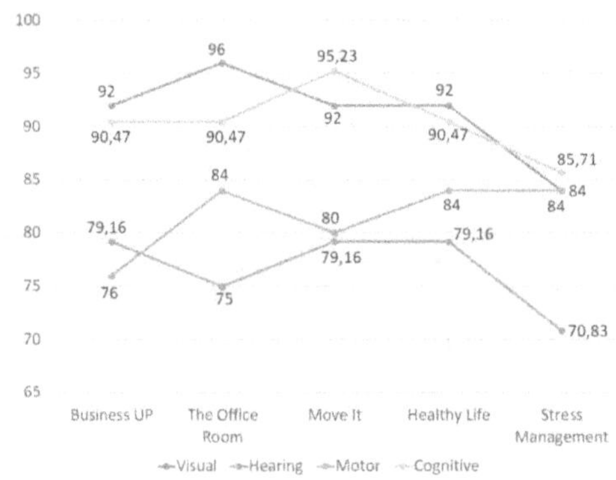

Considering that the serious games assessment was done by two experts, it is necessary to contrast the percentage of agreement that exists between both. For this, the authors consider the Cohen's Kappa coefficient that is frequently used to test inter-rater agreement for qualitative items. This coefficient is used when there are only two observers and can take values between +1 and -1. The closer to +1 or -1, the greater the degree of agreement or disagreement between observers, respectively (McHugh, 2012).

The Cohen's Kappa coefficient is applied in each level of accessibility assessed as well as in a general consolidation of all levels for each impairment. The results are shown in Table 6, Table 7, Table 8 and Table 9 for each impairment.

Once the values of the Cohen's Kappa coefficient are calculated, the authors can obtain the percentage of agreement of the results reflected by the two evaluators. Figure 6 shows the percentage of agreement of the five video games taking into account the assessed disability.

In the next sections, the results of the accessibility evaluation carried out will be analyzed and discussed.

DISCUSSION

Each game complies with many of the accessibility guidelines defined for mobile devices. In the Low Level - Good, the evaluation in the four disabilities allows to appreciate that it is the level with the highest number of compliances with accessibility guidelines. This fact may correspond that these guidelines have a greater ease of implementation in video games. On the other hand, the High Level - Best has hardly any compliance with the guidelines proposed for this level. This may correspond to the fact that the guidelines at this level are more complex to implement. The Medium Level - Better has very scattered assessments in the evaluations of the four disabilities.

Particularizing in the proposed guidelines, at Low Level all the games make use of a simple language that supports the development of the game. In addition, three games have in-game tutorials that offer help to the player while advancing in the game. At this same level, no game considers font customization, whether in size, color or type. Likewise, none of them has alternative configurations or accessible menus to provide a simplified interface that displays only the most commonly used controls in the menus. Considering the Medium Level - Better, three games offer the possibility for repetition and save settings features. In this level, barely one game allows movable or re-sizable user interface. In the High Level - Best, the scenario is minimal because most of the assessed games do not comply with the guidelines of this level. Only four games do not consider timing an essential feature to gameplay.

Considering two evaluators in the process requires a mechanism to monitor that there is no significant deviation in the results of their evaluations, in this case the Cohen's Kappa coefficient. Cohen suggested the Kappa result be interpreted as follows: values £ 0 as indicating no agreement and 0.01–0.20 as none to slight, 0.21–0.40 as fair, 0.41– 0.60 as moderate, 0.61–0.80 as substantial, and 0.81–1.00 as almost perfect agreement (McHugh, 2012). The calculated Cohen's Kappa coefficient allows us to appreciate that the percentage of agreement of the evaluators is generally adequate. The lowest values obtained correspond to the evaluation of the guidelines for hearing disabilities while the highest correspond to the guidelines for visual disabilities. It is observed that the game *The Office Room*, in all the evaluation of guidelines, is the game with the lowest value of compliance with accessibility guidelines. On the other hand, the game that has the highest value of compliance with accessibility guidelines is *Healthy Life*. These results allow us to understand that mobile video games in some cases lack accessibility features and in others, they comply fairly. Regarding the percentage of agreement, it is in an acceptable level but it can be seen that the evaluations of the guidelines for visual and cognitive disabilities have a higher percentage of agreement than the guidelines for hearing and motor disabilities.

To finalize this analysis, the authors should consider that the mobile video games analyzed are only an example of assessment of the accessibility guidelines. It is important to note that the results may vary from one game to another. With this analysis, the authors want to emphasize the importance of considering this kind of guidelines in the mobile serious game development. On the other hand, this analysis allows us to compare the compliance of the different levels of accessibility for each disability in each mobile video game.

FUTURE RESEARCH DIRECTIONS

As future work, the authors plan to use the accessibility evaluation tool to evaluate a greater number of mobile video games. This analysis aims to determine a current state of accessibility levels of mobile video games and add new ones. Finally, it is important to highlight that in a next version of the evaluation tool, the suitability of the categorization made in order to polish the analysis method, must be validated.

On the other hand, the authors plan to develop mobile serious games considering accessibility features to increase inclusion in education. Finally, it is important to highlight that in a next version of the evaluation tool, the suitability of the categorization made in order to polish the analysis method, must be validated. The long-term objective is to propose a holistic method of analysis and development of accessible serious games for any type of disability.

CONCLUSION

This research aims to provide general guidelines that support the development of accessible mobile video games for people with impairments to improve the inclusion in education. The growth of mobile video games leads to consideration of accessibility parameters in their design and implementation. Non-accessible mobile video games are a limitation for people with disabilities, especially in education.

On the other hand, the use of mobile devices has increased in recent years and this has motivated the development of more applications that may be available to more people. Video games are widely used by users of mobile devices and mobile video games market can be very attractive for this segment. Taking this premise into account, many initiatives are defining good practices for the development of video games for people with disabilities. However, these guidelines have not consolidated a formal model that allows the development of accessible video games. W3C is beginning to focus on defining guidelines for web applications on mobile devices through WCAG 2.1 but not focusing on video games.

The analysis of accessibility guidelines of several authors allows us to consolidate a guide with those related to the development of accessible video games, especially on mobile devices. It is important to consider that there are more guidelines and that they could be applied in the development of video games for other platforms. Likewise, accessibility is a key and a necessary aspect to reach an adequate UX and usability, it means, a technological solution that is easy to use and intuitive for all users, regardless of their capabilities, experience or the device they are using.

Categorizing the guidelines according to the complexity of implementation and the benefit it provides to the person with disabilities is strategic. In this way, it is possible that the developer can identify the guidelines that are most necessary or those that take less time to implement. In a mobile video game development project, these criteria can be useful in the planning stage of activities.

There are accessibility guidelines that are usually good practices used by software developers, especially those categorized as Low Level - Good. For this reason, when the authors apply the evaluation of accessibility guidelines, the highest compliance value is concentrated in those that belong to this category. On the contrary, those of High Level - Best have a lower, or almost zero, compliance value.

On the other hand, there is no doubt that accessibility is a very important factor for any type of application at present, and education is not the exception. The availability of a tool to evaluate the accessibility of a video game is more than relevant. With this tool, a person with a disability could properly select video games for their condition.

The Cohen's Kappa coefficient has been applied to assess the degree of agreement between the two evaluators. Two evaluators were used to avoid or minimize the subjectivity that could exists in the evaluation tool.

This study leaves open the opportunity to generate a methodology to develop accessible mobile serious games in the future that considers components of accessibility that satisfy the needs of people with impairments. In addition, it will be possible to test, with people with impairments, the effectiveness of the features of the mobile video games.

Finally, it is clear that people with disabilities require initiatives that improve the conditions of their daily lives and education is not the exception. For this reason, the authors consider important the development of tools that allow evaluating the accessibility of educational applications such as mobile serious games. This study supports the initiative of inclusion in education.

REFERENCES

Accessible University. (2016). *Defining Accessibility - Accessible University*. Retrieved July 11, 2017, from http://www.accessibleuniversity.com/accessibility-basics/defining-accessibility

Aguado, J., & Estrada, F. (2017). *Guía de accesibilidad de aplicaciones móviles (apps)*. Retrieved from https://administracionelectronica.gob.es/pae_Home/pae_Estrategias/pae_Accesibilidad/pae_documentacion/pae_eInclusion_Accesibilidad_de_apps.html#.Wv5i60jt7IU

Akkerman, S., Admiraal, W., & Huizenga, J. (2009). Storification in History education: A mobile game in and about medieval Amsterdam. *Computers & Education*, *52*(2), 449–459. doi:10.1016/j.compedu.2008.09.014

Callaghan, M., Savin-Baden, M., McShane, N., & Eguiluz, A. G. (2017). Mapping Learning and Game Mechanics for Serious Games Analysis in Engineering Education. *IEEE Transactions on Emerging Topics in Computing*, *5*(1), 77–83. doi:10.1109/TETC.2015.2504241

CISCO. (2017). *Cisco Visual Networking Index: Global Mobile Data Traffic Forecast Update, 2016–2021 White Paper - Cisco*. Retrieved July 11, 2017, from http://www.cisco.com/c/en/us/solutions/collateral/service-provider/visual-networking-index-vni/mobile-white-paper-c11-520862.html

Colour Blind Awareness. (n.d.). *What is Colour Blindness? — Colour Blind Awareness*. Retrieved July 11, 2017, from http://www.colourblindawareness.org/colour-blindness/

Confederación Española de Organizaciones Empresariales (CEOE). (n.d.). *Serious Games CEOE - Aplicaciones de Android en Google Play*. Retrieved July 12, 2017, from https://play.google.com/store/apps/details?id=com.prevencontrol.seriousgamesceoe&hl=es

Criollo-C, S., & Lujan-Mora, S. (2017). M-Learning and Their Potential use in the Higher Education: A Literature Review. In *2017 International Conference on Information Systems and Computer Science (INCISCOS)* (pp. 268–273). IEEE. 10.1109/INCISCOS.2017.43

Criollo-C, S., Lujan-Mora, S., & Jaramillo-Alcazar, A. (2018). Advantages and Disadvantages of M-Learning in Current Education. In *2018 IEEE World Engineering Education Conference (EDUNINE)* (pp. 1–6). IEEE. 10.1109/EDUNINE.2018.8450979

DeShazo, J., Harris, L., & Pratt, W. (2010). Effective Intervention or Child's Play? A Review of Video Games for Diabetes Education. *Diabetes Technology & Therapeutics*, *12*(10), 815–822. doi:10.1089/dia.2010.0030 PMID:20807119

Developer, A. (n.d.). *Accessibility on iOS*. Retrieved July 15, 2017, from https://developer.apple.com/accessibility/ios/

Developers, A. (n.d.). *Accessibility in Android*. Retrieved July 15, 2017, from https://developer.android.com/guide/topics/ui/accessibility/index.html

Game accessibility guidelines. (2017). Retrieved June 30, 2017, from http://gameaccessibilityguidelines.com/ensure-no-essential-information-is-conveyed-by-a-colour-alone

Ghannem, A. (2014). Characterization of Serious Games Guided by the Educational Objectives. *Proceedings of the Second International Conference on Technological Ecosystems for Enhancing Multiculturality*, 227–233.

Gikas, J., & Grant, M. M. (2013). Mobile computing devices in higher education: Student perspectives on learning with cellphones, smartphones & social media. *The Internet and Higher Education*, *19*, 18–26. doi:10.1016/j.iheduc.2013.06.002

Grammenos, D., Savidis, A., & Stephanidis, C. (2007). Unified Design of Universally Accessible Games. In Universal Access in Human-Computer Interaction. Applications and Services (pp. 607–616). Berlin: Springer Berlin Heidelberg. doi:10.1007/978-3-540-73283-9_67

Grammenos, D., Savidis, A., & Stephanidis, C. (2009). Designing universally accessible games. *Computers in Entertainment*, *7*(1), 1. doi:10.1145/1486508.1486516

Guillén-Nieto, V., & Aleson-Carbonell, M. (2012). Serious games and learning effectiveness: The case of It's a Deal! *Computers & Education*, *58*(1), 435–448. doi:10.1016/j.compedu.2011.07.015

International Game Developers Association (IGDA) — Game, & Accessibility SIG. (2004). *Accessibility in Games: Motivations and Approaches*. Retrieved February 5, 2018, from http://g3ict.org/download/p/fileId_776/productId_50

International Standard Organization. (2018). *ISO 9241-11:2018 - Ergonomics of human-system interaction -- Part 11: Usability: Definitions and concepts*. Retrieved from https://www.iso.org/standard/63500.html

International Standard Organization. (2019). *ISO 9241-210:2019 - Ergonomics of human-system interaction -- Part 210: Human-centred design for interactive systems*. ISO.

Jaramillo-Alcazar, A., Guaita, C., Rosero, J. L., & Lujan-Mora, S. (2018). Towards an Accessible Mobile Serious Game for Electronic Engineering Students with Hearing Impairments. In *2018 IEEE World Engineering Education Conference (EDUNINE)* (pp. 1–5). IEEE. 10.1109/EDUNINE.2018.8450948

Jaramillo-Alcázar, A., & Luján-Mora, S. (2017). Mobile Serious Games: An Accessibility Assessment for People with Visual Impairments. In Proceedings of the 5th International Conference on Technological Ecosystems for Enhancing Multiculturality - TEEM 2017 (pp. 1–6). New York: ACM Press. 10.1145/3144826.3145416

Jaramillo-Alcázar, A., & Luján-Mora, S. (2018). *An Approach to Mobile Serious Games Accessibility Assessment for People with Hearing Impairments*. Cham: Springer; doi:10.1007/978-3-319-73450-7_52

Jaramillo-Alcázar, A., Luján-Mora, S., & Salvador-Ullauri, L. (2017a). A Mobile Serious Games Assessment Tool for People with Motor Impairments. *International Conference on Education Technology and Computers*. doi:10.1145/3175536.3175569

Jaramillo-Alcázar, A., Luján-Mora, S., & Salvador-Ullauri, L. (2017b). Accessibility Assessment of Mobile Serious Games for People with Cognitive Impairments. *International Conference on Information Systems and Computer Science*. doi:10.1109/INCISCOS.2017.12

Koster, R. (2013). *A theory of fun for game design.*

La Presidencia, M. D. E., & Con Las Cortes Igualdad, R. E. (2018). *I. Disposiciones generales ministerio de la presidencia, relaciones con las cortes e igualdad.* Retrieved from http://www.boe.es

Markets and Markets. (n.d.). *Serious Game Market worth $5,448.82 Million by 2020.* Retrieved July 14, 2017, from http://www.marketsandmarkets.com/PressReleases/serious-game.asp

McHugh, M. L. (2012). Interrater reliability: The kappa statistic. *Biochemia Medica*, *22*(3), 276–282. doi:10.11613/BM.2012.031 PMID:23092060

Media, L. T. (2004). *Guidelines for the development of entertaining software for people with multiple learning disabilities.* Retrieved July 12, 2017, from http://www.medialt.no/rapport/entertainment_guidelines/index.htm

Michael, D., David, R., & Chen, S. L. (2006). *Serious games : games that educate, train and inform.* Thomson Course Technology. Retrieved from https://dl.acm.org/citation.cfm?id=1051239

Milne, L. R., Bennett, C. L., Ladner, R. E., & Azenkot, S. (2014). BraillePlay. In *Proceedings of the 16th international ACM SIGACCESS conference on Computers & accessibility - ASSETS '14* (pp. 137–144). New York: ACM Press. 10.1145/2661334.2661377

Pérez-Castilla Alvarez Colaboradores, L., Abenójar Agudo, V., Arribas Rincón, F., Aymerich Sabariego, M., Badia Corrons, A., Baldassarri, S., … Villegas Portero Rocío Zaragoza Martín, E. (2012). *Buenas prácticas de accesibilidad en videojuegos.* Retrieved from http://www.imserso.es

Rusu, C., Rusu, V., Roncagliolo, S., & González, C. (2015). Usability and User Experience. *International Journal of Information Technologies and Systems Approach*, *8*(2), 1–12. doi:10.4018/IJITSA.2015070101

Salvador-Ullauri, L., Jaramillo-Alcázar, A., & Luján-Mora, S. (2017). *A Serious Game Accessible to People with Visual Impairments.* 84-88. 10.1145/3175536.3175576.

Sánchez, J., & Olivares, R. (2011). Problem solving and collaboration using mobile serious games. *Computers & Education*, *57*(3), 1943–1952. doi:10.1016/j.compedu.2011.04.012

Sauve, L., Senecal, S., Kaufman, D., Renaud, L., & Leclerc, J. (2011). The Design of Generic Serious Game Shell. In *2011 International Conference on Information Technology Based Higher Education and Training* (pp. 1–5). IEEE. 10.1109/ITHET.2011.6018675

Sik, C., David, L., & Brown, J. (2010). *Design of Serious Games for Students with Intellectual Disability.* Retrieved from http://goet-project.eu/

Song, D., Karimi, A., & Kim, P. (2011). Toward designing mobile games for visually challenged children. In *Proceeding of the International Conference on e-Education, Entertainment and e-Management* (pp. 234–238). IEEE. 10.1109/ICeEEM.2011.6137794

The AbleGamers Foundation. (2012). *A Practical Guide to Game Accessibility*. Retrieved from http://includification.com/AbleGamers_Includification.pdf

The Radicati Group. (2014). *Mobile Statistics Report, 2014-2018*. Retrieved from http://www.radicati.com

Torrente, J., del Blanco, Á., Moreno-Ger, P., & Fernández-Manjón, B. (2012). *Designing Serious Games for Adult Students with Cognitive Disabilities* (pp. 603–610). Berlin: Springer. doi:10.1007/978-3-642-34478-7_73

World Health Organization. (2001). *International Classification of Functioning, Disability and Health*. ICF.

World Health Organization. (2011). *World Report on Disability*. Retrieved from http://www.who.int/disabilities/world_report/2011/report.pdf

World Health Organization. (2016a). WHO | Grades of hearing impairment. *WHO*. Retrieved from http://www.who.int/pbd/deafness/hearing_impairment_grades/en/

World Health Organization. (2016b). WHO | Visual impairment and blindness. *WHO*. Retrieved from http://www.who.int/mediacentre/factsheets/fs282/en/

World Wide Web Consortium. (2016). *Mobile Accessibility: How WCAG 2.0 and Other W3C/WAI Guidelines Apply to Mobile*. Retrieved May 15, 2018, from http://w3c.github.io/Mobile-A11y-TF-Note/

World Wide Web Consortium. (2018). *Web Content Accessibility Guidelines (WCAG) 2.1*. Retrieved May 15, 2018, from https://www.w3.org/TR/WCAG21/#cc2

Yuan, B., Folmer, E., & Harris, F. C. (2011). Game accessibility: A survey. *Universal Access in the Information Society*, *10*(1), 81–100. doi:10.100710209-010-0189-5

ADDITIONAL READING

EtnasSoft. (2014). OpenLibra | Desarrollo de Videojuegos: un enfoque práctico (3a Ed.). Retrieved from https://openlibra.com/es/book/desarrollo-de-videojuegos-un-enfoque-practico-3a-ed

Rogers, S. (2014). *Level up!: the guide to great video game design. Wiley. Chou, Y. K. (2013). Octalysis: Complete gamification framework*. Yu-Kai Chou & Gamification.

KEY TERMS AND DEFINITIONS

Accessibility: Ability of an object to be used regardless of the capacity and condition of a person.
Impairment: Persons having a disability of a specified kind.
Mobile Accessibility: The grade in which a mobile app is accessible to diverse users.
Mobile Serious Game: Mobile video game with educational features.

Chapter 4
UDL in Action:
Implementing Strategies in a Large Online Course

Aisha S. Haynes
University of South Carolina, Columbia, USA

ABSTRACT

This chapter discusses universal design strategies that could be implemented in online courses. The author discusses the application of universal design (UD) principles in a large (180 students) online Computer Applications in Hospitality, Retail, and Sport Management course. A survey was completed by students to determine the impact of UD strategies that were incorporated in the course. The results showed the ability to use learning aids when completing assignments, receiving instant feedback on assignments and the ability to complete course assignments unlimited times before the due date are impactful to student learning. The purpose of this chapter is to provide educators with a bank of UD strategies that can be used in online courses.

INTRODUCTION

Many educators design, develop, and deliver online courses without considering the needs of diverse learners. With over 7.1 million students enrolled in online courses nationwide, it is important for educators to consider diverse learners when designing, developing, and teaching online courses (Allen & Seaman, 2014; United States Department of Education, 2010). Educators do not know the characteristics of students who will be enrolling in their classes each semester. In most instances, instructors do not know if students have disabilities before the start of the course (Rao, Edelen-Smith and Wailehau, 2015). Many faculty and staff at the University of South Carolina - Columbia are committed to accomplishing the university's mission of designing quality and accessible distributed learning courses (Moorefield-Lang, Copeland, and Haynes, 2016). Consequently, with continuous improvement in mind, faculty and instructional designers from the Center for Teaching Excellence collaborate to implement Universal Design for Learning (UDL) principles to enhance online courses. This chapter discusses ways to create

DOI: 10.4018/978-1-7998-2325-4.ch004

accessible and universally designed courses and highlights data collected from a *Computer Applications in Hospitality, Retail and Sport Management* online course. The instructor collected information on the students' perceptions regarding the impact of implementing UDL principles to create an inclusive and accessible online learning environment. The objective of this chapter is to determine the impact of UDL strategies and provide educators with a bank of UD strategies that can be used in online courses.

BACKGROUND

Universal Design for Learning

It's important for educators to assess their instructional approaches and course design in face-to-face, blended, flipped and online learning environments. A first step to designing a universally designed course is to create a syllabus that clearly states the course learning outcomes and policies (Izzo, Murray & Novak, 2008). Implementing the principles of Universal Design for Learning provides all individuals equal opportunities to learn (Burgstahler, 2012; CAST, 2011; Coombs, 2010; McGuire and Scott, 2006; Meyer, Rose & Gordon, 2013; Rao, Edelen-Smith, & Wailehua, 2015; Simoncelli & Hinson, 2008; Tobin, 2014; Rogers-Shaw, Carr-Chellman, & Choi, 2018). The guidelines increase accessibility for all students, not just students with disabilities.

UDL stems from Universal Design (UD) principles. "Universal Design" was created by Ron Mace to create physical spaces that are accessible to a wide range of individuals (Rao & Tanners, 2011). There are three educational models that were created from UD principles – Universal Design for Learning (UDL), Universal Design for Instruction (UDI) and Universal Instructional Design UID) (Rao & Tanner, 2011). The three models complement each other.

The concept of UDL proactively considers students with disabilities when designing curriculum instead of reactively considering students who may have special needs (Kennedy & Yun, 2019). Courses that include universal design features can minimize the needs of accommodations for students with disabilities and create an inclusive course – no matter the background of the students (Rao & Tanners, 2011). Proactively creating universally designed lesson plans have the potential to reduce the time that instructors need to modify the plans (Spooner, Baker, Harris, Ahlgrim-Delzell & Browder, 2007). Spooner et al. also noted how implementing UDL strategies during the creation of lesson plans has the potential to include all students. Applying UDL principles reduce barriers to students engaging in and grasping course materials. The UDL principles can be used to plan learning opportunities for students, design learning materials and assess student learning (Geogan, Radil & Daniels, 2008). According to Gradel and Edson (2009), educators who apply UDL principles use "multiple goals, methods, tasks, materials, and assessments to meet students' needs" (p.112).

The United States Department of Education (2012) defined UDL as follows:

The term Universal Design for Learning means a scientifically valid framework for guiding educational practice that:

1. Provides flexibility in the ways information is presented, in the ways students respond or demonstrate knowledge and skills, and in the ways students are engaged; and
2. Reduces barriers in instruction, provides appropriate accommodations, supports, and challenges, and maintains high achievement expectations for all students, including students with disabilities and students who are limited English proficient.

The three key principles of UDL are multiple means of representation (what of learning), multiple means of action and expression (how of learning), multiple means of engagement (why of learning) (CAST, 2018). UDL provides learners with multiple ways to practice different skills (Kennedy & Yun, 2019) and present acquired knowledge (Rogers-Shaw et al., 2018). Applying UDL strategies provides a structure that includes increased flexible course options, easy to navigate course structures, and choices for students enrolled in the course (Rao, Edelen-Smith, & Wailehua, 2015). Even though implementing UDL increase opportunities for all students to learning, students with disabilities may need additional support (Rao, Edelen-Smith, & Wailehua, 2015).

Fidalgo and Thormann (2017) found that using alternative formats to present content and directions for assignments, using videos to support student learning, providing students options for how they submit assignments and using alternative formats to serve as a model is beneficial to students. Scott, Temple and Marshall (2015) studied three online courses to see how the courses aligned with UDL principles. The researchers found out that UDL enhanced the coursework and preparation of students and noted that incorporating UDL principles positively impacted the learning of students. Findings from He (2014) indicated that students benefited from prompt feedback from the instructor and having a consistent course organization. In addition, He noted that having weekly announcements and providing students the option to learn materials at their own pace was a success indicator. Smith (2012) analyzed a college course where UDL strategies were implemented. Participants stated that having access to rubrics, examples of assignments, hands-on activities and multiple ways to learn course content (lectures and handouts) were most beneficial to them. Snow (2018) implemented UDL strategies in a liberal arts seminar course and indicated how including rubrics lead to strong learning outcomes and guidance through assignments for students. Haynes (2019) conducted a study on an asynchronous *Introduction to Women's and Gender Studies* course and found that having a course broken into small segments positively impacted the learning of students. Study results from Haynes (2019) indicated that weekly checklists helped students stay on track in the course. Applying UDL principles to courses has the potential to have a major impact on improving access to curriculum and meeting the needs of all students.

Universal Design for Instruction

The Center of Postsecondary Education and Disability (2012) defined Universal Design for Instruction as follows:

Universal Design for Instruction (UDI) is an approach to teaching that consists of the proactive design and use of inclusive instructional strategies that benefit a broad range of learners including students with disabilities. The nine Principles of UDI provide a framework for college faculty to use when designing or revising instruction to be responsive to diverse student learners and to minimize the need for "special" accommodations and retrofitted changes to the learning environment. UDI operates on the premise that the planning and delivery of instruction, as well as the evaluation of learning can incorporate inclusive attributes that embrace diversity in learners without compromising academic standards.

UDI maximizes the learning of students by applying universal design principles to all parts of instruction. This includes class climate, interaction, physical environments and products, delivery methods, information resources and technology, feedback, assessment and accommodation (Burgstahler, 2009). Burgstahler (2012) noted that instructors should consider the variety of students that may be enrolling in courses. This includes, but is not limited to, age, gender, sexual orientation, learning styles and cultures. Burgstahler (2012) also stated that instructors should identify the course, define the universe, involve students, adopt instructional strategies, apply instructional strategies, plan for accommodations and evaluate. Below are specific ways to implement UDL strategies listed by Burgstahler (2012):

- Identify the course
  - Describe the course, the course learning outcomes and all the content.
- Define the universe
  - Describe the students who may enroll in the course and then examine their potential characteristics.
- Involve students
  - Involve potential students in the design of the course or consider the perspectives of potential students.
- Adopt instructional strategies
  - Adopt a variety of teaching methods in the course.
- Apply instructional strategies
  - Apply good instructional strategies to all aspects of the course. This can include instructional materials, assessments, discussions, group work and online materials.
- Plan for accommodations
  - Research accommodations that are available on campus and provide the information in syllabi.
- Evaluate
  - Monitor the instruction by gaining feedback from students and modify the course based on the feedback.

Universal Instructional Design

Universal Instructional Design proactively places accessibility as an essential part of instructional design (Silver, Bourke, & Strehorn, 1998). Fox, Hatfield and Collins (2003) noted how UID's principles are based on the work of Chickering and Gamson (1987). Chickering and Gamson (1987) created seven good practices in undergraduate education. The principles include (1) encourages contacts between students and faculty; (2) develops reciprocity and cooperation among students; (3) uses active learning techniques; (4) gives prompt feedback; (5) emphasizes time on task; (6) communicates high expectations and (7) respects the diverse talents and ways of learning.

The UID principles discussed by Fox, Hatfield and Collins (2003), based on the seven good practices in undergraduate education, include (1) creating welcoming classrooms; (2) determining the especial components of a course; (3) communicating clear expectations; (4) providing constructive feedback; (5) exploring the natural support of learning to enhance opportunities for all; (6) designing teaching methods that consider diverse styles, abilities, ways of knowing and previous experiences and background knowledge; (7) creating multiple ways for students to demonstrate their knowledge; and (8) promoting interaction among and between faculty and students.

MAIN FOCUS OF THE CHAPTER

Issues, Controversies, Problems

Silver, Bourke and Strehorn (1998) conducted a pilot study to introduce faculty to the concept of universal instructional design and identify barriers to faculty implementing the concept in their courses. Faculty in the study noted that time, attitudes, the lack of pedagogical knowledge of faculty and perceived faculty freedom were barriers to implementing UID. The faculty suggested support for implementing UID, including training on UID strategies, sample syllabi and suggestions from support service offices (Silver, Bourke, & Strehorn, 1998).

Students enrolled in online courses can have anytime/anywhere access to course materials. The online learning medium has the potential to include diverse learners (Kinash, Crichton & Kim-Rupnow, 2004). Proactively designing online courses that are universally designed is very important. Rao and Tanners (2015) conducted a study on 25 students who were enrolled in a master's level course to examine how UID and UDL guidelines could be implemented in the design of an online course. The researchers also examined the most valued elements in the course that were stated by the students. Rao and Tanners (2015) expressed how students appreciated having UDL and UDI features within the course. More specifically, students appreciated (1) having options and choices for engaging in course materials; (2) having brief weekly assignments over high stakes assessments; (3) consistent instructor feedback; (4) the clear and consistent layout of the course and (5) regular online interactions with the instructor. Instructors should consider designing online course materials that can be accessed in multiple formats and assignments that can be completed by students in various formats (Rao & Tanners, 2015).

A student with a disability can enrolled in a course at any time, and instructors should be ready to instruct a variety of students. Some students with disabilities do not register with the university's student disability office. This was discussed by Rao and Tanners (2015) and Schelly, Davies and Spooner (2011). Schelly, Davies and Spooner (2011) noted that 80% of the students who participated in their study on UDL did not report their disability to the university. In the study by Rao and Tanners (2015), three students had disabilities, but none of them registered with the student disability office. The students disclosed to the instructor during the class. One student with a disability expressed how the structure of the course made the course more manageable. All three of the students stated that the course being easy to navigate, having multiple ways to access information and having shorter assignments made the course more accommodating (Rao & Tanners, 2015). Instructors in a study by Izzo, Murray and Novak

(2008) desired training on how to meet the needs of students who do not disclose their disability to the university. Instructors also desired more professional development on UDL.

Strategies to Create Accessible and Inclusive Online Courses

With multiple means of representation, instructors should present information and content and different ways.

Below are strategies to implement "Multiple Means of Representation":

- Caption videos/transcribe audio.
- Don't just lecture. Utilize multiple mediums to present content.
- Give student textbook options – printed/accessible e-text.
- Provide students with outlines.
- Create accessible learning materials.
- Give directions in multiple ways.
- Don't use color alone to convey messages.
- Create easy to navigate courses.
- Share definitions of unknown terms.
- Include guest speakers.
- Use audio/video to explain major assignments.
- Chunk information into smaller segments.

With multiple means of action and expression, instructors should differentiate the ways that students can express what they know. Below are strategies for implementing "Multiple Means of Action and Expression":

- Give student choices for completing assignments.
- Use multiple types of assessments.
- Provide students with checklists.
- Provide students with rubrics and/or samples assignments.
- Allow students to share resources with classmates.
- Provide feedback in a variety of ways.
- Ensure keyboard only access for course materials.

With multiple means of engagement, educators should stimulate interest, motivation and persistence in learning. Below are strategies for implementing "Multiple Means of Engagement":

- Provide frequent and timely feedback.
- Use peer assessments.
- Have flexible formats for office hours.
- Break large assignments into smaller parts.
- Use multiple pathways to engage students.
- Provide students with a list of questions to answer while engaging in materials.
- Allow students to design class activities.

- Design assignments to encourage the use of multimedia.
- Conduct formative and summative evaluations.
- Integrate learning with beyond the classroom experiences.
- Allow students to select preferred topics when completing assignments.

Below are additional UD strategies:

- Encourage interactions.
- Employ interactive teaching techniques.
- Avoid using unnecessary jargon.
- Use student names.
- Provide feedback on a regular basis.
- Have grading rubrics.
- Have measurable learning outcomes.
- Avoid lengthy online exams.
- Include a "Getting Started" or "Start Here" section in the course.
- Limit instructor created videos to 20 minutes or less.

Many instructors include Word documents, PowerPoint presentations and PDF files within their courses. It is important that files uploaded to the learning management system are accessible, usable and universally designed. Haynes (2019) listed strategies for creating accessible Microsoft Word documents.

Microsoft Word

- Properly format headings to structure documents.
- Add alternative (alt-text) text to images.
- Properly label links with meaningful descriptions.
- Use pre-formatted list styles when making lists.
- Indicate column headers for tables and check the reading order of tables.
- Select "Repeat Header Row" for tables.
- Do not use color alone to convey messages.
- Use sufficient color contrast.
- Use consistent and easy to read font types.
- Use at least a 12-point font size.

Microsoft Office products include a built-in accessibility checker that can be used to check the accessibility of documents, presentations and spreadsheets.

Haynes (2019) also listed strategies for creating accessible PowerPoint presentations.

Microsoft PowerPoint

- Check the reading order of slide contents.
- Add alternative text to images, graphs, charts, tables, SmartArt.
- Properly label links with meaningful descriptions.
- Use the provided PowerPoint slide layouts.
- Include unique titles for slides.
- Use pre-formatted list styles when making lists.
- Indicate column headers for tables.
- Use sufficient color contrast.
- Do not use color alone to convey messages.
- Use consistent and easy to read font types.
- Use at least a 24-point font size.

Portable Document Format (PDF)

Text in PDF files should be searchable. If the text is not searchable, Optical Character Recognition (OCR) should be performed on the document. Tags should be checked. If tags are not included, they should be added. The reading order of document contents should also be checked. Adobe PDF has an accessibility checker. The checker should be performed on documents and the accessibility issues should be fixed.

Accessible Videos

In addition to creating accessible documents, it's important for videos to be accessible. Captions should be included for video content and a transcript should be provided for audio content. A best practice is to create a script first and use the script to create the video or audio clip. Video/audio clips should be short (7 minutes is ideal; no more than 20 minutes) and based on topics. Dragon Naturally Speaking is a tool that can be used to create transcripts. YouTube automatically captions uploaded videos. Additionally, users can upload a transcript to YouTube with a video and the captions will sync with the video. Amara can be used to caption videos that are created by other users and uploaded to video platforms like YouTube.

General UD/Accessibility Techniques

Below are general universal design and accessibility techniques that can be implemented in courses:

- Create easy to navigate courses.
- Include the institution's accessibility policy in syllabus.
- Include accessibility policies for all technologies.
- Have a course design that facilitates readability.
- Include clearly written course content. There should be no punctuation or grammatical errors.
- Create courses that can be navigated with a keyboard – without the use of a mouse.
- Do not use blinking or flashing animations within the course.
- Include page numbers in documents.
- Include instructor contact information in syllabus.

- Include textbook information in syllabus.
- Don't type sentences in all caps.

SOLUTIONS AND RECOMMENDATIONS

Course Context

An instructor of one large enrollment undergraduate course (180 students) at the University of South Carolina – Columbia applied UD principles in a Microsoft Excel and Access course. SPTE 274 (Computer Applications in Hospitality, Retail and Sport Management) is a required course for all College of Hospitality, Retail and Sport Management (HRSM) students at the University of South Carolina – Columbia. HRSM areas of study include Hotel, Restaurant and Tourism Management, Interdisciplinary Studies, Retailing, and Sport and Entertainment Management.

The SPTE 274 course specifically focuses on Microsoft Excel and Access and allows students to develop core skills and techniques that can be applied to the workplace. There are no prerequisite courses or knowledge needed to enroll in the course. However, after completing the course students should be able to correctly use computer terminology related to Microsoft Excel and Access programs, efficiently prepare Excel spreadsheets; efficiently develop Access databases, integrate Excel and Access components with each other and create effective presentation tutorials pertaining to Excel and Access software. Work for most of the course was completed in Pearson's MyITLab. MyITLab is an online platform that includes instructional content and activities for Microsoft Office and computer concepts. The study focused on one semester of the course.

Course Design and Delivery

The instructor sent a welcoming email to students a month before the class began. The email noted that the course was a fully online course, the start date and that the course was up and running if students wanted to get an early start on the course. The email also included textbook information. Students were officially welcomed to the class on the first day of the course. The email included a list of 15 items for students to read. Below are the items that were included in the email:

1. You should enter MyITLab through Blackboard. Please view the directions on page 2 of the syllabus.
2. This course is based on Microsoft Office for Windows. This course is best completed using a Windows computer. If you have a Mac and have trouble completing Excel assignments, I strongly recommend trying the assignments on a PC. Access capstone grader projects cannot be completed on a Mac.
3. Sign up for Remind. Sign up for important updates from me. Get information (assignment and test reminders, etc) right on your phone via text message!
4. I will respond to all questions within 24 hours Monday-Thursday and 48 hours on Friday-Sunday.
5. Before you begin working on assignments, please view the "START HERE!" section of the course.
6. Please complete your own work. If you submit the work of another student (or copy information from another student) from a previous semester, or another institution, your work will be flagged.

You will automatically receive a 0 on the assignment and will be reported to the Office of Academic Integrity.

7. Save all of your work on a flash drive or in the cloud (Dropbox, Google Drive, etc). It's important to have a backup copy of your assignments.
8. All course related questions, that are not personal in nature, should be posted on the proper discussion board in the "Discussion Boards" section of the course.
9. If you answer questions on the discussion board posted by other students, you will receive extra credit points (up to 10).
10. If you have trouble with MyITLab, please visit the Pearson MyITLab help website.
11. If you don't have your textbook yet, you can use the 14-day trial of MyITLab. Pages 2 and 3 of the syllabus include the directions.
12. What is due by Thursday?
    a. Buy your book and access to Pearson's MyITLab
    b. Review the Start Here section of the course
    c. Edit your email address in Blackboard
    d. Read the syllabus and review all due dates
    e. Complete the Introduce Yourself assignment
    f. Complete the orientation assessment
    g. Complete the Academic Integrity assessment
    h. Read Excel Chapter 1
    i. Complete the Excel Chapter 1 Simulation Training in MyITLab
    j. Complete the Excel Chapter 1 Grader Project in MyITLab
        i. All course assignments can be completed unlimited times before the due dates except the Exams, the Final Project and the Video Tutorial Assignment.
13. The quizzes, exams and the video tutorial assignments can be found in the "Course Modules" section of the course.
14. Feel free to work ahead in this course. Be sure to complete all assignments by the due dates.
15. Late work will not be accepted in this course.

The course was structured to begin with Excel chapter 1 (Introduction to Excel). Students completed Excel chapters 1-8 and Access chapters 1-4. The course topics include: formulas and function, depicting data visually, datasets and tables, subtotals, PivotTables and Pivot Charts, what-if analysis, specialized functions, statistical functions, finding your way through an Access database, designing databases and extracting data, using queries to make decisions, performing calculations and summarizing data using queries, and creating and using professional forms and reports. The typical class structure consists of course modules, which include the following:

- **Student Introductions:** Students introduced themselves to each other at the beginning of the course.
- **Simulations:** Students had an option to use learning aids, which included reading the e-text, watching the steps via video and practicing techniques step-by-step.
- **Grader Projects:** Students downloaded a spreadsheet/database and directions and followed the directions to manipulate the spreadsheet/database for each chapter. Students uploaded the spreadsheet or database into Pearson's MyITLab and received instant feedback.

Table 1.SPTE 274: Universal Design Strategies

•Provided students with textbook options	•Used a variety of evaluation methods
•Gave directions in multiple ways	•Allowed students to post and answer questions on the Blackboard discussion board
•Utilized multiple mediums to present content	•Used student names when communicating with students
•Created accessible course materials	•Provided feedback in a variety of ways
•Created easy to navigate course	•Provided frequent and timely feedback
•Chunked information into smaller segments	•Provided students with a rubric
•Designed activities that encouraged multimedia	•Included flexible format for office hours
•Provided students with textbook options	•Used a variety of evaluation methods

- **Quizzes:** Students completed quizzes (multiple choice and true/false questions) in the Blackboard Learning Management System. A test pool was used and students received different questions each time they completed the quiz. Students instantly received feedback on quizzes.
- **Exams:** Students had one opportunity to complete each exam (multiple choice and true/false questions) in Blackboard. Students instantly received feedback on the exams.
- **Video Tutorials:** Using PowerPoint, Jing, Screencast-o-Matic, Camtasia Studio or any other familiar technology, students showed the excel and access screen and provided voice over instructions on how to do a task in each program.
- **Final Project:** Students completed a final project that covered all chapters in the course. The project was similar to the grader projects mentioned above.

The instructor sent an email to students twice a week. Announcements were posted on the Blackboard Learning Management system twice a week. *Remind*, a communication tool that allows educators to send text messages to the cell phones of students, was also used in the course. Within the course, students asked questions on the Blackboard discussion board instead of emailing the instructor. The instructor answered all questions posted to the discussion boards within 24 hours during the week and within 48 hours during the weekend. Students also had the ability to answer questions on the discussion board and received extra credit points (up to 10) for answering questions correctly.

In-person one-on-one and drop-in tutoring was available to students through the University's Student Success Center (SSC). The SSC provides academic support services for undergraduate students. All of the programs and initiatives were free. Teaching assistants for the course held online drop-in sessions via Adobe Connect. Open labs were held in a computer lab on campus. The online drop-in sessions were held twice a week for an hour each day. Open labs were held once a week for an hour.

The course was created with UD strategies in mind. The universal design strategies in Table 1 were implemented within the design and delivery of the course:

Provided Students with Textbook Options

Students in the class had an opportunity to purchase the all-digital access to the course or the printed textbook. The all-digital access included the eText and MyITLab. The printed textbook option included a physical textbook and access to MyITLab. This option also included the eText. If students were unable to purchase the textbook immediately, they were able to access the eText and MyITLab for 14 days. At the end of the 14 days, the all-digital access needed to be purchased.

Gave Directions in Multiple Ways

Directions were provided to students in multiple ways. Students were provided with written directions, as well as video directions. They were able to choose the format of the directions that suited them best. In MyITLab, students had the ability to read instructions, watch videos on how to complete steps, and practice.

Utilized Multiple Mediums to Present Content

Multiple mediums to present content was utilized. The instructor also created step-by-step and video tutorials for students on how to complete various steps.

Created Accessible Course Materials

The instructor created accessible materials for students. The Microsoft accessibility checker was performed on all Word documents. The Word documents were saved as PDF and uploaded to Blackboard. Students had an opportunity to select the document format that they wanted.

The audio PowerPoint instructional presentations were transcribed. Students were able to hear the presentation, see the presentation and view the "Notes" for the presentation. The "Notes" section of the presentation included the transcript.

Created Easy to Navigate Course

The course was easy to navigate. The Blackboard menu included the following items:

- Announcements
- START HERE!
- About your Instructor and TA
- Syllabus and Schedule
- Discussion Boards
- Pearson MyITLab
- Course Modules
- Chapter Notes/Presentations
- MAC Compatibility Notes
- MyITLab & Blackboard Help
- Free Tutoring/Drop-in Sessions/Open Lab
- Check Grades
- Send Email

As noted above, announcements were sent twice a week. There were times when more announcements were sent to students. Assignments were due Wednesdays by 5pm, Eastern Time. Announcements were typically sent on Thursdays and Mondays. A copy of the announcements was emailed at the same time.

The "START HERE!" section of the course included the following:

- Link to sign up for Remind
- Note about the course
- Free tutoring, online drop-in session and open lab information
- List of getting started tasks
- Instructions on purchasing the textbook and MyITLab
- Video on how to purchase the all-digital option of MyITLab and eText
- Video on how to access the simulations and grader projects in MyITLab
- Video on how to view correct and incorrect work in MyITLab and how to re-submit the work
- How to edit email addresses in Blackboard
- Attachments of the Word and PDF versions of the syllabus
- Link to complete the Introduce Yourself Assignment
- Link to complete the Academic Integrity Assessment
- Links to become familiar with MyITLab
- Next Steps

The "About Your Instructor and TA" section included images of the instructor and the TA. The section also included information about the instructor and the TA and contact information for both individuals.

The Word and PDF versions of the syllabus and course schedule was included in the "Syllabus and Schedule" section of the course. The syllabus was very detailed. It included the following:

- Instructor contact information
- Notes about the course
- Course description
- Pre-requisites
- Course learning outcomes
- FAQs
- Textbook information
- Information on MyITLab
- Course overview and purpose
- Tips for being successful in the course
- Overall structure of the course
- Optional resources
- Minimal technical skills
- Technical support information for Blackboard and MyITLab
- Course communications
- Netiquette statements
- How grades will be calculated
- Grading scale
- How to submit assignments

- Detailed information on all assignments
- Late work/make up policy
- Disability and other student support services
- Academic honesty
- Course outline and due date checklist

The "Discussion Boards" section of the course included an "Introduce Yourself" and "FAQ-General Course Questions" discussion boards. There were an additional 24 discussion boards that were dedicated to questions pertaining to the simulation trainings and the grader exercises. Students were instructed to post questions on the proper discussion board instead of emailing the instructor directly. The instructor or TA answered questions on discussion boards. If students answered questions on the discussion boards correctly, they received up to 10 extra credit points.

Pearson's MyITLab was linked within Blackboard. Students could access MyITLab from within Blackboard. Grades from MyITLab were automatically synced with Blackboard.

The "Course Modules" section of the course included folders that pertained to each module. The module dates and topics were listed on the outside of each folder. In addition, a motivational tip of the week was located on the outside of each folder. The module learning objectives and a to-do list was included within each folder. Module folders also included optional voiceover PowerPoint presentations and optional notes. Quizzes, based on two chapters, were located within every other modular folder. Lastly, a "Next Steps" note was located at the end of each module.

As mentioned previously, optional chapter voiceover PowerPoint presentations and chapter notes were located within each module. These instructional materials were also located in the "Chapter Notes/ Presentations" section of the course.

Many students in the class use Mac computers. The course covered Excel and Access for Windows. Some of the functionality is different on Mac computers vs PCs. Therefore, the instructor included a "MAC Compatibility Notes" section within the course. The "Mac Compatibility Notes" information was provided by Pearson within MyITLab.

The "MyITLab & Blackboard" section of the course included the following:

- How to get started in the course
- MyITLab technical Support
- Technology and Blackboard Help
- MyITLab error message help
- MyITLab browser tune up
- Information about tutoring, open lab and online drop-in sessions
- Video on how to purchase the all-digital option of MyITLab and eText
- Video on how to access the simulations and grader projects in MyITLab
- Video on how to view correct and incorrect work in MyITLab and how to re-submit the work
- Videos on how to access quizzes and exams
- Videos on how to post to discussion boards
- Link to download Excel and Access for free from the University
- Link for Blackboard help
- Document for how students upgrade from temporary access to MyITLab to full access

The "Check Grades" section of the course allowed students to keep track of their grades in the course. Students always knew their current grade in the course. The "Send Email" section of the course allowed students to send emails to the instructor, teaching assistant and other students enrolled in the course.

Chunked Information into Smaller Segments

The course was chunked into manageable segments in weekly folder. Each folder included information for one chapter. Assignments were due weekly. Students had an opportunity to work ahead in the course, but work had to be completed by certain due dates.

Designed Activities that Encouraged Multimedia

Students completed simulation trainings within the course. They had the ability to read instructions, watch videos on how to complete steps, and practice. Audio PowerPoint presentations were utilized in the course. Students created two video presentations at the end of the course.

Used a Variety of Evaluation Methods

Students in the class completed a variety of assignments. They completed 12 simulations, 12 grader projects, six quizzes, two exams, a three-part final exam and created two video tutorials. The simulations, grader projects and quizzes could have been completed unlimited times before the due date. The three-part final exam could have been completed twice. The highest grade counted towards the student grades.

Allowed Students to Post and Answer Questions on the Blackboard Discussion Board

The class size for the course was 180. Instead of students emailing the instructor directly, they were instructed to post questions on FAQ discussion boards in Blackboard. Many students had the same questions. Having all questioned posted where everyone in the class can see helped multiple students – instead of the one person that would have been helped via email. The instructor and TA answered questions on the discussion boards multiple times a day. Students in the class had an opportunity to answer questions for up to 10 extra credit points.

Used Student Names when Communicating with Students

The instructor used names when communicating with students by email, on discussion boards and when providing feedback on assignments.

Provided Feedback in a Variety of Ways and Provided Frequent and Timely Feedback

Feedback was provided to students in a variety of ways. Immediate feedback was provided on simulations and grader projects. For the grader projects, students were able to immediately see correct and incorrect steps on a detailed score card in MyITLab. The score card provided feedback on how to fix steps that were done incorrectly. Students also had the ability to download a Live Comments Report that detailed errors and ways to fix the errors. The instructor also provided feedback to students via text and/or video.

Provided Students with a Rubric

A rubric was provided to students for the video tutorial. The rubric was in the syllabus and weekly module in Blackboard. The instructor and TA used the rubric feature in Blackboard to grade the video tutorials and provide students with feedback.

Included Flexible Format for Office Hours

Students had the ability to meet with the instructor in person on campus or by using Adobe Connect or Blackboard Collaborate. The office hours were "by appointment".

Survey Results for SPTE 274

All students had an opportunity to benefit from the course structure and design. There were 180 students enrolled in the course. One hundred and twenty-six (70%) participated and completed the survey. Most students (48%) logged into the course 3-4 times per week. Before the end of the semester, the instructor distributed a survey to all enrolled students. The survey consisted of questions related to UDI and UDL strategies and techniques used in the course. Students were asked to respond to 17 questions regarding elements of the course design. All questions began with "Based upon your experiences in this course, how did the elements below impact your learning in this course?"

In terms of demographic data, 98% of the students were between the ages of 18-24. There were more females (53%) than males (47%) enrolled in the sections. Eight-one percent of the students were white; 10% black, 1% Hispanic, 1% Hispanic or Latino, and 8% Asian or Pacific Islander. Students from 14 different majors were enrolled in the class. Ninety percent of the students were enrolled in a major in the College of HRSM. The majority of the class consisted of sophomores (38%) and juniors (26%). Fifty-eight percent of the students took an online course before enrolling into the SPTE 274 course. Eighteen percent of the students who were enrolled in the class identified themselves as having a disability. When asked "Do you live with one or more of the following characteristics? Please select all that apply", students selected the following:

- Blindness/Visual Impairment – 5%
- Cognitive Impairment - 1%
- Corrected Vision (e.g. Glasses, contact lenses) - 37%
- Deafness/Hearing Impaired - 1%
- Hearing loss – 1%
- Head/Brain Injury – 3%
- Mental Illness – 5%
- Mobility or Orthopedic Impairment, or Arthritis - 1%
- Learning Disability/Learning Difference – 11%
- Post-Traumatic Stress Disorder (PTSD) – 1%
- Speech/Communication Impairment - 2%

Low Impact Instructional Techniques	Major Impact	Moderate Impact	Neutral
1. The ability to utilize the online drop-in sessions with the TA.	10%	13%	34%
2. The ability to attend Open Lab with the TA.	10%	10%	39%
3. The ability to utilize tutoring services through the Student Success Center.	17%	13%	33%

Table 3

High Impact Instructional Techniques	Major Impact	Moderate Impact	Neutral
1. The ability to use learning aids for simulation activities ("read", "watch" and "practice") in MyITLab.	66%	16%	10%
2. The ability to receive instant feedback on the capstone grader projects in MyITLab.	65%	19%	10%
3. The ability to complete chapter quizzes in Blackboard unlimited times before the due date.	61%	23%	9%
4. The ability to complete capstone grader projects unlimited times before the due date.	58%	26%	8%
5. The ability to view instant feedback on quizzes in Blackboard.	58%	23%	10%
6. The ability to complete simulation assignments unlimited times before the due date.	55%	25%	11%
7. The ability to receive weekly updates via text messages.	51%	19%	17%
8. The ability view questions and answers to questions posted by other students and the instructor on the Blackboard discussion board.	50%	22%	15%
9. The ability to receive weekly updates via emails and announcements through Blackboard.	50%	32%	13%
10. The ability to ask questions on the Blackboard discussion board.	47%	20%	17%
11. The ability to complete coursework at your own pace (but before due dates).	33%	38%	19%

- Other – 6%

Students were asked if the following strategies had an impact on their learning:

1. The ability to complete coursework at your own pace (but before due dates).
2. The ability to receive weekly updates via emails and announcements through Blackboard.
3. The ability to receive weekly updates via text messages.
4. The ability to complete simulation assignments unlimited times before the due date.
5. The ability to use learning aids for simulation activities ("read", "watch" and "practice") in MyITLab.
6. The ability to use the "accessibility" feature for simulation activities in MyITLab.
7. The ability to complete capstone grader projects unlimited times before the due date.
8. The ability to receive instant feedback on the capstone grader projects in MyITLab.
9. The ability to complete chapter quizzes in Blackboard unlimited times before the due date.
10. The ability to view instant feedback on quizzes in Blackboard.

11. The ability to ask questions on the Blackboard discussion board.
12. The ability view questions and answers to questions posted by other students and the instructor on the Blackboard discussion board.
13. The ability to answer questions on the Blackboard discussion boards for extra credit points.
14. The ability to utilize tutoring services through the Student Success Center.
15. The ability to utilize the online drop-in sessions with Frances.
16. The ability to attend Open Lab with Julian.
17. The ability to view optional Voiceover PowerPoint presentations with scripted notes in Blackboard.
18. The ability to view optional chapter notes in Blackboard.
19. The ability to utilize the eText in MyITLab.

Results displayed in Table 2 indicate the techniques that had the least impact on student learning. Results presented in Table 3 indicate the techniques that had the most impact on student learning: Below are the results for the remaining five survey items that relate to the course design:

1. The ability to answer questions on the Blackboard discussion boards for extra credit points. (29% Major Impact, 20% Moderate Impact, 28% Neutral)
2. The ability to use the "accessibility" feature for simulation activities in MyITLab. (29% Major Impact, 27% Moderate Impact, 25% Neutral)
3. The ability to utilize the eText in MyITLab. (25% Major Impact, 21% Moderate Impact, 25% Neutral)
4. The ability to view optional chapter notes in Blackboard. (23% Major Impact, 29% Moderate Impact, 19% Neutral)
5. The ability to view optional Voiceover PowerPoint presentations with scripted notes in Blackboard. (19% Major Impact, 29% Moderate Impact, 25% Neutral)

DISCUSSION

Utilizing universal design strategies in online courses is valuable and beneficial to all students. The results of the study indicate that the ability to use learning aids for simulation activities in MyITLab and the ability to receive instant feedback on the capstone grader projects were the most impactful strategies for students. In addition, the ability to complete assignments unlimited times before the due date was impactful for students. This strategy allowed students to complete their work, learn from their mistakes and then re-attempt assignments. Study results also indicated that communication from the instructor was important. Students in the course were able to learn from the instructor, TA or a peer in the course. Instead of having to reach out the instructor, students had the ability to learn from questions posed by other students. Students felt that having the ability to complete the course at their own pace (but before due dates) was impactful. This strategy allowed students to work ahead.

Less impactful strategies were utilizing the online and in-person assistance on campus. This was provided as an option for students who desired one-on-one or group help with course assignments. This option also provided students an opportunity to have face-to-face time with a TA or a tutor. Students may not have attended the sessions because of the times offered. The "anytime, anywhere" nature of the course allowed students to work on course assignments at a time convenient for them.

CONCLUSION

This chapter discussed universal design for learning, universal design for instruction and universal instructional design and how universal design strategies can be implemented in online courses. Findings from the study complement results from similar studies done in the past (Fidalgo & Thormann, 2017; Rao, Edelen-Smith, & Wailehua, 2015; Schelly, Davies, & Spooner, 2011). According to survey results, students perceived some of the strategies implemented within the course as more impactful than others. The information presented in this chapter can assist educators with implementing universal design strategies in online courses.

REFERENCES

Allen, I. E., & Seaman, J. (2014). *Grade change: Tracking online education in the United States*. Babson Survey Research Group and Quahog Research Group, LLC. Retrieved from http://sloanconsortium.org/publications/survey/grade-change-2013

Burgstahler, S. (2009). *Universal design of instruction (UDI): Definition, principles, guidelines, and examples*. Seattle, WA: DO-IT, University of Washington. Retrieved from http://www.washington.edu/doit/Brochures/Academics/instruction.html

Burgstahler, S. (2012). *Equal access: Universal design of instruction*. Seattle, WA: DO-IT, University of Washington. Retrieved from www.uw.edu/doit/equal-access-universal-design-instruction

CAST. (2011). *Universal Design for Learning Guidelines version 2.0*. Wakefield, MA: Author.

CAST. (2018). *Universal Design for Learning Guidelines version 2.2*. Retrieved from http://udlguidelines.cast.org

Chickering, A. W., & Gamson, Z. F. (1987). Seven principles for good practice in undergraduate education. *AAHE Bulletin*, *39*(7), 3–7.

Coombs, N. (2010). *Making Online Teaching Accessible: Inclusive Course Design for Students with Disabilities*. San Francisco, CA: Jossey-Bass.

Fidalgo, P., & Thormann, J. (2017). Reaching student in online courses using alternative formats. *International Review of Research in Open and Distributed Learning.*, *18*(2), 139–161. doi:10.19173/irrodl.v18i2.2601

Fox, J. A., Hatfield, J. P., & Collins, T. C. (2003). Developing the Curriculum Transformation and Disability Workshop Model. In J. L. Higbee (Ed.), *Curriculum transformation and disability: Implementing Universal Design in higher education* (pp. 23–39). Minneapolis, MN: University of Minnesota, General College, Center for Research on Developmental Education and Urban Literacy. Retrieved from http://cehd.umn.edu/CRDEUL/books-ctad.html

Goegan, L. D., Radil, A. I., & Daniels, L. M. (2018). Accessibility in Questionnaire Research: Integrating Universal Design to Increase the Participation of Individuals with Learning Disabilities. *Learning Disabilities (Weston, Mass.)*, *16*(2), 177–190.

Gradel, K., & Edson, A. J. (2009). Putting Universal Design for Learning on the Higher Ed Agenda. *Journal of Educational Technology Systems*, *38*(2), 111–121. doi:10.2190/ET.38.2.d

Haynes, A. S. (2019). Establishing Considerations for Universal Design for Learning and Accessibility in Online Courses. In M. Khosrow-Pour, D.B.A. (Ed.), Handbook of Research on Challenges and Opportunities in Launching a Technology-Driven International University (pp. 69-90). Hershey, PA: IGI Global. doi:10.4018/978-1-5225-6255-9.ch005

He, Y. (2014). Universal Design for Learning in an Online Teacher Education Course: Enhancing Learners' Confidence to Teach Online. *Journal of Online Learning and Teaching / MERLOT*, *10*(2), 283–298.

Izzo, M. V., Murray, A., & Novak, J. (2008). The Faculty Perspective on Universal Design for Learning. *Journal of Postsecondary Education and Disability*, *21*(2), 60–72.

Kennedy, W., & Yun, J. (2019). Universal Design for Learning as a Curriculum Development Tool in Physical Education. *Journal of Physical Education, Recreation & Dance*, *90*(6), 25–31. doi:10.1080/07303084.2019.1614119

Kinash, S., Crichton, S., & Kim-Rupnow, W. S. (2004). A Review of 2000-2003 Literature at the Intersection of Online Learning and Disability. *American Journal of Distance Education*, *18*(1), 5–19. doi:10.120715389286ajde1801_2

McGuire, J. M., & Scott, S. S. (2006). Universal Design for instruction: Extending the universal paradigm to college instruction. *Journal of Postsecondary education and Disability*, *19*(2), 124–134.

Meyer, A., Rose, D. H., & Gordon, D. (2013). *Universal design for learning. Theory and practice*. Wakefield, MA: Center for Applied Special Technology. Retrieved from http://udltheorypractice.cast.org/login

Moorefield-Lang, H., Copeland, C. A., & Haynes, A. (2016). Accessing abilities: Creating innovative accessible online learning environments and putting quality into practice. *Education for Information*, *32*(1), 27–33. doi:10.3233/EFI-150966

Rao, K., Edelman-Smith, P., & Wailehua, C. (2015). Universal design for online courses: Applying principles to pedagogy. *Open Learning*, *20*(1), 35–52. doi:10.1080/02680513.2014.991300

Rao, K., & Tanners, A. (2015). Curb Cuts in Cyberspace: Universal Instructional Design for Online Courses. *Journal of Postsecondary Education and Disability*, *24*(3), 211–229.

Rogers-Shaw, C., Carr-Chellman, D. J., & Choi, J. (2018). University Design for Leanring: Guidelines for Accessible Online Instruction. *Adult Learning*, *29*(1), 20–31. doi:10.1177/1045159517735530

Schelly, C. L., Davies, P. L., & Spooner, C. L. (2011). Student perceptions of faculty implementation of Universal Design for Learning. *Journal of Postsecondary Education and Disability*, *24*, 17–30.

Scott, L. A., Temple, P., & Marshall, D. (2015). UDL in Online College Coursework: Insights of Infusion and Educator Preparedness. *Online Learning*, *19*(5), 99–119. doi:10.24059/olj.v19i5.623

Silver, P., Bourke, A., & Strehorn, K. C. (1998). Universal Instructional Design in Higher Education: An Approach for Inclusion. *Equity & Excellence in Education*, *2*(31), 47–51. doi:10.1080/1066568980310206

Simoncelli, A., & Hinson, J. M. (2008). College students' with learning disabilities personal reactions to online learning. *Journal of College Reading and Learning*, *38*(2), 49–62. doi:10.1080/10790195.2008.10850308

Smith, F. G. (2012). Analyzing a college course that adheres to the Universal Design for Learning (UDL) framework. *The Journal of Scholarship of Teaching and Learning*, *12*(3), 31–61.

Snow, H. K. (2018). High-Impact Practices, Universal Design and Assessment Opportunities in Liberal Arts Seminars. *ASIANetwork Exchange, 25*(2), 117-135.

Spooner, F., Baker, J. N., Harris, A. A., Ahlgrim-Delzell, L., & Browder, D. M. (2007). Effects of Training in Universal Design for Learning on Lesson Plan Development. *Remedial and Special Education*, *28*(2), 108–116. doi:10.1177/07419325070280020101

The Nine Principles of UDI. (2012). Center on Postsecondary Education and Disability, University of Connecticut. Retrieved from http://udi.uconn.edu/index.php?q=node/12

Tobin, T. J. (2014). Increase online student retention with universal design for learning. *The Quarterly Review of Distance Education.*, *15*(3), 13–24.

U. S. Department of Education. (2010). *Transforming American Education: Learning Powered by Technology*. Washington, DC: Office of Educational Technology.

U. S. Department of Education. (2012). *Higher Education Opportunity Act - 2008.* Retrieved from http://www2.ed.gov/policy/highered/leg/hea08/index.html

KEY TERMS AND DEFINITIONS

Accessibility: Ensuring access course materials to all learners.

Disability: Impairment that can makes routine tasks more difficult.

Online Learning: Anytime/anywhere access to education made available through the internet.

Universal Design for Instruction: Guidelines for applying universal design principles to all parts of instruction.

Universal Design for Learning: Providing equal access to curriculum for all students.

Universal Instructional Design: Principles to create accessible and inclusive learning environment.

Usability: Ease of use of course components.

Chapter 5
HCI and User Experience Design Education:
Principles for Ethical and Responsible Practices in Inclusive Research and Application

Troy Abel
https://orcid.org/0000-0002-5854-679X
University of North Texas, USA

Debra Satterfield
https://orcid.org/0000-0001-9962-0864
California State University, Long Beach, USA

ABSTRACT

A thorough and robust understanding of responsible and ethical practices in UX is essential to user experience designers. Ethical UX practices include authentic inclusion, vulnerability in participants, the inclusion of IRB-protected groups in research, tolerance for risk and motivation, truth in research, fair and respectful conduct, informed consent, cultural sensitivity, accessibility in UX processes, stigmatized populations, idiosyncratic populations, right to privacy, and an understanding of ADA-compliant accommodations by UX researchers and participants. This chapter will introduce these principles as well as demonstrate one possible application in an undergraduate design classroom.

INTRODUCTION

This chapter presents the reader with twelve (12) ethical principles which can be applied to the field of User Experience Research and Design. The objectives of this chapter are not only to introduce these principles to the reader, but also an application of these principles in an undergraduate classroom.

DOI: 10.4018/978-1-7998-2325-4.ch005

BACKGROUND

There is a historical lack of ethics in research on a global basis from the late 20th and persisting into the 21st century. Predominantly conducted by and/or on behalf of U.S. researchers in the name of scientific and medical advancement, this lack of ethical standards and conduct produced a wide range of issues that require professional oversights and protocols.

All scientific researchers must be aware of these egregious activities and understand the necessary responsibilities of themselves and ethical standards for which they must uphold. Researchers in the social sciences (which User Experience Research is a part of) must look to the medical professions as well as governmental oversight to begin informing guiding principles and codes of conduct to uphold while conducting their research.

The following discusses foundational understandings of ethics, the need for ethics and inclusion in UX, introduces the 12 Guiding Principles for Ethical and Inclusive Research (E-UX), and applies these to a typical undergraduate research exercise in creating a user persona. These E-UX principles are proposed by compiling best practices and ethical standards from a variety of organizations, federal and professional, who have already successfully incorporated ethical standards into their disciplines.

ETHICS OVERVIEW

Ethics, or moral philosophy, is a branch of philosophy that involves systematizing, defending, and recommending concepts of right and wrong conduct. ("Internet Encyclopedia of Philosophy: A Peer-Reviewed Academic Resource," n.d.)

The 3 major areas of Ethical study

Three major areas of study within ethics recognized today are: ("Internet Encyclopedia of Philosophy: A Peer-Reviewed Academic Resource," n.d.):

1. Meta-ethics, concerning the theoretical meaning and reference of moral propositions, and how their truth values (if any) can be determined,
2. Normative ethics, concerning the practical means of determining a moral course of action,
3. Applied ethics, concerning what a person is obligated (or permitted) to do in a specific situation or a particular domain of action

"In recent years applied ethical issues have been subdivided into convenient groups such as medical ethics, business ethics, environmental ethics, and sexual ethics." (Internet encyclopedia) Moreover, applied ethics is a discipline that attempts to apply ethical theory to real-life situations. This discipline has many specialized fields, such as engineering ethics, bioethics, geoethics, public service ethics and business ethics. Applied ethics involves examining specific controversial issues, such as abortion, infanticide, animal rights, environmental concerns, homosexuality, capital punishment, or nuclear war. ("Internet Encyclopedia of Philosophy: A Peer-Reviewed Academic Resource," n.d.)

Applied ethics is used in some aspects of determining public policy, as well as by individuals facing difficult decisions. The sort of questions addressed by applied ethics include: "Is getting an abortion immoral?" "Is euthanasia immoral?" "Is affirmative action right or wrong?" "What are human rights, and how do we determine them?" "Do animals have rights as well?" and "Do individuals have the right of self-determination?"

A more specific question could be: "If someone else can make better out of his/her life than I can, is it then moral to sacrifice myself for them if needed?" Without these questions, there is no clear fulcrum on which to balance law, politics, and the practice of arbitration—in fact, no common assumptions of all participants—so the ability to formulate the questions are prior to rights balancing. But not all questions studied in applied ethics concern public policy. For example, making ethical judgments regarding questions such as, "Is lying always wrong?" and, "If not, when is it permissible?" is prior to any etiquette.

People, in general, are more comfortable with dichotomies (two opposites). However, in ethics, the issues are most often multifaceted, and the best-proposed actions address many different areas concurrently. In ethical decisions, the answer is almost never a "yes or no", "right or wrong" statement. Many buttons are pushed so that the overall condition is improved and not to the benefit of any particular faction.

Unethical human experimentation in the United States can be demonstrated through several well-known and well-cited research studies. Such tests and experiments have been considered unethical, and were often performed illegally, without the knowledge, consent, or informed consent of the test subjects. Such tests have occurred throughout American history, but particularly in the 20th century. The experiments include: the exposure of humans to many chemical and biological weapons, human radiation experiments, injection of toxic and radioactive chemicals, surgical experiments, interrogation and torture experiments, tests involving mind-altering substances, and a wide variety of others. Many of these tests were performed on children, the sick, and mentally disabled individuals, often under the guise of "medical treatment". In many of the studies, a large portion of the subjects were poor, racial minorities, or prisoners.

The ethical, professional, and legal implications of this in the United States medical and scientific community were quite significant and led to many institutions and policies that attempted to ensure that future human subject research in the United States would be ethical and legal.

The Child Willowbrook Experiments

Willowbrook State School was a state-supported institution for children with intellectual disabilities located on Staten Island in New York City from 1947 until 1987.

Throughout the first decade of its operation, outbreaks of hepatitis, primarily hepatitis A, were common at the school. Between the 1950's and the 1970's Researchers Saul Krugman (New York University) and Robert W. McCollum (Yale University), monitored subjects to gauge the effects of gamma globulin in combating hepatitis. One result of the research was a better understanding of the differences between serum hepatitis, which is spread by blood transfusions, from infectious hepatitis, which is spread directly from person to person and is the more common form. Once discovered and made public, an outcry forced the research project and medical studies to be discontinued.

Paul A. Offit described Krugman's studies as follows:

In an effort to control outbreaks of hepatitis, the medical staff at Willowbrook consulted Saul Krugman.... Krugman found that hepatitis developed in 90 percent of children admitted to Willowbrook soon after their arrival. Although it was known that hepatitis was caused by a virus, it wasn't known how hepatitis virus spread, whether it could be prevented, or how many types of viruses caused the disease. Krugman used the children of Willowbrook to answer those questions. One of his studies involved feeding live hepatitis virus to sixty healthy children. Krugman watched as their skin and eyes turned yellow and their livers got bigger. He watched them vomit and refuse to eat. All the children fed hepatitis virus became ill, some severely. Krugman reasoned that it was justifiable to inoculate retarded children at Willowbrook with hepatitis virus because most of them would get hepatitis anyway. But by purposefully giving the children hepatitis, Krugman increased that chance to 100 percent. (Offit, n.d.)

Tuskegee Experiments

Another example of an unethical clinical study was conducted between 1932 and 1972 titled The Tuskegee Study of Untreated Syphilis. This study targeted African American men who were told they were receiving free health care from the United States government, when in actuality over 200 of them were intentionally infected with syphilis. The purpose of the study was to observe the natural course of untreated syphilis.

The study was run in collaboration with Tuskegee University, a historically black college in Alabama. Investigators enrolled in the study a total of 600 impoverished, African-American sharecroppers from Macon County, Alabama. Of these 600 enrolled in the study, only 201 did not have syphilis. The men were given free medical care, meals, and free burial insurance for participating in the study. The men were told that the study was only going to last six months, but it actually lasted 40 years. After funding for treatment was lost, the study was continued without informing the men that they would never be treated. None of the men were told that they had the disease, and none were treated with penicillin even after the antibiotic was proven to successfully treat syphilis. According to the Centers for Disease Control, the men were told that they were being treated for "bad blood", a colloquialism that described various conditions such as syphilis, anemia, and fatigue. "Bad blood"—specifically the collection of illnesses the term included—was a leading cause of death within the southern African-American community at the time.

This 40-year study is unethical for reasons related to common ethical standards. The number one reason being researchers *knowingly* failed to treat patients appropriately after the 1940s validation of penicillin was found as an effective cure for the disease. The Tuskegee Syphilis Study, has been cited as "arguably the most infamous biomedical research study in U.S. history" (Katz et al., 2006)

In 1972 whistleblower, Peter Buxtun, revealed the major failures of the study study which led to major changes in U.S. law and regulation on the protection of participants in clinical studies. In 1979 the Belmont Report led to the establishment of the Office for Human Research Protections and also to federal laws and regulations requiring Institutional Review Boards (IRB) for the protection of human subjects in studies involving them. The OHRP manages this responsibility within the US Department of Health and Human Services (HHS). IRB's generally only exist in academies of higher education and serve to protect the human test participants.

The Monster Study

The only written record of this research project being conducted is a thesis project by Mary Tudor of the University of Iowa. Mary worked under the tutelage of Wendell Jonson. The research surrounded stuttering in children and was conducted in Davenport, Iowa in 1939 with a total of 22 orphan children.

The methodology for this research was to supply half of the children with positive speech therapy, praising the fluency of their speech, and the other half, negative speech therapy, belittling the children for speech imperfections. It was later named the "Monster Study" as some of Johnson's peers were horrified that he would experiment on orphan children to confirm a hypothesis. This particular experiment was kept hidden for fear Johnson's reputation would be affected in the wake of the discovery of human experiments conducted by the Nazis during World War II. Because the results of the study were never published in any peer-reviewed journal, Mary Tudor's thesis is the only official record of the details of the experiment.

The research began with a selection of twenty-two subjects from a veterans' orphanage in Iowa. None were told the intent of her research, and they believed that they were to receive speech therapy. Tudor was trying to induce stuttering in healthy children and to see whether telling stutterers that their speech was fine would produce a change. Graduate students working with Jonson were assigned to the groups of children.

The results of the study were freely available in the library of the University of Iowa, but Johnson did not seek publication of the results. The experiment became national news in the wake of a series of articles conducted by an investigative reporter at the San Jose Mercury News in 2001, and a book titled *Ethics: A Case Study from Fluency* was written to provide an impartial scientific evaluation. The panel of authors in the book consists mostly of speech pathologists who fail to reach any consensus on either the ethical ramifications or scientific consequences of the Monster Study. Richard Schwartz concludes in Chapter 6 of the book that the Monster Study "was unfortunate in Tudor and Johnson's lack of regard for the potential harm to the children who participated and in their selection of institutionalized children simply because they were easily available. The deception and the apparent lack of debriefing were also not justifiable." (Goldfarb, 2006)

Other authors concur claiming the orphan experiment was not within the ethical boundaries of acceptable research. Others, however, felt that the ethical standards in 1939 were different from those used today. Some felt the study was poorly designed and executed by Tudor, and as a result the data offered no proof of Johnson's subsequent hypothesis that "stuttering begins, not in the child's mouth but in the parent's ear" (Tudor, 1939)-- i.e., that it is the well-meaning parent's effort to help the child avoid what the parent has labeled "stuttering" (but is in fact within the range of normal speech) that contributes to what ultimately becomes the problem diagnosed as stuttering.

On 17 August 2007, seven of the orphan children were awarded a total of $1.2M by the State of Iowa for lifelong psychological and emotional scars caused by six months of torment during the University of Iowa experiment. ("Huge payout in US stuttering case," n.d.)

ETHICAL STANDARDS IN SCIENTIFIC RESEARCH

Ethical standards are critical to safeguarding the public in the face of advancements in science and medical research. A well-vetted set of ethical standards that can be applied uniformly and overseen by an independent body of evaluators is critical to maintaining public safety. The standards govern the procedures, processes and subjects that can be involved in the research. In addition, protected populations are subjected to greater safeguards. These independent observations are conducted by groups of knowledgeable third-party evaluators.

The Government on Ethics and Research

On July 12, 1974, the National Research Act was signed into law, thereby creating the National Commission for the Protection of Human Subjects of Biomedical and Behavioral Research. One of the charges to the Commission was to identify the basic ethical principles that should underlie the conduct of biomedical and behavioral research involving human subjects and to develop guidelines which should be followed to assure that such research is conducted in accordance with those principles.

The Belmont Report is the outgrowth of an intensive four-day period of discussions that were held in February 1976 at the Smithsonian Institution's Belmont Conference Center supplemented by the monthly deliberations of the Commission that were held over a period of nearly four years. It is a statement of basic ethical principles and guidelines that should assist in resolving the ethical problems that surround the conduct of research with human subjects

The Belmont Report was completed and submitted in 1978 and immediately made publically available by the Superintendent of Documents, U.S. Government Printing Office. The short document (19 pages including cover, appendices and references) set-forth 3 guiding principles for ethical research: 1) Respect for Persons, 2) Beneficence, and 3) Justice. Researchers have referred to the Belmont Report for guidance when conducting research involving human subjects.

Basic Ethical Principles were laid out in the Belmont Report "The expression 'basic ethical principles' refers to those general judgments that serve as a basic justification for the many particular ethical prescriptions and evaluations of human actions. Three basic principles, among those generally accepted in our cultural tradition, are particularly relevant to the ethics of research involving human subjects: the principles of respect for persons, beneficence and justice." (Department of Health, Education, and Welfare & National Commission for the Protection of Human Subjects of Biomedical and Behavioral Research, n.d.)

Research in Higher Education

Academic and medical research and government funded research are strictly monitored by Institutional Review Boards (IRB). These boards oversee and govern research in these venues. There are policies that govern the use of human subjects in research, pathogens and medical procedures. Special safeguards are put in place with regard to invasive research and vulnerable populations including children under age 18, persons with cognitive impairments, illnesses, pregnant women, persons who are incarcerated and others who are unable to adequately understand and give consent to participate. IRB approvals oversee the number of participants, the research protocols, research communications with the human subject participants, and the length of time during which the study can be conducted prior to reapproval.

CURRENT ETHICAL AND CODES OF CONDUCT IN PARALLEL DISCIPLINES

ACM's Ethical Code

The Association for Computing Machinery has created, and continues to curate, a code of ethical principles in their disciplines. These principles fall under four (4) main categories: ((Gotterbarn, Miller, & Rogerson, 1997)

1. General ethical principles.
2. Professional responsibilities.
3. Professional leadership principles.
4. Compliance with the code.

Category 1 outlines fundamental ethical principles that form the basis for the remainder of the Code. Category 2 addresses additional, more specific considerations of professional responsibility. Category 3 guides individuals who have a leadership role, whether in the workplace or in a volunteer professional capacity. Finally, commitment to ethical conduct is required of every ACM member, and principles involving compliance with the Code are given in Section 4. (ACM, n.d.)

Each category is subdivided into several principles to consider under the umbrella of each category. The introduction to the ethical principles states:

The [ACM] Code as a whole is concerned with how fundamental ethical principles apply to a computing professional's conduct. The Code is not an algorithm for solving ethical problems; rather it serves as a basis for ethical decision-making. When thinking through a particular issue, a computing professional may find that multiple principles should be taken into account, and that different principles will have different relevance to the issue. Questions related to these kinds of issues can best be answered by thoughtful consideration of the fundamental ethical principles, understanding that the public good is the paramount consideration. The entire computing profession benefits when the ethical decision-making process is accountable to and transparent to all stakeholders. Open discussions about ethical issues promote this accountability and transparency. (ACM, n.d.)

American Psychological Association Ethical Principles of Psychologists and Code of Conduct

The first version of the APA Ethics Code was published in 1953. (Hobbs, 1948) The need for such a document came after psychologists were taking on more professional, public, and scientific roles post-World War II. (Hobbs, 1948) A committee was convened and collected ethical questions from the field of psychology. This committee organized these situations into themes and included them in the first document which was 170 pages in length. (Hobbs, 1948) Over the years, a distinction was made between aspirational principles and enforceable standards. Since, there have been nine revisions with the most recent published in 2002 and amended in 2010. ("APA Ethics Code," 2019)

"There are five general principles that serve as the ideals to which psychologists should aspire within the profession. The principles represent ethical goals but do not explicitly inform or instruct adherence to the goals; instead, the principles aim to influence and to guide professional behavior with respect to the psychologist, research subjects, students, and the individuals who seek psychological services." ("APA Ethics Code," 2019)

- **Principle A:** Beneficence and nonmaleficence
- **Principle B:** Fidelity and responsibility
- **Principle C:** Integrity
- **Principle D:** Justice
- **Principle E:** Respect for people's rights and dignity

Principle A: Beneficence and Nonmaleficence

The beneficence and nonmaleficence principle of the APA general principles guides psychologists to perform work that is beneficial to others yet does not hurt anyone in the process of carrying out that work. Psychologists are to remain aware of their professional influence and the potential consequences therein on individuals and groups who seek counsel with the psychologist, especially with respect to preventing misuse or abuse, while additionally maintaining awareness of how the psychologist's own physical and mental health may influence their work. Among professional interactions and research, psychologists ought to respect and protect the rights and welfare of patients and participants.

Principle B: Fidelity and Responsibility

The fidelity and responsibility principle of the APA general principles inspires psychologists to cultivate a professional and scientific environment built upon trust, accountability, and ethical considerations. Psychologists are bound to the community by way of their profession and must conduct themselves in a responsible and ethical manner while also maintaining a similar check on colleagues. Furthermore, psychologists are expected to altruistically devote some of their time to the community.

Principle C: Integrity

The integrity principle of the APA general principles aims to encourage psychologists to engage in honest, transparent practices within all aspects of the field of psychology. That is, psychologists should not engage in behavior that could be misconstrued as dishonest, exploitative, or otherwise malicious. When deception is appropriately used (most likely during psychological research), psychologists have a responsibility to mitigate the effects of its use on the overall field.

Principle D: Justice

The justice principle of the APA general principles states that people are entitled to the advances made within the field of psychology and to the services offered by professionals within the field. Furthermore, psychologists should prevent unjust practices by remaining aware of their biases, level of competence, and area and limits of expertise.

Principle E: Respect for People's Rights and Dignity

The APA general principle concerning respect for people's rights and dignity recognizes individuals' rights to privacy and confidentiality. Psychologists are to respect the individuals' rights while also acknowledging the worth of the individual by taking judicious precautions and engaging in positive, professional interactions, avoiding the influence of any personal bias towards the individual or group. This entails awareness of the vulnerabilities experienced by any particular population of people and necessitates understanding of and respect for diversity, including, but not limited to, factors concerning gender, race, religion, disability, and socioeconomic status. ("APA Ethics Code," 2019)

THE NEED FOR ETHICAL RESEARCH IN UX

The ability to adequately understand the cognitive, social, emotional, motivational and behavioral tendencies of a target audience are the important underpinnings of user experience (UX) research and design. However, not all members of a target audience are equally willing or able to participate in all forms of UX research. People with disabilities and mental illness are often subject to high levels of stigma by society. In healthcare, stigma is considered to be one of the biggest obstacles in their care and quality of life. (Sartorius, 2007) The target audience may believe that they either are not able to adequately perform the necessary tasks because of idiosyncratic skills or beliefs or because they believe that their participation would put them in a position of significant personal risk due to disabilities or stigmatizing beliefs or conditions. In addition, failing to include all members of the target audience because of disability or stigma can introduce significant bias into the research due to oversampling of normative populations and under sampling of idiosyncratic, atypical, or outlier populations. Therefore, there is a critical need to develop Ethical and Inclusive principles for the purpose of more robust risk management and mitigation strategies to improve inclusion and accurate representation in their research.

One particular need for ethical standards in UX can be examined when UX researchers are selecting and recruiting for studies. An initial literature search for research relating to usability studies participant selection, resulted in very little research and writing on the process of, or guidelines for the selection process. Currently, normative practitioners rely on the business unit to define the target audience and/or developed personas to include in the study as research participants. These methods can introduce bias into the testing results by eliminating or under representing specific user groups or over representing specific user groups. These biases may be based on each group's ability to perform the test, their ability to comply with the research requirements; a group's lack of willingness to participate based on anxiety, a group's predisposition to lie or please the researcher, or based on the researcher's convenient access to one group over another group. The target audience's own perception of themselves and their situation may differ from the perception of the same person and situation as identified from a researcher's point of view

Very little literature exists with regard to selecting participants, especially from marginalized populations; however, Rubin states "the selection and acquisition of participants whose background and abilities are representative of your products' intended user is a crucial element of the testing process." (Rubin & Chisnell, 2008) Moreover, "Selecting participants involves identifying and describing the relevant behavior, skills, and knowledge of the person(s) who will use your product. This description is known as the user profile…" (Rubin & Chisnell, 2008) Finally, "...your test results will only be valid if the people who participate are typical users of the product, or as close to that criterion as possible."

(Rubin & Chisnell, 2008) We, as practitioners, must strive to be as inclusive as possible when selecting participants for usability testing in any given system. We also must consider guidelines for inclusion and selection of marginalized populations to ensure our system is of greater use to more members of our initially identified audience, as well as marginalized audience members who may otherwise go unnoticed in persona development, especially by the business and marketing units.

INTRODUCING THE 12 E-UX PRINCIPLES TO UNDERGRADUATE AND GRADUATE CURRICULUM

The ***12 Guiding Principles for Ethical and Responsible Practices in Inclusive UX Research*** (E-UX) apply to research that can be applied to user groups that are typical in that they require little or no additional accommodations or modifications to the traditional UX tools and strategies. However, they are specifically designed to give guidance that also applies when designing UX protocols, strategies and tools that can be modified to accommodate persons with a wide variety of temporary or permanent disabling physical, psychological, social, emotional, intellectual or developmental conditions. In addition, guidelines are given that can be applied to situations where differences in culture or other social constructs may impede the UX process. The guidelines can be shared with UX participants so that they may be an active participant in creating the best accommodation for this unique situation. The guidelines can be applied without the necessity for the research participant to divulge the specific nature of their condition or situation to the research team thereby avoiding the introduction of unnecessary bias with regard to any participant. They are meant to provide a foundational guideline for authentic inclusion in the UX process and form a basis for further development and refinement as guidelines with applications in UX and AI.

The 12 Guiding Principles for Ethical UX Research and Design;

1. **Authentic Inclusion:** Authentic inclusion is reaching a representative stakeholder group that includes all of the impacted groups in ways that are accurate and appropriately nuanced. It strives to eliminate stereotypical representation and to acknowledge the actual lived experiences of the stakeholders. It captures the true identity of the user groups in ways that are consistent with their perceptions of themselves.
2. **Vulnerability:** Stakeholders may have actual or perceived vulnerability due to the circumstances of their relationship to the context of the study. Vulnerability may be in the form of perceived or actual harm from participation in the study either from the act of participation or from possible harm due to the information they provide. Examples of vulnerability include risk of identification, relationship to the researcher or the research subject, or the desperation of the subject. An example is a person who suffers from a serious condition under study who may feel compelled to participation due to their own vulnerability from the fear of dying. Another example of vulnerability might be experiencing a strong social push to participate in a study due to fear of retribution from the researchers. Vulnerability comes in the form of the participant's relationship to the study question or from their relationship to the study researchers.
3. **Tolerance for Risk:** Participants with a greater than normal tolerance for risk may be vulnerable from their inability to appropriately assess their own risk from participation. An increased tolerance for risk may be related to the participants level of cognitive understanding of the research, a greatly increased level of motivation to participate due to real or perceived vulnerability, or a predisposi-

tion to risk taking behavior. Increased tolerance for risk may be allowable when the participant demonstrates an ability to understand the context of the study and all possible consequences. If the participant does not demonstrate a thorough understanding and ability to accept all possible consequences, then tolerance for risk should be evaluated by a designated legal representative that is deemed able to evaluate all possible outcomes.

4. **Motivation:** Participant motivation may vary from highly unmotivated to highly motivated. The motivation may be intrinsic or extrinsic. The participants may have a real or perceived benefit from the research. Motivation may positively impact participation with regard to willingness and willingness to supply detailed information. Negative motivation averts participation and may affect the quality and nature of the information provided.
5. **Truth in Research**: It is the responsibility of the researcher to identify and adequately explain to the participants if deceit will be an integral part of the research process and data collection. If deceit is required to obtain the necessary data, then a thorough debriefing process should be developed as part of the research protocol. It should be clearly explained in the exit process what deceit was included in the research, why the deceit was necessary, and how the data will be used.
6. **Fair and Respectful Conduct:** The persons conducting the research should be fair in how they conduct the study and compensate participants. The conduct with research participants should be respectful of their time and their treatment. Researchers should be aware of the expectations of the participants and consciously abide by conduct that respects all participants. Fair compensation should be provided to the participants.
7. **Informed Consent:** It is the responsibility of the researcher to give clear written and verbal descriptions of the reason for the research, the protocol, and the role and expectations of the participant. The descriptions should be written in a way that is easy to read and understand by the participant. The participant should clearly understand what will be done with the data they provide, how their identity will be protected, the lifecycle of the data with regard to storage and when it will be destroyed, and how to indicate they wish to stop participation if necessary. If the participant is unable to read, the process will include and informed consent process to be completed by a legal guardian and a second consent process given to the participant in a manner that they can understand.
8. **Cultural Sensitivity:** The researchers need to have a genuine sensitivity to the culture of the participants. This includes an understanding of common practices for names and language, attire, and social gestures or cues. Cultural sensitivity should be maintained throughout the UX process from the first invitations to participate, informed consent, data collection, and data interpretation.
9. **Accessibility in UX Processes:** UX researchers need to thoroughly understand and comply with ADA accommodations throughout the invitation and data collection process. The impact of a disability on the proposed UX should be fully researched and reasonable accommodations should be readily available. In addition, each disability has many ways in which it may impact a proposed research protocol. For example, a person with low vision might need adaptations to printed materials or additional time in responding. Each person, even with the same or similar impairments, may require or prefer a different type of accommodation. It should also be noted that frequently a person may have multiple impairments that all require accommodations. The researcher must prepare and test accommodations ahead of the data collection phase and should allow the participant to choose what accommodations best fit their situation at the time of data collection. In addition, the participant is not required to fully disclose the nature of their disabling condition to the research team only the need for an accommodation and the type of desired accommodations. The accom-

modations should be appropriate to the data collection and in some cases appropriate to the actual use situation of the person with the disabling condition. This could include but is not limited to:

a. Modified size, color or contrast in written, digital, or print materials;
b. Changes to the physical testing environment in terms of space layout, accommodations for mobility, or a different location;
c. Modified or augmented lighting conditions;
d. Sound control or customization;
e. Private, semi-private or distraction free testing environment;
f. ADA compliant websites or data input accommodations;
g. Increased time or no timing of responses;
h. Customizable audio or printed descriptions;
i. Braille;
j. Use of interpreters for language translation, language assistance or sign language;
k. Assisted support from a caregiver or attendant for data input or free discussion;
l. Ability to spend time to become familiar with the test site, materials or situation;
m. Access to more detailed explanations or demonstrations of the testing procedures;
n. Ability for the participant to use their own assistive devices as needed for mobility, speech, fine or gross motor tasks, reading, grasping, or other devices as needed for participation in the UX process;
o. The option to suggest any additional or modified accommodation; and
p. A fully explained process and welcomed option to discontinue the testing at any point should the research participant choose to quit the study without any form of a penalty.

10. **Right to Privacy:** The UX team has the responsibility to protect the privacy of the research participants. This includes using the least invasive practices when collecting and storing data. Researchers should only collect necessary identifiable data and have a protocol for de-identifying data for public dissemination. Data including photos or video of participants, voice recording, handwriting, self-identification in survey responses, small data sets, and combining data sets call unintentionally identify participants. This can have devastating consequences in cases where the ramifications of the data have the potential to cause real or perceived harm to the participants. Combining data sets may lead to inaccurate or speculative data interpretation. Small data sets can lead to situations where the data itself can identify a person through a series of unrelated questions that single out one person by their characteristics.
11. **Stigmatized Populations:** Some research participants may feel a sense of stigma with regard to how they identify for a research study. This stigma whether actual or perceived may impact the nature of how they participate in UX research. It is critical that the research team understand the nature of stigma and how it may manifest itself in their research participants. Stigma may be associated with medical conditions such as epilepsy, HIV, mental illness or other well documented conditions. It may also be associated with social conditions such as in a society with a caste system, socio-economic factors, gender identity or sexual orientation, age, occupational status or other socially comparative factors. When stigma is not understood and mitigated, it may lead to serious issues in data collection or data interpretation.
12. **Idiosyncratic Populations:** Some UX research populations may be highly idiosyncratic in their social, emotional, physical or behavioral characteristics. Often times the research being conducted may be for the express purpose of better understanding the population with regard to the very issue

of its idiosyncratic nature. However, when working with a population that does not have a strong cohesive set of defining characteristics, it is important to choose the best research strategies that perform well without a normative standard. An example of a highly idiosyncratic population is children or adults on the autism spectrum. This is a highly researched group however studies that do not control for the variability of symptoms and behaviors may have findings that are largely inconclusive. Some mitigation strategies include:

a. Highly controlled inclusion criteria;
b. Descriptive research methodologies such as a case study or a qualitative or mixed method approach that allows for descriptive data to explain outliers or anomalous data;
c. Incorporate known descriptive or diagnostic tools into the methodology such as using the DSM-V categories to create a more homogenous group for study; and
d. Combine data sets for more accurate analysis such as combining a written survey with video data or combining EEG with a focus group or analysis by an expert or professional.

THE 12 GUIDING PRINCIPLES AS A FRAMEWORK FOR E-UX IN THE COLLEGE CURRICULUM

UX education is a new field in the areas of design, computer science, ergonomics, business, human computer interaction (HCI) and business. As UX evolves so do the core concepts in the curriculum. Ethics as it applies to the field of UX is an important part of the evolving curriculum. In addition, the way in which ethics are introduced and woven into the fabric of the educational experience for graduate and undergraduate students is an important consideration. In many cases, students in these areas of study may have only a rudimentary introduction to the concepts of ethics in their general education curriculum. Therefore, ethics in UX (E-UX) education includes:

- An introduction to fundamental ethical models;
- The 12 guiding principles of E-UX; and
- Case studies from UXD that relate to the individual ethics and E-UX concepts.

A complete E-UX curriculum needs to examine the various ethical frameworks in society as part of a comprehensive approach. The distinctions between Consequentialists Theories of Morality and Non-consequentialist theories as they apply to Ethical Egoism, Utilitarianism, Care Ethics, Intuition, Duty Ethics, and Divine Command Ethics are important to a discussion about the impact of ethics on UX. In addition, the distinctions between models and the impact of implicit ethical biases in the design of products, services and communities must be explored and discussed with regard to overall ramifications in UX. Community, in-groups, and culture also play a large role in the way ethics manifest themselves in society and on an interpersonal level. The 12 guiding principles of E-UX exist within the larger society level ethical models. These principles are specific guidelines to the treatment and inclusion of participants in the UX process. They are designed to be used as part of the UX process specifically and insure fair and equitable treatment of the participants.

The role of E- UX is to guide UX researchers with regard to best practices in terms of ethical data collection processes. It provides guidelines for inclusion, motivation, fair practices, safety, accessibility, and cultural sensitivity. In addition, stigma and idiosyncratic populations are addressed to increase awareness and authentic inclusion of these marginalized groups within the UX data collection process.

REFERENCES

ACM. (n.d.). *ACM Code of Ethics*. Retrieved from https://www.acm.org/code-of-ethics

APA Ethics Code. (2019). In *Wikipedia*. Retrieved from https://en.wikipedia.org/w/index.php?title=APA_Ethics_Code&oldid=899653507

Department of Health, Education, and Welfare. (n.d.). *The Belmont Report. Ethical principles and guidelines for the protection of human subjects of research. National Commission for the Protection of Human Subjects of Biomedical and Behavioral Research.*

Goldfarb, R. (2006). *Ethics: A case study from fluency*. San Diego, CA: Plural Publishing.

Gotterbarn, D., Miller, K., & Rogerson, S. (1997). Software Engineering Code of Ethics. *Communications of the ACM*, *40*(11), 110–118. doi:10.1145/265684.265699

Hobbs, N. (1948). The development of a code of ethical standards for psychology. *The American Psychologist*, *3*(3), 80–84. doi:10.1037/h0060281

Huge payout in US stuttering case. (n.d.). *BBC World News*. Retrieved from http://news.bbc.co.uk/2/hi/americas/6952446.stm

Internet Encyclopedia of Philosophy. A Peer-Reviewed Academic Resource. (n.d.). Retrieved from https://www.iep.utm.edu/ethics/

Katz, R. V., Kegeles, S. S., Kressin, N. R., Green, B. L., Wang, M. Q., James, S. A., ... Claudio, C. (2006). The Tuskegee Legacy Project: Willingness of Minorities to Participate in Biomedical Research. *Journal of Health Care for the Poor and Underserved*, *17*(4), 698–715. doi:10.1353/hpu.2006.0126 PMID:17242525

Offit, P. (n.d.). *Vaccinated: One Man's Quest to Defeat the World's Deadliest Diseases. Academic Press.*

Rubin, J., & Chisnell, D. (2008). *Handbook of usability testing: How to plan, design, and conduct effective tests*. Indianapolis, IN: Wiley Pub.

Sartorius, N. (2007). Stigma and mental health. *Lancet*, *370*(9590), 810–811. doi:10.1016/S0140-6736(07)61245-8 PMID:17804064

Tudor, M. (1939). *An experimental study of the act of evaluative labeling of speech fluency*. Iowa City, IA: University of Iowa.

ADDITIONAL READING

Fansher, M., Chivukula, S. S., & Gray, C. M. (2018, April). # darkpatterns: UX Practitioner Conversations About Ethical Design. In *Extended Abstracts of the 2018 CHI Conference on Human Factors in Computing Systems* (p. LBW082). ACM.

Fordham, M. J. (2019). *The importance of ethics in UX design*. Retrieved from: https://uxdesign.cc/the-importance-of-ethics-in-ux-design-378468935703

Gray, C. M., & Chivukula, S. S. (2019, April). Ethical Mediation in UX Practice. In *Proceedings of the 2019 CHI Conference on Human Factors in Computing Systems* (p. 178). ACM.

Kelly, A. (2019). *UX Ethics*. Retrieved from: https://blog.prototypr.io/ux-ethics-317b6f2b7116

Kiess, C. (2019). Building an Ethics Framework for UX Design. *User Experience Magazine, 18*(5). Retrieved from: http://uxpamagazine.org/building-an-ethics-framework-for-ux-design/

Mulvenna, M., Boger, J., & Bond, R. (2017, September). Ethical by Design: A Manifesto. In *Proceedings of the European Conference on Cognitive Ergonomics 2017* (pp. 51-54). ACM. 10.1145/3121283.3121300

Newell, A. F., Gregor, P., Morgan, M., Pullin, G., & Macaulay, C. (2011). User-sensitive inclusive design. *Universal Access in the Information Society, 10*(3), 235–243. doi:10.100710209-010-0203-y

Read, J. C., & Fredrikson, M. (2011). What do we take? What do we keep? What do we tell? Ethical concerns in the design of inclusive socially connected technology for children. *The Social Impact of Social Computing*, 392.

Scherling, L., & DeRosa, A. (Eds.). (2020). *Ethics in Design and Communication: Critical Perspectives*. Bloomsbury Publishing.

Shamonsky, D. (2018). Developing a Code of Ethics for UX Design: What We Can Learn from the Field of Architecture. *User Experience Magazine, 18*(4). Retrieved from https://uxpamagazine.org/developing-a-code-of-ethics/

KEY TERMS AND DEFINITIONS

Design Education: Design education is the teaching of theory and application in the design of products, services and environments. It encompasses various disciplines of design, such as concept design, architecture, landscape architecture, graphic design, user interface design, web design, packaging design, industrial design, fashion design, information design, interior design, sustainable design, transgenerational design, and universal design. The values and attitudes which underlie modern design schools differ among the different design schools.

Ethical Research: Norms, codes, policies that distinguish between acceptable and unacceptable behavior when conducting a research. The following is a rough and general summary of some ethical principles that various codes address: Honesty, Objectivity, Integrity, Carefulness, Openness, Respect for Intellectual Property, Confidentiality, Responsible Publication, Responsible Mentoring, Respect for colleagues, Social Responsibility, Non-Discrimination, Competence, Legality, Animal Care, Human Subjects Protection, among others.

Ethical UX: Involve several principles (strongly related to ethical research principles) to encourage a correct conduction of UX methodologies.

Ethics: At its simplest, ethics is a system of moral principles. They affect how people make decisions and lead their lives. Ethics is concerned with what is good for individuals and society and is also described as moral philosophy. The term is derived from the Greek word ethos which can mean custom, habit, character or disposition.

Inclusive Design: Inclusive design is a methodology, born out of digital environments, that enables and draws on the full range of human diversity. Most importantly, this means including and learning from people with a range of perspectives.

User Experience (UX): User experience (UX) focuses on having a deep understanding of users, what they need, what they value, their abilities, and also their limitations. It also takes into account the business goals and objectives of the group managing the project. UX best practices promote improving the quality of the user's interaction with and perceptions of your product and any related services.

Chapter 6
Physical Access Difficulties at Educational Institutions Experienced by People With Visual Impairment

Paola Manquillo-Manquillo
Universidad de La Rioja, Spain

Katerina Psegiannaki
Universidad Internacional de La Rioja, Spain

ABSTRACT

The objective of this chapter was to assess the impact that haptic tools have on the experience of people with some kind of visual impairment when accessing a building. The analysis was performed through the application of a case study carried out in the facilities of the Center for Teleinformatics and Industrial Production of the National Learning Service in Popayán, Colombia with the participation of five people. Taking into account the principles of universal design, the analysis considered people with total blindness, partial blindness, and people without visual limitation. Participants provided feedback and insights on their experience locating the designated area with and without the support of defined haptic tools. The study resulted in a set of drawbacks that influence the location of visually impaired people. Such findings can be taken into account by people who wish to make projects of access to physical spaces of visually impaired people.

INTRODUCTION

The National Apprenticeship Service (SENA, for its Spanish acronym) is a national public institution that offers free job training to millions of Colombians without distinction as to race, creed, economic status, age or political affiliation.

DOI: 10.4018/978-1-7998-2325-4.ch006

As a work training entity, SENA has a constitutional duty to serve vulnerable populations including people with disabilities but, in a city like Popayán, whose well-preserved colonial architecture has given it the title of "white city", much remains to be done in terms of accessibility and particularly inside the buildings considered as architectural heritage, which were built hundreds of years ago without taking into account accessibility considerations.

BACKGROUND

While it is true that design considerations are important to provide an adequate experience to the users of any product, the creation of haptic tools requires greater attention to design specifications to ensure that users' interaction with the tool is appropriate.

Considering the above, there are a number of concepts that are important to keep in mind during the design process that were implemented in this work and are described below.

The term "haptic" has its origin in the Greek word ἁπτικός (haptikós), which means "related to the ability to touch" (Capitulo II - Tecnología Háptica, n.d.); in human terms, perception refers to the process in which stimuli received by the senses become an organized experience, that is, it is the way the brain organizes and gives meaning to the information it receives from the different sensory organs (Dezcallar Sáez, 2012).

Bearing this in mind, we can infer that haptic perception refers to that which uses touch as a source of information and comprises tactile, cutaneous or static perception in which we feel the consistency and temperature of what we touch, and kinesthetic or dynamic perception in which movement provides information such as form, texture and hardness ("Educación Inclusiva - Módulo 9: Adaptación del material - Percepción táctil y háptica", n.d.).

The title of the first person to use tactile characters for reading is attributed to Al-Imam Al-Amadi in the mid-13th century. Al-Amadi was a book salesman who, being blind, used a series of embossed characters to recognize the price and title of each book (García Rubio, 2006).

Louis Braille's attendance at the Royal Institute for Young Blind People, a school founded by Valentin Haüy who developed the method of printing in relief on paper (Alvarez Gámez et al., 2000), and Charles Barbier's sonograph, which consisted of a matrix of 6 lines and 2 columns to represent the letters of the alphabet and some frequent sounds, inspired him to create what is now known as Braille language.

Braille language

Braille is a system that allows blind people to read and write by touch using raised dots distributed in a space known as a braille box or cell whose size is the same for all users of that system ("El código Braille", n.d.). The presence and location of the dots inside the box can represent up to 64 different combinations including the empty cell, which represents a space or separation between words.

Because of this, and bearing in mind that more than 64 different combinations are needed to express, in addition to letters, characters such as numbers, mathematical operations, punctuation marks and even musical symbols, double or complementary symbols are used which, introduced before a certain combination of points, transforms it into a number, a capital letter, italics or even a musical note ("Educación Inclusiva - Módulo 9: Adaptación del material - Percepción táctil y háptica", n.d.).; In addition, the

Braille system does not remain static but adapts to communication needs as they arise over time, i.e. it is flexible ("Educación Inclusiva - Módulo 9: Adaptación del material - Percepción táctil y háptica", n.d.).

Universal Design, Design for All or Inclusive Design

The Universal Design concept was created more than 30 years ago by Ron Mace, an American wheelchair-user architect, and is based on the idea of designing and creating environments and products that, without the need to be adapted or have specialized designs, can be used by as many people as possible (Borau, Hernández Galán & Álvarez Ilzarbe, 2011). Mace said that, instead of considering only aesthetics and considering disabilities as anomalies, fields such as product design and development, architecture, and interior and exterior design should, in the first instance, analyze the needs of their different users whether young, older adults, people with temporary or permanent disabilities, etc. and, taking these findings into account, create products that are usable by a wider range of people (Mcguire, Scott and Shaw, 2006).

In 1997 a team of architects, engineers, product designers and environmental design researchers established what would become known as universal design principles which could be used to evaluate existing designs or as a guide in the process of designing new products (Connell et al., 1997).

The principles of Universal Design are guidelines that allow designers to incorporate specific features into designs that meet the needs of as many users as possible; although in some cases, the design process also needs to take into account issues such as economic, cultural, environmental, engineering and gender (Connell et al., 1997).

The 7 principles of Universal Design (Connell et al., 1997), each with its corresponding guidelines, are the following:

PRINCIPLE ONE: Equitable Use
The design is useful and marketable to people with diverse abilities.
Guidelines:
1a. Provide the same means of use for all users: identical whenever possible; equivalent when not.
1b. Avoid segregating or stigmatizing any users.
1c. Provisions for privacy, security, and safety should be equally available to all users.
1d. Make the design appealing to all users.
PRINCIPLE TWO: Flexibility in Use
The design accommodates a wide range of individual preferences and abilities.
Guidelines:
2a. Provide choice in methods of use.
2b. Accommodate right- or left-handed access and use.
2c. Facilitate the user's accuracy and precision.
2d. Provide adaptability to the user's pace.
PRINCIPLE THREE: Simple and Intuitive Use
Use of the design is easy to understand, regardless of the user's experience, knowledge, language skills, or current concentration level.
Guidelines:
3a. Eliminate unnecessary complexity.
3b. Be consistent with user expectations and intuition.
3c. Accommodate a wide range of literacy and language skills.

3d. Arrange information consistent with its importance.
3e. Provide effective prompting and feedback during and after task completion.
PRINCIPLE FOUR: Perceptible Information
The design communicates necessary information effectively to the user, regardless of ambient conditions or the user's sensory abilities.
Guidelines:
4a. Use different modes (pictorial, verbal, tactile) for redundant presentation of essential information.
4b. Provide adequate contrast between essential information and its surroundings.
4c. Maximize "legibility" of essential information.
4d. Differentiate elements in ways that can be described (i.e., make it easy to give instructions or directions).
4e. Provide compatibility with a variety of techniques or devices used by people with sensory limitations.
PRINCIPLE FIVE: Tolerance for Error
The design minimizes hazards and the adverse consequences of accidental or unintended actions.
Guidelines:
5a. Arrange elements to minimize hazards and errors: most used elements, most accessible; hazardous elements eliminated, isolated, or shielded.
5b. Provide warnings of hazards and errors.
5c. Provide fail safe features.
5d. Discourage unconscious action in tasks that require vigilance.
PRINCIPLE SIX: Low Physical Effort
The design can be used efficiently and comfortably and with a minimum of fatigue.
Guidelines:
6a. Allow user to maintain a neutral body position.
6b. Use reasonable operating forces.
6c. Minimize repetitive actions.
6d. Minimize sustained physical effort.
PRINCIPLE SEVEN: Size and Space for Approach and Use
Appropriate size and space is provided for approach, reach, manipulation, and use regardless of user's body size, posture, or mobility.
Guidelines:
7a. Provide a clear line of sight to important elements for any seated or standing user.
7b. Make reach to all components comfortable for any seated or standing user.
7c. Accommodate variations in hand and grip size.
7d. Provide adequate space for the use of assistive devices or personal assistance.

MAIN FOCUS OF THE CHAPTER

Issues, Controversies, Problems

People with disabilities face a number of challenges on a daily basis, which is why it is particularly important to provide them with the tools to enable them to inclusion and to enable them to be productive and self-sufficient people. In this sense, education plays a fundamental role since it not only allows people to have similar knowledge to people without disabilities, but also makes it possible to acquire knowledge, skills and techniques that allow them to do paid work. This is not necessarily an easy task as it involves locative (Congreso de Colombia, 1997), technological and curricular adaptations (Corte Constitucional, Consejo Superior de la Judicatura, Sala Administrativa, Centro de Documentación Judicial, 1991) in addition to a change of mentality that no longer sees disability as an inability to do something but as a difficulty that can be solved through the use of specialized tools for that purpose, such as assistive technology ("Discapacidades: MedlinePlus en español", 2019)

At the moment of receiving training for work in the CTPI of SENA, the first difficulty to face for a visually impaired person would be to find the right place to ask questions, resolve doubts and even make registrations by having to be located in an area of almost 20 hectares of which are estimates that there are 14181 square meters built shared between CTPI and the Agricultural Center.

SOLUTIONS AND RECOMMENDATIONS

As mentioned above, a combination of haptic tools was implemented, for which the following phases were taken into account: Documentation, Experimentation and Interpretation. This section will describe the implementation of each phase directly in the case study.

To recognize the experience of users in finding a place with and without the help of haptic tools a case study was carried out whose scenario was the CTPI. Due to the difficulty of having blind people who had knowledge of Braille language and willingness to participate in the case study, 5 people participated: 4 users with visual impairment and an elderly person without disability.

Phase 1: Documentation: in this phase a documentary research is carried out in order to obtain basics about the topics to be dealt with.

- It begins with an exploration of the types of visual limitations and their percentage of occurrence in the Colombian and Caucan population.
- Later, the topic of the legislation related to accessibility at the level of the country and of the entity in which the case study is going to be carried out is touched upon.
- Finally, there is an inquiry into haptic perception, Braille language, the principles of Universal Design and the history of models.

Phase 2: Experimentation: in this phase the scale model and haptic aids are designed and tests are carried out with users to find out the perception of the participants when they use the experimental prototype and when they do not.

- In the beginning, the recommended characteristics for certain parts of the prototype are investigated:

At this stage, several Colombian technical standards related to accessibility and signage issues were consulted so that the prototype designed would comply with the following requirements with the minimum characteristics to make it accessible for persons with visual impairment; as it was evidenced that the information recorded with respect to measures, colors and so on is very poor and short was attempted to access the Spanish standard AENOR 170002 that regulates these issues, but it was impossible so it was chosen to appeal to the document 'Technical requirements for the production of plans accessible to the visually impaired' of the Spanish National Organization of the Blind (Baldrich Caselles et al.,

2012), which compiles general aspects and elements to be taken into account when creating a model or haptic plane.

Taking into account the considerations of the previous document, it was decided to make the haptic model with the following characteristics:

- **Dimensions of the Plan:** Although the document suggests a size of 60 cm, x 45 cm., due to the geographical distance between offices that made it difficult to correctly represent them in a small space, it was decided to make the plan in the maximum size which is 80 cm. x 60 cm.
- **Spatial Location:** The plane was placed horizontally located near the goal, this with the intention of not disrupting the flow of people and for the tranquility and safety of participants.
- **Typography and Size of the Letter:** it was chosen to use a typography "sans-serif" (without serifs) to facilitate the reading and, considering that it is recommended that the size of the capital letter should not be less than 7 mm. for capital letters and 6mm. for lower case, sizes these corresponding to the Arial of 28 and 32 points respectively, was chosen a typography Dsignes of 48 points.

In addition, the following considerations were taken into account for information written in Braille:

- **Braille Cell Height:** Between 6.2 and 7.1 mm.
- **Braille Cell Width:** Between 3.7 and 4.5 mm.
- The elements written in Braille were placed near the entrance of the place on which they warn.

Concerning several other considerations, the following was defined:

- The guide path would be made using an elevated filament since, due to the size of the area represented, the corridors in the model are very narrow and this makes it difficult for the participant's fingers to touch it properly.
- Because the environment represented in the model is not uniform, to maximize its size without neglecting the dimensions of the base was placed diagonally, this directly influenced the location of the legends, so we chose to place the legend in visual characters to the left and messages in Braille in each of the locations they represented. In addition, a support with color under the Braille messages was used to help people without visual limitations to orient themselves.

The prototype to use was made in a material called Medium Density Fiberboard (MDF for its Spanish acronym ("Tablero de fibra de densidad media - MDF", 2016)) which was chosen taking into account the following considerations:

- Due to the budgetary inconveniences caused by the absence of financial support from CTPI for the realization of the experiment, and being a prototype, the use of acrylic had to be discarded and a cheaper option was chosen.
- The MDF has a surface that is smooth and compact enough for a person to touch it without harming themselves.
- The MDF can be milled, cut, laser cut or manually which facilitates prototyping and reduces the possibility of sharp or imperfect edges that could injure the hands of the participants.

- Items can be glued with glue (messages in visual characters) or with liquid silicone (pieces of wood).

Then the construction and installation of the parts that are part of the prototype is described, taking into account some limitations and the solutions proposed in this respect:

The following steps were carried out for the design and construction of the model:

1. Obtaining the map of the facilities of the CTPI, which was provided in PDF version and later with DWG extension.
2. Creation of the model design, which took into account the above-mentioned considerations.
3. Cutting and turning of the parts of the prototype from the designs already made.
4. Creation of messages written in Braille.
5. Creation of messages written in ink.
6. Fine-tuning and assembly.

As tools to support the model, and in order to facilitate the location of people, signs were made that said the name of the office in normal text with its corresponding representation in Braille, on the other hand was devised a type of "path guide" made in such a way that present a notorious relief but, as far as possible, did not affect the transit of people without limitations.

To make the writing in Braille, and by recommendation of the typhologist, the material chosen was sheet of acetate caliber 0.8 because its thickness allows the marks to be in relief but the material does not break when punctured.

To make the tactile guide Yumbolon (polyethylene foam ("Espuma de Polietileno Superlon y Yumbolon", n.d.)) was used, covered by a yellow adhesive tape; it had been thought at first to use Balso wood tablets (Ochroma Pyramidale (Angel, n.d.).)) but another element was chosen due to its low tolerance to water (Popayán is characterized by being a very rainy city) and fragility (as it was necessary to carry out the "guide line" in different spaces such as corridors, stairs, platforms and even an open-air parking lot, there was a high probability that the tablets would break). The color of the ribbon was chosen to make it more noticeable to people with low vision or no visual limitations.

In the first instance the CTPI plan was obtained in .dwg format for Autocad, which was modified to remove the contour lines and moved to Corel Draw so that the file could be read by the cutting machine. later the model was cut, for this a part of the plan was selected, which represented the area in which they were going to perform tests with users and was cut with laser seeking to generate the least amount of possible imperfect surfaces that could confuse or injure the blind.

In order to enhance the haptic quality of the plane, it was built in levels such as the represented sector is constructed; in addition, figures made of wood were placed that symbolize the presence of stairs. On the other hand pieces of wood were put to represent the walls and spaces were left to simulate the existing doors.

An itinerary for users was designed taking into account the offices and places to which they would need to go in the first instance and, from there on, the path was marked on the model using yellow wool. It is important to bear in mind that a pilot test was previously carried out with a participant to find out his or her appreciation of this type of representation. A very low fidelity representation of what the participants were going to find in the model was created and two guideline options were placed: a strand of yellow wool suspended in the air between two pushpins and a piece of acetate with dots in relief and adhered to the base; although the pilot participant, after using the existing options, declared that both seemed easy to use and that he had no preference for any of them; It was decided to use the yellow wool because it was evident that the participant had to use his little finger in order to experience the acetate line, in addition to the fact that the wool presented a more inclusive aspect because due to its color and location it could be seen on the model by people without visual limitations.

In order to help blind people or people with low vision problems to locate themselves, signs were created, both for the identification of the offices and for representation on the model; these labels were created in transparent acetate and written in Braille on them using a Perkins Brailler Braille typewriter. However, taking into account that the case study was governed by the policy of designing for as many people as possible, the labels for the offices also had the name "in ink" (a term used by blind people to refer to the letters used by people without visual limitations) both in Spanish and in English; color legends were also used on the model so that visually impaired people could recognize the locations represented.

In order to facilitate the movement of blind and low vision people, and trying to emulate the idea of the tactile paving but incorporated into the interior of buildings, Yumbolon lines were cut 1 cm. high by 2 cm. wide approximately, covered with yellow adhesive tape, color that had been used in the model to represent the path to follow. Once the Yumbolon was cut into strips and covered by the yellow tape, these strips were fixed to the floor with transparent tape (in the ceramic) and with liquid silicone and transparent tape (in the cement and asphalt); this was done with the intention that the blind had a stop that indicated where they could pass even if they were in a space devoid of walls, and that people with low vision or without visual limitations also could make use of this aid to locate themselves thanks to the contrast of the yellow tape with the floor (asphalt, ceramic and cement).

The typography used to make the signs and signage was Dsignes (downloaded from http://es.ffonts.net/Dsignes-Regular.font.download) because it is one of the typographies specially designed for signaling (García Moreno, 2012) and that, unlike the other suggested typographies, is free to use.

Finally, the execution of the tests with and without the help of the experimental prototype is reported:

Due to the absence of documentation on how to carry out usability tests on tangible elements, we resorted to adapting recommendations to carry out usability tests of computer applications, both for people without disabilities and for people with visual impairments and to complete what was necessary. In this respect the most inconveniences were found because the test was not carried out inside a laboratory with a controlled environment, nor was it carried out in a place known to the participant as their home, but the participants had to face a place unknown to them and help themselves with things that were not familiar to them such as the model and the guide line.

Based on the information presented "Simply Ask: Integrating accessibility into design" (Henry, 2008) and making the necessary adaptations, the following was defined:

- **Conditioning the Environment:** Although it is true that the tests were not going to be carried out inside a laboratory, it was considered important to condition the testing environment, i.e., to keep the parking area clear; in addition, elements that could hinder the movement of the participants, such as stones, rubbish or branches, were removed. This was done to avoid confusion or accidents.

Figure 1. Haptic map construction and usage

- **Orientation to the Participants:** For this purpose, the objectives and the procedure to be carried out in each test were explained, the people who were going to serve as companions for each one of the participants were introduced and the haptic aids available were explained, i.e. the model, the signage and the guide line.
- **Procedures:** In this case, and at the suggestion of the typhologist, the documents written in Braille were not provided but were read and doubts were resolved. In order to sign the consent form, the typhologist was asked to carry a signature guide.
- **To Carry out the Tasks:** In this part it was where more adaptations had to be made due to the absence of documentation on the matter. This is included:
  - Creation of the guide line with its corresponding representation in the model o Use of companions for each one of the participants whose mission was to document all their appreciations and problems and, in addition, to serve as support to keep blind people safe in the strange environment they faced.
  - Explanations and change of language of the formats for those participants who needed them, such as the child who participated in the experience.

- **Data Collection:** The following actions were carried out in this section:
    - Video and/or audio recordings (in the case of the participants who authorized it) and transcription by the companions of facial expressions and thoughts of the participants who were asked to say aloud what they thought. In this part, attendees were asked to write down exactly what the participant said and, in case of doubt, to ask the participant to repeat or explain what he or she had said.
    - Completion of different questionnaires according to the stage of the test; this was done after each task to avoid intentional or involuntary forgetfulness and modifications of the information.

Seeking to diminish the possible factors that could produce erroneous results in the tests, and based on the experience reported in "Contrasting usability evaluation methods with blind users" (Miao et al., 2014), it was required that the participants with visual limitations have sufficient knowledge about Braille language, were born in a Spanish-speaking country, did not have previous experiences with this type of tests and did not have any other physical or mental limitation that could harm them in the performance of the activities to be performed. Due to the difficulty in obtaining people whose profile coincided with the one specified above and who wanted to take part in the study, and according to the recommendations of (Nielsen, 2012), the tests were carried out with 5 participants: 4 visually impaired (3 blind people and 1 person with low vision) and 1 person without visual impairment.

In order to avoid possible dangers for the participants of the tests, and in order to guarantee the continuity of the guideline, the parking area through which the personnel were going to mobilize was delimited using tape tied between five delimiting posts and the guide line was installed inside the delimited area. There were many drawbacks in the areas without ceramics, since the tape did not have enough adherence, so in the first instance the entire area was swept and later, for cement and asphalt, liquid silicone was used to join the guide line with the ground and it was finished off with adhesive tape, while in the case of ceramics, only adhesive tape was used to avoid leaving residues.

A sign containing information in ink (printed on paper) and Braille (written on acetate) was placed in the locations shown on the model. Both materials were glued with transparent tape so that they would remain in a single element which was glued to the surface with tape and the model was installed next to the entrance so that the participants could manipulate it.

Once the participants arrived, they were welcomed and given an explanation of the intention of the test; in addition, questions were resolved and doubts were clarified; then the consent form was read and signed, taking into account which issues were accepted and which were not. They were not given the questionnaire written in Braille at the suggestion of the typhologist and in order to reduce the time that the participants were going to spend on each test, the previous questionnaire was then applied to each of the people present in order to have an idea of their particular situation and once all the participants had finished answering the questions in the questionnaire, the procedure for carrying out the tests was explained.

Procedure Using the Model and Haptic Aids

- Based on a thorough analysis of the model, the participant had to get an idea of the location of the 4 offices he would be asked to arrive at.
- The person who would accompany him was introduced and it was explained to him that this person would be in charge of documenting his experience through video or audio (in case the participant had expressly accepted to be recorded) and transcribing his perceptions, suggestions, thoughts and inconveniences in each one of the proposed activities; in addition this person would act as assistant in case of need and would keep the participant with a feeling of security in an unknown environment.
- It was explained to them that they should not feel guilty if they had any kind of inconvenience because it would be due to an inadequate design.
- They were asked to verbalize any thoughts, problems, doubts or opinions that came up along the way.
- It was warned that the guide line should always be on the left side of the road, with the intention of preventing the participant from stumbling over obstacles on the right.
- They were asked in principle to go to the secretariat and return to the starting point, where the model was located.
- Later they were asked to go up to the coordination, the women's bathroom and the photocopier in an uninterrupted way and, once they arrived at the end of the route, back to the starting point.

Once the activities to be carried out using the model were finished, the participants were invited to the cafeteria to have a snack while they answered the questionnaire for location using the model and, after completing the questionnaires for location using the model, the participants were explained the actions to be carried out next:

Procedure Without Using the Model or Haptic Aids

- They were asked to verbalize any thoughts, problems, doubts or opinions that arose along the way.
- They were reminded that a person would continue to accompany them and document their experience through video or audio (if the participant had expressly agreed to be recorded) and transcribe their perceptions, suggestions, thoughts and inconveniences in each of the proposed activities; in addition, that person would act as an assistant in case of need and would keep the participant with a sense of security in an unfamiliar environment.
- They were initially asked to go to the chapel, then to the men's room and back to the starting point.
- They were then asked to go to the treasury.

The questionnaire was then filled out to locate the model without using it and, after the corresponding acknowledgements and farewells, the experience was terminated.

Phase 3: Interpretation: at this phase the results obtained in the tests are examined and some conclusions are generated from them.

In the first instance, the different questionnaires are reviewed and the answers given by the interviewed persons are compared, using and not using the model and other haptic aids.

The following 6 questions are part of the previous questionnaire that sought to have a basic knowledge of the population to be surveyed:

- For the question "Type of visual impairment" 3 of the 5 participants state that they are totally blind, one has partial blindness and one has no visual limitation whatsoever.
- In the question "Have you had any inconvenience when accessing a public or private entity? 60% of the interviewees answered yes, 20% answered that they do not know and 20% answered that they do not apply. In this regard, it must be borne in mind that, in the case of the person without visual limitation, the question does not apply; this is the case with several of the following questions. In addition, two of the participants have very specific characteristics that directly affect the answers given: one of them is an 11-year-old boy (who is partially blind), so many times he does not want to answer and the other is a person who, despite having lost his sight several years ago, until recently began to assume it so he usually goes out accompanied by another person, so his use of the cane is deficient and it is strange for him to have to locate himself alone.
- For the question "Have you had any problems related to your visual condition?" 60% of the participants answered yes, 20% did not know and 20% did not apply; in this question only one person with total blindness did not answer because, as explained in the previous answer, it does not go out alone, and for the person without visual impairment the question does not apply.
- The question "What kind of inconvenience have you had in accessing a public or private entity" was exclusive to those who said they had inconvenience because of their visual condition; of the three people who answered this question, one selected the option "The care provided by staff is discriminatory", two selected the option "You have difficulty finding the place you are going to", all three selected the option "The documents are not accessible to you" and none selected the option "Others, which?
- In the question "Have you needed to use Braille? 60% of the answers indicate yes, 20% indicate no, and for the remaining 20% do not apply; here it is evident that the majority of respondents have needed to use Braille since the person who answers "No" is the participant who does not mobilize alone and who has had difficulty accepting his new condition and, for the person without visual impairment, this question would not apply.
- For the question "Do you consider that entities, both public and private, are accessible for people with visual impairments? 60% of those surveyed answered no and the remaining 40% do not know what to answer; the people who did not answer in an affirmative manner were the child and the adult who is not autonomous; both have as a particularity the fact that they are always accompanied to the different places to which they need to go so their perception of the accessibility of these sites is different because they have not experienced in a direct way the possible barriers that others have noticed. It is worth highlighting as a curious fact that the person without visual limitations considers that there are accessibility problems for people who are blind or have low vision in public and private entities.

The following results were obtained in the questionnaires applied after the tests were carried out:

- The question "Did you make it to the specified place?" was answered positively by all participants, the reasons that the number of answers is the same both using the model and extra aids and not using it is that:
    - Although the participants did not actually arrive exactly at the requested site when they did not have the help of the model, they were close to achieving it.
    - The interviewees were always accompanied so they asked.
    - The indications given were EXTREMELY punctual (number of meters, turns, number of doors, etc.) so the possibility of error was drastically reduced.

Even so, the comments and perceptions regarding the haptic aids used were quite positive, as will be evident later.

- In the question "How easy was it to get to the specified place? 80% of the evaluated participants consider that it was relatively easy to get to the specified place using the model and other aids provided while 60% consider that, without haptic aids, it was not so easy or difficult to locate the locations. As explained above, these responses were influenced by the permanent company and the extremely specific explanations.
- For the question "Did you need outside help to get to the specified location?"100% of the interviewees needed external help to reach a location when they did not have the model and other haptic aids to show them the way while 60% of the 5 participants said they needed help "Sometimes" when making use of the haptic aids; it should be noted that this measure symbolizes, in the words of one participant, that "5 times, I needed help on one occasion" which implies that there is a high level of autonomy on the part of people evaluated when trying to locate a place using the aids.
- The question "Were the indications given by the model useful for you to reach the specified place?" had a forceful answer since all participants, regardless of their visual condition, consider that the model was helpful.
- In the question "How useful was the haptic model for you? 80% of the participants consider that the haptic model was useful, where 20% think that it was very useful; only 20% of the total of participants consider that the model was neither useful nor useless.
- All participants answered yes to the question "Was the existence of the guideline helpful to you?
- For the question "How useful was the guideline for you? 40% of those evaluated responded that it was very useful, while 60% considered that it was relatively useful; this implies that the guideline (tactile routing) was very well received by the participants, even by the person without visual limitations.
- 80% of the interviewees answered yes to the question "Was the existence of Braille/Ink signage helpful to you?" while 20% answered that they do not know; in this respect it is important to bear in mind that the person who does not respond is the 11-year-old child who, due to his shyness, sometimes does not know what to answer.
- For the question "How useful was the Braille/Ink signage for you? 60% of the people responded that it was very useful while the other 40% considered that it was relatively useful; this reflects the great acceptance of this support tool.

The following is a description of the appreciations given by the participants throughout the experience.

Through the completion of the questionnaires, the permanent presence of companions with each participant with their consequent notes and recordings (in the cases of allowed), the following assessments were collected:

- The participants with visual limitations consider that the repetition of routes is the best way to improve their experience when looking for a specific place since they feel safer when they learning the route and they can arrive more quickly at their destination.
- The majority of respondents feel that there is no progress in accessibility policies because, although there are laws and regulations on the subject, in many cases they are not applied.
- According to the visually impaired people interviewed the greatest inconvenience to reach a particular site, especially without the support of the model, the line and signage, is the presence of obstacles that can misplace them or cause them harm.
- The participants consider that it is very important the help of other people to improve their experience and to make it easier for them to locate themselves. This help can be reflected in giving correct, concrete and specific indications, in helping them to arrive or simply in having some empathy and not hindering access.
- At the time of performing the test without the use of haptic aids, the use of the guideline was one of the most repeated comments on how the experience could be improved. In this regard, specific suggestions were even made about what the guide line should look like, for example, a type of carpet between 10 and 20 cm.

FUTURE RESEARCH DIRECTIONS

Improve the prototype based on obtained feedback after the study, conduct more case studies with other groups and in other contexts in order to compare results, ideation of new haptic tools that can be used by blind people without previous knowledge in Braille nor in the use of the white cane, development of hardware and software that facilitates the location of people in buildings or specific environments and finally the creation of a strategy that defines the procedure for conducting physical usability tests in uncontrolled environments, that is, outside laboratories..

CONCLUSION

Although there are guidelines to be taken into account when evaluating the level of accessibility (such as the Web Content Accessibility Guidelines (WCAG) given by the W3C (W3.org, 2008) through the Web Accessibility Initiative (WAI) and there are also guides for testing with users, these are generally aimed at software products so adaptation to physical products becomes very complicated.

Moreover, for visually impaired people the accuracy and specificity of the indications is of paramount importance as they create a mental model according to what they hear and feel, which is why incomplete or low fidelity physical representations or sketchy and incomplete indications make it difficult (or even impossible) the proper location of a place. This was evidenced by the fact that, although a communication was sent by the deputy director authorizing the partial closure of the parking lot during the day of application of the tests, upon arrival at the CTPI facilities, it was necessary to 'negotiate' with instructors who had left their car in the designated parking space for the participants to travel (in which approximately one hour of work was lost); In fact, it was impossible to find the owner of a car that was parked all day in front of the stairs and that made the installation of the guide line in reality differ from the representation of it in the model, which was noticed and commented by the participants.

On the other hand, the use of haptic models must be combined with signage strategies (such as Braille/ Ink signs and tactile routes) that allow the visually impaired person to know where the bends and accesses are specifically located and thus facilitate their safe movement, especially important when there is an environment such as CTPI, in which there are wall elements that can represent inconveniences or even dangers for blind people; On the other hand, it is also very useful in open spaces with irregular surfaces or without boundaries that can increase the chances of an accident. For the present case study in particular and without underestimating the model and the signage, the guide line represented an enormous support for the participants since it allowed them to know if they were on the right track and, in this specific case, to move them away from the possible obstacles that could represent a danger for them; in addition, this was especially useful in open spaces where the blind person could not make use of reference points to locate themselves nor were there walls that would help them to follow a specific path.

Finally, the difficulties in building haptic aids, recruiting participants and carrying out tests reflect the absence, at the local level, of entities related to goods, products and services for people who are blind or have low vision, which makes their independence and integration into society even more difficult.

REFERENCES

Alvarez Gámez, F., Cantalejo Cano, J., Duran Vélez, J., Gómez Viñas, P., González Paredes, P., & Sánchez, Á. (2000). *Aspectos evolutivos y educativos de la deficiencia visual - Volumen II* (1st ed.). Madrid: Organización Nacional de Ciegos Españoles (ONCE). Retrieved from http://bibliorepo.umce.cl/libros_electronicos/diferencial/edtv_8.pdf

Angel, J. (n.d.). *Maderas de Colombia: Balso*. Retrieved from http://infomaderas.com/2014/09/11/maderas-de-colombia-balso/

Baldrich Caselles, M., Blanco Zárate, L., Consuegra Cano, B., Díez Álvarez, M., Sánchez Abietar, J., & García Soria, F. (2012). Requisitos técnicos para la confección de planos accesibles a personas con discapacidad visual (1st ed.). Academic Press.

Borau, J., Hernández Galán, J., & Álvarez Ilzarbe, F. (2011). *Accesibilidad universal y diseño para todos - Arquitectura y Urbanismo* (1st ed.). Madrid: Fundación ONCE. Retrieved from http://www.upv.es/contenidos/CAMUNISO/info/U0578035.pdf

Capitulo II - Tecnología Háptica. (n.d.). Retrieved from https://htid3.files.wordpress.com/2013/04/tecnologia-haptica.pdf

Connell, B., Jones, M., Mace, R., Mueller, J., Mullick, A., & Ostroff, E. (1997). *The Center for Universal Design - Universal Design Principles*. Retrieved from https://projects.ncsu.edu/ncsu/design/cud/about_ud/udprinciplestext.htm

Constitucional, C. (1991). *Consejo Superior de la Judicatura, Sala Administrativa, Centro de Documentación Judicial.* Constitución Política de Colombia.

de Colombia, C. (1997). *Ley 361 de 1997.* Retrieved from http://www.secretariasenado.gov.co/senado/basedoc/ley_0361_1997_pr001.html

Dezcallar Sáez, T. (2012). *Relación entre procesos mentales y sentido háptico: emociones y recuerdos mediante el análisis empírico de texturas. Doctorado. Universidad Autónoma de Barcelona; Facultad de Psicología.* Departamento de Psicología Básica, Evolutiva y de la Educación.

Discapacidades: MedlinePlus en español. (2019). Retrieved from https://medlineplus.gov/spanish/disabilities.html

Educación Inclusiva - Módulo 9: Adaptación del material - Percepción táctil y háptica. (n.d.). Retrieved from http://www.ite.educacion.es/formacion/materiales/129/cd/unidad_9/m9_percepcion_tactil.htm

El código Braille. (n.d.). Retrieved from http://instructorbraille.blogspot.com.co/p/el-codigo-braille.html

Espuma de Polietileno Superlon y Yumbolon. (n.d.). Retrieved from http://www.plastempack.com/empaque-y-embalaje/espuma-de-polietileno-superlony-jumbolon.html

García Moreno, D. (2012). *Diseño de Sistemas de Orientación Espacial: Wayfinding* (p. 32). Madrid: Laboratorio Wayfinding. Retrieved from http://riberdis.cedd.net/bitstream/handle/11181/4640/dise%c3%b1o%20de%20sistemas%20de%20orientaci%c3%b3n%20espacial.pdf?sequence=1&rd=0031227065841978

García Rubio, J. (2006). *Historia de la lectoescritura en relieve.* Alicante: ONCE - C.R.E "Espíritu Santo" - Servicio de Producción de Recursos Didácticos y Tecnológicos. Retrieved from https://acce-doalicante. wikispaces.com/file/view/Historia.pdf

Henry, S. (2008). *Realización de las pruebas de usabilidad | La accesibilidad en el proceso de DCU | Simplemente pregunta: Integración de la accesibilidad en el proceso de diseño.* Retrieved from http://www.uiaccess.com/JustAsk/es/ut_conduct.html

Mcguire, J., Scott, S., & Shaw, S. (2006). Universal Design and Its Applications in Educational Environments. *Remedial and Special Education*, *27*(3), 167. Retrieved from http://journals.sagepub.com/doi/pdf/10.1177/07419325060270030501

Miao, M., Pham, H., Friebe, J., & Weber, G. (2014). Contrasting usability evaluation methods with blind users. *Universal Access in the Information Society*, *15*(1), 66.

Nielsen, J. (2012). *How Many Test Users in a Usability Study?* Retrieved from https://www.nngroup.com/articles/how-many-test-users/

Tablero de fibra de densidad media - MDF. (2016). Retrieved from https://es.wikipedia.org/wiki/Tablero_de_fibra_de_densidad_media

Web C. A. G. (WCAG) 2.0. (2008). Retrieved from https://www.w3.org/TR/WCAG20/

ADDITIONAL READING

Edler, D., Bestgen, A., Kuchinke, L., & Dickmann, F. (2015). True-3D Accentuating of grids and streets in urban topographic maps enhances human object location memory. *PLoS One*, *10*(2), e0116959. doi:10.1371/journal.pone.0116959 PMID:25679208

Gual, J., Puyuelo, M., & Lloveras, J. (2015). The effect of volumetric (3D) tactile symbols within inclusive tactile maps. *Applied Ergonomics*, *48*, 1–10. doi:10.1016/j.apergo.2014.10.018 PMID:25683526

Holloway, L., Marriott, K., & Butler, M. (2018). Accessible maps for the blind: comparing 3D printed models with tactile graphics. 1-13. doi: . doi:10.1145/3173574.3173772

Holloway, L., Marriott, K., Butler, M., & Reinders, S. (2019). 3D printed maps and icons for inclusion: testing in the wild by people who are blind or have low vision. doi: 183-195. . doi:10.1145/3308561.3353790

Jehoel, S., Sowden, P., Ungar, S., & Sterr, A. (2009). Tactile elevation perception in blind and sighted participants and its implications for tactile map creation. Human Factors: the journal of the human factors and ergonomics society, 51(2), 208-223. doi:10.1177/0018720809334918

Lee, C. (2019). An evaluation of tactile symbols in public environment for the visually impaired. *Applied Ergonomics*, *75*, 193–200. doi:10.1016/j.apergo.2018.10.003 PMID:30509527

Sung Ho, Y. (2012). A study on the tactile map with tactile symbols for visually impaired people. Journal of digital design, 12(2), 103-112. doi:10.17280/jdd.2012.12.2.010

Watanabe, T., & Yamaguchi, T. (2017). Six-and-a-half-year practice of tactile map creation service. *Studies in Health Technology and Informatics*, *242*, 687–694. PMID:28873872

KEY TERMS AND DEFINITIONS

CTPI: Of the existing training centers in Popayán together with the agricultural center and the trade and services center.

DWG: Extension used by Autocad for computer drawing files.

Haptic Tools: Tools that provide information through the use of touch.

MDF: Medium density fiberboard, panels made of wood decomposed into fibers and compressed with synthetic resin.

SENA: A public training institution that promotes labor inclusion by providing free work skills training.

W3C: International community that seeks the standard in the use of the internet.

WAI: An initiative that promotes accessibility on the web.

WCAG: International guidelines that seek to ensure the accessibility of web content.

Chapter 7
Attention as the Base of the Development of Learning Supported by UXD Technologies

Samirna Collazos
Independent Researcher, Colombia

Bayron Mauricio Mazabuel
Universidad Del Cauca, Colombia

ABSTRACT

This chapter was intended to emphasize the need of user-centered technology for the current generation of learners: "Multipotentielites." The scenario suggests that fostering attention in Multipotentialites is required for effective learning being empathy and emotions the key to achieve it. Important concepts such as user experience design (UXD) and learning experience design (LXD) where analyzed here as pivotal aspects to envision both new educational/learning processes and the environments/technologies that support them. Under this context, the chapter summarized several perceptions from experts by highlighting those Multipotentialites' qualities and skills that should be strengthen and exploited during learning processes where attention appears to be the new IQ.

INTRODUCTION

The advances of the new technologies nowadays work like anthropological prostheses in the human beings, these amplify for good or for bad what already exists in each one of us. We are facing a paradigm change in terms of education and knowledge. We are in the process of abandoning the models based on the Gaussian's bell and Intellectual coefficient and we are reaching the new challenges of personalized education that opens up a new vision towards the detection of what would be called the personal taste of each one, something like their individual brand, route by which it is arrived to detect the significant and non-anecdotal capacities that each one of us possesses (Zgurovsky & Zaychenko, 2016).

DOI: 10.4018/978-1-7998-2325-4.ch007

Since this is a new factor in the challenges brought by the paradigm change, there is an essential ability to be able to develop these capacities, this ability is called Attention. Attention is a mechanism that is achieved when we direct our attention resources towards a specific focus at a specific moment (Nobre & Van Ede, 2018). This activity involves that the brain can only perceive what is in the focus of attention. It is also a limited resource and there are different processes at the time of the implementation of this ability and it requires particular and complex brain mechanisms developed especially in the frontal and parietal lobe, through which different ways in which our brain develops the various moments of attention activity as appropriate, for example there are different types of attention depending on the situation such as selective attention, sustained attention, divided Attention (Abdelrahman et al., 2019).

- **Selective Attention:** This is the one that is able to filter irrelevant stimuli to be able to perform the focus for example, when we want to hear someone speaking in a noisy environment.
- **Sustained Attention:** This one appears when we're studying or playing an instrument.
- **Divided Attention:** In this type of attention, the brain is able to focus on more than one task at a time, for example when we're studying and listening to radio.

This ability becomes the new frontier of knowledge and science, with the brain since the evolutionary era. Without attention there is no memory and without memory there is no learning. It is impossible to remember what we do not pay attention to. This tool is totally indispensable to perceive the world around us, if we go back to the primitive era, the attention was developed as a method of survival from the body brain mind unit, therefore, the one who pays first attention and evaluates survives and learns, being able to detect threats and rewards starting from the instinctive areas of the human being adapting it and developing this ability as a method of recognition evolution and adaptation to the environment.

According to (Posner, Rothbart & Ghassemzadeh, 2019), one of the most outstanding researchers in the area of attention, he argues, the human being has the ability to regulate thoughts, emotions and actions through "executive attention" in other words as thinking and rational beings, human beings have the ability to decide where we put the focus, through this, perform a self-regulation that leads to the choice of assertive thoughts and in turn, it leads us to the generation of emotions that involve us towards the focus of attention through the achievement of specific objectives and selected goals to obtain measurable and sustainable results over time through the regulations and variations that we are able to develop for the generation of knowledge. That's why, it is important to highlight that the concept of intelligence is changing, which it conveys to replace the definition of the idea of the pedagogical system.

There are many definitions of intelligence. The American Psychological Association (APA) report on intelligence acknowledges that *"individuals differ from one another in their ability to understand complex ideas, to adapt effectively to the environment, to learn from experience, to engage in various forms of reasoning, to overcome obstacles by taking thought*" (Neisser, et al., 1996). In this context, could be inferred that intelligence consists in the ability through which individuals are able to understand complex things and face certain complications through reasoning. According to the capacity of each person it is said that he/she is more or less intelligent than another.

With these new concepts, it should be noted that there are currently huge changes in the educational field and this change is leveraged by a proposed gear from a theory that has come to revolutionize the way in which learning and education are conceived and as a result, it involves enormously, the skill of attention (Abdelrahman, et al., 2019). This theory is the called *multiple-intelligences* and leads us to a change in the look towards the ways in which we learn and how we do it individually (Gardner, 2018;

Abdelrahman, et al., 2019). This change leads us to rethink the way in which we can broaden our vision and try to see to everyone in its entirety and not in a transversal way, leaving aside the social limits which we fit, qualify and select in relative ways that ultimately lead to personal limits (Abdelrahman, et al., 2019).

Capacities that people had are considered as talents, stories such as sports, music and drawing are not recognized as intelligence, but before continuing with this approach, the following question could be noted, who could say that Einstein was smarter than Beethoven or that Cervantes was less intelligent than Darwin, but each one of them have developed a type of individual intelligence. In our era, success is still being valued only from two types of knowledge, verbal and mathematical logical intelligence (Kerr & Gahm, 2018). Hence, the classrooms have not functioned as a predictor of intelligence that is the reason why, many of these brilliant minds were not outstanding in these places (Chestnut, et al., 2018).

BACKGROUND

The IQ, also known as Intellectual Quotient, is a number that results from the performance of a standardized assessment, which allows measuring the cognitive abilities of a person in relation to their age group, this result is abbreviated as CI or IQ (Quotient Intelligence).

The theory of multiple intelligences was presented as critical of the standard IQ. This valuable tool guides us towards the individualization of each person becoming the guide route of effective education by opening a universe of resources and technologies that make this task much easier.

With the new current concept of pedagogical system and generation of the new paradigm, we are faced with the new conductor (for calling it in a metaphorical way), because this ability allows us to develop intelligence that is capable of making decisions and that applies Optimally, the rest of its resources such as intellectual and emotional services at the service of the organization of human talent.

According to (Gardner, 2011), we have nine different types of intelligences which are: Linguistic Intelligence, Logical Mathematical, Bodily Kinesthetic, Spatial, Musical, Interpersonal, Intrapersonal Existential, and Naturalist. Following definitions were extracted from an infographic constructed by Mark Vital (Vital, 2014), an information designer and hacker who clearly synthesize Gardner's work.

- **Linguistic Intelligence:** Also known as Word Smart, it applies for those ones who optimally dominate the ability to communicate. According to (Vital, 2014) "*Linguistic intelligence is the ability to think in words and to use language to express and appreciate complex meanings. Linguistic intelligence allows us to understand the order and meaning of words and to apply meta-linguistic skills to reflect on our use of language. Linguistic intelligence is the most widely shared human competence and is evident in poets, novelists, journalists, and effective public speakers. Young adults with this kind of intelligence enjoy writing, reading, telling stories or doing crossword puzzles*".
- **Logical mathematics:** Or Number/Reasoning Smart. This one appears when your way of learning is through seeing things sequentially. (Vital, 2014) states that "*Logical-mathematical intelligence is the ability to calculate, quantify, consider propositions and hypotheses, and carry out complete mathematical operations. It enables us to perceive relationships and connections and to use abstract, symbolic thought; sequential reasoning skills; and inductive and deductive thinking patterns. Logical intelligence is usually well developed in mathematicians, scientists, and detec-*

tives. Young adults with lots of logical intelligence are interested in patterns, categories, and relationships. They are drawn to arithmetic problems, strategy games and experiments".

- **Bodily kinesthetic:** Also named Body Smart; it is characterized because of the ease of learning is through moving, touching and manipulating. According to (Vital, 2014), "*Bodily kinesthetic intelligence is the capacity to manipulate objects and use a variety of physical skills. This intelligence also involves a sense of timing and the perfection of skills through mind–body union. Athletes, dancers, surgeons, and crafts people exhibit well-developed bodily kinesthetic intelligence*".
- **Spatial:** Also known as Picture Smart. You need to see things globally for learning. (Vital, 2014) explains that "*Spatial intelligence is the ability to think in three dimensions. Core capacities include mental imagery, spatial reasoning, image manipulation, graphic and artistic skills, and an active imagination. Sailors, pilots, sculptors, painters, and architects all exhibit spatial intelligence. Young adults with this kind of intelligence may be fascinated with mazes or jigsaw puzzles, or spend free time drawing or daydreaming*".
- **Musical:** Also known as Sound Smart refers that people need information to enter through the ear. In this context, (Vial, 2014) summarize that "*Musical intelligence is the capacity to discern pitch, rhythm, timbre, and tone. This intelligence enables us to recognize, create, reproduce, and reflect on music, as demonstrated by composers, conductors, musicians, vocalist, and sensitive listeners. Interestingly, there is often an affective connection between music and the emotions; and mathematical and musical intelligences may share common thinking processes. Young adults with this kind of intelligence are usually singing or drumming to themselves. They are usually quite aware of sounds others may miss*".
- **Interpersonal:** Sometimes known among experts as People Smart. It could be perceived as to open that beautiful window you have to feel connected to another human being. According to (Vital, 2014), "*Interpersonal intelligence is the ability to understand and interact effectively with others. It involves effective verbal and nonverbal communication, the ability to note distinctions among others, sensitivity to the moods and temperaments of others, and the ability to entertain multiple perspectives. Teachers, social workers, actors, and politicians all exhibit interpersonal intelligence. Young adults with this kind of intelligence are leaders among their peers, are good at communicating, and seem to understand others' feelings and motives*".
- **Intra-personal:** Also known as Self Smart, means that some people have to reflect before understanding. In this case, (Vital, 2014) define this type as "*Intra-personal intelligence is the capacity to understand oneself and one's thoughts and feelings, and to use such knowledge in planning and directioning one's life. Intra-personal intelligence involves not only an appreciation of the self, but also of the human condition. It is evident in psychologist, spiritual leaders, and philosophers. These young adults may be shy. They are very aware of their own feelings and are self-motivated*".
- **Naturalist:** Is also known as Nature Smart. Many people are able to activate that moment of learning much better when they are in contact with nature. In this vein, (Vital, 2014) emphasize that "*Naturalist intelligence designates the human ability to discriminate among living things (plants, animals) as well as sensitivity to other features of the natural world (clouds, rock configurations). This ability was clearly of value in our evolutionary past as hunters, gatherers, and farmers; it continues to be central in such roles as botanist or chef. It is also speculated that much of our consumer society exploits the naturalist intelligences, which can be mobilized in the discrimination among cars, sneakers, kinds of makeup, and the like*".

- **Existential:** Also named Life smart. Is defined by (Vital, 2014) as "*Sensitivity and capacity to tackle deep questions about human existence, such as the meaning of life, why we die, and how did we get here*".

Developing learning based on each of our intelligences leads us to change the perspective of the teaching exercise. This cannot be to continue performed or developed in the same way, because we are in the era of the revolution and digital technological versatility of information. It is absurd to think that we all have to learn in the same way. We have enough technological tools to develop versatile platforms that adapt to individual needs. The serious questions it would be, what is the way in which we have been able to learn something? And, in which way have we felt really comfortable? Answers could help in identifying the route to follow, that would be the key that opens the window towards collective decentralization of learning, guiding us towards the individual discovery of it, because there are things that we should definitely all learn but there is no reason why we should all do it in the same way.

The environment and technologies play an important role in this scenario because should be integrated to people activities and encourage empathy and interest in students for engaged experiences. The User eXperience (UX) will be a pivotal aspect to cover. User eXperience (UX) was coined by Donald Norman for his working group at Apple Computers in 1993, but definitely the are some background, nevertheless "*It's hard to draw the line between traditional human factors and what we might call 'user-experience', aimed at human-centered design of interactive systems. Bell Labs was one of the pioneers in making this transition, starting with the first psychologist hired to design telephone systems in 1945: John E. Karlin. By the 1950s, Bell Labs definitely did UX work, in particular on the design of the touchtone keypad. That we use its design to this day is proof of how important it is to get the UX right in the first place*" (Nielsen, 2017). In fact, there are other historical events that suggest that discipline and interest by Scientists are more than a century old; by example, Frederick Taylor published Principles of Scientific Management that describes time and movement studies and methods to improve industrial efficiency (Taylor, 1911). Another famous example is the one that appeared in1936 when Alan Turing developed what we know as the Turing Machine and some years later discovered what it would change everything, the famous Turing Test, the basis of Artificial Intelligence and intelligent machines (Saygin, Cicekli, & Akman, 2000). In the same way, in 1954, the industrial designer Henry Dreyfuss writes "Designing for People", one of the classic texts of User eXperience and Usability (Dreyfuss, 2003). In late 50's Dieter Rams, perhaps one of the most influential designers in history, stated "10 principles of Good Design" (Bhowmik, 2012). In 1967 Micheal Scriven writes about formative and summative assessments in educational literature applied to the learning and evaluation of the students (Scriven, 1991). These terms will subsequently apply to different types of usability assessments. And in the final example, Ericsson and Simon publish "Verbal Reports as Data" in 1980 which focuses on the use of the Think Aloud method that in the future would dominate usability tests (Ericsson & Simon, 1980).

In the beginning it was the technology that commanded how users had to interact with it, for example in order to interact with computers you had to learn commands and programming languages. Between the years 1984 and 1985 Apple revolutionized with more intuitive graphic user interfaces integrating icons related to daily common objects according to their functional purposes, e.g. the recycle bin icon associated to a common trash can. This process continues to rise until what we know as the modern desktop interface in every personal computer and many mobile devices. Currently, computers are closer to people, to life, they are in clothes, smartphones, watches, appliances, cars, airplanes and many other many other daily things and artifacts; they are even around us everywhere in the ecology. Experiences are created through technology and due to this, the context of use is understood in a much clearer and more dynamic way from the point of view of the users taking into account their experience from beginning to end according to how they decide to live an experience. From UXD perspective, the idea is to create designs from the vantage point and focus from the users by researching and understanding what people needs and what they expect from these experiences within this broad framework offered by technology. UXD directs its efforts towards effective interactions and usability implementation for an easiest and more enjoyable experiences to help people to do specific activities by means of a large number of taylor-made products and services.

MAIN FOCUS OF THE CHAPTER

Issues, Controversies, Problems

Given the above, the learning exercise is closely related to the conscious process of attention, because as was mentioned earlier, without attention there is no memory, without memory there is no learning and without learning there is no knowledge generation, so we do not come programmed, we don't carry concentration models. It is a skill that must be developed to improve the possibilities of increasing talents, focusing on what is being done, followed by insistence, willingness and interest. Those are factors that have been difficult to maintain in environments currently saturated with distractors, such as emotional, sensory, and auditory, typical of this era.

This way of learning would be, not the new way of winning information, but to learn to filter the relevant information and try to link it with the existing one, looking for the optimal way to achieve it to find answers to specific questions. Also try to sow or instill multiple options and other forms or moments by which you can also learn, and by supporting the development of new technologies such as those ones based on User eXperience Design (UXD) which could be perceived as "*User experience (UX) design is the process design teams use to create products that provide meaningful and relevant experiences to users. This involves the design of the entire process of acquiring and integrating the product, including aspects of branding, design, usability and function*" (IDF, 2018).

UX in learning context had been a concern among experts from early this decade and many strategies have emerged. By example, (Peters, 2012) explains the relation between UX and Learning through the term Learning eXperience Design (LXD) which could be interpreted as follows: "*In much of design, we aim to craft a user experience that meets business or communication goals. In learning experience design, the goal is to help someone learn something. It's about improving learning outcomes and the quality of the learning experience. A big part of LXD is designing a user interface in a way that supports and enhances the cognitive and affective processes that learning involves*". (Peters, 2012), proposed fourteen design guidelines for the design of learning interfaces: 1) The multimedia principle: People learn better from a combination of text and visuals rather than text alone; 2) Graphics should be relevant, not merely decorative; 3) Use animations to teach physical procedures and still images to teach processes; 4) To promote understanding, simplify visuals or make them abstract; 5) Don't separate related text and visuals; 6) Use virtual agents to deliver instructional content; 7) Break complex information into chunks and provide pre-training; 8) Avoid irrelevant video, audio, stories, and text; 9) Set learning in a real-world context to facilitate knowledge transfer; 10) Provide informative feedback; 11) Choose your tools based on learning activities; 12) Know when to give learners control; 13) Design learning games and simulations in strict alignment with learning goals; and 14) Be aware of the expertise reversal effect.

Alternatives like LXD propose and promote an educational system that spread the feeling of freedom, of not only learning what we like but also what we are good for or even those areas out from our strengths. As pointed by (Silver, Strong, & Perini, 1997) "*We believe that the integration of learning styles and multiple intelligence theory may minimize their respective limitations and enhance their strengths, and we provide some practical suggestions for teachers to successfully integrate and apply learning styles and multiple intelligence theory in the classroom*". This fits us and positions us in a place where the same thing would definitely like us for the rest of our life.

Taking into account the previous paragraph, it is important to highlight a new topic that is being known little by little in the field of learning. This new topic is related to the high capacity to know and explore the multiple intelligences being able to combine them, through the different forms of learning, this concept is called multipotentiality. Tamara Fisher expert in learning and teaching strategies explains that "*Multipotentiality is the state of having many exceptional talents, any one or more of which could make for a great career for that person. Gifted children often (though of course not always) have multipotentiality. Their advanced intellectual abilities and their intense curiosity make them prime candidates for excelling in multiple areas. This can be both a blessing and a curse. On the bright side, they have many realistic options for future careers. But on the downside, some of them will struggle mightily trying to decide which choice to make. Particularly in the last couple years of high school and the first couple years of college, this monumentous decision with so many great possible outcomes can be a source of debilitating stress. The choice is "exhausting and stressful," as one of my students said this year*".

This topic comes to give a way, a route to meet the new information and learning knowledge guides. A multipotential person, it would be the one who is able to make the best of each of his intelligences in an optimal and effective way. Similarly, Heather Nester and Melanie Buford from University of Cincinati cites Emilie Wapnick founder of Puttylike "*An educational and psychological term referring to a pattern found among intellectually gifted individuals. [Multipotentialites] generally have diverse interests across numerous domains and may be capable of success in many endeavors or professions, they are confronted with unique decisions as a result of these choices*" (Nester & Bufford, 2018, p.70). In this context, (Nester & Bufford, 2018) emphasize three challenges of multipotentiality:

1. **Self-Esteem and Normalization:** To provide the concept of Multipotentiality to students, parents, professors, colleagues, friends, and other people involved in educational process, and emphasize that it is not wrong to have a variety of interests and goals.
2. **Quality Experiences:** It is crucial to provide quality experiences to students with Multipotentiality through environments and technologies.
3. **Making Decisions:** To realize strategies to help Multipotential students in selecting a career path in order to make them confident and comfortable.

This action would be enhanced through the ways of learning and move from one to the other, in a harmonic tuning when facing new challenges. There are four learning styles to be considered according to Emilie Wapnick:

1. **Active Learning:** It is the one that occurs when we encourage to try things, touching, testing and discovering.
2. **Reflective Learning:** it is what you get when you reflect on something. It is the question of why, the facts happen or why the things work.
3. **Theoretical Learning:** It elaborates theories on the subjects looking for some type of hypothesis, it is a type of learning that is related to the scientific method.
4. **Pragmatic Learning:** It is the learning that is achieved by wanting to check things through practice.

Learning strategies should be oriented to support previous learning styles and to foster development of inner skills from Multipotentialite. Under this context (Wapnick, 2012) states that Multipotentialites are skilled with seven abilities or powers:

1. **Contextual Thinking:** "*Multipotentialites are able to see the broader implications of a problem, and can therefore make smarter, more informed decisions.*"
2. **Translating between Modes of Thought:** "*A background of multidisciplinary exploration means that multipotentialites are able to "speak the language" of people in different fields. The ability to shift between modes of thought allows us to translate between groups, help them understand each other, and work with big teams*".
3. **Wearing Many Hats:** "*Multipotentialites know how to do many things well, which means that we rarely have to seek outside help (we may want to, but rarely do we have to). So while I may not have enough legal knowledge to be a lawyer, I do have enough skill for it to be a real asset in my business*".
4. **Fast Skill Acquisition:** "*Multipotentialites are so accustomed to diving into new disciplines and acquiring knowledge, that we become skilled at the process of learning. The more experience you have being a beginner, the faster "getting good" becomes*".
5. **Impact/Inspiration:** "*Being passionate doesn't just lead to fast skill acquisition. The enthusiasm that multipotentialites have for their interests makes them excellent leaders that other people want to band around. Knowledge is important, but I would argue that enthusiasm is more valuable since it reaches people on an emotional level*".
6. **Concoction:** "*Multipotentialites are schemers. We love coming up with new ideas and bringing projects to life. When I was a kid, I was constantly inventing awesome projects. There were plays, gymnastic shows, a kids news program, fortune telling and origami in the park, punk bands, websites, short films, and clubs. This pattern has continued throughout my life. Often when I look around and feel displeased with the existing options, I create my own. Multipotentialites are constantly looking to invent better, more fun ways of doing things*".
7. **Idea Synthesis:** "*Probably the coolest multipotentialite super power is the ability to combine disparate fields and create something entirely new at the intersection*".

When Multipotential people find out that they are to be able to use the four learning styles and identify patterns at the moment of learning help them to develop qualities such as:

- **Accelerated Learning:** People move by the curiosity to learn new things.
- **Adaptability:** People would shape thoughts towards different areas, with a learning style assuming different and general roles in a specific topic.
- **Overview:** People would develop the ability to see problems in a broad context, finding domino patterns and effects.
- **Translation Between Areas:** People would have the ability to analyze similarities and parallels between different areas, establishing tunnels through which they connect skills in different areas.

The frame described in this section points out issues, controversies, and problems, which need to be solved or reduce as soon as possible since represents daily barriers for new people's generation. In this scenario Users-Centered technologies get crucial importance.

SOLUTIONS AND RECOMMENDATIONS

All previous qualities and skills are developed based on the ability to increase and exercise the level of attention considered by various authors as the new IQ. This term is explained by the Thinker J. Bruce Stewart, "*The New IQ refers to inclusive intelligence and consists of 20 questions identified through a rigorous factor analysis trial of the Office of Personnel Management's (OPM is the human resources arm of the federal government) Employee Viewpoint Survey (EVS) questions. These 20 EVS questions had the highest correlation to inclusive environments of the 87 questions tested. The 20 questions are grouped into 5 Habits of inclusion, "F.O.C.S.E" (Fair, Open, Cooperative, Supportive, Empowering). Furthermore, the 20 EVS questions are referred to in our research as "behaviors". The New IQ is built upon the concept that individual behaviors, repeated over time, form the habits that create essential building blocks of an inclusive environment. These behaviors can be learned, practiced, and developed into habits of inclusiveness and subsequently improve the inclusive intelligence of organizational members*" (Stewart, 2018).

Around this ability, there are several instruments such as the attentional networks that work in our brain independently, with the ability to interact and perform different functions (Posner & Dehacne, 1994; Fan, et al., 2005). As the Spanish philosopher, Gregorio Luri said "*La capacidad de una persona para moverse de una manera inteligente en la sociedad de la información va a depender de su capacidad atencional* ("*The ability of a person to move intelligently in the information society will depend on their attention capacity*").

Nowadays, that ability is a great differentiator between achieving specific goals and objectives or wandering between the seas of information and existing possibilities. It is a reality which it must be accompanied by a guide from the classroom, producing focus tools and from technology, catching and exercising the attention, providing to the students an orientation to results that help them to develop their skills, abilities and competencies of multiple intelligences.

In this measure, the concept of intelligence is expanded and from this new area it is worth highlighting the great importance of recognizing this new and wide expansion platform to transmit and not only that but also to make new generations feel that there is no particular kind of correct person. We are all intelligent from our different types of intelligences, which are independent among them, but totally indispensable for development as human being in a whole and of course, the society needs multiple profiles through which, the different ways of processing regarding the others, it will make us valuable, and it will be our ability or inability to react to the new challenges that will have a differentiating value.

Cooperating with tools through which not only the new generations but also all generations can have equal opportunities in which there is an integration of all our intelligences that as human beings we have. In this way, we are (without exception) actively participating in the new information society, taking these opportunities as a privilege when cooperating, developing and sponsoring the potential and brilliance that we have and not taking full advantage of them. It is in this way that the new UXD-based technology for learning designs (Including obviously Learning eXperience Design, LXD) can provide us with that bridge that finds a catalyst through which the person achieves a filter of information more dynamic and useful that supports as a guide in the structure of a particular and individual formula that accompanies the achievement of objectives, using the development of UXD/ LXD tools and also increasing the educational and learning experiences. See by example (Villanueva & Vaidya, 2019) and (Hudson, 2017).

This scenario requires not only hardware and software development but also by implementing strategies such as frameworks, models, methodologies, models, among others, addressed to change and move towards new workspaces, environments, and processes based on the central development of the new horizon and the importance of new changes in the paradigms as regards attention as a platform in knowledge generation, learning and ways of educating. See by example (Hanauer, 1999) and (Flavell, Green, & Flavell, 1995). Combining these valuable tools co-create the new way of learning and teaching, it could be the bridge that unites and adapts to the vertiginous change of technology and information with the new needs of new users and providing improvements in existing ones, resulting in a valuable gear that gives a significant contribution to the new horizon in the way we generate nothing less the new society.

Taking the development of attention to identify how to work constantly and how to maintain the focus over time, this exercise would lead to the development of a disciplined mind, highlighting that in the new era of information, it is urgent to transform it, towards the generation of knowledge and we need to understand that the students are not only recipients but also generators of a social transformation through these spaces, making contributions from the development of their individual abilities and multiple intelligences, producing their own intellect.

It is here that through the development of attention as an ability to enhance the particular multiple intelligences and that technology plays an indispensable role in the service of education and learning. It is a fact that the technology has been evolving and as we know, it has been existing for several decades throughout the twentieth century, beginning in the thirties. The attempts to create spaces that generate the ease of the exercise of learning have been diverse, for example projector, films, videos, cassettes, record players, educational programs, radio, assisted teaching by computers, CD room and educational multimedia have always been trying to do a complete search so that the technological process as a support tool be effective in the implementation of the learning exercise.

FUTURE RESEARCH DIRECTIONS

Near future technologies for learning should be thought as a support suport for emerging learning processes by encouraging attention in order to take advantage of nature skills and qualities from current and new students (e.g. Multipotentialites). Under this context would be necessary to provide design guidelines, interactive patterns, evaluation methods (e.g. Heuristic Evaluation), and other user-oriented alternatives (including Design Thinking, DT; UXD; and LXD) that help in developing technology compatible with users' activities by understanding their associated needs. Accessibility, responsiveness, and mobility should be imperative features for all technological solutions.

Designer Suman Shrestha quotes Donald Norman, inventor of term User eXperience, stating that "*No product is an island. A product is more than the product. It is a cohesive, integrated set of experiences. Think through all of the stages of a product or service — from initial intentions through final reflections, from first usage to help, service, and maintenance. Make them all work together seamlessly*" (Suman, 2018).

Strategies such as User Experience Design (UXD) and Learnining eXperience Design (LXD), should be implemented in order to ensure designs in function of user experience based on the development of a product or service that is functional and allows a good experience at the time of use and accessibility.

CONCLUSION

Everything concerning technology has been advancing by leaps and bounds in the last half century. Nevertheless, in the field of education teaching and learning processes remain almost without changes for over 100 years, spirit of many recent methodologies derives in doing things in the same way: The same classroom, the same board, the students sitting and the teachers in front of the class. We continue using papers, pencils and notebooks, the same schedules, the same way to evaluate and the same way to transmit information. In other words, the same experience for students and teachers.

The idea is to apply all the tools offered by the technology through the User eXperience Design (UXD) and Learning eXperience Design (LXD) taking all the information regarding the new change of idea related with intelligence, multiple intelligences, multipotentials and attention development that undoubtedly divert us towards the change in the form of the exercise of learning and teaching all this, facing the new challenge of the vertiginous development of technological contexts.

The proposal is to take advantage of all the information we have in all these fields and start creating environments that allow a meeting that brings together all these disciplines in the field of education for example, taking advantage of a tool that allows to detect which within the eight multiple intelligences in an individual is a strength and which within the four ways of learning is facilitated more and develop tools and resources that allow to improve the development of the skill of attention in a society that lacks active attention generating environments relevant enough for an individual to connect and discover in a more agile clear way and also easy and versatile within their own capabilities. The help of these tools will increase and expand the adaptation to the new era.

For instance, the implementation and deployment of prediction of consumer tastes through information collected by social networks and trend searches are a clear way to show how technology can help us predict behavior patterns when it comes to buying preferences.

From this premise, it would be possible to contribute to the development of the new concept of intelligence. The new generation structure their experiences around new technologies and education customized to people, dynamically directed towards individual education and not to the current obsolete system.

REFERENCES

Abdelrahman, Y., Khan, A. A., Newn, J., Velloso, E., Safwat, S. A., Bailey, J., . . . Schmidt, A. (2019). Classifying Attention Types with Thermal Imaging and Eye Tracking. *Proceedings of the ACM on Interactive, Mobile, Wearable and Ubiquitous Technologies, 3*(3), 69. 10.1145/3351227

Arcibniegas, J. C., Cano, J. M., Carvajal, N. V., Lorente, C. G., & Jaramillo, M. N. (2019). Attention to individual differences in early education? The talented child. *Dilemas Contemporáneos: Educación, Política y Valores*, *6*(3).

Bhowmik, R. (2012). *How Dieter Rams' 10 Principles of Good Design can impact UX*. Retrieved from: https://medium.com/swlh/how-dieter-rams-10-principles-of-good-design-can-impact-ux-c2f369218a08

Chestnut, E., Lei, R., Leslie, S. J., & Cimpian, A. (2018). The myth that only brilliant people are good at math and its implications for diversity. *Education in Science*, *8*(2), 65. doi:10.3390/educsci8020065

Dreyfuss, H. (2003). *Designing for people*. Skyhorse Publishing Inc.

Ericsson, K. A., & Simon, H. A. (1980). Verbal reports as data. *Psychological Review*, *87*(3), 215–251. doi:10.1037/0033-295X.87.3.215

Fan, J., McCandliss, B. D., Fossella, J., Flombaum, J. I., & Posner, M. I. (2005). The activation of attentional networks. *NeuroImage*, *26*(2), 471–479. doi:10.1016/j.neuroimage.2005.02.004 PMID:15907304

FisherT. (2010). *Multipotentiality*. Retrieved from: http://blogs.edweek.org/teachers/unwrapping_the_gifted/2010/08/multipotentiality.html

Flavell, J. H., Green, F. L., & Flavell, E. R. (1995). The development of children's knowledge about attentional focus. *Developmental Psychology*, *31*(4), 706–712. doi:10.1037/0012-1649.31.4.706

Gardner, H. (2011). *Frames of mind: The theory of multiple intelligences*. Hachette.

Gardner, H. (2018). Multiple approaches to understanding. In K. Illeris (Ed.), *Contemporary Theories of Learning* (pp. 129–138). Routledge. doi:10.4324/9781315147277-9

Gomez, S. (2006). *Aproximaciones a una antropología del diseño*. Universidad Nacional de Colombia (Unimedios). Retrieved from: http://historico.unperiodico.unal.edu.co/Ediciones/95/15.html

Hanauer, D. (1999). Attention and literary education: A model of literary knowledge development. *Language Awareness*, *8*(1), 15–29. doi:10.1080/09658419908667114

Hudson, J. (2017). Putting learning experience design into workplace learning. *Training & Development*, *44*(5), 7.

Interaction Design Foundations. (2018). *User Experience (UX) Design*. Retrieved from: https://www.interaction-design.org/literature/topics/ux-design

Kerr, B. A., & Gahm, J. (2018). *Developing talents in girls and young women*. Academic Press.

Moran, S., & Gardner, H. (2018). *Hill, skill, and will: executive function from a multiple-intelligences perspective*. Academic Press.

Neisser, U., Boodoo, G., Bouchard, T. J. Jr, Boikin, A. W., Brody, N. C., Stephen, J., ... Sternberg, R. (1996). Intelligence: Knowns and Unknowns. *The American Psychologist*, *51*(2), 77–101. doi:10.1037/0003-066X.51.2.77

Nester, H., & Buford, M. (2018). *Multipotentiality: Finding a career path that reflects who you truly are.* Retrieved from: https://www.ceiainc.org/wp-content/uploads/2018/02/Exp_Spring18_07_Nester-Buford.pdf

Nielsen, J. (2017). *A 100-Year View of User Experience*. Retrieved from: https://www.nngroup.com/articles/100-years-ux/

Nobre, A. C., & Van Ede, F. (2018). Anticipated moments: Temporal structure in attention. *Nature Reviews. Neuroscience*, *19*(1), 34–48. doi:10.1038/nrn.2017.141 PMID:29213134

Peters, D. (2012). *UX for Learning: Design Guidelines for the Learner Experience*. Retrieved from: https://www.uxmatters.com/mt/archives/2012/07/ux-for-learning-design-guidelines-for-the-learner-experience.php

Posner, M. I., & Dehaene, S. (1994). Attentional networks. *Trends in Neurosciences*, *17*(2), 75–79. doi:10.1016/0166-2236(94)90078-7 PMID:7512772

Posner, M. I., Rothbart, M. K., & Ghassemzadeh, H. (2019). Focus: Attention Science: Restoring Attention Networks. *The Yale Journal of Biology and Medicine*, *92*(1), 139. PMID:30923481

Saygin, A. P., Cicekli, I., & Akman, V. (2000). Turing test: 50 years later. *Minds and Machines*, *10*(4), 463–518. doi:10.1023/A:1011288000451

Scriven, M. (1991). Evaluation thesaurus. *Sage (Atlanta, Ga.).*

Silver, H., Strong, R., & Perini, M. (1997). Integrating Learning Styles and Multiple Intelligences. *Educational Leadership*, *1*(55), 22–27.

Stewart, J. B. (2018). *The New IQ: A New Kind of Intelligence for a New Kind of World*. Retrieved from: https://medium.com/@j_brucestewart/the-new-iq-a-new-kind-of-intelligence-for-a-new-kind-of-world-72d453b3ada3

Suman, S. (2018). *UX 101: Basic Understanding*. Retrieved from: https://medium.com/nyc-design/ux-101-basic-understanding-11cf993f0e99

Taylor, F. W. (1911). The principles of scientiðc management. New York: Academic Press.

Villanueva, K., & Vaidya, J. (2019). Power up Learning With Mobile Games: The Educational Arcade–An Innovative Approach to Learning. In *Advancing Mobile Learning in Contemporary Educational Spaces* (pp. 209–242). IGI Global. doi:10.4018/978-1-5225-9351-5.ch008

Vital, M. (2014). *9 Types of Intelligence – Infographic*. Retrieved from: https://blog.adioma.com/9-types-of-intelligence-infographic/#bodily

WapnickE. (2012). *The 7 Multipotentialite Super Powers*. Retrieved from: https://puttylike.com/the-7-multipotentialite-super-powers/

Zgurovsky, M. Z., & Zaychenko, Y. P. (2016). Inductive Modeling Method (GMDH) in Problems of Intellectual Data Analysis and Forecasting. In *The Fundamentals of Computational Intelligence: System Approach* (pp. 221–260). Cham: Springer. doi:10.1007/978-3-319-35162-9_6

ADDITIONAL READING

Gardner, H. (1998). A Reply to Perry D. Klein's" Multiplying the Problems of Intelligence by Eight". *Canadian Journal of Education/Revue canadienne de l'éducation, 23*(1), 96-102.

Luri, G. (2018). *Attention, the new IQ* (In Spanish). Video. Retrieved from: https://www.youtube.com/watch?time_continue=39&v=uy4FIv-9Yew&feature=emb_logo

Mora, F. (2018). *What is Neuroscience?* (In Spanish). Video. Retrieved from: https://www.youtube.com/watch?v=d2Fud46xFPQ

Norman, D. (2016). *The term: UX.* (Video). Retrieved from: https://www.youtube.com/watch?time_continue=1&v=9BdtGjoIN4E&feature=emb_logo

Posner, M. I. (2003). Neural Systems and Individual Differences: A Commentary on Frames of Mind: The Theory of Multiple Intelligences.

Regader, B. (2014*). The Gardner's Theory of Multiple Intelligences* (In Spanish). Retrieved from: https://psicologiaymente.com/inteligencia/teoria-inteligencias-multiples-gardner

Triglia, A., Regader, B., & García-Allen, J. (2018). *What is Intelligence? From IQ to Multiintelligences.* EMSE Publishing. (In Spanish)

KEY TERMS AND DEFINITIONS

Multipotentialites: People with multiple passions and interests in life.

Pragmatic Learning: Provide structure, rules, logic, order, and systematic approaches that students follow to learn.

Reflective Learning: According to Researchers from Kent University, reflective learning derives from students' experiences and could be constantly updated. Retrieved from: https://www.kent.ac.uk/learning/PDP-and-employability/pdp/reflective.html

Chapter 8
Educational Applications as a Support for Reading Disability at Elementary School

Jaime Muñoz-Arteaga
https://orcid.org/0000-0002-3635-7592
Universidad Autónoma de Aguascalientes, Mexico

ABSTRACT

Reading is an important competency to be developed for children in the first years of elementary school. Reading becomes a mechanism that allows the children to interact with the world and identify their characteristics. Dyslexia is one learning disability frequently manifested in elementary school, and to identify it, teachers require extra educative resources, in particular educational applications. This work proposes a process model to design and develop educational applications considering the learning needs of children with dyslexia. It involves a user-centered approach because different perceptions of several actors are considered. The performance of the proposed model is explored in a case study and an evaluation, taking into account usability and accessibility factors.

INTRODUCTION

The educational applications also known as educational apps, they are interactive applications that promote the use multimedia content notably under mobile devices easy to use beyond the classroom walls in the education in schools (Ciullo et al. 2018). The software for this educational application encompasses a variety of forms, platforms, and purposes. These applications can be used in several domains for example to teach individual letter names, phonics and grammar in a certain language (Dore et al. 2019). Other educational applications introduce mathematical concepts for all grades or are aimed at helping to develop logical skills (Herro 2013). Nowadays, the elementary school has created inclusive programs in order to offer educative support for children with learning disable such as dyslexia, dysgraphia, and dyscalculia (Zikl 2015) (Uloyol & Sahin 2014). These children require an efficient learning method, teachers using educative resources can innovative teaching methods specific to the context of children

DOI: 10.4018/978-1-7998-2325-4.ch008

so that even they motivating differently and can be self-paced learning at the level that corresponds to their chronological age (Ciullo et al. 2018) (Mize et al. 2019a).

Nowadays, the elementary school has been created inclusive programs, which are dedicated offer support for children with learning disable such as dyslexia, dysgraphia, and dyscalculia (Zikl 2015). This work is interesting in the study of dyslexia; this is a specialized term for a specific set of traits in the reading process that it falls under the general category of specific learning disability in reading. Someone with dyslexia may be identified with disabilities in basic reading skills, reading comprehension and reading fluency as dyslexia often affects all three aspects. Individuals with specialized training can offer remedial techniques for dyslexia in a highly structured, multisensory approach to teaching reading.

This work is interested in the study of dyslexia; this is a specialized term for a specific set of traits of reading disability. Dyslexia is related to reading difficulties frequently identified at elementary school (Cook, L. & Dakin, K. 2007). Some of most common learning difficulties related to dyslexia are: misunderstand words with similar pronunciation, poor reading comprehension, slowness in reading, difficulty identifying the letters, delay to memorize the numbers, the alphabet, the days of the week, colors and shapes. These kind of difficulties in general affect the academic performance of a child (Turner & Greaney, 2009), arising several learning issues that are reflected in behavior, socialization, academic desertion among others (Tamboer et al., 2016). A teacher at elementary school spends time to prepare educational resources and it becomes difficult to find specific educational content as a support to reading disability. The instructional design for teaching reading for children with dyslexia requires to prepare additional educational applications in order to help the students to achieve their learning needs and these strategies can be incorporated into the child's education.

An alternative solution is the use of educational applications as educational content to help reading according to the learning needs. In general, children at the school can use several technological resources as complementary support for learning activities, then children with learning disabilities require a larger diversity of resources in order to support the acquisition of knowledge (Dore et al. 2019) (Gaggi et al. 2012). In addition, when there are groups with a large number of students for the teachers are not always possible to offer a personal teaching. Then, the interactive applications can be an efficiently support to mitigate some issues of learning problem in particular for reading.

Teachers can use their educative material accompanied by educational applications to gain visual interactive communication with the children and a greater understanding of what they are being taught. The cognitive processes of children with learning disability is taken into account in attention, memory, perception, and language and, on encountering a word and images that represents a certain concept; these can help to process the symbols and letters, extracting characteristics such as shape or position and the sound of the words by the verbal processing code (Quispe et al. 2017). The process at the cognitive level can be positive, since the children try to recognize, find and analyze information. The student is motivated to continue to have a better understanding of word using friendly and accessible user interface of an educational application as seen in the assessment carried out on evaluating a set of learning activities (Chelkowski et al. 2019).

The software production for educational applications does not necessarily have to start from scratch, it can be used standards that guide the construction of the product, some of these alternatives can be achieved through the partial representation of information, or by using efficient abstractions that can be applied to describe different approaches to software development (Somerville 2015). This paper proposes a software process model to develop educational applications to be used for teachers as a useful educational resource for help children with learning difficulties in particular with dyslexia; it involves a user-centered approach because different perceptions of several actors are considered, such as teacher, psycho-pedagogues and software engineer.

Current work is structured in six sections; section two presents some general challenges about teaching reading for children with reading disability. Next section identifies some reading disability issues at elementary school. Section three proposes a process model to design, develop and evaluate educational patterns. Section four presents a case study that was carried out to produce two educational applications. The activities have carried out throughout the phases of process model, the models are detailed and results of the case study. Section five presents an analysis of result in order to appreciate the performance of proposal. Finally, the conclusion and future works are described in section six.

PROBLEM OUTLINE

Several works in the e-learning and human computer-interaction literature have presented several successful experiences using the technology in order to tackle reading disability have considered the use of educational resources as an alternative supporting in learning problems at elementary school. (Atehortúa, 2010) has proposed a serious game improving the spelling of children with dyslexia, by means activities interactive where it achieves obtained favorable outcomes in reducing of misspellings. Other authors (Chelkowski et al. 2019) have developed a survey about use of mobile devices with students with disabilities. Quispe (Quispe et al. 2017) propose applications for helping children/adolescents with intellectual disability to instilling healthy eating habits. The application is based on a set of video games with different functionalities, which include a piece of advices for the eating process, where a pet has been designed with the aim of making the application more attractive in the interest of motivation. The authors of work of Rodríguez (Mize et al. 2019b) suggests that using the appropriate teaching methods, children could facilitate the learning processes and enhance the cognitive ability; (Rodríguez et al. 2013) proposed to combine iPad-assisted and peer-assisted instruction to foster their learning capability in children. The work (Charlton and Williams 2005) proposes a study to evaluate the effects of educational resources on the performance of eight elementary school students with learning disabilities; the results indicated that each student improved their performance on reading when educational video games were in effect.

However no there a lot works for help teachers to adapt designing educative resources in terms of pedagogical as well as technological aspects. Here a list of identified issues such as:

- Dyslexia is a very common problem that affects between 10 and 15 percent of the school population, reflecting a low academic performance in the child with the possibility of academic desertion (Antognazza & González 2011) (Uloyol & Sahin 2014)
- Most educational applications already designed to support learning difficulties arising from dyslexia don't give information about an effective use in a teaching session. In addition, teachers spend time in the identification of educational applications according to learning needs of students (Das et al. 2013) (Zikl 2015).
- Educational application development requires different perspectives of stakeholders since the early phases such as teachers, psychologists, programmers, students, IT analysts, etc., therefore. it is essential to have a software engineering process that integrates in an orderly manner (analysis, design, development, evaluation, among others) the participation of each role at different stages of the process model (Herro et al. 2013).

- Key activities of process such as design and test of traditional development of educational application are under the responsibility of software engineer (Kangas and Kinnunen 2005)
- Children at elementary school can use several technological resources as complementary support for learning activities, but for children with learning disabilities require a larger diversity of technological resources
- When there are groups with a large number of students for a teacher is not always possible to offer a personal teaching.
- Teachers of children with learning disabilities require continuous training programs about the use of ICT inside and outside the classroom (Quispe et al. 2017). This represents a drawback cause teachers does not have access to the wide range of interactive applications.

PROCESS MODEL

This paper proposes a software process model (see figure1) to design and develop educational applications to be used for teacher as a useful educational resource for help children with learning difficulties in particular with dyslexia. This process model advocates a user-centered approach because the users (such as teachers and children with dyslexia) can participate in most phases of development of an educational application (analysis, design, development, prototyping, evaluation and launching). Different roles of actors (such as teachers and children with dyslexia) are taken account in several phases of process model (for example analysis, prototyping, launching and evaluation) represented by modules (see figure 1). In addition, this process advocates a model-based design where the models are refined by interactive and incremental activities. In addition, the accessibility and usability are considered as key factors during the evaluation phase, in a similar from MPIU+a model of Granollers (Granollers et al. 2003). The user activities and artifacts are developed in the seven phases composing the process model, se next figure:

A description of every phase of process model is given in the next paragraphs:

1. **Requirements Analysis Phase:** This phase defines the requirements for an educational application where it is necessary to describe explicitly the problem to solver and user needs. User task analysis, usability guidelines, Person technique, use case diagram are examples of software artifacts to get in this phase.
2. **Prototyping Phase**: In this phase can be developed partial or complete prototypes for describing educational applications. These prototypes can bas sketches, mockup, wireframe, user interface and functional prototypes.
3. **Design Phase:** This phase specifies the solution in terms of models considering the requirements defined of previous level. Several design models are required to represent the structure as well as the behavior of an educational application. The architecture model, flowchart and class diagram describe the structural aspects. The behavior aspects can be specified by state chart, automats and activity diagrams etc.
4. **Development Phase**: This development of educational application considered the collected information in the requirements and design phases. Some examples of software artifacts are design patterns, algorithms and the source code under a programming language.

Figure 1. Process model to develop educational applications for help children with learning disabilities such as dyslexia
Source: Modified from Granollers et al. 2003

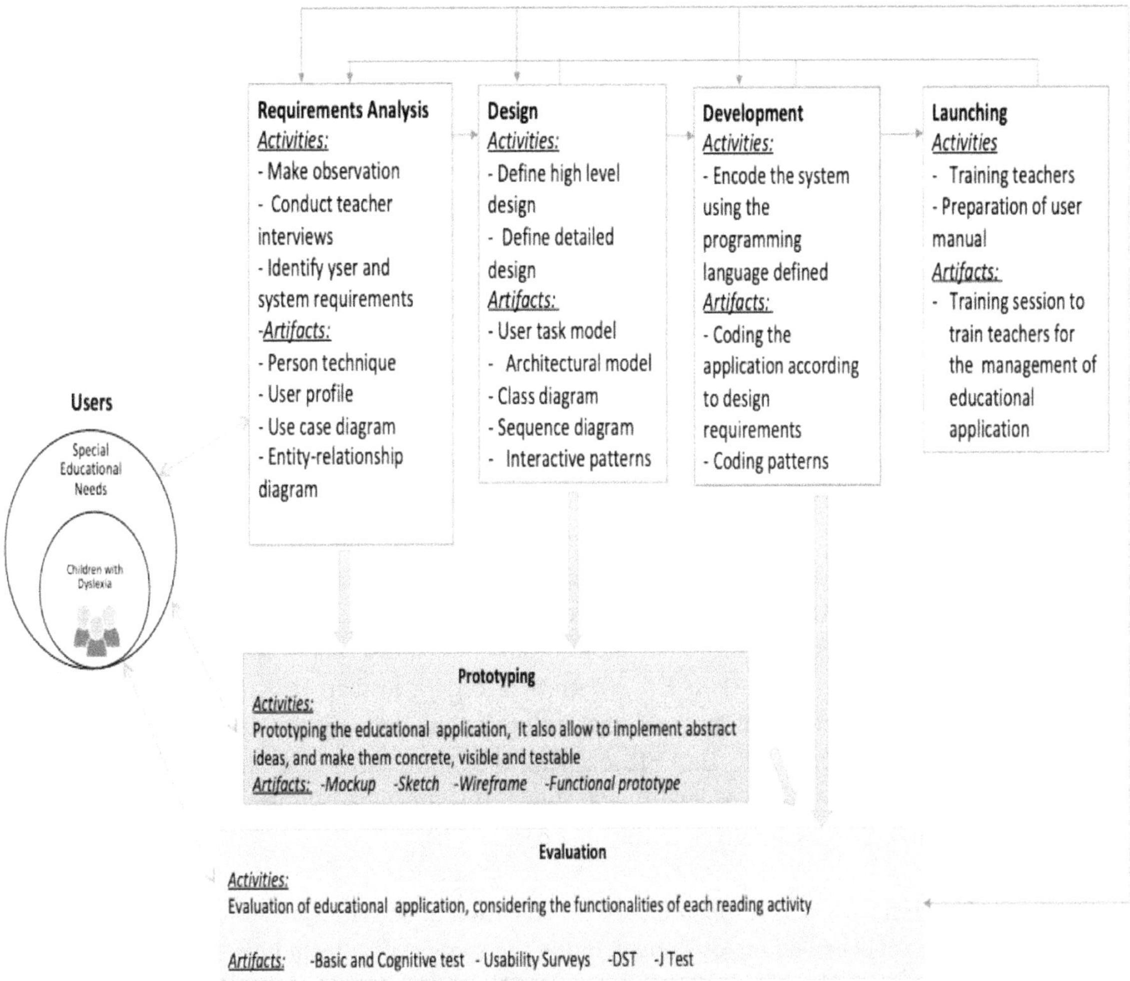

5. **Evaluation Phase**: The evaluation phase has the purpose of evaluating usability of educational application aspects as well the user experience in order to verify the requirement have been satisfied. It is necessary to conduct usability assessment, because it requires a certain way to ensure the proposed interactive applications were designed to assist reading through play for children with learning disabilities; some examples of usability testing such as dyslexia screening, test-junior and cognitive skills. Then, it is possible to provide a fun and innovative educational resource to promote the acquisition of reading skills.
6. **Launching Phase:** Once educational applications have been evaluated, they can be delivered for a large number of users with similar learning needs. This phase preconizes training programs for teachers in order they know the use effective of new educational applications.

The process model gives space for the interaction of pedagogical and technological areas to design and develop educational applications. The pedagogical area is responsible for studying and analyzing educational phenomena, providing systematic and intentional solutions using the instructional design, in order to support education in all its aspects for the improvement of the human being (Gómez 2008). The instructional design is a process where specific environmental situations can be specified and produced, promoting to the student to interact with the teaching system, generating a specific change in the student behavior (Martinez 2009). Several actors require to be involved during the production of software for educational applications. The technological area is responsible for providing the most appropriate process to manage the human factor and the organizational factor, to produce software that satisfy user requirement (Sommerville 2015). Teacher and pedagogical actors requires identify the user profile as well as the learning difficulties of children presenting dyslexia at elementary school.

CASE STUDY

A case study was conducted to apply and evaluate the proposed process model of figure 1. Some educational applications were developed as help in a specific reading difficulty of a group of 5 children with dyslexia between 6 and 8 years old at the elementary school. It was conducted by the UAA (Universidad Autónoma de Aguascalientes) team (software analyst, software designer, programmer) and a team of assistant teachers of USAER ("Unidades de Servicio y Apoyo a la Educación Regular" this means Service Units as a Support for Regular Education) of an elementary school located in Aguascalientes city in Mexico during five months (USAER 2019) (SEP 2019). In fact, USAER teachers conforms a multidisciplinary team composed of teachers, psychologists and pedagogues. In this case study, it was possible to offer a training course to USAER teachers, they have learned to handle mobile devices in order to offer their students an easy access to educational resources in/ out the classroom.

A short description of roles are given in the next paragraphs:

- Special education teacher is responsible for the selection of activities, resources and strategies that are the most appropriate taking on consideration the student profile and his/her grade of dyslexia.
- Pyscho-pedagogue is the actor who carrying out the pedagogical tests to determine if a student presents some level of dyslexia. He/she is also responsible for specifying the child profile, this profile has information regarding dyslexia problems, in which, the child has more difficulties, it contains an assessment of skills that are meaningful to measure the child's performance.
- The student represents the child who has been detected with some grade of dyslexia. The student use the educational application proposed by the teacher.
- Software analyst is the person who is responsible for interacting with the teacher and the student in order to facilitate the use of technology.
- Software designer is responsible for establishing the interactive application design; considering the specific children with dyslexia needs.
- Programmer is responsible for coding, based on the requirements expected to be in the educational application.

Figure 2. Profile of student A

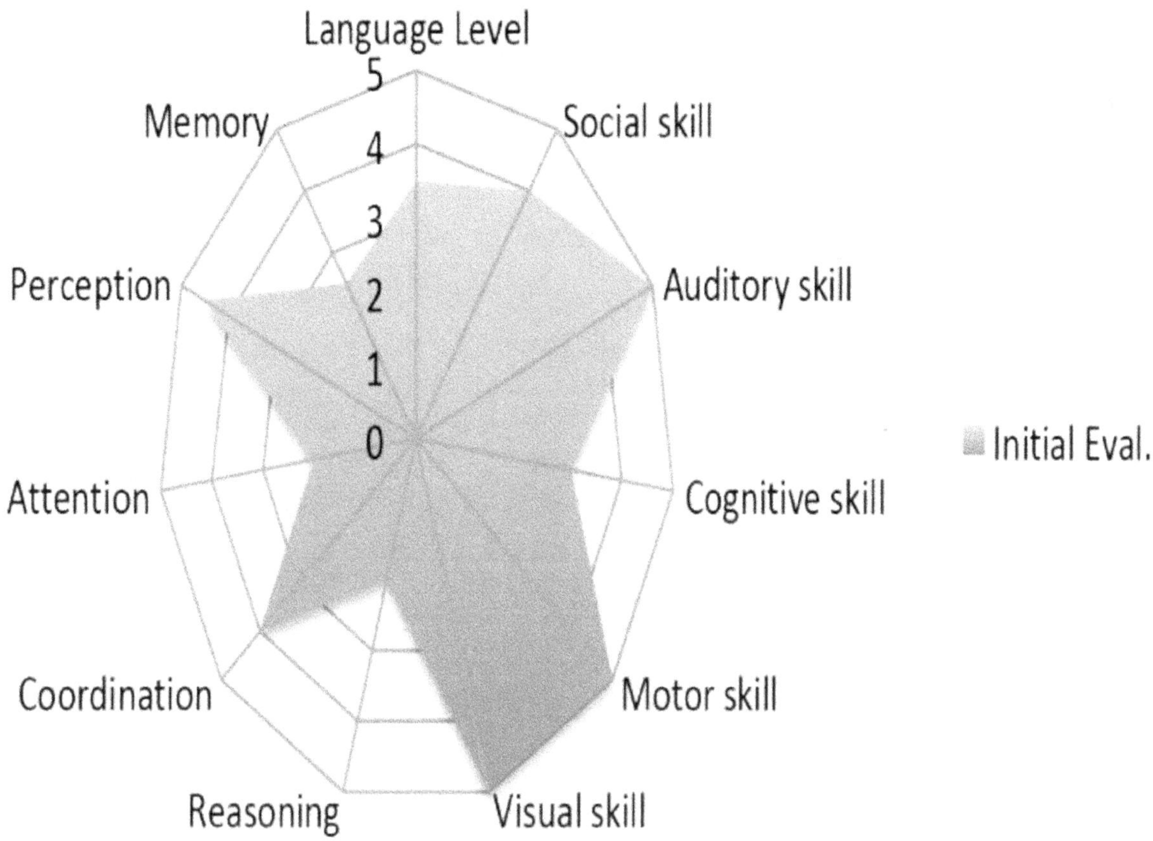

In fact, a multidisciplinary team work is necessary to design a solution for reading difficulties such as: omission, additional and substitution letters, irregular fluency, misunderstanding word, lack of memorization, poor comprehension, mispronounce of words, lack of order and structure when writing then some trouble learning numbers, days of the week, colors and shapes (Antonenko 2016).

No enough room here for all activities have carried out in each phase of process model, then current work only presents in this section some activities for two students called here A and B.

Requirements Analysis Phase

This phase defines the user requirements (such as user profile and the skill levels of students) and also the system requirements (such as sketches and wireframes)

User Profile

The user profile of every student was defined by a quest based on the DST-J test (Dyslexia Screening Test - Junior) (Fawcett & Nicolson 2016). This kind of test was proposed by a psycho-pedagogue of USAER team in order to identify the dyslexia level.

Figure 3. Profile of student B

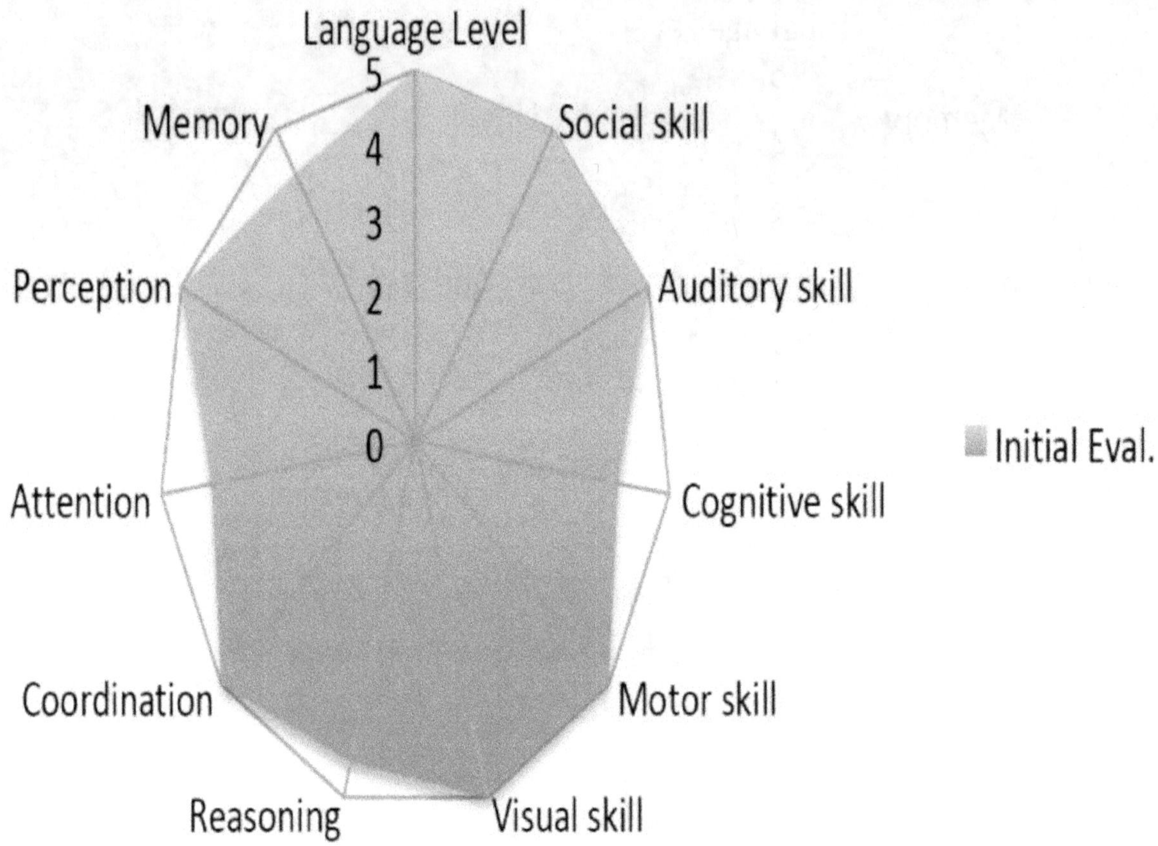

The series of values of a user profile are represented here in terms of a radar representation; these values correspond to cognitive skills (perception, attention, coordination, reasoning and language level) as well as basic skills (motor skill, auditory ability, visual ability, social ability, cognitive ability). The radar representation presents certain difficulties for the student A with low value in attention, memory, cognition and reasoning. The student B had presented also some difficulties to reading comprehension caused by light difficulties related to attention, memory and cognitive skills.

Once the user profiles has defined by the USAER teachers, it was possible to represent the reading level where the result could be basic, intermediate or advanced level (see next figure). The basic level is when a child presents elementary skills to start to read such attention, perception, memory and localization. Intermediate level is when a child has a preliminary grammatical level for reading such as pres-syllabic, syllabic and syllabic-alphabetic levels. The advanced level concerns the interpretation and the composition of several words to compose simple phrases.

According to figure 4, the student A presents a basic reading level because the low value in attention, memory, orientation and perception. The student B has an intermediate reading level because it is necessary to rise up the syllabic and syllabic-alphabetic skills for a better comprehension of phrases.

Figure 4. Reading skill levels for students A (Basic level) and B (Intermediate level)

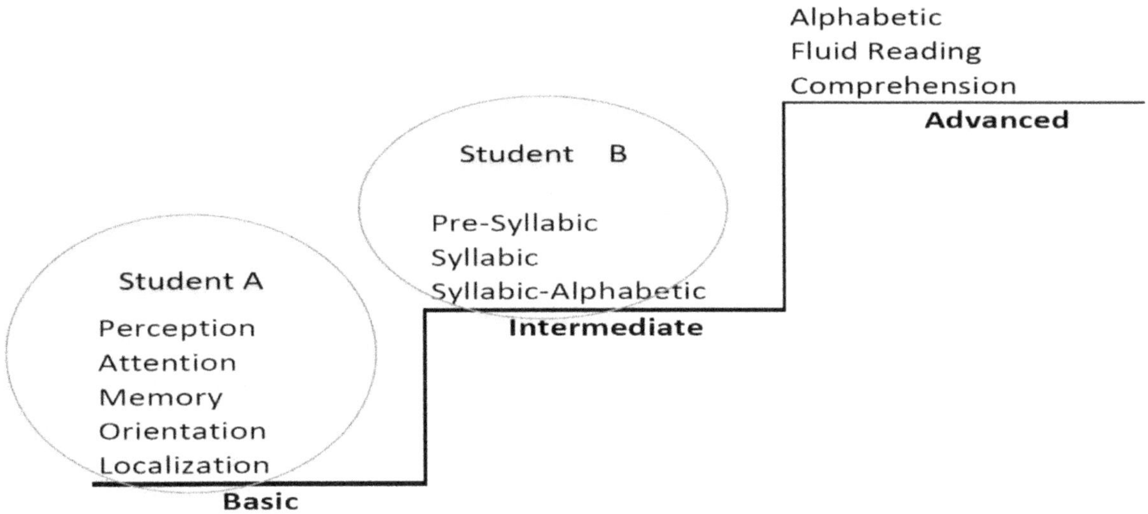

Prototyping Phase

Sketch and Wireframe

Once software analyst has known the user requirements and profiles, this analyst has proposed a prototype of educational application to USAER teacher in terms of sketch and wireframe. The figure 5 shows the proposed sketch for a user interface where the designer can identify the direction and a list of options to build phrases that better describe the meaning of images. It is possible to have the control of volume and navigation of content.

The wireframe of figure 6 is derived from the sketch of figure 5, the wireframe specifies the distribution of basic icons in the user interface for a new educational application to assist students to build phrases. This wireframe defines also a kind of icons to have the control of volume and the navigation of content.

Design Phase

In this phase the solution are specified under a user task model and educational application are specified under the design pattern approach, these are the best practice to recommend for the learning difficulties arising from dyslexia of student A and B, the guideline about letter omission was recommend to teachers to use.

User Task Model

The learning activities of students using the educational application as a support to dyslexia is specified here under a user tasks model using the CTT (Concur Task Trees) notation (Manca, Paternò et al. 2014). There are several notations for task modeling but CTT is a good option because is an expressive

Figure 5. Sketch of an educational application as a support to build phrases

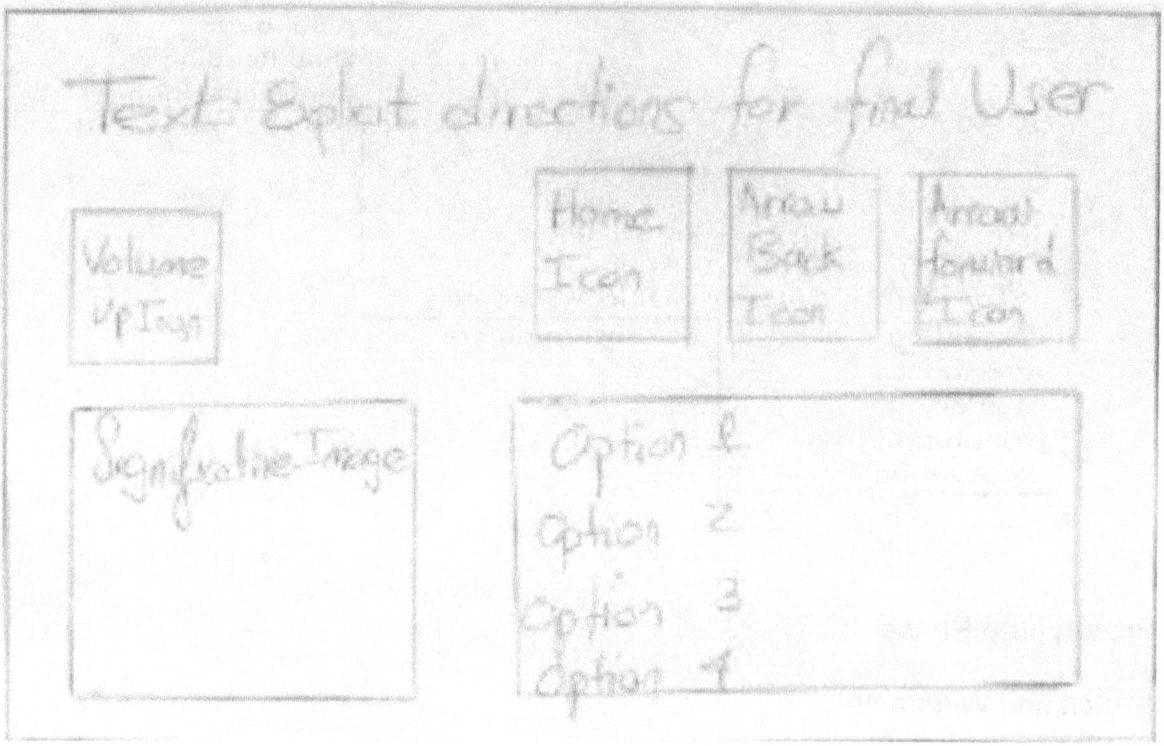

and flexible notation able to represent concurrent and interactive activities, also with the possibility to specify the user activities that needs to be done by teachers as well as students.

The task model of figure 7 specifies how the new educational application can help the student A to build syllables. The application presents several images and syllables in order to be selected by the user. Then, it matches the selected syllables versus a list of concepts associated to every image. Next, the application notifies if the user option is right or wrong. For a right option the application gives to user a confirmation of a good learning activity (*Well Formed Syllables icon*), and for a wrong option the application send to user a message error with some reading advices (*Advice to Have Well Formed Syllables* icon).

The task model of figure 8 specifies how the new educational application can help the student B to build syllables. The application presents first a list of phrases in order to be selected by the user, then it matches the selected phrase versus a reading scenario. Next, the application notifies if the user option is right or wrong. For a right option the application gives a confirmation to user of good job (*Good Job Well Formed Phrase* icon), and for a wrong option the application send to user a message error with some reading recommendations (*Recommendation to Have Well Formed Phrase* icon).

Figure 6. Wireframe of an educational application as a support to build phrases

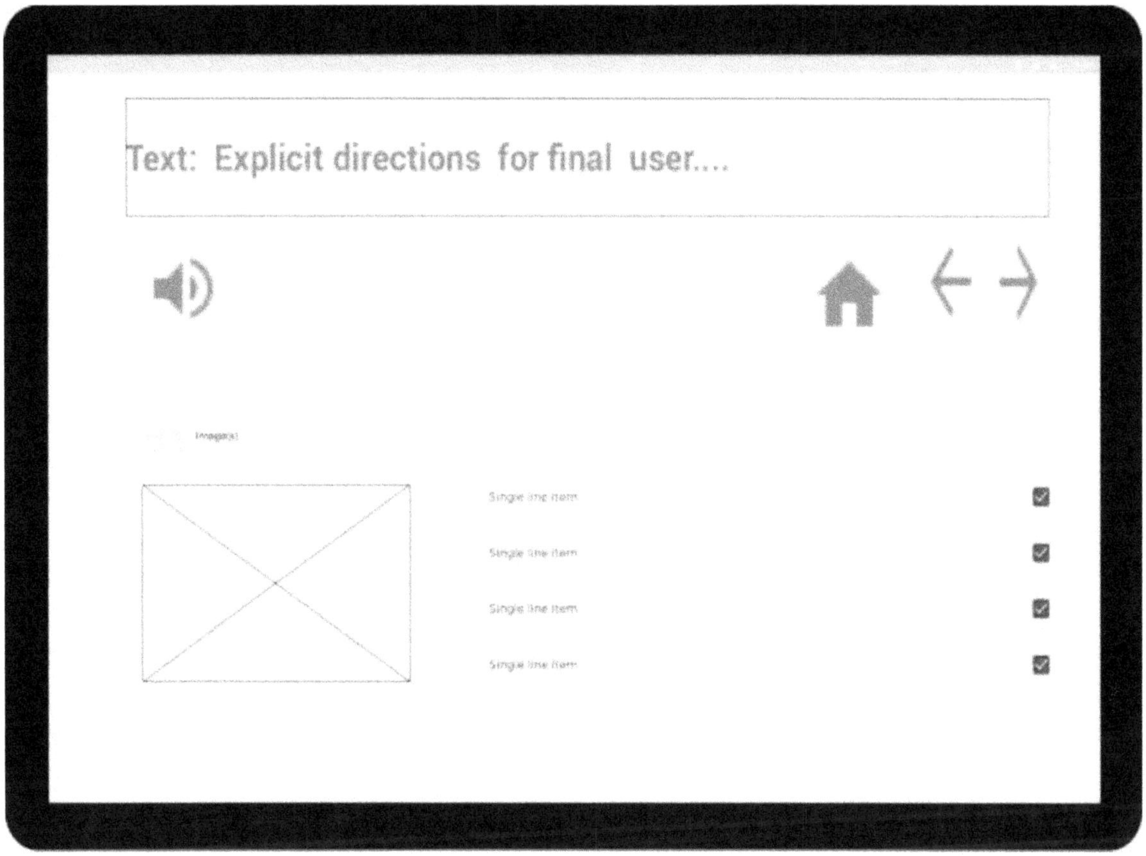

Figure 7. User task model for a new educational application to be used by student A

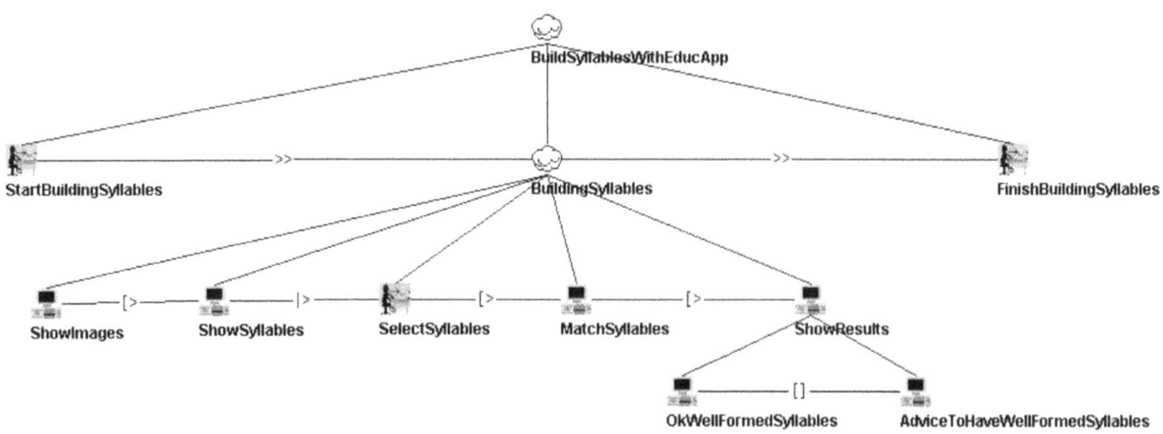

Figure 8. User task model for a new educational application to be used by student B

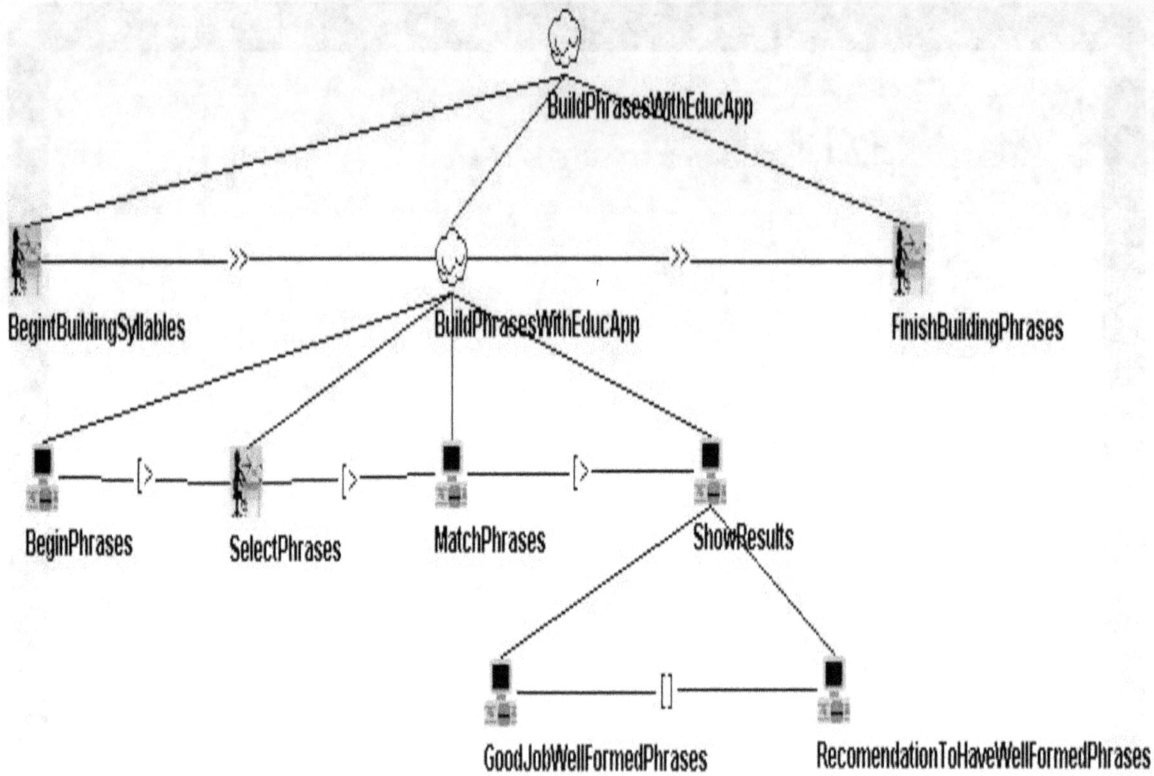

Usability Guideline

A usability guideline is presented here in terms of interactive design patterns. A pattern is a systematic approach to capture the experience of experts throughout a reusable solution to a recurrent problem within a given context (Gamma et al. 1995). In a similar way the pedagogical patterns (Bergin et al. 2012), the author propose the interaction design patterns to give a conceptual solution to a recurrent problem but in the domain of user interfaces for educational applications.

The table 1 presents the interactive pattern related to the educational application that helps to build syllables required for the student A (Table 1), the other pattern is proposed for the educational application to build phrases required for the student B (Table 2). According to the table 1 and 2, the structure of each interaction design pattern is composed of technological and pedagogical elements to assist any reading trouble. The first row of these tables specifies the name of the pattern. Next five rows concern to pedagogical elements as follows: the reading trouble, the reading level, a learning goal, and the expected learning. The last three rows show technological elements as follow: the first row present the name, icon, and link of an educational application, the second row give some teaching activities using previous educational application. The last row displays information about other educational applications useful also to raise the reading trouble related to dyslexia.

Table 1. Interaction design pattern for an educational application for student A<Tbl_Large></Tbl_Large>

Name	Mismatch syllables		
Reading trouble	The student does not get to match the phoneme of a syllable with a pertinent grapheme.		
Reading level	Syllabic level		
Goal	The student match phonemes with its corresponding grapheme of syllables.		
Context	-When a child can spell every syllable of a word then a child get a correct pronunciation by facilitating the language when reading.		
Expected learning	- The student can match the sound of a syllable with its grapheme		
Educatio -nal appli- cations	**Name**	**Icon**	**Link**
	Aprender a Leer – Silabario		https://play.google.com/store/apps/details?id=com.eduapps.silabario
Activities	Some activities are possible to do with the application "Aprender a Leer Silabario". A teacher can select a set of words with syllables which a child has learning troubles:  In this activity, a child can choose the syllable from the previous user interface that matches better with the word "1ducat".  A child can choose three syllables corresponding to the word "co-ne-jo" in the previous interface. Each time the user clicks in every syllable with the corresponding sound. Then a child can easier match the grapheme of the syllable with its phoneme.		
Other 1ducatio n-nal appli- cations	**Name**	**Icon**	**Link**
	Learn to read		https://play.google.com/store/apps/details?id=com.Company.aprenderjugando
	Hector, the passionate reader		http://www.genmagic.net/educa/mod/forum/discuss.php?d=214

Table 2. Interaction design pattern for an educational application for student B

<table>
<tr><td>Name</td><td colspan="3">Misunderstanding simple phrases</td></tr>
<tr><td>Reading trouble</td><td colspan="3">The student has some troubles for reading phrases</td></tr>
<tr><td>Reading level</td><td colspan="3">Alphabetic level</td></tr>
<tr><td>Goal</td><td colspan="3">- A phrase with a simple structure with a subject, a verb and predicate, they can be read by the student
-The student can understand the meaning of phrase</td></tr>
<tr><td>Context</td><td colspan="3">- It is possible to understand in a phrase every word in a fluent manner</td></tr>
<tr><td>Expected learning</td><td colspan="3">The students can spell and understand the word of a phrase. They can also identify the structure of a phrase</td></tr>
<tr><td rowspan="2">Educational applications</td><td>Name</td><td>Icon</td><td>Link</td></tr>
<tr><td>Tico</td><td></td><td>https://sourceforge.net/projects/tico/</td></tr>
<tr><td>Activities</td><td colspan="3">The TICO is an educational application to generate interactive communication boards where with two main sections: an editor and an interpreter.
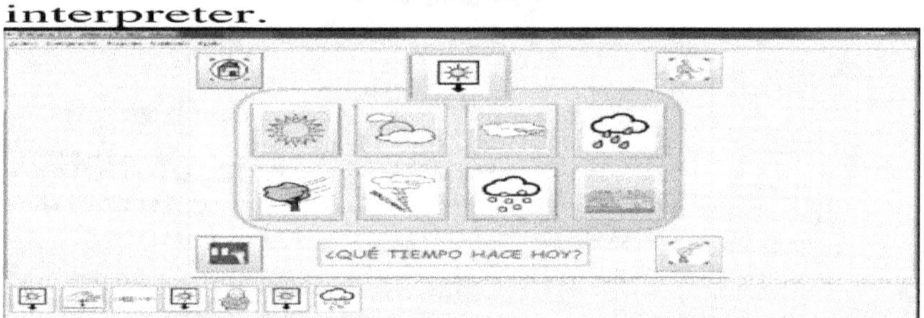

-The teacher can create the boards that will contain all visual, auditory or control elements of environment. The elements of the board of this application can be grouped to build sentences. For example a teacher can use this application in order to help the students for a better building and understanding some phrases related to the local weather.</td></tr>
<tr><td rowspan="3">Other educational applications</td><td>Name</td><td>Icon</td><td>Link</td></tr>
<tr><td>Classic tales</td><td>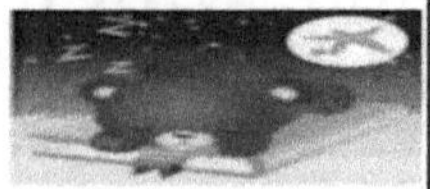</td><td>https://play.google.com/store/apps/details?id=es.lacaixa.mobile.android.cuentosclasicos</td></tr>
<tr><td>Piruletras</td><td>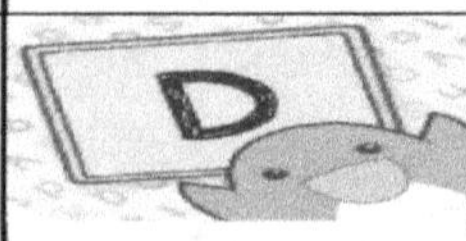</td><td>https://itunes.apple.com/mx/app/piruletras/id534986729?mt=8</td></tr>
</table>

Development Phase

The development of two educational applications for this case study has carried out considering the software artifacts defined in the previous phases such as analysis and design phases. The source code has written using the Android Studio development platform. In addition, some design patterns have been applied for the source the code such as Iterator and Command (Gamma et al. 1995).

Both educational applications were programmed according the previous models from analysis and design phases. The figure 9 shows a snapshot for a new educational application to help to build syllables required for student A, where the student can choice the syllable is common for both images. Teacher has decided to use this user interface in order to assist their students to compare and select the letters in the table versus a main letter (in this case the syllable *fan*) with symbol and sound representation. Note, the figure 10 shows a snapshot of a new application as a support to build phrases required for student B according the image of children listening music. The user interaction is according to the specification of models of previous sections such as sketch, wireframe and user task models.

Figure 9. User interface of educational application as a support to build syllables required for student A

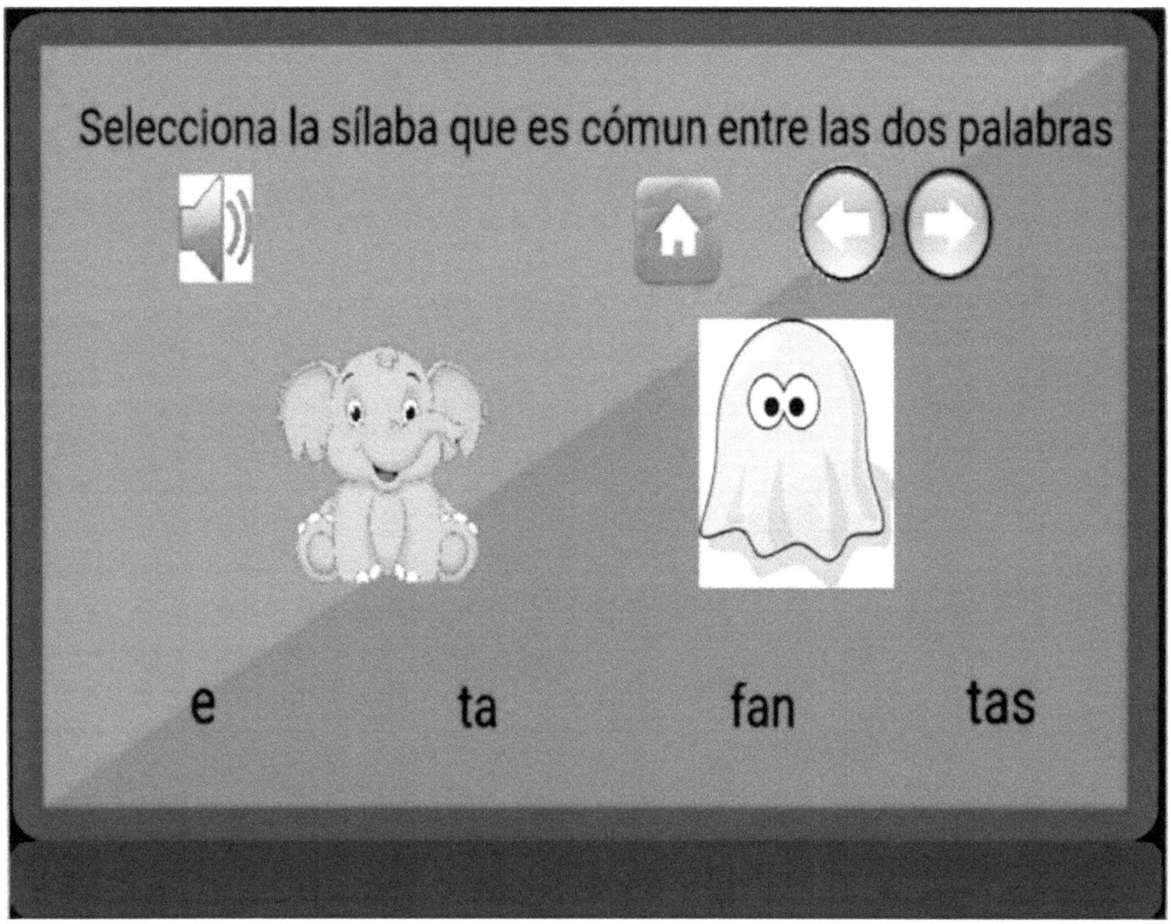

Figure 10. User interface of educational application as a support to build phrases required for student B

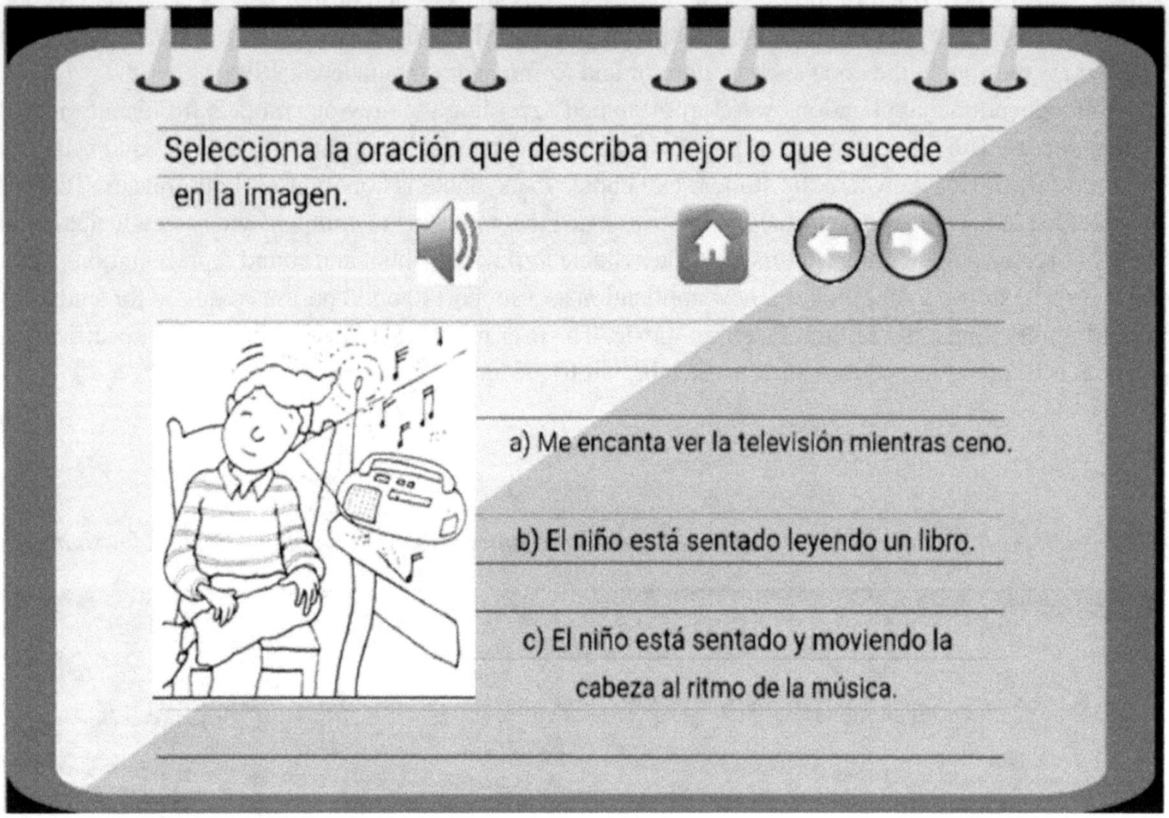

Table 3. Extract of usability questionnaire

Instructions. Answer the following questions based on your experience using the educational application. Scale: 1. Terrible 2. Poor 3. Improvable 4. Good 5. Excellent.					
Usability Aspects	**Scale**				
Efficiency	1	2	3	4	5
How do you evaluate the time when the application takes to respond an activity?				x	
How do you evaluate the time when the application takes to load the activities?					x
How do you evaluate the time when the application takes to start					x
Learnability					
Do you think the game is easy to learn?				x	
Does the application emphasize the answers for user?					x
Does the game facilitate the learning to final user?				x	
Are useful the pedagogical contents?					x
Is it easy for the child to remember what each of the application commands is for?				x	

Figure 11. A usability evaluation of an educational application by the child A

Figure 12. A usability evaluation of an educational application by the child B

Figure 13. A training session to use education applications by special education teachers

Evaluation Phase

The evaluation phase has the particular purpose of evaluating the usability and accessibility of educational applications.

Taking into account the usability test of Nielsen (Nielsen 1994), a usability questionnaire was developed in order to measure different usability aspects of educational application. Table 3 shows an extract of usability questionnaire that was applied to children, the questionnaire includes characteristic such as: usability, memory, effectiveness, misunderstanding, efficiency, content, satisfaction, accessibility and learnability.

Several sessions were planned together with the children and the USAER teachers in order to evaluate different elements such as: content, teaching activities, user requirements, user interface etc. The figure 11 shows one of session where the teacher observes the user tasks when the student A is using the developed educational application to build syllables. Teacher reads the directions required to develop the learning activity; the student can also listen every syllable using the sound of tablet. At the end of evaluation sessions, the teacher has passed to answer the usability questionnaire.

Launching Phase

In this final phase some training sessions has given to teachers and psycho-pedagogue participating in this case study. Some training sessions allow teachers (see figure 13) to access content in internet, use mobile devices, use ofs some educative resources (such as learning objects and educational applications) related to learning disability from a repository developed at Universidad Autónoma de Aguascalientes (UAA).

Next, the teachers have defined an instructional design selecting several educational applications as an educative support for help reading child with reading disability. Finally, the teachers have known the use of usability and accessibility evaluation of selected educational applications (see figure 14).

RESULTS

Quantitative methods were used during the case study to understand the different perspectives that USAER teachers have regarding technology, such as: interviews. Observation has also used to detect behaviors of interest in students and special education teachers, during training and collaborative interaction. To carry out the training, the necessary material was prepared, such as the classroom, computers, tablets, preparing the support material, planning the training, etc.

This section presents some results from the data analysis of evaluation phase; this analysis has carried out by the teacher, psycho-pedagogue and software designer.

Next two questions has posed in this case study as follows:

Figure 14. Teacher using an educational application designed to help children with dyslexia

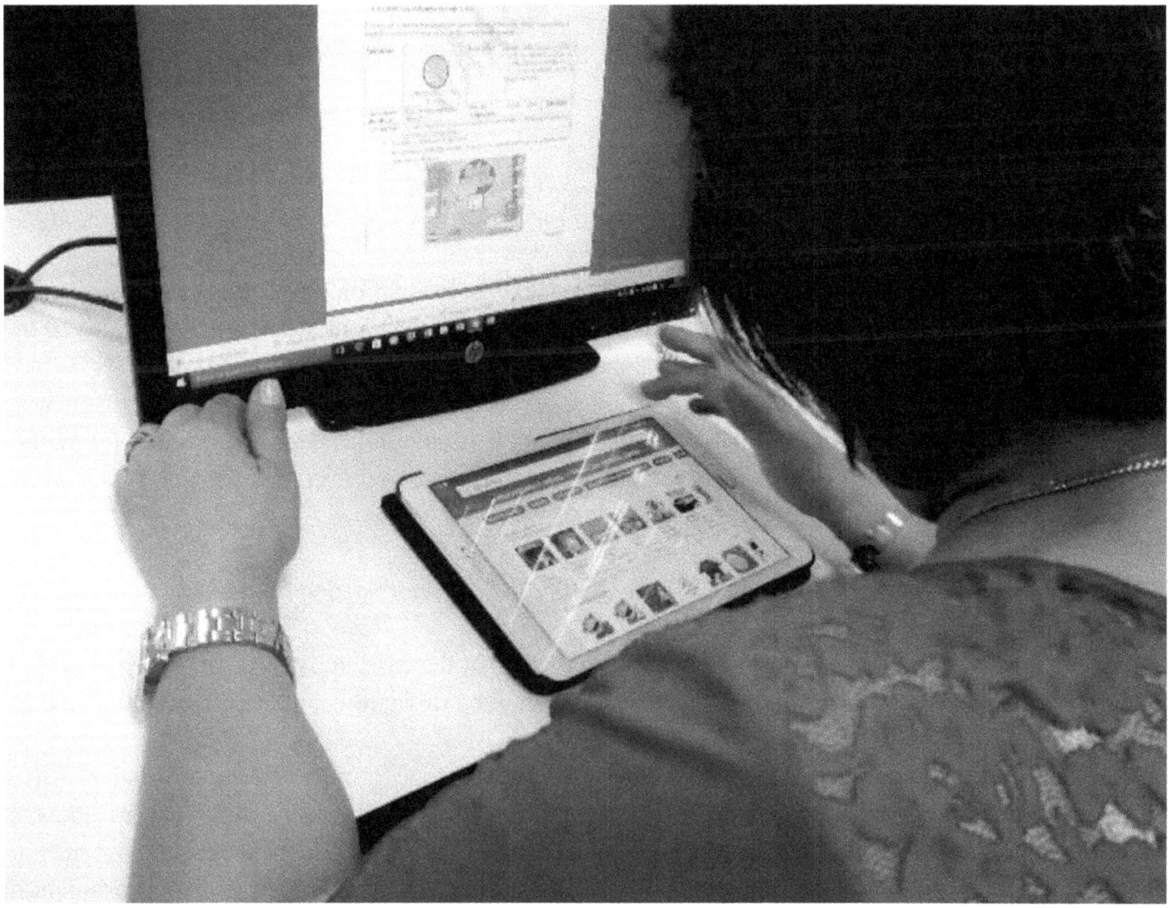

Figure 15. Usability evaluation of educational application designed to help building syllables for student A

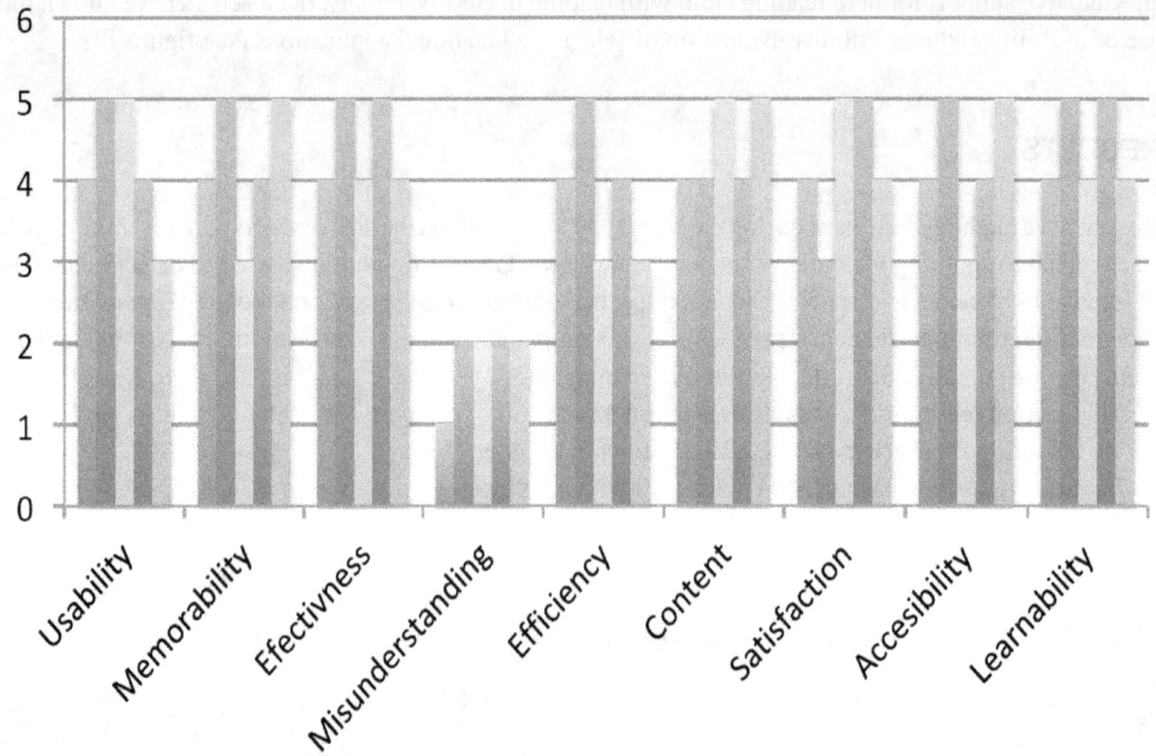

- *What is the usability level for the new educational application?*
- *Does any learning improvement was presented for the children participating in the case study?*

The first question related to usability test (Nielsen 1994) of evaluation phase, the answer is given by a representation under clustered column; the two educational applications were evaluated between the "Good" and "Excellent" according the questionnaire of Table 3.

Note, the educational application to help building phrases (see figure 16) has a better usability acceptation than the application to build syllables (figure 15), in particular it have excellent values for memorability, content, accessibility, learnability and efficiency; the rest of values they have an score of Good.

Concerning to second question:

- *Does any learning improvement was presented for the children participating in the case study?*

The answer is positive to this question because at the end of the case study some improvements were identified. Here some common improvements in the following difficulties: memory, reasoning and attention.

The comparative evolution in terms of a radar representation of figure 17 where the student A has some improvement in memory, reasoning and attention, social and cognitive skills. This student A requires to continue to work other educational applications recommended by the teachers in order to reduce much more the dyslexia troubles. The figure 18 shows the student B has some improvement in

Figure 16. Usability evaluation of educational application designed to help building phrases for student B

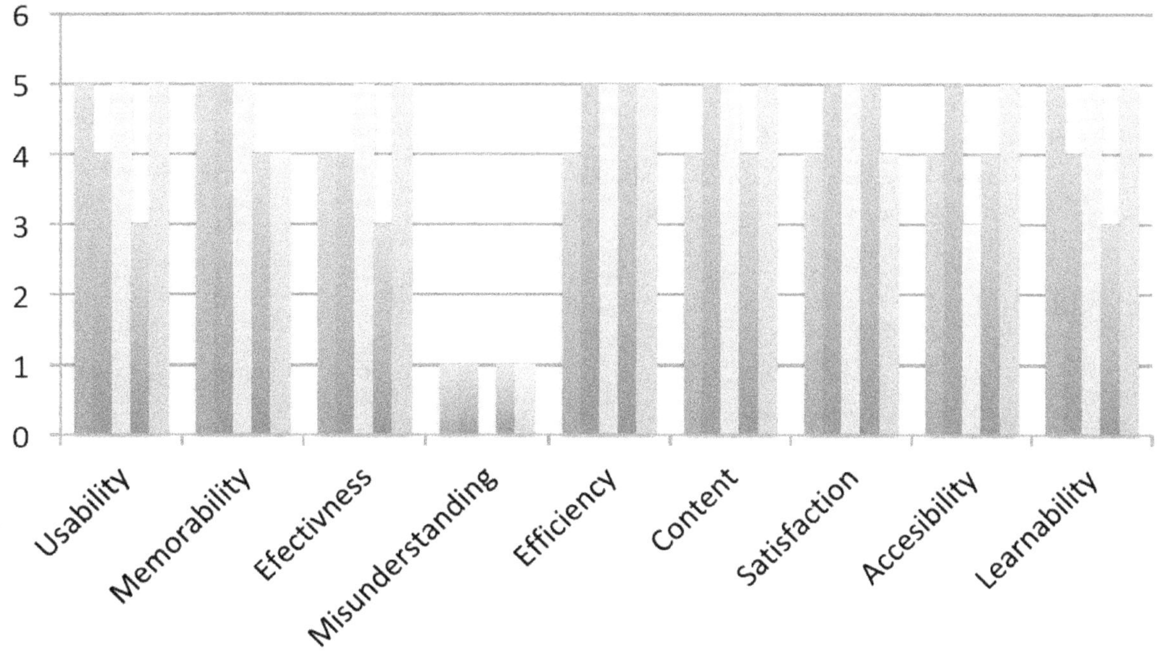

Figure 17. Comparative radar chart related to student A

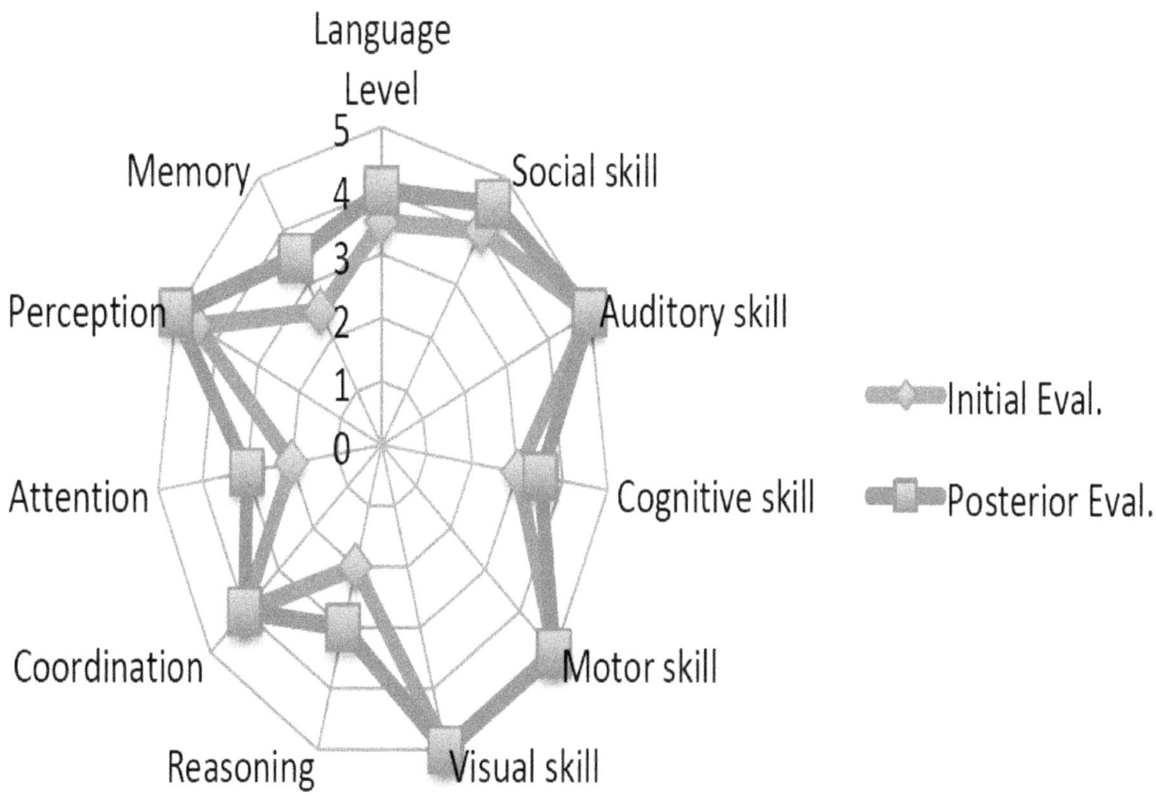

Figure 18. Comparative radar chart related to student B

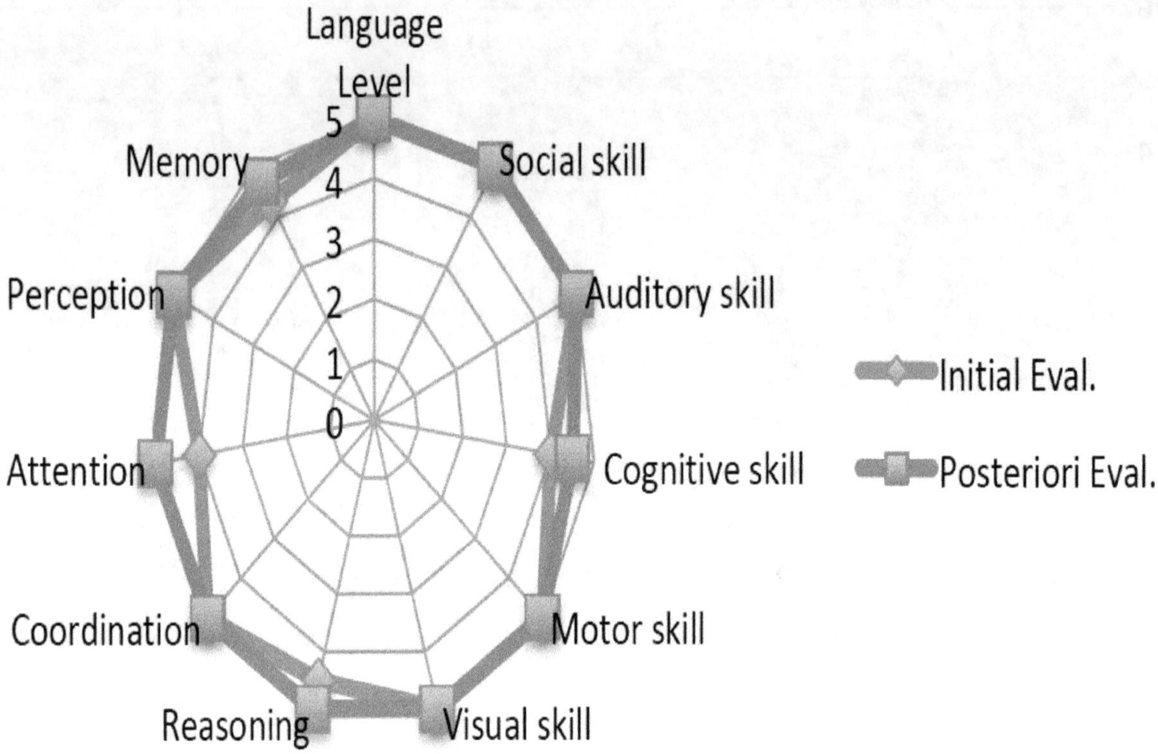

memory, reasoning and attention and cognitive skills. It is possible to say the educational application build phrases could help to student B to mitigate the dyslexia trouble. According the teacher of UR, this student has passed to next level in order to start to read at alphabetical level at elementary school.

CONCLUSION

Current work preconizes the children at elementary school can take advantages of certain amount of educational applications as complementary support for learning activities, then children with learning disabilities could require a larger diversity of these kind of resources in order to support the acquisition of knowledge.

A software process model of figure is proposed here in order to design, develop and evaluate educational applications that support dyslexia. The process helps to identify the reading skill levels of children, select educative resources according their skills identified as basic, intermediate and advanced level. It is possible to say that the process is also useful for teachers to identify different aspects to evaluate in the child progress of their activities with the use of interactive applications where children can learn in a ludic manner. The software process model can be identified with the following characteristics:

- **Iterative**: The process model has the flexibility to perform as many iterations of the process as desired, the iteration in a model allows a temporal application to occur with each iteration of the process, until attain the final version of the educational application
- **User-Centered Design:** The process model incorporates in the phases the participation of teachers and end-users, in this way, in the early stages of the process model (analysis and design) the participation of teachers is encouraged to cover the children with dyslexia learning needs, and in later stages (prototyping and evaluation) verify that these needs have considered.
- Best Practices for developing educative applications are identified to support learning difficulties related to dyslexia. Best practices respond to a specific learning related to dyslexia.
- **Training for Teachers**: Training course for the teachers can offer useful information about the use of new educational applications and it is space to answer questions in case of doubt. Whit this is more likely that the educational application will be integrated as an effective educational resource.

Finally, as future work is considered to use the proposed process model to other learning disability, such as dyscalculia, dysgraphia and attention deficit disorder with hyperactivity. It is also considered to extend the proposed model integrating parental requirements (Zosh et al. 2018). Other initiative as future work is the user experiences design incorporating the gratification techniques using tangible user interface in particular to support reading, mathematics and writing skills for children with learning disability at elementary school.

REFERENCES

Antognazza, M. P., & González, M. (2011). The dyslexic child and his educational enviroment perceptions and representations on the dyslexia. Ciencias Psicológicas, (2), 193-200.

Antonenko, P., Dawson, K., & Sahay, S. (2016). A Framework for aligning needs, abilities and affordances to inform design and practice of educational technologies. *British Journal of Educational Technology*, *48*(4), 916–927. doi:10.1111/bjet.12466

Bergin, J., Eckstein, J., Manns, M., Sharp, H., Marquardt, K., Chandler, K., … Wallingford, E. (2012). Pedagogical Patterns: Advice For Educators. CreateSpace.

Bery, Ch., & Randy, W. (2005). Educational Games: A Technique to accelerate the acquisition of reading skills of children with learning disabilities. *International Journal of Special Education*, *2*(20), 66–72.

Chelkowski, L., Yan, Z., & Asaro-Saddler, K. (2019). The use of mobile devices with students with disabilities: A literature review. *Preventing School Failure*, *63*(3), 277–295. doi:10.1080/1045988X.2019.1591336

Ciullo, S., Ely, E., McKenna, J. W., Alves, K., & Kennedy, J. K. (2018). *Reading Instruction for Students With Learning Disabilities in Grades 4 and 5: An Observation Study*. SAGE Publications Inc.

Cook, L., & Dakin, K. (2007). *Basic Facts About DYSLEXIA & Other Reading Problems*. International Dyslexia Association.

Dore, R.A., Shirilla, M., Hopkins, E., Collins, M., Scott, M., & Schatz, J. (2019). Education in the app store: using a mobile game to support US preschoolers' vocabulary learning. *Journal of Children and Media*, 1-20.

Fawcett, A., & Nicolson, R. (2016). *Test para la detección de la dislexia en niños (DST-J). 4ta. Edición.* Madrid: TEA Ediciones.

Gamma, E., Helm, R., Vlissides, J., & Johnson, R. (1995). *Design Patterns: Elements of Reusable Object-Oriented Software*. Addison-Wesley Proffessional Computing Series.

Gómez, L. (2008). El desarrollo de la competencia lectora en los primeros grados de primaria. *Revista Latinoamericana de Estudios Educativos (México)*, *18*(4), 95–126.

Granollers, T., Lorés, J., & Perdrix, F. (2003). Usability Engineering Process Model. *Integration with Software Engineering. Proceeding HCI-International.*

Herro, D., Kiger, D., & Owens, C. (2013). Mobile technology: Case-Based Suggestions for Classroom Integration and Teacher Educators. *Journal of Digital Learning in Teacher Education*, *30*(1), 30–40. do i:10.1080/21532974.2013.10784723

Kangas, E. and Kinnunen, T. (2005). Applying user-centered design to mobile application development. *Communications of the ACM-Designing for the Mobile Device, 48*(7), 55-59.

Manca, M., & Paternò, F. (2014) Considering task pre-conditions in model-based user interface design and generation. *Proceedings ACM SIGCHI Symposium on Engineering Interactive*, 149-154. 10.1145/2607023.2610283

Martínez, A. (2009). El diseño instruccional en la educación a distancia. Un acercamiento a los Modelos. *Apertura Review, 9*(10), 104-119.

Mize, M., Bryant, D. P., & Bryant, B. R. (2019b). Teaching reading to students with learning disabilities: Effects of combined iPad-assisted and peer-assisted instruction on oral reading fluency performance. *Assistive Technology Journal*, *15*, 1–8. PMID:30640569

Mize, M., Park, Y., & Schramm-Possinger, M. (2019a). *Developing a Rubric for Evaluating Reading Applications for Learners With Reading Difficulties, Intervention in School and Clinic*. SAGE Publications Inc.

Nielsen, J. (1994). *Usability Engineering*. Academic Press.

Quispe, A., Bernal, C., & Salazar, G. (2017). Use of applications for children with learning dificulties. *CAMPUS Revista, 12*(23), 13-26.

Rodríguez, I. A., López, B. A., Mendez, Z. A., & García, Z. B. (2013). *Helping children with Intellectual Disability to understand healthy eating habits with an IPad based serious game. In Computer Games: AI, Animation* (pp. 169–173). Mobile: Interactive Multimedia, Educational & Serious Games.

SEP-Secretaria de Educación Pública. (2019). *Educación especial*. Retrieved from https://www.educacionespecial.sep.gob.mx/2016/index_disca.html

Sommerville, I. (2015). *Software Engineering* (10th ed.). Person Editorial.

Tamboer, P., Vorst, H. C., & Oort, F. J. (2016). Five Describing Factors of Dyslexia. *Journal of Learning Disabilities*, *49*(5), 466–483. doi:10.1177/0022219414558123 PMID:25398549

Turner, W., & Greaney, K. (2009). Defining Dyslexia. *Journal of Learning Disabilities*, *43*(3), 229–243. PMID:19834134

Uluyol, C., & Sahin, C. (2014). Elementary school teachers' ICT use in the classroom and their motivators for using ICT. *British Journal of Educational Technology*, *47*(1), 65–75. doi:10.1111/bjet.12220

USAER. (2019). *Instituto de Educacion del Estado de Aguascalientes*. Retrieved from http://www.iea.gob.mx/webiea/sistema_educativo/sistema_eduespecial.aspx

Zikl, P., Bartošová, I. K., Víšková, K. J., Havlíčková, K., Kučírková, A., Navrátilová, J., & Zetková, B. (2015). The possibilities of ICT use for compensation of difficulties with reading in pupils with dyslexia. *Procedia: Social and Behavioral Sciences*, *176*, 915–922. doi:10.1016/j.sbspro.2015.01.558

Zosh, M. J., Hirsh-Pasek, K., Hopkins, J. H., Jensen, H., Liu, C., Neale, D. S., ... Whitebread, D. (2018). Accessing the inaccessible: Redefining play as a spectrum, Journal. *Frontiers in Psychology*, 9.

ADDITIONAL READING

Begoña, G., Escofet, A., & Marimon, M. (2016). The design patterns as tools to guide the practice of teachers. *Revista Latinoamericana de Tecnología Educativa*, *15*(3), 11–25.

De Raffaele, C., Smith, S., & Gemikonakli, O. (2017). Enabling the Effective Teaching and Learning of Advanced Robotics in Higher Education using an Active TUI Framework. En *Proceedings of the 3rd Africa and Middle East Conference on Software Engineering* (7-12). Cairo, Egypt: ACM. 10.1145/3178298.3178299

Laurillard, D. (2012). Teaching as a Design Science: Building Pedagogical Patterns for Learning and Technology. British Journal of Educational Studies. *Taylor and Francis Editorial*, *60*(4), 448–450.

Madeira, J., Silva, C., Marcelino, L., & Ferreira, P. (2015). Assistive Mobile Applications for Dyslexia. *Procedia Computer Science*, *64*, 417–424. doi:10.1016/j.procs.2015.08.535

Mekar-Sari, I., Sulistiyo-Kusumo, D., & Sabariah-Kaniz, M. (2017). Analysis of Interaction Design Patterns on Drawing Application for Early Preschool Children using Inductive Approach (Case Study: ABC Coloring Book for Toddlers and Tracer-hand Writing Pattern Drawing Application). *Journal of Computational Science*, *13*(12), 728–734. doi:10.3844/jcssp.2017.728.734

KEY TERMS AND DEFINITIONS

Accessibility: Accessibility in the sense considered here refers to the design of products, devices, services, interactive system, or application so as to be usable by people with disabilities.

Dyslexia: Dyslexia is a learning disorder that affects your ability to read, spell, write, and speak. Kids who have it are often smart and hardworking, but they have trouble connecting the letters they see to the sounds those letters make.

Interaction Design Patterns: An interaction design pattern is a general repeatable solution to a commonly-occurring usability problem in interface design or interaction design. They specify interaction models that make it easier for users to understand an interface and accomplish their tasks.

Pedagogical Patterns: Deals with pedagogical problems regarding the practice of teaching and learning. s focus on practices that have been thoroughly tested and proven useful by several people in different contexts rather than on new ideas.

Process Model: A software process model is a description of the sequence of activities carried out in an software engineering project, and the relative order of these activities. It provides a fixed generic framework that can be tailored to a specific project.

Usability: Usability is a quality attribute that assesses how easy user interfaces are to use. The word "usability" also refers to methods for improving ease-of-use during the design process.

User Task: A user task is used to model work that needs to be done by a human actor. When the process execution arrives at such a User Task, a new task is created in the task list of the user(s) or group(s) assigned to that task.

User-Centered Approach: This approach requires a design which is based upon an explicit understanding of users, tasks, and environments; is driven and refined by user-centered evaluation; and addresses the whole user experience. The process involves users throughout the design and development process, and it is iterative. And finally, the team includes multidisciplinary skills and perspectives.

Chapter 9
Analysis of the Use of VR and Haptic Devices in the Teaching-Learning Process for Blind People

Mitsari Lucio Alonso
Tecnológico Nacional de México IT Aguascalientes, Mexico

Hugo I. Medellin-Castillo
https://orcid.org/0000-0002-2827-9547
Universidad Autónoma de San Luis Potosí, Mexico

ABSTRACT

The inclusion of people with disabilities in society is an issue that is currently becoming relevant. This is why technology is in a constant struggle to develop tools that meet the needs of this sector of the population and with it fulfill this objective. One of these disabilities is blindness. Therefore, this chapter shows an analysis of the application of virtual reality (VR) and haptic devices as support tools in the teaching-learning of people with such disabilities through the study of various projects that have implement these technologies, obtaining the advantages and disadvantages offered by these resources. For this, an analysis is made from the point of view of accessibility that it presents as well as the approach of the user-centered design (UCD).

INTRODUCTION

Such has been the evolution that technology has experienced over the years that, currently, there are very few areas that are not yet under its influence. However, the goal is always the same: to make life easier for users. And with the passage of time, people who have a disability are given more opportunity, new strategies for accessibility and inclusion in society are sought.

DOI: 10.4018/978-1-7998-2325-4.ch009

Today, computers, video games, mobile phones and mobile devices instant access to information from around the world. There are a wide variety of options available to make information accessible to people with visual impairments, so many that choosing one can often seem daunting to someone new in the area of accessibility.

It is known that ninety percent of children with blindness or low vision do not go to school, and the unemployment rate among blind or low vision adults ranges between 75 and 90 percent. Experts believe that this situation is due, among other things, to the shortage of teaching equipment (SightFirst, 2010). The visual deficit translates into a reduction in the amount of information that the subject receives from the environment, restricting the number of keys offered by the natural environment and that are of great importance for the construction of the outside world. The specific educational needs presented by blind and low vision students are directly related to the implications that result from visual impairment.

The research on the accessibility of information for people with visual disabilities is wide, however, with the rapid pace that technology changes, it is important for researchers and developers, providing abstract solutions that do not depend on specific technologies, for Accessibility of all the presentation of information can be achieved in the future.

For example, smart glasses use a combination of artificial vision algorithms and cameras to record scenes in front of an individual, and then exaggerate certain details, such as increasing the contrast of the image, highlighting specific features or creating "representations of reality," depending on the user requirements.

The success of the culture of education lies in the inclusion of both non-blind and blind people. The importance of involving in educational materials aspects that allow blind people to perceive information, which is training and / or education, to the same extent as non-blind people, is equivalent to enabling the level of learning to be equitable.

Currently, traditional teaching and learning methods for blind people people are complex and inefficient because there are elements that require the perception and visualization of objects or images, so the resulting learning is minimal or low.

Multisensory stimulation is particularly useful for a person blind or weak visual because it allows them to raise awareness about the presence of different sensations, acquiring this information way through parts of his body. The development of technologies allowing to generate multisensory stimuli during the process of teaching-learning of blind or weak-sighted people, is therefore of the utmost importance. This involves exposing the student to situations requiring an activity of exploration, search for alternatives various, reflection on forms and conduct of personal and group activities (Medellin & Nieto, 2015). Most modern computer systems is considered the sight as the most important sense. However, the other senses also play an important role when it comes to virtual systems develop the closest to reality, and may even be more important than the view. The haptic system is fundamental in the adaptation of the individual in the world that surrounds him, that through him you get general information about the environment and the possibility to evaluate surfaces, sizes, shapes, textures and qualities of how hard, soft, viscous, consistency perception of temperature and pressure that can exert an object on the skin (Hidalgo & Mendez, 2000).

Touch development represents a complex psychology of development case, since it covers two functions, one driving and the other sensory or haptic. This last function is associated with the deployment of exploratory behaviour and develop perceptual skills related to the recognition of objects (Iñesta, 2002). Sensory perception, is the Foundation of knowledge for persons with low vision, blind or normal, given that all undergo the same process in their development.

Hav been proposed and developed various applications of virtual reality focused on auditory and tactile stimulation of blind and weak sighted people, and with the birth of devices haptic emerges the possibility of touch and feel objects in environments virtual, so it is possible to use virtual reality and haptic devices for teaching and learning of the blind and weak-sighted people; However arises the question "what so efficient is the combination of these technologies for this purpose?", therefore the objective of this chapter is to identify the advantages and disadvantages offered by these technologies through the analysis of various projects which have been developed systems for this purpose. For this, it is important to analyze the satisfaction and acceptance that these projects have generated users (students and teachers), the level of accessibility that these present as well as the level of inclusion to society that they achieve after being used. Different points are considered on the use of an approach based on user-centered design (UCD) and user experience.

BACKGROUND

People with low vision and blind people do not reach a normal development in its evolutionary process if not provoked a satisfactory situation for it to occur. The authors Hoolbrook and Koening (Holbrook & Koening, 2003) point out that "the academic success of students with visual impairment depends largely on access to training and teaching materials". Likewise Stratton (Stratton, 1990), says that in order to meet the student's needs and make the most of their skills, it is important to provide support and adaptations that are really necessary, considering that "an excessive adaptation separates the student your environment while a lack inhibits her learning". The two specified contributions are key to begin to enter the inclusive education of blind people (Organization, 2011). The probability that children with disabilities go to school is reduced; In addition, they have lower rates of retention and progress in the institutions (Nations, 2015). In this way, promoting the accessibility to education is the best way to change these statistics: "around the world, the accessibility varies from country to country, and there are different cultural values that come into play, as well as change the legal aspects from region to region, having an impact on the way in which accessibility is provided", said Scott Ready, and perform full inclusion in the classroom.

The participation of teachers and parents in the design process is crucial, but in order to understand and identify the needs and expectations of end users it is important to involve these users in the design process. All these needs of the blind and low vision students must be valued and considered at different levels of curricular implementation: from the curricular project to the classroom programming which includes the curricular adaptation made for the visually impaired student integrated in the group. The teacher is the key element in the educational inclusion process. A deep conviction is necessary that the participation of the student with visual impairment is possible in the school context. Hence the importance of being able to receive initial and ongoing training in evolutionary and educational aspects of visual impairment as well as inform you of the specific benefits and services complementary to your educational work. (Liébana, 2000).

"A lot of today's culture is based either in view or in the audio," says Nordvall (ZonaFrancaMX, 2015). "You are going to a concert or listen to the radio or going to the cinema", and if one of the senses involved is missing, it is compensated with other. Predominantly visual interfaces such as surfing the web are presented to blind people through screen readers who speak the text on a page, while television programs and movies can be viewed with subtitles for the deaf.

When users legally blind but with visual remains interact with video games with visual clues they take advantage of their rest of vision in order to achieve better results in the interaction. In the case of totally blind users do not have this possibility and it is necessary to provide all the information of the environment through other sensory channels such as touch and audio.

Thanks to haptic, a video game, for example, "could have a bit of vibration that indicates what the north is, so you don't have to look at a mini-map all the time," Nordvall adds (ZonaFrancaMX, 2015). None of these methods has been thoroughly explored, and the latter is especially conducive to attention. Users may have access to unique experiences that are only possible with haptic, Nordvall suggests or reinvent existing technologies. Meanwhile, it is a fact that this technology is maturing rapidly, and it is making its way into the mass market on a scale worthy of developer attention. Now what is needed is that the interfaces that need it be applied to catch up.

The term "haptic device" refers to those systems that allow the user to touch, feel or manipulate simulated objects in virtual environments and teleoperated systems. In other words, a haptic device / system adds the sense of touch to human-computer interaction, in this way if the pointer in the virtual environment is on a flat and solid surface, the haptic system will exert a force on the hand of the user such that he perceives it as the solid surface (Doñate, 2015).

According to Burdea (Burdea, 1996), haptic devices allow to obtain in general three types of feedback:

- Touch or skin feedback, which is useful for recognizing the texture, shape or even the temperature of virtual objects.
- Kinematic force feedback, which allows to recognize the weight, inertia and hardness of virtual objects, and where appropriate, collisions with other virtual objects.
- Feedback proprioceptive, which allows to capture the position and orientation of the virtual object in three-dimensional space.

Haptic interfaces are commonly used to enable the sense of touch and kinesthesia when manipulating virtual objects in an VR environment. However, these can also be used for remote manipulation of real systems. Haptic interfaces behave like a small robot that exchanges mechanical energy with the user. Although these interfaces could interact with any part of the human body, manual interfaces have been the most developed and used to date. There are currently several haptic devices on the market, including the Phantom Omni, Phantom Desktop de Sensable®, Falcon de Novint®, Virtuose de Haption® and Dexta Robotics.

Similar to computational graphing, computational haptic rendering provides the projection of objects to people in an interactive way, but with the difference that virtual objects can be touched or palpated. Haptic rendering is the general process of feeling or touching virtual objects, and includes tactile feedback to feel properties such as surface texture and shape, as well as kinesthetic feedback to feel the hardness, weight and inertia of objects.

As can be analyzed in previous paragraphs, the haptic goes hand in hand with another technology, virtual reality (VR), this allows to simulate a real environment through images, audio and their respective processing on a computer. The user can interact with this virtual environment in different degrees and ways, this being what defines the degree of immersion of said virtual environment.

In recent years, there has been a trend towards the use of virtual reality (VR) technologies for rehabilitation and disability support. This is partly due to lower costs and better access to technology, but also to the increase in the experience of researchers and virtual rehabilitation professionals. There are several definitions of VR, for example, Ellis (1994) defines it as "the interactive projection of improved virtual images and the use of non-visual modalities, such as haptic and auditory feedback, to make the user believe that he is interacting with real objects". Jayaram (Jayaram, Connacher, & Lyons, 1997) defines it as "the use of computer-generated synthetic environments and associated hardware to provide the user with the illusion of physical presence within that environment." The VR comprises the man-machine interface, which allows the user to immerse themselves in a 3D graphic simulation generated by the computer, and navigate and interact in it in real time, from a user-centered perspective (Pérez, 2011). A virtual environment or virtual reality is the technology which refers to schemes and interactive scenarios generated by computer in which users are involved, and where the information displayed is perceived as natural, although the settings are modified Depending on the user's movements (Ferrier, 2006). The fundamental concept behind the VR is the "immersion". The degree of immersion in a VR system refers to so deeply the user is sensory involved in the virtual environment, i.e., that you can both see, hear, feel and even smell or taste the virtual objects. There are different levels of immersion; for example, at the highest level of immersion, the user would be completely insulated from the real world and would use the five senses (sight, hearing, touch, smell and taste) to interact with the virtual environment. To date there is no system of VR that allows a total immersion with all your senses.

Within Virtual Reality we can find everything, such as various types of glasses, a host of leading applications and different types of devices for sensory channels other than the eyes. And, that is, the really immersive virtual reality cannot focus only on the view.

With devices such as Phantom Omni and Novint Falcon, which deliver great feedback to the user in their interaction with virtual objects, surfaces, objects and graphics can be represented, which are recognized by blind users thanks to the information transmitted by them (The global disability crisis, 2017). Another use of these devices is the representation of virtual spaces as training blind users to perform an increasingly autonomous navigation in the real environment. Through the Phantom Omni and Novint Falcon the user receives haptic feedback from the virtual environment, with which he can recognize objects, walls and corridors, managing to generate a mental map of the space traveled (Organization, 2011).

VR AND HAPTIC DEVICES IN THE PROCESS OF TEACHING-LEARNING

Analysis of Similar Projects

For some years now have been proposed and developed various projects to support the teaching and learning of blind and weak sighted people, some of them are mentioned below, through which different characteristics are analyzed which they are both in their development and in their application.

Nian-feng y Li-rong (Nian-Feng, 2011) made a proposal aimed at the translation of text in braille to Chinese characters, a model that could be extrapolated to any other language. Experiments showed that the methods described in this document can identify and remove effectively the Braille and, finally, to translate it into Chinese.

In the study by Smith y Smothers (Smith & Smothers, 2012) the translation of mathematical graphics was evaluated to Braille. The study was conducted with 598 graphics from data obtained of 10 books of mathematics. The researchers validated the results through comparative analysis of tactile graphics.

Figure 1 . Evaluation with a blind person using a Braille learning haptic device
Source: (Medellin, Gallegos, & Espinoza, 2015).

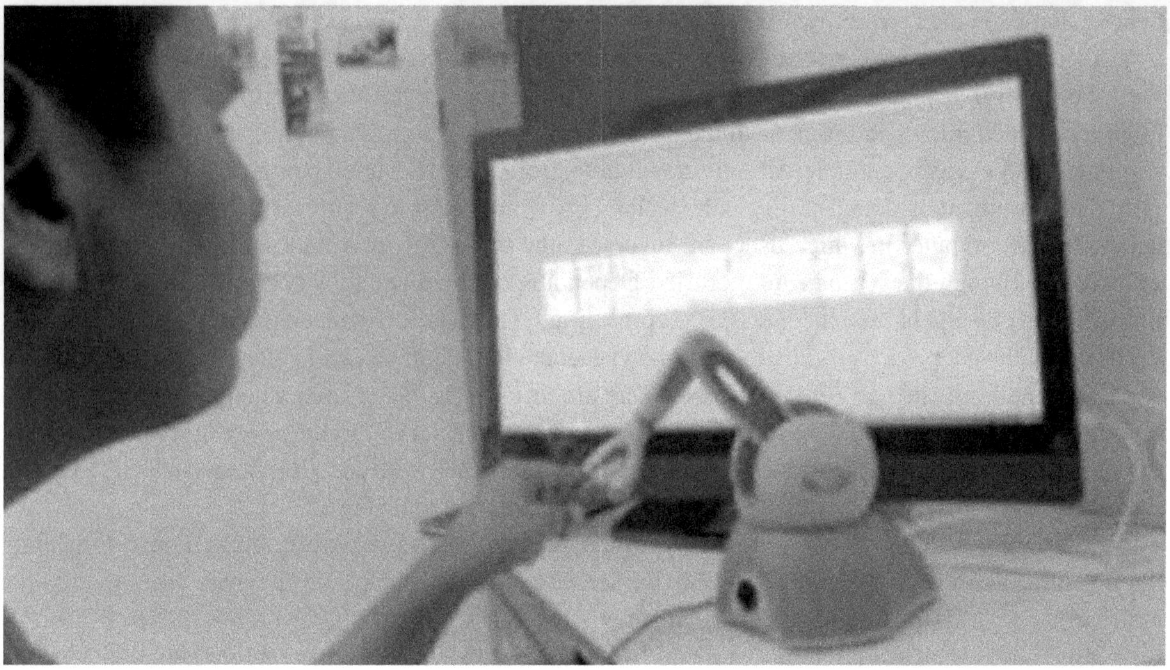

In another project, a new computer system based on the use of virtual reality technologies and haptic systems was proposed and developed. The main function of the proposed system shows different Braille texts for 3D objects, so that the user (blind person) can touch and feel them virtually using a haptic device. Virtual Braille texts are represented by sets of 3D tabs corresponding to the letters of the alphabet; Each letter is a 3D tab with embossed edges and dots according to the Braille system. The results of the system evaluation tests have demonstrated the functionality and usefulness of the new system as an effective teaching and learning tool for the Braille system process (Medellin, Gallegos, & Espinoza, 2015). Figure 1 shows a blind person using the system.

The Haptic Assistance System (HAT) proposed by Kim et al. (Kim, Collins, Bulmer, Sharma, & & Mayrose, 2016) consists of a workstation's feedback for the transfer and the improvement of handwriting. This is the first handwriting training system whose ease of use was tested in education classrooms of a local school district. A comparative study was conducted on the writing performance of twenty participants grouped into four categories according to the type of education (special vs. typical) and haptic devices (Phantom Omni ™ vs. Novint Falcon ™). As a result, it was observed that children quickly adapted to the system. The HAT system can play an important role in school programs, not only to improve handwriting skills, but also for learning various pencil-based activities. For example, it can be used for teaching an art of writing, such as cursive writing, a skill that is rapidly disappearing from schools in the United States (Rizzo, 2012)

Gómez et al. (Gomez, Bologna, & Pun, 2012) created an interface for the improvement of spatial perception and intelligibility for blind users through audio and touch signals. The core part of this interface was the coding of color and depth in sounds of musical instruments, which provides a spatial image of the environment, the limits and obstacles. This allowed blind people selectively explore environments, explore, and develop custom navigation strategies.

Petridou et al. (Petridou, Blanchfield, Alabadi, & Brailsford, 2011) describes the development of a framework for a set of educational feedback design so blind students can practice and learn about 3D free-space objects. Ultimately, this is a step in the process of developing games that help blind students learn more complex mathematical concepts that seem to need a visual understanding, such as geometry and graphics. The design of this game was derived from the expectations and needs of end users. The ultimate goal was to use the same channel used in real objects haptic exploration. A UCD approach is used to prepare a detailed specification of the virtual learning environment (VLE) and development of prototype revision using Novint Falcon. In this work the results of experiments are presented with visually impaired users, as well as interviews with these users, their parents and teachers to establish the framework of design. We discuss the first results obtained from the phase of testing in the handling and recognition of 3D geometric primitives by a focus group and highlights the improvements that must be made.

Lucio (Lucio, Juárez, & Medellín, 2015) developed a learning environment of different areas of study including art, biology and mathematics, among others. This system allows the user to interact with various 3D virtual models, being able to touch and feel through the support of a haptic device, which allows the person to create some idea of what the real object is in terms of shape, strength and texture. The system process is based on the activation of the haptic system and the loading of a 3D model from the menu, as well as the different current configuration options for interaction with it, the appreciation of its shape, texture, hardness and strength present from the movement of the cursor along the model.

The system allows loading and displaying 3D models in various formats for analysis and exploration through the use of the haptic system to obtain information regarding shape, texture and strength. However, no real people were tested, so the final results are unknown.

Figure 2 shows the use of the haptic device and one of the models used for the teaching of Art.

Simonnet and his team (Simonnet, Guinard, & Tisseau, 2006) developed a study on the use of software that implements an audio and haptic navigation system using the Phantom Omni, which was effective in training blind people in the generation of ship route itineraries, through the use of haptic strategies in order to build representations of spaces using maps. Georgios (Georgios, Tzovaras, Moustakidis, & Strintzis, 2004) developed an interactive virtual reality tool integrating Phantom Omni and CyberGrasp (virtual glove) that allows blind users to study and interact with various virtual objects specially designed for that purpose.

Gómez et al. (Gomez, Bologna, & Pun, 2012) created an interface for the improvement of spatial perception and intelligibility for blind users through audio and touch signals. The core part of this interface was the coding of color and depth in sounds of musical instruments, which provides a spatial image of the environment, the limits and obstacles. It was also observed that the user tends to get lost within the virtual environment by having all the degrees of freedom available in the space (6 degrees of freedom). In fact, the participating blind into his comments suggested to restrict movement of the haptic device to only the plane where is reading the text or touching any object; This in order to reduce the times of reading and recognition. General comments provided by participants was very positive. First of all it is considered that the system has great potential as a tool for teaching and learning.

Audiopolis is a video game based on audio and haptic whose purpose is to improve the skills of blind users. Audiopolis represents virtually a fictional open navigation environment in the city for a blind apprentice. The video game is developed in the first person, where the user can move freely through space,

Figure 2. Project design with haptic device and VR a) 3D model of "Emperor Augustus" applying Coulomb effect, b) System hardware
Source (Lucio, Juárez, & Medellin, 2015).

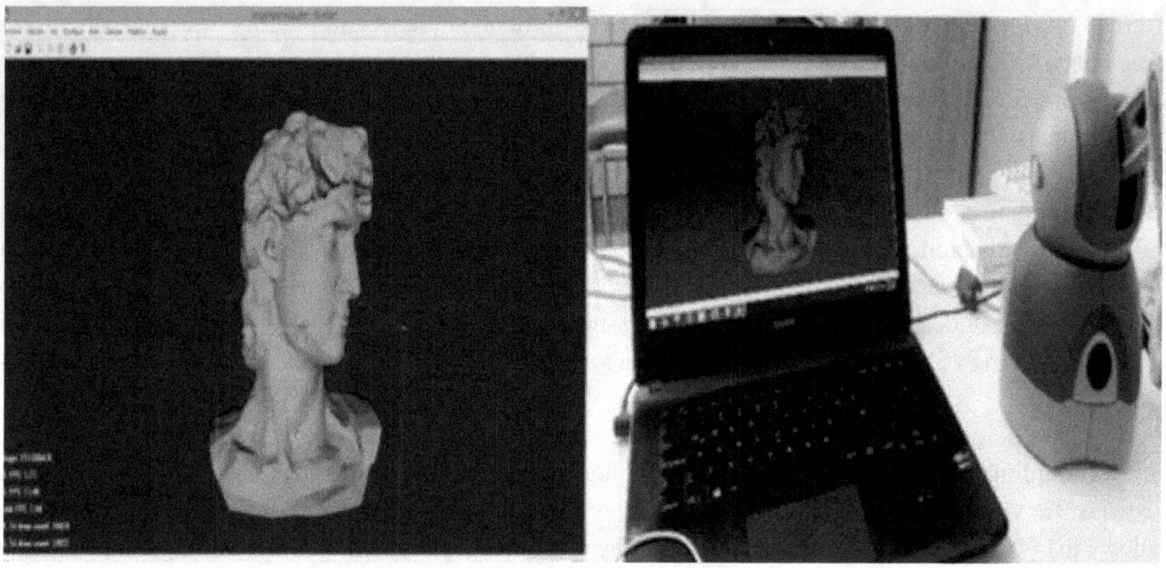

being able to move forward, backward and turn, recognizing either auditively and / or haptically, the different surfaces on which he moves and the different obstacles with those he meets. This was designed so that the user can move independently and get to know the entire map according to established routes. The sample obtained a satisfactory performance in the sizing tasks, achieving an average of over 90%. In general, the good development of proposed activities prepared apprentices for the application of cognitive tasks. Then, throughout the development of Cognitive Tasks, the percentage of achievement remained high and homogeneous (between 78% and 85%). The trainees were able to create new strategies to solve displacement problems at the virtual level (Sánchez, Espinoza, & De Borba Campos, 2014).

The Spanish company NeuroDigital (NeuroDigital, 2018), in collaboration with the multinational Geometry and the Czech Leontinka Foundation, it has developed an experience that allows people with low visibility to enjoy art with all five senses. What differentiates this project from its partners is not to resort to the traditional virtual reality helmet. On this occasion, the use of special gloves with haptic reaction provided the subject with the ability to touch works of art with their own hands. Although both not included the same physical space. Through a complex system of sensors around the interior of the glove, whose function is to capture the movements of the hand and then control them to the digital universe. Once this process is completed, the system reproduces vibrations that give the user the session to be able to touch the elements. . In this way, a blind person can feel in the air the recreation in three dimensions, while the technology installed in the gloves allows him to distinguish all the details of the sculpture. In figure 3 you can see the example of using this technology with a blind person, you can see that he has the gloves on while in the back there is a monitor where you can see the element that simulates the user being playing.

Another device of equal purpose and scope is e-Glance (e-Glance, 2016), an augmented reality system that gives blind people a mental image of the space around them. All this, from a virtual map that is accessed from the mobile phone. This technique is known as typhlotechnology and is based on the use

Figure 3. Example of use of the "Touching masterpiece" system

of a cognitive, sensitive and proximity interface that allows the patient to direct their attention to distant points and notice the presence of all those obstacles present around them.

Braille EDGE 40 (Hims, 2019) is not only the most reliable and high-performance upgradeable Braille display, but also helps you manage your daily activities. Create and save notes, or read books and documents with the notebook. It allows to program and remember important dates. Braille EDGE 40 contains 2 four-way navigation keys and 8 function keys (Escape, Tab, Control, Alt, Shift, Insert, Windows and Applications) that combine the convenience of entering Braille text with the intuitive functionality of a keyboard PC.

From a different perspective, there is The Dot Watch (Nobbot, 2019), the world's first smart watch based on the braille system, so that blind people can enjoy all the advantages offered by these wearables. This allows smartphone users (Android and iPhone) to receive and view their notifications on the smart watch in Braille. Other features are: battery level, bluetooth connection with the mobile, alarm, stopwatch and timer, time, GPS indications, among others.

Microsoft created a virtual reality system that allows blind people to interact with virtual reality objects through a cane. The device allows not only to detect the collision with objects, but also to distinguish objects and surfaces of different types through vibration and sound. The system consists of a metal rod attached to the belt, and a cane that is attached to it at the end but that can move freely along the rod. The cane is equipped with a vibration motor and a sensor that controls the position of the cane in relation to the virtual reality helmet. In addition, there is a brake installed at the base of the rod, which can stop its horizontal movement.

The user walks through the room and moves the cane to the left and right, which in virtual reality is much longer. When the cane collides with a virtual object, the brake stops the movement of the rod and, therefore, of the cane, and creates a real collision sensation. In addition, the engine in the cane produces a vibration, and the speakers in the helmet produce a sound that corresponds to a specific object. For example, the sound of a blow with a garbage can differs from the sound of a blow on the floor. In addition, the system can create a different tactile response for different surfaces (Kopiev, 2019).

Smartphones are also a great help in the daily life of people with visual disabilities. Applications such as Text Detective or Prizmo scan texts, business cards, menus or package labels and read it aloud through the VoiceOver (iPhone) or TalkBack (Android) function (Therapy, 2019).

The ONCE Digital Book Manager (GOLD) enables the download and accessible management of digital books in Daisy format. This system allows you to scroll through the content by chapters, subchapters, pages or even search for specific words. That is, it goes far beyond the traditional audiobook (Barrio, 2019).

As it can be observed, more and more work is being carried out in the development of support technology for blind people, both for the development of learning and for a correction inclusion to society, in addition there are other tools whose objective is to achieve the partial or total recovery of people.

Advantages of the Use of VR and Haptic Devices in the Process of Teaching-Learning for Blind People

Analyzed several investigations involved in the subject, a series of advantages have been identified that are obtained with the implementation of VR technologies and haptic devices in the teaching and learning process in people with visual disabilities, before, during and after use.

- Numerous studies have witnessed the ability of blind people to navigate complex environments
- The use of these technologies enables revolutionize various methods of teaching and learning and check that while the sense of sight can be considered as the most important on an issue of this magnitude it is learning, can be supplemented with the support of other senses that also manage to provide relevant information, in this case it was touch
- When blind and low vision people begin to receive services on a continuous basis, they have the opportunity and the necessary skills to participate fully in and contribute to society
- Interaction with multimodal interface offers a new experience for end-users
- A series of experiments have been carried out to determine the ease of use of the interface and compare its performance to that of a traditional screen reader. The results have defined the advantages that the interface offers for the blind and visually impaired. This includes the intensification of the spatial perception of web page design and navigation to the elements on a page
- The user can obtain general information about the environment and the possibility of being able to evaluate surfaces, sizes, shapes, textures, consistency qualities such as hard, soft, viscous, temperature and pressure perception that an object can have. on the skin since students perceive real objects or models better, simple two-dimensional representations with very different elements, static figures, as well as figures that are not superimposed or with perspective

- Allows autonomy because fewer and fewer projects require the help of another personYou can work on objects and real-life situations
- It respects the rhythm of the user
- The integration of video games in education and learning has had a significant impact on the learning of children, helping to make learning an even more pleasant experience
- The size of some of the devices are so small that portability is allowed
- The use of video games allow a better user experience
- The ease of use allows fast learning
- The connection you get with virtual reality is deeper and motivates students to learn more about a particular topic through their own means by directing their attention to other activities.
- By implementing the game as a way of learning in children, it allows them to learn faster and without knowing what they are learning
- Being a specific sector of the population, a study is made for a correct UCD
- Social inclusion is always a pressing objective in the development of these projects
- The implementation can be done through previously developed devices with another objective such as video game consoles

Disadvantage of the Use of RV and Haptic Devices in the Process of Teaching-Learning for Blind People

- Like any project, the implementation of these technologies for the purpose of teaching blind people also presents disadvantages, although over time these are reduced, a few are mentioned below:
- There are different types and levels of blindness, so it becomes difficult to create general or standard technology for this sector of the population.
- When it is desired to invent a new device, the manufacturing process can be slow
- In some cases the costs can be high and not very affordable
- An electronic device is needed for this to work (it is not autonomous)
- Some models are not small and are heavy
- The user may become confused to the point of not distinguishing the real from the fictitious
- May cause physical problems or discomfort in some users
- They fail to implement actions of total accessibility
- There are devices that can only be used through public or private institutions
- VR is becoming increasingly common, but programmers are still dealing with how to interact with virtual environments.

SOLUTIONS AND RECOMMENDATIONS

It has been suggested that immersion in virtual reality (VR) technology allows the construction of knowledge and, thus, provides an alternative to the educational process. Multi-sensory VR technology is very well suited to the needs of the sciences that require a higher level of visualization and haptic interaction, which refers to the physical interactions with the virtual environments (VEs) which can be coupled with other sensory modalities such as vision and hearing, and is associated with other channels such as the olfactory feedback.

Improve the information touch the consumer technology will be crucial to the efforts to reduce the gap between all that is physical and tangible, and everything else is digital and virtual.

The specific educational needs presented by blind and low vision students are directly related to the implications that result from visual impairment.

When you want to develop technology for these people it is very important to be aware of their needs for a correct UCD, below are some general action recommendations that will have to be taken into account when contacting these users:

- It is essential, to establish with him a link from the personal and not from the deficit. This gives you permission to differentiate and integrate your own feelings.
- Do not deny your limitations. Ask about your needs. If you want to know something about him, you should ask him directly
- Say things clearly. Do not avoid words related to vision
- In short, to know the characteristics of this deficit, to act naturally and give the student the image of a valuable person in himself, above his deficiency

Observe with attention and detail the way in which you perform the activities, this in order to seek to emulate these actions through the device or devices that you will later use

Take into account which are the channels to be able to obtain information from the world in which they live and with which they have to interact and consequently how they should obtain the maximum use from them

Know the student's visual situation and its implications from an educational and functional point of view

Once the development of the environment and the devices is started, a multisensory stimulation must be required, which allows and favors the use of all the senses, especially touch and hearing.

- Work on real life objects and situations
- Verbalize all situations using a specific language

It is important to keep in mind that the user perceives real objects or models better, simple two-dimensional representations with very different elements, static figures, figures that are not superimposed or with perspective.

In the process of testing and / or implementation you should be allowed autonomy. Do not help if you do not need it. Make him see his real possibilities.

- Anticipate some facts verbally, especially if the environment is poorly understood. Avoid surprises.
- Give additional information in cases where the user cannot perceive the significant data by himself.
- Have control over the noise level in the environment as well as the sounds and music in case these are used
- Keep in mind that haptic perception is analytical, so the student needs more time than is needed visually to mentally compose globality, once he has touched the object in a successive and organized way; Something that needs training.

FUTURE RESEARCH DIRECTIONS

This analysis can derive future projects such as the redesign of any of these projects or the generalization of characteristics for the creation of patterns, standards or design guides. As well as the creation of new tools to support blind people, making a complete analysis of needs and carrying out an approach based on the UCD.

And finally, it is desired to carry out an analysis of the technologies developed to achieve the total or partial recovery of sight and the way in which these can be complemented with the technologies previously analyzed in this chapter.

CONCLUSION

It should be noted that in most investigations the results of the evaluation have been positive, demonstrating not only the need for this type of research, but also the relevance of the specific proposals presented, however, many years have passed Of those rudimentary innovations, we are now more aware that haptic technology could be the missing piece of the puzzle in the virtual reality space. The problem is that virtual reality now looks and sounds so real that it instinctively feels as if it were physically in the virtual space, which means that the user wants to touch things and feel that they touch it. But without haptic (or a wide variety of accessories and careful planning), none of these options is possible.

The haptic is emerging as the next major trend in humanity's interactions with the digital world. With it you can put surround sound effects on the headphones and record audio in high fidelity with the help of smartphones. Similarly, you can touch, pinch and zoom in everything that appears on the screen. However, this still feels flat and lifeless because a very small effort has been made in this branch, leaving a very large hole, especially if you keep in mind that the human body has a highly sophisticated ability to recognize and respond to textures, the vibrations and all kinds of external forces that bind to the receptors in our sensory system.

Technology continues to advance at a rapid pace and one of its biggest challenges is the development of tools that help in the inclusion of people with visual disabilities in society.

As we could see, the combination of these technologies has many advantages both in use and in development, but it also has disadvantages in which designers and creators of technology must work, especially in the field of accessibility.

as mentioned above, there are many advances but much remains to be done; possibly in a short time the total immersion will be achieved and with it the support not only for the blind but for people who have some other disability, both physical and mental.

ACKNOWLEDGMENT

First author gratefully acknowledge CONACyT (Consejo Nacional de Ciencia y Tecnología, Mexico) for financial supporting her MSc studies.

REFERENCES

Barrio, C. (2019). *Con discapacidad visual, pero con visión de futuro*. Retrieved from https://www.nobbot.com/personas/tecnologia-ciegos-apps-herramientas/

Burdea, G. (1996). *Force and touch feedback for virtual reality*. New York: John Wiley & Sons, Inc.

Doñate, M. (2015). Interfaces Hápticos. Aplicaciones en entornos virtuales. e-Glance. *e-Glance*. Retrieved from e-Glance: http://eglance.ctb.upm.es/es/eglance/

Ellis, S. R. (1994). What are virtual environments? *IEEE Computer Graphics and Applications*, *14*(1), 17–22. doi:10.1109/38.250914 PMID:7757252

Ferrier, E. (2006). Multi-modal virtual environments for education with haptic and olfactory feedback. *Virtual Reality (Waltham Cross)*, 207–225.

Georgios, N., Tzovaras, D., Moustakidis, S., & Strintzis, M. (2004). Cybergrasp and PHANTOM integration: enhanced haptic access for visually impaired users. *SPECOM-2004*, 507-513.

Gomez, J., Bologna, G., & Pun, T. (2012). Spatial awareness and intelligibility for the blind: Audio-touch interfaces. *Human factors in computing systems*, 1529 – 1534.

Hidalgo, M., & Mendez, B. (2000). *Detección de Problemas de Aprendizaje*. San José, Costa Rica: Universidad Estatal a Distancia.

Hims. (2019). *Braille EDGE*. Retrieved from http://www.hims-inc.com/product/braille-edge-40/

Holbrook, M. C., & Koening, A. J. (2003). Foundations of education.: Vol. II. *Instructional Strategies for Teaching Children*. New York: AFB Press.

Iñesta, R. (2002). *Psicología del Aprendizaje*. El Manual Moderno.

Jayaram, S., Connacher, H., & Lyons, K. (1997). Virtual assembly using virtual reality techniques. *Computer Aided Design*, *29*(8), 575–584. doi:10.1016/S0010-4485(96)00094-2

Kim, Y.-S., Collins, M., Bulmer, W., Sharma, S., & Mayrose, J. (2016). Haptics Assisted Training (HAT) System for children's handwriting. *IEEE World Haptics Conference*, 6.

KopievG. (2019). *N+1*. Retrieved from https://nmas1.org/news/2018/02/16/realidadvirtual-ciegos

Liébana, M. (2000). *Aspectos evolutivos y educativos de la deficiencia visual*. Madrid: ONCE.

Lucio, M., Juárez, R., & Medellín, C. (2015). Desarrollo de Algoritmos de Manipulación e Interacción Háptica para la Enseñanza-Aprendizaje de personas con Discapacidad Visual. *Inducción a la Ciencia, la tecnología y la innovación en la UASLP*, 918-924.

Medellin, C., Gallegos, N., & Espinoza, C. (2015). Desarrollo de un sistema de realidad virtual asistido por dispositivos hápticos para la enseñanza-aprendizaje del sistema Braille. *Revista de Prototipos Tecnológicos*, *1*(1), 10–22.

NeuroDigital. (2018). *Touching Master Pieces*. Retrieved from https://touchingmasterpieces.com/

Nian-Feng, L.-R. (2011). A kind of Braille paper automatic marking system. *Conference on Mechatronic Science, Electric Engineering and Computer*. 10.1109/MEC.2011.6025553

Nobbot. (2019). *Dot Watch, el primer reloj inteligete en braille*. Retrieved from https://www.nobbot.com/general/dot-watch-braille/

Pérez, M. F. (2011). Presente y futuro de la tecnología de la realidad Virtual. *Revista Creatividad y Sociedad C/ Salud*, *15*(5).

Petridou, M., Blanchfield, P., Alabadi, R., & Brailsford, T. (2011). *User centred design and development of an educational force-feedback haptic game for blind students*. Academic Press.

Rizzo, J. (2012). Disappearing Act. *National Geographic*.

Sánchez, J., Espinoza, M., & De Borba Campos, M. (2014). *Videojuego Audio/Háptico para Desarrollar Habilidades de Navegación en Aprendices que son Ciegos*. Academic Press.

SightFirst. G. d. (2010). *Educación y rehabilitación para personas ciegas y con baja visión*. Retrieved from http://www.e-district.org/userfiles/357/file/Educaci%C3%B3n%20y%20rehabilitaci%C3%B3n%20para%20personas%20ciegas%20y%20con%20baja%20visi%C3%B3n.pdf

Simonnet, M., & Guinard, J.-Y., & Tisseau. (2006). Preliminary work for vocal and haptic navigation software for blind sailors. *6th International Conference on Disability, Virtual Reality and Associated Technologies, ICDVRAT*, 255-262. 10.1109/ICTTA.2006.1684489

Smith, D. W., & Smothers, S. M. (2012). The role and characteristics of tactile graphics in secondary mathematics and science textbooks in braille. *Journal of Visual Impairment & Blindness*, *106*(9), 543–554. doi:10.1177/0145482X1210600905

Stratton, J. (1990). The principle of test restrictive materials. *Journal of Visual Impairment & Blindness*, 3–5.

The global disability crisis. (2017). Retrieved from https://www.add.org.uk/why-disability/global-disability-crisis

Therapy, M. (2019). *Tecnología y apps accesibles que rompen las barreras de la discapacidad visual*. Retrieved from de https://www.mytherapyapp.com/es/blog/aplicaciones-tecnologia-accesible-discapadidad-visual

United Nations. (2015). *Global Status Report on Disability and Development*. Author.

World Health Organization. (2011). *World report on disability*. Retrieved from http://apps.who.int/iris/bitstream/10665/70670/1/WHO_NMH_VIP_11.01_eng.pdf

ZonaFrancaMX. (2015). *La revolución táctil llegó; la háptica se apunta como la próxima tendencia tecnológica*. Retrieved from https://zonafranca.mx/cultura-y-entretenimiento/la-revolucion-tactil-llego-la-haptica-se-apunta-como-la-proxima-tendencia-tecnologica

ADDITIONAL READING

Espinosa Castañeda, R. Y., & Medellín Castillo, H. I. (2014). Análisis Y Evaluación De La Generación De Iconos Mentales En Personas Invidentes A Partir De La Percepción Virtual Táctil Utilizando Realidad Virtual Y Sistemas Hápticos. *Icono*, *14*(12), 295–317. doi:10.7195/ri14.v12i2.695

Fuentes, R. (2003). Adaptaciones Curriculares Para Alumnos Con Baja Visión e Invidentes. *Enseñanza*, *21*, 275–298.

Raya, L. (2017) Dispositivos hápticos para ciegos. Retrieved from https://www.realovirtual.com/articulos/5043/dispositivos-hapticos-ciegos

Sánchez, J. (2007). User-Centered Technologies for Blind Children. *Human Technology Journal*, *45*(2), 96–122.

KEY TERMS AND DEFINITIONS

Accessibility: Possibility of accessing a certain thing or facility to do so.

Blindness: Disease that causes loss of vision in one or both eyes.

Braille System: It is a method of reading and writing for blind people based on an arrangement of raised dots that the blind person can touch or feel.

Haptics: Comes from the Greek word "haptesthai" which means to touch, or which is related to the sense of touch.

Immersion: Perception of being physically present in a non-physical world.

Tiflotechnology: A set of theories, knowledge, resources and techniques that enable the practical use of the technological knowledge applied to people who are blind or with low vision.

Touch: you can perceive through touch.

Section 2

Design, Assessment, and Redesign of Technology for Accessible Education

Chapter 10
Design Process for Accessible Virtual Reality Learning Environments:
A First Approach

Zeoli Antonio Maldonado
Tecnológico Nacional de México IT Aguascalientes, Mexico

ABSTRACT

Virtual reality has captured the attention of people. Since virtual reality has become more realistic, with the evolution of the technology like the innovation of smartphones, it has been more accessible for society, and many industries have begun research on the application of VR for training and for learning about certain specific topics as it allows reducing accidents and maximizes safety. Their use in the education industry has been best seen as a tool to complement certain issues that may be difficult to understand since it can allow one to virtually move to certain areas from safe areas. However, the development virtual environments is not fully specialized to implicitly include and promote learning, much less the consideration of people with disabilities. The main objective of this chapter is the presentation of a design process for the development of virtual learning environments that allows accessibility.

INTRODUCTION

New technologies like Virtual Reality (VR) bring us a new kind to explore digital content trough the user's interaction with the digital environment. VR offers the skill to explore a lot of world felt experiences without the need of leaving a safety place. VR is a technology that depends on audio, images and sensors mainly for the user's interaction with the virtual objects. These make it inaccessible to people with any impairments like visual or motor. The VR focus is the sensorial stimulation, but with people with impairment is difficult give them the complete experiences only with the tradition sensors, if have visual weakness, astigmatism, deafness, between others; for these kind, there is other ways to give the user the necessary stimulation for her VR experiences like smell, sense of touch by example.

DOI: 10.4018/978-1-7998-2325-4.ch010

The accessibility inside VR platforms is an issue that has been explored in some investigation areas. The education is a field that is exploring the development of applications to approach the great characteristics of VR to use it on learning environments. (Rosa, Laura, & Mauro, 2016). There are previous works that deal design process for virtual environments as topic. These previous researches pointed exist a strong relation between VR and Constructivism. The same nature of VR foments the use of Constructivism as educational theory in the learning that involve this technology. The accessibility in VR is one specific topic that is explored too. There are some VR guidelines that consider people with impairment. However, there is no design process for VR applications that includes both issues in question, from the promotion of learning through educational theories, to the consideration of techniques to provide an accessible application. It is because of this situation that it has been decided to develop a design process that helps integrate these two important points and that the process works harmoniously.

The aim of this chapter is providing an overview of an accessibility virtual reality learning design process, this design process has the propose of integrate educational theories like Constructivism and Cognitivism with user-centered design process, taking an emphasis about how include techniques for accessibility during the development of the virtual environment. The emphasis of the chapter will be describing the design process and explain how the components are important for the development of VR platforms. Also, to include and consider the impairment each phase and activity of the process show how to affront different impairments and implement a solution for them.

BACKGROUND

Virtual Reality technology is always associated with headsets and many kinds of inputs, which are needed for the interaction with the Virtual Environment (VEs). VEs are 3D scenes computer-generated and presented at the user on a screen, in the case of head mounted display (HMD), the screen is inside the VR's headset. VEs respond to movement and interaction with the user thought inputs like gloves, phones, game controllers, etc. These devices receive and send data between the environment and the user. This exchange of information made the illusion of interaction and generate sense of immersion and thanks this characteristic that Human Computer Interfaces for VR has become more and more adaptive and complete for the user. In the area of education, VR has become a topic recently discussed, both for institution education and for training (Laura & Michela, 2015)According to Freina and Ott, there are some investigations about rehabilitation of people with disabilities using VR applications.

The design of environments for these RV applications are mostly carried out through software development methodologies such as SCRUM, by following methodologies of this type that although they are capable of adapting to the required process and complying with the final product, they do not have approaches with the correct emphasis on users, and details could be found later like users who are not totally satisfied with the application since it does not cover their needs, such as from the perspective of view, the arrangement of objects in the virtual environment, the ease of interaction with objects necessary for the user. However, there are investigations that have carried out the development of processes so that the design of virtual environments is more complete, taking into account users and their needs, the presences of objects and their distributions throughout the scenario (Kaur, 1998). All this is possible with the proper integration of User-Centered Design (UCD) and Human-Computer Interaction (HCI).

Education is a complex issue to include in the development of applications, however, the application of a complete educational theory is not possible through the development of an application, so these are only used as a means to encourage learning that is according to the characteristics of the educational theory that it is proposed to use (Dale S. & Trish, 2000). According to certain characteristics that define RV, it is possible to determine what types of educational paradigms are easier to promote. In the case of the RV with its immersion qualities, its ease to simulate certain scenarios, its interaction of the user with the surrounding environment, it is possible to highlight that there are two educational paradigms that are compatible for its integration, the Constructivism (Huang & Liaw, 2018) and Cognitivism (Alvaro, Jose, & Victor, 2000). However, although it is possible to promote these educational paradigms through the use of this VR technology, it is necessary to provide the appropriate way to help it develop jointly with the proposed scenarios and its activities to be carried out for users within the virtual environment. Even if this inclusion can be carried out correctly in a design or development process, it would only be possible to help them be promoted in a certain proportion, since these include not only a way of carrying out actions or activities, but also consider psychological aspects, so the resulting applications are used as complementary tools of the study.

VR is a technology that is not widely researched, either for its current main entertainment industry or for the education industry. But in recent years VR research and development for learning has been carried out (Laura & Michela, 2015). Many methodologies have been carried out to work on the design and development of virtual environments (Kaur, 1998), and some methodologies for the development of virtual learning environments have subsequently appeared, however, many of these technologies focus directly on the field of development of software, therefore, most of its tasks specified in the process place special emphasis on how to perform good practices for software development adapted to the new Virtual Reality technology (Samperio, Arcega, Sanchez, & Navarrete, 2017). Now, with the popularity that VR has achieved, many have shown their interest in how to adapt development styles to make use of this in accessible education. Accessible education has been a subject that is constantly addressed by the UCD, UX and HCI, so it is not uncommon to think that the use of these branches techniques for accessible education can be well used in conjunction with RV to promote Learning and accessibility (Roberth, 2018).

MAIN FOCUS OF THE CHAPTER

Taking as a starting point the characteristics mentioned above regarding the current processes for the design of virtual learning environments that include accessibility as part of their measures during the tasks to be performed, we have noticed that there is no complete guideline about of how to carry out this process in an orderly manner. Therefore, this chapter presents a process for the design of virtual environments that facilitate both learning and accessibility. For the development of the design process for virtual learning environments, the User-Centered Design and Human-Computer Interaction techniques have been considered as the basis for achieving good designs. Using the techniques of UCD and HCI as a base will allow us to know in a more conscious way the true needs of our users in order to take into account the characteristics that should be included in our design of a virtual learning environment (Nadine, 2017). The use of these techniques helps to reduce development times, given that the early integration of the different characteristics that the user really needs is sought when making appropriate observations and bringing an order to the moment of obtaining objectives to be met. Although one of the issues for which many work teams are not using this type of techniques is because they find their integration complicated to their current style, and that they persist that they have to perform many more tasks before starting with the development of the application (Nadine, 2017). However, certainly including practices of this type can be difficult for teams that have become accustomed to software development without considering certain emphasis on which UCD focus, but in a cost-benefit relationship you can appreciate that including UCD techniques increases the time devoted to the analysis of user needs and the planning of a good design, but greatly reduces the time needed for development since the amounts of interactions for the correction of errors and characteristics that were not taken into account early (Izumi, Hiroko, Satoshi, & Masahiro, 2013).

Subsequently, the unique characteristics of the RV applications and their related concepts have been analyzed to be able to relate them to educational methodologies and in this way be able to ensure that following the fundamentals of the same technology and not neglecting its main characteristics, proper learning can be promoted to the users. However, can be users who suffer from a disability, whether visual or motor, and may not take advantage of certain features offered by VR technology. The methodologies mentioned in the previous section, including many of the methodologies not intended for the specific development of Virtual Reality Environments, do not have a section that helps implement support for this type of people with disabilities, therefore, it is important to highlight that one of the main features of the design process presented in this chapter tries to help solve this problem. For now, one of the most common practices in the work teams that carry out this type of VR applications is to use methodologies destined mainly for software development, although these include steps that suggest a previous planning to be able to take them to In a satisfactory manner, many times these work teams omit these work sections as it would mean extending the work time of the team. Therefore, the purpose of this chapter is to emphasize the need for a design process for these VR applications, and specify the work for the education and accessibility industry, providing easy-to-understand guides that do not require too much time to carry them out, but maintaining the integrity of a correct design process according to what the UCD techniques mention.

SOLUTIONS AND RECOMMENDATIONS

Currently the development of applications for virtual reality are being carried out through software development methodologies mostly, although there are some methodologies exclusively developed to perform work on this type of technologies. However, none of these options is highly targeted to the education industry, much less in the consideration of people with disabilities. As mentioned above, this chapter proposes as a solution a design process for learning environments in Virtual Reality. This design process has been developed taking into consideration the design guides for virtual reality environments (Microsoft Corporation, 2019), UCD and UX techniques, for its elaboration, and to include tools that allow the promotion of various educational paradigms such as Constructivism (Granja, 2015) and Cognitivism (Leiva, 2016). Certain activities have been determined that help us to implement tools within the Virtual Learning Environment that allow users with disabilities to be able to use the application that is currently being developed, this inclusion is done in various ways from the consideration of external devices that facilitate the use and interaction of the user with the environment, as well as virtual techniques to facilitate the understanding of the context of the activities in the proposed scenarios.

Table 1. Accessibility virtual learning environment design process

Phase	Stages	Activities
Conceptualization	User requirements	User Definition
		User Activities Definition
	Virtual Environment Conceptualization	Object Arrangement
Virtual Environment Design	Dynamic Modeling and Interactions	Agency Specification
		Navigation Mechanism and Interaction
	Low Fidelity Prototyping	Sketch VR
	Expert Evaluation	Score Checklist
		Evaluator's Notes
Design Implementation	High Fidelity Prototyping	Digital Prototyping
	User Evaluation	User perception
		Usability Study

The design process has been divided into three main phases, which in turn contain stages and activities as can be seen in Table 1, even in some recommendations are made of some specific tasks to support users who make use of this guide to Your carry out your design and have better references as to how to perform your work in an orderly and safe manner. Each corresponding part is explained in detail below.

Conceptualization Phase

The first phase to carry out our design of a learning environment for Virtual Reality is the conceptualization, this phase has the responsibility of carrying out the collection of data necessary for the general idea of how the design of the learning environment will be carried out.

In order to collect information in an organized and adequate manner, two stages have been established that consider the main aspects to be taken into account in order to elaborate the main idea of the design, taking into account the good design of the learning environment were divided into the categories of "User requirements" and "Virtual Environment Conceptualization", which are explained in more detail in their corresponding sections. This collection of information, is carried out mostly through observations of the real environment that you want to simulate in a virtual way, or the study of these real scenes, it is often possible that the scenarios that you want to simulate are difficult access or that use very expensive materials for which reason, simulation through RV is one of the most feasible solutions, to which to be able to correctly obtain information from these inaccessible or difficult to access scenarios, bibliographic research will be necessary instead of field observation.

User Requirements

During the User requirements stage, it is necessary to collect information about everything related to the user, that is, from their needs in accordance with the application that you want to prepare with Virtual Reality, to the characteristics that determine how to carry out their activities involved with learning and the physical characteristics that we want to be able to include in our design, considerations of use of the applications and some techniques that complement the possible lack of some sense in the user.. The user and everything related to this is too much information to collect, therefore, it has been divided into activities to organize correctly how to carry out this stage and consider everything relevant to the user.

User Definition

The definition of the users, one of the main sources of information that we need to be able to develop a good design is to determine what our target users will be, during this activity it will be determined who will be the users involved with the use of the virtual environment, determine their characteristics, meet their learning needs and develop their profiles According to the information that is observed of the user, their interests, what emotion is planned that the user has when using our design, what the design that is tried to elaborate would provide the user, among others.. These profiles are recommended to use the technique Person, since it contains the standards that are required to be able to properly profile our users.

User Activities Definition

It is necessary to carry out the compilation of the steps involved in carrying out the activity or activities that you want to simulate within the virtual environment, this is carried out so that the learning that is obtained with the use of the virtual environment is the most similar to a real situation. In order to carry out this activity, it is proposed to perform:

- **Interviews with The Teacher or Instructor**: The person in charge of applying the activities has a broad knowledge of the process to carry it out, from the steps to follow to the tools necessary to complete it.
- **Observation:** Observe the realization of the real activities and take notes on how these are carried out, all the tools that are used, how the user interacts with them and what are the steps in an organized way to complete the activity.

Since in order to be able to make the correct collection of information on how to carry out the activities to be simulated, it is necessary to obtain information not only on the way in which the activities are carried out, but also on all the elements with which the user interacts during the activity, the various tools that are used to carry it out, the way in which the tools are used, among others; Two tasks are proposed to carry out this collection.

- **Specification of Used Tools:** It is necessary to have a specification on all the tools that interact with the user to be able to complete the activity, from the strictly required tools with which most of the steps are made and of which if they were needed it is not could advance, to tools that are occasional or situational use but that may be required at any given time.
- **Detailed Specification of the Activity's Tasks:** This specification is recommended to have a record on how the user interacts with the elements around him, from the tools he uses to complete his activity, to the elements that surround him, since these can Be indirectly supportive of your learning. Likewise, it is important to specify the correct way to carry out the steps to complete the activity so that learning is organized since many times people tend to skip certain important parts of the process to complete an activity.

Subsequently, having obtained the detailed description of the different elements that make up everything related to the user, a VR Storyboard (Vincent, 2016) is proposed for verification. Carrying out this will give us a feedback with the teachers and / or in charge of imparting the activity to know if it is necessary to take certain characteristics into account to include within our requirements.

Virtual Environment Conceptualization

With the obtaining of the data related to the user, many times in the design of software applications it is all that is necessary to begin to realize an application design, but dealing with technologies such as Virtual Reality in which not only the It is also necessary to take into account the environment that surrounds it, the learning of people is often related to the elements that surround it and which are not taken into great consideration. Therefore, this stage has been specified during the virtual learning environment design process to conceptualize in the same way all the elements that make up the environment in which the user will develop to perform their learning activity.

Object Arrangement

An important part that composes the environment that surrounds the user is the arrangement of the objects in it, it is possible to represent a Field of Vision (FOV) (Facebook Technologies, LLC., 2019) with the current Virtual Reality technologies, composed of 110° horizontally and 90° vertically, so it is essential to establish the elements that are of highest priority to the user and place them in their main field of vision. Having a list of all the tools that are necessary to perform the tasks that make up the user's learning and its importance classification, it is now necessary to establish that other elements of the environment are needed so that the user has a correct understanding of the activity, these elements can be from lighting, objects with which the user does not interact directly but that are necessary, for example some tables, chairs, trays to store their tools, among others.

Virtual Environment Design Phase

For the second phase of this design process, the conceptualization of the virtual learning environment that is expected to be obtained according to the data collected in the previous phase is considered. During its stages the mechanics that will be used will be stipulated as well as the development of small rapid prototypes to be able to evaluate and feedback what is being done and thus be able to make necessary adjustments without going back so much in the activities that make up this process.

Dynamic Modeling and Interactions

During this stage there is the specification of the user's interactions with their environment and the objects that are in it, with the previous collection of the tools with which the user interacts to be able to solve the problems that they want to simulate, it is possible to determine the necessary Agency level, in the same way you can establish the physical criteria that will interact with the objects collisions, the use of dialogues, among others. The interactions that must be placed to provide users with a fluid experience with a fluid experience should consider the use of external devices in case there are users with motor

disabilities. This is with the idea of providing a totally equal experience to all types of possible users that may have.

Agency Specification

The specification of the Agency can be considered one of the main points to elaborate the design of the learning environment, different levels of Agency can be determined, depending on the number of things that it is desired that the user can freely manipulate within the scenario. Two extreme levels are considered, the Low Agency that indicates that the user has few permissions to modify the scenario at will, so that their interaction with the objects would be minimal or only presented as a spectator, and the High Agency which allows the user has total control over each element that composes the surrounding environment, from manipulating the shape of things, to permanently deleting them from the stage. Playing with the Agency's specifications can result in various ways of interacting with the stage, it can be determined that the user can have a high agency with certain elements, or a low agency with environmental objects that should not be modified at all by the user. This opens up to the possibility of determining and prioritizing what elements the user must control and not control so that their learning is satisfactory and representative with the real world.

Navigation Mechanism and Interaction

Navigation mechanisms are one of the most complicated issues to carry out in the realization of virtual environments. For this it is necessary to consider how much we want or can alter the reality that surrounds the user to facilitate their learning by obtaining information from the surrounding environment, although in the previous phase we obtain a collection of the information of the objects that surround the user, their interaction with the environment and how things are distributed in order to make the real environment as similar as possible, during this stage we must take into account how much help we will provide directly or indirectly. The direct way known as Diegetic, presents the information to users directly by means that are not possible in real scenarios, these can be through dialog boxes or even through information windows displayed above key objects to the realization of the activity. The indirect way known as Non-Diegetic, does not indicate that the relevant information on the performance of certain tasks within the virtual scenario can be presented to the user in subtle manners, either by highlighting the objects with a distinctive contour that tells the user that they are objects of interest and allow them to investigate their use and the relationship they have with the tasks they are doing on their own. In consideration for users who have disabilities which do not allow them to obtain information from the visual navigation and interaction systems such as those described above, it is recommended to take as a measure the following tasks to be performed during this activity, in order to compensate and cover the user needs and that they can obtain the expected learning.

- **Auditory Instructions**: Users who are visually impaired, may have many problems with the use of Diegetic and Non-Diegetic since these are mainly aimed at visual interaction with the user, therefore, it is recommended to integrate the design into auditory instructions so this type of user can enjoy and obtain the same quality of interaction. You can even consider providing the user with a "Virtual Guide Dog", these types of systems provide users with auditory information that allows them to know the directions they must take in order to continue with their activity, instructions and information required for them and that it is impossible for them to obtain sometimes given their visual impairment.

- **Textual Instructions:** This may be the case in which we encounter users with hearing impairment or deafness, for these cases the use of Diegetic is one of the ways in which we can counteract its impediment and provide the necessary information so that it can interact properly with the objects and their surroundings.
- **Navigation Through Visual Interaction:** We may encounter users with motor problems who cannot interact with sensory devices properly, it may even happen that we do not have the necessary equipment to provide this type of sensory interaction to users. For these situations it is possible to implement a navigation system that allows users to interact with the environment using only their vision. By establishing a Gaze Targeting, this will allow the user to interact with the elements found on the stage and even scroll through it.

Low Fidelity Prototyping

If the above points have been carried out correctly, by this time to reach this stage you should already have enough material to be able to perform a low quality prototyping and check if what has been done so far has been carried out correctly, from obtaining the user's needs to the design of the virtual environment. There are many tools to be able to make these prototypes, however, for our design process one in particular has been selected, which we consider may be too useful to later evaluate the progress of the design, the Sketch VR (Saara, 2017).

Sketch VR

This technique to make rapid prototypes adapts to the phase in which we are, since the time necessary to perform them is very little and the details that have to be placed are very basic. Sketch VR is a technique where a template of a sheet of paper is used to make a quick drawing of our design so far to later digitize it and test it on an HMD as a static image but that you can already observe a few features of what We have been working so far. By making this type of prototype on paper it is possible to obtain feedback to improve what we have done so far, it may not even be necessary to go back to the user requirements but only to go back within this same second phase of the process to make the changes, this gives us greater agility and that we do not take so much time to redo all the above.

Expert Evaluation

Once all of the above has been done and we have approved that the changes we make thanks to the rapid prototype made with Sketch VR in case we find some necessary changes, now the following is the evaluation of what we have with experts on the subject. In this case the evaluation can be with the teacher or instructor who is responsible for delivering the activity that we are simulating to provide us with necessary feedback if everything we have done at the moment adapts to the needs that we have specified previously. There are several ways to carry out these evaluations, in this chapter only two are presented that have been considered to be of greater use to be able to continue working in a fluid manner and to provide us with fast feedback. It is important that the evaluations presented below be carried out by experts in the field, since it is required that the results obtained from them be reliable to establish if changes to the design that has been made are required and in what way they are necessary.

Score Checklist

The Score Checklist is a very useful tool to evaluate our current design with the experts, we have to choose as evaluation points some of our main requirements so that the evaluator can decide how reliable is what we have done with what the user required. At the end of the evaluation it is advisable to allow the evaluator to place a recommendation since this can be useful to improve our design and be as real as possible to what our users need. Another way to carry out this type of evaluation is to know the weak points that our design has, which, knowing them, we can include improvements that satisfactorily comply with everything necessary to finalize our application design process.

Evaluator's Notes

Although as its name indicates directly, it is an evaluation method that allows the evaluator to make notes on different topics of our design, it is recommended that these topics be related to the main requirements that were obtained during the first phase of the process, adding some on usability and the considerations that the evaluator may have regarding the use of design as a tool for learning. Being a more open evaluation regarding the feedback obtained from this type of evaluation, it is possible that the changes have to be organized and prioritized, some may even be ruled out since they can be considered not of great importance but it is recommended take all comments that are received in consideration to include.

Design Implementation

With the second phase of the design process we can consider that our design is almost ready for implementation, during this third phase we will carry out some final evaluations with users in order to obtain feedback and decide if it is necessary to return to the previous phase and make some changes to the work We have done so far. To carry out these evaluations it is possible to do it in several ways but in this chapter, we only present some that have been considered more agile to carry out. The phase is divided into two main stages, the first is responsible for making a prototype of higher quality than the one developed in the previous phase in order to evaluate our design in all its aspects, from usability, the promotion of learning, the characteristics of the environment, the ease of use, navigation and all the points that have been considered during the whole process that has been carried out at the moment.

High Fidelity Prototyping

Making a High Fidelity Prototype is important to correctly evaluate all the changes we have made thanks to the previous phase, previously we evaluated the conditions according to the experts of the subject, so we focus on complying with the learning requirements Expected and user needs. Now at this point with the high fidelity prototype we have to evaluate with users how easy it is to be able to use this design for their activities, the ease they have of moving through the environment, among other considerations that will be mentioned later. Many applications can be found that provide us with the necessary tools to make this prototype, for this chapter we recommend the digital prototypes explained below.

Digital Prototyping

The digital prototype is one of the most viable ways to evaluate this type of Virtual Reality technology, it is currently possible to find applications that allow us to perform these with the use of few resources, they even provide us with 3D models of common elements to use them in the prototype although later we replace them with our own 3D models in the development of the application. Many of these tools mentioned have costs for their use, however, it is possible to find some that have an open source license, as to which we wish to use to evaluate our design, will depend strictly on the resources we have. In the same way it is possible to use the development tools that are commonly used for the formal development of VR applications such as game engines to make a digital prototype of the design, taking into account that being a quick prototype some functionality may be implemented limited or the low quality of the designs.

User Evaluation

The evaluation with users would be the last stage to later consider that our design is finished and meets the necessary characteristics to promote learning and accessibility that was included through the process for its design. This evaluation through users will allow us to know if our design meets the real satisfaction of their needs, if the design we have made is easy to use for them, as they consider that the elements are organized in the stage, if it is easy interact with the tools we provide, and if they consider that with this they can obtain a complement for their learning related to the topic that is being simulated with this virtual environment.

User Perception

With all the points that are tried to be understood with this evaluation, this stage has been divided into two activities to complete it, firstly the perception that the user has when using the design will be evaluated, as he considers the environment and the elements that are They understand, what is the level of immersion that we are providing, the quality of the environment compared to the real scenario, if the visual elements that were added to help in the activities are important enough for this to understand the situations and help you to continue with its activities, the sounds that were used, among other features that you wanted to place.

Usability Study

The second activity that complements the feedback that we require to be able to satisfactorily evaluate our design and decide if changes are necessary and to what extent we should return in the design process, is the usability study. With the usability study we will rate according to the opinions of our users that they consider it so easy to use our design to carry out the activity that we are simulating, if the accessibility elements that we have integrated are consistent and allow users with disabilities to be able to have access to this type of technology. The usability study will allow us to know if it is necessary to make improvements in certain specific areas of our design, it is recommended that users who carry out the usability study are divided into groups according to various considerations that were taken into account when preparing the design, that is, if measures were taken for an accessible design of people with motor disabilities, it will be necessary to include evaluators who have any of these disabilities, to really have reliable feedback.

FUTURE RESEARCH DIRECTIONS

Although it has been possible to develop a process for the design of accessible virtual learning environments, but it is still possible to include other types of disabilities, in the current design process some have been taken into account, however, with more work it is considered that It is possible to integrate even more considerations for inclusion in the work. Even as for the educational paradigms that have been reflected so that the resulting design encourages, only two have been taken into account, which are given thanks to the same characteristics that Virtual Reality technology provides us, therefore we consider that It is possible to include more educational paradigms when conducting a study and how to integrate them correctly within each stage and define the activities involved to reflect them. Subsequently, it is desired to improve the design process proposed in this chapter in order to reduce if possible, some work times, to be able to carry out more forceful evaluations regarding the feedback that may be necessary for users who wish to implement it as part of their application development processes. Similarly, an evaluation of this design process will be implemented with experts currently working in this type of industry to obtain feedback on a real work area and possibly improve the processes we already have.

CONCLUSION

The use of Virtual Reality learning environments are tools that complement teachers or instructors to carry out various practices. This does not mean that they replace the person in charge of instructing or educating their work, since they are still strictly necessary. These are due to the fact that although features are introduced in the methodology presented in this chapter, they only help to promote learning following certain educational paradigms, but it is impossible to include these entireties. It is possible to include even more features that help the inclusion of people with different disabilities, however, it is a work that still has to be considered to match the different stages that make up the good designs and design of applications for Virtual Reality. Likewise, it is important to mention that carrying out a design process prior to a development can help improve and simplify the steps of the software development part, it can even provide a reduction in working times, since it comes to a reduction in errors and less amount of feedback with previous stages in the software development process. So having a design process can significantly help work teams that want to dabble in the work of these new technologies that are becoming a trend for their ease of presenting people with scenarios that can often be hard to imagine seeing in person.

REFERENCES

Bottino, R., & Freino, L. & Mauro, T. (2016). From e-learning to VR-learning: An example of learning in an immersive virtual world. *Journal of E-Learning and Knowledge Society,* 101-113.

Chochoiek, N. (2017). Explaining the Success of User-Centered Design - An Empirical Study across German. *Junior Management Science,* 81-116.

Dorys, G. (2015). Constructivism as theory and teaching method. *Sophia, Colección de Filosofía de la Educación,* 93-110.

Facebook Technologies, L. L. C. (2019). *Oculus Developers.* Retrieved from https://developer.oculus.com/documentation/

Freina, L., & Ott, M. (2015). A Literature Review on Immersive Virtual Reality in Education: State Of The Art and Perspectives. *The International Scientific Conference eLearning and Software for Education*, 133-141.

Hsiu-Mei, H., & Shu-Sheng, L. (2018). An Analysis of Learners' Intentions Toward Virtual Reality Learning Based on Constructivist and Technology Acceptance Approaches. *International Review of Research in Open and Distributed Learning,* 91-115.

Kamppari-Miller, S. (2017, April 6). *Vr Sketch Sheets.* Retrieved from Prototypr.io: http://blog.prototypr.io/vr-sketch-sheets-4843fd690c91

Kohno, I., Yasu, H., & Sugawara, S. (2013). Design, A proposal and validation of cost benefit analysis method of User-Centered. Design, Chiba University, 1-10.

Kulwinder, K. (1998). *Designing Virtual Environments for Usability.* PhD Thesis.

Leiva, C. (2016). Conductismo, cognitivismo y aprendizaje. *Tecnología en Marcha*, *18*, 66–73.

McCurley, V. (2016, May 22). *Storyboarding in Virtual Reality.* Retrieved from Virtual Reality Pop: http://virtualrealitypop.com/storyboarding-in-virtual-reality-67d3438a2fb1

McLaren, R. (2018). *Virtual Learning Environments Making the most of the new regulations.* Technology & Innovation at Policy Connect.

Microsoft Corporation. (2019). *Mixed Reality Design.* Retrieved from https://docs.microsoft.com/en-us/windows/mixed-reality/design

Niederhauser, D., & Stoddart, T. (2000). Teachers' instructional perspectives and use of educational software. *Teaching and Teacher Education*, 15–31.

Samperio, G., & Arceaga, A., & Anilu, F. C. C. (2017). Metodología Para El Modelado De Sistemas De Realidad Virtual Para El Aprendizaje En Dispositivos Móviles. *Pistas Educativas*, 518-534.

Sanchez, A., Barreiro, J., & Maojo, V. (2000). Design of Virtual Reality Systems for Education: A Cognitive Approach. *Education and Information Technologies*, *5*(4), 345–362. doi:10.1023/A:1012061809603

ADDITIONAL READING

Bottino, R., & Freino, L. & Mauro, T. (2016). From e-learning to VR-learning: An example of learning in an immersive virtual world. *Journal of E-Learning and Knowledge Society,* 101-113.

Cromby, J., Standen, P., & Brown, D. (1996). The potentials of virtual environments in the education and training of people with learning disabilities. *Journal of Intellectual Disability Research*, *40*(6), 489–501. doi:10.1111/j.1365-2788.1996.tb00659.x PMID:9004109

Folmer, E. (2005). *Virtual World Accessibility: Directions for Research University of Nevada, Reno.* Reno: Department of Computer Science and Engineering.

Freina, L., & Ott, M. (2015). A Literature Review on Immersive Virtual Reality in Education: State Of The Art and Perspectives. *The International Scientific Conference eLearning and Software for Education*, 133-141.

Sanchez, A., Barreiro, J., & Maojo, V. (2000). Design of Virtual Reality Systems for Education: A Cognitive Approach. *Education and Information Technologies*, *5*(4), 345–362. doi:10.1023/A:1012061809603

KEY TERMS AND DEFINITIONS

Agency: The capacity of an entity (a person or other entity) to act in, and influence, an artificial environment.

Data Glove: An interactive device—often resembling a glove worn on the hand—that connects to a computer system and facilitates fine-motion control within virtual reality.

Diegetic: Is one kind of navigation system that show illustrative information to the user using elements that no exit on the real world.

Field of View (FOV): Is the view that is visible to the user while rotating their head from a fixed body position.

Gaze Targeting: It is a navigation system that consists of observing certain objects through a visual pointer that appears on the screen to be able to interact with them.

Head Mounted Display (HMD): A set of goggles or a helmet with tiny monitors in front of each eye to generate images seen by the wearer as three-dimensional.

Immersion: A psychological sense of being in a virtual environment.

Non-Diegetic: Is one kind of navigation system that subtly indicates the information to the user.

Presence: A feeling of being in and of the virtual world, and the ignoring of physical world distractions.

Virtual Reality (VR): Virtual reality (VR) places the experiencer in another location entirely. Whether that location has been generated by a computer or captured by video, it entirely occludes the user's natural surroundings.

Chapter 11
Redesigning the User Interface of a Learning Platform for Social Engineering Integrating Web Accessibility Basics

José Guadalupe Arceo-Olague
https://orcid.org/0000-0002-7240-8158
Universidad Autónoma de Zacatecas, Mexico

Jorge Ortiz-Reyes
Universidad Autónoma de Zacatecas, Mexico

Roberto Solís-Robles
https://orcid.org/0000-0001-6629-1048
Universidad Autónoma de Zacatecas, Mexico

Huizilopoztli Luna-García
Universidad Autónoma de Zacatecas, Mexico

Oscar Osvaldo Ordaz-García
Universidad Autónoma de Zacatecas, Mexico

Hamurabi Gamboa-Rosales
https://orcid.org/0000-0002-9498-6602
Universidad Autónoma de Zacatecas, Mexico

Carlos Eric Galván-Tejada
Universidad Autónoma de Zacatecas, Mexico

Jorge Issac Galván-Tejada
Universidad Autónoma de Zacatecas, Mexico

José María Celaya-Padilla
CONACyT, Universidad Autónoma de Zacatecas, Mexico

Manuel Agustín Ortiz-López
https://orcid.org/0000-0001-8312-1729
Universidad de Córdoba, Spain

ABSTRACT

The objective of this chapter is to identify web accessibility problems in order to fulfill the design guidelines. According to the proposal, accessibility is assessed through easy checks of the implementation of the social engineering educational platform. As a first phase, the developer carries out this evaluation and his results are analyzed. The second phase solves the identified problems or at least tries to give them a solution implementing a redesign on the platform; in the same way, the results are analyzed. In the third phase, a proposal is made of the improvements that can be introduced in the redesign of the user interface in a way that best complies with the web accessibility. The problem identified shows the difficulty of implementing the accessibility guides and the need to propose accessibility implementation guidelines that guarantee their compliance.

DOI: 10.4018/978-1-7998-2325-4.ch011

INTRODUCTION

The general perspective of this chapter is to establish aspects of web accessibility in an educational platform given the need for technological tools that are focused on online learning. There are papers that report the lack of compliance with accessibility guides on the websites of educational institutions. Some of the important aspects to be integrated in educational environments go from the interaction and processes necessary to acquire knowledge to the cognitive development (Jiménez-González, Mendoza-González, & Luna-García, 2018) and for this reason studying educational website is of interest to the community. Another point of view in the observation of educational environments are the Learning Content Management Systems (LCMSs), which have also been subject to study in terms of accessibility and have encountered difficulties for user interaction and therefore, the assurance and monitoring of accessibility in LCMSs is vital to guarantee universal access to education (Iglesias, Moreno, Martinez, & Calvo, 2014). Libraries also need to integrate aspects of accessibility because users nowadays access more services through the web, consequently, having good practices in usability, accessibility and universal design will allow libraries to offer accessible content, which is its main purpose (Riley-Huff, 2012). According to a study carried out on websites of top universities in Kyrgyzstan, Turkey, among others, the universities in several countries still have difficulties in meeting the criteria of web accessibility that allows providing services effectively for the entire group of users in those who also consider disabled users (Ismailova & Inal, 2018)

In an evolutionary field of what accessibility implies and how it is visualized, it makes it difficult for the web accessibility community to interact, agree or share the way it is understood. In addition to the above, one thing that is of importance outside the community is the difficulty they may have in understanding, planning or meeting the accessibility requirements given the conflict of ideas they have and what they really mean (Yesilada, Brajnik, Vigo, & Harper, 2015). For higher education, providing a properly designed website must be a good practice and a requirement to be met. The above is related to the fact that in universities there is an interest to place some undergraduate, and the entire graduate courses online (Floyd & Santiago, 2007). With the integration of new technologies, there is a lot of work to be done on e-learning websites, which should focus on how to make their websites accessible so that they can also serve disabled students (Shawar, 2015).

The use of tools to support the evaluation of aspects related to web pages is something that has been used in different works in aspects of usability (Kaur, Kaur, & Kaur, 2016) or accessibility as is the case of (Floyd & Santiago, 2007; Riley-Huff, 2012; Maisak & Brown, 2014; Iglesias et al., 2014; Shawar, 2015; Ismailova & Inal, 2018), applying the Web Content Accessibility Guidelines (WCAG). However, web accessibility evaluation tools can not determine the accessibility of web sites; they can only help us to determine if that is the case (Floyd & Santiago, 2007). In this sense, it is commented that technology cannot identify or solve all possible problems or situations in a way that replaces human evaluation. Consequently, the use of help tools for compliance with web accessibility guidelines can be a first step, but the second step, human judgment, is a critical part, which involves careful observation by web developers to identify and resolve situations that may arise. Finally, according to the work presented by Lee, in the context of higher education and long distance education, the increase in access to university education through online education is not automatic; furthermore, increasing accessibility is in fact, a complex and challenging process (Lee, 2017).

BACKGROUND

Currently, universities are focused on bringing higher education closer to more students who are interested in acquiring a bachelor's degree training or in topics of specialization (Lee, 2017). Similarly, basic education institutions have taken interest in using technologies for the training of students. Consequently, in education institutions in Mexico, efforts are made to reduce educational lags at different levels, at basic levels, for example, attempts are made to incorporate technological tools that allow communication with parents to notify of homework, and send reminders or messages about school activities. In institutions of higher education such as the Autonomous University of Zacatecas, open source learning platforms are used, being Moodle the predominant one. The Moodle platform is used in courses of the academic units of Health Sciences, High School, Physics, Letters and Engineering, to name a few.

The use of a learning platform helps teachers in the management of daily activities, better attendance control, homework evaluation and record of grades. In addition, as aspects of interest, there is the possibility of adding educational resources for student learning, such as internet pages, class presentations, videos, examples and any other resource related to the topics taught. Related to the above, different works comment that the site of a higher education institution may have different approaches depending on the group of target students, that is, face-to-face students who take courses daily or, distance students who acquire knowledge in the time they have available (Floyd & Santiago, 2007; Christopher, 2013; Iglesias et al., 2014; Shawar, 2015; Kaur et al., 2016; Lee, 2017). Taking into account the type of target student has its particularities to consider, however, nowadays in certain aspects, it is reported that students who are taking their courses on a daily basis face problems of poor performance or poor cognitive skills resulting from a poor training in previous educational levels. This problem is generated in the eagerness to increase the number of students entering an educational program instead of rejecting them for their low academic level. In addition, government requirements emphasize accepting all applicants to reduce social security problems, keeping students in a study program even though they have few skills or abilities to learn specific subjects. In this sense, an educational platform can contribute to the training of students who require additional support by reviewing class topics that can be provided by the teacher to improve skills with specific content. Li agrees that the main aim of e-Learning is that the *Learning process can be carried at any time, anywhere, by any one via any media and anyway.* According to this, e-learning websites should allow learners to access more materials and work more independently (Shawar, 2015).

There is no doubt that a quick way to provide resources for learning is through a website. Higher education institutions make use of platforms to get closer to students and maintain permanent contact as they progress in their studies. As mentioned before, Moodle is a widely used platform for the administration of the courses; however, it is interesting to develop other platforms that complement Moodle and that are online. Consequently, it is important that the design of these complementary platforms for the support of the institutions have the basic elements of accessibility. In this regard, different works mention this need for accessible educational sites (University, n.d.; Floyd & Santiago, 2007; Iglesias et al., 2014; Maisak & Brown, 2014; Ortiz, 2014; Shawar, 2015; Kaur et al., 2016; Lee, 2017; Ismailova & Inal, 2018).

A feature very important to mention is the Web accessibility concerns of building websites that are accessible by all people regardless of their ability or disability (Shawar, 2015). The W3C Web Accessibility Initiative (WAI) has been established to develop guidelines to ensure that Web pages are accessible. This is even more important in the case an assistive technology is used to improve the accessibility for disabled persons, executing tasks that are difficult or impossible to do without technical aid. Some disabilities in learners are Vision or Hearing problems and Cognitive o neurological disability. As stated in (Columbia, 2019) Web Accessibility refers to the inclusive practice of making websites usable by people of all abilities and disabilities. Almost every modern browser and operating system offers built-in features with assistive technologies. As examples, we can use screen readers like Microsoft Narrator or Mac OS X VoiceOver, Magnify the screen or customize your mouse pointer settings, but only if accessibility guidelines are complied.

An e-learning platform is used to provide educational content, storing information about users and monitoring the learning process, as well as make possible communication and cooperation between students and teachers. Based on this, the web is considered one of the main channels to deliver educational materials, which require applying WAI guidelines to make learning materials accessible to learners. The W3C WAI consider that the Web Accessibility also benefits people without disabilities, for example (WAI, 2019):

1. People using mobile phones, smart watches, smart TVs, and other devices with small screens, different input modes, etc.
2. Older people with changing abilities due to ageing
3. People with “temporary disabilities” such as a broken arm or lost glasses
4. People with “situational limitations” such as in bright sunlight or in an environment where they cannot listen to audio
5. People using a slow Internet connection, or who have limited or expensive bandwidth

Accessibility supports social inclusion for people with disabilities as well as others, such as:

1. Older people
2. People in rural areas
3. People in developing countries

As we can see, web accessibility is useful even for people without disabilities, as is stated at the beginning of this section. To assess the accessibility of a web page and in this case a learning platform, we follow the WAI guidelines by means of easy checks to get an idea of whether or not the accessibility is addressed in a basic way.

Social engineering is the art of skillfully manipulating people through psychology techniques and social skills to meet specific goals. Some main objectives of social engineering include people in charge of an organization, users with high economic status, tech support executives, system administrators etc. (Hadnagy, 2010). Social engineering is effective because there are many users who get lost in the issue of security in digital environments since they do not always understand the abstraction that this reality is showing them (Foozy, Ahmad, Abdollah, Yusof, & Masud, 2012). The impact of the attack that social engineering has on organizations is economic loss, loss of privacy, damage of goodwill, temporary or permanent closure, danger of terrorism.

The behavior vulnerable for this not technical attacks is to abuse people’s trust, not knowing about the types of social engineering attacks make organization an easy target. Imposing fear on users means that they become more vulnerable. Some social engineer promises great recommendations to users in exchange for information, all of this creates a vulnerability in the security against social engineering (Digital, n.d.). That why social engineering is so effective, because humans are the most susceptible factor, it is very difficult to detect an attack of social engineering, since there are no methods to completely ensure the safety of social engineering attacks (Watson & Mason, 2014; Molist, 2014).

There are phases of a social Engineering attack (Hadnagy, 2010), this phases are performed by research on target company. Reacher phase includes gather all the necessary information about target organizations, this information can be collected by dumpster diving, finding information of internet, tour company, employees. Etc. the second phase is select victim. The social engineer selects the victim among other employees of an organization. This user must have several defects, so that when interacting with him will be easy to reveal information. The third phase consist in develop a relationship with the selected employees. Finally, the final phase exploit the relationship by a collection of sensitive information (Watson & Mason, 2014; Mouton, Leenen, & Venter, 2016).

Social engineering attack can be performed by different techniques (Patel, 2013; Ozkaya, 2018). These types of social engineering are classified into the following type:

Human-based Social Engineering, which consists in the collection of information by interacting. They are physical attacks where the social engineer creates a realization with the victim and then exploit it and get valuable information (Krombholz, Hobel, Huber, & Weippl, 2015). Social engineers perform technologies such as eavesdropping which consists in secretly listening to someone else's conversation; interception of audio, video, or written communication. Shoulder surfing consists of obtaining information from the victim by standing behind him. Dumpster Diving consists of the snooping process in the garbage containers to get contacts information, financial information, phone bills etc. Social Reverse Engineering is a technique where the user and the attacker must really be interacting, the attacker introduces himself to the victim as a trustworthy person offering help to solve some problem, it attack involves sabotage, marketing and tech support (Irani, Balduzzi, Balzarotti, Kirda, & Pu, 2011). Piggybacking and tailgating is similar technique; an authorized person allows (intentionally or unintentionally) an unauthorized person to pass through a secure door, sometimes the social engineer can wear a fake ID badge (Hadnagy, 2018; Hadnagy, Marin, & Wilson, 2011).

Computer-based Social Engineering attacks are all those that are carried out with the help of software, most attackers design such attacks. Once the attackers have obtained enough information from the victim they prepare different scenes of attacks including pop-up windows requires login credentials. Internet messaging and emails such as Hoax letters, chain letters, and spam. The technique most used by engineers is called phishing, is a technique in which fake Web page looks like a legitimate web page. It is shown to the victim and when the victim opens the page the victim provides all sensitive information because of its resemblance. Another technique used for the social engineer is spear phishing, unlike the phishing, the spear phishing consists of only one individual attacker to fulfill a specific objective (Long, 2008; Jakobsson & Myers, 2016).

MAIN FOCUS OF THE CHAPTER

Issues, Controversies, Problems

As presented in this chapter, web accessibility is the main problem to be considered in current websites since their content should be accessible for everyone, regardless of their ability or disability, (Shawar, 2015). For higher education, providing a properly designed, accessible website is not just a matter of good practice, it is a requirement, (Floyd & Santiago, 2007). A best practice method to create Web pages that are accessible to a wide range of users is to use the latest markup languages and apply the Web Content Accessibility Guidelines (WCAG), established to develop and maintain interoperable technologies to lead the World Wide Web to its full potential (Floyd & Santiago, 2007). Web Accessibility must be a topic considered in undergraduate courses in order to better understands what it implies to the users and how it impact if it isn't considered in the webpage development.

As suggest Yesilada in his work about the perception of web accessibility, it is very difficult for those outside this community to understand, plan, budget, enact policy or conform to accessibility requirements when the community itself has so many, and in some cases, conflicting definitions (Yesilada, Brajnik, Vigo, & Harper, 2015). The community should rethink the web accessibility problem and contribute to better understand the topic and train students and web designers. As suggested by Lee, we need to remind students in the field of higher education that increasing the accessibility of university education is a complex and multidimensional social issue, one which requires serious, and continuing, scholarly discussions, (Lee, 2017). Not only the web accessibility is applied in education, currently it is tried to be extended to every webpage, however, not always is correct the implementation of the WAI guidelines. If we only focus on Universities Web pages, in the study made by Floyd, the institutions failed to meet the minimum accessibility requirements and there is no significant difference between an institution ´s student population and Web Site Accessibility compliance (Floyd, & Santiago, 2007). It seems that larger and smaller organizations alike are not conforming to the standard and that the central problem is not the financial resources as a cause for lack of web accessibility compliance.

SOLUTIONS AND RECOMMENDATIONS

First, the easy checks where provided to the developer and by itself he filled-up the Tables with checks and comments. In a second step, we review the Tables and evaluate the checks and comments provided, as well as the modifications made by the developer to accomplish with the design guidelines for accessibility. Finally, our observations found in the filling of the Accessibility Tables and the modifications made are commented with the developer to develop a version where he properly implements the necessary basic accessibility aspects.

Phase One: Easy Checks for Web Page Accessibility

Considering the problem identified, we used the easy checks to evaluate basic accessibility issues and extract information about the compliance of the web page accessibility (Group, n.d.). According to the problem stated, we try to find if the developer includes the basic elements into the e-learning platform designed for the Social Engineering attacks topic in a web page. In this way, Easy Checks provides an idea of the web page accessibility compliance. The evaluated aspects are shown in Tables 1 to 5 and these aspects are grouped in Page Title, Image Text alternatives, Text, Interaction and General Page attributes. In each Table the following elements are considered: page attributes, web accessibility aspect, a check mark specifying if it complies the accessibility and Comments about the aspect evaluated.

First, the easy checks where provided to the developer and he filled-up the Tables with the checks and comments by himself. The Page Title attribute is evaluated in Table 1. We found that the designer put a title, however, such title does not describe adequately and briefly the content of the page. Moreover, all the web pages have the same title as shown in the top of Figure 1. This means that the designer used

Table 1. Page title accessibility check

Page's attributes	Web accessibility aspect	Check	Comments
Page title	There is a title that adequately and briefly describes the content of the page	No	There is a title "Ingeniería social", but it doesn't describe the content of the web page.
	The title is different from other pages on the website, and adequately distinguishes the page from other web pages	No	All the web pages have the same title

Figure 1. Titles of pages on the website

Table 2. Image text alternatives accessibility check

Page's attributes	Web accessibility aspect	Check	Comments
Image text alternatives ("alt text")	Every image has alt with appropriate alternative text	Yes	All images have Alt. The text is appropriate according to the image

these attributes without incorporating appropriate titles on each page and that they are not very descriptive. This aspect is important since the titles of the pages are shown in the windows, in the tabs of the browsers when multiple pages are opened, and in the results collected by the search engines, allowing the users to be oriented when they are moving between the open pages in the browser

In the case of image text alternatives, as shown in Table 2, the developer suggests that every image has an alternative text and that it is appropriate according to the image. In *Figure 2* we can see an example of some of the image text alternatives evaluating the web page with the WAVE (Web Accessibility Evaluation Tool) (University, n.d.). All the images has an "alt text", however, it is not appropriate to the images because its contents is useful only for the developer to control the design of his web page. The text (e.g. fotoUnidad01) just reflects the sequence or the order of the image instead of describing the contents or purpose of each image. If we think about the purpose of the alt tag, it has to be helpful to disabled persons, for example, for the blind, as they need to use assistive technologies in order to access a web page. The latter is a good example of the importance of accessibility.

The next aspect to evaluate is the headings, text contrast ratio and text resizing. The developer reported that his designs fulfill the headings, contrast and resizing aspects as summarized in Table 3. The pages have headings and the text that looks like a heading is marked up with a tag h1, h2 or h3 and is

Figure 2. Image text alternatives obtained by the WAVE tool

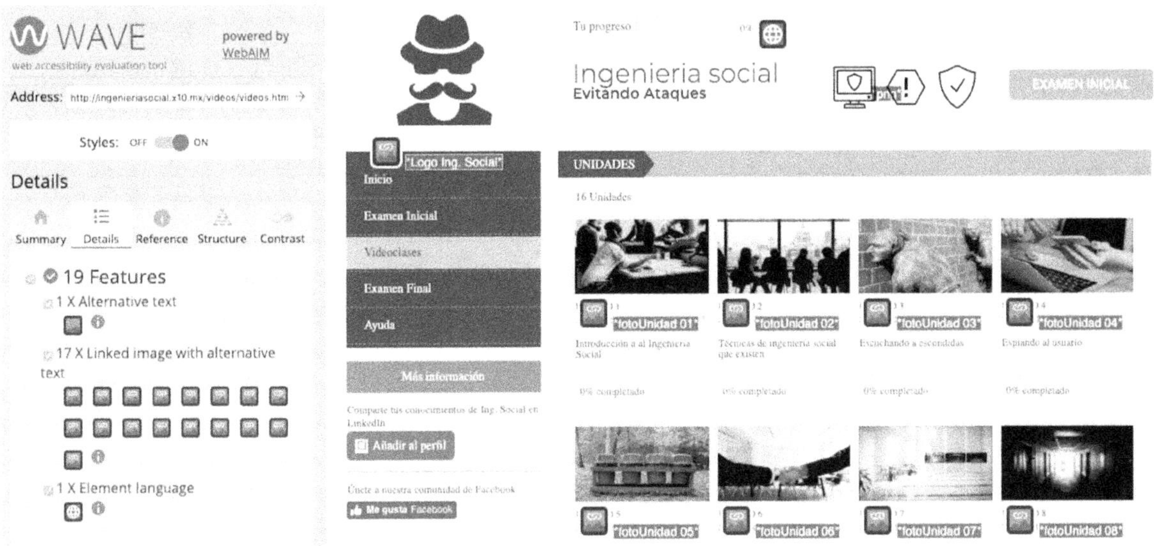

a conceptual section of the page, making it hierarchically meaningful. The evidence provided by the developer is shown in *Figures 3* and *4*, where the page contains some titles that are in the header section and at the top with the title of "Eavesdropping", "Videoclases..." or "Social Engineering", which are declared in the code with h2 or h3 tags. This evidence shows that the developer makes use of titles, however, proper use is discussed in the following phases.

In the same way, the developer comments that an adequate contrast ratio is achieved, although in some lines, the text has low contrast (see Figure 5). Finally, for this aspect of web accessibility, the page behaves appropriately in terms of text resizing. The text becomes larger when zooming and the text doesn't disappear and neither do the images and the text overlap. Additionally, all buttons or forms are visible and usable; therefore, scrolling is not required for viewing or reading the web page (see *Figure 6*).

The next accessibility aspect evaluated is the Interaction, which is focused on the keyboard use to interact with the web page. People with mobility impairments rely on the keyboard or on assistive technologies and strategies that rely on keyboard commands. Through a keyboard, accessible websites enable people to access all content and functionality to links, forms, media controls, etc. (Group, n.d.). In the first case, about the keyboard access and visual focus, the developer basically reported that he isn't using the keyboard accessibility tabbing through the web page. His answer is "No" in all checks and probably it means that he is not sure how to use or enable the keyboard functions on the browser, we will discuss later about the use of tabs and keyboard navigation. On the other hand, the platform has a few forms and all of them have a label and id that is positioned correctly. The problem in this aspect is the use of the keyboard for the accessibility in the web page.

The last web accessibility basic check is the evaluation of the general accessibility, which includes the moving, flashing or blinking content, multimedia alternatives and the basic structure check of the web page. In Table 5 the developer reported these evaluations. The web page contains few elements that are changing in an area at the top of the web page, they are random icons (see Figure 7) that are changing softly, but there is not a way for the user to stop the movement. Additionally, no other content is flashing or blinking because there are no elements that produce such effects.

Table 3. Text accessibility check

Page's attributes	Web accessibility aspect	Check	Comments
Headings	1. There is a heading in every page	Yes	All the pages have a heading.
	2. All text that looks like a heading, is marked up as a heading	Yes	The heading is marked up with a different color from the rest of the plåtform
	3. All text that is marked up as a heading, is a conceptual section heading	Yes	Each web page has a title in the header
	4. The heading is hierarchy meaningful	Yes	The page starts with an h2 since h1 is too big for the header
Contrast ratio ("color contrast")	5. The minimum contrast ratio is at least 4.5:1 for normal-size text?	Yes	Most text on web pages complies with a contrast ratio of 4.5: 1 for normal-size text. although some text lines have a very low contrast radio
Resize text	6. All text gets larger	Yes	The text gets larger when zooming.
	7. Text doesn't disappear or get cut off.	No	Zooming in on the text doesn't distort others texts.
	8. Text, images, and other content do not overlap.	No	The images and other content remain in place without being affected
	9. All buttons, form fields, and other controls are visible and usable	Yes	They are visible and usable because when zooming these are not affected
	10. Horizontal scrolling is not required to read sentences or "blocks of text"	No	The texts are very short and thematic content is distributed with videos

Figure 3. Heading for the section of video-class

Figure 4. Heading for unit 03 eavesdropping

Figure 5. Contrast ratio, first check

Figure 6. Resizing text in the web page

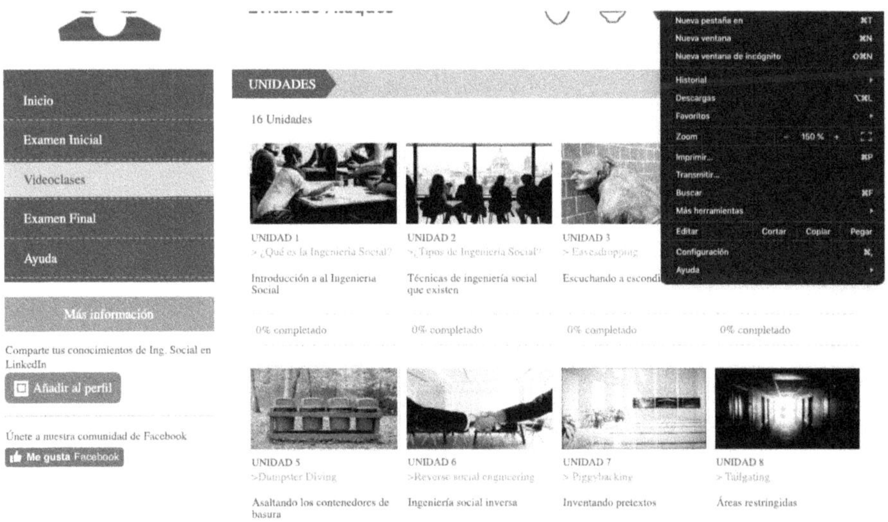

Table 4. Interaction accessibility check

Page's attributes	Web accessibility aspect	Check	Comments
Keyboard access and visual focus	1. Tab to all the elements	No	When pressing the tab key on the keyboard no fields are highlighted
	2. Tab away from all elements that you can tab into	No	None of the elements can tab away
	3. The tab order follows the logical reading order in sequence	No	As the tab function is not active the order is never followed
	4. Focus is clearly visible as you tab through the elements	No	There is no focus when tabbing through the elements
	5. All functionality by keyboard	No	There is no functionality to navigate the page through the keyboard
	6. Drop-down lists by using the arrow keys	No	There are not drop-down lists
	7. Clear visual focus and keyboard activation for image links	No	Image links don't work with keyboard keys
Forms, labels, and errors	1. All form controls are keyboard accessible	Yes	There is no way to activate a given button using the keyboard alone
	2. Every form control has a label associated with it using 'label', 'for', and 'id'	Yes	The main page has a form and each field has label and an id. The tests don't have a label
	3. Labels should be positioned correctly	Yes	Labels are positioned correctly

In the case of multimedia content, the e-learning platform has videos explaining some of the topics of Social Engineering. Such videos are not playing alone when the web page is loaded and opened in the user browser. The video starts once the user plays the video using the interface. Since the multimedia videos are stored in YouTube, the user has the option to activate subtitles to enable the transcription services as shown in Figure 8. In this way, the important audio information as dialogues and sound are transcripted in text to the screen. However, what is happening in the video scenes are not described and this makes difficult to understand for a person who cannot see.

For the last part of the general accessibility check, we review the developer answers for the first two aspects evaluated. The developer changed his mind because he misunderstood the questions. The fist two answers were:

- The texts are only readable on a computer, in case the content is seen on another screen the text does not adapt
- The alternative texts are not changing.

This observation doesn't affect our experiment, because the developer already presented this information in the previous aspects evaluated. The final answers are: the information makes sense as it is organized and shown in the web page, the alternative text isn't meaningful to the possible missing images because, as shown in Figure 2, the alternative text just shows the sequence order. To conclude the evaluation, the final aspect shows that the blocks of information have clear headings in the developed web page. In this case, we found a misunderstanding of some aspects evaluated, which can lead to a wrong application of the web accessibility guidelines.

Table 5. General accessibility check

Page's attributes	Web accessibility aspect	Check	Comments
Moving, Flashing, or Blinking Content	1. Looking for any moving, blinking, or scrolling information that starts automatically and lasts more than five seconds	Yes	There is an area where the icons are constantly changing so there is not a way for the user to pause, stop, or hide the movement
	2. Should be available a way for the user to pause, stop, or hide updated information, or for the user to control the frequency of the update	Yes	In multimedia content the user can take control
	3. No content should flash or blinks more than three times in one second	Yes	There is no content to flash or blink more than three times in a second.
Multimedia (video, audio) alternatives	1. All audio (including background noise and video with sound) should not to start automatically when a web page opens	Yes	The video starts once the user plays the video.
	2. Caption (subtitles) for videos should be turned on and off at any moment	Yes	Since multimedia videos are stored on YouTube, they have the option to activate and deactivate subtitles. The people who are speaking are identified when they speak
	3. If transcripts are available, should be easy to find near the audio/video itself and any links to the audio/video	Yes	As the videos are on YouTube, it offers video transcription services
	4. Transcripts should include all audio information, including dialogue with the speakers identified, and all important sound	Yes	Yes, the video transcript meets all the important sounds.
	5. Description of important visual information in a video should be available for help people who cannot see	No	There are scenes in the videos where it is not described what is happening in the content of the video and this makes it difficult for a person who cannot see.
Basic structure check	1. All information should make sense when read in the order it is shown	Yes	The information makes senses as is organized.
	2. Alternative text should provide adequate information for the missing images	No	Alternative text isn´t meaningful to the missing images
	3. Every block of information have clear headings	Yes	Blocks of information have clear headings

Figure 7. Changing icons

Figure 8. Video subtitles activation

Figure 9. Welcome and login page

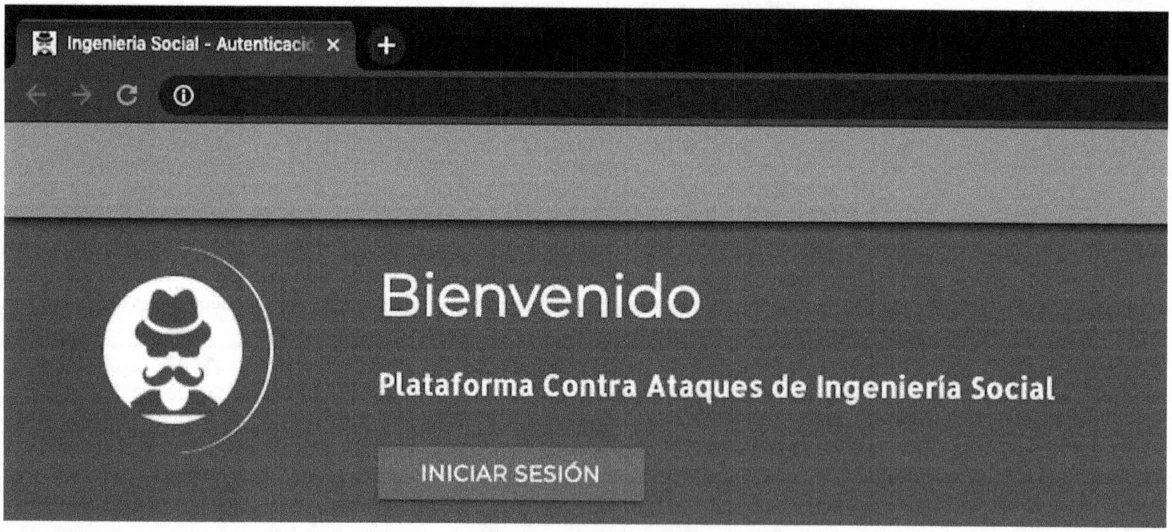

Phase Two: Discussion of the Developer´s Easy Checks Evaluations and Web Page Modifications

In this section we discuss the developer easy checks evaluations and the web page modifications. In this phase, an analysis of the evaluation carried out by the developer and of the way in which he implements these modifications in the redesign of the educational platform. In this way, we can see what his accessibility considerations are, and how he applies the design guidelines.

The page title wasn't adequate and it didn't describe the contents of the page; furthermore, he was using the same title for all web pages. This situation is difficult to evaluate with any accessibility evaluation tool, it just evaluates if there is page title. We observe the improvements of the page titles, changing

Figure 10. View of the titles of the pages at the top of the browser

their titles in all the pages of the e-learning platform; all of them are adequate according to the contents. In Figure 9 and 10 the page titles at the top of the browser are shown, indicating the purpose they have and that they are used for authentication (autenticación), main page of the platform (Página principal), video classes (Videoclases), SE Unit1 Video classes (Unidad1 - Video classes), etc.

The second aspect is the image alternative text. According to the developer's criteria, the alt tags didn't change because, due to the evaluation carried out by the developer, they properly fulfill their accessibility purposes. However, considering the use of assistive technologies for the disabled people, those tags probably are useless for accessibility and must be changed to comply with the guidelines. In the same way, he didn´t change the web page for the third aspect about text accessibility. The developer reported that the headings are correct and color contrast complies with most of the text on the web page. Although the web page has headings, we suggested that they should be improved as well as the contrast ratio that easily is resolved changing colors in buttons in light blue & white. The text resizing works adequately as is suggested in the accessibility guidelines; however, we detect horizontal scrolling when the text is very large and therefore, we suggest considering responsive design to resolve this problem, in order to avoid horizontal scrolling when adjusting the contents to the screen-size.

The fourth aspect considered is the capability of interaction using the keyboard. Tabbing on the web page was difficult. When pressing the tab key on the keyboard a few fields at the top of the page are highlighted and therefore not all the fields are accessible by the keyboard, including image links, buttons and forms. For the developer it was hard to find a solution to enable the keyboard interaction, and he reported no change about this functionality. Some guides to understand the keyboard accessibility are provided in (W3G, n.d.; WCAG, n.d.). First, it is highly recommended that styles are enabled for the links in the CSS file, so that they are displayed visually on the screen. In this case, this was the cause of the lack of compliance with accessibility through the keyboard. Another option to enable the keyboard accessibility is by means of activating such feature in the browser.

The last checks of accessibility to evaluate and resolve, are the description of important visual information in a video and heading and alternative text issues as mentioned at the end of the phase one. *Audio description sometimes known as video description or visual interpretation is important visual information in a video, in order to make it accessible to people who cannot see. For example, some videos start out with a title in text; have speaker names in the text as well as illustrations. That visual information needs to be provided to people who cannot see the video* (Group, n.d.). To include the audio description, it is suggested to review (W3C-WCAG, n.d.) to learn more about the topic. Finally, the problem about alternative text is not resolved yet and it must be resolved because it implies less effort to comply with the guidelines.

Phase Three: Redesign the User Interface to Implement Web Accessibility Basics

This section is dedicated to the redesign of the user interface to determine if the developer meets the basic aspects of web accessibility. Accordingly, it is determined whether the modifications made were appropriate, and if not, it indicates what adjustments must be made to fit the suggested design guidelines.

In the case of page titles, the redesign made by the developer was adequate, modifying the titles of each page in such a way that it now briefly describes the content or purpose of each page. Consequently, according to Figure 10, the different pages can be distinguished by the title in the corresponding browser tabs.

As can be seen in Figure 11, the WAVE tool shows the modified alt text tags. As an example, it can be seen that the broken image links for the "Imagen de Unidad 01 – Introducción" and "Imagen de Unidad 04 –Shoulder surfing" images. These images have a suitable alternative text, because they adequately describe the content of the images and in this case, they fulfill the purpose of accessibility.

Finally, Figure 12 shows some of the modifications made to the platform in terms of the titles and adaptation of the contrast ratio between the background color of the buttons and the color of the text, according to the background of the screen. When evaluating the page using the WAVE tool, it is observed that it adequately meets a contrast ratio of 8.59:1 (minimum contrast ratio is 4.5:1). In the case of the titles, the h1 title is used for the heading with the name of the site of social engineering attacks, for the h2 titles, they are used to show the welcome section, video lessons, exam, etc. h3 titles are used at a lower level of the pages in a way that improves accessibility in terms of organization of the pages.

FUTURE RESEARCH DIRECTIONS

To improve the design of web pages guarantee the implementation of web accessibility, a methodology is required to teach some strategies to students or developers in order to follow appropriately the guidelines implementation.

It is necessary to identify the main or common problems incurred by developers that cause accessibility aspects to fail on the websites and also develop implementation guidelines for accessibility. Specifically, will be crucial to identify the more complex accessibility aspects to be implemented by a developer and specify at least one implementation strategy for each one.

CONCLUSION

In this chapter, an analysis of the design of an educational web platform dedicated to the topic of Social Engineering is proposed, where compliance with the integration of web accessibility basics in the user interface is emphasized. According to the proposal presented, accessibility is assessed through easy checks of the implementation of the social engineering attacks educational platform. In the first phase, the developer carries out this evaluation and its results are analyzed. In the second phase, the identified problems, the developer either resolves or at least tries to by implementing a redesign of the platform; and the results are analyzed. In the third phase, a proposal is made for the improvements that can be introduced in the redesign of the user interface in a way that best complies with web accessibility.

Figure 11. Modified image text alternatives

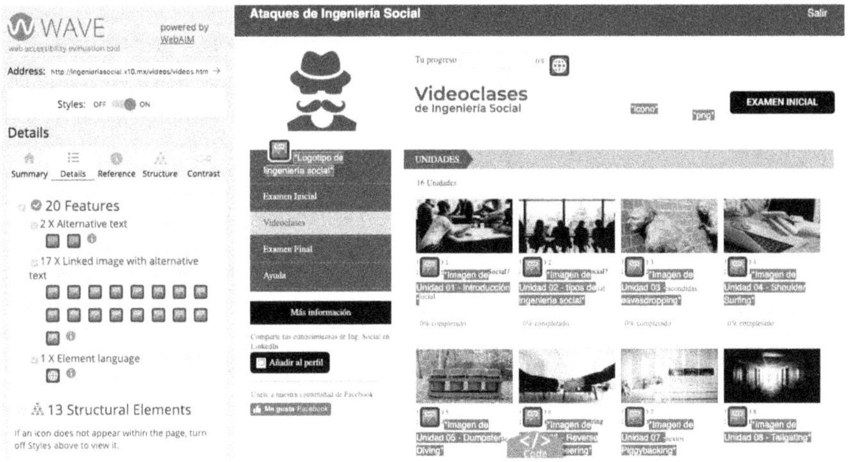

Figure 12. Headings and contrast ratio compliance

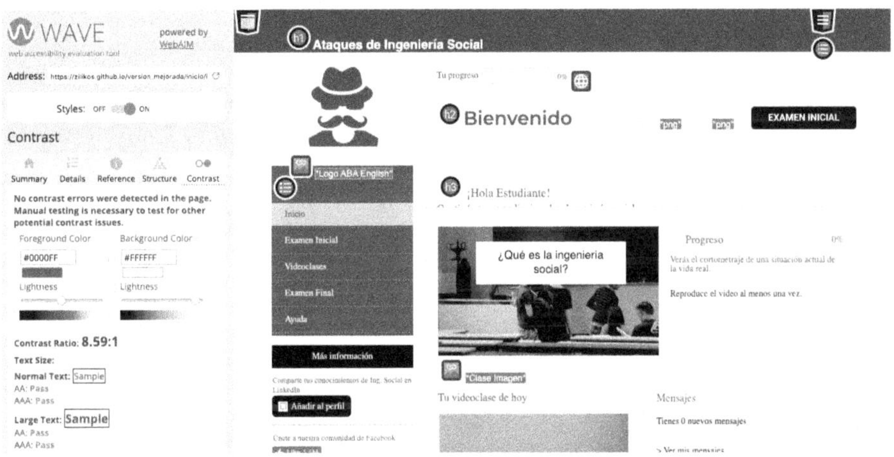

We found in the initial user interface that the developer had several accessibility problems that go from the inappropriate use of page titles to the lack of several aspects such as contrast ratio, alternative text, use of the keyboard for navigation on the page and the integration of descriptive text for the scenes in the videos. On the redesigned platform, the developer implemented improvements to solve most of the accessibility problems; however, some problems remain that prevent accessibility with the keyboard, the integration of descriptive text in the scenes of the videos to describe the scene environment and the possibility of improving the use of headings to provide a more adequate structure of the educational platform pages. All of the above show the difficulty of implementing the accessibility guides and the need to propose accessibility implementation guides that guarantee their compliance.

REFERENCES

W3C-WCAG. (n.d.). *Understanding Success Criterion 1.2.3: Audio Description or Media Alternative (Prerecorded)*. Retrieved November 18, 2019, from https://www.w3.org/WAI/WCAG21/Understanding/audio-description-or-media-alternative-prerecorded

W3G. (n.d.). *Keyboard Accessible: Understanding Guideline 2.1*. Retrieved November 12, 2019, from https://www.w3.org/TR/UNDERSTANDING-WCAG20/keyboard-operation.html

Christopher, B. (2013). *Learning about social learning in MOOCs: From statistical analysis to generative model*. Academic Press.

Columbia, T. U. of B. (2019). *Web accessibility*. Retrieved November 10, 2019, from https://www.ubc.ca/accessibility/

Digital, R. (n.d.). *Qué consecuencias puede tener un ciberataque para tu empresa*. Retrieved October 22, 2019, from https://www.reasonwhy.es/actualidad/digital/que-consecuencias-puede-tener-un-ciberataque-para-tu-empresa-2017-05-15

Floyd, K. S., & Santiago, J. (2007). The State Of Website Accessibility In Higher Education. *Proceedings of the 2007 Southern Association for Information Systems Conference*, 109–113. Retrieved from http://sais.aisnet.org/2007/SAIS07-25 Floyd-Santiago.pdf

Foozy, M. F. C., Ahmad, R., Abdollah, F., Yusof, R., & Masud, Z. M. (2012). *Generic Taxonomy of Social Engineering Attack and Defence Mechanism for Handheld Computer Study*. Retrieved from http://www.icact.org/upload/2012/0452/20120452_Abstract_B.pdf

Group, E. and O. W. (n.d.). *Easy Checks - A First Review of Web Accessibility*. Retrieved October 10, 2019, from https://www.w3.org/WAI/test-evaluate/preliminary/

Hadnagy, C. (2010). *Social engineering: The art of human hacking*. John Wiley & Sons.

Hadnagy, C. (2018). *Social Engineering: The Science of Human Hacking*. John Wiley & Sons. doi:10.1002/9781119433729

Hadnagy, C., Marin, A. M., & Wilson, P. (2011). *Ingeniería social. El arte del hacking personal*. Anaya Multimedia.

Iglesias, A., Moreno, L., Martinez, P., & Calvo, R. (2014). Evaluating the accessibility of three open-source learning content management systems: A comparative study. *Computer Applications in Engineering Education*, *22*(2), 320–328. doi:10.1002/cae.20557

Irani, D., Balduzzi, M., Balzarotti, D., Kirda, E., & Pu, C. (2011). Reverse social engineering attacks in online social networks. Lecture Notes in Computer Science, 6739, 55–74. doi:10.1007/978-3-642-22424-9_4

Ismailova, R., & Inal, Y. (2018). Accessibility evaluation of top university websites: A comparative study of Kyrgyzstan, Azerbaijan, Kazakhstan and Turkey. *Universal Access in the Information Society*, *17*(2), 437–445. doi:10.100710209-017-0541-0

Jakobsson, M., & Myers, S. (Eds.). (2016). *Phishing and Countermeasures: Understanding the Increasing Problem of Electronic Identity Theft*. Wiley.

Jiménez-González, S. G., Mendoza-González, R., & Luna-García, H. (2018). Guidelines Based on Need-Findings Study and Communication Types to Design Interactions for MOOCs. In F. Cipolla-Ficarra (Ed.), *Optimizing Human-Computer Interaction With Emerging Technologies*. doi:10.4018/978-1-5225-2616-2.ch008

Kaur, S., Kaur, K., & Kaur, P. (2016). An empirical performance evaluation of universities website. *International Journal of Computers and Applications*, *146*(15), 53–62.

Krombholz, K., Hobel, H., Huber, M., & Weippl, E. (2015). Advanced social engineering attacks. *Journal of Information Security and Applications*, *22*, 113–122. doi:10.1016/j.jisa.2014.09.005

Lee, K. (2017). Rethinking the accessibility of online higher education: A historical review. *The Internet and Higher Education*, *33*, 15–23. doi:10.1016/j.iheduc.2017.01.001

Long, J. (2008). No tech hacking: A guide to social engineering, dumpster diving, and shoulder surfing (Syngress, Ed.). Elsevier.

Maisak, R., & Brown, J. (2014). Web accessibility on Thai higher education Websites. *Proceedings of the Ninth International Conference on Software Engineering Advances.*

Molist, M. (2014). *El eslabón más débil en seguridad informática eres tú*. Retrieved October 20, 2019, from enero 20 website: https://www.elmundo.es/tecnologia/2014/01/18/52d90707ca4741f2798b4570.html

Mouton, F., Leenen, L., & Venter, H. S. (2016). Social engineering attack examples, templates and scenarios. *Computers & Security*, *59*(March), 186–209. doi:10.1016/j.cose.2016.03.004

Ortiz, T. R. (2014). *Accessibility in Distance Education: Implements of universal design for learning*. University of Hawai at Manoa.

Ozkaya, E. (2018). *Learn Social Engineering: Learn the art of human hacking with an internationally renowned expert*. Recuperado de https://books.google.com.mx/books?id=e_RZDwAAQBAJ

Patel, R. S. (2013). *Kali Linux Social Engineering*. Packt Publishing Ltd.

Riley-Huff, D. A. (2012). Web Accessibility and Universal Design: A Primer on Standards and Best Practices for Libraries. *Library Technology Reports*, *48*(7), 29–35. Retrieved from http://search.ebscohost.com/login.aspx?direct=true&db=ehh&AN=83242903&site=ehost-live

Shawar, B. A. (2015). Evaluating web accessibility of educational websites. *International Journal of Emerging Technologies in Learning*, *10*(4), 4–10. doi:10.3991/ijet.v10i4.4518

University, E. K. (n.d.). *Web Accessibility Basics & Guidelines Why Is Accessibility Important?* Retrieved from https://brand.eku.edu/sites/brand.eku.edu/files/files/cbm_web_accessibility_r1.pdf

University, U. S. (n.d.). *Web accessibiity evaluation Tool*. Retrieved November 10, 2019, from https://wave.webaim.org

WAI. (2019). *Introduction to Web Accessibility*. Retrieved October 10, 2019, from https://www.w3.org/WAI/fundamentals/accessibility-intro/

Watson, G., Mason, A, Ackroyd, R., (2014). *Social Engineering Penetration Testing: Executing Social Engineering Pen Tests, Assessments and Defense*. Syngress.

WCAG. (n.d.). *SCR29: Adding keyboard-accessible actions to static HTML elements*. Retrieved November 12, 2019, from https://www.w3.org/TR/2016/NOTE-WCAG20-TECHS-20161007/SCR29

Yesilada, Y., Brajnik, G., Vigo, M., & Harper, S. (2015). Exploring perceptions of web accessibility: A survey approach. *Behaviour & Information Technology*, *34*(2), 119–134. doi:10.1080/0144929X.2013.848238

ADDITIONAL READING

Batanero, C., Karhu, M., Holvikivi, J., Oton, S., & Amado-Salvatierra, H. R. (2014). A method to evaluate accessibility in E-learning education systems. *Proceedings - IEEE 14th International Conference on Advanced Learning Technologies, ICALT 2014*, 556–560. 10.1109/ICALT.2014.163

Da Silva, A. L. (2010). Comparative analysis of accessibility for blind digital environments for learning management for distance education. *Proceedings of the 5th Iberian Conference on Information Systems and Technologies, CISTI 2010.*

Dhanjal, A. S. (2019). Tools and Techniques of Assistive Technology for Hearing Impaired People. *2019 International Conference on Machine Learning, Big Data, Cloud and Parallel Computing (COMITCon)*, 205–210. 10.1109/COMITCon.2019.8862454

Dick, W., Golshani, F., & Beach, L. (2008). An Accessible Lane on the Information Superhighway. *IEEE MultiMedia*, *4*(15), 22–26. Retrieved from http://portal.computer.org/portal/cms_docs_multimedia/multimedia/mmgei0408.pdf. doi:10.1109/MMUL.2008.90

Gutierrez, Y., Restrepo, E. G., & Boticario, J. G. (2018). Responsive and responsible higher education through advanced technology Accessibility, empathy and diversity the keys of our future. *2017 International Conference on Engineering, Technology and Innovation: Engineering, Technology and Innovation Management Beyond 2020: New Challenges, New Approaches, ICE/ITMC 2017 - Proceedings, 2018-Januar*, 1552–1558. 10.1109/ICE.2017.8280067

Kowtko, M. (2012). Using assistive technologies to improve lives of older adults and people with disabilities. *2012 IEEE Long Island Systems, Applications and Technology Conference, LISAT 2012*, 1–6. 10.1109/LISAT.2012.6223205

Pühretmair, F., & Miesenberger, K. (2005). Making sense of accessibility in IT Design - Usable accessibility vs. accessible usability. *Proceedings - International Workshop on Database and Expert Systems Applications, DEXA, 2006*, 861–865. 10.1109/DEXA.2005.129

KEY TERMS AND DEFINITIONS

Assistive Technologies: Assistive technologies are software or equipment that people with disabilities use to improve interaction with the web.

Contrast Ratio: Is the rate of color between text and background in a web page to create a visual contrast.

Keyboard Access: It is used by people with or without disabilities to interact with the web interface. It allows you to navigate through the website using commands or tabbing in such a way that enables access to all of the contents and functionality that can be used by means of a mouse.

Social Engineering: Strategy that handles the vulnerabilities produced in people.

Social Engineering Attack: Exploiting vulnerabilities in a victim through some social engineering technique to extract valuable information.

Web Accessibility Evaluation Tool (WAVE): WAVE is a suite of evaluation tools that help authors make their web content more accessible.

Web Accessibility Guidelines: Is a series of guidelines to improve web accessibility.

Web Content: Web "content" generally refers to the information in a web page or web application, including text, images, forms, sounds, and such.

Chapter 12
A Software Testing Process Based in Gamification for Children With Down Syndrome

Alfredo Mendoza González
https://orcid.org/0000-0001-6608-046X
National Institute of Statistics and Geography, Mexico & Universidad Autónoma de Zacatecas, Mexico

ABSTRACT

Evaluating software implies challenging users' abilities during a period, applying several assessments, and analyzing their evolution. This process might turn unpleasant and stressful, especially to those susceptible to anxiety and stress, such as Down syndrome users. The poor performance of unpleasant users generates unreal results. A gamified approach for software testing is proposed that maintains user motivation and engagement and reduces anxiety and stress. Common behaviors expected are anxiety, stress, unwilling to work, and in general, lack of motivation. Using gamification, makes it possible to succeed in controlling these common negative behaviors and stimulating the positive ones including the MDA framework into a generic learnability evaluation process, linking these two elements with the psychological approach of gestalt therapy. Gamifying the testing experience increased the quality of communication between users and applicators; provided a friendly, motivational, and engaging environment; and increased the rate of testing success and the range of potential participants.

INTRODUCTION

When users of a software product start to interact with it, they begin a process that can be either the most pleasant experience or the worst. Usable software products are commonly perceived as the most useful, efficient, and lofty. To assure software usability, developers and designers must know how their products cover all learning needs of goal-users. User evaluation of software products has shown to enhance user-needs fitting in usability, accessibility, ergonomics and learning. Software evaluation involving

DOI: 10.4018/978-1-7998-2325-4.ch012

users means analysing the way users interact with it, and it is one of the most important aspects of User Centered Design (Barendregt, Bekker, Bouwhuis, & Baauw, 2007).

Testing in the software development process is mandatory; nevertheless, for some users the experience of being tested may turn unpleasant; in fact, all software testing involving users generate certain levels of anxiety and stress. Klemer explain that users might feel uncomfortable during evaluation due to (Klemer, 2016):

- Compromising to make things well
- Feeling of being observed
- Challenging of capabilities
- Error making afraid
- Changing of the ordinary working space

Users' discomfort may affect their performance in evaluation and reliability of resulting data. This is the reason of why is important to provide a friendly evaluation environment to users. Enhancing testing experiences, allow a deeper understanding of learning strategies and preferences of users (Kirijian, Myers, & Charland, 2007), and enhance reliability of the study results. This research presents a software testing process based on gamification -bringing the game experience to software evaluation. It allows maintaining the user's motivation and engagement, reducing anxiety and stress, during the whole testing process, and takes especially care of the Down syndrome users' characteristics in communication, socialization, and behaviour.

BACKGROUND

Testing With Users

User testing, can provide both quantitative and qualitative information about software's learnability. It depends of the technique(s) followed by applicators, the most common are:

Quantitative Information: In (Butler, 1985), authors presented a case of study where they test a financial system by analysing the users' performance (time to mastery and error avoidance/recovery) in a set of tasks with a predefined level of expected success. In (Baxter & Oatley, 1991) authors tested two spreadsheet software measuring the performance of 16 navy users and 16 experts in 14 tasks. They found that previous experience has a large effect on tasks scores not the brand of the software previously learned. Many other authors have used the method of task performance to assess learnability (Chapanis, 1991), (Davis & Wiedenbeck, 1998) (Raisamo & Räihä, 2000), (Elliott, 2002), (Ziefle M. .., 2002), (Rafique, Jingnong, Wang, Abbasi, & Lew, 2012), (Zbick, Nake, Milrad, & Jansen, 2015).

Qualitative Information: Authors complemented the qualitative data from the testing with a questionnaire about the quality of certain features of the system. Results of the performance testing let the authors know that the current version of the system surpassed the expectations in learnability. The questionnaire results let them to identify features of the system where improvement was needed. The think-aloud protocol consists basically in encourage users to verbalize the learnability experience. In (Mack, Lewis, & Carroll, 1983) authors asked ten novice users to verbalize they work while learning to use a word processor. As authors mentioned, they used this method because it did not impose limitations of more traditional ones, and because it was successfully used in cognitive psychology studies. This chapter shown how frustrating can be the process of learning to use a computer system, the method let the authors to know how users felt when troubles occurred, going from "what did I do?" to "Stupid stuff", and "I'm lost already". From this, authors detect behavioral patterns that let them to generalize characteristics in learning and features of the system that made learning difficult. Since this early research, the use of the think aloud protocol was also reported in (Kato, 1986), (Mack & Robinson, 1992), (Linja aho, 2006), (Grossman, Fitzmaurice, & Ramtin, 2009), among others.

These are the most common techniques employed to evaluate software products, nevertheless the use of other techniques has also been reported, for example in (Stickel, Fink, & Holzinger, 2007) authors study the correlation between brainwave patterns and the level of usability perceived. By analysing the rise and fall of brain signals through electroencephalographic records; (Pretorius, Gelderblom, & Chimbo, 2010) employed eye tracking to analyse the focus points and visual strategies of children and adults trying to learn the use of a computer game; focus groups, a method that involves a group of users working with the software and then having a moderated discussion, was applied by Fuhrmann to evaluate the learnability of a Geovirtual environments in (Fuhrmann & MacEachren, 2001).

Gamification

Gamification is about including the game thinking in non-gaming scenarios to change people behavior, i.e. to make activities more or less game-like in non-gaming contexts (Werbach, 2014) (Robson, Plangger, McCarthy, & Leyland, 2016), (Chee, 2016); but more than creating a game, gamification is creating a gamified experience in an optimized way (Zichermann & Cunningham, 2011). Also, the gamification of non-gaming processes means making them more fun and engaging without undermining their credibility (Muntean, 2011), (Dichev, Dicheva, Angelova, & Agre, 2015). Among the benefits of Gamification there are (Conger, 2016):

- Fun and pleasure
- Increase altruism
- Increase brainstorming and alternatives development
- Increase company loyalty
- Increase competition
- Increase effectiveness of learning
- Increase efficiency of learning
- Increase information dissemination
- Increase motivation
- Increase productivity
- Increase self-expression
- Increase skills
- Increase social capital
- Increase tasks engagement

- Obtain desired behaviors

Despite all advantages, there is a potential danger in applying Gamification in non-gaming process: Gamification turns to be successful in providing gameful experiences to users, but they are distracted by using the core service; when this happen, the whole process had failed (Huotari & Hamari, 2016).

One of the most used frameworks to apply gamification in non-game scenarios is referred as MDA: Mechanics, Dynamics, and Aesthetics, it refers to:

- **Mechanics:** The control mechanisms that rules the players' actions within a game context.
- **Dynamics:** The specific player actions and/or behavior triggered or motivated by a certain set of game mechanics.
- **Aesthetics:** The desired behavior evoked in the player by the game, resulting by certain dynamics.

These three elements of game design help understand players and apply the required techniques to generate the desired behaviors on them. In shortly, mechanics are the core elements of the game that guide players' actions; dynamics determine what players do in response to the mechanics; and aesthetics is the resulted behavior that mechanics and dynamics generate in players. The MDA Framework helps designers to understand how the elements of a Game will work to generate certain behavior in players. The art of applying gamification in non-gaming scenarios is how these three elements work together to evoke the design behavior in users.

Understanding Users' Stress

The prolonged exposure to a stressor results in suppression of the immune system and wear and tear of several body systems [Gillian, 2007]. That is why levels of stress must have much attention during Learnability studies. Based in [Gillian, 2013], stress is a process of how a person responses in Affection, Behaviour and Psychology to stimuli, all responses affect directly subject's health; Figure 1 shows graphically this process.

There is an approach in Psychology called The Gestalt Psychology which it has been recently used to treat mental blocks. Broadly speaking, it is a humanist focus of Psychology that claims any human bean can develop his/her maximum potential by him/her-self, and how the environment affects, and is affected, by him/her; therefore, any Gestalt intervention facilitate experience in where subjects grown their self-confidence and growth (Salama, 2012).

The Gestalt Cycle of Experience (Figure 2) represents clearly how these blocks are presented in any subject's experience dividing it in 8 stages: Repose, Sensation, Awareness, Energy, Action, Pre-contact, Full-contact, and Post-contact (Salama, 2012). By matching the 8 stages of the Gestalt Cycle of Experience with the Learnability Testing Process, we knew exactly how to treat each stress-risk point, depending on the block and that users experienced.

In (Salama, 2012) the author suggests that there are mental blocks commonly presented in each Gestalt stage, which difficult the flow of energy through the whole cycle and that, in consequence, stress subjects. In the next table, we present a set of good practices for each Gestalt stages that deal with respective mental blocks.

Figure 1. The stress process
Source: (based in Gillian, 2013, p.4)

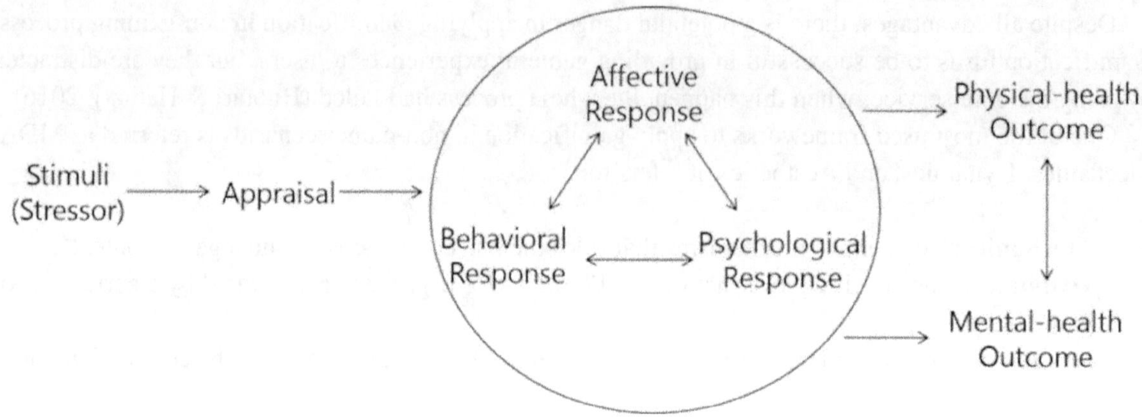

Figure 2. The gestalt cycle

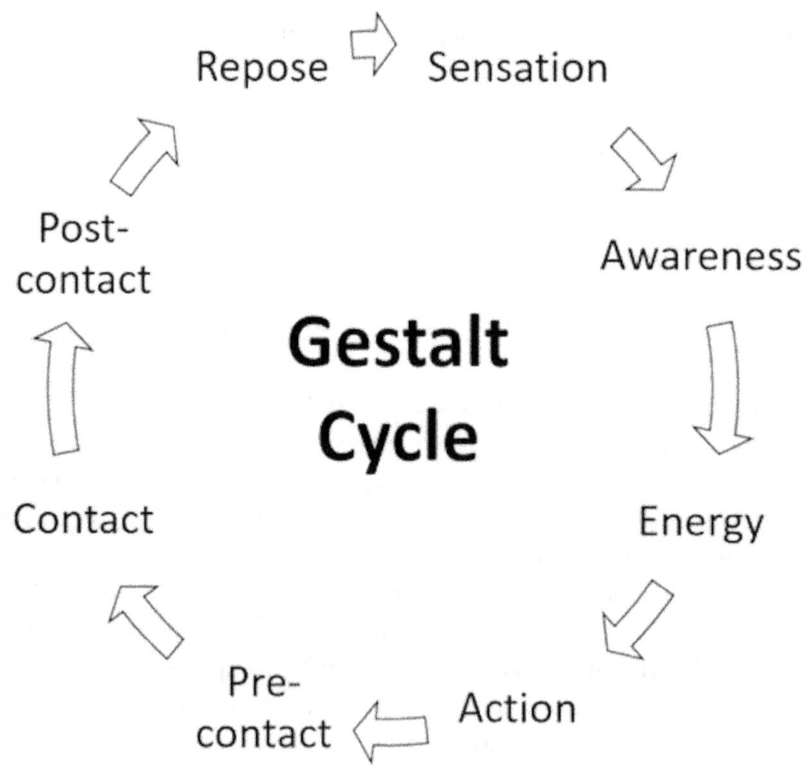

Table 1. Good practices for each Gestalt Stages

Gestalt Stage	Objective	Techniques
Repose	Motivate relaxation, decrease sloth	People commonly postpone new and difficult tasks because fear of falling; in this stage the objective is to connect previous success with the new activity.
Sensation	Motivate affection with the activity	Create an affective bound with the new activity by denoting the leadership of the subject by doing it.
Figure	Provide knowledge Increase security	Provide a general explanation of the new activity, assuring that subjects feels that he is the right person to do the job.
Energy	Help in accepting the role, increase confidence	Encourage the subject to do the best, assuring that this will be the only way to achieve the goals. Emphasize his qualities.
Action	Increase decision and expression	Motivate the subject to realize that soon is the moment to begin actions.
Pre-contact	Provide recognition of the activity.	It will help if this stage takes place in a different physical location from the previous. A more specific explanation of the activity must be provided. Subject must not feel alone.
Contact	Decrease shame Increase responsi-bility, membership.	Subject must be convinced that he can do it, that he is not alone and that mistakes are allowed.
Post-contact	Motivate independence decrease fixation	Subject must be motivated to separate from the activity. A physical separation between the space where the action takes place and the ending/closing activity will help to encourage it.

Down Syndrome

The functional activity of a person (user) can be restricted by 4 factors (WHO, 2016):

1. Health conditions
2. Contextual factors
3. Body structure and functions
4. Social Participation

Furthermore, there are 5 interaction limitations that, at some level, affect the Body structure and functions (Vanderheiden, 2012):

1. Vision impairments
2. Hearing impairments
3. Speaking impairments
4. Motor impairments
5. Learning impairments

Down syndrome is caused by a genetic anomaly, making an extra copy of chromosome 21 (Parker, 2004). Such genetic condition brings particular characteristics in learning, communicating and perceiving skills, Affective their performance in daily living, work, school, social interaction, etc. A study revealed that people with Down syndrome are more susceptible to have psychiatric disorders than other intellectual-disabled individuals, denoting bipolarity and impulse control disorder (Dykens, y otros, 2015).

Down syndrome affects physical, intellectual and behavioural capabilities in those who burn with it, affecting social interaction and work productivity (Chapman & Hesketh, 2000). Among the most common physical limitations of Down syndrome people there are difficulties in the fine motor skills, eye-hand coordination, eyesight, hearing. Around 80% of Down syndrome people have Intelligence Quotient average of 50, being in the rank of moderate intellectual disability (Parker, 2004), having commonly problems like low comprehension of abstract concepts, delay in expressive language, lack of concentration, problems in short-term memory, among others (Bruni, 2006) (Chapman & Hesketh, 2000) (Parker, 2004).

The very first challenge when testing software with Down syndrome users is the number of possible participants. The estimated incidence of Down syndrome is about 1 in 1000 worldwide, making homogeneous groups of users for software testing, or selecting only those best suitable for (the most communicative, participative, and committed users) is not option. In (Barendregt, Bekker, Bouwhuis, & Baauw, 2007) authors presented how neurotypical children can be better selected as participants in software testing based in their personality characteristics, at the end they optimize testing effort with this. Clearly with Down syndrome users we must find another way to do that.

There are a few papers in literature that inform about the software evaluation with Down syndrome users, among the common behaviours reported by researchers are: easy distraction, limited concentration time, difficulty in understanding instructions, difficulty in following a set of instructions, being not cooperative to work, and spontaneous and impulsive changes of mood. Feng in (Feng & Lazar, 2010) present a summary of difficulties experienced by Down Syndrome users using computers, among the most common are:

- Typing
- Frustration in navigation
- Frustration in trouble shooting
- Lack of patience
- Low error tolerance
- Frustration when excessive information was found
- Frustration in inconsistencies in interface design
- Frustration when there are too many windows opened

Caliz in (Cáliz, Martínez, Alamán, Terán, & Cáliz, 2016) presented a literature review of the experiences of researchers working with Down syndrome users in usability testing. From a systematic literature review, authors derived a 9 steps process for usability testing with Down syndrome users:

1. Recruit participants
2. Establish the users' tasks
3. Write the instructions
4. Define the test plan
5. Run a pilot test
6. Refine the test plan after the pilot tests
7. Run the test session.
8. Analyse the collected data
9. Report results

Authors of (Lazar, Kumin, & Feng, 2011) and (Kirijian, Myers, & Charland, 2007) gave an interesting list of good practices in evaluating software with Down syndrome users from two different cases of study:

- Be sure that users understand what they will do, when and what they would get when done; also explain them the kind of help they would get if needed.
- Visual learning strategies works better with Down syndrome users, take special care in the visual design of the test.
- Take care in details, individuals with Down syndrome methodically scan every piece of information, every variation in design will be interpreted in some way.
- The time of attention in a particular activity is around 10 to 15 minutes
- Use real examples
- Be flexible with participants
- Anticipate material required in testing
- Present satisfaction scales visually
- Instructions should be provided visually and verbally
- Create attractive tools to the study

Related Work

In (Butler, 1985), one of the first works about learnability, authors presented a case of study for the learnability of a financial system, analyzing the performance (time to mastery and error avoidance/recovery) of seven users (individually tested), in a set of tasks with a predefined level of expected success. Users had to solve one of the three proposed problems. These problems followed three criteria: They represented a typical problem that novice users often try to solve via a computer system, they were conceptually simple, and they sample a set of features of functionality and design. After the trial, users were provided with a questionnaire about the design quality of the system. Authors were surprised by how the users' tests and questionnaire provided information about the human factors involved and how they can be improved in application and research. Other studies reporting learnability evaluation have been presented in (Chapanis, 1991), (Davis & Wiedenbeck, 1998) (Raisamo & Räihä, 2000), (Elliott, 2002), (Ziefle, 2002), and (Zbick, Nake, Milrad, & Jansen, 2015); all of them followed the same approach of evaluating software by individually testing users' performance, and complementing it with questionnaires and interviews. With this, we can see that learnability evaluation process has not changed so much.

Scientific works about users with Down syndrome, in the Human-Computer bibliography are limited in number. An empirical study of three input techniques used by Down syndrome children and young adults were presented in (Hu, Feng, Lazar, & Kumin, 2013). They analyzed the use of the keyboard, word prediction and speech recognition to a group of 10 users with Down syndrome between 10 and 24 years old. Besides the surprising results of performance in keyboard and preference of speech recognition (see original paper for more details), the evaluation of the users implied the collection of demographic data. Authors also reported that some users were easily distracted during the evaluation and have fatigue and lack of patience. Authors suggested that the computer experience (number of years using computers) can be a good predictor of users' performance. Also, they suggested that low performance shown by users in some activities was due to lack of motivation, training, and exposure to technology, rather than limitations in ability.

In (Caliz, Martinez, Alaman, Teran, & Caliz, 2016) the author presented a process for usability testing with Users with Down syndrome consisting of 6 phases: Recruit participants, establish tasks, write instructions, pilot testing, and testing. This process was made from a previous literature review. Nevertheless, the literature review seems to be limited, the process considered only 5 papers from 2009 to 2013, and the process is not applied or validated. Still, authors presented the need for a process when working with Users with Down syndrome.

METHODOLOGY

The objective of this research is to provide a friendly environment during software testing where motivation, action, and commitment in users. All the advantages of applying Gamification appear to be clear: it engages, motivates, and makes users react in a better way to new, unknown and difficult situations. Before creating a gamified version of a learnability test, we must understand the context of being evaluated, from the user perspective. The process proposed by Caliz in (Caliz, Martinez, Alaman, Teran, & Caliz, 2016) for usability testing for Down syndrome users was taken as the baseline. It was enhanced by including a general process to game design and an analysis of users' behavior. The result was a gamified approach for learnability testing.

The Testing Process

Caliz in (Caliz, Martinez, Alaman, Teran, & Caliz, 2016) proposed a process for usability testing with Down syndrome users (figure 2), the 9 phases of the process are:

1. Recruit Participants: Define the goal users, and a multidisciplinary team of experts to better understand the desired aspect of the Down syndrome users learning.
2. Establish tasks: All testing sessions and tasks must be defined and specified at detail including objectives, times, evaluation, users' tasks, etc.
3. Write instructions: All the instructions that will be followed to collect data must be written to formally identify the techniques involved: interviews, expert opinions, family meetings, users' feedback, etc.
4. Define test plan: Including participants and roles, testing sessions, user's tasks,
5. Pilot testing: To clarify tasks, objectives, testing tools and evaluation methods; and to provide extra information about what to expect in the real test.
6. Refine test plan: All feedback collected in the previous step will enhance the testing.
7. Testing: Apply testing application over the goal population.
8. Analyze data: All information collected from testing must be analyzed according to the objective of the study.
9. Present result: Present results to the objective audience.

Table 2. Emotions in gestalt cycle

Gestalt Stage	Behavior
Repose	Motivate relaxation, decrease sloth
Sensation	Motivate affection with the activity
Figure	Provide knowledge Increase security
Energy	Help in accepting the role, increase confidence
Action	Increase decision and expression
Pre-contact	Provide recognition of the activity.
Contact	Decrease shame Increase responsibility, membership.
Post-contact	Motivate independence decrease fixation

Game Development Process

The generic process to develop games shown in Figure 3 was proposed by Purdue University's Department of Computer Graphics Technology (Purdue, 2016) for educational game development. It is divided in three phases: Pre-Production, Production and Post-Production. Chandler in (Chandler, 2009) mentioned that in Pre-Production phase is defined the objective and features of the game, the resources needed as the cost and people; i.e. the game plan. The Pre-production, according with Chandler, consists in:

- **Game Concept:** Find the solution of the problem, starts with the question: What the game would be like?
- **Design:** It start by figuring out the first game requirements. While the game features are defined, current technology is research to find out what is better for the proposed game. It must be defined a game plan to define how everything is going to be done.

The production phase is focused in the construction of the game by the production team, basically composed by graphical artists and programmers. Once the game is created, its effectiveness is tested in the Post-production phase (Purdue, 2016).

Behavioral Analysis

Our proposal to gamify the learnability testing process is based on motivating positive behavior and controlling the negative one. For this, we applied the Gestalt psychology approach, which is an approach which aims to heighten an individual's self-awareness and perception of the moment, especially in terms of their relationships with their environment (Bloom, 2006). In (Salama, 2012) was proposed a practical way to apply the Gestalt approach in order to know the emotional state of patients at any moment: The Gestalt Experience Cycle. It divides any experience into 8 phases: Repose, Sensation, Figure, Energy, Action, Pre-contact, Contact and Post-contact, in which, patients may experience mental blocks that difficult completing and closing such experience, generating stress and anxiety. Salama defined a set of emotions for each phase (table 2) which if stimulated in the right way, might help to face and overcome these mental blocks.

Table 3. Testing experience from the gestalt perspective

Testing experience	Gestalt Stage	Description
Welcome	Repose	The users change the current activity to start participation in the learnability test
Presentation	Sensation	Users actually knows that they are going to be involved in a new activity
Explanation	Figure	Users figure out what this new activity is all about.
	Energy	Users realize what they are going to need to do the new activity
Doing tasks	Action	Users start actions into the new activity
	Pre-contact	Users focus the attention in the new activity
	Contact	Users make the new activity
Finishing	Post-contact	Users end the new activity

We divided the experience of users being tested in a learnability study in 5 stages: Welcome, Presentation, Explanation, Task Development and Finishing, in which we can easily match the Gestalt Experience Cycle. Table 3 presents how a learnability testing experience may be seen from the Gestalt cycle approach. The eight phases focus around the participation of users in the testing, having an approximation to it, doing it, and moving away from it. Consequently, guided by the Gestalt cycle, we could identify the behavior that must be stimulated at each event of the learnability experience, this shown also in table 3.

A Gamified Approach For Learnability Evaluation

The gamified approach (figure 4) is based in the usability testing process for Down syndrome users proposed by (Cáliz, Martínez, Alamán, Terán, & Cáliz, 2016), the game development process proposed in (Purdue, 2016) and the Gestalt Experience Cycle of (Salama, 2012). It has seven phases:

Definition of the learnability test plan, including sessions, schedule, evaluation methods, and everything about the testing process. Definition of all participants such as users, users' relatives, expert consultants and members of the testing team, and their role in the process. Definition of the set of tasks to be developed by users and their proper evaluation method according with the study's objective.

1. Ethnographic Study

As mentioned in (Ladner, 2014) ethnography is used to understand participants' language, concepts, categories and opinions and use them to define the research. Methods used in ethnographic studies are designed to discover prior the testing (LeCompte & Schensul, 2010). The first step is to stop being a stranger to users, to take part in common activities with them, and to collect any useful data. Then, collect data about users' academics, capabilities and limitations, and technology usage.

2. Behavioral Analysis

A learnability test experience can be divided in five stages: Arrival, presentation, explanation, participation, and ending. The gestalt experience cycle applied to it can serve as a guide to desired behaviors to evoke in users during testing. A behavioral control can be defined from this and the behavioral data collected in the ethnographic study.

3. Gamification

Directly, from the last step we defined the Aesthetics of our Gamified Learnability Testing Experience. The game-play will be defined to let users develop all defined tasks guided by game mechanics and dynamics that generates the proper aesthetics previously defined.

4. Pilot Testing

Select a few participants, not limited to the user population, and apply the testing procedure in order to find out the pain points. All the feedback will enhance the actual testing application.

5. Testing

Apply the testing procedure to the user population according the testing plan. A common application of a learnability test consists in two stages: An explanation of the task given by the applicator, and the participation of the user.

6. Results

Analysis of all collected data and its proper arrangement that leads some concluding remarks.

EXPERIMENTAL WORK

Participants

10 users with Down syndrome between 15 and 20 years old $\left(\bar{X}=16, S=2.23\right)$ were involved in this study; 4 women and 6 men, all enrolled in a special school program in the same grade. All of them have basic reading and writing skills, and can develop a set of tasks derived from a set of instructions. Verbal communication is very limited. They have basic experience using computers, they usually play academic games using keyboard and mouse. They also have basic knowledge using tablet computers and smartphones, they know how open certain applications (usually games) which involve tapping and swiping.

Our first meeting with users was in their classroom, as a guest student. We (all members of the team that was in touch with users during testing) participated in both curricular and extracurricular activities during one week. We applied a survey to know about particular characteristics of users such as: social interaction, healthcare, daily living, computational skills, frequency of use of computers and other electronic, to parents, teachers and therapists. We also provide to parents the institutional document of consent participation, based on the *Informed Parental Consent for Research Involving Children* of the World Health Organization (WHO, 2016).

Table 4. Behaviour to evoke on users while tested

Testing Phase	Behaviour
Welcome	Willing to start a new activity
Presentation	Confidence with the test applicator and commitment with the study
Explanation	Concentration and attention to the instructions, commitment in making the best effort
Participation	Concentration and attention in making the task
	Proud of the work done
Finishing	Proud to have participated

Joining all data collected in the ethnographic study, the application of the Gestalt cycle in the testing experience (Table 4); together, researchers, therapists, teachers and psychologist consultants, defined the corresponding desired behavior to each of the stages of the learnability testing experience shown in Table 4.

Sessions and Materials

All the experiments were performed in a classroom specially adapted for the study, a table, a couple of seats and two video-cameras (in front and behind the user) conform the classroom environment. All tests were made over a mobile application running in a 10.1'' Samsung © Galaxy tablet computer with Android© 5.0.2 Lollipop. The mobile application tested was "Learn to read and write" v1.1.1 made by Endyanos-imedia and available in http://www.endyanosimedia.com/apps.

The main roles in the testing team was

- **Applicator:** Guides the users throughout testing, gives all the instructions and provide necessary help.
- **Assistant:** Helps applicator in several tasks, such as configuring the environment, providing material, setting devices, etc.
- **Psychologist:** Evaluates the users emotional state at each stage of the testing experience.

The testing plan was:

1. Application of the ethnographic study: Which included academic and social activities with potential users, interviews and application of the survey to parents, teachers and therapists.
2. Pilot testing: Applied to one user, one teacher, and one testing team member.
3. Testing: We selected a homogeneous group of 10 users (according the ethnographic study, age, skills and limitations) to apply the test. We applied eight individual sessions for each user, the same tasks were developed on each one, to analyze the learning evolution.

Table 5. Behaviour to evoke on users while tested

Testing experience	Behaviour
Welcome	Willing to start a new activity
Presentation	Confidence with the test applicator and commitment with the study
Explanation	Concentration and attention to the instructions, commitment in making the best effort
Participation	Concentration and attention in making the task
	Proud of the work done
Finishing	Proud to have participated

Three tasks were defined to the learnability test:

1. **Interaction with the Reading Part of the App:** Listen the letter and the word by touching the figures and use the "next" button to do it with the first five letters.
2. **Interaction With the Writing part of the App:** Paint in the blackboard following the writing pattern, erase, and use the "next" button to do it with the first five letters.
3. **Interaction With the App:** Close the current window, change between windows, open new window from the main menu, close the app, and open the app.

The variables measured in these tasks were:

1. Percentage of users that successfully completed each task at first try.
2. Percentage of users that fail in completing each task.
3. Average number of trials per task.
4. Average time expended to each task.

Ethnographic Study

Our first meeting with users was in their classroom, as a guest student. We (all members of the team that was in touch with users during testing) participated in both curricular and extracurricular activities during one week. We applied a survey to know about particular characteristics of users such as: social interaction, healthcare, daily living, computational skills, frequency of use of computers and other electronic, to parents, teachers and therapists. We also provide to parents the institutional document of consent participation, based on the *Informed Parental Consent for Research Involving Children* of the World Health Organization (WHO, 2016).

Behavioural Analysis

Joining all data collected in the ethnographic study, the application of the gestalt cycle in the testing experience (table 1); together, researchers, therapists, teachers and psychologist consultants, defined the corresponding desired behaviour to each of the stages of the learnability testing experience shown in table 5.

Gamification Implementation

The general objective of the game was set as engaging users into the study and making learnability testing a fun and great experience. People with Down syndrome usually feel great when they feel useful to others (Troncoso & Del Cerro, 2009), (Ruiz, 2012), from here that the game basically is about helping a character to achieve certain goal. In order to meet this very representative goal, the user must complete a set of challenges: the three tasks of the study.

The set of behaviors of table 2 as the Game aesthetics, thus these are the corresponding game Dynamics:

- **Happiness and Joy:** In order to motivate the users to start this new activity, no matter what they were doing, we must make them feel that this is a more pleasant one.
- **Affective Bound:** Creating an affective bound between the user and both, the applicator and the study, will result in trust and commitment.
- **Clear Understanding:** We motivate in the users their willing to pay attention to the set of instructions of a particular task, to facilitate their comprehension and let user to have a clear idea (Figure in the Gestalt cycle) about the effort required to accomplish it (Energy in the Gestalt cycle).
- **Working Hard:** In this game Dynamic motivate the users' willing to work, providing them self-confidence and enhancing concentration.
- **Rewarding:** We reward all users' effort, making them feel proud of the work they made.
- **Friendly Competition:** Since there is not winner and losers in this game, we do stimulate the feeling to being distinguished by their merits from the rest of them.

Finally, we defined the game mechanics that produce these dynamics. By searching in literature and specialized websites, 10 mechanics were selected to be included into the gamified learnability evaluation:

- **Discovery:** Encourage users to discover something, to be surprised.
- **Story:** A sequence of events involving the character. The story engages the character and the player.
- **Avatar:** A fictitious character that is affected by the player actions in the game-world. Avatars give the opportunity to create a commitment with the player.
- **Epic Meaning:** It enrolls player to believe they are working to make something great, inspiring, bigger than themselves.
- **Cascading Information:** Provides information in the minimum possible snippets to gain the appropriate level of understanding.
- **Blissful Productivity:** Keep users working hard doing meaningful and rewarding their work.
- **Permission to Fail:** It gives the opportunity to player to make mistakes with no point loss. Motivates player to do what he/she can without fear to lose.
- **Points:** They are cumulative rewards won by the proper actions of player during game.
- **Badges:** It is a label of distinction for certain qualities of the player during the game.
- **Leaderboards:** Compare the position of all best players in the game.

The application of the MDA framework is shown in table 6. Table 7 to 11 show the specification of each learnability testing experience phase.

Table 6. The MDA framework applied

Mechanics	Dynamics	Aesthetics
Discovery	Happiness and Joy	Willing to start a new activity
Story Avatar Epic meaning	Affective bound	Confidence with the test applicator and commitment with the study
Cascading Information Missions	Clear understanding	Concentration and attention to the instructions
Blissful Productivity Permission to fail	Working hard	Concentration and attention in making the task, commitment in making the best effort
Points Badges Leaderboards	Rewarding Friendly Competition	Proud of the work done

Table 7. Phase 1 The Welcome

Game Aesthetic:	Willing to start a new activity
Game dynamics:	Happiness and Joy
Game mechanics:	Discovery
Application	
1. Welcome 2. Presentation of the test applicator as the guide 3. Introduction of the study and its tasks	
Game-play	
The presentation of the game makes feel the users great to start a new activity. The test applicator is presented as a guide. inviting them to press a big red button to start.	

Table 8. Phase 2 The Presentation

Game Aesthetic:	Confidence with the test applicator and commitment with the study
Game dynamics:	Affective bound
Game mechanics:	Story, Avatar, Epic meaning
Application	
1. Present (remind) the story. 2. Present the avatars, or remind the chosen one. 3. Let the users choose one avatar. 4. Present (remind) a panoramic view of the whole scenario. 5. Remark the importance of completing the story.	
Game-play	
The character must collect eight stars in order to win a very big unknown price. Users must complete the three tasks in order to have one star.	

Table 9: Phase 3 the explanation

Game Aesthetic:	Concentration and attention to the instructions
Game dynamics:	Clear understanding
Game mechanics:	Cascading Information
Application	
1. Provide the user with the specific instructions to each Activity, one by one.	
Game-play	
The character receives a parchment that shares with the user. That is the key to complete the activity. The instructions are read to users.	

Table 10. Phase 4 the participation

Game Aesthetic:	Concentration and commitment in making the task
Game dynamics:	Working hard
Game mechanics:	Blissful Productivity, Permission to fail
Application	
1. Remind the user the price to complete the activity 2. Inform the user that they can make any mistake	
Game-play	
The applicator motivates the users to make the activity, he reminds them how the star will be filled with gold as they complete the activity.	

Table 11. Phase 5 the end

Game Aesthetic:	Proud of the work done
Game dynamics:	Rewarding, Friendly Competition
Game mechanics:	Points, Badges, Leaderboards
Application	
1. Give to users the corresponding golden star 2. Feedback the users about their progress in the game 3. Award the users with a great characteristic of their participation 4. Inform the users about the rest of them.	
Game-play	
The applicator gives to users the golden star and show how the character has got benefit with that. The applicator also highlights one characteristic in users' participation and finally presents the leaderboard with stars and badges earned by each of the other users.	

Table 12. Users' performance final session

Task	Completed at First Try	No Completed	Attempts Avg	Time Avg (secs)
Interaction with the reading part of the app	70%|▲40%	0%|▼40%	1.8|▼.5	93.4|▼15.3
Interaction with the writing part of the app	50%|▲30%	20%|▼30%	2.5|▼.9	218.7|▼11.4
Interaction with the whole app	30%|▲30%	50%|▼10%	2.8|▼.7	145.6|▼14.3

Table 13. Users' behavior change

	First Session	Final Session
% of users with negative emotion at the beginning of the test	40%	10%
% of users with neutral emotion at the beginning of the tests	30%	0%
% of users with negative emotion at the end of the tests	0%	0%
% of users with neutral emotion at the end of the tests	0%	0%
% of users requiring the behavioural control extra-actions	60%	20%

Pilot Testing

According with (Kumin, Lazar, Feng, Wentz, & Ekedebe, 2012) a pilot test is useful because it provides an overview of the whole study, and what to expect applying the evaluation protocol, it would may involve a couple of participants. We apply a pilot testing first with one member of the research team and then with one user with Down syndrome which have already participated in other tests. The feedback provided let us improve certain characteristics of the game play, specifically to remark the attitude of the applicator to interact with users. Also the testing schedule was adjusted due to the time that took the team to re-organized the game environment.

Testing

As mentioned before, we applied the study over 10 users with Down syndrome. We test eight users per day due to their school schedule. Although many data were coded during sessions, we recorded all users' activity to make a further analysis. The protocol of the test was: Users were received outside the classroom and invited to start their participation by pushing a red button, creating interest to participate. Next, we prepare users by explaining the story and the rules of the game at first session and reminding them in the subsequent. Then each task was explained once, and the user was encouraged to do it. When additional explanations were required, applicator avoided negative behaviour by diminishing the importance of have failed, and giving in to do it again. At the third fail we passed to the next activity avoiding negativity in the same way plus evoking independence to it. Once the three tasks of the session

Table 14. Comparison between first and final session

Testing experience Stage	Behaviour	
	First Session	Final Session
Welcome	Negative (40%)	Positive (100%)
Presentation	Neutral (50%)	Positive (100%)
Explanation	Neutral (40%)	Positive (80%)
Participation	Neutral (60%)	Positive (80%)
Finishing	Positive (60%)	Positive (100%)

Table 15. Failure analysis

	First Session	Final Session
Failed tasks	15	7
% of tasks failed due to task complexity	80%	90%
% of tasks failed due to misunderstanding	13%	5%
% of tasks failed due to giving up	8%	5%

were finished applicator give the corresponding feedback to users including points, badges and showing leaderboard. The next figure shows pictures of users being at each stage of the test.

Results

In order to know the evolution of the users' learning, we present how each of the four measured variables increase or decrease along the eight sessions. Table 12 presents for each variable the qualification obtained at the last session and the corresponding increment/decrement it underwent with respect to the first one.

The behaviour of users was analysed by a Psychology with more than 20 years of experience working with people with intellectual disabilities. She took check out how users start and end their participation, by considering three possible emotional states: Positive behaviour (happy, cooperative, friendly, etc.), neutral (staid, calmed, inexpressive, etc.) and negative behaviour (bored, angry, sad, etc.). These results are shown in the next table.

Psychology also coded the most common behaviour shown by users at each stage of the testing experience. Table 14 shows a comparison between first and final session.

Fails in a Learnability study may indicate how difficult is to achieve some knowledge in an interface, so that in (Tullis & Albert, 2013) is suggested to analyse the reason of why these fails happen. They define three types of fails: Due to the ability of the user, due to misunderstanding of the task, and due to the user gave up. The results for the failure analysis in our research is shown in the next table.

According to experts, the users gave up because they found too much difficult to do the task, they lost the interest or the motivation, and they were bored, tired and even angry, among a variety of negative feelings.

FUTURE RESEARCH DIRECTIONS

Reminding the challenges of testing software with Down syndrome users presented in 3.4, we know that it is very common that users stop test activities, to avoid challenge, frustration or boring; they feel anxious and stressed in new situations with strange people, they have limited verbal communication and effusive behaviour. We faced all these situations in our study but they were successfully managed.

After the definition of the plan study, we proposed to apply an ethnographic study over the goal population. Doing this we collect very useful data that help us in the definitions of further steps. Literature review about Down syndrome, interviews with participants' relatives, teachers and therapists, and our enrolment in curricular and extracurricular activities with them, summarize the activities made in the ethnographic study.

The gamification of the learnability testing process was relatively simple, since we had already know what behaviour we need to evoke in users at which time thanks to the prior application of the Gestalt cycle of experience. These were taken as the game aesthetics, then we select the proper dynamics and mechanics, put them all together into a simple story and play it with users.

Analysing results of users' behaviour gave us the chance to explore how the gamification enhance the learnability testing process. Data of table 11 show how even users that began their very first participation in the study with negative behaviour change it; having at the end of this first session the whole population of users finalizing it with positive behaviour. Also the percentage of users that required extra assistance in controlling their emotional state was reduce 40 percent, meaning that users feel more comfortable. This does not mean that users were always happy, but that gamification was working diminishing for example fear before making the tasks, creating independence from pleasant tasks, and overcoming fails.

The high percentage of failed tasks due to its complexity, in comparison with other causes, shown in table 12, let us see how gamification motivated users to keep working, maintained self-confidence and enhanced communication between applicator and users.

CONCLUDING REMARKS AND FUTURE WORK

In this chapter we proposed a gamified approach, consisting in seven steps, for learnability testing with Down syndrome users. Commonly, testing software with Down syndrome users turns to be an unpleasant experience to users and applicators. Our proposal in summary, increased the quality of communication between users and applicators, provided a friendly, motivational, and engaging emotional-environment, increased the rate of testing success and the range of potential participants; which is especially important due to the difficulty to find appropriate participants.

We did not try to enhance the learning environment, which in case, affect the learnability level of the system tested, giving unreal information; on the contrary, we create a friendly-user space, where users' ability to learn software was not affected in a bad way by their emotional state. We can highlight that applying an ethnographic study gave us great elements to better work with the goal population; applying a behavioural analysis to users gave us the understanding of how they usually react to specific stimulus; by applying gamification we successfully evoke positive emotions in users, maintaining engagement, commitment, and interest during all the testing process.

All the stages of our approach worth. Because it was not only the ethnographic study alone, nor the gamification, nor the Gestalt Cycle; it was the whole approach that takes the best of each individual method and joins it to work together. Thus, the behavioural study, the game, and the testing was enhanced by the ethnographic study, and all together enhanced the users' testing experiences.

Besides all information derived from results we cannot misprize the subjective appreciation of the study by users. We fortunately received many good comments by relatives of participants: *"what did you do with my kid yesterday? He was fascinated about this new class... he told everybody about it, all day long!"*, *"I thought tablet computers were a waste of time and money, but I'd never seen my boy so participative and happy to work!"*, *"... she actually learned the letters, she even practices them at home"*.

Finally, we derived a set of recommendations to researchers that face software testing with Down syndrome users:

- It is important to create a strong affective bound between the users and people that will interact with them (from the research team), in order to stop being strangers and affect users' performance and comfort.
- An affective bound with relatives, teachers and therapists will be as important as the one with the users.
- When users make mistakes, do not provide help immediately. Motivate them to continue working or close the experience by diminishing the error and enhancing the value of participation.
- Use comparison between other users to motivate, but avoid competition.
- Always remark the good things made by users in participation.
- The users must be convinced that their work is worthy.
- Do not use any text in the game,
- Uuse very understandable images.

REFERENCES

Barendregt, W., Bekker, M., Bouwhuis, D., & Baauw, E. (2007). Predicting effectiveness of children participants in user testing based on personality characteristics. *Journal Behaviour & Information Technology*, 133-147.

Baxter, I., & Oatley, K. (1991). Measuring the learnability of spreadsheets in inexperienced users and those with previous spreadsheet experience. *Behaviour & Information Technology*, *40*(6), 475–490. doi:10.1080/01449299108924305

Bloom, R. (2006). *The Handbook of Gestalt Play Therapy: Practical Guidelines for Child Therapists*. London: Jessica Kingsley.

Bruni, M. (2006). Fine Motor Skills for Children with Down Syndrome. Woodbine House Eds.

Butler, K. A. (1985). Connecting theory and practice: a case study of achieving usability goals. *SIGCHI Conference on Human Factors in Computing Systems*. 10.1145/317456.317472

Cáliz, D., Martínez, L., Alamán, X., Terán, C., & Cáliz, R. (2016). Usability Testing in Mobile Applications Involving People with Down Syndrome: A Literature Review. *Computer Science and Information Technology*, *8*(3), 117–131.

Caliz, D., Martinez, L., Alaman, X., Teran, C., & Caliz, R. (2016). Usability Testing Process with People with Down Syndrome Interacting with Mobile Applications: A Literature Review. *International Journal of Computer Science & Information Technology*, *8*(3), 117–131. doi:10.5121/ijcsit.2016.8309

Chandler, H. (2009). *The Game Production Handbook*. Jones & Bartlett Publishers.

Chapanis, A. (1991). Evaluating usability. In Human factors for informatics usability (pp. 359–398). Cambridge University Press.

Chapman, R., & Hesketh, L. (2000). Behavioral phenotype of individuals with Down syndrome. *Journal: Mental Retardation and Developmental Disabilities*, *6*(2), 84–95. PMID:10899801

Chee, Y. (2016). *Games-To-Teach or Games-To-Learn: Unlocking the Power of Digital Game-Based, Learning Through Performance*. Springer Singapore. doi:10.1007/978-981-287-518-1

Conger, S. (2016). Gamification of Service Desk Work. In The Impact of ICT on Work (pp. 151-172). Singapore: Springer Science+Business Media Singapore. doi:10.1007/978-981-287-612-6_8

Davis, S., & Wiedenbeck, S. (1998). The effect of interaction style and training method on end user learning of software packages. *Interacting with Computers*, *11*(2), 147–172. doi:10.1016/S0953-5438(98)00026-5

Dichev, C., Dicheva, D., Angelova, G., & Agre, G. (2015). *From Gamification to Gameful Design and Gameful Experience in Learning*. Academic Press.

Dykens, E., Shah, B., Davis, B., Baker, C., Fife, T., & Fitzpatrick, J. (2015). Psychiatric disorders in adolescents and young adults with Down syndrome and other intellectual disabilities. Journal of Neurodevelopmental Disorders, 7-9. doi:10.118611689-015-9101-1

Elliott, G. J., Jones, E., & Barker, P. (2002). A grounded theory approach to modelling learnability of hypermedia authoring tools. *Interacting with Computers*, *14*(5), 547–574. doi:10.1016/S0953-5438(02)00021-8

Feng, J., Lazar, J., Kumin, L., & Ozok, A. (2010). Computer Usage by Children with Down Syndrome: Challenges and Future Research. *ACM Transactions on Accessible Computing*, *2*(3), 13. doi:10.1145/1714458.1714460

Fuhrmann, S., & MacEachren, A. (2001). Navigation in Desktop Geovirtual Environments: Usability Assessment. *Proceedings of the 20th ICA/ACI International Cartographic Conference.*

Grossman, T., Fitzmaurice, G., & Ramtin, A. (2009). A survey of soft-ware Learnability: metrics, methodologies and guidelines. *Proceedings of the SIGCHI Conference on Human Factors in Computing Systems*.

Hu, R., Feng, J., Lazar, J., & Kumin, L. (2013). Investigating input technologies for children and young adults with Down syndrome. *Universal Access in the Information Society*, *12*(1), 89–104. doi:10.100710209-011-0267-3

Huotari, K., & Hamari, J. (2016). A definition for gamification: Anchoring gamification in the service marketing literature. *Electronic Markets*, 1–11.

Kato, T. (1986). What question-asking protocols can say about the user interface. *International Journal of Man-Machine Studies*, *25*(6), 659–673. doi:10.1016/S0020-7373(86)80080-3

Kirijian, A., Myers, M., & Charland, S. (2007). Web Fun Central: online learning tools for individuals with Down syndrome. In *Universal Usability: Designing Information Systems for Diverse User Populations*. Chichester, UK: John Wiley & Sons.

Klemer, S. (2016). *Human Centered Design Course: Design Principles, Class Notes*. Obtenido de Coursera Inc.: https://www.coursera.org/learn/design-principles

Kumin, L., Lazar, J., Feng, J., Wentz, B., & Ekedebe, N. (2012). Syndrome, A Usability Evaluation of Workplace-Related Tasks on a Multi-Touch Tablet Computer by Adults with Down. *Journal of Usability Studies*, *7*(4), 118–142.

Ladner, S. (2014). *Practical Ethinography: A guide to doing Ethnography in Private Sector*. Walnut Creek, CA: Left Coast Press, Inc.

Lazar, J., Kumin, L., & Feng, J. (2011). Understanding the computer skills of adult expert users with down syndrome: an exploratory study. International ACM SIGACCESS conference on Computers and Accessibility.

LeCompte, M., & Schensul, J. (2010). Designing & Conducting Ethnographic Research: The Ethnographer's Toolkit. Plymouth, UK: Rowman & Littlefield Publishers, Inc.

Linja aho, M. (2006). Creating a Framework for Improving the Learnability of a Complex System. *Journal of Human Technology, 2*(2), 202-224.

Mack, R., & Robinson, J. (1992). When novices elicit knowledge: question asking in designing evaluating and learning to use software. In The psychology of expertise: cognitive research and empirical AI (págs. 245-268). Springer-Verlag. doi:10.1007/978-1-4613-9733-5_15

Mack, R. L., Lewis, C. H., & Carroll, J. M. (1983). Learning to use word processors: Problems and prospects. *ACM Transactions on Information Systems*, *1*(3), 254–271. doi:10.1145/357436.357440

Muntean, C. (2011). Raising engagement in e-learning through gamification. *Proceedings of the 6th International Conference on Virtual Learning*, 323-329.

Parker, P. (2004). *Down Syndrome: A Bibliography and Dictionary for Physicians, Patients, and Genome Researchers*. Icon Group International Inc.

Pretorius, M., Gelderblom, H., & Chimbo, B. (2010). Using Eye Tracking to Compare how Adults and Children Learn to Use an Unfamiliar Computer Game. *Proceedings of the 2010 Annual Research Conference of the South African Institute of Computer Scientists and Information Technologists*, 275-283. 10.1145/1899503.1899534

Purdue, U. (2016). *Game Development Process*. Obtenido de Educational Games at Purdue: https://e-games.tech.purdue.edu/GameDevProcess.asp

Rafique, I., Jingnong, W., Wang, Y., Abbasi, M., & Lew, P. (2012). Software Learnability Evaluation: An overview of definitions and evaluation Methodologies for GIS applications. International Multi-conference on computing in the global in-formation technology.

Raisamo, K., & Räihä, K. (2000). Design and evaluation of the alignment stick. *Interacting with Computers*, *12*(5), 128–134. doi:10.1016/S0953-5438(99)00020-X

Robson, K., Plangger, K., McCarthy, I., & Leyland, P. (2016). Game on: Engaging customers and employees through gamification. *Business Horizons*, 26–36.

Ruiz, E. (2012). *Programación Educativa para Escolares con Síndrome de Down.* Madrid, España: Fundación Iberoamericana Down 21.

Salama, H. (2012). *Gestalt 2.0*. Alfaomega.

Stickel, C., Fink, J., & Holzinger, A. (2007). Enhancing Universal Access–EEG Based Learnability Assessment. *Universal Access in Human-Computer Interaction. Applications and Services*, 813-822.

Troncoso, M., & Del Cerro, M. (2009). *Síndrome de Down: Lectura y Escritura.* Madrid: Fundación Down 21.

Tullis, T., & Albert, B. (2013). *Measuring the User Experience: Collecting, Analyzing, and Presenting Usability Metrics*. Waltham, MA: Morgan Kaufmann.

Werbach, K. (2014). (Re)Defining Gamification: A Process Approach, Persuasive Technology. *Persuasive Technology*, *8462*, 266–272. doi:10.1007/978-3-319-07127-5_23

WHO. (2016). *Informed Consent Form Templates*. Obtenido de Informed Parental Consent for Research Involving Children (qualitative): http://www.who.int/rpc/research_ethics/informed_consent/en/

Zbick, J., Nake, I., Milrad, M., & Jansen, M. (2015). A web-based framework to design and deploy mobile learning activities: Evaluating its usability, learnability and acceptance. In *2015 IEEE 15th International Conference on Advanced Learning Technologies* (pp. 88-92). Hualien, Taiwan: IEEE Computer Society.

Zichermann, G., & Cunningham, C. (2011). *Gamification by Design*. Sebastopol, CA: O'Reilly Media, Inc.

Ziefle, M. (2002). The influence of user experience and phone complexity on performance easy of use and learnability of different mobile phones. *Behaviour & Information Technology*, *21*(5), 303–311. doi:10.1080/0144929021000048538

KEY TERMS AND DEFINITIONS

Accessible Design: The accessible design ensures unassisted and assisted-device compatibility to technology.

Alzheimer Disease: An irreversible, progressive brain disease that slowly destroys memory and thinking skills, and eventually even the ability to carry out the simplest tasks.

Anterograde Amnesia: A selective memory deficit, resulting from brain injury, in which the individual is severely impaired in learning new information.

Disability: Disability is the consequence of an impairment that may be physical, cognitive, mental, sensory, emotional, developmental, or some combination of these. A disability may be present from birth or occur during a person's lifetime.

Down Syndrome: A chromosomal condition that is associated with intellectual disability, a characteristic facial appearance, and weak muscle tone (hypotonia) in infancy. All affected individuals experience cognitive delays, but the intellectual disability is usually mild to moderate.

Interactive Element: An interactive element (in a user interface) is every component that implies any interaction with the user.

Usability: Usability means making products and systems easier to use, and matching them more closely to user needs and requirements.

User Interface: Everything designed into an information device with which a human being may interact – including display screen, keyboard, mouse, light pen, the appearance of a desktop, illuminated characters, help messages, and how an application program or a web site invites interaction and responds to it.

Chapter 13
Virtual Course of Accessibility of the Tecnológico Nacional de México and IT Aguascalientes:
Analysis and Improvement Proposal

Mitsari Lucio Alonso
Tecnológico Nacional de México IT Aguascalientes, Mexico

ABSTRACT

This chapter described an analysis and those derived design improvements for an accessibility course offered by Tecnológico Nacional de México/IT Aguascalientes (ITA). The course is addressed to train professors for awareness and implementation of educational strategies that allow an accessible and inclusive learning environment. Enhancements found were oriented to makes easier teachers' tasks when generating strategies for the creation of accessible educational content. All suggestions were derived from a usability analysis of both interactive elements and the structure of the course on the on-line learning platform Moodle. The study was performed by implementing several international standards and design guides such as the traditional web content accessibility guidelines (WCAG).

INTRODUCTION

Within education, the issue of *accessibility* is something that over time is becoming more important, in the case of information technologies there is the need for all websites to be visited by anyone, whether or not they have any physical or sensory disabilities and especially when they are E-Learning platforms.

Educational institutions must include accessible educational platforms, as they are a key resource for training. They allow access to a multitude of resources aimed at the management of training processes, such as content, activities, assessment tests, rubrics or the option of participation of members of the digital community: students, teachers, among others. So you can interact through video conferences and carry out monitoring and evaluation processes (Fernández, 2019).

DOI: 10.4018/978-1-7998-2325-4.ch013

The lines marked in the international sphere have a clear commitment towards different people and groups. Inclusion, equality and equity are the goal to be achieved for several decades. A democratic and egalitarian society must take into account all the people who constitute it. When we design a product, well or service, human diversity has to be present; thinking about *normal* or *frequent* means excluding different people and, therefore, harming their rights.

The first thing is to recognize those who are invisible in the institutions for physical, communicational and/or cultural reasons. They must be able to participate in equal opportunities and how this materializes in effectively solutions that allow collecting, the conditions of possibility for different people to participate in the construction of the community. It is not a situation that can be addressed only by thinking about the student body, but also the official and the academic (Parra, 2019).

Regarding *inclusion*, it is well known that is another of the issues that take importance in education, as it there are several factors that generate a degree of student marginalization, for example the physical, intellectual or learning conditions of individuals, therefore, it is necessary to identify if there are elements that allow the systems to be adapted to the diverse physical and cognitive needs of the students, such as those that present visual, auditory, speech or even motor problems; or adapt to the different ways of learning of each one. Full inclusion only occurs when the tool for accessibility is fully integrated with the rest of the educational platform, in this way no student who wants to use the resource is isolated.

According to (Fernández, 2019), when education directed to a standard subject is planned in education, exclusion processes are increased, especially for students with disadvantaged situations. From the design and planning of the curriculum, it is necessary to plan to meet everyone's needs, eliminating barriers to learning and participation, and especially, for those at greater risk of social exclusion for reasons such as disability, cultural origin, etc.

Access to inclusive education is a development objective that should involve organizations of all levels and all sectors, regardless of the regional context. The reality is that we are all different and we need the same opportunities, so accessibility is a requirement that we must see reflected in all areas of our environment (Pickard, 2018).

However, most education professionals are not sufficiently trained in these issues and their correct application, for this reason the Aguascalientes Institute of Technology (ITA) seeks to implement educational and infrastructure strategies to achieve greater accessibility for its students. An example of this is the implementation of an educational learning model through an E-Learning platform through which students can carry out all study activities from any point inside and outside the institution.

The ITA is part of the network of educational centers of the National Technological Institute of Mexico (TecNM), which implements a "Distance Education Model", which is a frame of reference and systematic operation for the offer of technological higher education in the non- distance and mixed school modalities, with the essential support of information and communication technologies. The objective of this model is to guarantee an increase in the coverage of educational services offered by institutes, units and centers, thus training professionals who are a determining factor in national and international development, with a broad perspective of accessibility, inclusion, equity and quality. Therefore, these qualities must be reflected in the same way on the platform, thus achieving an accessible and universal education. The foregoing, with the intention of strengthening the quality of professional training, generating a wide range of opportunities in the attention of students and creating favorable conditions for learning, within a framework of appreciation of individual differences with an inclusive, accessible attitude and innovative (ITA, 2019).

While this type of teaching-learning has many benefits for the student community, it is important that the needs of the students are taken into account in the first instance, as well as the diverse physical and educational capacities of them, This in order to provide adequate and accessible virtual resources and platforms for them, thereby achieving a correct user experience (UX).

This educational model allows a 100% online education through the study of the degrees of "Engineering in Business Management" and "Industrial Engineering", also has the modality of remote units, which allow the learning of these careers to students who found in some places outside the state capital. In addition to studying these professional careers, a series of training courses for the rest of the student community and teachers are also provided. The Accessibility course is currently in effect, which aims to inform teachers about accessibility and inclusion issues so that they begin to develop educational strategies to be implemented in the classroom and through the various media for distance education.

The institution has allowed access to this course to carry out an analysis of the content with the aim of studying the structure and topics that are presented so far, this with the purpose of creating a proposal to complement and improve said course by taking as reference similar studies carried out in other university institutions, as well as various regulations, design guides and international standards for the creation of accessible and inclusive educational content, inside and outside the virtual platform. In addition, an analysis is made of the structure of the platform in general to identify the tools with which the teacher has both for the study of this course and for the realization of content for students, identify those that allow better accessibility and propose The developers integrate some others that may be considered important or necessary so that it can be used by all students without finding any barrier or limitation that prevents them from continuing their learning. That is why, one of the most important premises is always to take into account the approach of a User Centered Design (UCD), so it is necessary to understand that one of the first points to attend is that not all students have the same skills based on the use of information technologies, so we begin with a study to analyze the UX that this platform offers, the ease with which it works and makes use of the various elements that the environment has.

BACKGROUND

Distance education is a form of teaching in which students do not need to physically attend the place of study. In this teaching system, the student receives the study material (personally, by mail, email or other possibilities through various digital platforms), allowing the educational act to use new learning techniques and strategies focused on the own student, thus promoting self-education and self-management, that is, it is a flexible and self-directed education, whose main tools are communication and information technologies.

The main objective of this educational model is to establish the definitions, guidelines and procedures to offer a wide educational coverage, which ensures equal opportunities for students residing anywhere. In addition, through accessibility, according to the Official Gazette of the Federation, to offer the possibility of combining the study with other activities, promoting equity, gender perspective, inclusion and diversity; promoting "the development and use of information and communication technologies" in institutes, units and centers "to support student learning, expand their life skills and promote their insertion into the knowledge society".

Based on accessibility in various situations such as physical, economic and temporary, this strategy offers a series of benefits such as:

- The reduction of expenses of transfer or change of residence, because it can be implemented from any place
- Overcome distance, time, place or cultural restrictions
- Be able to combine the study with other activities by being flexible with the schedules
- Develop the competence to work in both face-to-face and virtual teams
- Develop a high capacity to self-regulate their own learning to be autonomous
- Share ideas with people from different geographical areas
- To familiarize and develop the competence of the use of ICTs, to socialize knowledge through connectivity without spatial limits, a situation that facilitates access to consultation with online experts and the enormous volume of data on the network
- The recognition, accreditation and certification of the competences acquired from experience inside and outside the institution
- As well as attention to diversity through specific programs

Although this type of teaching-learning has many benefits for the student community, it is important that this takes into account, in the first instance, the needs of the students as well as knowing their diverse abilities, this in order to be able to provide the appropriate resources and virtual platforms accessible to them.

Accessibility has already been discussed, but it is important to define what we mean by this term. Accessibility indicates the ease with which something can be used, visited or accessed in general by all people, especially those who have some type of disability (BOE, 2003), it is important to keep in mind that this also requires knowing and understand the Universal Design paradigm, since it aims to reach accessibility in environments, spaces, services, goods, objects and devices, so that they can be used by the greatest number of people without the need to adapt or specialize for specific population sectors, contrary to Design without barriers that produces exclusive and exclusive accessibility.

There are two visions about accessibility, one focused on applications or services (web accessibility) and on the other as a relationship in a virtual environment between the educational offer and student preferences. Web accessibility refers to the ease that all people can perceive, understand, navigate and interact with the web. There are many norms and standards in the design of web pages aimed at facilitating the achievement of an adequate level of accessibility (Serrano, Moratilla, & Olmeda, 2010).

Both visions are complementary but it should be noted that when the approach emphasizes education and a virtual environment in particular, all the concepts that are handled come from the educational field, where there is an intricate relationship between the student, the teacher, the course, the virtual environment and a vision of inclusion that underlies the institution's policy and that makes the notion of accessibility more meaningful but also more complex.

People with disabilities when accessing Virtual Higher Education may encounter different barriers or experience very varied difficulties depending on the functional capacity and to mitigate these barriers they use physical devices (Hardware) and specialized software (Software). One of the needs identified from the ESVIAL project (Hilera, Motz, & Temesio Silvana, 2019) is the offer of virtual educational programs with accessible settings and designs that allow the inclusion of people with disabilities to Higher Education. This implies the implementation of virtual learning environments with adapted technological platforms and encouraging the use of support technologies that allow compensating for the need derived from a disability.

For example, people with physical disabilities regularly read the information on the output devices without problems but have difficulty using data entry devices such as the keyboard and mouse, and because of this there are technical supports such as push buttons, alternative keyboards, among others, which allow other body skills to be used to give an order to the browser. In the case of people with visual limitation or low vision they have difficulties with the output devices and need to make adaptations such as using magnifiers, magnifiers, voice synthesizers and screen readers, among others, that allow the use of other senses such as The audio and touch. In the case of people with auditory compromise, there are programs that emit visual signals or symbols that alternate the audio or simplify a text to make it understandable. It is essential for designers and administrators of virtual learning environments and Web pages to keep in mind a series of components that configure the universal design or design for all, because the context and use can vary significantly from one user to another. The key is to ensure that the contents and services allow usability for anyone regardless of the support products and / or applications used to navigate, that is, that the use of technical aids or specialized software does not generate incompatibility with the design, the coding of the contents or the virtual learning objects. With the continuous improvement and development of the wide range of learning technologies, new challenges arise constantly to allow for equal opportunities for learning and the achievements that will be provided for all students of a university.

Within an educational institution there is a virtual environment where each course has a series of associated educational resources and each of these resources has a web design that is where they apply accessible design standards and some features are optional or mandatory depending on the policies and plans Institutional Some of the guides and standards include the Web Accessibility Initiative of the World Wide Web Consortium (W3C, 2012) that seeks to establish recommendations for obtaining content, browsers and accessible web development environments. Among its recommendations are the Web Content Accessibility Guidelines (WCAG), sets of guidelines for obtaining accessible web pages including the user interface of the pages in which the contents are presented. The latest version of this recommendation is WCAG 2.0, adopted in 2012 by ISO as a standard (ISO, 2012). There is also the ATAG guide on accessibility requirements for authoring tools such as text editors. The UUAG guide to accessibility requirements for auxiliary tools such as video players, but also web browsers (W3C, 2012) and WAI-ARIA for dynamic content accessibility requirements and rich web interfaces in users enriched by widgets and complementary software integrated in the platform such as add-ons or multimedia applications such as Ajax, HTML5, JavaScript, Flash, Silverlight or similar (W3C, 2012). It is also advisable to take into account the ISO / IEC 24751 standard (ISO, 2008): Individualized adaptability and accessibility in e-learning, education and training, which presents an information model for both Student Preferences and Personal Needs (PPN).

Focused on digital platforms there are four general principles that are the basis of web accessibility:

1. Perceptible: the information and components of the user interface must be presented to users so that they can perceive them.
2. Operable: the components of the user interface and navigation must be operable.
3. Understandable: the information and management of the user interface must be understandable.
4. Robust: the content must be robust enough to be interpreted reliably by a wide variety of user applications, including technical aids.

Each principle is organized in a series of guidelines, which provide the basic objectives that must be achieved in order to create more accessible content for users with different disabilities. In total there are twelve guidelines that in turn are divided into 61 compliance criteria. The compliance criteria are organized into three levels of conformity: A (the lowest), AA and AAA (the highest). When all the compliance criteria of one level and the previous one are met, then it can be said that the website has reached that level of compliance. For example, if all the criteria for level A and level AA conformity are met on a page, the website has the level of compliance AA.

If any of these principles is not met, users with disabilities may have trouble accessing the web content.

Reason why it is important that the development of these platforms should always be linked to a UCD approach and the main step to achieve this is to understand the different types of users that exist in this environment, (González & Farnós, 2009) made a study through which they managed to classify students as follows:

- Cooperative students
- Students taken advantage of.
- Silent students.
- Absent students.
- Students with special educational needs (SEN).

However, according to E-Learn Team (Team, 2018) both software developers, program designers and teachers often make mistakes that go against accessibility mechanisms according to the type of disability, for example:

1. Hearing impairments:
   Content that only supports audio, such as videos with voices and sounds, without subtitles or transcriptions.
   Media players that do not have subtitles and that do not have volume controls.
   Services included in the Web, including web applications, which are based on interaction using voice.
   The lack of sign language for important complementary information.
2. Visual impairments:
   Images, and other structural elements that have no equivalent text alternatives.
   Designs, images and pages that cannot be resized, or that lose information when resized.
   Lack of visual and non-visual orientation signs, page structure, and other navigation aids.
   Media players that do not offer options to adjust text size and colors.
   Video content that has no text or audio alternatives, as well as descriptions of these.
   Websites, web browsers, and authoring tools that do not have support for using the full keyboard
3. Speech impairments:
   Services included in the Web, including web applications, which are based on interaction using voice.
   Websites that offer phone numbers as the only way to communicate with the organization
4. Impediments of motor actions:
   Websites, web browsers, and authoring tools that do not have full keyboard support.
   Insufficient deadlines for responding or completing tasks, such as filling out online forms.
5. Cognitive impairments:
   Complex navigation mechanisms and page layouts that are difficult to understand and use.

Complex phrases that are difficult to read and unusual words that are difficult to understand, long passages of text without images, graphics, etc.

Page designs that are not adaptable in different types of browser or device.

The platforms must be perfectly designed to meet the needs of each of these types of students, so it is also important that they be based on the following principles:

1. The design is based on an explicit understanding of users, tasks and environments.
2. Users are involved during design and development.
3. The design is directed and refined by user-centered assessments.
4. The process is iterative.
5. The design is aimed at the whole experience.
6. The design team includes multidisciplinary skills and perspectives.

Likewise, according to (Amado, Hernández, & Linares, 2017) the accessibility requirements for a virtual platform are divided and described as follows:

- General accessibility requirements of learning platforms
- Accessibility requirements for content and user interfaces
- Accessibility requirements for content authoring tools
- Accessibility requirements of content playback tools
- Accessibility requirements for dynamic content and rich user interfaces
- Accessibility requirements for Learning Objects
- General knowledge requirements that authors and users must have to generate accessible content for a virtual campus

Finally, according to (González & Farnós, 2009) a virtual teaching environment must contain the following elements:

- Resources. This should be handled by the teacher and presents the information that the teacher wants students to use
- Forums. Allows discussions between students and the teacher
- Chores. Allows the teacher to assign activities to their students
- Questionnaires. Through these, the teacher evaluates the knowledge acquired by the students
- Surveys. It is the means to provide feedback on the development of the course. It allows the teacher to know the personal opinions of the students and in this way adapt or redirect the teaching process if it requires it
- Lesson. Offer the content in a simple and enjoyable way to the student
- Statistics. It allows the teacher to control the work of each of the students, verify the number of accesses and activities carried out, the time spent on the platform, etc.

We must remember that accessibility is also linked to another social situation, inclusion. In this sense, the objective is to guarantee equity, equal opportunities for all, education in the most normal conditions and possible development despite the differences in the peculiar development of each person.

From this vision, inclusion is closely linked to other terms and concepts used, currently in education sciences and in specialized literature, such as: "inclusive education or inclusive school", "diversity education", "school open to diversity "and school integration of children with special educational needs (Viteri and Abilés, 2017).

In terms of content development for these platforms, a series of requirements must also be met which are:

- Know how to use educational content correctly in different digital multimedia formats.
- Create multimedia educational digital content.
- Be familiar with the digital formats of educational content.
- Know how to install and use open source tools for editing and playing digital multimedia content.
- Be able to organize plain textual content in the form of interactive web pages.
- Be able to edit and transform images.
- Basic sound editing capability.
- Basic video editing capability.
- Be able to create short-lived video tutorials subtitled.
- Understand and know how to apply the techniques to make educational digital content accessible to all.

And to ensure that this knowledge is applied in an appropriate form is important that various guidelines and general compliance criteria of WCAG 2.0 are taken into account for any website, in the case of learning platforms it could be synthesized in the following principles basic suggested in (MOODLE, 2012):

1. Allow users to customize based on their preferences.
2. Provide equivalents to visual and tempo-dependent elements.
3. Use different ways of presenting information in an interface.
4. Provide information compatible with technical assistance / support product.
5. Allow access to all functionalities through the keyboard.
6. Provide context information and user status information at all times.

The Learning Objects must meet accessibility requirements in order to allow access to students with different functional profiles. For this, the educational platform must store the Preferences and Personal Needs (PPN) of the student in its profile and based on these, it will search and select those OAs that meet the requirements for viewing.

For the correct application of the standard it is necessary to perform each of the following actions:

- Introduction of the profile by the student.
- Creation of the original resource (for example a video) and of the adapted resources (for example the subtitles of the video) by the content author.
- Introduction of accessibility metadata in learning objects (both in the original resource and in the adapted ones) by the content author.
- Installation of a software or plug-in on the educational platform that supports the completion of the entire process.

- Search and selection of digital resources that meet the requirements established in the educational plan.

The level of accessibility achieved in a virtual platform must be constantly maintained through the content and learning material periodically updated by teachers and administrators.

Several higher institutions are studying the accessibility of their online courses, one of the most recent is the one developed by the Gies College of Business at the University of Illinois Urbana-Champaign, where the digital media team for eLearning has overcome the challenge of creating accessible content. The team is working to implement a "master transcript" to accompany all the Geis Business MOOCs available in Coursera. To make the course content accessible, the team, which also included instructional designer Jinhee Choo and disability specialist Juliana García Jaramillo, began proactively creating universal and usable MOOC content. This was a departure from the usual reactionary approach in an individual with a disability in a "traditional" course on campus. A standard strategy to make web pages accessible to people with visual or physical disabilities is to use the "Tab" key to move between various elements of the page. However, in a course platform like Coursera, each page has many activities, which makes it difficult or confusing for a person with visual or physical disabilities to navigate the page using only the keyboard. In addition, the Coursera video player does not support the description of standard audio, extended audio or text descriptions of nonverbal critical information (Pickard, 2018).

MAIN FOCUS OF THE CHAPTER

As mentioned earlier, the TecNM has a distance education model that students and teachers use, both for learning and for the development of learning modules, for this reason in this section a brief analysis of the virtual platform is carried out of the ITA to identify the extent to which they comply with some of the general accessibility guidelines and standards discussed in the previous section and subsequently generate a series of recommendations to complement and/or improve both the course and the platform. The first consists of a general analysis of the educational platform divided into three sections:

1. Accessibility of all collaborative services offered
2. Editing services
3. Complementary services that require the activation of complementary software by the user

The second includes the analysis of electronic educational resources that are published on the learning platform. Recalling that if on a platform that meets the different accessibility conformance criteria, such as those mentioned, educational resources with non-accessible electronic content are published, the virtual campus is no longer accessible. It is very important to maintain a continuous training process so that the users involved in the use of the virtual campus that are going to publish content know that such content must be accessible, especially in this case where the main theme of the course is accessibility.

ITA DISTANCE EDUCATION MODULE ANALYSIS

The TecNM distance education service is through a Massive Online and Open Course (MOOC) known as MOODLE. The "Modular Object Oriented Dynamic Learning Environment" (MOODLE) is a software whose purpose is to help the creation of courses focused on the interaction and collaborative construction of content. The software has many capabilities to perform online assessments, deliver personal work, assessment correction assistant, instant messages between students, online calendars, news, and announcements, create custom wikis for courses and discussion forums for students and academics can talk about the contents of the courses

One of the reasons for the success of this platform is its flexibility: it is built to operate in different contexts such as education, training and professional training, development, business, among others. And in addition allows users to program modules and plugins that they can provide with necessary functionalities that they did not previously have (Trejos, 2014).

As MOOCs move from experimental technology to a more standard learning resource, course developers and MOOC platforms spend more time thinking about how to make MOOCs accessible. For example, under the Americans with Disabilities Act, colleges and universities must make their offers accessible to people with disabilities (Pickard, 2018).

Moodle is a platform in constant evolution and that allows external developers to complement and modify elements in it thanks to the facilities that it allows in its open source, however, since its initial creation it is governed in its development by a series of rules and standards internationals that allow better accessibility, such as WCAG 2.0, ATAG 2.0, ARIA 1.0 (Moodle, 2019) (Córdova, 2019).

Accessibility of all Collaborative Services Offered

As mentioned earlier, the Moodle platform is open source, which allows developers to adapt it to the needs and standards of the institution in operation, in this case it is possible to observe that the various services offered on the ITA platform are those presented by Moodle in its initial configuration, so there was no exhaustive analysis to verify if they meet the various accessibility standards described by other organizations. Figure 1 shows some of the resources and activities that are available to students and teachers.

Editing Services

To provide access to optimal learning, there is the possibility of holding web conferences through BigBlueBottom (BigBlueButton, 2019), this is an open source system for online learning. The goal is to provide remote students with a high-quality online learning experience, which allows the teacher to share audio, slides, chat, video and desk with students. Integrated surveys facilitate student participation and recording your lectures means that you can make them available for later review. By emphasizing the issue of accessibility, this tool complies with the W3C WCAG 2.0 guidelines. However, total accessibility cannot be guaranteed since this is a situation that also depends on the way in which the teacher shows the contents that will be taught.

Figure 1. Collaborative services
(Source: Course "Accessibility ITA, 2019")

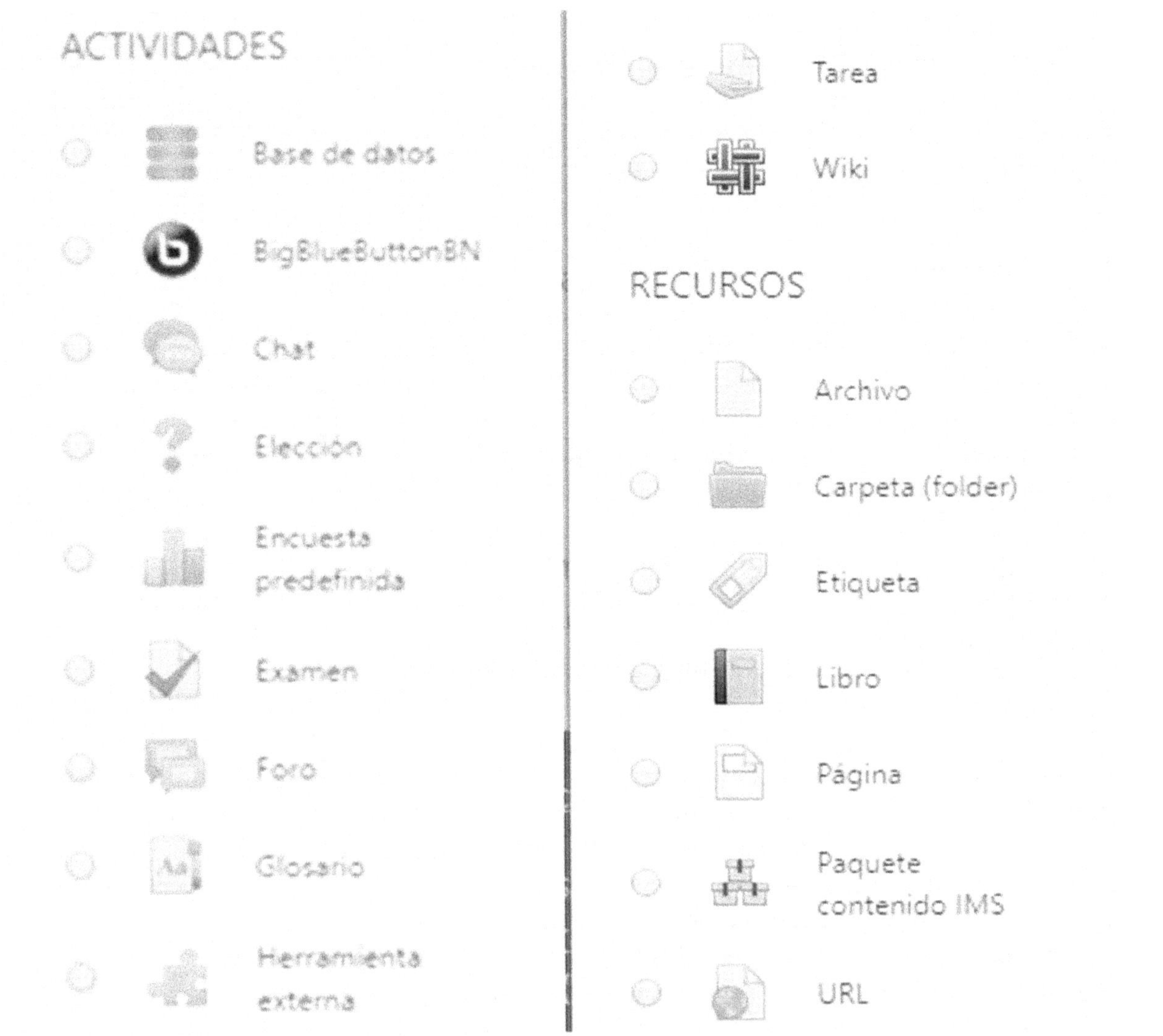

Complementary Services that Require the Activation of Complementary Software by the User

Within the platform there is the option to download and install an NVDA reader (NVDA, 2019), however, there is no information that allows to know a little more about its use, which although it seems simple, can be somewhat complex for some people. NVDA is a free screen reader for Microsoft Windows, this reader allows blind and visually impaired people to access and interact with the Windows operating system and many third-party applications.

The highlights include:

- Compatibility with popular applications, including web browsers such as Mozilla Firefox and Google Chrome, email clients, Internet chat software, music players and office programs such as Microsoft Word and Excel
- Built-in voice synthesizer that supports more than 50 languages, more compatibility with many other third-party voices.
- Report text format where available, such as name and font size, style and spelling errors.
- Automatic text announcement under the mouse and optional audible indication of the mouse position

Analysis of the Accessibility Course

Before doing the analysis on the resources available to the course, the content of the course was reviewed in order to correctly understand the objective for which it was developed and if the topics that compose it allow the user to meet that objective.

The *Accessibility* course is based on 4 modules through which it intends to provide information to users on various topics related to accessibility and inclusion, some of the topics it presents are the following:

- Strategies for inclusion and educational accessibility
- Concepts of Diversity, Segregation, Integration, Exclusion and Inclusive Education
- Learning barriers
- Motor, auditory, visual accessibility guidelines, among others
- •Special educational needs

At the end of each of the sections a series of activities are presented to reinforce the knowledge acquired from reading and writing activities, however, there are no activities that involve the direct application of the knowledge acquired, that is, the teachers they acquire the theory but not the practice to be able to implement this knowledge with their students inside or outside the classroom, for example the realization of accessible digital content.

When performing the analysis directly on the structure of the contents it is observed that there are Word documents, PDF, PowerPoint presentations, as well as a series of videos and it can be identified that some of these resources that were presented were not created directly for the course, but they have been extracted from other sources, so in some cases they do not fully comply with the rules for creating accessible content. Some of the details observed are:

The content of the texts is very extensive and in some cases does not comply with the rules of sizes and colors of the typography. Two examples of these situations are shown in Figure 2. It should be remembered that some users with vision problems, such as color blindness, can be found, and these features in the documents may be inconvenient for them.

There are tools that perform the accessibility analysis of the various objects, which is why one of these software was used to analyze some of the PDF documents that are available in the course, managing to observe that they practically do not cover any of the criteria that the tool presents, in Figure 3 it can be seen that the results obtained in two of the documents analyzed are negative.

In the case of graphic presentations there are the same situations. There are errors that prevent these from being accessible such as images, the background of the different slides, the text, among many other details.

Figure 2. Example of text documents in the accessibility course
(Source: Course "Accessibility ITA, 2019")

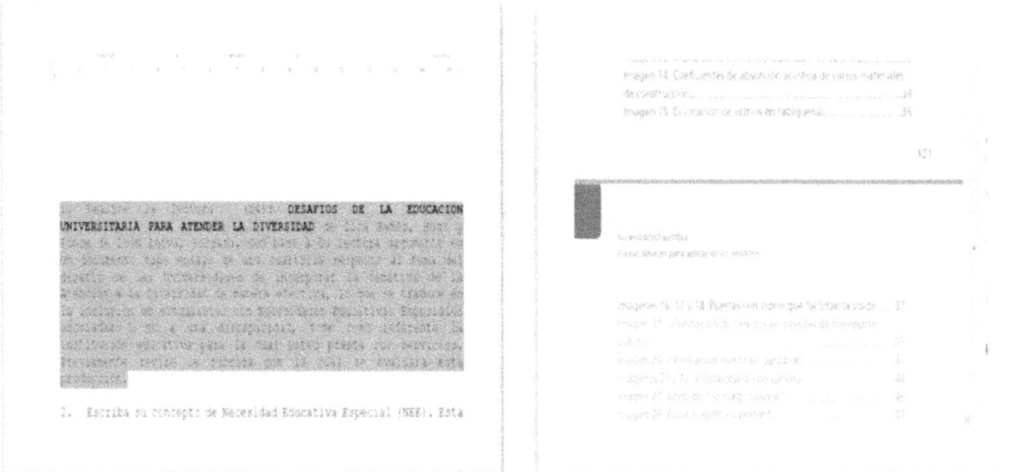

Figure 3. Results of accessibility analysis in PDF's
(Source: Course "Accessibility ITA, 2019")

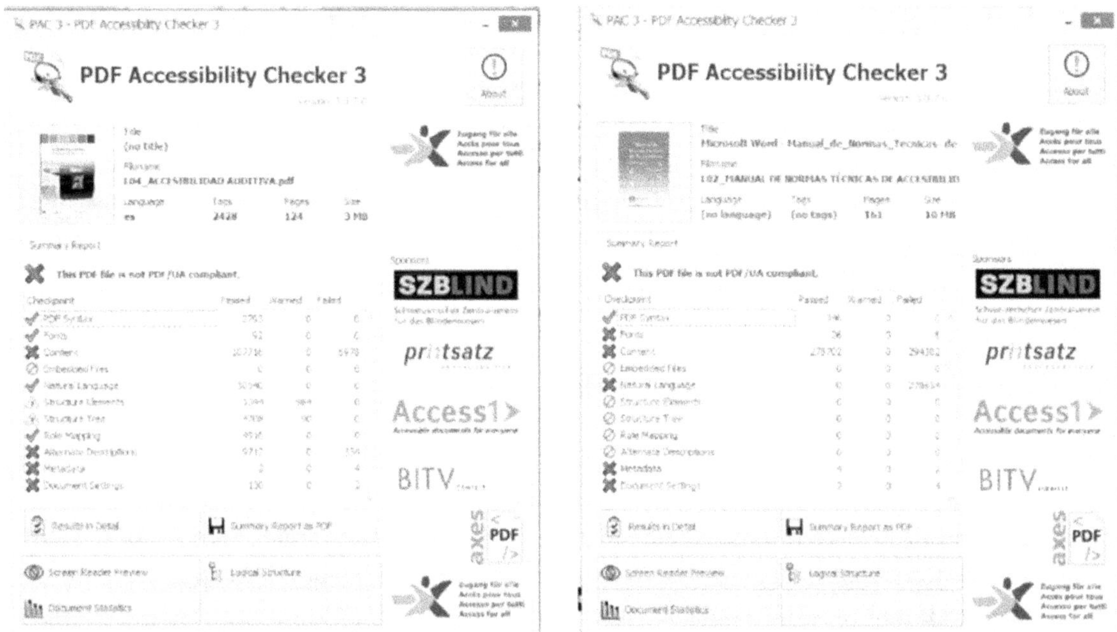

Figure 4. Video sample presented in the accessibility course
(Source: Course "Accessibility ITA, 2019")

Finally, the videos are clear, the images are readable and the volume of music and sound are adequate, they also help people with hearing impairment through the integration of a sign language translator in the video (Figure 4) However, you should keep in mind that there are people who may not use this language or that the video may not be available in the user's language, so some other support is required, such as subtitle integration.

SOLUTIONS AND RECOMMENDATIONS

When using the Moodle and not having made major configurations, the platform does not present situations that put accessibility at risk, however it is important that in case of wishing to make any modification or integrate a new element or resource ensure that it complies with The various norms and standards. It is also necessary to add some modules that allow the user to obtain help or information about the use of some of the objects and elements available on the platform.

Speaking directly about the course, as mentioned above, it only presents modules in which it shows the teacher the fundamentals, the characteristics as well as the way in which strategies to eradicate the problems of exclusion and inaccessibility within the institutes are begun to be implemented. However, it is important that topics that allow the teacher to develop content and educational material are also discussed, so below are some proposals for improvement for the creation of new modules and some recommendations of topics and elements that are considered necessary to include.

First of all it is important to point out that there are various ways to transmit information to the student, both on and off the platform, the most common are through text documents, graphic presentations and/or audiovisual content. Reason why it is necessary that there is a module that shows the teacher the guidelines to follow for the creation of these contents.

The contents made through text documents and graphic presentations developed in tools such as Microsoft Word, PowerPoint or PDF must have a correct analysis so that they can be used by all students taking into account conditions such as possible visual impairments, so It is necessary to know the rules based on size, type and font color in the texts. In this case, help can be obtained through Microsoft (Office, 2019) where you can find a series of guides and solutions for the correct implementation of accessibility in the development of texts.

Some of the modules and themes suggested to be implemented are the following:

1. Creating accessible Word documents
    a. Fundamentals of Accessibility in documents
    b. Document structure
    c. Graphics, images and multimedia content
    d. Checking the accessibility of a Word document
2. Creating accessible PowerPoint digital presentations
    a. Fundamentals of Accessibility in presentations
    b. Creation of accessible presentations
    c. Checking the accessibility of a presentation
3. Creation of accessible PDF documents
    a. Fundamentals of Accessibility in PDF documents
    b. Characteristics of a PDF document
    c. Checking through Adobe Acrobat
4. Multimedia Content
    a. Multimedia accessibility
    b. Video edition and audio
    c. Video titles and subtitles
    d. Animation Creation

On the other hand, you can also use a reading tool such as NVDA that is present on the platform to be downloaded and installed. In this case it is convenient to include a user guide, because despite appearing to be a simple tool to handle it can be confusing for any of the users. Some other tools for screen reading that can be used according to (Fernández, 2019) are:

- **JAWS:** Through a voice synthesizer, read texts in different languages (Spanish, English, German, Italian or Portuguese among others). They help people with visual difficulties to read or create web pages, social networks or documents.
- **Orca:** Extensible, open, flexible and free screen reader for Linux, which provides access to the graphic desktop via voice and Braille.
- **ZoomText:** Interact with the graphical output of the computer so that any content on the enlarged screen can be displayed, using it as if it were a magnifying glass, enlarging the entire screen or dividing it vertically or horizontally. It is intended for people with reduced vision.

Regarding audiovisual content, the accessibility concepts applicable to audio and video teaching materials, as well as how to convert text documents into audio files, should be studied. The platform must have greater access to tools that allow recording the computer screen, as well as editing videos and creating the different teaching content. Likewise, the course must present a section that allows teachers to learn how to use these tools. For example, there are numerous tools that allow you to record the computer screen, as well as edit the videos and create the different teaching content. Some of these recording tools are: CamStudio, Freeseer BBFlashBack Express Wink, Hypercam, and Screencast-O-Matic.

Previously it was mentioned that within the platform the BigBlueButton system is enabled, however within the course there is no user manual, so in case the user needs to use it, they should look for the documentation in another site. It is an excellent support tool, but it is important to know how to use it in order to obtain all the benefits it offers both students and teachers.

For the creation and development of animations, one of the simplest and most practical options is through Adobe Flash.

There is a mobile application that allows access to Moodle, so it is important that the teacher also knows how this application works and the accessibility possibilities that can be offered to the student if they want to enter from a mobile device, as well as the services and tools that you can provide to the student from the platform or those that you can recommend installing.

In addition, the teacher must adequately know the operation of each of the resources that he has within the platform and how he should apply them in a way that makes them accessible to all his students.

Finally, it is important to remember that for a course to be defined as accessible, all the elements that compose it must be accessible, so it is necessary that if it is a course of "Accessibility", each of the materials of Support are accessible, the best option is that all content be created by the institution and, in case of using external material, make sure that it meets all accessibility standards.

FUTURE RESEARCH DIRECTIONS

There are several actions that are intended to be carried out as future work, in the first place an analysis of the points proposed and described above is performed and then implemented within the course, for this it is important to meet with experts to restructure the course material, create new resources or modify existing ones to make them accessible.

The second action is to enable new tools that help students improve their learning, especially support tools for users with special disabilities. NVDA is a very functional resource knowing how to make use of this, so integrating new elements like this or some of the ones mentioned above can bring great benefits.

In addition, as mentioned in previous sections, the platform has not undergone considerable modifications, so it would be interesting to carry out an analysis that identifies whether the state in which it remains allows to fully comply with the teaching and learning objectives that the institution presents or if the ITA should request improvements and some new implementations that allow students to obtain better results. In addition, the ITA within its educational model also has remote units for students to learn from other places near the state capital, within this future work it is intended to move to one of these units in order to perform an analysis also to the hardware with which these students work, because it must be remembered that accessibility must occur at all levels and in every way.

And finally once these options are implemented to make a complete analysis of accessibility, usability and user experience of the platform, which could allow us to make this proposal for other educational sites or for the entire TecNM in general.

CONCLUSION

If it is intended to achieve the goals of equity, quality and expansion of access to higher education, accessibility should be the most important point in the design, implementation and evaluation of virtual environments for distance education and any proposal for mediated education for the tics. In this sense, we consider that the absence of accessibility conditions in any virtual environment constitutes a way to establish situations of exclusion, in this case, a digital, educational and social exclusion. Likewise, in virtual teaching-learning proposals, exclusion involves students, teachers as well as personnel involved in these proposals, such as developers, designers, etc.

Within an educational institution there is a virtual environment where each course has a series of associated educational resources, where, in turn, each of these resources has a web design that is where the accessible design standards of the W3C are applied, for example. Some of these characteristics are optional or mandatory depending on the policies and plans of the institution, so it can be seen in the enhanced analysis that the platform generated for the ITA meets some of these standards, however, it is far from many others, which must be implemented. In general terms, the planning of virtual courses implies the realization of a needs analysis to carry out the approach of educational projects within a given context.

ACKNOWLEDGMENT

First author gratefully acknowledge CONACyT (Consejo Nacional de Ciencia y Tecnología, Mexico) for financial supporting her MSc studies.

REFERENCES

W3C. (2012). Web Content Accessibility Guidelines (WCAG) 2.0. *World Wide Web Consortium*. Retrieved from http://www.w3.org/TR/WCAG/

Amado, H., Hernández, R., & Linares, B. (2017). Requisitos de accesibilidad indispensables para un campus virtual accesible. *ESVIAL*, 119-130.

BigBlueButton. (2019). *BigBlueButton*. Retrieved from https://bigbluebutton.org/about/

BOE. (2003). *Ley 51/2003, de 2 de diciembre, de igualdad de oportunidades, no discriminación y accesibilidad universal de las personas con discapacidad*. Academic Press.

Cano, C., Fernandez, L., & Pages, C. (2012). Modelos de madurez de la enseñanza virtual, ¿Consideran la accesibilidad? *IV Congreso Internacional ATICA*, 100-108.

Córdova, M. A. (2019). *MOODLE LTS 2.7 y estándares de accesibilidad web.* Retrieved from http://www.esvial.org/wp-content/files/CAFVIR2015pp67-74.pdf

E-Learning Team. (2018). *¿Qué saber, qué evitar, creando E-Learning accesible?* Retrieved from https://www.sicom.com.mx/e-learning/que-saber-que-evitar-creando-e-learning-accesible/

Fernández, J. M. (2019). *Formación del profesorado para la incorporación de las TIC en alumnado con diversidad funcional.* Barcelona: Octaedro. doi:10.36006/116162

González, A., & Farnós, J. D. (2009). Usabilidad y accesibilidad para un e-learning inclusivo. *Educació inclusiva*, 49-60.

Hilera, J. R., Motz, R., & Silvana, T. (2019). *Guía Metodológica para la Implantación de Desarrollos Curriculares Virtuales Accesibles.* Retrieved from www.esvial.org/

ISO. (2008). *ISO/IEC 24751-2:2008, Information technology -- Individualized adaptability and accessibility in e-learning, education and training -- Part 2: "Access for all" personal needs and preferences for digital.* Geneva, Switzerland: International Standard Organization.

ISO. (2012). *ISO/IEC 40500, Information technology -- W3C Web Content Accessibility Guidelines (WCAG) 2.0. Ginebra.* International Organization for Standardization.

ITA. (2019). *Modelo Educativo.* Retrieved from http://www.itaguascalientes.edu.mx/site/modelo.php

Marshall, S. (2006). *E-Learning Maturity Model Version Two: New Zealand Tertiary Institution E-Learning Capability: Informing and Guiding E-Learning Architectural Change and Development Project Report.* Report to the New Zealand Ministry of Education.

Microsoft Office. (2019). *Crear documentos de Word accesibles para personas con discapacidades.* Retrieved from https://support.office.com/es-es/article/crear-documentos-de-word-accesibles-para-personas-con-discapacidades-d9bf3683-87ac-47ea-b91a-78dcacb3c66d

Moodle. (2019). *Accesibilidad.* Retrieved from https://docs.moodle.org/all/es/Accesibilidad

Moodle. (2019). *Especificación de accesibilidad Moodle.* Retrieved from http://docs.moodle.org/dev/Moodle_Accessibility_Specification

NVDA. (2019). *NV Access LimitedNVDA.* Retrieved from https://www.nvaccess.org/about-nvda/

Parra, C. (2019). *Por una universidad para todas y todos: accesibilidad infraestructural universal.* Universidad de Chile.

Pickard, L. (2018). *How One University Tackles Accessibility in MOOCs.* Class Central.

Serrano, E., Moratilla, A., & Olmeda, I. (2010). Métrica para la evaluación de la accesibilidad en Internet: Propuesta y testeo. *Revista Espanola la de Documentacion Cientifica, 33*(3), 378–396. doi:10.3989/redc.2010.3.719

Trejos, A. (2014). *Evaluación de Usabilidad de un Masive Open Online Course (MOOC).* Santiago de Chile: Universidad de Chile.

Viteri, A., & Abilés, A. (2017). El uso de las TIC en la educación inclusiva. In F. Pesántez, R. Sánchez, & V. Robles (Eds.), *Inclusión, discapacidad y educación. Enfoque práctico desde las Tecnologías Emergentes (pp. 325-340)*. Quito, Ecuador: Universidad Politécnica Salesiana.

ADDITIONAL READING

Alcalá, M., Capdevila, J., & Ribera, M. (2012). *Guía de contenido digital accesible - Microsoft PowerPoint 2010*. Universidad de Barcelona.

ESVIAL. (2012) Informe de análisis de estándares, normas y modelos de capacidad de madurez relacionados con la calidad y accesibilidad de la educación virtual. *Proyecto ESVIAL*. Retrieved from http://www.esvial.org/

Henry, S. L. (2008) Simplemente pregunta: Integración de la accesibilidad en el diseño. Retrieved from http://www.uiaccess.com/justask/es/index.html

Hilera, J. R., & Campo, E. (2015) Guía para crear contenidos accesibles digitales. *ESVIAL*. Retrieved from http://www.esvial.org/wp-content/files/ESVIAL.LibroDigital_es_2015.pdf

Hilera, J. R., & Hoya, R. (2010) Guía de consulta de estándares de e-learning. Universidad de Alcalá. Retrieved from http://www.cc.uah.es/hilera/GuiaEstandares.pdf

INTECO. (2010) Guía de WAI ARIA. Instituto Nacional de Tecnologías de la Comunicación. Retrieved from http://www.inteco.es/file/cPaNoHmdaUbMlxpjOX2pMw ISO (2002) ISO/TR 16982:2002, Ergonomics of human-system interaction -- Usability methods supporting human-centered design. International Organization for Standardization.

ISO. (2005). *ISO/IEC 19796-1:2005, ITLET Quality management, assurance and metrics, Part 1: General approach*. International Organization for Standardization.

ISO. (2009). *ISO/IEC 19796-3:2009, ITLET Quality management, assurance and metrics, Part 3: Reference methods and metrics*. International Organization for Standardization.

Lujan, S. (2019). Accesibilidad Web. Retrieved from http://accesibilidadweb.dlsi.ua.es/?menu=guiabreve-1

Moreno, L. (2013) Recursos para elaborar documentación accesible. Universidad Carlos III, España. Retrieved from http://labda.inf.uc3m.es/doku.php?id=es:labda_personal:personal_lmoreno#ReDocuAcc

Poulson, D., Ashby, M., & Richardson, S. J. (1996) A practical handbook on user centered design for assistive technology. *HUSAT Research Institute for the European Commission*. Retrieved from http://www.education.edean.org/index.php?row=3&filters=f16&cardIndex=21

KEY TERMS AND DEFINITIONS

Design Without Barriers: It is an approach that proposes the design and construction of spaces and facilities for the exclusive use of people with disabilities, that is, functional environments for this population.

E-Learning: Virtual learning space aimed at facilitating the experience of distance training, both for companies and for educational institutions.

Exclusion: Situation of marginalization or segregation that affects specific groups of society.

Flexibility: Multiplicity of ways in which the user and the system exchange information.

Inclusion: It is a pedagogical concept that refers to the way in which the school should respond to diversity or the way in which society should consider citizens.

Universal Design: It constitutes a paradigm of design and a philosophical conception aimed at achieving accessibility in environments, spaces, services, goods, objects and devices, so that they can be used by the greatest number of people without the need to adapt or specialize to determined population sectors.

Usability: Measure of the degree of ease in the use of a type of product (in this case "technological") and the type of satisfaction generated by that use in the user.

Chapter 14
On the Development of Haptic-Virtual Learning Systems for the Education of Blind People

Raquel Espinosa Castañeda
https://orcid.org/0000-0003-4978-729X
Universidad Autónoma de San Luis Potosí, Mexico

Hugo Ivan Medellín Castillo
https://orcid.org/0000-0002-2827-9547
Universidad Autónoma de San Luis Potosí, Mexico

ABSTRACT

The concept of inclusive education goes beyond considering the needs of people with disabilities; it refers to the process of recognizing the students' learning needs and to act according to such needs. People with visual limitations do not necessarily require more attention and dedication than other people; they only need to be initially guided and to have accessible information. Thus, one of the main challenges of universal education is to generate inclusive and assistive educational technologies, which can be used for the teaching and learning of people with disabilities. In this chapter, the development and assessment of haptic-enabled virtual reality learning systems for the education of non-sighted people are presented and discussed. These virtual systems represent the research work conducted to promote the accessible education of blind people and to determine the effectiveness of virtual touch in the education of blind people.

INTRODUCTION

According to The United Nations Educational, Scientific and Cultural Organisation (UNESCO), Information and Communication Technologies (ICT) can contribute to universal access to education, equity in education, and delivery of quality learning and teaching (UNESCO, 2017). Thus, one of the main challenges of education is to generate inclusive and assistive educational technologies, which can be used for the teaching and learning of people with disabilities. However, although the use of ICT in

DOI: 10.4018/978-1-7998-2325-4.ch014

education has increased exponentially in the last two decades, little research efforts have been made in order to develop assistive technologies to enhance the educational process of people with disabilities, in particular blind people.

Since many years ago, several studies have shown that the human sense of touch is a psychological source of knowledge. Recently, the progress in computer technologies have led to the development of virtual reality and haptic systems, which are able to provide virtual touch and information about size, shape and physical properties of virtual objects. Moreover, computer haptic systems can also be used to generate mental representations of virtual objects. However, although virtual reality and haptic systems have been widely used in science and engineering, little research work has been done in the design and application of such systems in education; in particular, in the teaching and learning process of visually impaired individuals.

In this chapter the development and assessment of two haptic-enabled virtual reality learning systems for the education of non-sighted people are presented and discussed. These systems are designed considering the special educational needs of blind people, i.e. user centered-design (UCD), and aim to provide educational tools that are accessible to visually impaired people. The proposed virtual systems represent the research work that has been conducted in the last years by the authors to answer the research question: how effective can virtual touch (haptics) be used for the education of blind people?

The first system, named as CIGI, is a novel interactive cinematography system that incorporates the sense of touch in movies by using virtual reality and haptics devices, and aims to teach art and film to blind people. To do this, the system creates a virtual world for the blind user to explore, touch and feel by means of a haptic device that enables the sense of touch. The second system aims to improve the teaching and learning process of the Braille system. The main function of this system is to show on the computer screen different 3D virtual objects that correspond to Braille texts for the user (blind people) to feel and touch them by means of the haptic device.

BACKGROUND

Educational Process and Inclusive Education

West and Turner (2004) define the communication process as the social process in which individuals use symbols to establish and interpret the meaning of their environment. The four key terms of this conceptual perspective are: communication as a social process, as a symbol, as meaning and as an environment. On the other hand, the education is also a social process that involves the interaction between two or more people, the teacher and the student(s). Thus, the terms communication and education can be compared as shown in Figure 1.

The interaction among the teacher and the apprentices is part of the educational process, which is a dynamic, complex and continuously changing process. In both education and communication there is interaction between symbols, which are an arbitrary label or a representation of the phenomena where the message is extracted from manufactured or constructed meanings. Words are symbols that represent notions of concepts and things; for example, the word chair represents the object in which one can sit (West & Turner, 2004); and the word pyramid represents a geometric body that has a single base, and the side faces are triangles that meet at a vertex. However, the name of the pyramid will depend on the shape of its base because there are triangular, quadrangular, pentagonal, etc., pyramids. If a person has

Figure 1. Similarities between communication and education

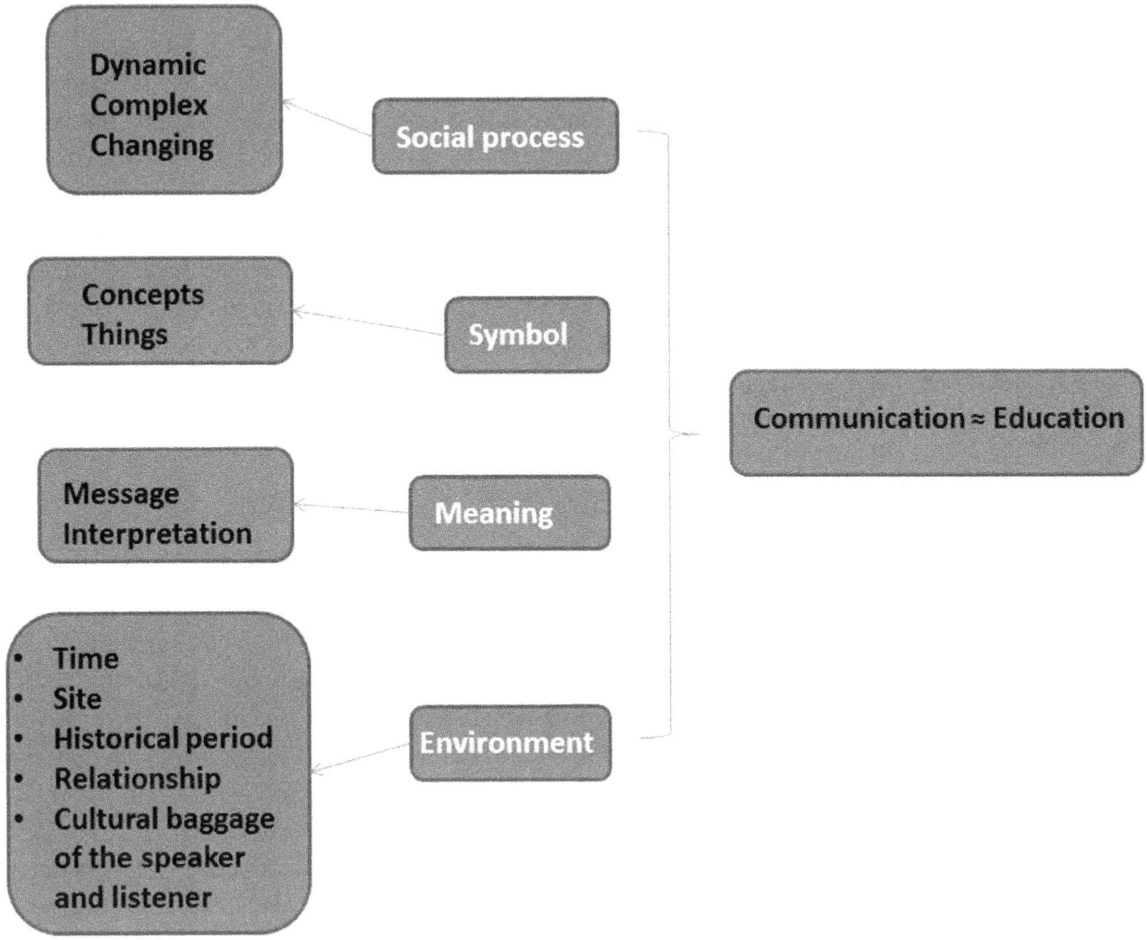

only been exposed to a quadrangular pyramid, the mental symbol will be based on his/her previous experiences and feelings. A teacher as a message sender or encoder must decide the best effective way to communicate and conceptualize the message. Therefore, an important element in communication and education is the meaning because it will be what the student will interpret from the teacher´s message. Likewise, the student, as a message receiver, will extract the meaning from the message. If the persons do not share the same meanings, they will have difficulties to speak and interpret the same fact (West & Turner, 2004). In such situations, the teacher must be able to explain, repeat and clarify the concepts. The environment is also important in the educational process since it refers to the situation or context in which the communication takes place. The environment in the communication process can also be mediated and established with technical support by email, chat rooms or Internet. These mediated environments necessarily influence the communication between two people (West & Turner, 2004).

Van Manen (1998) states that pedagogy is the art of tactfully mediating the possible influences of the world so that the child is constantly encouraged to assume a greater responsibility for their learning and personal development. However, this influence on learning and development must be also reflected in the education of people with special educational needs (SEN). The special education can be understood in a more dynamic way and it is focused on serving: a) the person with SEN, b) the educational situations that foster their development, c) the interdisciplinary of the professionals involved, and d) the contexts: social, family, school or community (Martínez, 2012).

In the educational process, it is very important to communicate the meanings and to generate the adequate didactic situations and environments that lead to a correct learning. However, the learning requirements differ from person to person regardless their physical and mental condition, or despite being considered statistically as a normal person. The concept of inclusive education refers to the process of recognizing the students' learning needs and to act according to such needs. The key premise is that everybody should learn the same but considering that everybody learns differently. For instance, in a mainstream education can be easily observed that the learning styles differ from student to student; however, it does not mean that they have an inability to learn. In the case of blind people, it is necessary to use nonvisual representations to enable the teaching-learning process and an inclusive education. Many of these didactic situations and environments are based on visual representations, which are impractical for blind and visually impaired people. With an appropriate support, pupils with visual impairment in mainstream schools can have an educational experience as rewarding as their sighted classmates (Salisbury, 2008).

A learning problem is a general term that describes specific learning difficulties that can cause a person to have learning conflicts and difficulties to develop certain skills. Blindness itself represents a learning problem, but it does not mean that they cannot learn, but it is necessary to figure out how to learn best. The skills that are most frequently affected when a person suffers from a learning problem are: listening, speaking, reasoning, reading, writing, and math learning. People with learning disabilities have no mental retardation or are not slow to learn, on the contrary, most of these people have a normal or above average normal intelligence (Romero & Lavigne, 2005). For a person with learning problems, the communicational or educational messages that reach his/her brain are confusing, resulting in difficulties to learn in one or more academic areas. However, they can learn and be very successful as in the case of well-known scientists and artists such as Thomas A. Edison, Albert Einstein, Beethoven, Louis Pasteur, Winston Churchill, and Nelson Rockefeller, who had learning problems but developed extraordinary skills and thinking ability.

User Centered-Design (Ucd) As A Support For Inclusive Education

Inclusive education is part of the dominant discourse around the world, but the terminology used in every country is different; for example, England uses the term special educational needs and disabilities (SEN) and Scotland uses the term additional support needs (ASN) (Riddell, Gillooly, Harris & Davidge, 2019A). Moreover, the analysis of administrative data suggested that there are important differences between England and Scotland regarding to the identification of children with SEN and ASN, and the provision of statutory support plans (Riddell, Gillooly, Harris & Davidge, 2019B). There also appear to be large differences in technology. Therefore, actual assistive educational technology centered-design for the blind user is often lacking. "In 1994, at the World Conference of Salamanca, for the first time, the problem of inclusion and special educational needs were addressed; thereafter, these subjects became two of the most important principles regarding educational policies" (Palmeros-Ávila, Pérez-Castro & Quiroz-Segura, 2017: 161). From then onwards, the discourse and jurisdiction has being part of a distinct narrative. At the beginning doctors used to be very involved in the education process, but now the roll has been given to teachers, and the focus has not to do with incapacity, but what is contending in the big umbrella of ASN (Riddell, Gillooly, Harris & Davidge, 2019A).

In Mexico, the attention of students with SEN represents a challenge for the National Education System. Currently, there are more and more schools that open their doors to these students and face the challenge of offering them an educational response with equity. In recent years and to promote the educational integration, basic education has assumed this responsibility of making the education accessible and inclusive to all persons. The attention of the students with SEN in Mexico meets what the National Education Program 2001-2006 points out in relation to the need to establish the regulatory framework, as well as the monitoring and evaluation mechanisms that will regulate the educational integration processes in all basic education schools in the country, in the area of equity, relevance and quality (SEP, 2006).

According to Roth, Ross and MacEachren, UCD describes the process of ensuring interface success by gathering input and feedback from target users throughout the design and development of the interface (2015: 262). Therefore, the focus of the research presented in this chapter is centered on the needs of blind students when conceptualizing knowledge by the use of Haptic and VR technology on the teaching and learning process. Immersive virtual environments (IVEs) have been studied as an experimental tool for fully sighted people in order to translate behavioral information into quantitative measures and incorporate user preference data for evaluating design alternatives with the objective of meeting end-user preferences (Heydarian, Pantazis, Wang, Gerber & Becerik-Gerbera, 2017: 56). IVEs had been also used with three-dimensional sounds as a guide for blind people to interact with conventional music games (De Oliveira, LottoCorrea, Taboada, Costa, & Lopes, 2016). Likewise, a system based on Virtual and Augmented Reality was proposed as an educational and support tool in everyday tasks for people with cognitive disabilities. In order to illustrate the usability and functionality of the system, they chose to train and support navigation skills on people with Down Syndrome based on a navigation task (Covaci, Kramer, Augusto, Rus, & Braun, 2015).

The reasons for deviating from a user-centered approach include different aspects such as lack of access to the target users, costs, limited resources, among others. However, a user-centered approach often saves project resources rather than wasting them (Roth, Ross & MacEachren, 2015). In particular, Yuan, Hanrahan, Lee, Rosson, and Carroll (2019) examined in detail how visually impaired people conduct grocery shopping with the help of different technologies; and claimed that participatory design (PD) can be an empowering method that democratizes the design environment by engaging and valuing the contributions of such individuals (or skateholders).

The standard ISO 9241-11 makes emphasis on usability measurement and defines usability in terms of effectiveness, efficiency and satisfaction in a particular context of use, making emphasis in that usability is an outcome of interaction rather than a property of a product (Bevan, Carter & Harker, 2015). Generally, teachers strive to serve the students' interests by promoting science and technology in a didactic manner. By being aware of the importance of the user's special educational needs (in this case blind people), some virtual educational material will allow teachers to create more effective information resources and to encourage and develop best learning practices. In this respect, noting the blind's educational special needs helps to emphasize the necessity of making even the most advanced technology easy to use in order to support their education. Virtual environments can be a potential learning resource to promote accessible and inclusive education. As an example, the online virtual world Second Life (2019) can be used to meet students, to create or visit labs and buildings, and to know and interact with virtual objects in order to learn different subjects and skills, including soft skills.

Blind People Education

Since human beings have the possibility of perceiving images through sensory substitution, a person with visual limitations depends mainly on the haptic (touch) and ear senses to obtain self-knowledge from the surrounding environment. In addition, the kinesthetic sense gives information about the position of the body and its parts, facilitating a greater spatial location. Thus, sensory perception is a source of knowledge for blind, partially sighted or fully sighted people, since everyone follow the same development process. If there is not a satisfactory situation incited to acquire knowledge, then visually impaired people do not reach a standard development in their educational evolutionary process. The multi-sensory approach is particularly useful to acquire information through the parts of the body.

The integral formation of blind students involves exposing the student to situations that require an activity of exploration, search of different alternatives, reflection on forms and conducts of personal and group activities. Information and Communication Technologies (ICTs) can be a useful multi-sensory tool to explore different concepts and reduce learning problems. Hoolbrook and Koening (2003) mentioned that the academic success of students with visual impairment depends on the information access and teaching materials. Stratton (1990) also emphasized that it is important to provide the help and adaptations that are necessary to meet the needs of the student and make the most of their skills. It is important to consider that extreme adaptation separates the students from their environment while a poor adaptation inhibits their learning.

Learning Objects, Virtual Reality and Haptics

Wiley (2000) defines a learning object as any structured digital resource that can be used and reused as a learning support. A learning object is characterized by its discoverability, reusability, and interoperability. The main components of a learning object are: general course descriptive data, instructional content, quizzes and assessments, typology and learning object metadata. Learning objects have been widely used for education and training in many areas. However, few research works have focused on the development of learning objects for people with visual disabilities. Vaspori and Arato (1995) highlighted the practical use of talking computer technologies by visually impaired people. However Kumar, Ramasamy and Stefanich (2001) did not designed a computer system, they proposed the use of universal instructional design for visually impaired people. On the other hand, Bayir, Keser and Numanoglu (2010) mentioned that empowering people with visual disabilities as computer literate with ICT skills is an improvement, though the benefits from these trainings are low and expensive.

Some other investigations have examined the learning process based on special software to allow blind people to independently enhance their knowledge, learning, and social skills. A generic human computer interface as an assistive technology for disabled people and elderly people to access internet was reported by Pieper and Hermsdorf (1997). Lahav, Hagab, Kader, Levy and Talis, (2018) demonstrated that the integration of sonified models with the Listening-to-Complexity (L2C), used as a compensatory aid, has a beneficial impact in the acquisition of scientific conceptual knowledge and systems reasoning for the Kinetic Molecular Theory (KMT), allowing blind students their inclusion in the academic curriculum on an equal basis. The Braille Score is a computer program that uses artificial intelligence methods to process music information and to support blind people to read music scores and operate music notation during music education (Macukow & Homenda, 2006). Borges and Tomé (2014) also presented a methodology for teaching music to blind children but based on the interaction with the Musibraille software. To improve access to educational courses and curriculum materials in Scotland, the use of synchronized audio books was proposed by McCreath and Cuthbertson (2005). On the other hand, the Sound Design 4.1 project aimed to approach science knowledge to blind children by means of friendly narrations and surround audio (Ortiz-Alvarado, Espinosa-Castañeda, Vargas-Neri & Rodríguez-Arellano, 2017; Ortíz et al., 2018).

New media technologies have become widely used and adapted to education in the last few years. Opie (2018) proposed an online unit as an expanded core curriculum component to educate teachers of visually impaired students in order to eliminate unintentional exclusion practices currently experienced and to encourage them to incorporate components of the expanded core curriculum into their everyday practices. The web, augmented reality, virtual reality, mixed reality and haptic technologies can be used as learning objects because they are flexible, adaptable and reusable. In the case of Virtual Reality (VR), it is defined as "the interactive projection of virtual images and the use of nonvisual modalities, such as haptic and audio feedback, to make the user feel that he/she is interacting with real objects" (Ellis, 1994). VR is also defined as "the use of computer-generated synthetic environments and the associated hardware, to provide the user with the illusion of physical presence within the artificial environment" (Jayaram, Connacher & Lyons, 1997). Although there are several definitions of VR, all of them agree that VR is a synthetic environment, generated by the computer and other external devices, that allows the user to interact with a 3D virtual world in which the objects behave and looks like if they were real. The fundamental concept behind VR is the illusion (Mujber, Szecsi & Hashmi, 2004).

There are different immersion levels; for instance, at the highest immersion level the user would be fully isolated from the real world and would be using the five senses to interact with the virtual environment. VR systems can be classified into three main types (Mujber, Szecsi & Hashmi, 2004): non-immersive (desktop systems), semi-immersive, and fully-immersive. To date, there is not any virtual environment able to fully immerse the user. On the other hand, a low immersion level involves only one or two senses, being the sight the most common.

One of the most important features of VR systems is that they can be used as tools for data, knowledge and abilities acquisition. They can also be used to represent and model concepts, ideas and places that could be impossible to represent or access in other ways. Thus, VR has a wide range of applications in different areas, from which the engineering area outstands.

The use of haptic devices that allow feeling the shape, texture, weight and inertia of virtual objects, is more common every day. The word "haptics" comes from the Greek haptesthai, which means to touch, or anything related the sense of touch. Haptics can be considered under different concepts such as: 1) human haptic perception, which refers to the process of perceiving objects by the sense of touch, 2) haptic feedback, which refers to the process of receiving a force or external signal to stimulate the sense of touch, and 3) haptic interface, which refers to the devices used to generate the haptic feedback signal. Haptic rendering is the name given to the general process of feeling or touching virtual objects. This comprises tactile feedback, to feel properties such as the superficial texture, and the kinesthetic feedback, to feel the shapes, sizes and weight of virtual objects. Similar to graphic rendering, haptic rendering provides interactive projections of virtual objects to the user, but with the difference that virtual objects can be touched. Haptic devices allow obtaining three different types of feedbacks (Burdea, 1996):

Figure 2. General architecture of VR systems with haptics

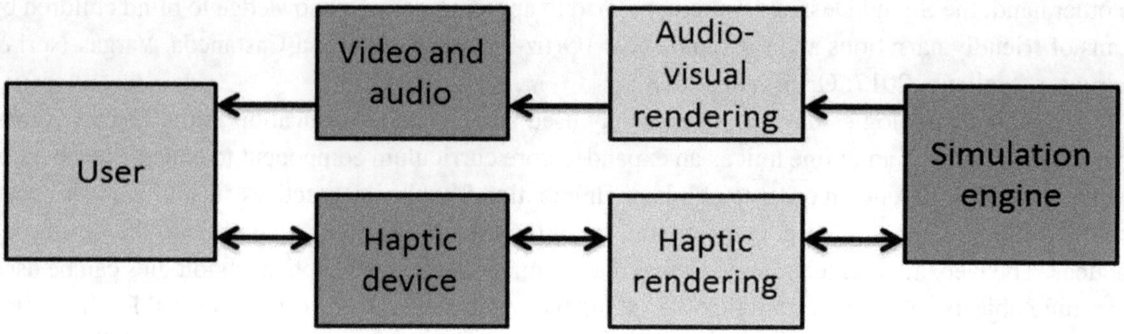

- Tactile or cutaneous feedback, useful to recognize textures, shapes or even temperatures of virtual objects.
- Kinematic force feedback, to recognize the weight, shape, inertia, hardness of virtual objects, and in some cases, the collisions among virtual objects.
- Proprioceptive feedback, to perceive the position and orientation of virtual objects in the space.

Haptic interfaces can be used for remote manipulation of real objects; for example, to control a robotic arm that manipulates hazardous materials or performs rehabilitation therapies. Haptic devices behave as a small robot that exchanges mechanical energy with the user. Although haptic devices could be designed to be in touch with any part of the user's body, manual devices have been the most developed and used haptic interfaces. Currently, there are several types of haptic devices, the most common are: the Geomagic Touch (formerly known as the Phantom Omni and Phantom desktop from Sensable), the Falcon from Novint and the Virtuose from Haption.

The force feedback characteristics of haptic devices allow the creation of more intuitive applications where users have a high level of interaction and influence on the virtual environment. Haptic feedback is essential to increase the immersion level and the user interaction with the virtual environment.

The main architecture of a virtual reality system with visual, auditory, and haptic rendering, comprises the following basic elements, Figure 2 (Salisbury, Conti, & Barbagli, 2004):

- Simulation engine, responsible for computing the physical behavior of virtual objects in the VE.
- Visual, audio and haptic rendering, responsible for calculating the graphics, audio and force feedbacks of the virtual environment (VE).
- Transducers or interfaces, responsible of converting the visual, audio and force feedback signals from the computer to the user.

Currently there are several companies and institutions working on the research and development of virtual reality applications in various areas such as medicine and engineering. Some of these applications include:

- **Medicine:** Design of prostheses and implants (Scharver, Evenhouse, Johnson & Leigh, 2004); development of computer systems for surgery planning (Girod, Keeve & Girod, 1995), (Bell R. B., DDS & MD., 2011), surgery training (Pohlenz, Gro¨, Petersik, Von, Pflesser, Pommert, Ho¨, Tiede, Springer & Heiland, 2010), rehabilitation, treatments and therapies for some particular illnesses such as phobias (Castañeda-Roldán & Vázquez-García, 2011).
- **Engineering:** Virtual design and manufacturing systems (Henderson & Kattethota, 1999), (Fischer, Vance & Vo, 2009); industrial processes simulation (Aras & Yip-Hoi, 2007), (Lim, Medellin, Sung, Ritchie & Corney, 2009); virtual training of workers (Pérez-Acal & Sanz-Lobera, 2007), (Brough, Schwartz, Gupta, Anand, Kavetsky & Pettersen, 2007); and virtual factories (Mujber, Szecsi & Hashmi, 2004).
- **Science:** Representation and simulation of physical, biological, and chemical phenomena and processes, and scientific data visualization.
- **Education:** Creation of nano, micro, macro and astronomic scale virtual scenarios for the students to experience various phenomena of the virtual world; e.g. primary school teaching of organic systems (Castañeda-Roldán & Espinosa-Victoria, 2008).
- **Entertainment:** Creation of videogames and simulations in which the user can feel and manipulate the virtual objects, or even to have a virtual second life (Elias, Batumalai and Azmi, 2019; Second life, 2019).
- **Art:** Virtual exhibitions of art, virtual museums, virtual concerts, virtual sculpting, etc.

Although VR has become an outstanding technology in many areas, including education, it is difficult to be used for blind people because it mainly relies on the sense of sight. However, with the development of modern haptic computer interfaces the virtual touch in VR systems is possible. Moreover, the combination of VR and haptics has proved to be effective to generate mental images in blind people (Espinosa-Castañeda & Medellin-Castillo, 2014). Also the orientation and mobility (O&M) through unfamiliar spaces is a complex task for blind people that require compensatory sensorial channels to collect information. Lahav & Mioduser (2008a) used VR to assist blind people in their anticipatory exploration and cognitive mapping of an unknown space. It was observed that virtual reality is effective in the construction of cognitive maps from the exploration of the VE, which can then be used to navigate in the real environment. In the Lahav's VE, auditory and haptic feedback were provided at different levels (e.g. the name of an object, indication of end points, indication of turning points), in order to assist the participants in the mapping of the virtual objects (Lahav et al., 2008b). Similarly, Sánchez (2012) developed a haptic-interface videogame, named as Audio Haptic Maze (AHM), to improve the O&M skills of blind people. The user interaction in the AHM system is by means of a standard computer keyboard, a Novint Falcon haptic device and headphones. The results of the AHM project showed that the haptic feedback is as effective as the audio feedback.

On the other hand, Gomez and Sandnes (2012) mentioned that it is harder to communicate the environment information, such as type of object, identity form and dimensions, by haptic feedback than by synthetic speech. Therefore, a hybrid strategy based on both haptic feedback and synthetic speech was proposed. The RoboGuideDog project (Gomez & Sandnes, 2012) aimed to transform the environment information into a description by means of a synthetic speech and/or a force feedback joystick, allowing blind people to navigate around physical spaces. The system HITPROTO enables users, such as mentors or support workers, to quickly create haptic interactions (with an emphasis on haptic data visualization) by means of a visual programming interface. Although the project is not specially orientated to blind people, it can produce tactile diagrams for blind users (Panëels, Ritsos, Rodgers & Roberts, 2013).

Konstantinos, Panagiotis, Eleni, Marina, Asimis and Valari (2015) examined the contribution of an audio-haptic aid to the O&M of blind people within a real environment. The audio-haptic aid consisted of 3 maps referring respectively to three residential areas. By controlling the handle in two dimensions (up – down and left – right), the participant could move through the streets, receive haptic and audio stimuli and form a cognitive map of the area. Koukourikos and Papadopoulos (2015) examined the spatial knowledge that blind people gain by studying an audio-haptic map of a multisensory application that included a Novint Falcon haptic device. They concluded that blind people were able to build significant spatial knowledge after using the proposed multisensory application.

From the literature review, it is observed that in order to facilitate the acquisition of knowledge by people with visual disabilities, access to educational materials through multisensory feedback or assistive technologies, including talking devices or physical tactile teaching material, must be developed. In addition, it is observed a clear consensus about the capability of haptic technologies to induce mental representations in blind people.

DEVELOPMENT OF HAPTIC-VIRTUAL LEARNING SYSTEMS

In order to promote the development of assistive technologies for the inclusive education of blind people, two virtual reality systems with haptic habilitation have been developed and are described in this section.

Cinematography System

Sight loss affects more than one million people in Mexico, a number that represents the 11.5 of the total population (INEGI, 2010). Losing sight can change many areas of a person's life, even apparently trivial things like being able to watch cinema. Having access to movies is part of the cultural conversation. Movies are made for everybody, just because somebody can't see, doesn't mean they can't enjoy a film (Ford & Spielberg, 2014). Science fiction cinema can become an excellent bearer for reflection and social dissemination of scientific technological advances (Marín-Ramos, 2018). In the area of arts, particularly in film, a novel interactive cinematography system for blind people has been proposed and developed (Medellín-Castillo, Martínez-Hernández, Espinosa-Castañeda & Castañeda-Roldán, 2011). The system, named as CIGI®, is a novel interactive cinematography system that incorporates the sense of touch to the movies by using virtual reality and haptic technologies. The CIGI system creates a virtual world for the blind user to explore, feel, and touch the scenarios by means of the haptic device. As the user explores the virtual world, the audio story corresponding to the film story is being played.

The general architecture of the CIGI system is shown in Figure 3, where it can be observed that besides the audio, the haptics, and the graphics rendering modules, the system incorporates a module corresponding to the cinematographic production. In this cinematographic production module the virtual scenes, audio stories, and virtual objects are defined and configured according to the cinematographic script. A physics simulation engine calculates the physical behavior and interaction of virtual objects in the virtual environment.

The CIGI system has been developed using Visual C++ and the following libraries:

Figure 3. CIGI system architecture.

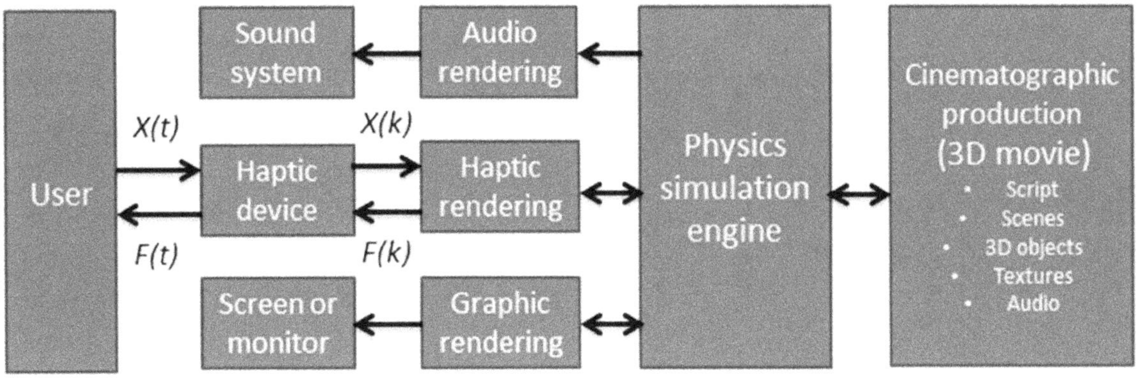

Figure 4. CIGI system: a) system integration; b) user interface and virtual scene

- OpenAL (open source 3D audio library, which can simulate the localization of sound in a 3D space of various channels),
- OpenHaptics (Haptic rendering library which integrates the basic steps for haptic and graphic configuration), and
- OpenGL (a standard specification that defines a multilanguage and multiplatform API to produce 2D and 3D graphics applications).

The haptic rendering is performed using a Phantom Omni haptic device. The CIGI system and the interactive-tactile 3D movie are shown in Figure 4. The haptic cursor is shown in Figure 4b as a blue sphere, which corresponds to the user position in the virtual environment.

Figure 5. Braille system and alphabet

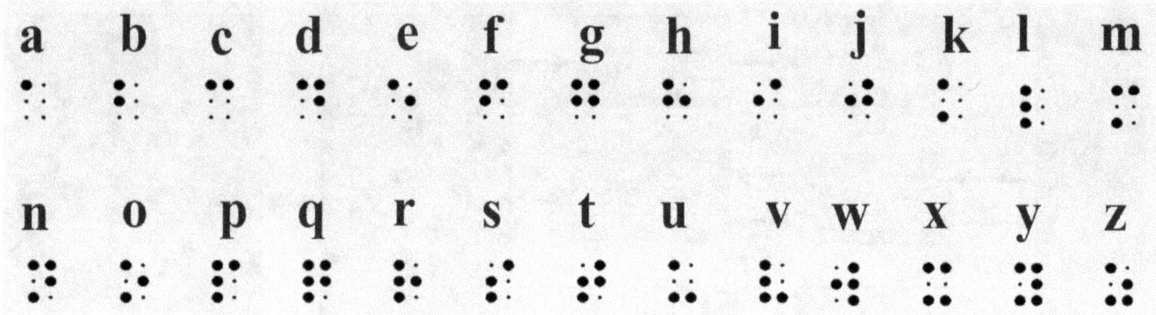

The main features of the CIGI system are:

- Virtual 3D objects can be freely explored by the user using the haptic device.
- Virtual scenes and audio stories can be forwarded or rewind according to the user's desire.
- The exploring time of virtual scenes and objects is not limited.
- It is possible to reproduce different movies, however the 3D modeling of the virtual scenes, objects, textures and audios is required, i.e. a 3D virtual-haptic movie must be created.

Braille System

The Braille system is the most widely used communication system for blind people to read and write. It is based on an array of superficial dots for the visually impaired people to feel and touch, and it was created in 1821 by Louis Braille, who was blinded by an accident in his father's workshop. The Braille system consists of cells with an arrangement of 6 raised points distributed in two columns and three rows to represent a letter, as shown in Figure 5. In addition, there are special arrangements for some symbols. To form words or sentences, the cells of each letter are placed consecutively. The Braille teaching-learning process comprises an identification stage where blind people touch the different cells to identify and learn the configurations of each letter of the alphabet.

UNESCO's concern with Braille dates back to 1949 when, upon a request from India, it undertook the pioneering task of adopting a uniform Braille system and creating a standard writing for blind people all over the world (1951). Current special education teachers uses synthetic trend methods (syllabic and phonetic) to teach the reading of the Braille system, while stimulating the lexical and sublexic pathways with the didactic activities proposed to blind students (Arroyo, Campos, Carballo, González, Solano, Vargas & Carpio, 2019). In order to improve the teaching and learning process of Braille, a haptic-enabled virtual system has been proposed and developed. The main function of the proposed system is to show on the computer screen different 3D virtual objects, corresponding to Braille texts, for the user (blind people) to virtually feel and touch them by means of the haptic device. The proposed system, named as SEAB® aims to explore the use of virtual reality and haptic technologies for teaching the Braille system to blind people. Figure 6 shows the general architecture of the proposed system, which comprises three main modules:

- **Graphic Module**: Responsible for the graphic rendering of virtual objects and the virtual environment, in this case Braille texts.
- **Haptic Module**: Responsible for haptic rendering that provides the sense of touch and force feedback so that the user can touch and feel virtual objects.
- **Braille Module**: Responsible for the generation of virtual objects corresponding to 3D texts in Braille, as well as the conversion of texts in Spanish to 3D texts in Braille. It also has a catalog that contains a wide variety of predefined 3D texts so that the user can select them and display them on the screen during the teaching-learning process.

The integration of these three modules allows the SEAB® system to carry out Braille teaching-learning tasks in an interactive way, where the user (blind person) can touch and feel the texts in Braille through a haptic device.

The SEAB® system has been implemented and developed in the MFC platform (Microsoft Foundation Classes) of Visual Studio 2010. For the graphic rendering the OpenGL libraries were used, while for the haptic rendering the OpenHaptics libraries and a Phantom Omni device from Sensable® were used. The virtual objects corresponding to braille texts are represented in the *.OBJ format, which is a format that is used to describe the surfaces of 3D objects, and which can be generated in geometric modeling systems such as CAD software. Figure 7 shows the user interface (GUI) of the SEAB® system, which consists of a main menu bar and a virtual stage area. Virtual objects are presented in the virtual scene (Braille texts), which can be touched and felt by the user through the haptic device. The main menu of the SEAB® application comprises nine options: File, Alphabet, Accented vowels, Numbers, Signs, Words, Sentences, Help and Haptic.

The main functionalities of the SEAB® system are:

- Conversion of texts into 3D Braille texts.
- Importing 3D objects corresponding to texts in Braille.
- Virtual reality environment for viewing 3D texts in Braille.
- User haptic manipulation and interaction with 3D texts in Braille.
- Extensive catalog of 3D texts in Braille comprising alphabet, accented vowels, numbers, signs, words and sentences.

One of the important features of the SEAB system is that it allows the displacement, rotation and scaling of the objects on the screen by means of the PC mouse, allowing the user to adjust them for greater comfort.

SOLUTIONS AND RECOMMENDATIONS

Cinematography System

In order to evaluate the performance and functionality of the CIGI system, a group of 8 young participants was selected as follows: 4 blind individuals, 3 partially blind individuals, and 1 low vision individual. Participants with different levels of blindness were considered in order to evaluate the influence of the

Figure 6. General architecture of the Braille teaching-learning system (SEAB®)

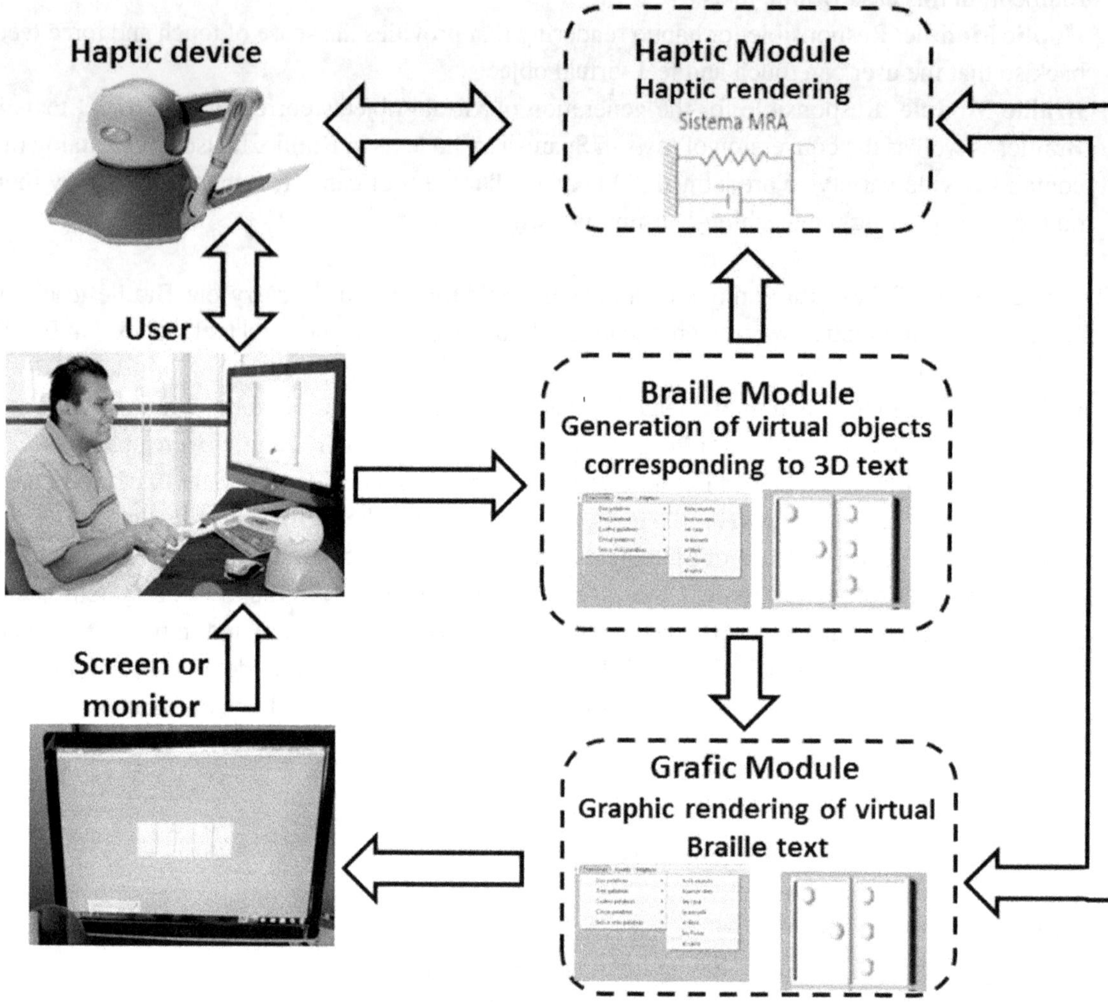

blindness level on the haptics recognition of 3D virtual objects. Therefore, none of the participants was allowed to see the screen during the test. Figure 8 shows one of the participants during the evaluation tests.

The facial expressions that participants showed during the haptics exploration and recognition of 3D virtual objects are presented in Table 1. From these results, it can be noticed that many of the facial expressions were smiles, eyebrow-lift and hands motion expressing surprise. All participants expressed great excitement.

At the end of the tests the users were asked: How was your experience when feeling geometrical objects using the CIGI system? The answers are shown in Table 2. From these results it can be observed that most of the users liked the experience of feeling 3D virtual objects in the CIGI system. The experience of knowing that they were touching the objects in the screen excited them the most, as it is observed in their comments about feeling surprised for having never felt that way. In addition, most of the participants used the two hands to look for a real object behind the haptic interface, and got surprised when no physical objects were founded.

Figure 7. Graphical user interface (GUI) of the SEAB® system

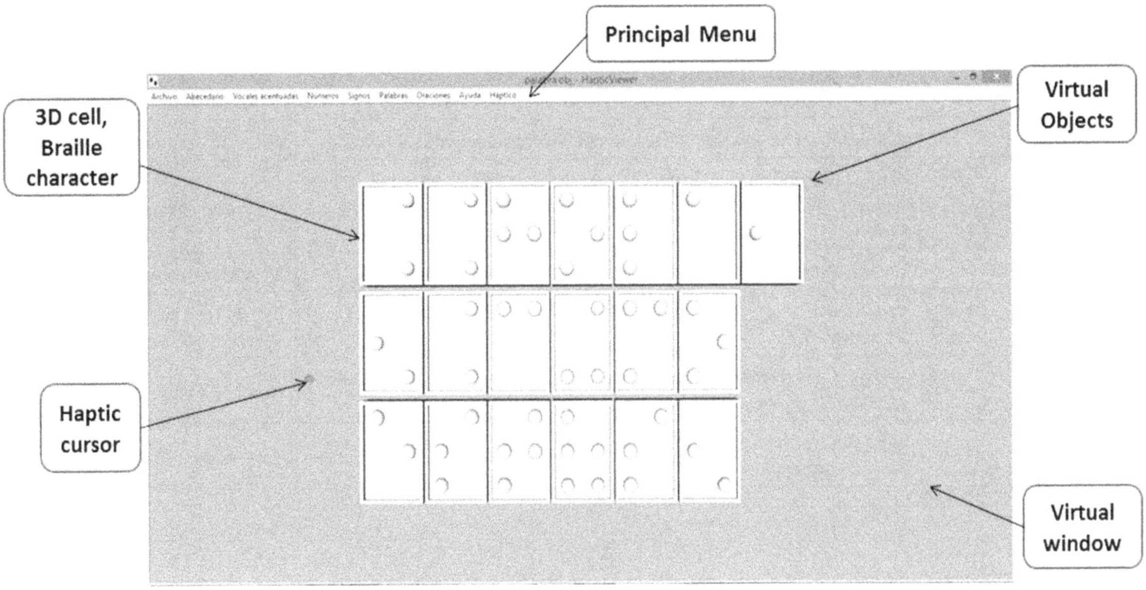

Figure 8. Participant during the evaluation of the CIGI system

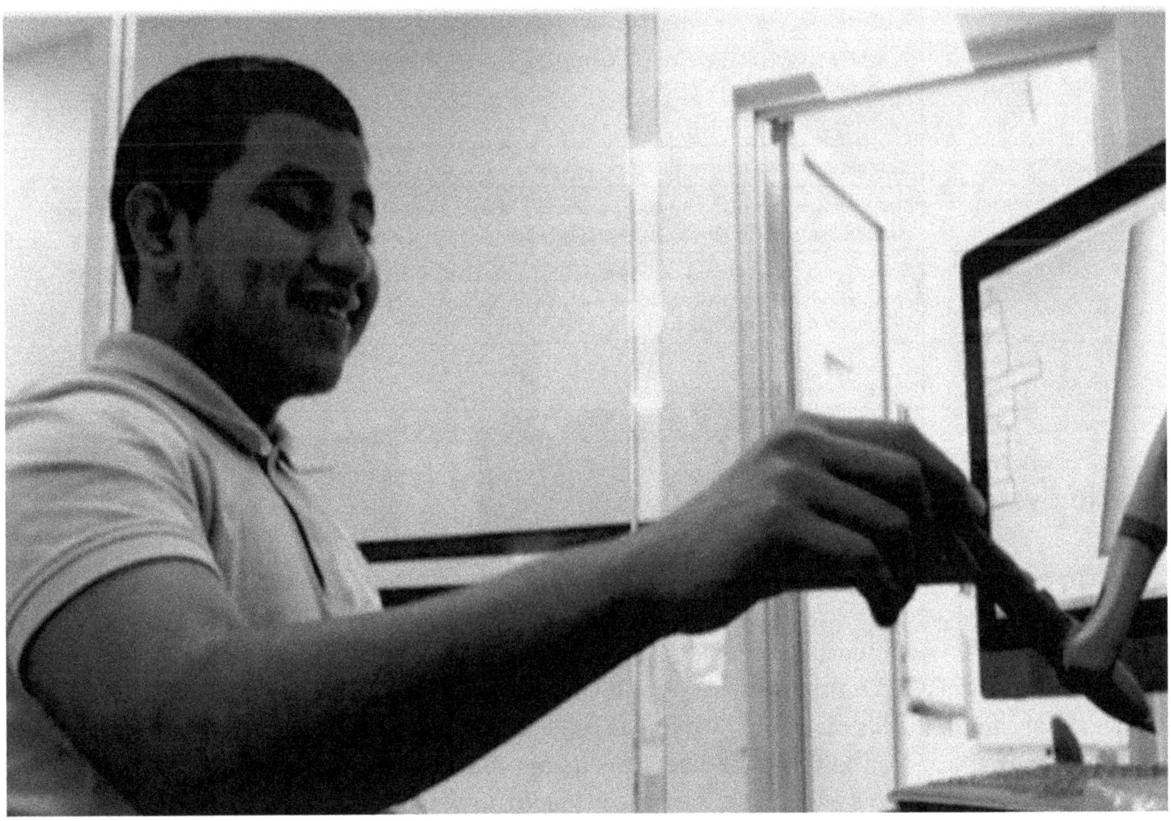

Table 1. Facial expression during haptics exploration and recognition of virtual objects

User	Facial expression	Verbal expression
1	Smiles and laughs, astonishment faces.	Cool! It feels!
2	Lots of smiles, close ups to the screen, excited hand movements.	¡It feels nice!
3	Astonishment, gentle movements, doubt when guessing the 3D object.	No verbal expression
4	Got lost in the virtual environment, this situation was reflected on his facial expression. Smile and laughs when making holes to virtual objects.	No verbal expression
5	Try to explore the object, jerking, laughs, and facial emotion.	No verbal expression
6	Very excited, smiles and laughs. Surprised when realizes that objects are hollowed.	It feels very nice! What happens if I push the object? It's very weird!
7	Surprised when realizing that his hand movements are in the air, and despite this, he does feel the objects.	How? Is it drawn on the screen?
8	When allowed to see, he explored the objects at 3 cm from the screen. Smiles when exploring.	So, it feels.

Table 2. Personal experiences of participants

User	Personal experience
1	I got surprised because I have never felt the figures in such a way, because other people can see the figures but I don't. It is interesting the way how the figures are presented.
2	It was nice because I´ve never experienced the way the images felt, then it was like a new experience.
3	I got little troubles because the pen was getting into the virtual object. I was having problems, but the experience was nice.
4	I did like it
5	Very excited, I liked it very much; however it was a bit difficult.
6	Her actions were: explore the Omni device arm, jerking, wait for the haptic device to move by itself and guide her through 3D objects. Very excited when identifying objects. The user found it difficult to use.
7	It was a bit difficult because as a blind people, I am used to touch embossed images, but not in the 3D space. However once you get the knowledge of how to use the pen (haptic cursor) to explore this type of figures, then it becomes easier.
8	It is not difficult for me to find the objects as long as I can see them. However when my eyes got covered, it was hard to recognize the objects.

Braille System

To evaluate the functionality of the SEAB® system, an experimental pilot test was conducted with a blind person with knowledge of the Braille language. First, an explanation was given to the blind participant about the SEAB® system and its functionality. Subsequently, some letters, numbers, words and sentences in Braille were displayed on the screen and read by the instructor, the participant was then asked to read the text by means of the haptic device (see Figure 9a). Finally, other letters, numbers, signs, words and sentences in Braille were shown on the screen again, but this time the instructor did not read the text shown in the screen, and the participant was asked to recognize and read the text by means of the haptic

Figure 9. Evaluation of the SEAB system: a) Braille reading, b) recognition of Braille texts

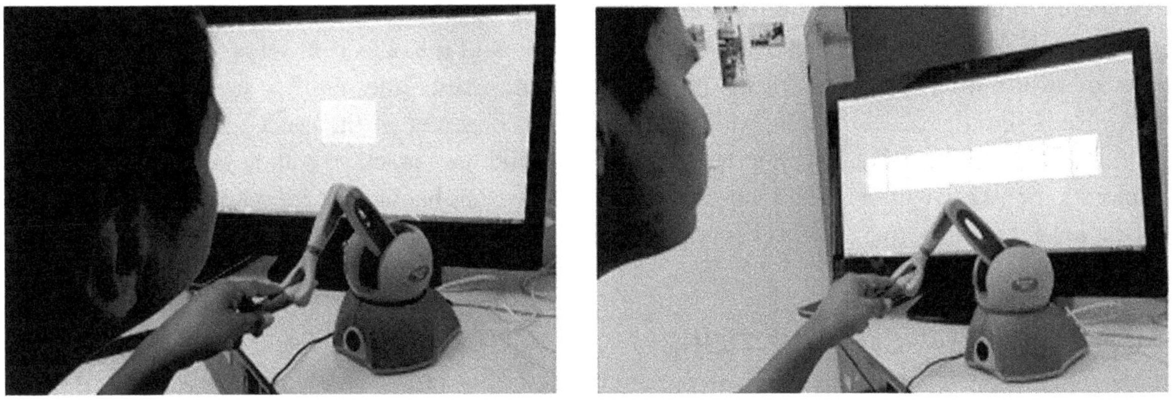

device (see Figure 9b). At the conclusion of the tests the participant was questioned about the utility and performance of the system, as well as their comments and feedback about the system.

The results obtained from the pilot test of the SEAB system with a blind person were satisfactory, the blind person was able to feel the Braille texts, as well as to recognize and read them. On average the blind person took 28 seconds to recognize and read a letter or number; a 4 letter word (LOVE) 2 minutes and 22 seconds; and a 2 word sentence (HELLO WORLD) 12 minutes and 29 seconds. From these results it was observed that the user required longer times to recognize and read Braille texts in the virtual environment than in the real world. This problem is because in the virtual system the haptic device only allows a single point contact, whereas in the real world the reading of Braille texts is done with the whole fingertip, touching or feeling all the points of a letter at the same time. Therefore, the use of a haptic interface with more contact points is considered as part of the future work.

It was also noted that the user tends to get lost in the virtual environment by having all the degrees of freedom available in the virtual environment (6 degrees of freedom). The general comments provided by the participant were very positive. In the first place, he considered that the system has a lot of potential as a teaching-learning tool of the Braille language. Second, he proposes its application as a general-purpose interface for the interaction of blind people with computers.

SOLUTIONS AND RECOMMENDATIONS

Virtual environments can be used to improve the educational process of people with visual disabilities. During the projection of tactile films through the CIGI system, blind people were able to recognize geometric shapes in the virtual environment. From the analysis of the results obtained from the experimental tests, it can be inferred that when touching 3D geometric bodies, there is a greater enrichment for the blind user in the construction of symbolic representations through virtual tactile perception. However, it is not only necessary to have the technological tool or system for inclusive education, but it is also essential that the shared meanings be the same between the teacher and the student(s). Additionally, it can be said that the CIGI system can be used as a technique for the development of thinking skills, helping to reduce learning problems caused by the lack of sight.

The participants, by exploring the geometric bodies in a virtual haptic way, generated mental imagery similar to the reality. The movement of the hand with the haptic device made the user aware of the properties of the presented object. Although the recognition of the objects in some of the users was not immediate, the similarity of the virtual object's form with reality allowed their correct identification. Likewise, a significant decrease in exploration times was observed as the users became more familiar with the system. Therefore, it is inferred that the more the user practice in the system, the faster the exploration process will be. Finally, it can be said that virtual haptic perception can generate mental tactile images of the virtual objects being explored by the blind user.

FUTURE RESEARCH DIRECTIONS

According to the standard ISO 9241-11, and the UCD principles, current research work is also focused on the development and evaluation of a new design methodology for blind people. The proposed methodology, shown in Figure 10, considers the use of virtual reality and haptic technologies to design and evaluate products or systems intended to be used by the blind. The design for the blind is based on the shape perception of the product; therefore the use of haptic technologies, which allows the user to touch virtual objects, represents a potential design evaluation tool for this type of design. This methodology was used in the design of the CIGI system, and it is meant to be extended to other type of products or systems for blind people.

The proposed methodology comprises two main stages: definition and design. At the definition stage the users' needs are identified by carrying out individual and group interviews. Based on this information, the design problem is established, and the requirements and characteristics defined according to the user experience. At the design stage, a user centered-design process is conducted and the solution developed. As a result, a prototype is created and evaluated by the user in order to provide feedback about the usability and experience. This information is the used to conducted, if necessary, a redesign process or optimization process.

CONCLUSION

The integration of virtual reality and haptic technologies by gathering input and feedback from target users represent a potential educational tool for visual impaired people. The results of this research centered the needs of blind students when conceptualizing knowledge and is demonstrated that blind people can learn and improve their skills by means of the virtual touch provided by haptic devices. Moreover, tactile mental images can be induced in blind people so they can recognize objects as in the real life. Two haptic-enabled virtual systems for the education of blind people were developed and evaluated. The results demonstrated that these systems can be used as assistive educational technologies for the inclusive education of blind people. However, most research work is needed in order to characterize and optimize the haptic-enabled virtual learning process of blind people. Current research work is focused on the development and evaluation of more 3D learning strategies for blind people but in different areas of knowledge and taking into consideration the lessons learnt from these first developments.

Figure 10. Proposed design methodology for blind people

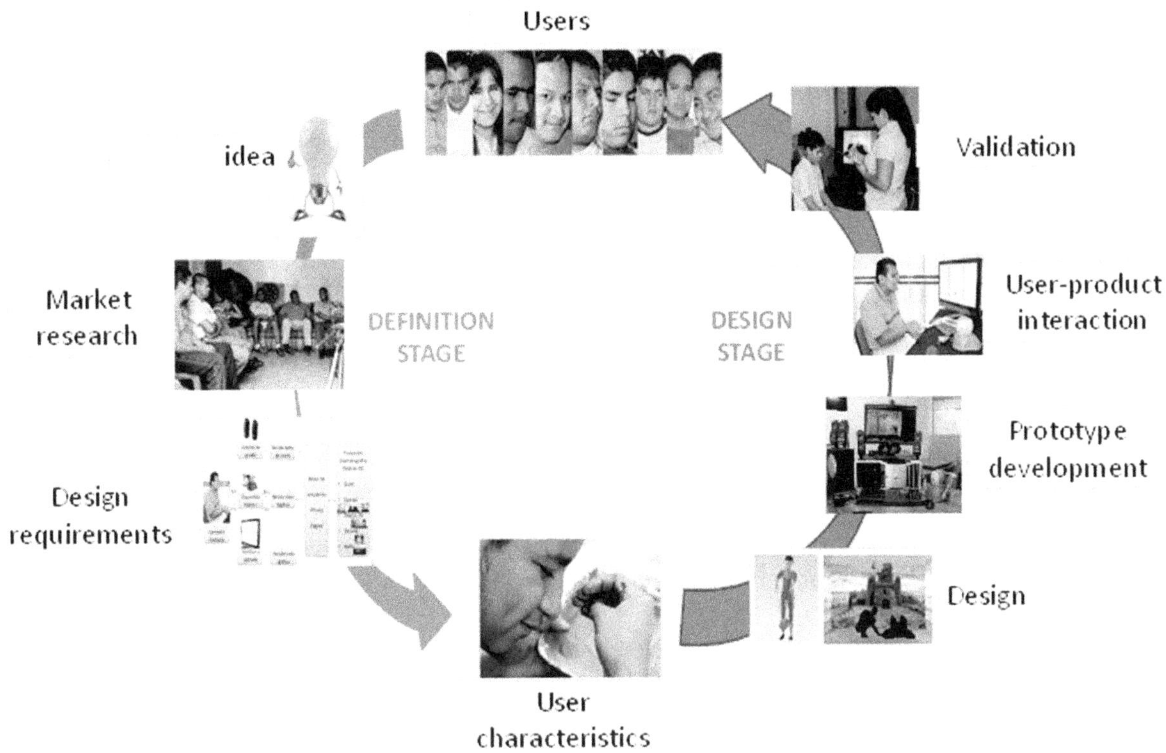

ACKNOWLEDGMENT

Authors acknowledge the support from CONACYT [Project #283503, Agreement C-252/2017], CONACULTA, and PROMEP from SEP.

REFERENCES

Aras, E., & Yip-Hoi, D. (2007). Geometric modeling of cutter/work piece engagements in 3-axis milling using polyhedral models. *ASME 2007 International Mechanical Engineering Congress and Exposition (IMECE2007).*

Arroyo, N., Campos, F., Carballo, M., González, G., Solano, A., Vargas, E., & Carpio, M. A. (2019) El Modelo dual de reconocimiento de la palabra en el Sistema Braille. *CienciAmérica*, *8*(1), 90-104. Available on: http://cienciamerica.uti.edu.ec/openjournal/index.php/uti/article/view/194

Bayir, S., Keser, H., & Numanoglu, G. (2010). General review on computer literacy of visually handicapped individuals in Turkey. *Procedia: Social and Behavioral Sciences*, *9*, 1475–1480. doi:10.1016/j.sbspro.2010.12.352

Bell, R. (2011). Computer Planning and Intraoperative Navigation in Orthognathic Surgery. *Journal of Oral and Maxillofacial Surgery*, *69*(3), 592–605. doi:10.1016/j.joms.2009.06.030 PMID:21353924

Bevan, N., Carter, J., & Harker, S. (2015). ISO 9241-11 Revised: What Have We Learnt About Usability Since 1998? In M. Kurosu (Ed.), Lecture Notes in Computer Science: Vol. 9169. *Human-Computer Interaction: Design and Evaluation. HCI 2015*. Cham: Springer.

Borges, J. A., & Tomé, D. (2014). Teaching music to blind children: New strategies for teaching through interactive use of Musibraille software. 5th International Conference on Software Development and Technologies for Enhancing Accessibility and Fighting Info-exclusion, DSAI 2013. *Procedia Computer Science*, *27*, 19–27. doi:10.1016/j.procs.2014.02.004

Brough, J., Schwartz, M., Gupta, S. K., Anand, D. K., Kavetsky, R., & Pettersen, R. (2007). Towards the development of a virtual environment-based training system for mechanical assembly operations. *Virtual Reality (Waltham Cross)*, *11*(4), 189–206. doi:10.100710055-007-0076-4

Burdea, G. C. (1996). *Force and touch feedback for virtual reality*. New York: John Wiley & Sons, Inc.

Castañeda-Roldán, C. Y., & Vázquez-García, F. E. (2011). Realidad Virtual, un apoyo en la Terapia de Acrofobia, Claustrofobia y Agorafobia. *Memorias del VIII Congreso Internacional sobre Innovación y Desarrollo Tecnológico (CIINDET 2011)*.

Castañeda-Roldán & Espinosa-Victoria. (2008, August). Realidad Virtual, una herramienta computacional para el estudio de Sistemas Orgánicos y los Sentidos del Tacto y Olfato a Nivel Primaria. *Impulso*.

Covaci, A., Kramer, D., Augusto, J. C., Rus, S., & Braun, A. (2015). Assessing Real World Imagery in Virtual Environments for People with Cognitive Disabilities. *2015 International Conference on Intelligent Environments*. 10.1109/IE.2015.14

De Oliveira, P. A., Lotto, E. P., Correa, A. G. D., Taboada, L. G. G., Costa, L. C. P., & Lopes, R. D. (2015). Virtual Stage: An Immersive Musical Game for People with Visual Impairment. *2015 14th Brazilian Symposium on Computer Games and Digital Entertainment (SBGames)*.

Elias, Z. M., Batumalai, U. M., & Azmi, A. N. H. (2019, November). Virtual reality games on accommodation and convergence. *Applied Ergonomics*, *81*. PMID:31422241

Ellis, S. R. (1994). What are virtual environments? *IEEE Computer Graphics and Applications*, *14*(1), 17–22. doi:10.1109/38.250914 PMID:7757252

Espinosa-Castañeda, R. & Medellín-Castillo, H. I. (2014). Análisis y evaluación de la generación de iconos mentales en personas invidentes a partir de la percepción virtual táctil utilizando realidad virtual y sistemas hápticos. *Revista ICONO14. Revista de estudios de comunicación y tecnologías emergentes*, *12*(2), 295-317.

Fischer, A., Vance, J. M., & Vo, D. M. (2009). Haptic feedback to guide interactive product design. *ASME-AFM 2009 World Conference on Innovative Virtual Reality (WINVR2009)*.

Ford, H., & Spielberg, S. (2014). *"Not Much To See": How the Blind Enjoy Movies* [Video Archive]. Retrieved from https://youtu.be/QJguIANUEX8

Girod, S., Keeve, E., & Girod, B. (1995). Advances in interactive craniofacial surgery planning by 3D simulation and visualization. *International Journal of Oral and Maxillofacial Surgery*, *24*(1), 120–125. doi:10.1016/S0901-5027(05)80872-0 PMID:7782646

Gomez, J. V., & Sandnes, F. E. (2012). RoboGuideDog: Guiding blind users through physical environments with laser range scanners. *Procedia Computer Science*, *14*, 218–225. doi:10.1016/j.procs.2012.10.025

Henderson, M., & Kattethota, G. (1999). Manufacturability evaluation for rapid fabrication: A system for traditional machining and layered manufacturing planning. *CAD Conference*, Neuchatel, Switzerland.

Heydarian, A., Pantazis, E., Wang, A., Gerber, D., & Becerik-Gerbera, B. (2017). Towards user centered building design: Identifying end-user lighting preferences via immersive virtual environments. *Automation in Construction*, *81*(September), 56–66. doi:10.1016/j.autcon.2017.05.003

Holbrook, M. C., & Koening, A. J. (Eds.). (2003). Foundations of education. Volume II. Instructional Strategies for Teaching Children and Youth with Visual Impairments. AFB Press.

INEGI. (2010). *Instituto Nacional de Estadística y Geografía.* INEGI.

ISO 9241-11: *Ergonomic requirements for office work with visual display terminals* (VDTs) - Part 11 Guidance on usability (1998) Retrieved from https://www.iso.org/standard/16883.html

Jayaram, S., Connacher, H. I., & Lyons, K. W. (1997). Virtual assembly using virtual reality techniques. *Computer Aided Design*, *29*(8), 575–584. doi:10.1016/S0010-4485(96)00094-2

Konstantinos, P., Panagiotis, K., Eleni, K., Marina, M., Asimis, V., & Valari, E. (2015). Audio-Haptic Map: An Orientation and Mobility Aid for Individuals with Blindness. *Procedia Computer Science*, *67*, 223–230. doi:10.1016/j.procs.2015.09.266

Koukourikos, P., & Papadopoulos, K. (2015). Development of Cognitive Maps by Individuals with Blindness Using a Multisensory Application. *Procedia Computer Science*, *67*, 213–222. doi:10.1016/j.procs.2015.09.265

Kumar, D. D., Ramasamy, R., & Stefanich, G. P. (2001). Science for Students with Visual Impairments: Teaching Suggestions and Policy Implications for Secondary Educators. *Electronic Journal of Science Education*, *5*, 3. Retrieved April 9, 2019, from http://unr.edu/homepage/crowther/ejse/kumar2etal.html

Lahav, O., Hagab, N., Kader, S. A. E., Levy, S. T., & Talis, V. (2018). Listen to the models: Sonified learning models for people who are Blind. *Computers & Education*, *127*, 141–153. doi:10.1016/j.compedu.2018.08.020

Lahav, O., & Mioduser, D. (2008a). Construction of cognitive maps of unknown spaces using a multi-sensory virtual environment for people who are blind. *Computers in Human Behavior*, *24*(3), 1139–1155. doi:10.1016/j.chb.2007.04.003

Lahav, O., & Mioduser, D. (2008b). Haptic-feedback support for cognitive mapping of unknown spaces by people who are blind. Int. *J. Human-Computer Studies*, *66*(1), 23–35. doi:10.1016/j.ijhcs.2007.08.001

Lim, T., Medellin, H., Sung, R., Ritchie, J. M., & Corney, J. (2009). Virtual bloxing assembly rapid prototyping of near net shapes. *ASME-AFM 2009 World Conference on Innovative Virtual Reality (WINVR2009).*

Macukow, B., & Homenda, W. (2006). Methods of Artificial Intelligence in Blind People Education. In L. Rutkowski, R. Tadeusiewicz, L. A. Zadeh, & J. M. Żurada (Eds.), Lecture Notes in Computer Science: Vol. 4029. *Artificial Intelligence and Soft Computing – ICAISC 2006. ICAISC 2006.* Berlin: Springer. doi:10.1007/11785231_123

Marín-Ramos, E. (2018). Blade Runner, de 2019 a 2049. El cine de ciencia ficción como divulgador de la ciencia. *InMediaciones de la Comunicación, 13*(2), 187–211. doi:10.18861/ic.2018.13.2.2873

Martínez, L. (2012). *Sistemas de educación especial.* Estado de México: Red Tercer Milenio.

McCreath, G., & Cuthbertson, J. (2005). Using digital technology to improve access to learning. *International Congress Series, 1282*, 956–959. doi:10.1016/j.ics.2005.05.144

Medellín-Castillo, H. I., Martínez-Hernández, C. A., Espinosa-Castañeda, R. & Castañeda-Roldán, C. Y. (2011). Desarrollo de un Sistema de Proyección de Películas Virtuales para Gente Invidente. *Impulso, 4*(2).

Mujber, T. S., Szecsi, T., & Hashmi, M. S. J. (2004). Virtual reality applications in manufacturing process simulation. *Journal of Materials Processing Technology, 155-156*, 1834–1838. doi:10.1016/j.jmatprotec.2004.04.401

Opie, J. (2018). Educating students with vision impairment today: Consideration of the expanded core curriculum. *British Journal of Visual Impairment, 36*(1), 75–89. doi:10.1177/0264619617730861

Ortiz-Alvarado, F., Espinosa-Castañeda, R., Vargas-Neri, J., & Rodrígues-Arellano, S. (2017). Divulgación científica y cultural: El diseño sonoro 4.1. *Revista de Sociología Contemporánea, 4*(12), 1–11.

Ortiz-Alvarado, F., Espinosa-Castañeda, R., Vargas-Neri, J., & Rodrígues-Arellano, S. (2018). Hacia una concepción del Diseño Sonoro 4.1 para personas con discapacidad visual. *Revista de Fisioterapia, 2*(3), 1–9.

Palmeros-Ávila, G., Pérez-Castro, J., & Quiroz-Segura, M. L. (2017). Educational Inclusion and Development of Strategies for Learning a Second Language. The Case Study of a Student with Visual Impairment. *International Journal of Humanities and Social Science, 7*(7), 161–170.

Panëels, S. A., Ritsos, P. D., Rodgers, P. J., & Roberts, J. C. (2013). Prototyping 3D haptic data visualizations. *Computers & Graphics, 37*(3), 179–192. doi:10.1016/j.cag.2013.01.009

Pérez-Acal, A., & Sanz-Lobera, A. (2007). Virtual reality simulation applied to a numerical control milling machine. *International Journal on Interactive Design and Manufacturing, 1*(3), 143–154. doi:10.100712008-007-0016-2

Pieper, M., & Hermsdorf, D. (1997). BSCW for disabled teleworkers: Usability evaluation and interface adaptation of an internet-based cooperation environment. *Computer Networks and ISDN Systems, 29*(8-13), 1479–1487. doi:10.1016/S0169-7552(97)00014-7

Pohlenz, P., Gro¨, B. A., Petersik, A., Von, S. N., Pflesser, B., Pommert, A., ... Heiland, M. (2010). Virtual Dental Surgery as a New Educational Tool in Dental School. *Journal of Cranio-Maxillo-Facial Surgery*, *38*(8), 560–564. doi:10.1016/j.jcms.2010.02.011 PMID:20303282

Riddell, S., Gillooly, A., Harris, N., & Davidge, G. (2019a). Autonomy, Rights and Children with Special Needs: A New Paradigm? Findings from an ESRC funded study. *ESRC Economic & Social Research Council*. Report Online. http://www.docs.hss.ed.ac.uk/education/creid/Projects/39_vi_ESRC_SENChildren_FinalRpt.pdf

Riddell, S., Gillooly, A., Harris, N., & Davidge, G. (2019b). Autonomy, Rights and Children with Special Needs: A New Paradigm? The Rights of Children with Special and Additional Support Needs in England and Scotland. *ESRC Economic & Social Research Council*. CREID Briefing 45. Retrieved from http://www.docs.hss.ed.ac.uk/education/creid/Briefings/Briefing45.pdf

Romero & Lavigne. (2005). Dificultades en el Aprendizaje Unificación de Criterios Diagnósticos. I. Definición, Características y tipos. Materiales para la Práctica Orientadora. *Consejería de Educación*, (1).

Roth, R. E., Ross, K. S., & MacEachren, A. M. (2015). User-Centered Design for Interactive Maps: A Case Study in Crime Analysis. *ISPRS International Journal of Geo-Information*, *4*(1), 262–301. doi:10.3390/ijgi4010262

Ruiz, Muñoz, & Álvarez. (2007). Evaluación de Objetos de Aprendizaje a través del Aseguramiento de Competencias Educativas. *Virtual Educa*.

Salisbury, K., Conti, F., & Barbagli, F. (2004). Haptic rendering: Introductory concepts. *Computer Graphics and Applications, IEEE*, *24*(2), 24–32. doi:10.1109/MCG.2004.1274058 PMID:15387225

Salisbury, R. (2008). *Teaching Pupils with Visual Impairment. A Guide to Making the School Curriculum Accessible*. Taylor & Francis Group.

Sánchez, J. (2012). Development of navigation skills through audio haptic videogaming in learners who are blind. *Procedia Computer Science*, *14*, 102–110. doi:10.1016/j.procs.2012.10.012

Scharver, C., Evenhouse, R., Johnson, A., & Leigh, J. (2004). Designing cranial implants in a haptic augmented reality environment. *Communications of the ACM*, *47*(8), 33–38. doi:10.1145/1012037.1012059

Second Life. (n.d.). Available: http://secondlife.com/

SEP. (2006). *Orientaciones generales para el funcionamiento de los servicios de educación especial. Coordinadores: Ernesto Castellano Pérez, María del Carmen Escandón Minutti*. Secretaría de Educación Pública.

Stratton, J. (1990). The principle of test restrictive materials. *Journal of Visual Impairment & Blindness*, (84): 3–5.

Sutherland, I. E. (1965). The ultimate display. *Proceedings of IFIPS Congress*, (2), 506–508.

UNESCO. (1951). UNESCO's work on Braille since 1949 and future activities of the World Braille Council. *Consultative Committee for the Creation of a World Braille Council*. MC/CONF.11/3, WS/111.178. Disponible en: https://unesdoc.unesco.org/ark:/48223/pf0000147824

UNESCO. (2017). ICT in Education. *UNESCO ICTs in Education website*. Retrieved 4 April 2019, from www.unesco.org/new/en/newdelhi/areas-of-action/special-themes/icts-in-education/

Van-Manen, M. (1998). *El tacto en la enseñanza*. Barcelona: Paidós Educador.

Vaspori, T., & Arato, A. (1995). Ten years of computer use by visually impaired people in Hungary. *Journal of Microcomputer Applications*, *18*(4), 313–317. doi:10.1016/S0745-7138(05)80030-2

West, R., & Turner, L. H. (2004). *Teoría de la Comunicación: Análisis y Aplicación*. Madrid: Mc Graw Hill.

Wiley, D. A. (2000). Connecting learning objects to instructional design theory: A definition, a metaphor, and a taxonomy. In *The Instructional Use of Learning Objects: Online Version*. Recuperado el 18 de 08 de 2006, de http://reusability.org/read/chapters/wiley.doc

Yuan, C. W., Hanrahan, B. V., Lee, S., Rosson, M. B., & Carroll, J. M. (2019, March). Constructing a holistic view of shopping with people with visual impairment: A participatory design approach. *Universal Access in the Information Society*, *18*(1), 127–140. doi:10.100710209-017-0577-1

ADDITIONAL READING

Bowman, D. A., Gabbard, J. L., & Hix, D. (2002). A Survey of Usability Evaluation in Virtual Environments: Classification and Comparison of Methods. *PRESENCE: Virtual and Augmented Reality*, *11*(4), 404–424. doi:10.1162/105474602760204309

Hervás, R., Bravo, J., & Fontecha, J. (2014). An Assistive Navigation System Based on Augmented Reality and Context Awareness for People With Mild Cognitive Impairments. *IEEE Journal of Biomedical and Health Informatics*, *18*(1), 368–374. doi:10.1109/JBHI.2013.2266480 PMID:24403436

Katz, B. F. G., Kammoun, S., Parseihian, G., Gutierrez, O., Brilhault, A., Auvray, M., ... Jouffrais, C. (2012). NAVIG: Augmented reality guidance system for the visually impaired. Combining object localization, GNSS, and spatial audio. *Virtual Reality (Waltham Cross)*, *16*(4), 253–269. doi:10.100710055-012-0213-6

Menelas, B. A. J., Picinali, L., Bourdot, P., & Katz, B. F. G. (2014). Non-visual identification, localization, and selection of entities of interest in a 3D environment. *Multimodal User Interfaces.*, *8*(3), 243–256. doi:10.100712193-014-0148-1

MIIPAT. (2019) Proyectos. *Museo Interactivo Incluyente de Producción Audiovisual Transmedia*. Retrieved from https://miipatfcc.wixsite.com/website-6/proyectos

MIIPAT. (2019) Canal de YouTube. *Museo Interactivo Incluyente de Producción Audiovisual Transmedia*. Retrieved from https://www.youtube.com/channel/UCiyklBa10HWqp86UyJJRyZg

SEP. (2019) *Educación Especial*. Retrieved from https://www.educacionespecial.sep.gob.mx/2016/index.html

KEY TERMS AND DEFINITIONS

Haptic-Virtual-Reality System: HVR systems allow to virtually touch objects through a robotic arm and at the same time see them on the screen.

HVR Teaching-Learning System: It is an HVR unit that incorporates all the teaching-learning aspects and parts, namely students, teachers, curriculum, content and evaluation of instructional objectives.

Immersion Level of a VR System: Refers to the level of how deeply the user is sensorial involved inside a virtual environment.

Inclusive Education: To have the ability to adapt educational content by accepting the SEN of the students.

Learning Systems: An ecosystem where teaching and learning can coexist along with several other functionalities of the didactic process.

Legally Blind Person: When the central visual acuity or ability to perceive figures and forms is 20/200.

SEN: Special educational needs.

Chapter 15
Towards a Role-Playing Game Procedural Dungeon Generation Strategy to Help Developing Working Skills

Esteban A. Durán-Yañez
Tecnológico Nacional de México IT Aguascalientes, Mexico

Mario A. Rodríguez-Díaz
Tecnológico Nacional de México IT Aguascalientes, Mexico

César A. López-Luévano
Universidad Politécnica de Aguascalientes, Mexico

ABSTRACT

This chapter describes the insights towards a proposal to integrate a procedural content generation strategy in a computer role-playing usable and accessible learning video game for gaining replayability to encourage engagement and motivation in learners. In order to explain the contextual issues of the topic, the chapter includes a discussion on how computer role-playing video games impact the skills considered crucial for the work in the future—abstraction, system thinking, experimentation, and collaboration—emphasizing the importance of usability and accessibility to ensure effectiveness of the proposal. A first approach of a computer role-playing video game is presented to provide an illustrative example. The prototype will serve for future evaluations with people for usability and accessibility.

INTRODUCTION

Role-playing is an activity that has been present in the development of the human being since the beginning of civilization, and nowadays takes several forms, including video games, that has become the biggest entertainment industry and has proved to be an important tool for education.

DOI: 10.4018/978-1-7998-2325-4.ch015

Video games for learning represents a power alternative to develop useful skills and competencies in students (Barr, 2018). Engagement becomes video games an effective learning tool which may be potentiated by blending it with face-to-face approaches, it seems that said strategy do enhance student motivation and can be associated with behavioural change (De Freitas, 2018). In this context, a "*critical component of an engaging game is delivering content to player with incrementally increasing the challenge*" (cited by Adellin, Khuan, & Gertrude, 2019, p. 1); this concept is strongly related to the concept replayability or reply value, which broadly speaking consist in provide gamers the possibility of continue playing a game after its first completion (Adellin, Khuan, & Gertrude, 2019). One important tool to give video games replayability is the use of procedural content generation (PPG), which is currently popular in industry since is suitable to generate several elements of video games with high cost-benefit value, these elements include the construction of levels for platform games, and dungeons (Volkmar, Mählmann, & Malaka, 2019).

Replayability could enhance the experience of players in role-playing video games for education but it is very important to reinforce said strategy with usability and accessibility aspects (Darin, Andrade, & Sánchez, 2018). In this scenario, traditional usability aspects (Nielsen, 1995) should be complemented by including important aspects in such as mobility, multiplayer interactions, enjoyability, fun, satisfaction, storyline, customization, social connectivity, multimodal interaction, among others (Yanez-Gomez, et al., 2019). The goal of usability in this context is to provide user-friendly environments that foster learning in a more attractive, intense, and challenging way to help students in learning a variety of complex skills and abilities (Slootmaker, et al., 2018). Additionally, role-playing videogames should consider the configuration and functionality of the interface within the same game, and control over scenarios (dungeons) and main and secondary characters (Lee & Song, 2019).

Accessibility lies in the same level of importance; in fact, a product cannot be called usable without consider accessibility basics in its design process. As explained in (Bierre et al. 2005) "*While specific needs vary from person to person, the common issue is the same. The need to address accessibility in gaming is real. The number of people interested in gaming transcends age, gender, income, and disability. The disabled are often misunderstood and underestimated in terms of potential and participation*". Accessibility directly affects players experience and, therefore, to the effectiveness of the video game's purpose. Designing accessible video games include devices for control and interactions with user interface (Compañ-Rosique, et al., 2019). Related to said requirements (Tyagi, Choudhary, & Majumdar, 2019) found three families of accessibility issues that players currently face: (1) Don't receive feedbacks; (2) No identification of in game responses; (3) No way to provide the input from the various input devices used. In this way it is necessary to have strategies, approaches, and/or tools that result in video games that can be enjoyed and played by people independently of their skills to operate or perceive things in order to them feel included (Cairns, et al., 2019). (Smith, & Abrams, 2019) particularly explained said general context of video games accessibility from the vantage point of educational perspective, emphasizing that the gamification of learning procedures should foster equity and access to instructional materials for all the students including those with auditory, cognitive, neurological, physical, speech, or visual disabilities.

Literature that integrate the whole context is limited and it has not been found researches that explain in detail the procedural dungeon generation that takes into consideration usability and accessibility aspects during settings of said scenarios. In order to contribute to filling this gap here is proposed first approach for a procedure that provide more control for players allowing the selection of the role that the player must take when using certain character class in a role-playing game having high replayability by adapting its game environment or dungeons considering the character classes. Additionally, multimodal interactions will be offered to users for comfortable control and configurations including narrative and affordances relating specific learning activities and character roles abilities. By doing this, the player could get a better experience intended for the character class chosen encouraging engagement.

BACKGROUND

Role-playing

Role-playing can be seen in several activities of human behavior, like childhood playing, arts, rituals and storytelling. People have always lived limited by constraints imposed by the time they live in, its geographical location, cultural, economic and political situation, so they often use fantasy for healthy development. As people are younger, they dream about their future, like kids wanting to be a superhero, a cowboy, a famous singer, etc. But as we grow, we often do not follow the path we fantasize about as children, adapting ourselves to the constraints imposed by adulthood reality.

Several artistic and cultural expressions offer a relaxation from the expectations imposed by the society, those expressions include theatre, movies, music and video games. Some cultural critics manifest that art offers a healthy liberation to the mind, while others consider that excessive indulgence in fantasy makes people forget about real-life problems. Regardless of opinion about fantasy and art, it is a strong element in culture, worthy of study and important for understanding how people develop its minds (Bowman, 2007, 2010).

Tabletop Role-Playing Games

Traditional tabletop role-playing games has its origins in Dungeons & Dragons, a tabletop game like others but radically different, it is a role-playing game, it is a game where its participants control fantastic characters in a world that exists only in the imagination of the players (Ewalt, 2013). Of course, there are several others tabletop role-playing games such as Shadowrun and The Dark Eye.

Dungeons & Dragons was created by Gary Gygax and Dave Arneson in 1974 (Gygax & Arneson, 1974) and gets its inspiration from several narratives and literary work sources, being the stories of J.R.R. Tolkien, like Lord of the Rings (Tolkien, 1954), its mayor influences, it is based mainly on stories of brave knights and wise and elder mages fighting against evil forces (Ewalt, 2013). A typical gaming session in a role-playing game, the players find themselves immersed in huge caves where they look for treasures and have to fight with terrible monsters, in this kind of game there is a very important figure known as the Dungeon Master, who is the person in charge to guide the players through their adventure.

A fundamental characteristic in role-playing games is that each player takes a special role from a character belonging to a certain class. A character class refers to the profession or the kind of adventurer, this determines not only the character role, but the possibilities that it has in the game. This can be defined as a subset of characteristics and abilities owned that differentiates it from the other characters (Pantaleev, 2012).

In Dungeons & Dragons there exist three main character classes: fighters, magic-users and clerics (Gygax & Arneson, 1974). The fighters character class defines brute force and high constitution, can use armors and has a lot of health points (Voorhees, 2009), the mages character class, on the other hand, needs intelligence, wisdom and dexterity, can not use armors and have few health points, the clerics character class is capable to use magic that restores its health and to give protection, they can use armors.

Video Games

Video games have their origins since the first days of modern electronic computers, being Alan Turing the first person to write a computer Chess Program in 1947. Through the industry of video games as we know nowadays has its roots in the 70s, with important pioneering engineers like Ralph Baer, Steve Russell and Nolan Bushnell (Kent, 2001).

Nowadays many consider the video games industry a young one, and that is truly being in its sixth decade, but are an economic sector encompassing dozens of job disciplines and employing thousands of people worldwide. As an industry it has grown from being a niche sector to the mainstream market, being the most profitable entertainment industry.

Modern devices for playing computer games owe many of its advances by the necessity for faster and better hardware, like sound cards, graphic cards and processors to play video games. Similarly, in the software part, the video games industry has motivated many innovations in the fields of graphics algorithms and artificial intelligence techniques.

There exists a lot of debate whether video games, as a whole medium, can be considered a form of art or not, though there is no doubt that video games include many forms of artistic expression: sculpture, painting, music, acting and literature. The hardware that runs video games is just a vehicle for the creativity and vision of creators (video games developers) where unlike other media, the consumer (player) is an active participant, rather than a passive observer (Donovan, 2010).

Nowadays exists several video games genres and subgenres, being the following the wider and most recognized:

1. **Action:** Games that emphasize hand-eye coordination and motor skills.
2. **Simulation:** Refer to those games that are designed to model natural or manmade systems or phenomena.
3. **Strategy:** The main objective is to think skillfully and make planification.
4. **Adventure:** The mechanics of adventure games are mainly to solve puzzles by interacting with the game world or characters.
5. **Sports:** Designed to model real-life or fictional sports, with competitivity in mind.
6. **Role-playing:** Role-playing video games are based on tabletop games.

Role-Playing Video Games

Computer role-playing video games are a very special video game genre that holds the traditional role-playing experience but presenting it by means of a computer screen instead with a bunch of miniature figures and a map as traditional games (Barton, 2007, 2019). With the combination of role-playing elements with video games, the pioneering designers of computer role-playing and their players realized that role-playing video games were more than the sum of their parts, those games were a lot more than role-playing games computerized equivalents.

Akalabeth: World of Doom is considered one of the earliest computer role-playing video game, it was released in 1979, this video game was designed by Richard Garriot, who was an experienced Dungeons & Dragons Dungeon Master and member of the Society of Creative Anachronisms and Renaissance Fairs. The video game industry has changed a lot since Garriot released Akalabeth, but the same foundations still remains leveling up characters, acquiring the best armors and weapons and fighting against ever more powerful enemies.

There is important to make a distinction between computer role-playing video games and Japanese role-playing video games, both genres share some characteristics, but there exist some key differences, being storytelling the principal: in computer role-playing video games, often the players control a single customizable avatar that along the way develops its abilities and end up meeting other characters that join their crew and form bonds with them, eventually progressing as a team through the main story, emphasis is often placed on choice, giving the player the opportunity to turn its actions towards evil or good, meanwhile in Japanese role-playing video games, rather than an avatar, the player is given a predefined main character or a group of main characters and the story is a quest from an ultimate evil, giving the player some choices to determine parts of the game, but it is usually a much more clear ending with a focus on a cinematic experience. So the main difference between those genres is the capacity to decide the type of character to play with and its development, as well as the capacity to decide what to do on the story, having a lot more freedom in computer role-playing video games.

MAIN FOCUS OF THE CHAPTER

Issues, Controversies, Problems

Education and Video Games

Video games is not an industry extent of controversy, through its history there have been blames for increasing aggressivity in users (Anderson, 2004; Anderson & Bushman, 2001), or being addicting (Toker & Baturay, 2016), causing in users difficulty in regulating the amount of time spending on playing (Ogletree & Drake, 2007) or even provoking different health issues like motion sickness and postural problems (Chang, Pan, Tseng, & Stoffregen, 2012; Merhi, Faugloire, Flanagan, & Stoffregen, 2007; Stoffregen, Faugloire, Yoshida, Flanagan, & Merhi, 2008).

On the other hand, a lot of research has been made to study the effect of videogames in education, showing that the support of education in video games helps students to learn better (McDaniel & Telep, 2009; Sevilla, Santini, Haya, Rodriguez, & Sacha, 2012; Vlachopoulos & Makri, 2017; Zheng & Gardner, 2017), considering the study of particular topics like English (Yang, Chen, & Chang Jeng, 2010; Yen, 2011), mathematics (Chiu & Hsieh, 2017), geology (Chen, Yeh, & Chang, 2016), even for human skills (Chiang, Lin, Cheng, & Liu, 2011; Daniau, 2016; Jang & Ryu, 2011; Su, Chiang, James Lee, & Chang, 2016).

When learning is active, experiential, situated, problem-based and provides immediate feedback it is most effective, according to modern theories of education (Boyle, Connolly, & Hainey, 2011). And video games appeared to offer those features. Education integrates new technologies to support its processes, nowadays technological applications, video games and simulations are widely used by formal education institutions (Vlachopoulos & Makri, 2017).

According to (Reich, 1991) on his book The Work of Nations, there are four basic skills that are critical for the workplace in the future:

1. **Abstraction:** Is the capacity for the human mind to put order in the chaotic, highly entropy, the world we live in, by the recognition of patterns and meanings and the classification of the information we receive by our senses, so it can be manipulated in new ways. Abstraction is the very essence of symbolic analysis.
2. **System Thinking:** This refers to the capacity to identify causes and consequences, to be able to see in the world the different systems interacting forming the reality, but also, being able to see the relationships between different systems identified by abstraction, seeing the world as a whole allows for new discover opportunities.
3. **Experimentation**: The capacity to test different options to note causes and effects in a systematic and orderly fashion allows to a better understanding of the world. In order to learn higher forms of abstraction and system thinking, the experimentation is imperative.
4. **Collaboration**: Being able to collaborate, communicate abstract concepts effectively, and achieve consensus is a skill very important for symbolic analyst, who seem to work in an unrelated way, but they must communicate their findings and ideas among the team.

Role-playing games generally are composed of rulebooks and bestiaries and are played by using miniature figures in maps previously defined where the players are situated, discover treasures, challenges and advance through a story (Gygax & Arneson, 1974). It those rulebooks are included data tables with ability points for each character class, this has allowed that the players experiment with those points and learn to play with each one of the character classes. This learning process is an empirical one, while it is true that the players know which character class is the most appropriate to perform (and they know how to do it), there is not documentation that cites each case or that facilitates the identification of the conditions where each character class is better than the others.

Most activities are better learned by doing, rather than just by studying. In computer role-paying video games normally the designers give few advices to players and encourage them to experiment with controls and commands, making this a process of discovery. The gamer that begins to play a new computer role-playing video game normally acts as a scientist, devising theories based on observations and then making experimentations, to understands how this virtual world works (Barton, 2019), this shows us two of Reich's skills: system thinking and experimentation (Reich, 1991). According to (Gee, 2003): "Video games situate meaning in a multimodal space through embodied experiences to solve problems and reflect on the intricacies of the design of imagined worlds and the design of both real and imagined social relationships and identities in the modern world."

Gaming experiences allow for better learning of game mechanics than reading the video game manual, by observing the effects of different parameters in the video game, the gamer can learn about its meaning in a better way than by reading its description in manual or tutorial. This works in the same way in much of a formal educational system: we may read an memorize facts, but outside of context or real experience they do not mean anything, and we do not get real understanding of underlying mechanics this way. This argument do not says that the videogames necessarily teach us how important concepts works, those concepts maybe do not have importance in the real world as they could be lore specific for the video game or something not very useful outside of the game world, the important thing is the teaching of mental habits that those games demand and reward that end being more important than much of the disembodied learning we get in formal learning systems. By instead of memorizing definitions of a textbook, the gamer thoroughly internalizes this critical thinking, getting better knowledge than a boring science class (Barton, 2019). The ability to abstract knowledge from a realm and apply it to another is a skill undervalued in formal education systems, and is another of the skills described in (Reich, 1991).

According to (Moses, 1986), statistics are a body of methods for learning from experience, this also applies to computer role-playing video games, that as been said before, are complicated statistical models that model the game mechanics, systems and simulations, using mathematical formulas with different parameters for computing probabilities. And allow the player to learn about how those mechanics work by playing the video game, the gamer normally is unable to know the exact formulas but get an idea of how they work by their experiences at playing. What happens at schools is the opposite, the students learn the formulas, but will hardly know what they model if they are not applied in a context.

The other skill described by (Reich, 1991) is collaboration. Countless education experts stress the importance of collaborative learning; students learn more by discussing topics among them, ratter than just listening a teacher. Players must frequently work together to learn to play a Massive Multiplayer Online Role Playing Game, a subgenre of computer role-playing video game, that one of their principal mechanics is the collaboration online of lots of gamers around the world, and differently to tabletop role-playing games, the online element facilitates the reunion of groups of players. One inconvenient, though, is that the online experience allows for anonymous usage, with the possibility to leading to problems of toxic communities (Paul, 2018). On the other hand, single player computer role-playing video games can also teach effective collaboration, in some occasions better than massive multiplayer online role playing games, as they allow the player to control more than a single character, in a crew of adventurers with complementing abilities, allowing for a tactical thought by using the different perks, making the successful party of adventurers the one that successfully leverage strengths and weakness of their members.

One problem with computer video games is that the experience they offer eventually can become boring or finally it ends, offering no more surprises to the player.

SOLUTIONS AND RECOMMENDATIONS

Computer role-playing video games are descendants form the tabletop role-playing games and are based on them, having inherited many of their characteristics, but as we commented before, there are fundamental differences. The tabletop role-playing games benefit enormously form the players and the Dungeon Master ability to improvise story and add surprising elements at any moment, this characteristic is limited for computer role-playing video games. On the other hand, computer role-playing video games can perform millions of complicated operations per second on its relying hardware, allowing the use of complicated systems of rules impractical for tabletop role-playing games. This allows for more complex game play (Pantaleev, 2013), allowing for several stats that the characters can have.

In role-playing tabletop games, the dungeons are designed by hand by the dungeon master. In Dungeons & Dragons, in the tome The Underworld & Wilderness Adventures it is shown how to create a dungeon with interconnected level segments (Appelcline, 2013).

Procedural Content Generation

The main idea behind procedural content generation is that an asset is not generated manually by human designers, but by computers executing a well defined procedure (X. Short & Adams, 2017). To avoid losing control over the design process, it is desirable that humans can still influence the final product by adjusting the parameters of the procedure (Hendrikx, Meijer, Van Der Velden, & Iosup, 2013). By content we can refer to several elements in a video game: levels, maps, game rules, textures, stories, items, quest, music, weapons, vehicles, characters, etc (Shaker, Togelius, & Nelson, 2016).

Vander Der Linden, Et. Al, (Van Der Linden, Lopes, & Bidarra, 2014) identifies five reasons to use procedural content generation in video games:

1. Agile content generation of content correctly structured (A. M. Smith & Mateas, 2011).
2. Replayability, with a big diversity of results (Hastings, Guha, & Stanley, 2009; G. Smith, Gan, Othenin-Girard, & Whitehead, 2011). Another reason to use procedural content generation is to increase the replayability, by allowing to generate new content in real time, if this new content has enough variety this can allow the creation of endless games (Togelius, Yannakakis, Stanley, & Browne, 2011).
3. Save time and money in videogames creation (Tutenel, Bidarra, Smelik, & Kraker, 2009). One of the main reasons to use procedural content generation in video games is to reduce production costs, nowadays video games industry has grown to the point that production is a bottleneck in both game budgets and product time to market (Iosup, 2009; Kelly & McCabe, 2007; Lefebvre & Neyret, 2003; Smelik, Kraker, Groenewegen, Tutenel, & Bidarra, 2009).
4. Generate the basis for the adaptability of video games to the players (Lopes & Bidarra, 2011; Yannakakis & Togelius, 2011).
5. The creation of designs that helps creativity (Shaker et al., 2016).

An important aspect to consider about procedural content generation is to perceive this as the solution to problems of content generation. This problem is defined as the necessity of being able to generate content under certain rules or through the fulfillment of definite properties. The following is a list of common properties that it is desirable to take into account in the procedural content generation (Shaker et al., 2016):

1. **Speed:** Speed requirement, when it is desirable that certain result is achieved in a specific time lapse.
2. **Reliability:** Is the capacity to be able to satisfy a given quality criteria.
3. **Controllability:** The generation of the content needs to be controllable in some sense, so there can be specified some aspects of the content to be generated.
4. **Expressivity and Diversity:** Being able to offer results that are enough different among themselves.
5. **Creativity and Credibility:** It is a good thing that the result not look like it has been designed by a procedural content generator.

Procedural Generation of Dungeons

Inspired by maps (dungeons) in tabletop role-playing games, the computer role-playing video game Rogue is created in 1980, developed by Michael Toy and Glenn Wichman; this video game is one of the first to employ procedural content generation of dungeons in real time (Hendrikx et al., 2013), from the release of this title on forward there have been a derivation for other video games that generate dungeons procedurally, creating a new genre of video games known as "Rogue-like" (M. R. Johnson, 2017). One of the most outstanding aspects of this genre of video games known as roguelikes is the creation of dungeons in an automatized way, without a doubt, this genre marked a milestone in procedural content in video games (Garda, 2013).

A dungeon can be defined as a labyrinthic environment, consisting mostly of interrelated challenges, rewards, and puzzles, tightly placed in time and space to offer highly structured gameplay progressions, this close control over gameplay pacing is an aspect which sets dungeons apart from other types of levels. In this sense, a dungeon is not only the physical structure of the gameplay space, but also the set of challenges and rewards that shape it. A kind of content generated procedurally that results very interesting is precisely the generation of levels for dungeons, this because to the peculiar relationship between Rhythm, Playability and Space. (Adams, 2002). As has been seen before, there exists diverse computer video games that use procedural content generation, and even there exists al whole genre of those (roguelikes). In all those cases the procedural generation comes from a set of parameters that try to control the result.

A well designed dungeon is the one that offer a good game play experience and has the next elements: interesting level architecture, adequate rhythm, realism, intelligent foes, advance previews, non linearity, takes care on the inclusion of new elements, balancing resources, adequate difficulty (Lopes & Bidarra, 2011).

There are used several techniques to generate dungeons procedurally, some of them are the following:

1. **Agent Based Dungeon Growing:** Usually, a single agent dig tunnels and create rooms in a sequence (Shaker et al., 2016).
2. **Space Partitioning Approach:** There is made a subdivision of the game play space into disjoint subsets so that any point in the space lies in exactly one of these subsets (Shaker et al., 2016).
3. **Cellular Automata:** Cellular automata are widely studied in computer science and other sciences as models of computation, growth, development, physical phenomena, etc. though somewhat simple to understands its basic concepts (L. Johnson, Yannakakis, & Togelius, 2010).
4. **Grammar Based Dungeon Generation:** Developed to formally describe structures in natural language are modeled by a finite set of recursive rules that describe linguistic structures in a way that also describes how to generate them (Adams, 2002; Dormans, 2010).
5. **Genetic Algorithms:** Search-based evolutionary algorithms that try to find an optimal solution to an optimization problem, a genetic representation and a fitness function are required (Ashlock, Lee, & Mcguinness, n.d.; Hartsook, Zook, Das, & Riedl, 2011; Valtchanov & Brown, 2012).
6. **Constraint Based Method:** Generation is based on a constraint solving approach where constraints are expressed as rules with parameters that place nodes in relation to fixed terminal nodes (Roden & Parberry, 2004).
7. **Machine Learning:** A relatively new paradigm to generate dungeons procedurally, it consists on machine learning models trained on existing content (Summerville et al., 2018).

For the development of the procedural dungeon generator, it is considered to use an artificial neural network because one of the key elements is the ability to learn. A neural network is not just a complex system, but a complex adaptive system, meaning it can change its internal structure based on the information flowing through it, typically it is achieved through the adjusting of weights. There is considered to use a reinforcement learning approach.

There has not been found evidence that procedural dungeon generated computer role-playing video games generate the dungeons considering the role or character class. There has only been found in some sources (Adams, 2002; Forsyth, 2016; Hendrikx et al., 2013) that the only considerations for dungeon generation are the same aspects: size, complexity, difficulty, realism, topology, etc.

Development of Procedural Dungeon Generator for Computer Role-Playing Video Games

Currently, a computer role-playing video games is in development by the indie games studio Ogre Pixel, the development team consist of nine specialists that include game designers, programmers, visual artists and artificial intelligence scientists. The project is called Swipy Fantasy. It is expected that the Swipy Fantasy video game to be released in the first quarter of 2021.

The video game Swipy Fantasy is a casual roguelike adventure game where the player fights nasty creatures by drawing swipes to perform attacks, the game perspective is a 2D top down view, its game mode is a single player adventure with a team or party of adventurers controlled by computer but with the direction of the player, the player can configure the kind of behavior it desires for its party members. The target audience is for people of approximately between the ages from 10 to 35 years old who are fans of fantasy casual mobile games and also for fans of classic roguelikes and computer role-playing video games like Rogue or Tibia.

In Swipy Fantasy video game there are several stats that will define the combat and mechanics results, being the following the most important:

- **Maximum Health Points:** Capacity to live for the character.
- **Maximum Magic Points:** Capacity to use magic movements by the character.
- **Regeneration of health:** How quickly the character recovers health points.
- **Regeneration of Magic:** How quickly the character recovers magic points.
- **Damage:** The basic damage the character can inflict when it attacks.
- **Armor:** The capacity to absorb damage when the character is attacked.
- **Evasion Rating:** The capacity to dodge attacks, making the enemies attack ineffective.
- **Dexterity:** How fast can the character attack.
- **Speed:** Movement speed in the game world.
- **Range:** How far the character can inflict damage.

The values of all those stats depends mainly of the character class, but also can be raised when the character gets experience and raises its level. Besides the stats can be modified positively or negatively by the equipment the character uses, for example, a heavy armor rises the player armor but reduces its speed and dexterity.

Figure 1. Knight, conceptual art.

Figure 2. Archer, conceptual art.

The character classes available are based in the classic Dungeons & Dragons classes. Their attributes are modeled by different value combinations of the stats previously described. The character classes can be also controlled by the computer, and are the following:

- **Knight:** The Knight, represented in Figure 1, is a strong melee attacking hero, with short range, has a high resistance to damage but is somewhat slow on its movement. Its artificial intelligence behavior consist on staying quiet and close range attack enemies one by one.

- **Archer:** The Archer, represented in Figure 2, is a hero that has medium attacking power with a very long range attack, have medium resistance to damage and is fast moving. Its artificial intelligence behavior consist on keeping distance form its closest enemies, its shooting long range attack simulates arrows.

- **Wizard:** The Wizard, represented in Figure 3, has a very powerful attack and also a long range of attack, but it is ratter weak to damage and slow on its movement. So its artificial intelligence behavior is to keep the distance from enemies and use its powerful long range attacks.

Figure 3. Wizard, conceptual art.

Figure 4. Healer, conceptual art.

- **Healer:** The Healer, represented in Figure 4, is mainly a support unit for its partners, it has a weak attack with short range, medium resistance to damage and medium speed of movement, though it has the capacity to improve his stats and from its party members, also can heal both partners and himself. The artificial intelligence tries to keep distance from enemies and concentrates on raising its partners abilities, also helps its partners with low health.

Swipy Fantasy video game will feature autonomous moving and behavior agents that will offer the player challenges in accordance with the game play style of the character class chosen. The foes will adapt their behavior depending on the class the character uses, trying to offer the player the best experience intended for the player character class. For this, there is in development a proprietary physics and artificial intelligence engine that models effectively the movement steering behavior for actions to seek, flee, arrive, pursuit, evade, wander, obstacle avoidance, wall avoidance, interpose, hide, path following and offset pursuit.

For the Swipy Fantasy video game there will be included both antagonist characters (enemies, bosses and non player characters), as well as good or neutral characters (shopkeepers, and other party members). The main gameplay revolves mainly in character interaction, either combat or otherwise, and each of these elements can be complex. The types of characters to be present and their artificial intelligence are the following:

- **Enemies:** The common enemies that are present in large quantities in the video game, they are the main source of experience for the character, have a statistical behavior that depends on their basic stats. There exists a vast variety of them. Can use complex behavior patterns, including running away, healing themselves, fighting in groups, surround the player, use complementary attach methods and so forth.
- **Bosses:** Larger, more complex game characters, either humanoid or creature, found at the end of sections or levels after defeating a horde of lesser enemies. Are very specific, usually unique characters that can break previous rules. That is why are heavily scripted with special attacks and behaviors that only they can perform.
- **Non Playable Characters:** Can be defined as anybody in the game that is not a human player. Usually refers to characters in the game that the player can interact with in ways other than combat. Non playable characters are generally not very intelligent; they usually do not have to be. Anything they add beyond information or story advancement is just flavor for the game. So their intelligence limits to path following and grammar systems.
- **Shopkeepers:** Special non player characters that do business with the player: buying and selling gear, teaching the player new skills, and so on. Shopkeepers usually are not much smarter than regular non player characters, but what differentiates from them is that they require special interfaces and additional programming, so they seem intelligent when doing transactions, they take in account for their prices if they like or dislike the player.
- **Party Members:** Members of a player´s adventuring party are also special non player characters, except that they travel with the player, and are either completely controlled by the player or have artificial intelligence code associated with them.

FUTURE RESEARCH DIRECTIONS

As future research directions, it is considered to:

1. Identify characteristics and game play ways for the different character classes of computer role-playing video games.
2. Identify key design elements for dungeons that can improve the game experience for each of the character classes in computer role-playing video games.
3. Identify a mechanic to measure the Flow (Borderie & Michinov, 2016; Cowley, Charles, Black, & Hickey, 2008; Csikszentmihalyi, 1991; Velikovsky, 2014) and the game experience through the data recompilation from the player.
4. Define an algorithm for the procedural dungeon generation with an approach to key design elements that can improve the game experience for each character classes of computer role-playing video games.
5. Examine the Flow and the game experience in a prototype where it is generated dungeons procedurally applying key design elements that can improve the game experience for each character classes of computer role-playing video games.

CONCLUSION

Role-playing is an activity performed historically by humans, since ancient times in the form of childhood playing, arts, rituals, storytelling, etc. It is considered that role-playing is an important activity for healthy brain development. In modern times there exists a subculture around role-playing that is expressed in performances, tabletop games and more recently in videogames.

Being, nowadays, video games the biggest entertainment industry in the world, it has a huge impact on culture and economics. Besides the doubtless importance on the economic aspect, video games also represent an important repository of creativity and a medium of artistic expression. Because of those both reasons, a lot of research has been made on the negative and the positive impacts of playing digital games. In the educational field, there exists a lot of research about the video games capacity to help students acquire values, skills and knowledge, that have demonstrated its utility on the field.

Computer role-playing video games help to the development of a set of skills considered as critical for the workplace in the future: abstraction, system thinking, experimentation and collaboration. In this case engagement is a feature to exploit from role-playing video games.

A constraint in video games is that eventually the game play becomes repetitive or it ends, an option to mitigate this is by using procedural content generation, that consist in creating new content by algorithmic means, this increases the replay value of the video games.

This in-progress computer role-playing video game will aimed to help developing learning skills previously mentioned. This video games will consider the use of procedural dungeon generation using artificial neural networks with a reinforced learning approach. This algorithm will take the character class chosen by the player to give it the best experience. Besides, the game in development will use a proprietary artificial intelligence engine that will enhance the player experience considering the chosen character class. The proposal will be oriented to integrate both traditional and video games usability aspects, together with accessibility elements addressed to encompass all disabilities including auditory, cognitive, neurological, physical, speech, and visual by considering multimodal interfaces, narrative, and affordances.

REFERENCES

Adams, D. (2002). *Automatic Generation of Dungeons for Computer Games*. University of Sheffield. Retrieved from https://pdfs.semanticscholar.org/2502/0f8d955aee07b7dd49a3ec23b1f2a8cf1d06.pdf

Adellin, R., Khuan, C. T., & Gertrude, L. D. (2019, May). Conceptual Framework Puzzle Game with High Replayability. *Journal of Physics: Conference Series*, *1228*(1), 012070. doi:10.1088/1742-6596/1228/1/012070

Anderson, C. A. (2004). An update on the effects of playing violent video games. *Journal of Adolescence*, *27*(1), 113–122. doi:10.1016/j.adolescence.2003.10.009 PMID:15013264

Anderson, C. A., & Bushman, B. J. (2001). Effects of violent video games on aggressive behavior, aggressive cognition, aggressive affect, physiological arousal, and prosocial behavior: A Meta-Analytic Review of the Scientific Literature. *Psychological Science*, *12*(5), 353–359. doi:10.1111/1467-9280.00366 PMID:11554666

Appelcline, S. (2013). *The (Not-So) Secret Origin of D&D*. Retrieved from http://dnd.wizards.com/articles/features/not-so-secret-origin-dd

Ashlock, D., Lee, C., & Mcguinness, C. (n.d.). *Search-Based Procedural Generation of Maze-Like Levels. Academic Press.*

Barr, M. (2018). Student attitudes to games-based skills development: Learning from video games in higher education. *Computers in Human Behavior*, *80*, 283–294. doi:10.1016/j.chb.2017.11.030

Barton, M. (2007). *The History of Computer Role-Playing Games Part 1: The Early Years (1980-1983)*. Retrieved from Gamasutra website: http://www.gamasutra.com/view/feature/132024/the_history_of_computer_.php

Barton, M. (2019). *Dungeons and Desktops Dungeons and Desktops The History of Computer Role-Playing Games (2nd ed.)*. Taylor & Francis. doi:10.1201/9781351273404

Bierre, K., Chetwynd, J., Ellis, B., Hinn, D. M., Ludi, S., & Westin, T. (2005, July). Game not over: Accessibility issues in video games. In *Proc. of the 3rd International Conference on Universal Access in Human-Computer Interaction* (pp. 22-27). Academic Press.

Borderie, J., & Michinov, N. (2016). Identifying Flow in Video Games. *International Journal of Gaming and Computer-Mediated Simulations*, *8*(3), 19–38. doi:10.4018/IJGCMS.2016070102

Bowman, S. L. (2007). The Psychological Power of the Roleplaying Experience. *Journal of Interactive Drama*.

Bowman, S. L. (2010). *The Functions of Role-Playing Games: How Participants Create Community, Solve Problems and Explore Identity*. Jefferson, NC: McFarland & Company, Inc., Publishers.

Boyle, E., Connolly, T. M., & Hainey, T. (2011). The role of psychology in understanding the impact of computer games. *Entertainment Computing*, *2*(2), 69–74. doi:10.1016/j.entcom.2010.12.002

Cairns, P., Power, C., Barlet, M., & Haynes, G. (2019). Future Design of Accessibility in Games: A Design Vocabulary. *International Journal of Human-Computer Studies*, *131*, 64–71. doi:10.1016/j.ijhcs.2019.06.010

Chang, C. H., Pan, W. W., Tseng, L. Y., & Stoffregen, T. A. (2012). Postural activity and motion sickness during video game play in children and adults. *Experimental Brain Research*, *217*(2), 299–309. doi:10.100700221-011-2993-4 PMID:22210118

Chen, C. L. D., Yeh, T. K., & Chang, C. Y. (2016). *The effects of game-based learning and anticipation of a test on the learning outcomes of 10 th grade geology students. Eurasia Journal of Mathematics, Science and Technology Education*. doi:10.12973/eurasia.2016.1519a

Chiang, Y. T., Lin, S. S. J., Cheng, C. Y., & Liu, E. Z. F. (2011). *Exploring online game players' flow experiences and positive affect. Turkish Online Journal of Educational Technology.*

Chiu, F. Y., & Hsieh, M. L. (2017). *Role-playing game based assessment to fractional concept in second grade mathematics. Eurasia Journal of Mathematics, Science and Technology Education*. doi:10.12973/eurasia.2017.00659a

Compañ-Rosique, P., Molina-Carmona, R., Gallego-Durán, F., Satorre-Cuerda, R., Villagrá-Arnedo, C., & Llorens-Largo, F. (2019). A guide for making video games accessible to users with cerebral palsy. *Universal Access in the Information Society*, *18*(3), 565–581. doi:10.100710209-019-00679-6

Cowley, B., Charles, D., Black, M., & Hickey, R. (2008). Toward an understanding of flow in video games. *Computers in Entertainment*, *6*(2), 1. doi:10.1145/1371216.1371223

Csikszentmihalyi, M. (1991). Flow: The psychology of optimal experience: Steps toward enhancing the quality of life. *Design Issues*, *8*(1), 80. doi:10.2307/1511458

Daniau, S. (2016). The Transformative Potential of Role-Playing Games—: From Play Skills to Human Skills. *Simulation & Gaming*, *47*(4), 423–444. doi:10.1177/1046878116650765

Darin, T., Andrade, R., & Sánchez, J. (2018, January). CLUE: A Usability Evaluation Checklist for Multimodal Video Game Field Studies with Children Who Are Blind. *Proceedings of the 51st Hawaii International Conference on System Sciences*. 10.24251/HICSS.2018.034

De Freitas, S. (2018). Are games effective learning tools? A review of educational games. *Journal of Educational Technology & Society*, *21*(2), 74–84.

Donovan, T. (2010). *Replay: The History of Video Games*. Yellow Ant Media Ltd.

Dormans, J. (2010). Adventures in level design: Generating missions and spaces for action adventure games. *Workshop on Procedural Content Generation in Games, PC Games 2010, Co-Located with the 5th International Conference on the Foundations of Digital Games*. 10.1145/1814256.1814257

Ewalt, D. M. (2013). Of Dice and Men: The Story of Dungeons and Dragons and the People Who Play It. In *American Journal of Play*. Scribner Book Company.

Forsyth, W. (2016). Globalized Random Procedural Content for Dungeon Generation. *Journal of Computing Sciences in Colleges*.

Garda, M. B. (2013). Neo-rogue and the essence of roguelikeness. *Homo Ludens*, *1*(5), 59–72.

Gee, J. P. (2003). *What video games have to teach us about learning and literacy*. New York: Palgrave Macmillan.

Gygax, B. G., & Arneson, D. (1974). *Dungeons & Dragons*. Academic Press.

Hartsook, K., Zook, A., Das, S., & Riedl, M. O. (2011). Toward supporting stories with procedurally generated game worlds. *2011 IEEE Conference on Computational Intelligence and Games, CIG 2011*, 297–304. 10.1109/CIG.2011.6032020

Hastings, E. J., Guha, R. K., & Stanley, K. O. (2009). Automatic content generation in the galactic arms race video game. *IEEE Transactions on Computational Intelligence and AI in Games*, *1*(4), 245–263. doi:10.1109/TCIAIG.2009.2038365

Hendrikx, M., Meijer, S., Van Der Velden, J., & Iosup, A. (2013). Procedural content generation for Games: A Survey. *ACM Transactions on Multimedia Computing Communications and Applications*, *9*(1), 1–22. doi:10.1145/2422956.2422957

Iosup, A. (2009). *POGGI: Puzzle-based online games on grid infrastructures*. Lecture Notes in Computer Science. doi:10.1007/978-3-642-03869-3_39

Jang, Y., & Ryu, S. (2011). Exploring game experiences and game leadership in massively multiplayer online role-playing games. *British Journal of Educational Technology*, *42*(4), 616–623. doi:10.1111/j.1467-8535.2010.01064.x

Johnson, L., Yannakakis, G. N., & Togelius, J. (2010). Cellular automata for real-time generation of infinite cave levels. *Workshop on Procedural Content Generation in Games, PC Games 2010, Co-Located with the 5th International Conference on the Foundations of Digital Games*. 10.1145/1814256.1814266

Johnson, M. R. (2017). The Use of ASCII Graphics in Roguelikes: Aesthetic Nostalgia and Semiotic Difference. *Games and Culture*, *12*(2), 115–135. doi:10.1177/1555412015585884

Kelly, G., & McCabe, H. (2007). Citygen: An interactive system for procedural city generation. *Fifth International Conference on Game Design and Technology*.

Kent, S. L. (2001). *The Ultimate History of Video Games: From Pong to Pokémon and Beyond - The Story Behind the Craze that Touched our Lives and Changed the World*. New York: Three Rivers Press.

Lee, S. H., & Song, D. H. (2019). Functional usability analysis of top Korean mobile role playing games based on user interface design. *Indones. J. Electr. Eng. Comput. Sci*, *13*(1), 123. doi:10.11591/ijeecs.v13.i1.pp123-128

Lefebvre, S., & Neyret, F. (2003). Pattern based procedural textures. Proceedings of the Symposium on Interactive 3D Graphics. 10.1145/641514.641518

Lopes, R., & Bidarra, R. (2011). Adaptivity challenges in games and simulations: A survey. *IEEE Transactions on Computational Intelligence and AI in Games*, *3*(2), 85–99. doi:10.1109/TCIAIG.2011.2152841

McDaniel, R., & Telep, P. (2009). Best Practices for Integrating Game-Based Learning into Online Teaching. *Journal of Online Learning and Teaching / MERLOT*.

Merhi, O., Faugloire, E., Flanagan, M., & Stoffregen, T. A. (2007). Motion sickness, console video games, and head-mounted displays. *Human Factors*, *49*(5), 920–934. doi:10.1518/001872007X230262 PMID:17915607

Moses, L. E. (1986). *Think and Explain with Statistics*. Penguin Books Australia.

Nielsen, J. (1995). *10 usability heuristics for user interface design*. Nielsen Norman Group.

Ogletree, S. M., & Drake, R. (2007). College students' video game participation and perceptions: Gender differences and implications. *Sex Roles*, *56*(7-8), 537–542. doi:10.100711199-007-9193-5

Pantaleev, A. (2012). In Search of Patterns: Disrupting RPG Classes Through Procedural Content Generation. Proceedings of the The Third Workshop on Procedural Content Generation in Games, 4:1-4:5. 10.1145/2538528.2538532

Pantaleev, A. (2013). *In Search of Patterns: Disrupting RPG Classes through Procedural Content Generation*. doi:10.1145/2538528.2538532

Paul, C. A. (2018). *The Toxic Meritocray of Video Games, Why Gaming Culture is the Worst.* Minneapolis, MN: University of Minnesota Press. doi:10.5749/j.ctt2204rbz

Reich, R. (1991). The Work of Nations: preparing ourselves for 21st century capitalism. In *The Work of Nations*. New York: Vintage Books.

Roden, T., & Parberry, I. (2004). From artistry to automation: A structured methodology for procedural content creation. *Lecture Notes in Computer Science*, *3166*, 151–156. doi:10.1007/978-3-540-28643-1_19

Sevilla, C., Santini, S., Haya, P. A., Rodriguez, P., & Sacha, G. M. (2012). Interdisciplinary design of videogames: A highly motivating method of learning. *2012 International Symposium on Computers in Education, SIIE 2012*.

Shaker, N., Togelius, J., & Nelson, M. J. (2016). Procedural Content Generation in Games. In Retrogame Archeology. doi:10.1007/978-3-319-42716-4

Short, X. T., & Adams, T. (2017). Procedural Content Generation in Game Design. Taylor & Francis.

Slootmaker, A., Nadolski, R., Kurvers, H. J., Hummel, H. G. K., & Koper, E. J. R. (2018). Usability of the EMERGO player environment for scenario-based serious games. *Human-Computer Interaction.*

Smelik, R. M., De Kraker, K. J., Groenewegen, S. A., Tutenel, T., & Bidarra, R. (2009). A survey of procedural methods for terrain modelling. *Proceedings of the CASA Workshop on 3D Advanced Media in Gaming and Simulation (3AMIGAS).*

Smith, A. M., & Mateas, M. (2011). Answer set programming for procedural content generation: A design space approach. *IEEE Transactions on Computational Intelligence and AI in Games*, *3*(3), 187–200. doi:10.1109/TCIAIG.2011.2158545

Smith, G., Gan, E., Othenin-Girard, A., & Whitehead, J. (2011). PCG-Based Game Design: Enabling New Play Experiences through Procedural Content Generation. *Proceedings of the 2nd International Workshop on Procedural Content Generation in Games Article No.* 7. 10.1145/2000919.2000926

Smith, K., & Abrams, S. S. (2019). Gamification and accessibility. *The International Journal of Information and Learning Technology*, *36*(2), 104–123. doi:10.1108/IJILT-06-2018-0061

Stoffregen, T. A., Faugloire, E., Yoshida, K., Flanagan, M. B., & Merhi, O. (2008). Motion sickness and postural sway in console video games. *Human Factors*, *50*(2), 322–331. doi:10.1518/001872008X250755 PMID:18516842

Su, Y. S., Chiang, W. L., James Lee, C. T., & Chang, H. C. (2016). The effect of flow experience on player loyalty in mobile game application. *Computers in Human Behavior*, *63*, 240–248. doi:10.1016/j.chb.2016.05.049

Summerville, A., Snodgrass, S., Guzdial, M., Holmgard, C., Hoover, A. K., Isaksen, A., ... Togelius, J. (2018). Procedural Content Generation via Machine Learning (PCGML). *IEEE Transactions on Games*, *10*(3), 257–270. doi:10.1109/TG.2018.2846639

Togelius, J., Yannakakis, G. N., Stanley, K. O., & Browne, C. (2011). Search-based procedural content generation: A taxonomy and survey. *IEEE Transactions on Computational Intelligence and AI in Games*, *3*(3), 172–186. doi:10.1109/TCIAIG.2011.2148116

Toker, S., & Baturay, M. H. (2016). Antecedents and consequences of game addiction. *Computers in Human Behavior*, *55*, 668–679. doi:10.1016/j.chb.2015.10.002

Tolkien, J. R. R. (1954). *The Lord of the Rings*. George Allen & Unwin.

Tutenel, T., Bidarra, R., Smelik, R. M., & De Kraker, K. J. (2009). *The role of semantics in games and simulations*. Computers in Entertainment. doi:10.1145/1461999.1462009

Tyagi, M., Choudhary, C., & Majumdar, R. (2019). A Study on Gaming Engines Accessibility. In *Advances in Interdisciplinary Engineering* (pp. 33–41). Singapore: Springer. doi:10.1007/978-981-13-6577-5_4

Valtchanov, V., & Brown, J. A. (2012). Evolving dungeon crawler levels with relative placement. doi:10.1145/2347583.2347587

Van Der Linden, R., Lopes, R., & Bidarra, R. (2014). Procedural generation of dungeons. *IEEE Transactions on Computational Intelligence and AI in Games*, *6*(1), 78–89. doi:10.1109/TCIAIG.2013.2290371

Velikovsky, J. (2014). *Flow Theory, Evolution & Creativity*. doi:10.1145/2677758.2677770

Vieira, E. A. O., Da Silveira, A. C., & Martins, R. X. (2019). Heuristic Evaluation on Usability of Educational Games: A Systematic Review. *Informatics in Education*, *18*(2), 427–442. doi:10.15388/infedu.2019.20

Vlachopoulos, D., & Makri, A. (2017). The effect of games and simulations on higher education: a systematic literature review. International Journal of Educational Technology in Higher Education, 14. doi:10.118641239-017-0062-1

Volkmar, G., Mählmann, N., & Malaka, R. (2019, November). Procedural Content Generation in Competitive Multiplayer Platform Games. In *Joint International Conference on Entertainment Computing and Serious Games* (pp. 228-234). Springer. 10.1007/978-3-030-34644-7_18

Voorhees, G. (2009). The character of difference: Procedurality, rhetoric, and roleplaying games. *Game Studies*. Retrieved from http://gamestudies.org/0902/articles/voorhees

Yanez-Gomez, R., Font, J. L., Cascado-Caballero, D., & Sevillano, J. L. (2019). Heuristic usability evaluation on games: A modular approach. *Multimedia Tools and Applications*, *78*(4), 4937–4964. doi:10.100711042-018-6593-1

Yang, J. C., Chen, C. H., & Chang Jeng, M. (2010). Integrating video-capture virtual reality technology into a physically interactive learning environment for English learning. *Computers & Education*, *55*(3), 1346–1356. doi:10.1016/j.compedu.2010.06.005

Yannakakis, G. N., & Togelius, J. (2011). *Experience-driven procedural content generation*. IEEE Transactions on Affective Computing. doi:10.1109/T-AFFC.2011.6

Yen, L. (2011). *Promotion of Student Problem-Solving Skills, Motivation, Knowledge Acquisition and English Proficiency level Using an Interactive Computer Game*. ED-MEDIA.

Zheng, R., & Gardner, M. K. (2017). *Handbook of Research on Serious Games for Educational Applications*. IGI Global. doi:10.4018/978-1-5225-0513-6

ADDITIONAL READING

Barton, M. (2019). *Dungeons and Desktops Dungeons and Desktops The History of Computer Role-Playing Games (Second edi)*. Taylor & Francis. doi:10.1201/9781351273404

Bowman, S. L. (2010). *The Functions of Role-Playing Games: How Participants Create Community, Solve Problems and Explore Identity*. Jefferson, North Carolina: McFarland & Company, Inc., Publishers.

Cowley, B., Charles, D., Black, M., & Hickey, R. (2008). Toward an understanding of flow in video games. *Computers in Entertainment*, *6*(2), 1. doi:10.1145/1371216.1371223

Donovan, T. (2010). *Replay: The History of Video Games*. Yellow Ant Media Ltd.

Ewalt, D. M. (2013). *Of Dice and Men: The Story of Dungeons and Dragons and the People Who Play It. American Journal of Play*. Scribner Book Company.

Gee, J. P. (2003). *What video games have to teach us about learning and literacy*. New York: palgrave macmillan.

Kent, S. L. (2001). *The Ultimate History of Video Games: From Pong to Pokémon and Beyond - The Story Behind the Craze that Touched our Lives and Changed the World*. New York, USA: Three Rivers Press.

Paul, C. A. (2018). *The Toxic Meritocray of Video Games, Why Gaming Culture is the Worst*. Minneapolis: University of Minnesota Press. doi:10.5749/j.ctt2204rbz

Reich, R. (1991). *The Work of Nations: preparing ourselves for 21st century capitalism. The Work of Nations*. New York: Vintage Books.

Shaker, N., Togelius, J., & Nelson, M. J. (2016). *Procedural Content Generation in Games*. Retrogame Archeology; doi:10.1007/978-3-319-42716-4

Short, X. T., & Adams, T. (2017). Procedural Content Generation in Game Design. Taylor & Francis.

KEY TERMS AND DEFINITIONS

Artificial Intelligence: According to many authors, artificial intelligence can be hard to be described, but we can reduce it to two actions: (1) a set of technics and methods used to allow any device to perceive its environment and make decisions that maximize its chance of successfully achieving its goals, mimicking a living being brain. (2) Capability of a machine to learn and perform narrow, repetitive and/or delicate tasks, for example an IA focused in predict words according to the context of the writer and previous sentences will not be able to predict the amount of money a person will spent next year.

Character: Is the complete simulation of a being (a person, an animal, an imaginary creature, etc) inside a computer game, this may include the ethnicity, height and weight, gender, psychological, cultural and regional properties, skills and abilities, dressing styles among other features. The equivalent in the real world would be an actor inside a theater play. Some characters are playable, and others have the purpose of give information, be the enemy or simply allow the player a better immersive experience of a simulation.

Education: Process which aim is to achieve the learning of a student, this can be measured as skills, values or knowledge that will help the student take the best possible decision in similar tasks reviewed in the educational system.

Flow: In terms of gaming, flow is a state of fulfillment where the player feels the game is in optimal conditions for his own level of experience, not too difficult nor too easy, increasing the loyalty and sense of personal achievement. There is an entire theory constructed around explaining this concept, it is not only limited to the field of games, any human activity can be described in terms of passion and boringness, concepts that are the pillars of this construct.

Game: Is the proposal of a fictional scenery that includes the goal(s), a set of rules and the structure of the development and the quantity of players per game (single person or by teams). A game can be played for fun or with educational purposes due the real-life simulation inside it. It can also represent unreal situations.

Indie Game Studio: It is an abbreviation of "independent game studio". This is a company that typically have fewer economic resources than a well know brand. However, many times an indie development disrupts the common constraints imposed by the market and the players achieve better experiences due the development of new technologies or styles.

Procedural Content Generation: A set of tools and methods that helps game developers the creation of sceneries algorithmically instead of manually. For example, if you have a set of three types of traps (mood, ice or fire) and you choose to put random traps in a narrow space like an aisle the software must be capable of adapt the space and the trap type and react according to the character approaching it.

Replayability: When a player has achieved all the goals of a game, if the game offers alternate endings, secret missions, additional characters, increasing scores and rewards or any other mechanism that keeps the interest of continue playing the game is called replayability.

Role Playing: Is the action of taking a certain job or activity inside a group of beings (teacher, student, janitor, policeman, etc.). Talking about games, it means specifically becoming a character inside a simulation. In computer science role playing will be selecting a certain type of warrior, agent, scientist, driver, or any other job description the game needs. The main purpose of taking a role in a game is develop the skills the character have, and make easier the task needed to achieve the games goal.

Video Game: In computer science, a game is a software that typically include graphical, sound, text and other multimedia combination aiming to simulate a real or unreal world situations to entertain the players in a single or collective way.

APPENDIX 1

Yuji Nakamura via bloomberg.com in his article "Peak Video Game? Top Analyst Sees Industry Slumping in 2019" has a deep analysis about the annual revenue of the videogame industry from 1971 to 2018, and if we compare this data with Pamela McClintock's article "Global Box Office Revenue Hits Record $41B in 2018" via the Hollywoodreporter.com about the film industry in the past 5 years we can clearly see that videogames surpass films by far, in fact, we can highlight that in 2014 Game industry revenue was 2.5 times the Films revenue globally speaking and by 2018 it has become 3.36 times, also we can see the film industry has reached a top and has flattened its incomes.
If we make a similar comparison with the music industry and using the data collected from IFPI (International Federation of the Phonographic Industry) Global Music Report 2019 // State of the Industry, we can clearly see that the differences are even more drastic going from 6.33 times in 2014 to 7.25 times in 2018 as can be seen in Table 1.

Table 1. Video games vs films and music revenues expressed in billions of US dollars.

Year	Video Games	Films	Music
2014	91.2	36.4	14.3
2015	97.1	38.4	14.8
2016	107.7	38.8	16.2
2017	122	40.5	17.4
2018	138.5	41.1	19.1

And if we express this data as a graphic, Figure 5, for visual comparison purposes we can point the fact how films are not growing at the same rate as videogames or music, even if music is the lower of the three of them it has a constant increase.

Figure 5. Video games vs. films and music revenues expressed in billions of US dollars.

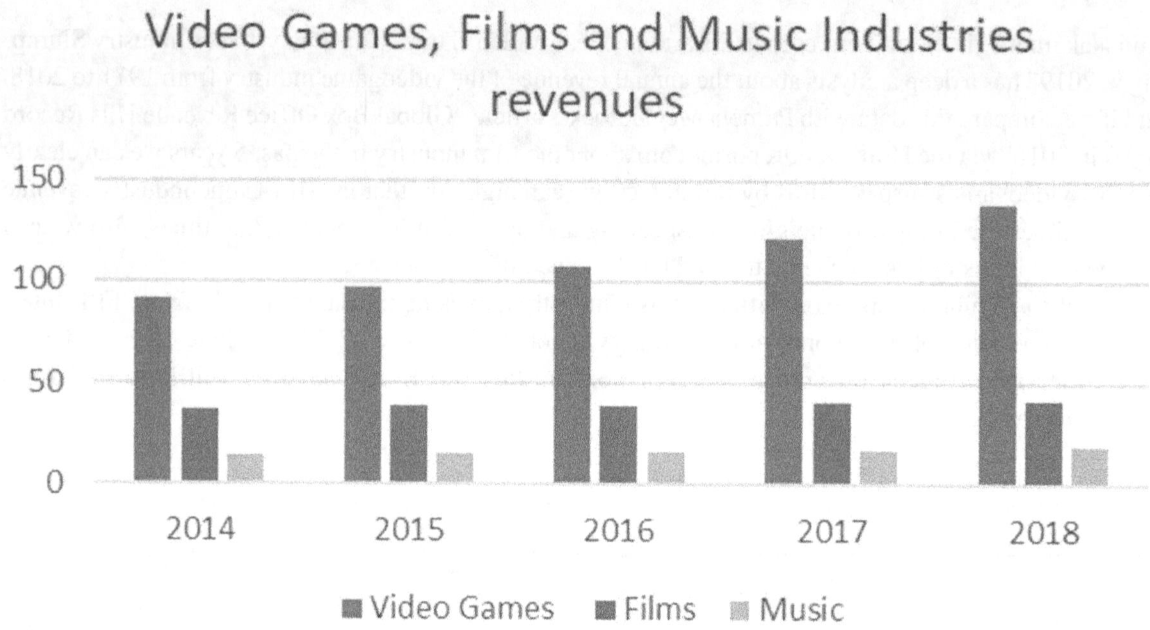

Compilation of References

Abdelrahman, Y., Khan, A. A., Newn, J., Velloso, E., Safwat, S. A., Bailey, J., . . . Schmidt, A. (2019). Classifying Attention Types with Thermal Imaging and Eye Tracking. *Proceedings of the ACM on Interactive, Mobile, Wearable and Ubiquitous Technologies, 3*(3), 69. 10.1145/3351227

Accessible University. (2016). *Defining Accessibility - Accessible University*. Retrieved July 11, 2017, from http://www.accessibleuniversity.com/accessibility-basics/defining-accessibility

ACM. (n.d.). *ACM Code of Ethics*. Retrieved from https://www.acm.org/code-of-ethics

Adams, D. (2002). *Automatic Generation of Dungeons for Computer Games*. University of Sheffield. Retrieved from https://pdfs.semanticscholar.org/2502/0f8d955aee07b7dd49a3ec23b1f2a8cf1d06.pdf

Adellin, R., Khuan, C. T., & Gertrude, L. D. (2019, May). Conceptual Framework Puzzle Game with High Replayability. *Journal of Physics: Conference Series, 1228*(1), 012070. doi:10.1088/1742-6596/1228/1/012070

Aguado, J., & Estrada, F. (2017). *Guía de accesibilidad de aplicaciones móviles (apps)*. Retrieved from https://administracionelectronica.gob.es/pae_Home/pae_Estrategias/pae_Accesibilidad/pae_documentacion/pae_eInclusion_Accesibilidad_de_apps.html#.Wv5i60jt7IU

Akkerman, S., Admiraal, W., & Huizenga, J. (2009). Storification in History education: A mobile game in and about medieval Amsterdam. *Computers & Education, 52*(2), 449–459. doi:10.1016/j.compedu.2008.09.014

Allen, I. E., & Seaman, J. (2014). *Grade change: Tracking online education in the United States*. Babson Survey Research Group and Quahog Research Group, LLC. Retrieved from http://sloanconsortium.org/publications/survey/grade-change-2013

Alvarez Gámez, F., Cantalejo Cano, J., Duran Vélez, J., Gómez Viñas, P., González Paredes, P., & Sánchez, Á. (2000). *Aspectos evolutivos y educativos de la deficiencia visual - Volumen II* (1st ed.). Madrid: Organización Nacional de Ciegos Españoles (ONCE). Retrieved from http://bibliorepo.umce.cl/libros_electronicos/diferencial/edtv_8.pdf

Amado, H., Hernández, R., & Linares, B. (2017). Requisitos de accesibilidad indispensables para un campus virtual accesible. *ESVIAL*, 119-130.

Anastasiou, D., & Vázquez, L. M. (2010). Localisation Standards and Metadata. In S. Sánchez-Alonso & I. N. Athanasiadis (Eds.), *Metadata and Semantic Research. MTSR 2010. Communications in Computer and Information Science* (Vol. 108). Berlin: Springer.

Anderson, C. A. (2004). An update on the effects of playing violent video games. *Journal of Adolescence, 27*(1), 113–122. doi:10.1016/j.adolescence.2003.10.009 PMID:15013264

Anderson, C. A., & Bushman, B. J. (2001). Effects of violent video games on aggressive behavior, aggressive cognition, aggressive affect, physiological arousal, and prosocial behavior: A Meta-Analytic Review of the Scientific Literature. *Psychological Science*, *12*(5), 353–359. doi:10.1111/1467-9280.00366 PMID:11554666

Angel, J. (n.d.). *Maderas de Colombia: Balso*. Retrieved from http://infomaderas.com/2014/09/11/maderas-de-colombia-balso/

Anido, L. E., Fernández, M. J., Caeiro, M., Santos, J. M., Rodríguez, J. S., & Llamas, M. (2002). Educational metadata and brokerage for learning resources. *Computers & Education, 38*(4), 351-374. doi:10.1016/S0360-1315(02)00018-0

Antognazza, M. P., & González, M. (2011). The dyslexic child and his educational enviroment perceptions and representations on the dyslexia. Ciencias Psicológicas, (2), 193-200.

Antonenko, P., Dawson, K., & Sahay, S. (2016). A Framework for aligning needs, abilities and affordances to inform design and practice of educational technologies. *British Journal of Educational Technology*, *48*(4), 916–927. doi:10.1111/bjet.12466

APA Ethics Code. (2019). In *Wikipedia*. Retrieved from https://en.wikipedia.org/w/index.php?title=APA_Ethics_Code&oldid=899653507

Appelcline, S. (2013). *The (Not-So) Secret Origin of D&D*. Retrieved from http://dnd.wizards.com/articles/features/not-so-secret-origin-dd

Aras, E., & Yip-Hoi, D. (2007). Geometric modeling of cutter/work piece engagements in 3-axis milling using polyhedral models. *ASME 2007 International Mechanical Engineering Congress and Exposition (IMECE2007).*

Arcibniegas, J. C., Cano, J. M., Carvajal, N. V., Lorente, C. G., & Jaramillo, M. N. (2019). Attention to individual differences in early education? The talented child. *Dilemas Contemporáneos: Educación, Política y Valores*, *6*(3).

Arroyo, N., Campos, F., Carballo, M., González, G., Solano, A., Vargas, E., & Carpio, M. A. (2019) El Modelo dual de reconocimiento de la palabra en el Sistema Braille. *CienciAmérica*, *8*(1), 90-104. Available on: http://cienciamerica.uti.edu.ec/openjournal/index.php/uti/article/view/194

Ashlock, D., Lee, C., & Mcguinness, C. (n.d.). *Search-Based Procedural Generation of Maze-Like Levels. Academic Press.*

Baldrich Caselles, M., Blanco Zárate, L., Consuegra Cano, B., Díez Álvarez, M., Sánchez Abietar, J., & García Soria, F. (2012). Requisitos técnicos para la confección de planos accesibles a personas con discapacidad visual (1st ed.). Academic Press.

Barendregt, W., Bekker, M., Bouwhuis, D., & Baauw, E. (2007). Predicting effectiveness of children participants in user testing based on personality characteristics. *Journal Behaviour & Information Technology*, 133-147.

Barrio, C. (2019). *Con discapacidad visual, pero con visión de futuro*. Retrieved from https://www.nobbot.com/personas/tecnologia-ciegos-apps-herramientas/

Barritt, C., & Alderman, F.L. (2004). *Creating a reusable learning objects strategy: Leveraging information and learning in a knowledge economy*. Pfeiffer & Company Editorial.

Barr, M. (2018). Student attitudes to games-based skills development: Learning from video games in higher education. *Computers in Human Behavior*, *80*, 283–294. doi:10.1016/j.chb.2017.11.030

Barton, M. (2007). *The History of Computer Role-Playing Games Part 1: The Early Years (1980-1983).* Retrieved from Gamasutra website: http://www.gamasutra.com/view/feature/132024/the_history_of_computer_.php

Barton, M. (2019). *Dungeons and Desktops Dungeons and Desktops The History of Computer Role-Playing Games (2nd ed.).* Taylor & Francis. doi:10.1201/9781351273404

Batanero, C., Karhu, M., Holvikivi, J., Otón, S., & Amado-Salvatierra, H. R. (2014, July). A method to evaluate accessibility in e-learning education systems. In *Advanced Learning Technologies (ICALT), 2014 IEEE 14th International Conference on* (pp. 556-560). IEEE. 10.1109/ICALT.2014.163

Batanero, C., Fernández-Sanz, L., Piironen, A. K., Holvikivi, J., Hilera, J. R., Otón, S., & Alonso, J. (2017). Accessible platforms for e-learning: A case study. *Computer Applications in Engineering Education*, *25*(6), 1018–1037. doi:10.1002/cae.21852

Baxter, I., & Oatley, K. (1991). Measuring the learnability of spreadsheets in inexperienced users and those with previous spreadsheet experience. *Behaviour & Information Technology*, *40*(6), 475–490. doi:10.1080/01449299108924305

Bayir, S., Keser, H., & Numanoglu, G. (2010). General review on computer literacy of visually handicapped individuals in Turkey. *Procedia: Social and Behavioral Sciences*, *9*, 1475–1480. doi:10.1016/j.sbspro.2010.12.352

Bell, R. (2011). Computer Planning and Intraoperative Navigation in Orthognathic Surgery. *Journal of Oral and Maxillofacial Surgery*, *69*(3), 592–605. doi:10.1016/j.joms.2009.06.030 PMID:21353924

Bergin, J., Eckstein, J., Manns, M., Sharp, H., Marquardt, K., Chandler, K., … Wallingford, E. (2012). Pedagogical Patterns: Advice For Educators. CreateSpace.

Bery, Ch., & Randy, W. (2005). Educational Games: A Technique to accelerate the acquisition of reading skills of children with learning disabilities. *International Journal of Special Education*, *2*(20), 66–72.

Bevan, N., Carter, J., & Harker, S. (2015). ISO 9241-11 Revised: What Have We Learnt About Usability Since 1998? In M. Kurosu (Ed.), Lecture Notes in Computer Science: Vol. 9169. *Human-Computer Interaction: Design and Evaluation. HCI 2015*. Cham: Springer.

Bhowmik, R. (2012). *How Dieter Rams' 10 Principles of Good Design can impact UX*. Retrieved from: https://medium.com/swlh/how-dieter-rams-10-principles-of-good-design-can-impact-ux-c2f369218a08

Bierre, K., Chetwynd, J., Ellis, B., Hinn, D. M., Ludi, S., & Westin, T. (2005, July). Game not over: Accessibility issues in video games. In *Proc. of the 3rd International Conference on Universal Access in Human-Computer Interaction* (pp. 22-27). Academic Press.

BigBlueButton. (2019). *BigBlueButton*. Retrieved from https://bigbluebutton.org/about/

Bloom, R. (2006). *The Handbook of Gestalt Play Therapy: Practical Guidelines for Child Therapists*. London: Jessica Kingsley.

BOE. (2003). *Ley 51/2003, de 2 de diciembre, de igualdad de oportunidades, no discriminación y accesibilidad universal de las personas con discapacidad*. Academic Press.

Borau, J., Hernández Galán, J., & Álvarez Ilzarbe, F. (2011). *Accesibilidad universal y diseño para todos - Arquitectura y Urbanismo* (1st ed.). Madrid: Fundación ONCE. Retrieved from http://www.upv.es/contenidos/CAMUNISO/info/U0578035.pdf

Borderie, J., & Michinov, N. (2016). Identifying Flow in Video Games. *International Journal of Gaming and Computer-Mediated Simulations*, *8*(3), 19–38. doi:10.4018/IJGCMS.2016070102

Borges, J. A., & Tomé, D. (2014). Teaching music to blind children: New strategies for teaching through interactive use of Musibraille software. 5th International Conference on Software Development and Technologies for Enhancing Accessibility and Fighting Info-exclusion, DSAI 2013. *Procedia Computer Science*, *27*, 19–27. doi:10.1016/j.procs.2014.02.004

Bottino, R., & Freino, L. & Mauro, T. (2016). From e-learning to VR-learning: An example of learning in an immersive virtual world. *Journal of E-Learning and Knowledge Society*, 101-113.

Bowman, S. L. (2007). The Psychological Power of the Roleplaying Experience. *Journal of Interactive Drama*.

Bowman, S. L. (2010). *The Functions of Role-Playing Games: How Participants Create Community, Solve Problems and Explore Identity*. Jefferson, NC: McFarland & Company, Inc., Publishers.

Boyle, E., Connolly, T. M., & Hainey, T. (2011). The role of psychology in understanding the impact of computer games. *Entertainment Computing*, *2*(2), 69–74. doi:10.1016/j.entcom.2010.12.002

Brahim, H. B., Jemaa, A. B., Jemni, M., & Laabidi, M. (2013, July). Towards the design of personalised accessible e-learning environments. In *Advanced Learning Technologies (ICALT), 2013 IEEE 13th International Conference* (pp. 419-420). IEEE. 10.1109/ICALT.2013.128

Brough, J., Schwartz, M., Gupta, S. K., Anand, D. K., Kavetsky, R., & Pettersen, R. (2007). Towards the development of a virtual environment-based training system for mechanical assembly operations. *Virtual Reality (Waltham Cross)*, *11*(4), 189–206. doi:10.100710055-007-0076-4

Bruff, D. (2012). *Teaching with MOOCs: Four Cases*. Retrieved from http://cft. vanderbilt. edu/2012/11/teaching-with-moocs—four-cases

Bruff, D. O., Fisher, D. H., McEwen, K. E., & Smith, B. E. (2013). Wrapping a MOOC: Student perceptions of an experiment in blended learning. *Journal of Online Learning and Teaching / MERLOT*, *9*(2), 187.

Bruni, M. (2006). Fine Motor Skills for Children with Down Syndrome. Woodbine House Eds.

Burdea, G. (1996). *Force and touch feedback for virtual reality*. New York: John Wiley & Sons, Inc.

Burgstahler, S. (2009). *Universal design of instruction (UDI): Definition, principles, guidelines, and examples*. Seattle, WA: DO-IT, University of Washington. Retrieved from http://www.washington.edu/doit/Brochures/Academics/instruction.html

Burgstahler, S. (2012). *Equal access: Universal design of instruction*. Seattle, WA: DO-IT, University of Washington. Retrieved from www.uw.edu/doit/equal-access-universal-design-instruction

Butler, K. A. (1985). Connecting theory and practice: a case study of achieving usability goals. *SIGCHI Conference on Human Factors in Computing Systems*. 10.1145/317456.317472

Cairns, P., Power, C., Barlet, M., & Haynes, G. (2019). Future Design of Accessibility in Games: A Design Vocabulary. *International Journal of Human-Computer Studies*, *131*, 64–71. doi:10.1016/j.ijhcs.2019.06.010

Cáliz, D., Martínez, L., Alamán, X., Terán, C., & Cáliz, R. (2016). Usability Testing in Mobile Applications Involving People with Down Syndrome: A Literature Review. *Computer Science and Information Technology*, *8*(3), 117–131.

Caliz, D., Martinez, L., Alaman, X., Teran, C., & Caliz, R. (2016). Usability Testing Process with People with Down Syndrome Interacting with Mobile Applications: A Literature Review. *International Journal of Computer Science & Information Technology*, *8*(3), 117–131. doi:10.5121/ijcsit.2016.8309

Callaghan, M., Savin-Baden, M., McShane, N., & Eguiluz, A. G. (2017). Mapping Learning and Game Mechanics for Serious Games Analysis in Engineering Education. *IEEE Transactions on Emerging Topics in Computing*, *5*(1), 77–83. doi:10.1109/TETC.2015.2504241

Cano, C., Fernandez, L., & Pages, C. (2012). Modelos de madurez de la enseñanza virtual, ¿Consideran la accesibilidad? *IV Congreso Internacional ATICA*, 100-108.

Capitulo II - Tecnología Háptica. (n.d.). Retrieved from https://htid3.files.wordpress.com/2013/04/tecnologia-haptica.pdf

CAST. (2011). *Universal Design for Learning Guidelines version 2.0*. Wakefield, MA: Author.

CAST. (2018). *Universal Design for Learning Guidelines version 2.2*. Retrieved from http://udlguidelines.cast.org

Castañeda-Roldán & Espinosa-Victoria. (2008, August). Realidad Virtual, una herramienta computacional para el estudio de Sistemas Orgánicos y los Sentidos del Tacto y Olfato a Nivel Primaria. *Impulso.*

Castañeda-Roldán, C. Y., & Vázquez-García, F. E. (2011). Realidad Virtual, un apoyo en la Terapia de Acrofobia, Claustrofobia y Agorafobia. *Memorias del VIII Congreso Internacional sobre Innovación y Desarrollo Tecnológico (CIINDET 2011).*

Caulfield, M., Collier, A., & Halawa, S. (2013). Rethinking online community in MOOCs used for blended learning. *Educause Review.* Retrieved from http://www.educause.edu/ero/article/rethinking-online-community-moocs-used-blended-learning

Chandler, H. (2009). *The Game Production Handbook*. Jones & Bartlett Publishers.

Chang, C. H., Pan, W. W., Tseng, L. Y., & Stoffregen, T. A. (2012). Postural activity and motion sickness during video game play in children and adults. *Experimental Brain Research*, *217*(2), 299–309. doi:10.100700221-011-2993-4 PMID:22210118

Chapanis, A. (1991). Evaluating usability. In Human factors for informatics usability (pp. 359–398). Cambridge University Press.

Chapman, R., & Hesketh, L. (2000). Behavioral phenotype of individuals with Down syndrome. *Journal: Mental Retardation and Developmental Disabilities*, *6*(2), 84–95. PMID:10899801

Chee, Y. (2016). *Games-To-Teach or Games-To-Learn: Unlocking the Power of Digital Game-Based, Learning Through Performance*. Springer Singapore. doi:10.1007/978-981-287-518-1

Chelkowski, L., Yan, Z., & Asaro-Saddler, K. (2019). The use of mobile devices with students with disabilities: A literature review. *Preventing School Failure*, *63*(3), 277–295. doi:10.1080/1045988X.2019.1591336

Chen, C. L. D., Yeh, T. K., & Chang, C. Y. (2016). *The effects of game-based learning and anticipation of a test on the learning outcomes of 10 th grade geology students. Eurasia Journal of Mathematics, Science and Technology Education.* doi:10.12973/eurasia.2016.1519a

Chestnut, E., Lei, R., Leslie, S. J., & Cimpian, A. (2018). The myth that only brilliant people are good at math and its implications for diversity. *Education in Science*, *8*(2), 65. doi:10.3390/educsci8020065

Chiang, Y. T., Lin, S. S. J., Cheng, C. Y., & Liu, E. Z. F. (2011). *Exploring online game players' flow experiences and positive affect. Turkish Online Journal of Educational Technology.*

Chickering, A. W., & Gamson, Z. F. (1987). Seven principles for good practice in undergraduate education. *AAHE Bulletin*, *39*(7), 3–7.

Chiu, F. Y., & Hsieh, M. L. (2017). *Role-playing game based assessment to fractional concept in second grade mathematics. Eurasia Journal of Mathematics, Science and Technology Education.* doi:10.12973/eurasia.2017.00659a

Chochoiek, N. (2017). Explaining the Success of User-Centered Design - An Empirical Study across German. *Junior Management Science,* 81-116.

Christopher, B. (2013). *Learning about social learning in MOOCs: From statistical analysis to generative model.* Academic Press.

CISCO. (2017). *Cisco Visual Networking Index: Global Mobile Data Traffic Forecast Update, 2016–2021 White Paper - Cisco.* Retrieved July 11, 2017, from http://www.cisco.com/c/en/us/solutions/collateral/service-provider/visual-networking-index-vni/mobile-white-paper-c11-520862.html

Ciullo, S., Ely, E., McKenna, J. W., Alves, K., & Kennedy, J. K. (2018). *Reading Instruction for Students With Learning Disabilities in Grades 4 and 5: An Observation Study.* SAGE Publications Inc.

Clark, D. (2013). *MOOCs: taxonomy of 8 types of MOOC.* Retrieved from http://donaldclarkplanb.blogspot.com/2013/04/moocs-taxonomy-of-8-types-of-mooc.html

Colour Blind Awareness. (n.d.). *What is Colour Blindness? — Colour Blind Awareness.* Retrieved July 11, 2017, from http://www.colourblindawareness.org/colour-blindness/

Columbia, T. U. of B. (2019). *Web accessibility.* Retrieved November 10, 2019, from https://www.ubc.ca/accessibility/

Combéfis, S., Bibal, A., & Van Roy, P. (2014). Recasting a Traditional Course into a MOOC by Means of a SPOC. *Proceedings of the European MOOCs Stakeholders Summit,* 205-208.

Compañ-Rosique, P., Molina-Carmona, R., Gallego-Durán, F., Satorre-Cuerda, R., Villagrá-Arnedo, C., & Llorens-Largo, F. (2019). A guide for making video games accessible to users with cerebral palsy. *Universal Access in the Information Society, 18*(3), 565–581. doi:10.100710209-019-00679-6

Confederación Española de Organizaciones Empresariales (CEOE). (n.d.). *Serious Games CEOE - Aplicaciones de Android en Google Play.* Retrieved July 12, 2017, from https://play.google.com/store/apps/details?id=com.prevencontrol.seriousgamesceoe&hl=es

Conger, S. (2016). Gamification of Service Desk Work. In The Impact of ICT on Work (pp. 151-172). Singapore: Springer Science+Business Media Singapore. doi:10.1007/978-981-287-612-6_8

Connell, B., Jones, M., Mace, R., Mueller, J., Mullick, A., & Ostroff, E. (1997). *The Center for Universal Design - Universal Design Principles.* Retrieved from https://projects.ncsu.edu/ncsu/design/cud/about_ud/udprinciplestext.htm

Conole, G. (2010). An overview of design representations. In *Proceedings of the 7th International Conference on Networked Learning* (pp. 482-489). Academic Press.

Conole, G. (2014). A new classification schema for MOOCs. *The International Journal for Innovation and Quality in Learning, 2*(3), 65-77.

Conole, G. (2008). Capturing practice: the role of mediating artefacts in learning design. In L. Lockyer, S. Bennett, S. Agostinho, & B. Harper (Eds.), *Handbook of Research on Learning Design and Learning Objects: Issues, Applications and Technologies* (pp. 187–207). Hersey, PA: IGI Global. doi:10.4018/978-1-59904-861-1.ch008

Constitucional, C. (1991). *Consejo Superior de la Judicatura, Sala Administrativa, Centro de Documentación Judicial.* Constitución Política de Colombia.

Cook, L., & Dakin, K. (2007). *Basic Facts About DYSLEXIA & Other Reading Problems*. International Dyslexia Association.

Coombs, N. (2010). *Making Online Teaching Accessible: Inclusive Course Design for Students with Disabilities*. San Francisco, CA: Jossey-Bass.

Córdova, M. A. (2019). *MOODLE LTS 2.7 y estándares de accesibilidad web*. Retrieved from http://www.esvial.org/wp-content/files/CAFVIR2015pp67-74.pdf

Covaci, A., Kramer, D., Augusto, J. C., Rus, S., & Braun, A. (2015). Assessing Real World Imagery in Virtual Environments for People with Cognitive Disabilities. *2015 International Conference on Intelligent Environments*. 10.1109/IE.2015.14

Cowley, B., Charles, D., Black, M., & Hickey, R. (2008). Toward an understanding of flow in video games. *Computers in Entertainment*, *6*(2), 1. doi:10.1145/1371216.1371223

Creelman, A., Ehlers, U., & Ossiannilsson, E. (2014). Perspectives on MOOC quality-An account of the EFQUEL MOOC Quality Project. *INNOQUAL-International Journal for Innovation and Quality in Learning*, *2*(3), 78–87.

Criollo-C, S., & Lujan-Mora, S. (2017). M-Learning and Their Potential use in the Higher Education: A Literature Review. In *2017 International Conference on Information Systems and Computer Science (INCISCOS)* (pp. 268–273). IEEE. 10.1109/INCISCOS.2017.43

Criollo-C, S., Lujan-Mora, S., & Jaramillo-Alcazar, A. (2018). Advantages and Disadvantages of M-Learning in Current Education. In *2018 IEEE World Engineering Education Conference (EDUNINE)* (pp. 1–6). IEEE. 10.1109/EDUNINE.2018.8450979

Csikszentmihalyi, M. (1991). Flow: The psychology of optimal experience: Steps toward enhancing the quality of life. *Design Issues*, *8*(1), 80. doi:10.2307/1511458

Dabbagh, N., & Kitsantas, A. (2012). Personal Learning Environments, social media, and self-regulated learning: A natural formula for connecting formal and informal learning. *The Internet and higher education*, *15*(1), 3–8. doi:10.1016/j.iheduc.2011.06.002

DAMA. (2009). *The DAMA Guide to the Data Management Body of Knowledge*. Technics Publications, LLC.

Daniau, S. (2016). The Transformative Potential of Role-Playing Games—: From Play Skills to Human Skills. *Simulation & Gaming*, *47*(4), 423–444. doi:10.1177/1046878116650765

Daniel, J. (2012). Making sense of MOOCs: Musings in a maze of myth, paradox and possibility. *Journal of Interactive Media in Education*, *2012*(3), 18. doi:10.5334/2012-18

Darin, T., Andrade, R., & Sánchez, J. (2018, January). CLUE: A Usability Evaluation Checklist for Multimodal Video Game Field Studies with Children Who Are Blind. *Proceedings of the 51st Hawaii International Conference on System Sciences*. 10.24251/HICSS.2018.034

Dasarathy, B., Sullivan, K., Schmidt, D. C., Fisher, D. H., & Porter, A. (2014). The past, present, and future of MOOCs and their relevance to software engineering. In *Proceedings of the on Future of Software Engineering* (pp. 212-224). ACM. 10.1145/2593882.2593897

Davis, S., & Wiedenbeck, S. (1998). The effect of interaction style and training method on end user learning of software packages. *Interacting with Computers*, *11*(2), 147–172. doi:10.1016/S0953-5438(98)00026-5

DCMI. (2009). *Dublin Core Metadata Initiative*. Retrieved from http://dublincore.org/

DCMI. (2012). *Learning Resource Metadata Initiative (LRMI)*. Retrieved from http://lrmi.dublincore.net/

DCMI. (2012). *LRMI Terms*. Retrieved from http://dublincore.org/specifications/lrmi/lrmi_terms/1.1/

de Colombia, C. (1997). *Ley 361 de 1997*. Retrieved from http://www.secretariasenado.gov.co/senado/basedoc/ley_0361_1997_pr001.html

De Freitas, S. (2018). Are games effective learning tools? A review of educational games. *Journal of Educational Technology & Society*, *21*(2), 74–84.

De Oliveira, P. A., Lotto, E. P., Correa, A. G. D., Taboada, L. G. G., Costa, L. C. P., & Lopes, R. D. (2015). Virtual Stage: An Immersive Musical Game for People with Visual Impairment. *2015 14th Brazilian Symposium on Computer Games and Digital Entertainment (SBGames)*.

de Waard, I., Gallagher, M. S., Zelezny-Green, R., Czerniewicz, L., Downes, S., Kukulska-Hulme, A., & Willems, J. (2014). Challenges for conceptualising EU MOOC for vulnerable learner groups. *Proceedings of the European MOOC Stakeholder Summit*, *2014*, 33–42.

Defaweux, V., Delbrassine, D., Dozo, B. O., Etienne, A. M., Centi, V., D'Anna, V., ... Wagener, A. (2019). To combine a MOOC to a regular face-to-face course–A study of three blended pedagogical patterns. *Proceedings of Work in Progress Papers of the Research. Experience and Business Tracks at EMOOCs*, *2019*, 210–217.

Department of Health, Education, and Welfare . (n.d.). *The Belmont Report. Ethical principles and guidelines for the protection of human subjects of research. National Commission for the Protection of Human Subjects of Biomedical and Behavioral Research.*

DeShazo, J., Harris, L., & Pratt, W. (2010). Effective Intervention or Child's Play? A Review of Video Games for Diabetes Education. *Diabetes Technology & Therapeutics*, *12*(10), 815–822. doi:10.1089/dia.2010.0030 PMID:20807119

Developer, A. (n.d.). *Accessibility on iOS*. Retrieved July 15, 2017, from https://developer.apple.com/accessibility/ios/

Developers, A. (n.d.). *Accessibility in Android*. Retrieved July 15, 2017, from https://developer.android.com/guide/topics/ui/accessibility/index.html

Dezcallar Sáez, T. (2012). *Relación entre procesos mentales y sentido háptico: emociones y recuerdos mediante el análisis empírico de texturas. Doctorado. Universidad Autónoma de Barcelona; Facultad de Psicología*. Departamento de Psicología Básica, Evolutiva y de la Educación.

Di Iorio, A., Feliziani, A. A., Mirri, S., Salomoni, P., & Vitali, F. (2006). Automatically producing accessible learning objects. *Journal of Educational Technology & Society*, *9*(4), 3–16.

Dichev, C., Dicheva, D., Angelova, G., & Agre, G. (2015). *From Gamification to Gameful Design and Gameful Experience in Learning*. Academic Press.

Digital, R. (n.d.). *Qué consecuencias puede tener un ciberataque para tu empresa*. Retrieved October 22, 2019, from https://www.reasonwhy.es/actualidad/digital/que-consecuencias-puede-tener-un-ciberataque-para-tu-empresa-2017-05-15

Discapacidades: MedlinePlus en español. (2019). Retrieved from https://medlineplus.gov/spanish/disabilities.html

Doñate, M. (2015). Interfaces Hápticos. Aplicaciones en entornos virtuales. e-Glance. *e-Glance*. Retrieved from e-Glance: http://eglance.ctb.upm.es/es/eglance/

Donovan, T. (2010). *Replay: The History of Video Games*. Yellow Ant Media Ltd.

Dore, R.A., Shirilla, M., Hopkins, E., Collins, M., Scott, M., & Schatz, J. (2019). Education in the app store: using a mobile game to support US preschoolers' vocabulary learning. *Journal of Children and Media*, 1-20.

Dormans, J. (2010). Adventures in level design: Generating missions and spaces for action adventure games. *Workshop on Procedural Content Generation in Games, PC Games 2010, Co-Located with the 5th International Conference on the Foundations of Digital Games*. 10.1145/1814256.1814257

Dorys, G. (2015). Constructivism as theory and teaching method. *Sophia, Colección de Filosofía de la Educación,* 93-110.

Downes, S. (2015). The Quality of Massive Open Online Courses. In International Handbook of E-Learning. Academic Press.

Dreyfuss, H. (2003). *Designing for people*. Skyhorse Publishing Inc.

Dykens, E., Shah, B., Davis, B., Baker, C., Fife, T., & Fitzpatrick, J. (2015). Psychiatric disorders in adolescents and young adults with Down syndrome and other intellectual disabilities. Journal of Neurodevelopmental Disorders, 7-9. doi:10.118611689-015-9101-1

Educación Inclusiva - Módulo 9: Adaptación del material - Percepción táctil y háptica. (n.d.). Retrieved from http://www.ite.educacion.es/formacion/materiales/129/cd/unidad_9/m9_percepcion_tactil.htm

El código Braille. (n.d.). Retrieved from http://instructorbraille.blogspot.com.co/p/el-codigo-braille.html

E-Learning Team. (2018). *¿Qué saber, qué evitar, creando E-Learning accesible?* Retrieved from https://www.sicom.com.mx/e-learning/que-saber-que-evitar-creando-e-learning-accesible/

Elias, Z. M., Batumalai, U. M., & Azmi, A. N. H. (2019, November). Virtual reality games on accommodation and convergence. *Applied Ergonomics*, *81*. PMID:31422241

Elliott, G. J., Jones, E., & Barker, P. (2002). A grounded theory approach to modelling learnability of hypermedia authoring tools. *Interacting with Computers*, *14*(5), 547–574. doi:10.1016/S0953-5438(02)00021-8

Ellis, S. R. (1994). What are virtual environments? *IEEE Computer Graphics and Applications*, *14*(1), 17–22. doi:10.1109/38.250914 PMID:7757252

Emanuel, E. J. (2013). MOOCs taken by educated few. *Nature, 503*, 342.

Ericsson, K. A., & Simon, H. A. (1980). Verbal reports as data. *Psychological Review*, *87*(3), 215–251. doi:10.1037/0033-295X.87.3.215

Espinosa-Castañeda, R. & Medellín-Castillo, H. I. (2014). Análisis y evaluación de la generación de iconos mentales en personas invidentes a partir de la percepción virtual táctil utilizando realidad virtual y sistemas hápticos. *Revista ICONO14. Revista de estudios de comunicación y tecnologías emergentes*, *12*(2), 295-317.

Espuma de Polietileno Superlon y Yumbolon. (n.d.). Retrieved from http://www.plastempack.com/empaque-y-embalaje/espuma-de-polietileno-superlony-jumbolon.html

Ewalt, D. M. (2013). Of Dice and Men: The Story of Dungeons and Dragons and the People Who Play It. In *American Journal of Play*. Scribner Book Company.

Facebook Technologies, L. L. C. (2019). *Oculus Developers*. Retrieved from https://developer.oculus.com/documentation/

Fan, J., McCandliss, B. D., Fossella, J., Flombaum, J. I., & Posner, M. I. (2005). The activation of attentional networks. *NeuroImage*, *26*(2), 471–479. doi:10.1016/j.neuroimage.2005.02.004 PMID:15907304

Fawcett, A., & Nicolson, R. (2016). *Test para la detección de la dislexia en niños (DST-J). 4ta. Edición*. Madrid: TEA Ediciones.

Feng, J., Lazar, J., Kumin, L., & Ozok, A. (2010). Computer Usage by Children with Down Syndrome: Challenges and Future Research. *ACM Transactions on Accessible Computing*, *2*(3), 13. doi:10.1145/1714458.1714460

Fernández, J. M. (2019). *Formación del profesorado para la incorporación de las TIC en alumnado con diversidad funcional*. Barcelona: Octaedro. doi:10.36006/116162

Ferrier, E. (2006). Multi-modal virtual environments for education with haptic and olfactory feedback. *Virtual Reality (Waltham Cross)*, 207–225.

Fidalgo, P., & Thormann, J. (2017). Reaching student in online courses using alternative formats. *International Review of Research in Open and Distributed Learning.*, *18*(2), 139–161. doi:10.19173/irrodl.v18i2.2601

Fischer, A., Vance, J. M., & Vo, D. M. (2009). Haptic feedback to guide interactive product design. *ASME-AFM 2009 World Conference on Innovative Virtual Reality (WINVR2009).*

FisherT. (2010). *Multipotentiality*. Retrieved from: http://blogs.edweek.org/teachers/unwrapping_the_gifted/2010/08/multipotentiality.html

Flavell, J. H., Green, F. L., & Flavell, E. R. (1995). The development of children's knowledge about attentional focus. *Developmental Psychology*, *31*(4), 706–712. doi:10.1037/0012-1649.31.4.706

Floyd, K. S., & Santiago, J. (2007). The State Of Website Accessibility In Higher Education. *Proceedings of the 2007 Southern Association for Information Systems Conference*, 109–113. Retrieved from http://sais.aisnet.org/2007/SAIS07-25 Floyd-Santiago.pdf

Foozy, M. F. C., Ahmad, R., Abdollah, F., Yusof, R., & Masud, Z. M. (2012). *Generic Taxonomy of Social Engineering Attack and Defence Mechanism for Handheld Computer Study*. Retrieved from http://www.icact.org/upload/2012/0452/20120452_Abstract_B.pdf

Ford, H., & Spielberg, S. (2014). *"Not Much To See": How the Blind Enjoy Movies* [Video Archive]. Retrieved from https://youtu.be/QJguIANUEX8

Forsyth, W. (2016). Globalized Random Procedural Content for Dungeon Generation. *Journal of Computing Sciences in Colleges.*

Fox, J. A., Hatfield, J. P., & Collins, T. C. (2003). Developing the Curriculum Transformation and Disability Workshop Model. In J. L. Higbee (Ed.), *Curriculum transformation and disability: Implementing Universal Design in higher education* (pp. 23–39). Minneapolis, MN: University of Minnesota, General College, Center for Research on Developmental Education and Urban Literacy. Retrieved from http://cehd.umn.edu/CRDEUL/books-ctad.html

Freina, L., & Ott, M. (2015). A Literature Review on Immersive Virtual Reality in Education: State Of The Art and Perspectives. *The International Scientific Conference eLearning and Software for Education*, 133-141.

Fuhrmann, S., & MacEachren, A. (2001). Navigation in Desktop Geovirtual Environments: Usability Assessment. *Proceedings of the 20th ICA/ACI International Cartographic Conference.*

Gagné, R. M., Briggs, L. J., & Wager, W. W. (1992). *Principles of instructional design* (4th ed.). Fort Worth, TX: Harcourt Brace Jovanovich College Publishers.

Game accessibility guidelines. (2017). Retrieved June 30, 2017, from http://gameaccessibilityguidelines.com/ensure-no-essential-information-is-conveyed-by-a-colour-alone

Gamma, E., Helm, R., Vlissides, J., & Johnson, R. (1995). *Design Patterns: Elements of Reusable Object-Oriented Software*. Addison-Wesley Proffessional Computing Series.

García Moreno, D. (2012). *Diseño de Sistemas de Orientación Espacial: Wayfinding* (p. 32). Madrid: Laboratorio Wayfinding. Retrieved from http://riberdis.cedd.net/bitstream/handle/11181/4640/dise%c3%b1o%20de%20sistemas%20de%20orientaci%c3%b3n%20espacial.pdf?sequence=1&rd=0031227065841978

García Rubio, J. (2006). *Historia de la lectoescritura en relieve*. Alicante: ONCE - C.R.E "Espíritu Santo" - Servicio de Producción de Recursos Didácticos y Tecnológicos. Retrieved from https://accedoalicante. wikispaces.com/file/view/Historia.pdf

García-Peñalvo, F. J., Fidalgo-Blanco, Á., & Sein-Echaluce, M. L. (2018). An adaptive hybrid MOOC model: Disrupting the MOOC concept in higher education. *Telematics and Informatics*, *35*(4), 1018–1030. doi:10.1016/j.tele.2017.09.012

Garda, M. B. (2013). Neo-rogue and the essence of roguelikeness. *Homo Ludens*, *1*(5), 59–72.

Gardner, H. (1983). Frames of Mind: The Theory of Multiple Intelligences. New York: Academic Press.

Gardner, H. (2011). *Frames of mind: The theory of multiple intelligences*. Hachette.

Gardner, H. (2018). Multiple approaches to understanding. In K. Illeris (Ed.), *Contemporary Theories of Learning* (pp. 129–138). Routledge. doi:10.4324/9781315147277-9

Gardner, H., & Hatch, T. (1989). Educational implications of the theory of multiple intelligences. *Educational Researcher*, *18*(8), 4–10.

Gasevic, D., Kovanovic, V., Joksimovic, S., & Siemens, G. (2014). Where is research on massive open online courses headed? A data analysis of the MOOC Research Initiative. *The International Review of Research in Open and Distributed Learning*, *15*(5). doi:10.19173/irrodl.v15i5.1954

Gee, J. P. (2003). *What video games have to teach us about learning and literacy*. New York: Palgrave Macmillan.

Georgios, N., Tzovaras, D., Moustakidis, S., & Strintzis, M. (2004). Cybergrasp and PHANTOM integration: enhanced haptic access for visually impaired users. *SPECOM-2004*, 507-513.

Ghannem, A. (2014). Characterization of Serious Games Guided by the Educational Objectives. *Proceedings of the Second International Conference on Technological Ecosystems for Enhancing Multiculturality*, 227–233.

Gikas, J., & Grant, M. M. (2013). Mobile computing devices in higher education: Student perspectives on learning with cellphones, smartphones & social media. *The Internet and Higher Education*, *19*, 18–26. doi:10.1016/j.iheduc.2013.06.002

Gil-Jaurena, I. (2015). MOOCs in Spain: preliminary lessons from UNED MOOCs experience. *MOOCs and educational challenges around Asia and Europe*, 191-204.

Girod, S., Keeve, E., & Girod, B. (1995). Advances in interactive craniofacial surgery planning by 3D simulation and visualization. *International Journal of Oral and Maxillofacial Surgery*, *24*(1), 120–125. doi:10.1016/S0901-5027(05)80872-0 PMID:7782646

Goegan, L. D., Radil, A. I., & Daniels, L. M. (2018). Accessibility in Questionnaire Research: Integrating Universal Design to Increase the Participation of Individuals with Learning Disabilities. *Learning Disabilities (Weston, Mass.)*, *16*(2), 177–190.

Goldfarb, R. (2006). *Ethics: A case study from fluency*. San Diego, CA: Plural Publishing.

Gomez, J., Bologna, G., & Pun, T. (2012). Spatial awareness and intelligibility for the blind: Audio-touch interfaces. *Human factors in computing systems*, 1529 – 1534.

Gomez, S. (2006). *Aproximaciones a una antropología del diseño.* Universidad Nacional de Colombia (Unimedios). Retrieved from: http://historico.unperiodico.unal.edu.co/Ediciones/95/15.html

Gomez, J. V., & Sandnes, F. E. (2012). RoboGuideDog: Guiding blind users through physical environments with laser range scanners. *Procedia Computer Science*, *14*, 218–225. doi:10.1016/j.procs.2012.10.025

Gómez, L. (2008). El desarrollo de la competencia lectora en los primeros grados de primaria. *Revista Latinoamericana de Estudios Educativos (México)*, *18*(4), 95–126.

González, A., & Farnós, J. D. (2009). Usabilidad y accesibilidad para un e-learning inclusivo. *Educació inclusiva*, 49-60.

Gotterbarn, D., Miller, K., & Rogerson, S. (1997). Software Engineering Code of Ethics. *Communications of the ACM*, *40*(11), 110–118. doi:10.1145/265684.265699

Gradel, K., & Edson, A. J. (2009). Putting Universal Design for Learning on the Higher Ed Agenda. *Journal of Educational Technology Systems*, *38*(2), 111–121. doi:10.2190/ET.38.2.d

Grammenos, D., Savidis, A., & Stephanidis, C. (2007). Unified Design of Universally Accessible Games. In Universal Access in Human-Computer Interaction. Applications and Services (pp. 607–616). Berlin: Springer Berlin Heidelberg. doi:10.1007/978-3-540-73283-9_67

Grammenos, D., Savidis, A., & Stephanidis, C. (2009). Designing universally accessible games. *Computers in Entertainment*, *7*(1), 1. doi:10.1145/1486508.1486516

Granollers, T., Lorés, J., & Perdrix, F. (2003). Usability Engineering Process Model. *Integration with Software Engineering. Proceeding HCI-International.*

Grossman, T., Fitzmaurice, G., & Ramtin, A. (2009). A survey of soft-ware Learnability: metrics, methodologies and guidelines. *Proceedings of the SIGCHI Conference on Human Factors in Computing Systems.*

Group, E. and O. W. (n.d.). *Easy Checks - A First Review of Web Accessibility.* Retrieved October 10, 2019, from https://www.w3.org/WAI/test-evaluate/preliminary/

Guàrdia, L., Maina, M., & Sangrà, A. (2013). MOOC design principles: A pedagogical approach from the learner's perspective. *eLearning Papers*, (33).

Guillén-Nieto, V., & Aleson-Carbonell, M. (2012). Serious games and learning effectiveness: The case of It's a Deal! *Computers & Education*, *58*(1), 435–448. doi:10.1016/j.compedu.2011.07.015

Gygax, B. G., & Arneson, D. (1974). *Dungeons & Dragons*. Academic Press.

Hadnagy, C. (2010). *Social engineering: The art of human hacking*. John Wiley & Sons.

Hadnagy, C. (2018). *Social Engineering: The Science of Human Hacking*. John Wiley & Sons. doi:10.1002/9781119433729

Hadnagy, C., Marin, A. M., & Wilson, P. (2011). *Ingeniería social. El arte del hacking personal*. Anaya Multimedia.

Haggard, S. (2013). Massive open online courses and online distance learning: review. *GOV. UK. Research and analysis, 18.*

Hanauer, D. (1999). Attention and literary education: A model of literary knowledge development. *Language Awareness*, *8*(1), 15–29. doi:10.1080/09658419908667114

Hartsook, K., Zook, A., Das, S., & Riedl, M. O. (2011). Toward supporting stories with procedurally generated game worlds. *2011 IEEE Conference on Computational Intelligence and Games, CIG 2011*, 297–304. 10.1109/CIG.2011.6032020

Hastings, E. J., Guha, R. K., & Stanley, K. O. (2009). Automatic content generation in the galactic arms race video game. *IEEE Transactions on Computational Intelligence and AI in Games*, *1*(4), 245–263. doi:10.1109/TCIAIG.2009.2038365

Haynes, A. S. (2019). Establishing Considerations for Universal Design for Learning and Accessibility in Online Courses. In M. Khosrow-Pour, D.B.A. (Ed.), Handbook of Research on Challenges and Opportunities in Launching a Technology-Driven International University (pp. 69-90). Hershey, PA: IGI Global. doi:10.4018/978-1-5225-6255-9.ch005

Henderson, M., & Kattethota, G. (1999). Manufacturability evaluation for rapid fabrication: A system for traditional machining and layered manufacturing planning. *CAD Conference*, Neuchatel, Switzerland.

Hendrikx, M., Meijer, S., Van Der Velden, J., & Iosup, A. (2013). Procedural content generation for Games: A Survey. *ACM Transactions on Multimedia Computing Communications and Applications*, *9*(1), 1–22. doi:10.1145/2422956.2422957

Henry, S. (2008). *Realización de las pruebas de usabilidad | La accesibilidad en el proceso de DCU | Simplemente pregunta: Integración de la accesibilidad en el proceso de diseño*. Retrieved from http://www.uiaccess.com/JustAsk/es/ut_conduct.html

Herro, D., Kiger, D., & Owens, C. (2013). Mobile technology: Case-Based Suggestions for Classroom Integration and Teacher Educators. *Journal of Digital Learning in Teacher Education*, *30*(1), 30–40. doi:10.1080/21532974.2013.10784723

He, Y. (2014). Universal Design for Learning in an Online Teacher Education Course: Enhancing Learners' Confidence to Teach Online. *Journal of Online Learning and Teaching / MERLOT*, *10*(2), 283–298.

Heydarian, A., Pantazis, E., Wang, A., Gerber, D., & Becerik-Gerbera, B. (2017). Towards user centered building design: Identifying end-user lighting preferences via immersive virtual environments. *Automation in Construction*, *81*(September), 56–66. doi:10.1016/j.autcon.2017.05.003

Hidalgo, M., & Mendez, B. (2000). *Detección de Problemas de Aprendizaje*. San José, Costa Rica: Universidad Estatal a Distancia.

Hilera, J. R., Motz, R., & Silvana, T. (2019). *Guía Metodológica para la Implantación de Desarrollos Curriculares Virtuales Accesibles*. Retrieved from www.esvial.org/

Hill, P. (2012). Online educational delivery models: A descriptive view. *EDUCAUSE Review*, *47*(6), 84–86.

Hims. (2019). *Braille EDGE*. Retrieved from http://www.hims-inc.com/product/braille-edge-40/

Hobbs, N. (1948). The development of a code of ethical standards for psychology. *The American Psychologist*, *3*(3), 80–84. doi:10.1037/h0060281

Holbrook, M. C., & Koening, A. J. (Eds.). (2003). Foundations of education. Volume II. Instructional Strategies for Teaching Children and Youth with Visual Impairments. AFB Press.

Holbrook, M. C., & Koening, A. J. (2003). Foundations of education.: Vol. II. *Instructional Strategies for Teaching Children*. New York: AFB Press.

Holotescu, C., Grosseck, G., Creţu, V., & Naaji, A. (2014). Integrating MOOCs in blended courses. *Elearning & Software for Education*, (1).

Howell, J., & Ostashewski, N. (2015). MOOCifying courses: real and authentic learning in higher education. In EdMedia+ Innovate Learning (pp. 1663-1668). Association for the Advancement of Computing in Education (AACE).

Hoyos, C. A., Ayres, I. M. E., Kloos, C. D., Román, J. V., Merino, P. J. M., & Pérez, E. L. (2019). Redesigning a freshman engineering course to promoteactive learning by flipping the classroom through thereuse of MOOcs. *International Journal of Engineering Education*, *35*(1), 385–396.

Hsiu-Mei, H., & Shu-Sheng, L. (2018). An Analysis of Learners' Intentions Toward Virtual Reality Learning Based on Constructivist and Technology Acceptance Approaches. *International Review of Research in Open and Distributed Learning*, 91-115.

Hudson, J. (2017). Putting learning experience design into workplace learning. *Training & Development*, *44*(5), 7.

Huge payout in US stuttering case. (n.d.). *BBC World News*. Retrieved from http://news.bbc.co.uk/2/hi/americas/6952446.stm

Huotari, K., & Hamari, J. (2016). A definition for gamification: Anchoring gamification in the service marketing literature. *Electronic Markets*, 1–11.

Hu, R., Feng, J., Lazar, J., & Kumin, L. (2013). Investigating input technologies for children and young adults with Down syndrome. *Universal Access in the Information Society*, *12*(1), 89–104. doi:10.100710209-011-0267-3

Iglesias, A., Moreno, L., Martinez, P., & Calvo, R. (2014). Evaluating the accessibility of three open-source learning content management systems: A comparative study. *Computer Applications in Engineering Education*, *22*(2), 320–328. doi:10.1002/cae.20557

IMS. (2003). IMS Global Learning Consortium (2003). *IMS Learner Information Package Accessibility for LIP. Version 1*. Retrieved from http://www.imsglobal.org/accessibility/#acclip

IMS. (2004). IMS Global Learning Consortium (2004). *IMS AccessForAll Meta-data Specification. Version 1*. Retrieved from http://www.imsglobal.org/accessibility/#accmd

IMS. (2009). IMS Global Learning Consortium (2012). *IMS AccessForAll v2.0 Final Specification*. Retrieved from http://www.imsglobal.org/accessibility/#accDRD

IMS. (2012). IMS Global Learning Consortium, Inc. (2012). *IMS Access For All Version 3.0*. Retrieved from http://imsglobal.org/accessibility

INEGI. (2010). *Instituto Nacional de Estadística y Geografía*. INEGI.

Iñesta, R. (2002). *Psicología del Aprendizaje*. El Manual Moderno.

Iniesto, F., & Rodrigo, C. (2018). YourMOOC4all: a MOOCs inclusive design and useful feedback research project. In 2018 Learning With MOOCS (LWMOOCS) (pp. 147-150). IEEE. doi:10.1109/LWMOOCS.2018.8534644

Iniesto, F., McAndrew, P., Minocha, S., & Coughlan, T. (2016). Accessibility of MOOCs: Understanding the Provider Perspective. *Journal of Interactive Media in Education*, *2016*(1), 20. doi:10.5334/jime.430

Institute of Electrical and Electronics Engineers (IEEE). (2002). *IEEE 1484.12.1-2002 Learning Object Metadata (LOM)*. Retrieved from http://ltsc.ieee.org

Interaction Design Foundations. (2018). *User Experience (UX) Design*. Retrieved from: https://www.interaction-design.org/literature/topics/ux-design

International Game Developers Association (IGDA) — Game, & Accessibility SIG. (2004). *Accessibility in Games: Motivations and Approaches*. Retrieved February 5, 2018, from http://g3ict.org/download/p/fileId_776/productId_50

International Standard Organization. (2008). *ISO/IEC 24751:2008, Information technology -- Individualized adaptability and accessibility in e-learning, education and training*. Author.

International Standard Organization. (2008a). *ISO/IEC 24751-1:2008, Information Technology -- Individualized Adaptability and Accessibility in e-Learning, Education and Training -- Part 1: Framework and Reference Model*. Retrieved from http://www.iso.org/cms/render/live/en/sites/isoorg/contents/data/standard/04/15/41521.html

International Standard Organization. (2008b). *ISO/IEC 24751-2:2008, Information Technology -- Individualized Adaptability and Accessibility in e-Learning, Education and Training -- Part 2: "Access for All" Personal Needs and Preferences for Digital Delivery.* Retrieved from http://www.iso.org/cms/render/live/en/sites/isoorg/contents/data/standard/04/36/43603.html

International Standard Organization. (2008c). *ISO/IEC 24751-3:2008, Information Technology -- Individualized Adaptability and Accessibility in e-Learning, Education and Training -- Part 3: "Access for All" Digital Resource Description.* Retrieved from http://www.iso.org/cms/render/live/en/sites/isoorg/contents/data/standard/04/36/43604.html

International Standard Organization. (2009). *ISO/IEC 19796-3:2009, Information Technology -- Learning, Education and Training -- Quality Management, Assurance and Metrics -- Part 3: Reference Methods and Metrics.* Retrieved from http://www.iso.org/cms/render/live/en/sites/isoorg/contents/data/standard/04/61/46159.html

International Standard Organization. (2012). *ISO/IEC 40500:2012, Information Technology -- W3C Web Content Accessibility Guidelines (WCAG) 2.0.* Retrieved from http://www.iso.org/cms/render/live/en/sites/isoorg/contents/data/standard/05/86/58625.html

International Standard Organization. (2015). *ISO/IEC 19778-3:2015, Information technology -- Learning, education and training -- Collaborative technology -- Collaborative workplace -- Part 3: Collaborative group data model.* Retrieved from http://www.iso.org/cms/render/live/en/sites/isoorg/contents/data/standard/06/50/65099.html

International Standard Organization. (2018). *ISO 9241-11:2018 - Ergonomics of human-system interaction -- Part 11: Usability: Definitions and concepts.* Retrieved from https://www.iso.org/standard/63500.html

International Standard Organization. (2018). *ISO 9241-11:2018, Ergonomics of human-system interaction -- Part 11: Usability: Definitions and concepts.* Retrieved from https://www.iso.org/standard/63500.html

International Standard Organization. (2019). *ISO 9241-210:2019 - Ergonomics of human-system interaction -- Part 210: Human-centred design for interactive systems.* ISO.

Internet Encyclopedia of Philosophy. A Peer-Reviewed Academic Resource. (n.d.). Retrieved from https://www.iep.utm.edu/ethics/

Iosup, A. (2009). *POGGI: Puzzle-based online games on grid infrastructures.* Lecture Notes in Computer Science. doi:10.1007/978-3-642-03869-3_39

Irani, D., Balduzzi, M., Balzarotti, D., Kirda, E., & Pu, C. (2011). Reverse social engineering attacks in online social networks. Lecture Notes in Computer Science, 6739, 55–74. doi:10.1007/978-3-642-22424-9_4

Ismailova, R., & Inal, Y. (2018). Accessibility evaluation of top university websites: A comparative study of Kyrgyzstan, Azerbaijan, Kazakhstan and Turkey. *Universal Access in the Information Society, 17*(2), 437–445. doi:10.100710209-017-0541-0

ISO 9241-11: *Ergonomic requirements for office work with visual display terminals* (VDTs) - Part 11 Guidance on usability (1998) Retrieved from https://www.iso.org/standard/16883.html

ISO. (2008). *ISO/IEC 24751-2:2008, Information technology -- Individualized adaptability and accessibility in e-learning, education and training -- Part 2: "Access for all" personal needs and preferences for digital.* Geneva, Switzerland: International Standard Organization.

ISO. (2012). *ISO/IEC 40500, Information technology -- W3C Web Content Accessibility Guidelines (WCAG) 2.0. Ginebra.* International Organization for Standardization.

ITA. (2019). *Modelo Educativo.* Retrieved from http://www.itaguascalientes.edu.mx/site/modelo.php

Izzo, M. V., Murray, A., & Novak, J. (2008). The Faculty Perspective on Universal Design for Learning. *Journal of Postsecondary Education and Disability, 21*(2), 60–72.

Jakobsson, M., & Myers, S. (Eds.). (2016). *Phishing and Countermeasures: Understanding the Increasing Problem of Electronic Identity Theft.* Wiley.

Jang, Y., & Ryu, S. (2011). Exploring game experiences and game leadership in massively multiplayer online role-playing games. *British Journal of Educational Technology, 42*(4), 616–623. doi:10.1111/j.1467-8535.2010.01064.x

Jaramillo-Alcázar, A., & Luján-Mora, S. (2017). Mobile Serious Games: An Accessibility Assessment for People with Visual Impairments. In Proceedings of the 5th International Conference on Technological Ecosystems for Enhancing Multiculturality - TEEM 2017 (pp. 1–6). New York: ACM Press. 10.1145/3144826.3145416

Jaramillo-Alcazar, A., Guaita, C., Rosero, J. L., & Lujan-Mora, S. (2018). Towards an Accessible Mobile Serious Game for Electronic Engineering Students with Hearing Impairments. In *2018 IEEE World Engineering Education Conference (EDUNINE)* (pp. 1–5). IEEE. 10.1109/EDUNINE.2018.8450948

Jaramillo-Alcázar, A., & Luján-Mora, S. (2018). *An Approach to Mobile Serious Games Accessibility Assessment for People with Hearing Impairments.* Cham: Springer; doi:10.1007/978-3-319-73450-7_52

Jaramillo-Alcázar, A., Luján-Mora, S., & Salvador-Ullauri, L. (2017a). A Mobile Serious Games Assessment Tool for People with Motor Impairments. *International Conference on Education Technology and Computers.* doi:10.1145/3175536.3175569

Jaramillo-Alcázar, A., Luján-Mora, S., & Salvador-Ullauri, L. (2017b). Accessibility Assessment of Mobile Serious Games for People with Cognitive Impairments. *International Conference on Information Systems and Computer Science.* doi:10.1109/INCISCOS.2017.12

Jayaram, S., Connacher, H., & Lyons, K. (1997). Virtual assembly using virtual reality techniques. *Computer Aided Design, 29*(8), 575–584. doi:10.1016/S0010-4485(96)00094-2

Jiménez-González, S. G., Mendoza-González, R., & Luna-García, H. (2018). Guidelines Based on Need-Findings Study and Communication Types to Design Interactions for MOOCs. In F. Cipolla-Ficarra (Ed.), *Optimizing Human-Computer Interaction With Emerging Technologies.* doi:10.4018/978-1-5225-2616-2.ch008

Johnson, L., Yannakakis, G. N., & Togelius, J. (2010). Cellular automata for real-time generation of infinite cave levels. *Workshop on Procedural Content Generation in Games, PC Games 2010, Co-Located with the 5th International Conference on the Foundations of Digital Games.* 10.1145/1814256.1814266

Johnson, M. R. (2017). The Use of ASCII Graphics in Roguelikes: Aesthetic Nostalgia and Semiotic Difference. *Games and Culture, 12*(2), 115–135. doi:10.1177/1555412015585884

Jordan, K. (2015). Massive open online course completion rates revisited: Assessment, length and attrition. *The International Review of Research in Open and Distributed Learning, 16*(3). doi:10.19173/irrodl.v16i3.2112

Kamppari-Miller, S. (2017, April 6). *Vr Sketch Sheets.* Retrieved from Prototypr.io: http://blog.prototypr.io/vr-sketch-sheets-4843fd690c91

Kangas, E. and Kinnunen, T. (2005). Applying user-centered design to mobile application development. *Communications of the ACM-Designing for the Mobile Device, 48*(7), 55-59.

Kato, T. (1986). What question-asking protocols can say about the user interface. *International Journal of Man-Machine Studies, 25*(6), 659–673. doi:10.1016/S0020-7373(86)80080-3

Katz, R. V., Kegeles, S. S., Kressin, N. R., Green, B. L., Wang, M. Q., James, S. A., ... Claudio, C. (2006). The Tuskegee Legacy Project: Willingness of Minorities to Participate in Biomedical Research. *Journal of Health Care for the Poor and Underserved, 17*(4), 698–715. doi:10.1353/hpu.2006.0126 PMID:17242525

Kaur, S., Kaur, K., & Kaur, P. (2016). An empirical performance evaluation of universities website. *International Journal of Computers and Applications, 146*(15), 53–62.

Kear, K., Rosewell, J., Williams, K., Ossiannilsson, E., Rodrigo, C., Sánchez-Elvira, P., … Mellar, H. (2016). *Quality assessment for e-learning: A benchmarking approach*. Academic Press.

Kelly, G., & McCabe, H. (2007). Citygen: An interactive system for procedural city generation. *Fifth International Conference on Game Design and Technology*.

Kennedy, W., & Yun, J. (2019). Universal Design for Learning as a Curriculum Development Tool in Physical Education. *Journal of Physical Education, Recreation & Dance, 90*(6), 25–31. doi:10.1080/07303084.2019.1614119

Kent, S. L. (2001). *The Ultimate History of Video Games: From Pong to Pokémon and Beyond - The Story Behind the Craze that Touched our Lives and Changed the World*. New York: Three Rivers Press.

Kerr, B. A., & Gahm, J. (2018). *Developing talents in girls and young women*. Academic Press.

Kim, Y.-S., Collins, M., Bulmer, W., Sharma, S., & Mayrose, J. (2016). Haptics Assisted Training (HAT) System for children's handwriting. *IEEE World Haptics Conference*, 6.

Kinash, S., Crichton, S., & Kim-Rupnow, W. S. (2004). A Review of 2000-2003 Literature at the Intersection of Online Learning and Disability. *American Journal of Distance Education, 18*(1), 5–19. doi:10.120715389286ajde1801_2

Kirijian, A., Myers, M., & Charland, S. (2007). Web Fun Central: online learning tools for individuals with Down syndrome. In *Universal Usability: Designing Information Systems for Diverse User Populations*. Chichester, UK: John Wiley & Sons.

Klemer, S. (2016). *Human Centered Design Course: Design Principles, Class Notes*. Obtenido de Coursera Inc.: https://www.coursera.org/learn/design-principles

Kohno, I., Yasu, H., & Sugawara, S. (2013). Design, A proposal and validation of cost benefit analysis method of User-Centered. Design, Chiba University, 1-10.

Koller, D. (2012). How online courses can form a basis for on-campus teaching. *Forbes*. Retrieved from http://www.forbes.com/sites/coursera/2012/11/07/how-online-courses-can-form-a-basis-for-on-campus-teaching/

Konstantinos, P., Panagiotis, K., Eleni, K., Marina, M., Asimis, V., & Valari, E. (2015). Audio-Haptic Map: An Orientation and Mobility Aid for Individuals with Blindness. *Procedia Computer Science, 67*, 223–230. doi:10.1016/j.procs.2015.09.266

KopievG. (2019). *N+1*. Retrieved from https://nmas1.org/news/2018/02/16/realidadvirtual-ciegos

Koster, R. (2013). *A theory of fun for game design*.

Koukourikos, P., & Papadopoulos, K. (2015). Development of Cognitive Maps by Individuals with Blindness Using a Multisensory Application. *Procedia Computer Science, 67*, 213–222. doi:10.1016/j.procs.2015.09.265

Krombholz, K., Hobel, H., Huber, M., & Weippl, E. (2015). Advanced social engineering attacks. *Journal of Information Security and Applications, 22*, 113–122. doi:10.1016/j.jisa.2014.09.005

Kulwinder, K. (1998). *Designing Virtual Environments for Usability*. PhD Thesis.

Kumar, D. D., Ramasamy, R., & Stefanich, G. P. (2001). Science for Students with Visual Impairments: Teaching Suggestions and Policy Implications for Secondary Educators. *Electronic Journal of Science Education*, *5*, 3. Retrieved April 9, 2019, from http://unr.edu/homepage/crowther/ejse/kumar2etal.html

Kumin, L., Lazar, J., Feng, J., Wentz, B., & Ekedebe, N. (2012). Syndrome, A Usability Evaluation of Workplace-Related Tasks on a Multi-Touch Tablet Computer by Adults with Down. *Journal of Usability Studies*, *7*(4), 118–142.

La Presidencia, M. D. E., & Con Las Cortes Igualdad, R. E. (2018). *I. Disposiciones generales ministerio de la presidencia, relaciones con las cortes e igualdad*. Retrieved from http://www.boe.es

Laabidi, M., Jemni, M., Ayed, L. J. B., Brahim, H. B., & Jemaa, A. B. (2014). Learning technologies for people with disabilities. *Journal of King Saud University-Computer and Information Sciences*, *26*(1), 29–45. doi:10.1016/j.jksuci.2013.10.005

Ladner, S. (2014). *Practical Ethinography: A guide to doing Ethnography in Private Sector*. Walnut Creek, CA: Left Coast Press, Inc.

Lahav, O., Hagab, N., Kader, S. A. E., Levy, S. T., & Talis, V. (2018). Listen to the models: Sonified learning models for people who are Blind. *Computers & Education*, *127*, 141–153. doi:10.1016/j.compedu.2018.08.020

Lahav, O., & Mioduser, D. (2008a). Construction of cognitive maps of unknown spaces using a multi-sensory virtual environment for people who are blind. *Computers in Human Behavior*, *24*(3), 1139–1155. doi:10.1016/j.chb.2007.04.003

Lahav, O., & Mioduser, D. (2008b). Haptic-feedback support for cognitive mapping of unknown spaces by people who are blind. Int. *J. Human-Computer Studies*, *66*(1), 23–35. doi:10.1016/j.ijhcs.2007.08.001

Lane, C. (2008). *The distance learning technology resource guide*. Retrieved from https://www.tecweb.org/styles/gardner.html

Lazar, J., Kumin, L., & Feng, J. (2011). Understanding the computer skills of adult expert users with down syndrome: an exploratory study. International ACM SIGACCESS conference on Computers and Accessibility.

LeCompte, M., & Schensul, J. (2010). Designing & Conducting Ethnographic Research: The Ethnographer's Toolkit. Plymouth, UK: Rowman & Littlefield Publishers, Inc.

Lee, K. (2017). Rethinking the accessibility of online higher education: A historical review. *The Internet and Higher Education*, *33*, 15–23. doi:10.1016/j.iheduc.2017.01.001

Lee, S. H., & Song, D. H. (2019). Functional usability analysis of top Korean mobile role playing games based on user interface design. *Indones. J. Electr. Eng. Comput. Sci*, *13*(1), 123. doi:10.11591/ijeecs.v13.i1.pp123-128

Lefebvre, S., & Neyret, F. (2003). Pattern based procedural textures. Proceedings of the Symposium on Interactive 3D Graphics. 10.1145/641514.641518

Leiva, C. (2016). Conductismo, cognitivismo y aprendizaje. *Tecnología en Marcha*, *18*, 66–73.

Letón, E., & Molanes-Lopez, E. M. (2014). Two New Concepts in Video Podcasts-Minimalist Slides and Modular Teaching Mini-videos. *CSEDU,* (2), 292-297.

Liébana, M. (2000). *Aspectos evolutivos y educativos de la deficiencia visual*. Madrid: ONCE.

Lim, T., Medellin, H., Sung, R., Ritchie, J. M., & Corney, J. (2009). Virtual bloxing assembly rapid prototyping of near net shapes. *ASME-AFM 2009 World Conference on Innovative Virtual Reality (WINVR2009).*

Linja aho, M. (2006). Creating a Framework for Improving the Learnability of a Complex System. *Journal of Human Technology, 2*(2), 202-224.

Littlejohn, A., Hood, N., Milligan, C., & Mustain, P. (2016). Learning in MOOCs: Motivations and self-regulated learning in MOOCs. *The Internet and Higher Education, 29*, 40–48. doi:10.1016/j.iheduc.2015.12.003

Liyanagunawardena, T. R., Parslow, P., & Williams, S. (2014). Dropout: MOOC participants' perspective. *Proceedings of the European MOOC Stakeholder Summit, 2014*, 95–100.

Long, J. (2008). No tech hacking: A guide to social engineering, dumpster diving, and shoulder surfing (Syngress, Ed.). Elsevier.

Lopes, R., & Bidarra, R. (2011). Adaptivity challenges in games and simulations: A survey. *IEEE Transactions on Computational Intelligence and AI in Games, 3*(2), 85–99. doi:10.1109/TCIAIG.2011.2152841

Lucio, M., Juárez, R., & Medellín, C. (2015). Desarrollo de Algoritmos de Manipulación e Interacción Háptica para la Enseñanza-Aprendizaje de personas con Discapacidad Visual. *Inducción a la Ciencia, la tecnología y la innovación en la UASLP*, 918-924.

Mack, R., & Robinson, J. (1992). When novices elicit knowledge: question asking in designing evaluating and learning to use software. In The psychology of expertise: cognitive research and empirical AI (págs. 245-268). Springer-Verlag. doi:10.1007/978-1-4613-9733-5_15

Mack, R. L., Lewis, C. H., & Carroll, J. M. (1983). Learning to use word processors: Problems and prospects. *ACM Transactions on Information Systems, 1*(3), 254–271. doi:10.1145/357436.357440

Macukow, B., & Homenda, W. (2006). Methods of Artificial Intelligence in Blind People Education. In L. Rutkowski, R. Tadeusiewicz, L. A. Zadeh, & J. M. Żurada (Eds.), Lecture Notes in Computer Science: Vol. 4029. *Artificial Intelligence and Soft Computing – ICAISC 2006. ICAISC 2006*. Berlin: Springer. doi:10.1007/11785231_123

Maisak, R., & Brown, J. (2014). Web accessibility on Thai higher education Websites. *Proceedings of the Ninth International Conference on Software Engineering Advances.*

Manca, M., & Paternò, F. (2014) Considering task pre-conditions in model-based user interface design and generation. *Proceedings ACM SIGCHI Symposium on Engineering Interactive*, 149-154. 10.1145/2607023.2610283

Manso-Callejo, M., Wachowicz, M., & Bernabé-Poveda, M. (2010). The Design of an Automated Workflow for Metadata Generation. In S. Sánchez-Alonso & I. N. Athanasiadis (Eds.), *In Metadata and Semantic Research. MTSR 2010. Communications in Computer and Information Science* (Vol. 108). Berlin, Heidelberg: Springer. doi:10.1007/978-3-642-16552-8_25

MARC21. (2010). *MARC 21 format for bibliographic records.* NIPO: 032-15-027-1. Retrieved from http://www.bne.es/es/Micrositios/Guias/

Marín-Ramos, E. (2018). Blade Runner, de 2019 a 2049. El cine de ciencia ficción como divulgador de la ciencia. *In-Mediaciones de la Comunicación, 13*(2), 187–211. doi:10.18861/ic.2018.13.2.2873

Markets and Markets. (n.d.). *Serious Game Market worth $5,448.82 Million by 2020.* Retrieved July 14, 2017, from http://www.marketsandmarkets.com/PressReleases/serious-game.asp

Marshall, S. (2006). *E-Learning Maturity Model Version Two: New Zealand Tertiary Institution E-Learning Capability: Informing and Guiding E-Learning Architectural Change and Development Project Report.* Report to the New Zealand Ministry of Education.

Martínez, A. (2009). El diseño instruccional en la educación a distancia. Un acercamiento a los Modelos. *Apertura Review, 9*(10), 104-119.

Martínez, L. (2012). *Sistemas de educación especial.* Estado de México: Red Tercer Milenio.

McCreath, G., & Cuthbertson, J. (2005). Using digital technology to improve access to learning. *International Congress Series, 1282*, 956–959. doi:10.1016/j.ics.2005.05.144

McCurley, V. (2016, May 22). *Storyboarding in Virtual Reality.* Retrieved from Virtual Reality Pop: http://virtualrealitypop.com/storyboarding-in-virtual-reality-67d3438a2fb1

McDaniel, R., & Telep, P. (2009). Best Practices for Integrating Game-Based Learning into Online Teaching. *Journal of Online Learning and Teaching / MERLOT.*

Mcguire, J., Scott, S., & Shaw, S. (2006). Universal Design and Its Applications in Educational Environments. *Remedial and Special Education, 27*(3), 167. Retrieved from http://journals.sagepub.com/doi/pdf/10.1177/07419325060270030501

McGuire, J. M., & Scott, S. S. (2006). Universal Design for instruction: Extending the universal paradigm to college instruction. *Journal of Postsecondary education and Disability, 19*(2), 124–134.

McHugh, M. L. (2012). Interrater reliability: The kappa statistic. *Biochemia Medica, 22*(3), 276–282. doi:10.11613/BM.2012.031 PMID:23092060

McLaren, R. (2018). *Virtual Learning Environments Making the most of the new regulations.* Technology & Innovation at Policy Connect.

Medellin, C., Gallegos, N., & Espinoza, C. (2015). Desarrollo de un sistema de realidad virtual asistido por dispositivos hápticos para la enseñanza-aprendizaje del sistema Braille. *Revista de Prototipos Tecnológicos, 1*(1), 10–22.

Medellín-Castillo, H. I., Martínez-Hernández, C. A., Espinosa-Castañeda, R. & Castañeda-Roldán, C. Y. (2011). Desarrollo de un Sistema de Proyección de Películas Virtuales para Gente Invidente. *Impulso, 4*(2).

Media, L. T. (2004). *Guidelines for the development of entertaining software for people with multiple learning disabilities.* Retrieved July 12, 2017, from http://www.medialt.no/rapport/entertainment_guidelines/index.htm

Merhi, O., Faugloire, E., Flanagan, M., & Stoffregen, T. A. (2007). Motion sickness, console video games, and head-mounted displays. *Human Factors, 49*(5), 920–934. doi:10.1518/001872007X230262 PMID:17915607

Meusel, R., Petrovski, P., & Bizer, C. (2014). The WebDataCommons Microdata, RDFa and microformat dataset series. In *13th International Semantic Web Conference (ISWC '14) - Part I,* 277-292. DOI: 10.1007/978-3-319-11964-9_18

Meyer, A., Rose, D. H., & Gordon, D. (2013). *Universal design for learning. Theory and practice.* Wakefield, MA: Center for Applied Special Technology. Retrieved from http://udltheorypractice.cast.org/login

Miao, M., Pham, H., Friebe, J., & Weber, G. (2014). Contrasting usability evaluation methods with blind users. *Universal Access in the Information Society, 15*(1), 66.

Michael, D., David, R., & Chen, S. L. (2006). *Serious games : games that educate, train and inform.* Thomson Course Technology. Retrieved from https://dl.acm.org/citation.cfm?id=1051239

Microsoft Corporation. (2019). *Mixed Reality Design.* Retrieved from https://docs.microsoft.com/en-us/windows/mixed-reality/design

Microsoft Office. (2019). *Crear documentos de Word accesibles para personas con discapacidades.* Retrieved from https://support.office.com/es-es/article/crear-documentos-de-word-accesibles-para-personas-con-discapacidades-d9bf3683-87ac-47ea-b91a-78dcacb3c66d

Milne, L. R., Bennett, C. L., Ladner, R. E., & Azenkot, S. (2014). BraillePlay. In *Proceedings of the 16th international ACM SIGACCESS conference on Computers & accessibility - ASSETS '14* (pp. 137–144). New York: ACM Press. 10.1145/2661334.2661377

Mirri, S., Pantieri, D., Roccetti, M., & Salomoni, P. (2006). A multimedia broker for accessible learning objects transcoding. In Information and Communication Technologies, 2006. ICTTA'06 (Vol. 1, pp. 641-646). IEEE. doi:10.1109/ICTTA.2006.1684447

Mirri, S., Salomoni, P., Roccetti, M., & Gay, G. R. (2011). *Beyond standards: unleashing accessibility on a learning content management system. In Transactions on edutainment V* (pp. 35–49). Berlin: Springer.

Mize, M., Bryant, D. P., & Bryant, B. R. (2019b). Teaching reading to students with learning disabilities: Effects of combined iPad-assisted and peer-assisted instruction on oral reading fluency performance. *Assistive Technology Journal, 15*, 1–8. PMID:30640569

Mize, M., Park, Y., & Schramm-Possinger, M. (2019a). *Developing a Rubric for Evaluating Reading Applications for Learners With Reading Difficulties, Intervention in School and Clinic.* SAGE Publications Inc.

Molist, M. (2014). *El eslabón más débil en seguridad informática eres tú.* Retrieved October 20, 2019, from enero 20 website: https://www.elmundo.es/tecnologia/2014/01/18/52d90707ca4741f2798b4570.html

Montgomery, A., & Mallette, L. (2018, October). Massive Open Online Courses: Misperceptions of Completion Rates The Misalignment of Measurements and Actual Participation. In *E-Learn: World Conference on E-Learning in Corporate, Government, Healthcare, and Higher Education* (pp. 850-857). Association for the Advancement of Computing in Education (AACE).

Moodle. (2019). *Accesibilidad.* Retrieved from https://docs.moodle.org/all/es/Accesibilidad

Moodle. (2019). *Especificación de accesibilidad Moodle.* Retrieved from http://docs.moodle.org/dev/Moodle_Accessibility_Specification

Moorefield-Lang, H., Copeland, C. A., & Haynes, A. (2016). Accessing abilities: Creating innovative accessible online learning environments and putting quality into practice. *Education for Information, 32*(1), 27–33. doi:10.3233/EFI-150966

Moran, S., & Gardner, H. (2018). *Hill, skill, and will: executive function from a multiple-intelligences perspective.* Academic Press.

Morrison, D. (2013). *A MOOC Quality Scorecard applied to Coursera Course.* Retrieved from http://onlinelearninginsights.wordpress.com/2013/06/15/a-mooc-quality-scorecard-applied-to-courseracourse

Moses, L. E. (1986). *Think and Explain with Statistics.* Penguin Books Australia.

Mouton, F., Leenen, L., & Venter, H. S. (2016). Social engineering attack examples, templates and scenarios. *Computers & Security, 59*(March), 186–209. doi:10.1016/j.cose.2016.03.004

Mudler, F. (2013). OER reflections on Opening up Education (OuE). In Neth-ER Seminar, EU Parliament, Brussels, Belgium.

Mujber, T. S., Szecsi, T., & Hashmi, M. S. J. (2004). Virtual reality applications in manufacturing process simulation. *Journal of Materials Processing Technology, 155-156*, 1834–1838. doi:10.1016/j.jmatprotec.2004.04.401

Muntean, C. (2011). Raising engagement in e-learning through gamification. *Proceedings of the 6th International Conference on Virtual Learning*, 323-329.

Navarrete, R., & Lujan-Mora, S. (2018). Microdata with Schema vocabulary: Improvement search results visualization of open educational resources. *13th Iberian Conference on Information Systems and Technologies (CISTI)*, 1-6. 10.23919/CISTI.2018.8399222

Neisser, U., Boodoo, G., Bouchard, T. J. Jr, Boikin, A. W., Brody, N. C., Stephen, J., ... Sternberg, R. (1996). Intelligence: Knowns and Unknowns. *The American Psychologist*, *51*(2), 77–101. doi:10.1037/0003-066X.51.2.77

Nester, H., & Buford, M. (2018). *Multipotentiality: Finding a career path that reflects who you truly are.* Retrieved from: https://www.ceiainc.org/wp-content/uploads/2018/02/Exp_Spring18_07_NesterBuford.pdf

NeuroDigital. (2018). *Touching Master Pieces.* Retrieved from https://touchingmasterpieces.com/

Nian-Feng, L.-R. (2011). A kind of Braille paper automatic marking system. *Conference on Mechatronic Science, Electric Engineering and Computer.* 10.1109/MEC.2011.6025553

Niederhauser, D., & Stoddart, T. (2000). Teachers' instructional perspectives and use of educational software. *Teaching and Teacher Education*, 15–31.

Nielsen, J. (1995). *10 usability heuristics for user interface design.* Nielsen Norman Group.

Nielsen, J. (2012). *How Many Test Users in a Usability Study?* Retrieved from https://www.nngroup.com/articles/how-many-test-users/

Nielsen, J. (2017). *A 100-Year View of User Experience.* Retrieved from: https://www.nngroup.com/articles/100-years-ux/

Nielsen, J. (1994). *Usability Engineering.* Academic Press.

NISO. (2004). Understanding Metadata. NISO Press.

Nobbot. (2019). *Dot Watch, el primer reloj inteligete en braille.* Retrieved from https://www.nobbot.com/general/dot-watch-braille/

Nobre, A. C., & Van Ede, F. (2018). Anticipated moments: Temporal structure in attention. *Nature Reviews. Neuroscience*, *19*(1), 34–48. doi:10.1038/nrn.2017.141 PMID:29213134

Nunez, J. L. M., Caro, E. T., & Gonzalez, J. R. H. (2016). From higher education to open education: Challenges in the transformation of an online traditional course. *IEEE Transactions on Education*, *60*(2), 134–142. doi:10.1109/TE.2016.2607693

NVDA. (2019). *NV Access LimitedNVDA.* Retrieved from https://www.nvaccess.org/about-nvda/

Offit, P. (n.d.). *Vaccinated: One Man's Quest to Defeat the World's Deadliest Diseases. Academic Press.*

Ogletree, S. M., & Drake, R. (2007). College students' video game participation and perceptions: Gender differences and implications. *Sex Roles*, *56*(7-8), 537–542. doi:10.100711199-007-9193-5

Opie, J. (2018). Educating students with vision impairment today: Consideration of the expanded core curriculum. *British Journal of Visual Impairment*, *36*(1), 75–89. doi:10.1177/0264619617730861

Ortiz-Alvarado, F., Espinosa-Castañeda, R., Vargas-Neri, J., & Rodrígues-Arellano, S. (2017). Divulgación científica y cultural: El diseño sonoro 4.1. *Revista de Sociología Contemporánea*, *4*(12), 1–11.

Ortiz-Alvarado, F., Espinosa-Castañeda, R., Vargas-Neri, J., & Rodrígues-Arellano, S. (2018). Hacia una concepción del Diseño Sonoro 4.1 para personas con discapacidad visual. *Revista de Fisioterapia*, *2*(3), 1–9.

Ortiz, T. R. (2014). *Accessibility in Distance Education: Implements of universal design for learning*. University of Hawai at Manoa.

Ostashewski, N., Howell, J., & Dron, J. (2016). *Crowdsourcing MOOC Interactions: Using a Social Media Site cMOOC to Engage Students in University Course Activities*. Academic Press.

Ostashewski, N., Howell, J., & Dron, J. (2017). MOOCifying Courses: Delivery of a MOOC to Enhance University Course Activities. *Journal of Learning for Development.*, *4*(2), 184–195.

Otón, S., Amado-Salvatierra, H., Hilera, J. R., García, E., & García, A. (2015). Considerations on Barriers to Effective E-learning toward Accessible Virtual Campuses. In *E-learning - Instructional Design, Organizational Strategy and Management*. IntechOpen. Retrieved from https://www.intechopen.com/books/e-learning-instructional-design-organizational-strategy-and-management/considerations-on-barriers-to-effective-e-learning-toward-accessible-virtual-campuses

Otón, S., Batanero, C., García, E., García, A., & Barchino, R. (2014). Description of accessible learning resources by using metadata. *16TH International Conference on Enterprise Information Systems Vol. 2 (ICEIS 2014)*, 620-626. DOI:10.5220/0004895606200626

Otón, S., García, A., García, E., Barchino, R., & Amado-Salvatierra, H. R. (2014). Transforming LOMPad to Support IMS Access for All v3.0. *2014 IEEE 14th International Conference on Advanced Learning Technologies*, 599-600. 10.1109/ICALT.2014.175

Otón, S., Gutiérrez de Mesa, J. A., & Batanero C. (2015). Una implementación de afa para la educación virtual accesible. *Revista Vínculos, 12*(1).

Otón, S., Ortiz, A., Hilera, J. R., Barchino, R., Gutiérrez, J. M., Martínez, J. J., & Gutiérrez, J. A. (2010). Service oriented architecture for the implementation of distributed repositories of learning objects. *International Journal of Innovative Computing, Information & Control, 6-3*(A), 843-854.

Ozkaya, E. (2018). *Learn Social Engineering: Learn the art of human hacking with an internationally renowned expert*. Recuperado de https://books.google.com.mx/books?id=e_RZDwAAQBAJ

Palmeros-Ávila, G., Pérez-Castro, J., & Quiroz-Segura, M. L. (2017). Educational Inclusion and Development of Strategies for Learning a Second Language. The Case Study of a Student with Visual Impairment. *International Journal of Humanities and Social Science*, *7*(7), 161–170.

Panëels, S. A., Ritsos, P. D., Rodgers, P. J., & Roberts, J. C. (2013). Prototyping 3D haptic data visualizations. *Computers & Graphics*, *37*(3), 179–192. doi:10.1016/j.cag.2013.01.009

Pantaleev, A. (2012). In Search of Patterns: Disrupting RPG Classes Through Procedural Content Generation. Proceedings of the The Third Workshop on Procedural Content Generation in Games, 4:1-4:5. 10.1145/2538528.2538532

Papathoma, T. (2019). *MOOC educators: who they are and how they learn* (Doctoral dissertation). The Open University.

Parker, P. (2004). *Down Syndrome: A Bibliography and Dictionary for Physicians, Patients, and Genome Researchers*. Icon Group International Inc.

Parra, C. (2019). *Por una universidad para todas y todos: accesibilidad infraestructural universal*. Universidad de Chile.

Parry, Z., & Baird, C. (2013). Should I, Could I MOOCify my course? In *INTED2013 Proceedings* (pp. 3669-3679). IATED.

Patel, R. S. (2013). *Kali Linux Social Engineering*. Packt Publishing Ltd.

Paul, C. A. (2018). *The Toxic Meritocray of Video Games, Why Gaming Culture is the Worst*. Minneapolis, MN: University of Minnesota Press. doi:10.5749/j.ctt2204rbz

Pérez, M. F. (2011). Presente y futuro de la tecnología de la realidad Virtual. *Revista Creatividad y Sociedad C/ Salud, 15*(5).

Pérez-Acal, A., & Sanz-Lobera, A. (2007). Virtual reality simulation applied to a numerical control milling machine. *International Journal on Interactive Design and Manufacturing, 1*(3), 143–154. doi:10.100712008-007-0016-2

Pérez-Castilla Alvarez Colaboradores, L., Abenójar Agudo, V., Arribas Rincón, F., Aymerich Sabariego, M., Badia Corrons, A., Baldassarri, S., … Villegas Portero Rocío Zaragoza Martín, E. (2012). *Buenas prácticas de accesibilidad en videojuegos*. Retrieved from http://www.imserso.es

Persson, H., Åhman, H., Yngling, A. A., & Gulliksen, J. (2015). Universal design, inclusive design, accessible design, design for all: Different concepts—one goal? On the concept of accessibility—historical, methodological and philosophical aspects. *Universal Access in the Information Society, 14*(4), 505–526. doi:10.100710209-014-0358-z

Peters, D. (2012). *UX for Learning: Design Guidelines for the Learner Experience*. Retrieved from: https://www.uxmatters.com/mt/archives/2012/07/ux-for-learning-design-guidelines-for-the-learner-experience.php

Petridou, M., Blanchfield, P., Alabadi, R., & Brailsford, T. (2011). *User centred design and development of an educational force-feedback haptic game for blind students*. Academic Press.

Pickard, L. (2018). *How One University Tackles Accessibility in MOOCs*. Class Central.

Pieper, M., & Hermsdorf, D. (1997). BSCW for disabled teleworkers: Usability evaluation and interface adaptation of an internet-based cooperation environment. *Computer Networks and ISDN Systems, 29*(8-13), 1479–1487. doi:10.1016/S0169-7552(97)00014-7

Pohlenz, P., Gro¨, B. A., Petersik, A., Von, S. N., Pflesser, B., Pommert, A., ... Heiland, M. (2010). Virtual Dental Surgery as a New Educational Tool in Dental School. *Journal of Cranio-Maxillo-Facial Surgery, 38*(8), 560–564. doi:10.1016/j.jcms.2010.02.011 PMID:20303282

Pons, D., Hilera, J. R., Fernández, L., & Pagés, C. (2016). A Learning Quality Metadata Approach: Automatic Quality Assessment of Virtual Training from Metadata. *Computer Standards & Interfaces, 45*, 45–61. doi:10.1016/j.csi.2015.12.001

Posner, M. I., & Dehaene, S. (1994). Attentional networks. *Trends in Neurosciences, 17*(2), 75–79. doi:10.1016/0166-2236(94)90078-7 PMID:7512772

Posner, M. I., Rothbart, M. K., & Ghassemzadeh, H. (2019). Focus: Attention Science: Restoring Attention Networks. *The Yale Journal of Biology and Medicine, 92*(1), 139. PMID:30923481

Pretorius, M., Gelderblom, H., & Chimbo, B. (2010). Using Eye Tracking to Compare how Adults and Children Learn to Use an Unfamiliar Computer Game. *Proceedings of the 2010 Annual Research Conference of the South African Institute of Computer Scientists and Information Technologists*, 275-283. 10.1145/1899503.1899534

Purdue, U. (2016). *Game Development Process*. Obtenido de Educational Games at Purdue: https://e-games.tech.purdue.edu/GameDevProcess.asp

Quispe, A., Bernal, C., & Salazar, G. (2017). Use of applications for children with learning dificulties. *CAMPUS Revista, 12*(23), 13-26.

Rafique, I., Jingnong, W., Wang, Y., Abbasi, M., & Lew, P. (2012). Software Learnability Evaluation: An overview of definitions and evaluation Methodologies for GIS applications. International Multi-conference on computing in the global in-formation technology.

Raisamo, K., & Räihä, K. (2000). Design and evaluation of the alignment stick. *Interacting with Computers*, *12*(5), 128–134. doi:10.1016/S0953-5438(99)00020-X

Rao, K., Edelman-Smith, P., & Wailehua, C. (2015). Universal design for online courses: Applying principles to pedagogy. *Open Learning*, *20*(1), 35–52. doi:10.1080/02680513.2014.991300

Rao, K., & Tanners, A. (2015). Curb Cuts in Cyberspace: Universal Instructional Design for Online Courses. *Journal of Postsecondary Education and Disability*, *24*(3), 211–229.

Read, T., & Rodrigo, C. (2014). Toward a quality model for UNED MOOCs. *eLearning Papers*. Retrieved from http:// www. openeducationeuropa. eu/en/elearning_papers

Reich, R. (1991). The Work of Nations: preparing ourselves for 21st century capitalism. In *The Work of Nations*. New York: Vintage Books.

Richardson, J. T. (2017). Academic attainment in students with autism spectrum disorders in distance education. *Open Learning: The Journal of Open, Distance and e-Learning, 32*(1), 81-91.

Riddell, S., Gillooly, A., Harris, N., & Davidge, G. (2019a). Autonomy, Rights and Children with Special Needs: A New Paradigm? Findings from an ESRC funded study. *ESRC Economic & Social Research Council*. Report Online. http:// www.docs.hss.ed.ac.uk/education/creid/Projects/39_vi_ESRC_SENChildren_FinalRpt.pdf

Riddell, S., Gillooly, A., Harris, N., & Davidge, G. (2019b). Autonomy, Rights and Children with Special Needs: A New Paradigm? The Rights of Children with Special and Additional Support Needs in England and Scotland. *ESRC Economic & Social Research Council*. CREID Briefing 45. Retrieved from http://www.docs.hss.ed.ac.uk/education/ creid/Briefings/Briefing45.pdf

Riley-Huff, D. A. (2012). Web Accessibility and Universal Design: A Primer on Standards and Best Practices for Libraries. *Library Technology Reports*, *48*(7), 29–35. Retrieved from http://search.ebscohost.com/login.aspx?direct=true&db =ehh&AN=83242903&site=ehost-live

Rizzo, J. (2012). Disappearing Act. *National Geographic*.

Robson, K., Plangger, K., McCarthy, I., & Leyland, P. (2016). Game on: Engaging customers and employees through gamification. *Business Horizons*, 26–36.

Roden, T., & Parberry, I. (2004). From artistry to automation: A structured methodology for procedural content creation. *Lecture Notes in Computer Science*, *3166*, 151–156. doi:10.1007/978-3-540-28643-1_19

Rodrigo, C., Read, T., Santamaria, M., & Sánchez-Elvira, A. (2014). OpenupEdLabel for MOOC quality assurance: UNED COMA initial self-evaluation. In *Actas del V Congreso Internacional sobre Calidad y Accesibilidad en la Formación Virtual (CAFVIR 2014)* (pp. 551-555). Academic Press.

Rodrigo, C., García-Serrano, A., Delgado, J. L., & Iniesto, F. (2016). Challenges while MOOCifying a HE eLearning course on Universal Accessibility. In *Proceedings of the XVII International Conference on Human Computer Interaction* (p. 44). ACM. 10.1145/2998626.2998659

Rodríguez, I. A., López, B. A., Mendez, Z. A., & García, Z. B. (2013). *Helping children with Intellectual Disability to understand healthy eating habits with an IPad based serious game. In Computer Games: AI, Animation* (pp. 169–173). Mobile: Interactive Multimedia, Educational & Serious Games.

Rogers-Shaw, C., Carr-Chellman, D. J., & Choi, J. (2018). University Design for Leanring: Guidelines for Accessible Online Instruction. *Adult Learning*, *29*(1), 20–31. doi:10.1177/1045159517735530

Romero & Lavigne. (2005). Dificultades en el Aprendizaje Unificación de Criterios Diagnósticos. I. Definición, Características y tipos. Materiales para la Práctica Orientadora. *Consejería de Educación*, (1).

Rosewell, J. (2013). *E-xcellence / OpenupEd Quality benchmarks for MOOCs*. Retrieved from http://www.openuped.eu/images/docs/e-xcellence-MOOC-benchmarks-v09.pdf

Rosewell, J., & Barefoot, H. (2013). MOOCs and Quality Issues – QAQE Steering Group. *QAA*. Retrieved from http://www.slideshare.net/J.P.Rosewell/rosewell-barefootmoo-csandqualityissues

Roth, R. E., Ross, K. S., & MacEachren, A. M. (2015). User-Centered Design for Interactive Maps: A Case Study in Crime Analysis. *ISPRS International Journal of Geo-Information*, *4*(1), 262–301. doi:10.3390/ijgi4010262

Rubin, J., & Chisnell, D. (2008). *Handbook of usability testing: How to plan, design, and conduct effective tests*. Indianapolis, IN: Wiley Pub.

Ruiz, E. (2012). *Programación Educativa para Escolares con Síndrome de Down*. Madrid, España: Fundación Iberoamericana Down 21.

Ruiz, Muñoz, & Álvarez. (2007). Evaluación de Objetos de Aprendizaje a través del Aseguramiento de Competencias Educativas. *Virtual Educa.*

Rusu, C., Rusu, V., Roncagliolo, S., & González, C. (2015). Usability and User Experience. *International Journal of Information Technologies and Systems Approach*, *8*(2), 1–12. doi:10.4018/IJITSA.2015070101

Salama, H. (2012). *Gestalt 2.0*. Alfaomega.

Salisbury, K., Conti, F., & Barbagli, F. (2004). Haptic rendering: Introductory concepts. *Computer Graphics and Applications, IEEE*, *24*(2), 24–32. doi:10.1109/MCG.2004.1274058 PMID:15387225

Salisbury, R. (2008). *Teaching Pupils with Visual Impairment. A Guide to Making the School Curriculum Accessible*. Taylor & Francis Group.

Samperio, G., & Arceaga, A., & Anilu, F. C. C. (2017). Metodología Para El Modelado De Sistemas De Realidad Virtual Para El Aprendizaje En Dispositivos Móviles. *Pistas Educativas*, 518-534.

Sánchez, J., Espinoza, M., & De Borba Campos, M. (2014). *Videojuego Audio/Háptico para Desarrollar Habilidades de Navegación en Aprendices que son Ciegos*. Academic Press.

Sanchez, A., Barreiro, J., & Maojo, V. (2000). Design of Virtual Reality Systems for Education: A Cognitive Approach. *Education and Information Technologies*, *5*(4), 345–362. doi:10.1023/A:1012061809603

Sanchez-Gordon, S., & Luján-Mora, S. (2018). Research challenges in accessible MOOCs: A systematic literature review 2008-2016. *Universal Access in the Information Society*, *17*(4), 775–789. doi:10.100710209-017-0531-2

Sanchez-Gordon, S., & Luján-Mora, S. (2018b). Technological Innovations in Large-Scale Teaching: Five Roots of MOOCS. *Journal of Educational Computing Research*, *56*(5), 623–644. doi:10.1177/0735633117727597

Sanchez-Gordon, S., & Luján-Mora, S. (2018c). Lifecycle for MOOC Development and Management. In R. Queirós (Ed.), *Emerging Trends, Techniques, and Tools for Massive Open Online Course (MOOC) Management* (pp. 24–48). IGI Global. doi:10.4018/978-1-5225-5011-2.ch002

Sánchez, J. (2012). Development of navigation skills through audio haptic videogaming in learners who are blind. *Procedia Computer Science, 14*, 102–110. doi:10.1016/j.procs.2012.10.012

Sánchez, J., & Olivares, R. (2011). Problem solving and collaboration using mobile serious games. *Computers & Education, 57*(3), 1943–1952. doi:10.1016/j.compedu.2011.04.012

Sandeen, C. (2013). Integrating MOOCs into traditional higher education: The emerging "MOOC 3.0" era. *Change: The Magazine of Higher Learning, 45*(6), 34-39.

Sartorius, N. (2007). Stigma and mental health. *Lancet, 370*(9590), 810–811. doi:10.1016/S0140-6736(07)61245-8 PMID:17804064

Sauve, L., Senecal, S., Kaufman, D., Renaud, L., & Leclerc, J. (2011). The Design of Generic Serious Game Shell. In *2011 International Conference on Information Technology Based Higher Education and Training* (pp. 1–5). IEEE. 10.1109/ITHET.2011.6018675

Saygin, A. P., Cicekli, I., & Akman, V. (2000). Turing test: 50 years later. *Minds and Machines, 10*(4), 463–518. doi:10.1023/A:1011288000451

Scharver, C., Evenhouse, R., Johnson, A., & Leigh, J. (2004). Designing cranial implants in a haptic augmented reality environment. *Communications of the ACM, 47*(8), 33–38. doi:10.1145/1012037.1012059

Schelly, C. L., Davies, P. L., & Spooner, C. L. (2011). Student perceptions of faculty implementation of Universal Design for Learning. *Journal of Postsecondary Education and Disability, 24*, 17–30.

Schema.org. (2019). Retrieved from https://schema.org/

Scott, L. A., Temple, P., & Marshall, D. (2015). UDL in Online College Coursework: Insights of Infusion and Educator Preparedness. *Online Learning, 19*(5), 99–119. doi:10.24059/olj.v19i5.623

Scriven, M. (1991). Evaluation thesaurus. *Sage (Atlanta, Ga.)*.

Second Life. (n.d.). Available: http://secondlife.com/

SEP. (2006). *Orientaciones generales para el funcionamiento de los servicios de educación especial. Coordinadores: Ernesto Castellano Pérez, María del Carmen Escandón Minutti.* Secretaría de Educación Pública.

SEP-Secretaria de Educación Pública. (2019). *Educación especial.* Retrieved from https://www.educacionespecial.sep.gob.mx/2016/index_disca.html

Serrano, E., Moratilla, A., & Olmeda, I. (2010). Métrica para la evaluación de la accesibilidad en Internet: Propuesta y testeo. *Revista Espanola la de Documentacion Cientifica, 33*(3), 378–396. doi:10.3989/redc.2010.3.719

Sevilla, C., Santini, S., Haya, P. A., Rodriguez, P., & Sacha, G. M. (2012). Interdisciplinary design of videogames: A highly motivating method of learning. *2012 International Symposium on Computers in Education, SIIE 2012.*

Shaker, N., Togelius, J., & Nelson, M. J. (2016). Procedural Content Generation in Games. In Retrogame Archeology. doi:10.1007/978-3-319-42716-4

Shawar, B. A. (2015). Evaluating web accessibility of educational websites. *International Journal of Emerging Technologies in Learning, 10*(4), 4–10. doi:10.3991/ijet.v10i4.4518

Short, X. T., & Adams, T. (2017). Procedural Content Generation in Game Design. Taylor & Francis.

Sicilia, M. A. (2006). Metadata, semantics and ontology: Providing meaning to information resources. *International Journal of Metadata, Semantics and Ontologies, 1*(1), 83–86. doi:10.1504/IJMSO.2006.008773

SightFirst. G. d. (2010). *Educación y rehabilitación para personas ciegas y con baja visión*. Retrieved from http://www.e-district.org/userfiles/357/file/Educaci%C3%B3n%20y%20rehabilitaci%C3%B3n%20para%20personas%20ciegas%20y%20con%20baja%20visi%C3%B3n.pdf

Sik, C., David, L., & Brown, J. (2010). *Design of Serious Games for Students with Intellectual Disability*. Retrieved from http://goet-project.eu/

Sikos, L. F. (2015). *Mastering Structured Data on the Semantic Web: From HTML5 Microdata to Linked Open Data*. New York: Apress. doi:10.1007/978-1-4842-1049-9

Silver, H., Strong, R., & Perini, M. (1997). Integrating Learning Styles and Multiple Intelligences. *Educational Leadership*, *1*(55), 22–27.

Silver, P., Bourke, A., & Strehorn, K. C. (1998). Universal Instructional Design in Higher Education: An Approach for Inclusion. *Equity & Excellence in Education*, *2*(31), 47–51. doi:10.1080/1066568980310206

Simoncelli, A., & Hinson, J. M. (2008). College students' with learning disabilities personal reactions to online learning. *Journal of College Reading and Learning*, *38*(2), 49–62. doi:10.1080/10790195.2008.10850308

Simonnet, M., & Guinard, J.-Y., & Tisseau. (2006). Preliminary work for vocal and haptic navigation software for blind sailors. *6th International Conference on Disability, Virtual Reality and Associated Technologies, ICDVRAT*, 255-262. 10.1109/ICTTA.2006.1684489

Slootmaker, A., Nadolski, R., Kurvers, H. J., Hummel, H. G. K., & Koper, E. J. R. (2018). Usability of the EMERGO player environment for scenario-based serious games. *Human-Computer Interaction*.

Smelik, R. M., De Kraker, K. J., Groenewegen, S. A., Tutenel, T., & Bidarra, R. (2009). A survey of procedural methods for terrain modelling. *Proceedings of the CASA Workshop on 3D Advanced Media in Gaming and Simulation (3AMIGAS)*.

Smith, A. M., & Mateas, M. (2011). Answer set programming for procedural content generation: A design space approach. *IEEE Transactions on Computational Intelligence and AI in Games*, *3*(3), 187–200. doi:10.1109/TCIAIG.2011.2158545

Smith, D. W., & Smothers, S. M. (2012). The role and characteristics of tactile graphics in secondary mathematics and science textbooks in braille. *Journal of Visual Impairment & Blindness*, *106*(9), 543–554. doi:10.1177/0145482X1210600905

Smith, F. G. (2012). Analyzing a college course that adheres to the Universal Design for Learning (UDL) framework. *The Journal of Scholarship of Teaching and Learning*, *12*(3), 31–61.

Smith, G., Gan, E., Othenin-Girard, A., & Whitehead, J. (2011). PCG-Based Game Design: Enabling New Play Experiences through Procedural Content Generation. *Proceedings of the 2nd International Workshop on Procedural Content Generation in Games Article No.* 7. 10.1145/2000919.2000926

Smith, K., & Abrams, S. S. (2019). Gamification and accessibility. *The International Journal of Information and Learning Technology*, *36*(2), 104–123. doi:10.1108/IJILT-06-2018-0061

Snow, H. K. (2018). High-Impact Practices, Universal Design and Assessment Opportunities in Liberal Arts Seminars. *ASIANetwork Exchange, 25*(2), 117-135.

Solomou, G., Pierrakeas, C., & Kameas, A. (2015). Characterization of Educational Resources in e-Learning Systems Using an Educational Metadata Profile. *Journal of Educational Technology & Society*, *18*(4), 246–260.

Sommerville, I. (2015). *Software Engineering* (10th ed.). Person Editorial.

Song, D., Karimi, A., & Kim, P. (2011). Toward designing mobile games for visually challenged children. In *Proceeding of the International Conference on e-Education, Entertainment and e-Management* (pp. 234–238). IEEE. 10.1109/ICeEEM.2011.6137794

Sooryanarayan, D. G., & Gupta, D. (2015). Impact of learner motivation on mooc preferences: Transfer vs. made moocs. In *2015 International Conference on Advances in Computing, Communications and Informatics (ICACCI)* (pp. 929-934). IEEE. 10.1109/ICACCI.2015.7275730

Spooner, F., Baker, J. N., Harris, A. A., Ahlgrim-Delzell, L., & Browder, D. M. (2007). Effects of Training in Universal Design for Learning on Lesson Plan Development. *Remedial and Special Education*, *28*(2), 108–116. doi:10.1177/07419325070280020101

Stewart, J. B. (2018). *The New IQ: A New Kind of Intelligence for a New Kind of World.* Retrieved from: https://medium.com/@j_brucestewart/the-new-iq-a-new-kind-of-intelligence-for-a-new-kind-of-world-72d453b3ada3

Stickel, C., Fink, J., & Holzinger, A. (2007). Enhancing Universal Access–EEG Based Learnability Assessment. *Universal Access in Human-Computer Interaction. Applications and Services*, 813-822.

Stoffregen, T. A., Faugloire, E., Yoshida, K., Flanagan, M. B., & Merhi, O. (2008). Motion sickness and postural sway in console video games. *Human Factors*, *50*(2), 322–331. doi:10.1518/001872008X250755 PMID:18516842

Stratton, J. (1990). The principle of test restrictive materials. *Journal of Visual Impairment & Blindness*, 3–5.

Suman, S. (2018). *UX 101: Basic Understanding*. Retrieved from: https://medium.com/nyc-design/ux-101-basic-understanding-11cf993f0e99

Summerville, A., Snodgrass, S., Guzdial, M., Holmgard, C., Hoover, A. K., Isaksen, A., ... Togelius, J. (2018). Procedural Content Generation via Machine Learning (PCGML). *IEEE Transactions on Games*, *10*(3), 257–270. doi:10.1109/TG.2018.2846639

Sutherland, I. E. (1965). The ultimate display. *Proceedings of IFIPS Congress*, (2), 506–508.

Su, Y. S., Chiang, W. L., James Lee, C. T., & Chang, H. C. (2016). The effect of flow experience on player loyalty in mobile game application. *Computers in Human Behavior*, *63*, 240–248. doi:10.1016/j.chb.2016.05.049

Tablero de fibra de densidad media - MDF. (2016). Retrieved from https://es.wikipedia.org/wiki/Tablero_de_fibra_de_densidad_media

Tamboer, P., Vorst, H. C., & Oort, F. J. (2016). Five Describing Factors of Dyslexia. *Journal of Learning Disabilities*, *49*(5), 466–483. doi:10.1177/0022219414558123 PMID:25398549

Taylor, F. W. (1911). The principles of scientiðc management. New York: Academic Press.

The AbleGamers Foundation. (2012). *A Practical Guide to Game Accessibility*. Retrieved from http://includification.com/AbleGamers_Includification.pdf

The global disability crisis. (2017). Retrieved from https://www.add.org.uk/why-disability/global-disability-crisis

The Nine Principles of UDI. (2012). Center on Postsecondary Education and Disability, University of Connecticut. Retrieved from http://udi.uconn.edu/index.php?q=node/12

The Radicati Group. (2014). *Mobile Statistics Report, 2014-2018*. Retrieved from http://www.radicati.com

The Xerte Project. (2008). *Learning Technology*. University of Nottingham. Retrieved from http://www.nottingham.ac.uk/xerte/index.aspx

Therapy, M. (2019). *Tecnología y apps accesibles que rompen las barreras de la discapacidad visual.* Retrieved from de https://www.mytherapyapp.com/es/blog/aplicaciones-tecnologia-accesible-discapadidad-visual

TILE. (2004). *The Inclusive Learning Exchange.* University of Toronto. Retrieved from http://inclusivelearning.ca/tile/servlet/showtemplate?template=rswi/AboutTILE

Tobin, T. J. (2014). Increase online student retention with universal design for learning. *The Quarterly Review of Distance Education., 15*(3), 13–24.

Togelius, J., Yannakakis, G. N., Stanley, K. O., & Browne, C. (2011). Search-based procedural content generation: A taxonomy and survey. *IEEE Transactions on Computational Intelligence and AI in Games, 3*(3), 172–186. doi:10.1109/TCIAIG.2011.2148116

Toker, S., & Baturay, M. H. (2016). Antecedents and consequences of game addiction. *Computers in Human Behavior, 55*, 668–679. doi:10.1016/j.chb.2015.10.002

Tolkien, J. R. R. (1954). *The Lord of the Rings.* George Allen & Unwin.

Torrente, J., del Blanco, Á., Moreno-Ger, P., & Fernández-Manjón, B. (2012). *Designing Serious Games for Adult Students with Cognitive Disabilities* (pp. 603–610). Berlin: Springer. doi:10.1007/978-3-642-34478-7_73

Trejos, A. (2014). *Evaluación de Usabilidad de un Masive Open Online Course (MOOC).* Santiago de Chile: Universidad de Chile.

Troncoso, M., & Del Cerro, M. (2009). *Síndrome de Down: Lectura y Escritura.* Madrid: Fundación Down 21.

Tudor, M. (1939). *An experimental study of the act of evaluative labeling of speech fluency.* Iowa City, IA: University of Iowa.

Tullis, T., & Albert, B. (2013). *Measuring the User Experience: Collecting, Analyzing, and Presenting Usability Metrics.* Waltham, MA: Morgan Kaufmann.

Turner, W., & Greaney, K. (2009). Defining Dyslexia. *Journal of Learning Disabilities, 43*(3), 229–243. PMID:19834134

Tutenel, T., Bidarra, R., Smelik, R. M., & De Kraker, K. J. (2009). *The role of semantics in games and simulations.* Computers in Entertainment. doi:10.1145/1461999.1462009

Tyagi, M., Choudhary, C., & Majumdar, R. (2019). A Study on Gaming Engines Accessibility. In *Advances in Interdisciplinary Engineering* (pp. 33–41). Singapore: Springer. doi:10.1007/978-981-13-6577-5_4

U. S. Department of Education. (2010). *Transforming American Education: Learning Powered by Technology.* Washington, DC: Office of Educational Technology.

U. S. Department of Education. (2012). *Higher Education Opportunity Act - 2008.* Retrieved from http://www2.ed.gov/policy/highered/leg/hea08/index.html

Uluyol, C., & Sahin, C. (2014). Elementary school teachers' ICT use in the classroom and their motivators for using ICT. *British Journal of Educational Technology, 47*(1), 65–75. doi:10.1111/bjet.12220

UNESCO. (1951). UNESCO's work on Braille since 1949 and future activities of the World Braille Council. *Consultative Committee for the Creation of a World Braille Council.* MC/CONF.11/3, WS/111.178. Disponible en: https://unesdoc.unesco.org/ark:/48223/pf0000147824

UNESCO. (2017). ICT in Education. *UNESCO ICTs in Education website.* Retrieved 4 April 2019, from www.unesco.org/new/en/newdelhi/areas-of-action/special-themes/icts-in-education/

United Nations. (2015). *Global Status Report on Disability and Development*. Author.

University, E. K. (n.d.). *Web Accessibility Basics & Guidelines Why Is Accessibility Important?* Retrieved from https://brand.eku.edu/sites/brand.eku.edu/files/files/cbm_web_accessibility_r1.pdf

University, U. S. (n.d.). *Web accessibiity evaluation Tool*. Retrieved November 10, 2019, from https://wave.webaim.org

USAER. (2019). *Instituto de Educacion del Estado de Aguascalientes*. Retrieved from http://www.iea.gob.mx/webiea/sistema_educativo/sistema_eduespecial.aspx

Valiente, M.-C., Sicilia, M.-A., Garcia-Barriocanal, E., & Rajabi, E. (2015). Adopting the metadata approach to improve the search and analysis of educational resources for online learning. *Computers in Human Behavior*, *51*, 1134–1141. doi:10.1016/j.chb.2014.12.059

Valtchanov, V., & Brown, J. A. (2012). Evolving dungeon crawler levels with relative placement. doi:10.1145/2347583.2347587

Van Der Linden, R., Lopes, R., & Bidarra, R. (2014). Procedural generation of dungeons. *IEEE Transactions on Computational Intelligence and AI in Games*, *6*(1), 78–89. doi:10.1109/TCIAIG.2013.2290371

Van-Manen, M. (1998). *El tacto en la enseñanza*. Barcelona: Paidós Educador.

Vaspori, T., & Arato, A. (1995). Ten years of computer use by visually impaired people in Hungary. *Journal of Microcomputer Applications*, *18*(4), 313–317. doi:10.1016/S0745-7138(05)80030-2

Velikovsky, J. (2014). *Flow Theory, Evolution & Creativity*. doi:10.1145/2677758.2677770

Vieira, E. A. O., Da Silveira, A. C., & Martins, R. X. (2019). Heuristic Evaluation on Usability of Educational Games: A Systematic Review. *Informatics in Education*, *18*(2), 427–442. doi:10.15388/infedu.2019.20

Villanueva, K., & Vaidya, J. (2019). Power up Learning With Mobile Games: The Educational Arcade–An Innovative Approach to Learning. In *Advancing Mobile Learning in Contemporary Educational Spaces* (pp. 209–242). IGI Global. doi:10.4018/978-1-5225-9351-5.ch008

Vital, M. (2014). *9 Types of Intelligence – Infographic*. Retrieved from: https://blog.adioma.com/9-types-of-intelligence-infographic/#bodily

Viteri, A., & Abilés, A. (2017). El uso de las TIC en la educación inclusiva. In F. Pesántez, R. Sánchez, & V. Robles (Eds.), *Inclusión, discapacidad y educación. Enfoque práctico desde las Tecnologías Emergentes (pp. 325-340)*. Quito, Ecuador: Universidad Politécnica Salesiana.

Vizoso, S. (2017). Metadatos de accesibilidad en recursos educativos: análisis y propuesta. *Palabra Clave; Ensenada*, *7*(1). doi:10.24215/18539912e040

Vlachopoulos, D., & Makri, A. (2017). The effect of games and simulations on higher education: a systematic literature review. International Journal of Educational Technology in Higher Education, 14. doi:10.118641239-017-0062-1

Volkmar, G., Mählmann, N., & Malaka, R. (2019, November). Procedural Content Generation in Competitive Multiplayer Platform Games. In *Joint International Conference on Entertainment Computing and Serious Games* (pp. 228-234). Springer. 10.1007/978-3-030-34644-7_18

Voorhees, G. (2009). The character of difference: Procedurality, rhetoric, and roleplaying games. *Game Studies*. Retrieved from http://gamestudies.org/0902/articles/voorhees

W3C. (2012). Web Content Accessibility Guidelines (WCAG) 2.0. *World Wide Web Consortium*. Retrieved from http://www.w3.org/TR/WCAG/

W3C-WCAG. (n.d.). *Understanding Success Criterion 1.2.3: Audio Description or Media Alternative (Prerecorded).* Retrieved November 18, 2019, from https://www.w3.org/WAI/WCAG21/Understanding/audio-description-or-media-alternative-prerecorded

W3G. (n.d.). *Keyboard Accessible: Understanding Guideline 2.1.* Retrieved November 12, 2019, from https://www.w3.org/TR/UNDERSTANDING-WCAG20/keyboard-operation.html

WAI. (2019). *Introduction to Web Accessibility.* Retrieved October 10, 2019, from https://www.w3.org/WAI/fundamentals/accessibility-intro/

WapnickE. (2012). *The 7 Multipotentialite Super Powers.* Retrieved from: https://puttylike.com/the-7-multipotentialite-super-powers/

Watson, G., Mason, A, Ackroyd, R., (2014). *Social Engineering Penetration Testing: Executing Social Engineering Pen Tests, Assessments and Defense.* Syngress.

WCAG. (n.d.). *SCR29: Adding keyboard-accessible actions to static HTML elements.* Retrieved November 12, 2019, from https://www.w3.org/TR/2016/NOTE-WCAG20-TECHS-20161007/SCR29

Web C. A. G. (WCAG) 2.0. (2008). Retrieved from https://www.w3.org/TR/WCAG20/

Web-4-All. (2003). *Web Accessibility through sight, sound and touch.* Adaptative Technology Resource Centre, ATRC. University of Toronto. Retrieved from http://www.web4all.ca

Weller, M. (2013*). MOOCs & Quality.* MOOC Quality Project, week 7. Retrieved from http://mooc.efquel.org/week-7-moocs-quality-by-martin-weller

Werbach, K. (2014). (Re)Defining Gamification: A Process Approach, Persuasive Technology. *Persuasive Technology, 8462*, 266–272. doi:10.1007/978-3-319-07127-5_23

West, R., & Turner, L. H. (2004). *Teoría de la Comunicación: Análisis y Aplicación.* Madrid: Mc Graw Hill.

WHO. (2016). *Informed Consent Form Templates.* Obtenido de Informed Parental Consent for Research Involving Children (qualitative): http://www.who.int/rpc/research_ethics/informed_consent/en/

Wiley, D. A. (2000). Connecting learning objects to instructional design theory: A definition, a metaphor, and a taxonomy. In *The Instructional Use of Learning Objects: Online Version.* Recuperado el 18 de 08 de 2006, de http://reusability.org/read/chapters/wiley.doc

World Health Organization. (2001). *International Classification of Functioning, Disability and Health.* ICF.

World Health Organization. (2011). *World report on disability.* Retrieved from http://apps.who.int/iris/bitstream/10665/70670/1/WHO_NMH_VIP_11.01_eng.pdf

World Health Organization. (2011). *World Report on Disability.* Retrieved from http://www.who.int/disabilities/world_report/2011/report.pdf

World Health Organization. (2016a). WHO | Grades of hearing impairment. *WHO.* Retrieved from http://www.who.int/pbd/deafness/hearing_impairment_grades/en/

World Health Organization. (2016b). WHO | Visual impairment and blindness. *WHO.* Retrieved from http://www.who.int/mediacentre/factsheets/fs282/en/

World Wide Web Consortium. (2016). *Mobile Accessibility: How WCAG 2.0 and Other W3C/WAI Guidelines Apply to Mobile.* Retrieved May 15, 2018, from http://w3c.github.io/Mobile-A11y-TF-Note/

World Wide Web Consortium. (2018). *Web Content Accessibility Guidelines (WCAG) 2.1*. Retrieved from https://www.w3.org/TR/WCAG21/

World Wide Web Consortium. (2018). *Web Content Accessibility Guidelines (WCAG) 2.1*. Retrieved May 15, 2018, from https://www.w3.org/TR/WCAG21/#cc2

Yanez-Gomez, R., Font, J. L., Cascado-Caballero, D., & Sevillano, J. L. (2019). Heuristic usability evaluation on games: A modular approach. *Multimedia Tools and Applications*, *78*(4), 4937–4964. doi:10.100711042-018-6593-1

Yang, D., Sinha, T., Adamson, D., & Rosé, C. P. (2013, December). Turn on, tune in, drop out: Anticipating student dropouts in massive open online courses. In *Proceedings of the 2013 NIPS Data-driven education workshop* (*Vol. 11*, p. 14). Academic Press.

Yang, J. C., Chen, C. H., & Chang Jeng, M. (2010). Integrating video-capture virtual reality technology into a physically interactive learning environment for English learning. *Computers & Education*, *55*(3), 1346–1356. doi:10.1016/j.compedu.2010.06.005

Yannakakis, G. N., & Togelius, J. (2011). *Experience-driven procedural content generation*. IEEE Transactions on Affective Computing. doi:10.1109/T-AFFC.2011.6

Yen, L. (2011). *Promotion of Student Problem-Solving Skills, Motivation, Knowledge Acquisition and English Proficiency level Using an Interactive Computer Game*. ED-MEDIA.

Yesilada, Y., Brajnik, G., Vigo, M., & Harper, S. (2015). Exploring perceptions of web accessibility: A survey approach. *Behaviour & Information Technology*, *34*(2), 119–134. doi:10.1080/0144929X.2013.848238

Yousef, A. M. F., Chatti, M. A., Schroeder, U., & Wosnitza, M. (2014). What drives a successful MOOC? An empirical examination of criteria to assure design quality of MOOCs. In *2014 IEEE 14th International Conference on Advanced Learning Technologies* (pp. 44-48). IEEE. 10.1109/ICALT.2014.23

Yuan, L., & Powell, S. (2013). MOOCs and disruptive innovation: Implications for higher education. *eLearning Papers, In-Depth, 33*(2), 1-7.

Yuan, B., Folmer, E., & Harris, F. C. (2011). Game accessibility: A survey. *Universal Access in the Information Society*, *10*(1), 81–100. doi:10.100710209-010-0189-5

Yuan, C. W., Hanrahan, B. V., Lee, S., Rosson, M. B., & Carroll, J. M. (2019, March). Constructing a holistic view of shopping with people with visual impairment: A participatory design approach. *Universal Access in the Information Society*, *18*(1), 127–140. doi:10.100710209-017-0577-1

Zbick, J., Nake, I., Milrad, M., & Jansen, M. (2015). A web-based framework to design and deploy mobile learning activities: Evaluating its usability, learnability and acceptance. In *2015 IEEE 15th International Conference on Advanced Learning Technologies* (pp. 88-92). Hualien, Taiwan: IEEE Computer Society.

Zgurovsky, M. Z., & Zaychenko, Y. P. (2016). Inductive Modeling Method (GMDH) in Problems of Intellectual Data Analysis and Forecasting. In *The Fundamentals of Computational Intelligence: System Approach* (pp. 221–260). Cham: Springer. doi:10.1007/978-3-319-35162-9_6

Zheng, R., & Gardner, M. K. (2017). *Handbook of Research on Serious Games for Educational Applications*. IGI Global. doi:10.4018/978-1-5225-0513-6

Zichermann, G., & Cunningham, C. (2011). *Gamification by Design*. Sebastopol, CA: O'Reilly Media, Inc.

Ziefle, M. (2002). The influence of user experience and phone complexity on performance easy of use and learnability of different mobile phones. *Behaviour & Information Technology*, *21*(5), 303–311. doi:10.1080/0144929021000048538

Zikl, P., Bartošová, I. K., Víšková, K. J., Havlíčková, K., Kučírková, A., Navrátilová, J., & Zetková, B. (2015). The possibilities of ICT use for compensation of difficulties with reading in pupils with dyslexia. *Procedia: Social and Behavioral Sciences*, *176*, 915–922. doi:10.1016/j.sbspro.2015.01.558

ZonaFrancaMX. (2015). *La revolución táctil llegó; la háptica se apunta como la próxima tendencia tecnológica.* Retrieved from https://zonafranca.mx/cultura-y-entretenimiento/la-revolucion-tactil-llego-la-haptica-se-apunta-como-la-proxima-tendencia-tecnologica

Zosh, M. J., Hirsh-Pasek, K., Hopkins, J. H., Jensen, H., Liu, C., Neale, D. S., ... Whitebread, D. (2018). Accessing the inaccessible: Redefining play as a spectrum, Journal. *Frontiers in Psychology*, 9.

Zweifler, S. (2013). Study: MOOC students are highly educated, job-oriented. *The Daily Pennsylvanian.* Retrieved from http://www.thedp.com/article/2013/11/new-penn-study-moocs-far-from-revolutionizing-higher-education

About the Contributors

Ricardo Mendoza-González is a full-time professor at the Tecnológico Nacional de México/ IT Aguascalientes. Member of the National Research System (Level 1) from the National Council of Science and Technology (SNI, CONACyT, Mexico). His current research interests include several topics on: Human-Computer Interaction, User Research, User-Centered Design, Usability, Accessibility and Equity in technology, Design Thinking, Interfaces Design, Educational Technology, Open Educational Resources, Software Engineering and Artificial Intelligence

Huizilopoztli Luna-García is professor in Computer Science at Universidad Autónoma de Zacatecas, Campus Jalpa, México. Currently he is a Ph.D. student in Computer Science at Instituto Tecnológico de Aguascalientes; he holds a Master's degree in Sciences and Information Systems (Universidad Autónoma de Aguascalientes, with honor: Summa Cum Laude), and a Bachelor of Engineering in Computer Systems (Instituto Tecnológico de Zacatecas). MC Luna-García collaborates with important researchers of the University of Ontario Institute of Technology (UOIT, Canada), and Universidad Autónoma de Aguascalientes (México). He has reported his work in journals, book chapters, conference papers (Best Paper Award in MexIHC´14), and research seminars. His research interests include educational technology, design patterns, mobile technology, human-computer interaction, usability, user centered design, groupware, graphical-user interfaces and software engineering.

Alfredo Mendoza-González is a research professor at the Autonomous University of Aguascalientes, an associate professor at the Polytechnic University of Aguascalientes and the Technological University of Aguascalientes. He is a Computer Systems Engineer from the Autonomous University of Aguascalientes (2008), a Master in Computational Sciences from the Autonomous University of Aguascalientes (2013) and a Doctor in Computer Science from the Universidad Juárez Autónoma de Tabasco (2017). He is a founding member and Director of Linking of the Institute for Research, Development and Innovation in Interactive Technologies, A. C. (IIDITI). He has published scientific articles in international conferences and journals in the area of Artificial Intelligence on Genetic Algorithms and Algorithms of Estimation of Distribution, and in the area of Human-Computer Interaction on accessibility and adaptation and evaluation of interfaces for people with cognitive disabilities. He has written book chapters on evaluation of users with Down syndrome and accessibility for people with visual impairment. His topics of interest include: Human-Computer Interaction, Usability and User Experience, Human-Machine Interaction, Accessibility for people with cognitive disabilities, Internet of Things, Software Engineering, mobile interface design, wearable technology, brain-computer interfaces , educational technology and green technology.

* * *

Troy Abel received his PhD in Human Computer Interaction and MFA in Graphic Design, both from Iowa State University. He has 25+ years of industry, and 10+ years of academic experience, in Graphic Design, User Experience Design, Usability Testing, Design Education, and Human Computer interaction. He is currently an Assistant Professor of User Experience Design at University of North Texas and is also the director of the new Eye Tracking and Usability Testing lab (ETUT) at UNT (etut.unt.edu). He has worked with a wide range of industry clients on high-level usability testing and iterative agile-design methodologies. These clients include Southwest Airlines, Citibank, Kaspersky Labs, Belk, ADP, and Bose to name a few. His experience with eye-tracking technology also includes creating new methods to incorporate eye-tracking into traditional usability testing methods. His current research areas investigate Ethics in User Experience and design education, as well as the intersection of perception and usability evaluation methodologies utilizing multiple data-streams including eye tracking, qualitative data and facial reading. Additionally, his lab is exploring new participatory design methods within Human Centered Design which create novel inter-disciplinary knowledge. He is also interested in alternative assisted communication (AAC) for individuals with communication challenges and cognitive impairments, health-care experience design, social-network experience design, graphic design pedagogy, human computer usability testing and graphic design methodology.

José Guadalupe Arceo-Olague is a full-time professor and researcher at the Academic Unit of Electrical Engineering, Universidad Autónoma de Zacatecas (UAZ). He is the leader of the Academic Body of Emerging Technologies of Communications and Computation. Graduated as an Engineer in Communications and Electronics, UAZ, Master with Specialization in Digital Systems by CITEDI-IPN and PhD in Communications and Electronics, graduated from the IPN. His main interests are the integration of computational and electronic features in the design of digital systems. He is currently developing research on the Internet of Things, Wireless Sensor Networks and open source technologies.

José María Celaya-Padilla was born in Zacatecas, México, on February 16, 1985. He earned the bachelor degree in computer engineering and his Master degree in engineering from the Universidad Autónoma de Zacatecas in 2008 and 2010. Recently he earned his PhD in Information Technologies and Communications. As today, he is full time research at CONACyT - Autonomous University of Zacatecas. His research interests include: BioInformatics, Computer vision, Artificial Intelligence, IoT, Activity recognition, Automotive application development.

Samirna Collazos is Colombian independent researcher interested in several topics related to cognitive learning and technology.

Santiago Criollo-C was born in Quito, Ecuador, in 1984. He received the B.S. degree in electronics and information networks engineering from National Polytechnic School in Quito, in 2010 and the M.S. degree in communication networks from Pontificia Universidad Católica del Ecuador, in 2015. He is currently pursuing the Ph.D. degree in computer science at University of Alicante in Alicante, Spain, where he has oriented his research to the use of mobile devices as support in higher education. Since 2013, he has been professor of information technology in Universidad de Las Américas in Quito, Ecuador.

Esteban A. Durán-Yañez graduated from Informatics at the Instituto Tecnológico de Aguascalientes (ITA) in 2010, currently he is studying MSc Engineering at ITA. Is founder of the Inde Game Development Studio Ogre Pixel, that has published several successful video games. His main interests are artificial intelligence, computer programming and video games development.

Raquel Espinosa Castañeda is a professor and a researcher at the Communication Science Faculty at the Universidad Autonoma de San Luis Potosi. She did her degree in Communication Sciences at the Universidad de las Americas Puebla, Mexico. She graduated from master in Film Production and Direction from the Edinburgh College of Art, Scotland UK. She studies a PhD in Education. Her research and publication interests include inclusive education, special educational needs, blind people, virtual reality and haptics, assistive educational and recreational technologies.

Carlos E. Galván-Tejada, a full-time professor and researcher at the Academic Unit of Electrical Engineering, received his degree in Computer Engineering and his Master's Degree in Engineering with specialization in Digital Signal Processing by the Universidad Autónoma de Zacatecas. The degree of doctor in Information Technology and Communications with specialty in Artificial Intelligence granted by the Tecnológico de Monterrey Monterrey campus. His interests include environmental intelligence, signal processing, context research, Context-Aware computing and video game development.

Jorge Issac Galván-Tejada is an Engineer in Communications and Electronics and a Master in Engineering with orientation in PDS by the Autonomous University of Zacatecas (2004 and 2007). He is Doctor in Philosophy with orientation in Bioinformatics by the Technological Institute and Superior Studies of Monterrey (2016). He is currently a full-time Professor and Researcher at the Autonomous University of Zacatecas. His areas of interest are Bioinformatics and PDS.

Hamurabi Gamboa-Rosales is electronics and communications engineer graduated from the Faculty of engineering of the Universidad Autónoma de Guadalajara in 2000. He studied his master studies from 2001 to 2003 in Digital signal processing at the University of Guanajuato. He got his PhD degree at the Technical University of Dresden, Germany in the area of voice processing in 2010. He currently works as a professor and researcher in the academic Division of electrical engineering in the Universidad Autónoma de Zacatecas, Mexico.

Ana Garcia-Serrano is a permanent professor at ETSI Informática (UNED). She has a Ph.D. in Computer Science from the (UPM). Since 1995 she succeeded in having rather stable project funding from European and National research projects, and the results have been published in more than 100 papers related to topics as Natural Language Processing, Information Retrieval, eLearning and others. She has supervised eight doctoral and 20 official master's theses. She has been vice-President of the Spanish Association for Artificial Intelligence for eight years, and member of the standing committee of the Spanish Association of Natural Language Processing for 16 years.

Aisha S. Haynes is the Assistant Director at the Center for Teaching Excellence (CTE): University of South Carolina – Columbia. She oversees the CTE's instructional design team. Haynes is a certified

Quality Matters Peer and Master Reviewer, and has earned Online Teaching certifications from the Online Learning Consortium. She is Graduate Associate Faculty in the College of Education at UofSC-Columbia. Haynes also teaches courses for the College of Hospitality, Retail and Sport Management at UofSC-Columbia and UofSC-Union. Her research interests include: instructional design in online learning environments, online course accessibility, Universal Design for Learning (UDL), learning styles, and collaboration and engagement in online learning environments.

Paola Ingavelez is a Systems Engineer of the Army Polytechnic School. Postgraduate in: Multimedia Design, Evaluation of Higher Education, Intellectual Development, Public Policy and disability. Current candidate for PhD at the University of Alcalá - Spain. I have been a university teacher for 20 years. I have worked as a teacher at Polytechnic School of the Army, Universidad Tecnológica América and at the Salesian Polytechnic University where I currently work as director of the Biomedical Engineering degree.

Francisco Iniesto is a Ph.D. candidate by a Leverhulme Trust Doctoral Scholarship in Open World Learning based in The Open University researching accessibility in MOOCs. Francisco's background is as a Computer Engineer from UAM with a M.Sc. in Educational Technology from UNED. Francisco is a member of the Global OER Graduate Network and collaborates with the Digital Inclusion UNED-Vodafone Foundation Research Chair.

Angel Jaramillo-Alcázar was born in Quito, Ecuador, in 1985. He received the B.S. degree in electronics and information networks engineering from National Polytechnic School in Quito, in 2010 and the M.S. degree in systems and information technologies management from Universidad de Las Américas in Quito, in 2014. He is currently pursuing the Ph.D. degree in computer science at University of Alicante in Alicante, Spain, where he has oriented his research on accessibility for people with impairments in serious games. Since 2008, he has been professor of information technology in Universidad de Las Américas in Quito, Ecuador.

César A. López-Luévano is currently studying to get his PhD from the Instituto Tecnológico de Aguascalientes (ITA). Received his MSc Engineering with specialty in the field of Networking and Computer Systems in 2013 from the Universidad Politécnica de Aguascalientes (UPA). Received his BSc in Computer Systems Engineering in 2006 from the Universidad Autónoma de Aguascalientes (UAA). Currently he works at the UPA where he gives postgraduate and undergraduate courses, does academic management and does research. He has more than 10 years of experience in the educational field. His main interests are computer science, cyber security, networking, image processing and pattern recognition.

Sergio Luján-Mora was born in Alicante, Spain, in 1974. He received the Ph.D. degree in Computer Engineering from the Department of Software and Computing Systems at the University of Alicante, Alicante, Spain, in 2005. He received the Computer Science and Engineering degree at the University of Alicante in 1998. He is currently a senior lecturer of the Department of Software and Computing Systems at the University of Alicante. His main research interests include web applications, web development, and web accessibility and usability. In recent years, he has focused on e-learning, Massive Open Online Courses (MOOCs), Open Educational Resources (OERs), and the accessibility of video games. He is the author of several books and many published articles in various conferences (ER, UML, DOLAP) and high-impact journals (DKE, JCIS, JDBM, JECR, JIS, JWE, IJEE, UAIS).

Paola Andrea Manquillo-Manquillo has a master's degree in User Experience Design from the International University of La Rioja, Spain and holds a Bachelor's degree in Electronic and Telecommunications Engineering from the University of Cauca, Colombia. Her research interests are User Experience, Accessibility, Usablity, Human-Technology Interaction, User Centered Design and Educational Technology.

Hugo Iván Medellín Castillo is currently Full-time Professor in the Mechanical and Electrical Engineering department and Research Coordinator at Universidad Autonoma de San Luis Potosí. He completed his undergraduate studies in Mechanical and Electrical Engineering in 1999 at Universidad Autónoma de San Luis Potosí, Mexico. Later, he received his Master degree in Mechanical Engineering in 2001 at Universidad de Guanajuato, Mexico. After concluding his master studies, he joined Comisión Federal de Electricidad as a design engineer before receiving a Doctorate Scholarship. He completed his PhD studies in Mechanical Engineering in 2005 at Heriot-Watt University, Scotland, UK. Since 2006 he has been working as full time lecturer and researcher in Mechanical Engineering at Universidad Autonóma de San Luis Potosí, Mexico. He is member of the National System of Researchers (SNI) in México. His research interests includes virtual design and manufacturing, analysis and computational modeling, human biomechanics, virtual surgery, and inclusive education.

Jaime Muñoz Arteaga is a research professor at Universidad Autonoma de Aguascalientes (UAA) in Mexico. He got his phd in computer science at Université Toulouse III, in France. He got a postdoc of two years. Nowadays, He is member of SNI I in Mexico, and his research topics are in the domain of human-computer interaction, e-learning and web engineering. The doctor has managed several research projects about digital divide, collaborative production of text book and secure Interactive system. Finally, the Dr. Muñoz has published two books about Software Engineering, one book about Human-Computer Interaction and two books about learning object technology

Oscar Osvaldo Ordaz-García is a full-time professor and researcher at the Academic Unit of Electrical Engineering, Universidad Autónoma de Zacatecas (UAZ). Graduated as Engineer in Communications and Electronics, UAZ, with Specialization in Computing, UAZ, Master in Administrative information from the UAD-CZ, and PhD candidate in Computer Architecture and Electronic Technology, from the University of Córdoba (Spain). His main interests are the integration of computational and electronic features in the design of digital systems. He is currently developing research on the Wireless Sensor Networks, Internet of Things and open source technologies.

Manuel Agustín Ortiz-López is Associate Professor at the Dept. of Electronics and Computers Engineering, University of Córdoba (Spain) since 1996. Received his M.Sc. in Physics Electronics, University of Granada, Spain, in 1987 and his PhD. Degree in the University of Cordoba in 2013. Since 1987 till 1996 he worked in the R&D department of Fujitsu, in the R&D of TECOSA (a Siemens group company) and for the department of Computer Communications & Networks in Telefonica. His research work is related to the development of low-power embedded systems for use in sensor networks, the implementation of redundant arithmetic in FPGAs and HW/SW codesing. He has authored or co-authored several monographs, technical papers and articles covering topics on embedded system and wired and Wireless networks applied to communications for energy management systems and applications. He has been General Chair of 26th Intl. Annual Seminar on Automation, Industrial Electronics and Instrumentation (Seminario Anual de Automática, Electrónica Industrial e Instrumentación -SAAEI 2019). Since June 2017 he is the Head of the Department of Electronics and Computer Engineering in the University of Cordoba.

Jorge Ortíz-Reyes is a CTF player in Mayas-CTF team in binary analysis category. Graduated as Computer Engineer, UAZ, with more than 2 years in the security field, first place winner in HackDef Capture The Flag Mexico 2018 (HackDef CTF). He is currently interested in reverse engineering, vulnerability discovery, and all forms of ethical hacking.

Salvador Otón Tortosa has a Computer Sciences Engineering degree from the University of Murcia (1996) and a PhD from the University of Alcalá (2006). Currently, he is an Associate Professor in the Computer Science Department of the University of Alcalá. He coordinates the Master on Software Engineering for the Web. He is author or co-author of more than 80 scientific works (books, articles, papers and research projects), the majority of them directly related to Learning Technology, Accessibility and Interoperability. His research interests are focused on learning objects and e-learning standardization and mainly in accessibility, metadata, distributed learning objects repositories, interoperability and enterprise architectures.

Katerina Psegiannaki is an architect from the Democritus University of Thrace (2005) and PhD Architect from the E.T.S.A. of Madrid, UPM (Cum Laude, 2015). She is teaching in the Camilo José Cela University in Madrid in Bachelor in Urban Management and Digital Arts Degree. She has collaborated with the University of La Rioja as a Final Thesis Supervisor at the Online Master in User Experience Design. Since 2009 she is a founding member and co-director of HipoTesis magazine and since 2016 of KUNE Office whose main practice focuses on exploring the architectural possibilities of being together.

Covadonga Rodrigo holds a Ph.D. in Telecommunications from the Universidad Politecnica de Madrid (1999). In 2000 she joined the Department of Languages and Computer Systems of UNED (Universidad Nacional de Educacion a Distancia). She has held various academic positions being Vice Chancellor of Technology in the period 2010-2013 and director of the Accessible Technology UNED-Vodafone Foundation Research Chair. She currently leads the Digital Inclusion Lab.

Mario A. Rodríguez-Díaz recieved his PhD and MSc in Exact Sciences, Systems and Information in 2009 and 2015 and BSc in computer systems engineering in 2006, all from the Universidad Autónoma de Aguascalientes (UAA). Currently, he works at Instituto Tecnológico de Aguascalientes (ITA), where he gives postgraduate courses, does academic management, and does research. He has more than 10 years of professional experience at software industry. He has developed successful systems for binary document image compression that achieves better compression than the international standards and state of the art methods in literature, also developed computer vision systems for vehicle plate recognition. His main interests are image processing, computer vision, pattern recognition, information theory, automata theory and artificial intelligence in videogames.

Mary Sánchez-Gordón is an Associate Professor at the Computer Science Department of the Østfold University College. Formerly she worked at Universidad Central del Ecuador. Her research interests are software process, software process improvement and knowledge management. She holds a Ph.D. and

Master's degree in Information Science and Technology from Universidad Carlos III de Madrid.She also holds a Master's in Education and a bachelor's degree in Informatics from Universidad Central del Ecuador. She has been working as Software Engineer, Project Manager and Software Engineering Consultant in several companies.

Sandra Sánchez-Gordón holds a PhD in Applications of Informatics by University of Alicante, Spain. Sandra is researcher and professor of the Department of Informatics and Computer Sciences of National Polytechnic School of Ecuador. Her main research interests include MOOCs, web accessibility, software requirements engineering, software testing engineering, software quality assurance, and IT governance. She has twenty-one years of experience in teaching at graduate and undergraduate level. She has twenty-three years of experience in development and implementation of software solutions in Ecuador, Panama and USA. She practices Yoga, Tai-Chi, and Zazen Meditation.

Debra Satterfield has extensive research and publication in design for social inclusion, design for behavioral change, and the design of educational learning experiences for children with autism and other cognitive and physical disabilities. She has published this work through the Design Research Society (DRS), the International Association of Societies of Design Research (IASDR), and Interaction Design and Children (IDC). She has taught courses on smart home technologies, human computer interaction, experience design, and design ethics. She is currently conducting research on quality of life issues for children with autism spectrum disorders and the implications it has for the design of products, services and environments for persons with ASD.

Roberto Solís-Robles holds a Ph.D. degree in Computer Science from the University of Illinois at Urbana-Champaign, United States, where he also completed a postdoctoral degree at the Coordinated Science Laboratory (CSL). Previously, he obtained a Master's degree in Computer Science from ITESM and a degree in Computer Systems Engineering from the Technological Institute of Zacatecas. He is a member of the Academic Body CA-231 Emerging Communications and Computing Technologies in the Academic Unit of Electrical Engineering of the Autonomous University of Zacatecas, where he currently works as a teacher-researcher in the academic programs of Software Engineering and Computer Engineering. He is a site director for the International ICPC Programming Contest in the Mexico Region and a leader of the Zacatecas Delegation for Mexican Olympiad of Informatics. He has published technical articles on topics related to sensor networks and mobile applications. As a researcher, his areas of interest are: Software Engineering, Internet of Things and Cloud Computing. He holds various certifications such as PSP, Software Engineering Master, Java Programming and MySQL among others.

Index

V

W

www.ingramcontent.com/pod-product-compliance
Lightning Source LLC
LaVergne TN
LVHW060414300926
849162LV00006B/1427
9781799823254